Lecture Notes in Electrical Engineering

Volume 1007

The book series *Lecture Notes in Electrical Engineering* (LNEE) publishes the latest developments in Electrical Engineering—quickly, informally and in high quality. While original research reported in proceedings and monographs has traditionally formed the core of LNEE, we also encourage authors to submit books devoted to supporting student education and professional training in the various fields and applications areas of electrical engineering. The series cover classical and emerging topics concerning:

- Communication Engineering, Information Theory and Networks
- Electronics Engineering and Microelectronics
- Signal, Image and Speech Processing
- Wireless and Mobile Communication
- Circuits and Systems
- Energy Systems, Power Electronics and Electrical Machines
- Electro-optical Engineering
- Instrumentation Engineering
- Avionics Engineering
- Control Systems
- Internet-of-Things and Cybersecurity
- Biomedical Devices, MEMS and NEMS

For general information about this book series, comments or suggestions, please contact leontina.dicecco@springer.com.

To submit a proposal or request further information, please contact the Publishing Editor in your country:

China

Jasmine Dou, Editor (jasmine.dou@springer.com)

India, Japan, Rest of Asia

Swati Meherishi, Editorial Director (Swati.Meherishi@springer.com)

Southeast Asia, Australia, New Zealand

Ramesh Nath Premnath, Editor (ramesh.premnath@springernature.com)

USA, Canada

Michael Luby, Senior Editor (michael.luby@springer.com)

All other Countries

Leontina Di Cecco, Senior Editor (leontina.dicecco@springer.com)

** This series is indexed by EI Compendex and Scopus databases. **

Koushlendra Kumar Singh · Manish Kumar Bajpai · Akbar Sheikh Akbari

Editors

Machine Vision and Augmented Intelligence

Select Proceedings of MAI 2022

Springer

Editors
Koushlendra Kumar Singh
Department of Computer Science
and Engineering
National Institute of Technology
Jamshedpur
Jamshedpur, India

Manish Kumar Bajpai
Department of Computer Science
and Engineering
IIITDM Jabalpur
Jabalpur, India

Akbar Sheikh Akbari
Leeds Beckett University
Leeds, UK

ISSN 1876-1100   ISSN 1876-1119 (electronic)
Lecture Notes in Electrical Engineering
ISBN 978-981-99-0191-3   ISBN 978-981-99-0189-0 (eBook)
https://doi.org/10.1007/978-981-99-0189-0

This Springer imprint is published by the registered company Springer Nature Singapore Pte Ltd.
The registered company address is: 152 Beach Road, #21-01/04 Gateway East, Singapore 189721,
Singapore

Contents

About the Editors

Koushlendra Kumar Singh is currently working as an assistant professor in the Department of Computer Science and Engineering at the National Institute of Technology, Jamshedpur, India. He completed his doctoral degree and master's program at the Indian Institute of Information Technology, Design, and Manufacturing, Jabalpur, India, in 2016 and 2011, respectively. Dr. Singh graduated in computer science and engineering from Bhagalpur College of Engineering, Bhagalpur, in 2008. He has published several papers in international refereed journals and conferences. His current research interest areas are image processing, biometrics, different applications of fractional derivatives, computational modeling, epidemic forecasting, etc.

Manish Kumar Bajpai is an Assistant Professor in the Department of Computer Science and Engineering at the Indian Institute of Information Technology Design and Manufacturing, Jabalpur, India. He completed his Ph.D. from IIT Kanpur in image reconstruction and parallel algorithm design. Dr. Bajpai has published over 50 publications in international journals and conferences. He has several sponsored research and consultancy projects funded by agencies such as SPARC, MHRD, DST, USIEF, ATAL, BRNS, and NVIDIA. Eleven students have completed/pursuing their Ph.D. under his supervision. His research areas are augmented intelligence, machine vision, brain-computer interface, medical imaging, and parallel algorithms design. Dr. Bajpai is a senior member of IEEE and a life member of the Indian Science Congress and Indian Nuclear Society.

Dr. Akbar Sheikh Akbari is an associate professor (Reader) of Electronic Engineering in the School of Built Environment, Engineering and Computing. He has a B.Sc. (Hons), M.Sc. (distinction), and Ph.D. in Electronic and Electrical Engineering. After completing his Ph.D. at Strathclyde University, he joined Bristol University to work on an EPSRC project in stereo/multi-view video processing. Dr. Sheikh Akbari's main areas of research are: biometric identification techniques, e.g., iris, ear, and face recognition, image resolution enhancement (super-resolution) methods, image source camera identification, color constancy (white balancing) techniques, standard and non-standard image/video codecs, e.g., H.264 and HEVC, multi-view image/video processing, video analytics and real-time embedded systems, edge detection in low SNR environments, compressive sensing, retro-reflective materials, online camera calibration. Dr. Sheikh Akbari was the academic supervisor for the following KTP project: Omega Security Systems/Leeds Beckett University, "Research, develop and implement a scalable and modular system which monitors and analyses individual behavioural patterns and movements in a range of environments", Funder: innovate UK, 24 months, £122,040, which was graded outstanding by innovate UK.

Detection of Physical Impairments on Solar Panel Using YOLOv5

Ashutosh Kumar Sahoo, Swagatika Behera, Shivam Maurya, and Paresh Kale

1 Introduction

A crystal solar panel's lifespan is often guaranteed for 25–30 years, but having 30 years of performance would not be the same as in the beginning. Due to unavoidable conditions such as UV exposure and weather cycles, solar cells suffer degradation and performance declines. Short-circuiting in the module, shadowing effect, inverse diode bypass, and shunted diode bypass are severe faults in the PV cell plant [1]. Efficiency is also reduced because of scattering, reflection, and absorption at the PV cell surface, which happens because of printed patterns and dust [2]. Overheating and maloperation of the cell occur because of partial shading that affects the PV cell performance, as shown in [3] using artificial neural network. It is considered a failure if there is a 20% decline. It is difficult to determine what constitutes a failure, since a 50% degradation of a high-efficiency module may still be as efficient as a nondegraded module from a less efficient technology [4]. Three types of product failures are distinguished: infant failures, midlife failures, and wear-out failures. Delamination, cracked cell isolation, and PID are the common PV failures that belong to midlife and wear-out failure [5], leading to heavy power losses.

Image processing is an advancing method to perform some operations on an image to extract image-based defects on the solar cell. Solar cell quality inspection improves production quality and helps in the lifetime of the photovoltaic module. Labeling of images stands out to be the crucial part of this as the images are nontextured. LabelImg is a software that focuses on where the defect happens and does the pre-processing by selecting and extracting that filters out redundant features and creates a brand of datasets [6]. It also encodes categorical variables into continuous variables and aggregates a smaller set of features for better model training.

A. K. Sahoo · S. Behera · S. Maurya · P. Kale (✉)
Department of Electrical Engineering, National Institute of Technology Rourkela, Rourkela, India
e-mail: pareshkale@nitrkl.ac.in

© The Author(s), under exclusive license to Springer Nature Singapore Pte Ltd. 2023
K. Kumar Singh et al. (eds.), *Machine Vision and Augmented Intelligence*, Lecture Notes in Electrical Engineering 1007, https://doi.org/10.1007/978-981-99-0189-0_1

By performing bounding box prediction and class label prediction, the YOLOv5 model generates a differentiable end-to-end network [7]. It is the translation of the Darknet research framework into PyTorch 1.8 framework written in C that provides fine-grained control over the operations encoded in the network that is the most significant contribution made by YOLOv5 [8]. The PyTorch 1.8 framework comprises convolutional layers with other layers like focus, maxpooling, bottleneck CSP, SPP, upsample, and concat [9–11].

2   Image Pre-Processing Parameters and Algorithm

Image processing methods effectively obtain the defects in solar cells such as cracks, delamination, hotspot, snail trail, and PID effect. The algorithms use matching methods between the present image and the self-produced image by functions.

2.1   Collection of Specimen Images Data

The images taken from various sites and references have been subjected to correctness. Different cell defects have different results like a crack can cause a reduced power output in the future. Hence, the classification of defect cells into various defect categories is essential. Roboflow, a computer vision developer framework used for better pre-processing collected data, performs binary and multi-classification. There are many steps involved, such as image orientations, resizing, contrasting, and data augmentations. Labeling images play a crucial role which is done with the help of LabelImg software in Python. Labeling is drawing bounding boxes to get the notations where the object is precisely present in the image and correct annotation errors. Various steps are involved in a health check of the dataset to ensure if datasets are imbalanced for classification models. But the farthest cells may suffer as small defect structures may be hidden and hard to detect, making it more challenging.

2.2   Detection of Object Using YOLOv5 Algorithm

For object detection, we adapted YOLOv5, which is implemented in the PyTorch 1.8 framework. It uses Cross Stage Partial Network (CSP), which reduces the computation cost significantly. It is better at detecting small and far away objects and uses little to no overlapping boxes. The core architecture for YOLOv5 is the convolutional layer, the pooling layer, and the output layer, which is generally a fully connected layer. The convolutional layer applies the convolution operation to the input, passing the result to the next layer, and the result is usually referred to as a feature map. Three major advantages of the convolution operation include its ability to reduce parameter numbers by utilizing weight sharing on the same feature map. In local connectivity, pixels are connected by learning correlations among them and their variation with respect to their location.

The neural network has three different output layers at 82, 94, and 106, as shown in Fig. 1. The network operates like a typical CNN, using the first convolutional layers to extract features from the input image while reducing spatial dimensions. The first detection is made at layer 82, applying a 1×1 kernel to the previous layer's resulting feature map. If the input image has a dimension of 416×416, the resulting feature map would have a 13×13 dimension, as the layer has a stride of 32. After applying the detection kernel, the resulting feature map would be $13 \times 13 \times N$, where N is the Nth number of filters in the layer. YOLO algorithm has a fixed size prediction, with being $S \times S \times (C + (5 \times B))$, with B being the number of predictions per grid cell, and C being the number of classes. In YOLOv5, the feature map is divided into an $S \times S$ grid shown in Fig. 2, and all the tests done in [12] used $B = 3$, which means each block can only predict three objects and $C = 80$, because of the COCO dataset, making the first detection feature map $13 \times 13 \times 255$. After predicting the first scale, the feature map from the 79th layer is subjected to a few convolutional layers before being upsampled by two times, making the resultant feature map 26×26. The feature map is concatenated with a feature map from a previous layer of the network, precisely layer 61, allowing the feature map to get more meaningful information. The same procedure is done at layer 94, resulting in a detection feature map of $26 \times 26 \times 255$, which is precisely two times the dimension of the previous detections, making it suitable for detecting objects with smaller sizes. The process is repeated at the last layer, the 106th, with an output shape of $52 \times 52 \times 255$, resulting in three different output shapes for detection, allowing the network to extract more minor features and thus better detect smaller objects compared to previous versions of the algorithm.

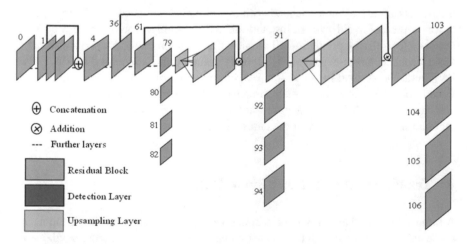

Fig. 1 Schematic of the architecture of various block layers in YOLOv5

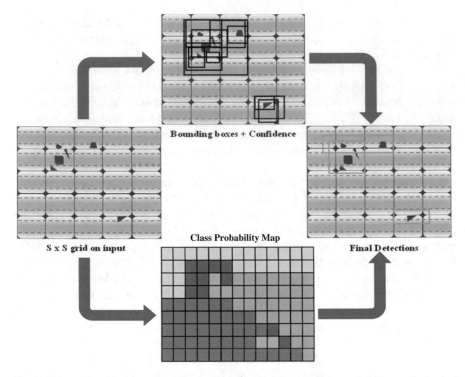

Fig. 2 Schematic of input grid with proposed bounding boxes, class probability, and physical damage detection

2.3 Data Augmentation for Accuracy Improvement

Small datasets are often associated with low classification accuracy. Data augmentation is used to avoid over-fitting and make the training process more robust and better at generalizing predictions. The data augmentation methods used are similarly described in the original paper [13]. One of its methods is to diversify data in random horizontal and vertical image flipping. Arbitary scaleing and translations are introduced up to 10% and random adjustments to the color saturation and intensity by a factor of 0.5. All bounding boxes are automatically updated with this process, maintaining the authenticity of the dataset (Table 1).

3 Training and Loss Function of Datasets

A large volume of data for both networks must learn how to process their inputs and make an accurate prediction to train neural networks. For every picture available for training, the label must be available and match the network output. The datasets were

Table 1 Frequency of each class of physical damages

Class name	No. of occurrence
Crack	92
Hotspot	43
Delamination	41
Snail trail	44
PID effect	36

divided into two subsets: training and validation. The dataset was 256 images, with 80% destined for training and 20% for validation. The training stage of the object detector is similar to the one described in the original paper [13]. Since the scope of the dissertation is to infer the accuracy of an object detection algorithm in a solar panel, the training is done using transfer learning.

The network is pre-trained in the COCO dataset, where a mAP has reached 31.0% [14], and these weights are available. The rationale behind using these weights is to initialize the network's parameters and speed up the training process. The pre-trained network can successfully do the detection and classification of objects. The main task of the training process is to retrain the detector to only classify in the desired class range and to retrain the last convolutional layers to learn the high-level features associated with the desired dataset class. The training process will not significantly affect the lower convolutional layers because they detect low-level features like edges or corners. Those features are transversal for nearly all detectors. The training dataset was taken of 256 images, taking 16 images per batch of training up to 300 epochs, a validation dataset of 55 images, and an augmented dataset of 3105 batches which was given to the neural network to produce the result.

With the pre-trained weights, the network can detect simple objects such as boats from the beginning with relatively high accuracy regarding the bounding box local-ization. So, the main focus of the training is emphasized on classification detection, which led to small changes in the loss function, as detailed below. Regarding the hyperparameters, the training was done using a batch size of 16, the learning rate of 0.001 using the stochastic gradient descent optimizer with momentum $= 0.9$, and weight decay $= 0.0005$. As given in (1), the loss function is used for training the convent, where $l1, l2, l3$, and $l4$ are tunable parameters to balance the loss function.

$$\text{Loss} = \lambda_1 \sum \left[(x - \hat{x})^2 + (y - \hat{y})^2 \right] + \lambda_2 \sum \left[\left(h - \hat{h} \right)^2 (w - \hat{w})^2 \right]$$
$$+ \lambda_3 \sum -y \times \log(1 - \hat{y}) + \lambda_4 \sum y \times \log(\hat{y}) + (1 - y) \times \log(1 - \hat{y})$$
$$(1)$$

The first two elements of the function are related to the bounding box regression, the first one is related to the center-x and center-y coordinates, and the second one is related to the height and width of the bounding box. Since the pre-trained network is already accurate in locating objects, these portions of the (1) will have less impact on the sum. The objective is to retrain the network to re-learn how to classify objects by changing the dataset; these parameters were changed against the original paper where the actual loss function was proposed in [13]. More emphasis was put on the third and fourth elements of the loss functions: class confidence and object confidence, respectively. The grid search method was applied to achieve the optimal values for the loss function, providing the best combination of these hyperparameters that result in the best network accuracy. So, the values used for $l1$, $l2$, $l3$, and $l4$ were 8, 4, 2, and 64.

The main issue regarding the training is using the pre-trained network because the model was trained to extract features necessary to locate and classify 80 different classes. In doing so, the appearance of false positives could lead to the additional training provided by the developed module. However, the scope of the system's application is limited to a natural environment, significantly reducing the probability of occurrence of such incidents.

4   Evolution Metrics for Damage Detection

The evaluation metrics are parameters used to help find the bounding boxes, the exact location of labeled images, and helpful to see the positive detection in an image. There are many parameters used, but here, we chose only four parameters based on the below.

4.1   Object Detection Using Intersection Over Union (IoU)

Intersection over union, as given in (2), is a metric used to measure the accuracy of an object detector. To apply the IoU metric, the ground truth and the predicted bounding box is necessary. It is almost impossible to have a pixel-perfect match between an expected and a ground-truth bounding box. Because of the difficulty, the IoU metric calculates how much the predicted bounding box overlaps with the ground-truth one. With the metric, object detection algorithms have a metric that rewards predicted bounding boxes for heavily overlapping with the ground-truth boxes.

$$\text{IoU} = \frac{\text{Area of Union}}{\text{Area of Overlap}} \tag{2}$$

4.2 Precision of Prediction of Damage Class

As given in (3), the precision metric infers how accurate the predictions are, where TP = True Positive and FP = False Positive.

$$\text{Precision} = \frac{\text{TP}}{\text{TP} + \text{FP}} \text{ or } \frac{\text{TP}}{\text{Actual Results}} \tag{3}$$

A TP occurs when a prediction matches ground-truth data. When a sample is miss-predicted; i.e., the prognosis does not match the correct class. An FP occurs when the classifier makes a wrong prediction regarding the ground-truth data. In the scope of the dissertation, a prediction is considered a true positive if the bounding box has an IoU > 0.5 and the predicted class matches the ground-truth counterpart.

4.3 Recall of Total Relevant Result

As given in (4), the recall metric measures the percentage of total relevant results correctly classified, where FN = False Negative. An FN occurs when a ground-truth sample is not detected.

$$\text{Recall} = \frac{\text{TP}}{\text{TP} + \text{FN}} \text{ or } \frac{\text{TP}}{\text{Predicted Results}} \tag{4}$$

4.4 Mean Average Precision (mAP) of Precision–Recall Curve

The formal definition for the mean average precision (mAP), as given in (5), is finding the area under a curve denoted as the precision–recall curve. However, some authors replace the integral with a finite sum of the interpolated precision, as given in Eq. (6). The average accuracy by averaging the precision over eleven evenly spaced recall levels [15].

$$\text{mAP} = \int_0^1 p(r)\mathrm{d}r \tag{5}$$

$$\text{mAP} = \frac{1}{11} \sum_{r \in \{0,0.1,\dots,1\}} P_{\text{interp}}(r)\mathrm{d}r \tag{6}$$

The precision is interpolated by taking the maximum precision value, as given in (7), whose recall value is more significant than r, where $P(\bar{r})$ is the measured precision–recall $\bar{r} \geq r$.

$$P_{\text{interp}} = \max p(\bar{r}) \tag{7}$$

The method of computing the AP metric has changed. Instead of calculating the interpolation over only 11 evenly spaced points, the interpolation is done over all data points, as given in (8) and (9).

$$mAP = \sum_{0}^{1} (r_{n+1} - r) P_{\text{interp}}(r_{n+1}) \tag{8}$$

$$P_{\text{interp}}(r_{n+1}) = \max p(\bar{r}) \tag{9}$$

The average precision is obtained by interpolating the precision at each level r, taking the maximum accuracy whose recall value is greater or equal to $r + 1$ [16, 17].

5 Training Results

The training was done during 300 epochs, with a training dataset of 256 images and a validation dataset of 55 images. The training was done using 16 images per batch of training, resulting in 3105 batches of images after augmentation, which is fed into the neural network producing the result.

In Fig. 3, the box, classification, and objectness decrease because the box's location is easily found with less search. The objectness is nearly 3%, and those of the COCO dataset is 5%. Identification of bounding box depends on the boxing parameter; lesser the boxing, nearer the bounding box to each other. The precision and recall graphs are similar, around 30–25% with 3% error, which shows optimistic prediction.

The network's giou_loss has reached around less than 0.04 and only came a MAP of only 25% across the validation set. Although the result is within the range of values achieved by the same algorithm on the COCO dataset, a difference in our dataset has 8× fewer classes. The loss of IoU is also shown in Fig. 3.

The labeled boxes cannot correctly classify the cracks and snail trail type. The labeled boxes are dependent upon the probability distribution of the images and the precision of all the images.

Several algorithms can be implemented for object detection; the YOLOv5 algorithm for object detection and LabelImg software for image pre-processing are done. All the images are labeled and processed for augmentation where the photos are crop, brighten, tilted, sheared, and many more. The enlargement and link for the dataset

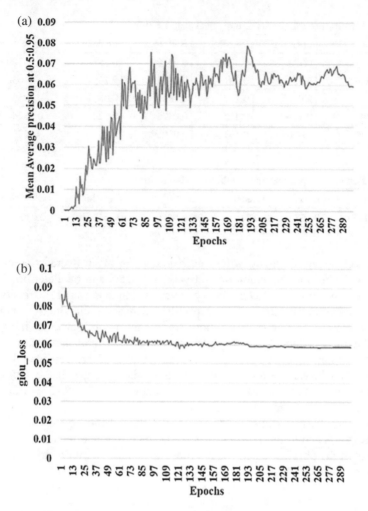

Fig. 3 **a** mAP of the general classification and **b** training losses

are formed with the help of Roboflow [18]. Roboflow is a website where the augmentation of data with validation of data is done. Link is generated with trained, test, and validation dataset processed through the trained model with the help of the YOLOv5 algorithm. The activation function should be maximum for object detection.

The error happens due to spatial constraints as well as proximity to other damages. In Fig. 3, the crack and snail trail is not fully boxed, leading to inaccurate detection of the damages. The differences between the individual and general/multi-labeling classifications are shown in Tables 2 and 3. The significant damages classification has been shown in Table 2, and the rest of the damage classification has been shown in Table 3.

Table 2 Performance parameters of individual classification

Damages	mAP	Recall	Box	Precision	Objectness
Crack	0.121	0.301	0.03689	0.151	0.04109
Delamination	0.32	0.381	0.0329	0.265	0.03036
Hot spot	0.0563	0.167	0.03489	0.0811	0.0259
Snail trail	0.124	0.455	0.0326	0.124	0.03242
PID effect	0.0987	0.191	0.02904	0.153	0.03339

Table 3 Performance parameters of multi-level classification

Damages	mAP	Recall	Box	Precision	Objectness
Multi-label	0.157	0.264	0.02983	0.251	0.03038

To conclude the accuracy within each class, the mean average precision of each class within the validation dataset was calculated and tabulated in Tables 2 and 3. Here, hotspot and PID effects have very negligible average precision over-classification of other damages. Each physical damage is classified separately to detect to remove the drawback. A more significant number of data (images) are required to meet the goal to obtain better results in the general classification.

All predictions that have an IoU with a target over 0.5 are considered accurate detection. And the value is divided by the total number of targets in the dataset used. MAP shows around 25 and 30% of the COCO dataset. Around 83.33% of accuracy is obtained from all the average precision.

Results are classified into single and multi-classification depending upon the damages that occurred on the solar panel. The precision and recall of the training model detect the physical cracks with utmost accuracy and minimum losses. Some results are shown in Fig. 4.

6   Conclusion and Future Work

The proposed system can be used as a real-time 'Physical damages detection system', capable of measuring the relative distance of each target. One significant conclusion is the algorithm does not perform well in the multi-label classification problem. Two different approaches are sufficient and valid to improve the result in future work. One could simplify the dataset, having only classes with distinctive features, which would enhance the learning curve and the mean average precision within the dataset. The second approach could consist of reverting the YOLOv5 change for the multi-labeling classification. A different sigmoid function can be used, and the convolutional layer can be used, and most importantly, the size of the image depends upon better accuracy.

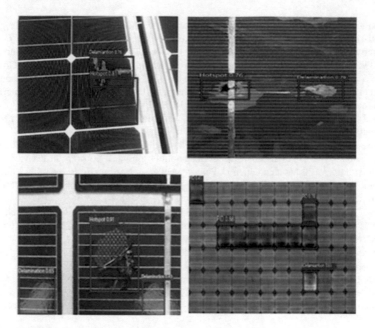

Fig. 4 High probability physical damage detection

The approach should be more prominent toward the dataset; more the data, more accurate is the detection. For example, the crack dataset has many images, so the detection results are high. Not only does the number matter but also the quality of images is essential also. If the requirement is met, better results can be achieved. The multi-level or general classification, the mixture of all data, makes it complicated to classify between the images. So, the average precision is less. So the accuracy of detection is less than of the individual result.

References

1. Mandal RK, Kale PG (2021) Assessment of different multiclass SVM strategies for fault classification in a PV system, pp 747–756. https://doi.org/10.1007/978-981-15-5955-6_70
2. Kale PG, Singh KK, Seth C (2019) Modeling effect of dust particles on performance parameters of the solar PV module. In: 5th International conference on electrical energy systems, ICEES 2019. https://doi.org/10.1109/ICEES.2019.8719298
3. Mohanty R, Sahoo MK, Kale P (2020) Estimation of partial shading and soiling percentage for a solar panel using an artificial neural network model. In: PIICON 2020—9th IEEE power India international conference. https://doi.org/10.1109/PIICON49524.2020.9112892
4. Jordan DC, Kurtz SR (2012) Photovoltaic degradation rates—an analytical review NREL/JA-5200-51664

5. Köntges M, Kurtz S, Packard C, Jahn U, Berger KA, Kato K, Friesen T, Van Iseghem M (2014) Performance and reliability of photovoltaic systems subtask 3.2: review of failures of photovoltaic modules. In: IEA PVPS task 13 external final report IEA-PVPS March 2014. ISBN: 978-3-906042-16-9. SUPSI ISAAC, TÜV Rheinland Energie und Umwelt GmbH
6. Yu CW, Chen YL, Lee KF, Chen CH, Hsiao CY (2019) efficient intelligent automatic image annotation method based on machine learning techniques. In: 2019 IEEE international conference on consumer electronics-Taiwan (ICCE-TW). IEEE, pp 1–2
7. Yao J, Qi J, Zhang J, Shao H, Yang J, Li X (2021) A real-time detection algorithm for Kiwifruit defects based on YOLOv5. Electronics 10(14):1711
8. Li S, Zhao Y, Varma R, Salpekar O, Noordhuis P, Li T, Chintala S et al. (2020) Pytorch distributed: experiences on accelerating data parallel training. arXiv preprint arXiv:2006.15704
9. Mohiyuddin A, Basharat A, Ghani U, Peter V, Abbas S, Naeem OB, Rizwan M (2022) Breast tumor detection and classification in mammogram images using modified YOLOv5 network. Comput Math Methods Med 2022
10. Toha TR, Rahaman M, Salim SI, Hossain M, Sadri AM, Al Islam AA (2021) DhakaNet: unstructured vehicle detection using limited computational resources. In: 2021 IEEE international conference on data mining (ICDM). IEEE, pp 1367–1372
11. Peng P, Liu Y, Lv X (2021) MLFF: a object detector based on a multi-layer feature fusion. In: 2021 International joint conference on neural networks (IJCNN). IEEE, pp 1–8
12. Redmon J, Farhadi A (2018) Yolov3: an incremental improvement. arXiv:1804.02767
13. Redmon J, Divvala S, Girshick R, Farhadi A (2016) You only look once: unified, real-time object detection. In: Proceedings of the IEEE conference on computer vision and pattern recognition, pp 779–788
14. Redmon J, Farhadi A (2017) Yolo9000: better, faster, stronger. In: 2017 IEEE conference on computer vision and pattern recognition (CVPR). https://doi.org/10.1109/CVPR.2017.690
15. Everingham M, Van Gool L, Williams CK, Winn J, Zisserman A (2010) The pascal visual object classes (VOC) challenge. Int J Comput Vis 88(2):303–338
16. Everingham M, Ali Eslami SM, Van Gool L, Williams CKI, Winn J, Zisserman A (2015) The pascal visual object classes challenge: a retrospective. Int J Comput Vis 111(1):98–136. https://doi.org/10.1007/s11263-014-0733-5
17. Padilla R (2019) Most popular metrics are used to evaluate object detection algorithms: Rafael Padilla/object-detection-metrics. Original-date: 2018-05-23T17:51:15Z. https://github.com/rafaelpadilla/Object-Detection-Metrics
18. Solawetz J, Nelson J (2020) How to train YOLOv5 on a custom dataset. Roboflow-https://blog.roboflow.com/

Image Processing Techniques on Porous Silicon to Estimate Porosity and Pore Size

Meenakshi Panigrahy, Shivam Maurya, and Paresh Kale

1 Introduction

Porous silicon (PS) application has sensors, electroluminescent devices, photodetection, biochemistry, medicines, and solar cells. Canham and Leigh [1] mention around 30 PS formation techniques for different pore size categories. For macroporous, mesoporous, and microporous PS formation, anodization is the most popular method used. The oldest process for preparing PS Anodization is carried out in 'anodization cells' consisting of an HF-resistant chamber mainly made up of Teflon, which contains the HF-based electrolyte with the silicon wafer and the counter electrode, mostly a platinum electrode, dipped in the solution. The type of pores formed depends on the HF concentration, the resistivity of the wafer, type of doping, current, time of etching, temperature, and illumination [2]. The pore size, porosity, and pore shape are the major PS characteristics. The pore size can vary from 1 nm to 50 μm. The classification of PS based is microporous (< 2 nm), mesoporous (2–50 nm), and macroporous (> 50 nm) in IUPAC. The pores can be of varied morphology like simple, branched, tilted, and perpendicular. Porosity is the ratio of the total volume of the pores to the total volume of the wafer [3].

Porosity dramatically affects the mechanical, electrical, optical, and thermal properties of the PS. Porosity is commonly determined by the physical processes of gravimetric analysis or gas adsorption. The gas adsorption method involves the quantitative analysis of the volume of gas adsorbed by the porous surface at low temperatures to determine the porosity of PS [4]. The gravimetric method is given by Burmhead et al. [5]. The gravimetric method of calculating the porosity uses the weight of the wafer before anodization (m_1), weight after anodization (m_2), and weight of the wafer after the dissolution (m_3) given by Eq. (1).

M. Panigrahy · S. Maurya · P. Kale (✉)
Department of Electrical Engineering, National Institute of Technology Rourkela, Rourkela, India
e-mail: pareshkale@nitrkl.ac.in

© The Author(s), under exclusive license to Springer Nature Singapore Pte Ltd. 2023　　13
K. Kumar Singh et al. (eds.), *Machine Vision and Augmented Intelligence*, Lecture Notes in Electrical Engineering 1007, https://doi.org/10.1007/978-981-99-0189-0_2

$$\%p = \frac{m_1 - m_2}{m_1 - m_3} \times 100\% \tag{1}$$

The proposed method uses image processing algorithms on scanning electron microscope (SEM) images of PS to determine the porosity and the pore size of the PS. Thus, a more straightforward process for porosity determination compared to the gravimetric analysis and gas adsorption method.

Different thresholding methods segmented the PS SEM images into porous and non-porous surfaces. The ratio of the surface area of the pores to the total surface area gave the calculated porosity value for each thresholding method. The difference between porosity values calculated by each of these methods and those determined by the gravimetric analysis method showed the effectiveness of each thresholding method. The adaptive thresholding method gave the most accurate results as the algorithm segments the image based on local threshold pixel values rather than a single global threshold pixel value. The average major axis lengths of the pores in the segmented image gave the pore size. The use of image processing enables to take into account hundreds of pores in calculating average pore size compared to the limitations of a few pores in the manual determination of average pore size.

2 Image Processing of Porous Silicon SEM Images

A scanning electron microscope (SEM) is a microscope that uses electrons rather than light to form images. Electron microscopy was widely used to investigate the structure of PS layers. Top-view images provide visual information about the geometry of the layers, while cross-section images exhibit their morphology. Digital image processing can provide additional quantitative information, such as the pore size and density, size distribution, and structural parameters. For porous silicon layers, the image shows the porous areas clearly distinguished from the substrate. IP is based on segmentation, which is the partitioning of images between the pores and the solid surface. An image consists of an array of pixels. A group of numbers, given by the imaging device, defines the characteristics of each pixel. But errors are introduced during the number allocation due to environmental conditions, object movement or imaging device movement, faulty equipment, or image compression and transmission.

2.1 Image De-noising and Filtration to Reduce Error

Noise is the additional unwanted signal in the image. Noise in the image may lead to erroneous results, which necessitate the removal of noise signals from an image. Noise in an image can be of two types; impulse noise or additive noise [5]. The impulse noise drops the original data value of the affected image pixel and replaces the pixel with a black or white pixel and is also termed as salt 'n' pepper noise or spike noise. The additive noise is evenly distributed over the frequency domain of the image and mainly consists of high-frequency components. Gaussian noise and Poisson noise are examples of additive noise [6]. Removal of noise from an image is the de-noising or image filtration process. Filtration can be of two types, linear filtration and nonlinear filtration. Linear filters apply the de-noising function on all the image pixels irrespective of corrupted or not. The linear filter removes discontinuities in an image and blurs the edges. The nonlinear filter is better at preserving the edges that act on the noisy pixels than on all the images' pixels. The various types of filters remove different types of noise. Linear filtration methods mean and median filters remove the impulse noise. The Gaussian filter eliminates the noise following the Gaussian curve, like the Gaussian and Poisson noise.

2.2 Morphological Operations of Images

Morphological operations use the structuring element (SE) to probe the image. A structuring element is a small template of a given shape and a defined origin deciding the size and shape of the neighborhood of the target pixel. The target pixel value is tweaked according to its neighborhood pixel values during a morphological operation. The two basic types of morphological operations are erosion and dilation. Erosion is the process of eroding or shrinking the foreground elements. Dilation is the opposite of the erosion process and dilates or expands the foreground elements. The erosion and dilation operations performed sequentially do the morphological opening operation, which removes the unwanted foreground elements in the image. The reverse, first dilation and then erosion, gives the morphological closing. The closing operation eliminates the light-colored elements within the foreground components of image [7].

2.3 Image Thresholding

The SEM images are in three-channel RGB format, which is first converted to a single-channel grayscale image. A grayscale image has every pixel value within 0–255, where zero-pixel value denotes black, and 255 denotes white. After obtaining a grayscale image, an automatic thresholding method binarizes the image. Thresholding or binarization is the process of separating the foreground of an image from the background. Figure 1 shows the binarized SEM image with pores as black in the foreground and white background. The process involves selecting a threshold pixel value and then assigning the values of 0 or 1 to all other pixels in the image depending on if they are less than or more than the selected threshold value, respectively. Thresholding techniques are broadly grouped as global and local thresholding. Global thresholding techniques select one threshold value for the entire image and are

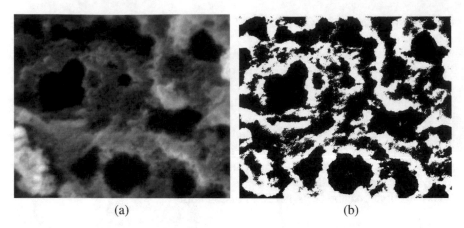

(a)   (b)

Fig. 1 **a** Top-view SEM image of porous silicon, **b** separation of foreground pores from the wafer surface by image thresholding

most efficient for cases where there is one prominent peak in the gray level histogram of the image. On the other hand, local thresholding techniques determine threshold values for each pixel based upon the properties of the neighboring pixels. These are most efficient when there are distinct local peaks in the gray level histogram.

Mean thresholding is the simplest thresholding method and uses the mean pixel value as the global threshold. Otsu devised a discriminant analysis method to determine the threshold, minimize the within-class variance, and maximize the between-class variance [8] of the foreground and background pixels. The iterative self-organizing data analysis techniques algorithm (ISODATA) uses the mean of the average grayscale values of the background and the foreground classes to find the threshold value for every iteration [9]. The process repeats till there is no change in the binary output image of the next iteration. In the minimum cross-entropy global thresholding method [10], the threshold value minimizes the cross-entropy between the background and foreground classes. In the above-mentioned global thresholding methods, the threshold value was constant for the entire image. The process is unable to account for the changes in illumination [11] across the image. Local adaptive thresholding overcomes the change in illumination ten across the image as the threshold value for a pixel is set depending upon its neighborhood pixel values. In PS SEM images, a pixel darker than or lighter than the neighboring pixels is set as a black pore pixel or a white background pixel, respectively. The formed microstructural pore distribution is uneven with a size range of 12–27 nm because of uneven current distribution and irregular resistivity [12]. The adaptive thresholding method was more promising than the global thresholding methods in PS image segmentation. The ratio of the number of black pixels in the threshold image to the total number of pixels in the image gave the porosity.

3 Parameter Selection for Noise Filtration and Closing Operation

The image de-noising and morphological operations removed the unwanted components of the images and reduced the errors in the results. The images were first subjected to median filtering to remove any impulse noise if present, Gaussian filtering to remove any noise following the Gaussian curve, closing operation to close the small white elements present within the pores of the SEM image of the PS surface. The structuring elements for the median filter and the closing operation and the sigma value for the Gaussian filter are the different parameters used in the entire operation. These three parameters were varied, keeping the other two constants and the porosity variation plotted for each case.

For sigma varying from 0.25 to 5 for Gaussian filter applied on the PS SEM images to remove noise, the porosity value increased steadily for PS image sample numbers 01_001, 01_002, and 01_127. It decreased steadily for another set of PS samples 01_049 and 01_047, Fig. 2. The change in porosity values calculated from sigma value 0.25 to sigma value 5 is 1.60%, 4.31%, 1.03%, 22.66%, and 25.87%, respectively, for PS image samples 01_001, 01_002, 01_127, 01_047, and 01_049. The change for calculated porosity for variation of sigma from 0.25 to 5 was thus maximum for PS images with ~ 33% porosity and was minimum for PS images of ~ 60% porosity. The calculated porosity values for all the image samples were close to the values determined by gravimetric analysis for sigma value 0.5, keeping SE sizes for median and closing operations constant.

The variation of calculated porosity with the change in the size of the SE for the median filter was plotted against different square SE sizes keeping sigma and size of SE for closing operation constant. Figure 3 showed a repeating trend. The porosity

Fig. 2 Porosity calculated by varying sigma; keeping structuring element for closing and median filtering as 2 * 2 square

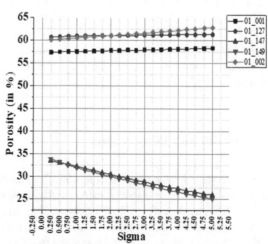

Porosity values by Gravimetric Analysis:
01_001: 59.9537; 01_002: 59.9537; 01_127: 61.03679; 01_047: 32.84314; 01_049: 32.84314

Fig. 3 Porosity calculated by varying size of structuring element for median filter; keeping sigma as 0.5 and structuring element for closing operation as 2 * 2 square

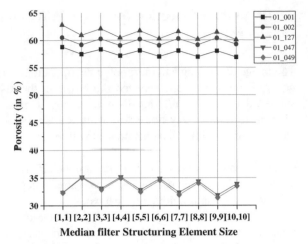

Porosity Calculated by Gravimetric Analysis:
01_001: 59.9537; 01_002: 59.9537; 01_127: 61.03679; 01_047: 32.84314; 01_049: 32.84314

values calculated were similar for SE with an even and odd number of pixels. The change in porosity value in adjacent SE size was in the range of 2–5% for 01_001, 01_002, and 01_127 sample images and around 5–10% for 01_049 and 01_047 sample images.

Figure 4 shows the change in the calculated porosity value by varying SE's size for closing operation, keeping the sigma value for Gaussian filtration constant at 0.5 and SE size for median filter consistent at 2 * 2 square. The porosity calculated value remained almost the same for PS sample images 01_001, 01_002, and 01_127, which have porosity values in the range of 55–65% for increasing the size of the SE from (1 * 1) to (10 * 10). The change in value is 2–5% from (1 * 1) SE to (10 * 10) SE. But for PS samples 01_049 and 01_047, the overall change in value was 5–10%. The observed pattern may be due to smaller pores as dark patches in images 01_047 and 01_049, getting closed by the increase in the size of SE. The declination in calculated porosity may be due to the closing of smaller pores with the increase in the size of SE.

4 Results and Discussions

Figures 2, 3 and 4 show the variation of SE size for closing operation, and sigma value for Gaussian filter has a more profound effect on the calculated porosity value for PS image samples with 30–40% porosity. The image samples with higher porosity values at 60–70% showed lesser variation. Also, the graphs confirmed lesser variation in the porosity values calculated by image processing and gravimetric analysis with a sigma value as 0.5 for Gaussian filtration and SE size as 2 * 2 square element for both median filtration and closing operation forming a chain of connectivity.

Fig. 4 Porosity calculation by varying size of structuring element for closing operation; keeping sigma for Gaussian filter as 0.5 and size of structuring element for the median filter as 2 * 2 square

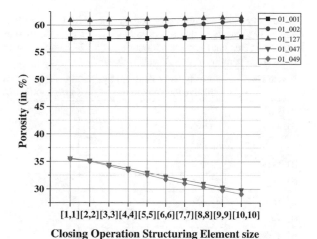

Closing Operation Structuring Element size

Porosity Calculated by Gravimetric Analysis:

01_001: 59.9537; 01_002: 59.9537; 01_127: 61.03679; 01_047: 32.84314; 01_049: : 32.84314

Table 1 shows the porosity values calculated using the above parameters. The average pore size of PS from SEM images is manually done by directly measuring each image for a few pores and finding the mean values. Automation of the measurement process gives a more accurate measurement of the pore diameters by considering more pores of PS SEM images clicked under different resolutions. Thus, the average calculated is closer to the actual pore size. The segmented binary image of a PS substrate may have hundreds of pores on the image surface. Pores make the black objects of the binary image, and the non-porous white part makes the background. The number of connected components in the thresholded image gives the number of pores in the image surface. The connected pixels in a binary image are pixels in each other's neighborhoods, forming a chain of connectivity.

The average of the sizes of the determining connected components of an image should give the average pore size of the PS. Each image has hundreds of pores on its surface, ranging from very small to large ones detected as the connected components. The main focus is measuring the maximum distance between two points of the most significant related members representing the pores of interest. The 'MajorAxisLength' attribute of the 'Regionprops' function in MATLAB gave the maximum lengths of the connected components. The program returns the table of the maximum lengths of all the objects as pixels. The average size of a certain number of the most prominent pores multiplied with the calibration factor gave pore size in nano-meters or micro-meters.

To determine the number of the most prominent pores of an image should be considered to estimate the average pore size accurately. The average pore size calculations were plotted against the most prominent pores taken to find the average for different magnifications of the same PS sample. In Fig. 5, the average pore size was calculated for PS formed from a 0.01 to 0.02 mho resistivity wafer. It was done under anodization conditions of 2:8 HF and ethanol ratio for 20 min. As the pores on the

Table 1 Porosity calculated for porous silicon SEM images using local adaptive image thresh-olding. The pre-processing image parameters are set as; Gaussian filter sigma value as 0.5, size of structuring element for median filtration as (2 * 2) square element, and size of structuring element for closing operation as (2 * 2) square element

Image No.	Porosity (%) calculated by adaptive thresholding	Porosity (%) calculated by gravimetric method	Error (%)
01_001	57.7738	59.9537	3.64
01_002	59.7809		0.288
01_003	66.6882		11.23
01_005	52.4045		12.59
01_045	32.5657	32.84314	0.844
01_046	27.7617		15.47
01_047	32.6953		0.450
01_048	21.2775		35.21
01_049	32.6324		0.641
01_050	28.9610		11.82
01_127	61.6801	61.03679	1.05
01_130	67.1814		10.07
01_132	58.9198		3.47
01_134	58.8657		3.56
01_135	68.5338		12.28

SEM image decreased with increased magnification, fewer pores were averaged for higher magnification images. Averaging 90, 190, and 300 pores for embellishments 200, 100, and 50 K gave the correct results for pore size. The average pore sizes calculated for SEM images of various magnifications of PS prepared under different etching conditions, and resistivity is given in Table 2. The percentage deviation of the calculated values from the manually calculated values was less than ~ 5% and thus is in the acceptable range.

5   Conclusion

Adaptive thresholding on porous silicon SEM images proved to be the most effi-cient method for image segmentation. The ratio of the surface area of the pores to the total surface area in the segmented images gave the porosity. The image pre-processing steps included image de-noising by median and Gaussian filtering and closing morphological operation. The sigma value was fixed at 0.5 for Gaussian filtration and structuring element size as 2 * 2 square elements for median filtration and closing operation. The difference between the calculated porosity and porosity by gravimetric analysis gave the error within the acceptable range of around ~ 5%.

Fig. 5 Calculated pore sizes for SEM images of same porous silicon sample taken under three different magnifications by varying the number of pores averaged

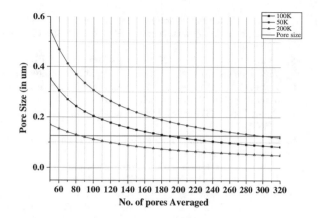

Table 2 Calculated average pore values for different SEM images of porous silicon prepared under various anodization conditions and the error percentage with the actual value

Preparation conditions	Magnification of image (10^3)	Actual pore size (μm)	Calculated avg. pore size (μm)	Error (%)
0.01–0.02Ω cm HF:EtOH = 2:8	50	0.126	0.1258	0.16
	100	0.126	0.1249	0.87
	200	0.126	0.1212	3.80
0.01–0.02Ω cm HF:EtOH = 3:7	25	0.130	0.1356	4.31
	50	0.130	0.1313	1.00
0.01–0.02Ω cm HF:EtOH = 3:7	50	0.041	0.0420	2.38
	100	0.043	0.0420	2.34

Then, the region properties of the connected components of the segmented image gave the major axis lengths of the pores. The mean of a certain number of most prominent pores for each magnification gave the average pore size.

References

1. Canham L (2014) Handbook of porous silicon, pp 1–1017. https://doi.org/10.1007/978-3-319-05744-6
2. Sahoo MK, Kale P (2019) Restructured porous silicon for solar photovoltaic: a review. Microporous Mesoporous Mater 289. https://doi.org/10.1016/j.micromeso.2019.109619
3. Kale P, Gangal AC, Edla R, Sharma P (2012) Investigation of hydrogen storage behavior of silicon nanoparticles. Int J Hydrogen Energy 37(4):3741–3747. https://doi.org/10.1016/j.ijhydene.2011.04.054

4. Bomchil G, Herino R, Barla K, Pfister JC, Soc JE (1983) Pore size distribution in porous silicon studied by adsorption isotherms. J Electrochem Soc 130:1611–1614. https://doi.org/10.1149/1.2120044
5. Brumhead D, Canham LT, Seekings DM, Tufton PJ (1993) Gravimetric analysis of pore nucleation and propagation in anodised silicon. Electrochim Acta 38(2–3):191–197
6. Joshua O, Ibiyemi T, Adu B (2019) A comprehensive review on various types of noise in image processing. Int J Sci Eng Res 10:388–393
7. Davies ER (2018) Image filtering and morphology. https://doi.org/10.1016/b978-0-12-809284-2.00003-4
8. Otsu N (1979) A threshold selection method from gray-level histograms. IEEE Trans Syst Man Cybern 9(1):62–66
9. Ridler TW, Calvard S (1978) Picture thresholding using an iterative selection method. IEEE Trans Syst Man Cybern SMC-8 630–632. https://doi.org/10.1109/tsmc.1978.4310039
10. Li CH, Lee CK (1993) Minimum cross entropy thresholding. Pattern Recogn 26(4):617–625
11. Bradley D, Roth G (2007) Adaptive thresholding using the Integral Image. J Graph Tools 12:13–21. https://doi.org/10.1080/2151237x.2007.10129236
12. Kale PG, Solanki CS (2010) Synthesis of si nanoparticles from freestanding porous silicon (ps) film using ultrasonication. In: Conference record of the IEEE photovoltaic specialists conference, pp 3692–3697. https://doi.org/10.1109/PVSC.2010.5617016

Solar PV System Fault Classification Using Machine Learning Techniques

Chisola Nyala, Vinayaka K. Hiremath, and Paresh Kale

1 Introduction

The world's energy crisis can be successfully vanquished by photovoltaic (PV) systems. [1]. As a renewable energy source, the solar industry is rising in popularity because of the maturity in the existing non-renewable energy sources. However, because of the outdoor installation of PV system, it is not economical due to the high capital and maintenance costs [2]. In addition to the cost, installing PV system outdoor results in hotspots, power losses, and complications during fire outbreaks leading to the breakdown of the entire plant.

Compared to conventional energy conversion systems, PV system delivers considerable advantages. The PV system also has the option of secure expansion of the plant, based on the increase in demand [3]. Apart from the high initial capital cost for setting up a PV power system plant, there is no other machinery cost such as transformer, generator, and transmission line. Therefore, the expansion of the solar PV industry has risen exponentially in India since 2010. Majorly, the solar power is expected to fulfill the total electricity demand by 2030 [4].

The PV system faults may propagate within the PV modules and cause a complete failure of the PV array in an unmonitored system [5]. Therefore, fault classification along with monitoring of the PV system is highly essential. The fault detection methods for the PV system are classified in various ways [6], such as (i) visual analysis, (ii) thermal analysis, and (iii) electrical fault analysis. Electrical fault analysis is more effective and promising because of efficient monitoring and diagnostics. Here, the single diode model is used for solar cell modeling, which works on no recombination at the junction region [7].

C. Nyala · V. K. Hiremath · P. Kale (✉)
Department of Electrical Engineering, National Institute of Technology Rourkela, Rourkela, Odisha 769008, India
e-mail: pareshkale@nitrkl.ac.in

© The Author(s), under exclusive license to Springer Nature Singapore Pte Ltd. 2023
K. Kumar Singh et al. (eds.), *Machine Vision and Augmented Intelligence*, Lecture Notes in Electrical Engineering 1007, https://doi.org/10.1007/978-981-99-0189-0_3

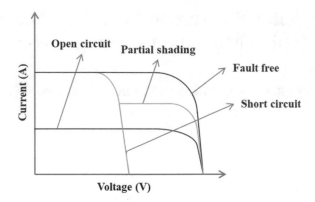

Machine learning techniques are widely being exploited virtually by every sector due to the self-learning attribute by supervised and unsupervised learning techniques. Because of the complexity in applications involving highly nonlinear relations like finding the influence of different factors on the generation of PV systems, conventional computations are tedious. Still, they can be easily solved using machine learning techniques [8]. For the prediction and classification of faults, several machine learning techniques have been used, such as decision tree [9], support vector machines (SVMs) [10], and multiclass SVM strategies [11] aided with preprocessing of data by principal component analysis (PCA).

The PV system faults can be classified into two types, i.e., reversible and irreversible faults. Mechanical stress (due to module aging) or electrical stress (e.g., open circuit, short circuits) is responsible for irreversible faults. The reversible or temporary faults are due to structures or cloud shadows. Figure 1 gives a brief description of common faults in the PV system. The PV system faults change the I-V characteristic [12], as shown in Fig. 1. A short circuit fault occurs due to reduced open-circuit voltage. The mismatch and the open-circuit faults produce similar characteristics with an inflection point but different I-V curve parameters [13].

The occurrence of faults decreases the efficiency of PV systems leading to severe damage to property and human life. To prevent such destruction, the location and classification of the faults are highly essential. The paper introduces a new method to analyze the plant faults based on the I-V curve analysis. The model identifies the types of fault based on the monitored plant parameters. Once the model gives an alarm for a potential fault, a diagnostic process begins for quick troubleshooting. In the diagnostic process, a controller can acquire the I-V curve of the whole array and compare it with the standard short circuit current (I_{sc}) and open voltage (V_{oc}). Figure 2 presents the general methodology for the work.

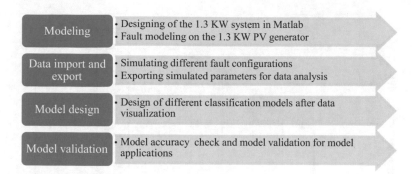

Fig. 2 Work methodology of detecting and classifying the fault

2 Simulation of the 1.3 KW PV-System for Synthetic Data Generation

The initial process of the model design is data generation. Actual weather conditions are incorporated based on the locality to capture the 1.3 kW (average household demand) PV system's characteristics. For simulation, the research includes Rourkela, India, weather conditions [14], as shown in Fig. 3. The first step is to identify the sunrise and sunset hour to consider only the power plant's generation period. In the winter of 2019 in Rourkela, the sunrise and the sunset occurred at 7 am and 4 pm, respectively. Average measurements may not precisely provide the plant's actual behavior but give an overall behavior. The measurements consist of two months' data that offer the average irradiance level corresponding to the time and temperatures of the day. The irradiance is minimum during morning time and maximum at noontime.

As recorded from the location, the irradiance and temperature are varied for simulation of all fault configurations [15]. All the possible configurations of the faults within the plant are simulated. Table 1 shows the different fault configurations introduced in the plant for data generation. Eight different fault conditions consisting of OP, LG, LL, and shading have been considered. Previously established predictive models using simplified model (SFM) and further simplified model (FSFM) [16], and radial basis neural network [17] designed to predict the energy output of PV systems can be integrated as a reference for more precise outcomes.

Based on a single diode model, the proposed model (Fig. 4) was implemented in MATLAB using the inbuilt solar module by '1-Soltech' (simulation in the Sims-cape toolbox), which offered a flexible interface for modeling numerical and electrical systems [18]. The 1.3 kW power generating unit comprises two strings with three modules in series in each string. Each module generates an optimum current of 7.47 A at an optimum voltage of 29.3 V. Table 2 gives all the module parameters associated with the PV panel. A variable DC source was used as the load that consumed the PV system's generated energy. Blocking diodes and bypass diodes were used to improve panel utilization by reducing the shading effect and preventing hotspots (Fig. 4).

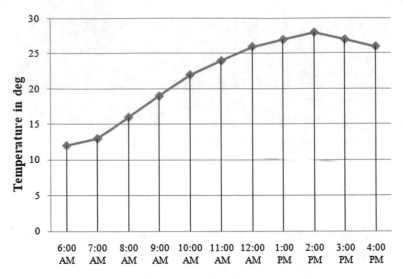

Fig. 3 Measured average temperatures in Rourkela during the winter of 2019

Table 1 Different fault conditions considered for the study and their respective code and count

Type of fault	Code	Count
Open circuit	OP	11
Lower line to ground	LLG	11
Upper line to ground	ULG	11
Low voltage difference line to line	LLL	11
High voltage difference line to line	HLL	11
20% shading	S20	11
30% shading	S30	11
50% shading	S50	11

Table 2 Specifications of the module (manufactured by 1-Soltech)

Parameter	Value
V_{oc}	36.6 V
I_{sc}	7.79 A
Maximum voltage (V_{mp})	29.3 V
Current (I_{mp})	7.47 A
Solar PV efficiency	14%
System voltage	600 V

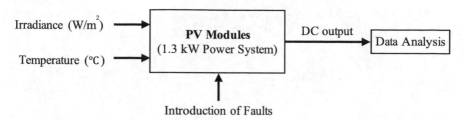

Fig. 4 Schematic for a design flow of data analysis using temperature and irradiance as variables

A successful fault classification in a PV system is essential for reliability in power production. Any fault configuration results in a shift from the power plant's optimal operating point, reducing the plant capacity, and potentially causing a total power system breakdown. Fast identification and isolation of the fault [19] to ensure satisfactory customer service depends on identifying the exact type of fault with great accuracy. The simulated results of a healthy and faulty plant are discussed in the following sections.

2.1 Healthy Condition

The power capacity during the regular operation of the '1-Soltech' solar plant is 1.3 kW, as shown in Fig. 5; the generation resides around the capacity during good sunshine hours. The standard operating voltage generation is 87.8 V for efficient panel utilization of the plant. A fault in the power system results in a shift from the optimum operation point that reduces the plant capacity and underutilizes the solar panels.

2.2 Shading Faults

The shading effect on the PV system generation depends on the shading percentage on the panels. Shading occurs when structures like trees and buildings hinder radiation from reaching the surface of the panels. Shading also occurs due to cloudy weather conditions [20]. The shading effect shifts the PV system operating point and affects the efficiency of the plant. Figure 6 shows the simulation results for 30% shading on the plant, for which the capacity reduces to 435.98 W.

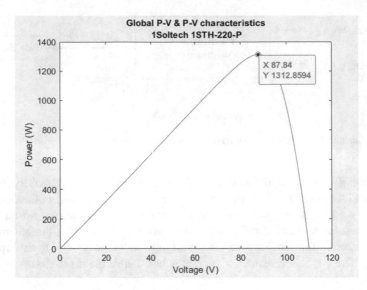

Fig. 5 Simulation of a healthy 1.3 kW PV power system

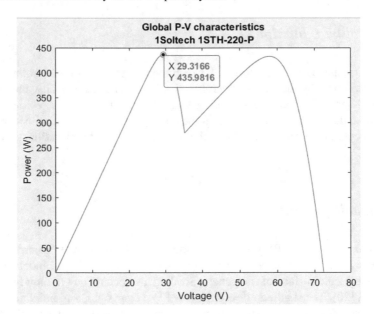

Fig. 6 Simulation of 1.3 kW PV power plant with 30% shading

2.3 Line-To-Line Fault

The line-to-line faults result in an additional current path away from the load. The additional current path shifts the operating point of the PV system, causing under-utilization [21]. The line faults heat the insulations attached to the conductors, which damages the insulation. All line-to-line faults simulated on the 1.3 kW system resulted in reduced plant capacity, i.e., 914 W, as shown in Fig. 7. The line-to-line faults are less frequent than the line-to-ground faults resulting in a significant loss in the plant capacity. In the same manner, the other faults are simulated for data visualization and model design. The generated data represent the plant's system behavior, and the model learns the behavior to predict future fault instances.

3 Machine Learning Techniques

The PV system is simulated under different fault configurations to capture the system characteristics. The generated data are exported to design an intelligent model for predicting fault conditions in the PV system using a decision tree, ANN, support vector machine, and random forest algorithm. The accuracy of each model depends on the data; hence, data visualization is an essential part of the design process to ensure the best algorithm for that particular dataset is selected. The learning process ensures that the model explores the data and captures hidden patterns and characteristics.

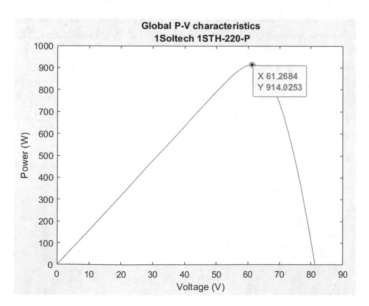

Fig. 7 Simulation of the 1.3 kW PV power system for a line-to-line fault

Fig. 8 Sequential steps of proposed model design

The design is dependent on an extensive database accumulating data for various conditions for versatility [12]. The classification process involves splitting the data frame into the target element versus the rest (mapping between the target and the selected feature). In general, 80% of the data is used for training, and 20% is used for testing the trained model to predict the fault type correctly [13] occurring in the system by quick troubleshooting. The design needs to be validated to cut down the power outages. Figure 8 shows the sequential steps for implementing the process using anaconda's Jupyter notebook.

The highly correlated features suggest dropping to improve the model's ability to retain accuracy. Table 3 gives the correlation data, and the highest correlation is 0.844 between temperature and irradiance, confirming a strong relationship between the two parameters. A correlation value of 0.733 asserts the dependency of current on irradiance. In situations where the database is enormous, feature engineering [22] involves dropping off the highly correlated features as they indicate almost the same information about the system. Temperature and voltage show a negative correlation indicating inverse relation, i.e., a temperature rise reduces the cell voltage however increases the generated current. Both voltage and current show a high correlation with the maximum power (P_{max}). The correlation between voltage and P_{max} is 0.726, and that between current and P_{max} is 0.671. The correlation between different features is essential for feature engineering to reduce redundancy in the data. Feature engineering reduces the overfitting of the model, improving model performance.

Table 3 Feature correlation of various PV system parameters

	Irradiance (W/m^2)	Temperature (°C)	I_{mp} (A)	V_{mp} (V)	P_{max} (W)
Irradiance (W/m^2)	1	0.844	0.733	− 0.032	0.408
Temperature (°C)	0.844	1	0.621	− 0.040	0.340
I_{mp} (A)	0.733	0.621	1	− 0.084	0.671
V_{mp} (V)	− 0.032	− 0.040	− 0.084	1	0.721
P_{max} (W)	0.408	0.340	0.671	0.726	1

3.1 Accuracy Check and Results

After designing the models, the best fit model is selected by checking the accuracy using the accuracy score command. The accuracy score validates the performance of the design and determines the model's excellency. The exact process is repeated further for feature engineering and analysis.

Confusion matrix, $CM(i, j)$, also referred to as error matrix, checks the accuracy score. The confusion matrix uses a table to describe the efficiency of a model based on data with known outcomes. Table 4 shows a typical confusion matrix of a binary classifier, clarifying the errors that a particular model makes, representing the classifier's efficiency in the prediction process.

The diagonal and the off-diagonal elements indicate the correctly predicted parameters and the misclassified classes, respectively. The elements i and j of n_{ij} in Eq. (1) indicate the row and the column number and show the cases of class i identified as class j. The total cases 'N' is given by (1).

$$N = \left(\sum_{i=0}^{M} \right) \sum_{j=0}^{M} n_{ij} \tag{1}$$

In various applications, the normalization of the confusion matrix is helpful for quick analysis and understanding of data. As given in Eq. (2), normalization is calculated by dividing each element of $CM(i, j)$ by the total number of samples in the dataset.

$$CM_n(i, j) = \frac{CM(i, j)}{\left(\sum_{m=1}^{N_c} \right) \sum_{n=1}^{N_c} CM(m, n)} \tag{2}$$

The class-specific measure, which describes how well the classification algorithm performs on each class, includes recall ($R_e(i)$), precision ($P_e(i)$), and accuracy ($Acc(i)$). These measures are defined in Eqs. (3–5) and are critical in the model design analysis to validate the designed model performance, where $\sum_{m=1}^{N_c} CM(i, j)$ represents the total number of samples belonging to class i. If the confusion matrix is row-wise normalized, then $\sum_{m=1}^{N_c} CM(i, m) = 1$ giving $R_e(i) = CM(i, i)$, implying that the diagonal elements of the matrix are the recall values. Precision is a fraction of correctly classified samples in class i for all the samples in the class. Precision measures accuracy on a class basis and is defined by in Eq. (3). The recall is the proportion of data with true class labels i that were correctly assigned to class i and is represented in Eq. (4).

Table 4 Binary classifier confusion matrix

	Predicted class 1	Predicted class 0
Actual class 1	True positive	False negative
Actual class 0	False positive	True negative

$$P_e(i) = \frac{CM(i, i)}{\sum_{m=1}^{N_c} CM(m, i)} \tag{3}$$

$$R_e(i) = \frac{CM(i, i)}{\sum_{m=1}^{N_c} CM(i, m)} \tag{4}$$

$$Acc = \frac{\sum_{m=1}^{N_c} CM(m, m)}{\left(\sum_{m=1}^{N_c}\right) \sum_{n=1}^{N_c} CM(m, n)} \tag{5}$$

3.2 Prediction Results

The dataset of 1062 data points is split, with 80% of the training data and around 20% for testing. Using the test data, performance of the model is validated. The obtained confusion matrix using the decision tree (DT) algorithm is shown in Table 5. Equation 5 calculates the accuracy for the four algorithms, and the highest score is selected. Data from the other three algorithms' confusion matrices are reported in Table 6, with Table 5 showing the detailed confusion matrix for the DT since it gives the highest score. Using Eq. (5) for the obtained matrix, the summation of the diagonal elements is 31 indicating the correctly predicted classes, and the prediction count is equal to 36. The obtained accuracy score (Acc) is 0.8611 (Table 7).

Similarly, Table 4 accumulates all the accuracy of the other classifiers. Equation 5 also calculates the accuracy score of each classifier, as given in Table 7.

Table 5 Obtained confusion matrix from decision tree algorithm

4	0	0	0	0	0	0	0	0	0	0	0	0	0	0
0	2	0	0	0	0	0	0	0	0	0	0	0	0	0
0	0	2	0	0	0	0	0	0	0	0	0	0	0	0
0	0	0	4	0	0	0	0	0	0	0	0	0	0	0
0	0	0	0	4	0	0	0	0	0	0	0	0	0	0
0	0	0	0	0	0	0	0	0	0	0	0	0	0	0
0	0	0	0	0	0	3	0	0	0	0	0	0	0	0
0	0	0	0	0	0	0	1	0	0	0	0	0	0	0
0	0	0	0	0	0	0	0	3	0	0	0	0	0	0
0	0	0	0	0	0	0	0	0	1	0	0	0	0	0
0	0	0	0	0	0	0	0	0	0	1	0	0	0	0
0	0	0	0	0	0	0	0	0	0	0	5	0	0	0
0	0	0	0	0	0	0	0	0	0	0	0	0	0	0
0	0	0	0	0	0	0	0	0	0	0	0	0	0	0
0	0	0	0	0	0	0	0	0	0	0	0	0	0	1

Table 6 Data obtained from the confusion matrix of random forest, ANN, and SVM algorithm

Element	Random forest	ANN	SVM
Non-zero diagonals	[2,2,3,4]	[2,2,4,1,5]	[2,2,4,1,1,1,1,1,5,1]
Non-zero off-diagonals	[1,2,2,3,1,1,1,1,1,3,1, 2,3,1,1,1]	[1,1,2,1,1,2,2,3,2,3, 1,1,1,1]	[2,3,3,1,2,2,4]

Table 7 Performance table of the four classifiers

Parameter	DT	Random forest	ANN	SVM
$\sum_{m-1}^{N_c} CM(m,m)$	31	11	14	19
$\sum_{m=1}^{N_c} CM(m,i)$	5	25	22	17
$\left(\sum_{m=1}^{N_c}\right)\sum_{n=1}^{N_c} CM(m,n)$	36	36	36	36
$\dfrac{\sum_{m=1}^{N_c} CM(m,m)}{\left(\sum_{m=1}^{N_c}\right)\sum_{n=1}^{N_c} CM(m,n)}$	0.8611	0.3056	0.388	0.5277

Table 8 Modelwise summary of classifier performance

Model	Testing accuracy (%)
Decision tree	86
Random forest	31
ANN	38
Support vector machine	53

Table 8 shows the summary of the performance by each classifier used for the classification process, with the decision tree giving the highest score of 86%, which is good enough for model designing.

4 Conclusion

The main contribution is an automatic fault detection and location method to replace the traditional manual methods. The challenge is to collect all the possible fault configurations for capturing the entire system behavior. Hence, the model may not effectively classify instances that may represent fault conditions previously untrained during model training, which is the biggest throwback of using synthetic data rather than real-time data from a plant collected over the years. The method applies to both small-scale and large-scale PV systems.

References

1. Luque A, Hegedus S (2010) Handbook of photovoltaic science and engineering. Wiley, Chichester
2. Reichelstein S, Yorston M (2013) The prospects for cost-competitive solar PV power. Energy Policy 55:117–127. https://doi.org/10.1016/j.enpol.2012.11.003
3. Mandal R, Panja S (2016) Design and feasibility studies of a small scale grid connected solar PV power plant. Energy Procedia 90:191–199. https://doi.org/10.1016/j.egypro.2016.11.185
4. Africa-EU Renewable Energy Cooperation Programme (RECP) (2017) Global market outlook—for solar power/2017–2021
5. Sabbaghpur Arani M, Hejazi MA (2016) The comprehensive study of electrical faults in PV arrays. J Electr Comput Eng 2016:1–10. https://doi.org/10.1155/2016/8712960
6. Mellit A, Tina GM, Kalogirou SA (2018) Fault detection and diagnosis methods for photovoltaic systems: a review. Renew Sustain Energy Rev 91:1–17. https://doi.org/10.1016/j.rser.2018.03.062
7. Ghani F, Rosengarten G, Duke M, Carson JK (2014) The numerical calculation of single-diode solar-cell modelling parameters. Renew Energy 72:105–112. https://doi.org/10.1016/j.renene.2014.06.035
8. Mohanty R, Kale PG (2021) Influence of wind speed on solar pv plant power production—prediction model using decision-based artificial neural network. Adv Intell Syst Comput 1086:3–16. https://doi.org/10.1007/978-981-15-1275-9_1
9. Zhao Y, Yang L, Lehman B, De Palma JF, Mosesian J, Lyons R (2012) Decision tree-based fault detection and classification in solar photovoltaic arrays. In: Conference proceedings—IEEE applied power electronics conference and exposition—APEC, pp 93–99. https://doi.org/10.1109/APEC.2012.6165803
10. Mandal RK, Anand N, Sahu N, Kale P (2020) PV system fault classification using SVM accelerated by dimension reduction using PCA. In: PIICON 2020—9th IEEE power India international conference, pp 3–8. https://doi.org/10.1109/PIICON49524.2020.9112896
11. Mandal RK, Kale PG (2021) Assessment of different multiclass SVM strategies for fault classification in a PV system, pp 747–756. https://doi.org/10.1007/978-981-15-5955-6_70
12. Russell S, Norvig P (2010) Artificial intelligence: a modern approach, 3rd edn
13. Petrone G, Ramos-Paja CA (2011) Modeling of photovoltaic fields in mismatched conditions for energy yield evaluations. Electr Power Syst Res 81(4):1003–1013. https://doi.org/10.1016/j.epsr.2010.12.008
14. The weather channel, Bondamunda, Odisha (2020). Retrieved from https://weather.com/
15. Nieto Vallejo AE, Ruiz F, Patiño D (2019) Characterization of electric faults in photovoltaic array systems. DYNA. 86(211):54–63. https://doi.org/10.15446/dyna.v86n211.79085
16. Tarai RK, Kale P (2016) Validation of predictive models to estimate annual PV production: a case study of Odisha. Int J Smart Grid Clean Energy 160–167. https://doi.org/10.12720/sgce.5.3.160-167
17. Mandal RK, Kale P (2018) Development of a decision-based neural network for a day-ahead prediction of solar PV plant power output. In: International conference on computational intelligence and communication technology, CICT 2018, pp 1–6. https://doi.org/10.1109/CIACT.2018.8480396
18. Ding K, Bian X, Liu H, Peng T (2012) A MATLAB-simulink-based PV module model and its application under conditions of nonuniform irradiance. IEEE Trans Energy Convers 27(4):864–872. https://doi.org/10.1109/TEC.2012.2216529
19. Zhao Y (2010) Fault analysis in solar photovoltaic arrays. Northeastern University
20. Massi Pavan A, Tessarolo A, Barbini N, Mellit A, Lughi V (2015) The effect of manufacturing mismatch on energy production for large-scale photovoltaic plants. Sol Energy 117:282–289. https://doi.org/10.1016/j.solener.2015.05.003

21. Yi Z, Etemadi AH (2016) A novel detection algorithm for line-to-line faults in photovoltaic (PV) arrays based on support vector machine (SVM). In: 2016 IEEE Power and energy society general meeting (PESGM), pp 1–4. https://doi.org/10.1109/PESGM.2016.7742026
22. Witten IH, Frank E, Hall MA, Pal CJ (2011) Data mining: practical machine learning tools and techniques. Elsevier

A Lightweight Network for Detecting Pedestrians in Hazy Weather

Balaram Murthy Chintakindi and Farukh Hashmi Mohammad

1 Introduction

The World Health Organization (WHO) updates the statistics of injured people in traffic accidents every year. As per the WHO statistics in 2018, an annual road traffic death was 1.35 million [1], of which 50% of the traffic road accidents were pedestrians and cyclists. Though some of the safest roads in the world are in nations of the European Union, every year more than 25,000 [2] people lose their lives.

The major cause of traffic road accidents is bad weather condition. Various environmental factors such as rain, fog and snow affect visibility and act on driver psychology, which are increasing traffic road accident rate. So, there is a need to detect pedestrians effectively in adverse weather conditions which would improve driver safety in both semi-autonomous and autonomous vehicles.

Over two decades, tremendous growth and success have been achieved in pedestrian detection area, using both traditional machine learning [3–6] and deep learning-based methods [7]. Generally, pedestrian detection models are classified into two types: one-stage detectors and two-stage detectors. Although two-stage detectors [7] achieve higher detection accuracy, they are typically slower, while one-stage detectors [8–12] might lose detection accuracy, but they are much faster compared to two-stage detectors.

However, most of the existing pedestrian detection models have been trained and tested only in clear-day conditions. Therefore, these models fail to detect pedestrians effectively in hazy weather conditions. In general, the number of traffic road accidents in hazy weather is higher compared to the number of traffic road accidents in clear

B. M. Chintakindi (✉) · F. H. Mohammad
Department of Electronics and Communication Engineering, National Institute of Technology, Warangal, Telangana 506004, India
e-mail: balu1602@student.nitw.ac.in

F. H. Mohammad
e-mail: mdfarukh@nitw.ac.in

weather. Commonly, denser haze increases the accident rate. So, it is particularly challenging to detect pedestrians effectively in hazy weather because of blurred appearance of pedestrians, sandstorm, undesirable color cast and degraded visibility which make it very difficult to distinguish pedestrians from the complex background.

A dehazing algorithm based on dark-channel priori was proposed [13] to solve this problem. Huang et al. [14] proposed an effective "Laplacian-based visibility restoration (LVR)" method to handle inadequate haze thickness problem. Zhao et al. [15] proposed a two-stage weakly supervised RefineDNet dehazing network, which combines the merits of prior-based and learning-based approaches. However, existing methods mainly are applicable only in clear-day scenarios, under the constraint of uniform light distribution. Intuitively, these algorithms are unsuitable, because most of the hazy weather occurs only under dim light.

To solve this problem, we proposed a lightweight network which can detect pedestrians effectively in severe hazy weather conditions. To build more efficient, faster and accurate model, we selected MobileNetv2 [16] as a feature extractor and YOLOv2 [9] as a detector. In order to improve detection performance, Convolutional Block Attention Module (CBAM) [17] was introduced in the proposed model, and to improve the loss function, we applied normalization on the anchor box loss error [12]. In the proposed paper, prior to the model training, we applied K-means clustering to figure out the optimal number of anchor boxes to improve precise detection.

The contributions of the proposed work are as follows:

(1) We introduced CBAM attention module in the proposed model, which would improve the network feature map by recalibrating the feature map via learning weights.
(2) As the height of the pedestrian is more compared to the width of the pedestrian, we reduce the anchor box loss error by applying normalization on the loss function [9].
(3) We applied seven data augmentation techniques such as multiply, contrast, affine, flip, crop and Gaussian noise + blur to enhance the robustness of the proposed model.

The organization of this paper is as follows: Sect. 2 covers related work on the pedestrian detection in hazy weather. Sections 3 and 4 cover the proposed methodology, experiments and results on both hazy and INRIA pedestrian datasets. Finally, conclusion and future work were discussed.

2   Related Work

As one-stage detectors achieve better detection accuracy and run faster with real time, we have adopted YOLOv2 [9] as our detection model.

YOLO [8] is a simple and extremely fast object detector. This model treats object detection task as a regression problem and predicts anchor boxes and respective class probabilities simultaneously in one evaluation. YOLO detector consists of a total of

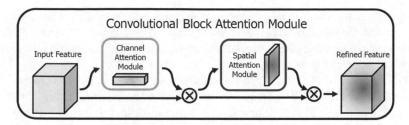

Fig. 1 Structure of convolutional block attention module (CBAM)

26 layers, of which 24 are convolutional layers and two are fully connected layers. The detailed architecture of YOLO is presented in [8]. YOLO divides an input image into $S \times S$ grid cells, and each cell predicts 'B' anchor boxes and 'C' confidence scores for those anchor boxes. If the object center falls within a grid cell, then that cell is responsible for detecting that object. For example, while evaluating YOLO on that dataset, the final prediction output is $7 \times 7 \times 30$, by considering $S = 7$, $B = 2$ and $C = 20$ (since $S \times S \times (B * 5 + C)$) attributes. This model was trained to detect only 20 different objects and also gives relatively high localization error.

YOLOv2 [9] is the improved version of YOLO [8] and focuses mainly on improving recall and localization error, without losing any classification accuracy. To achieve better performance in YOLOv2, batch normalization was applied in all YOLO layers, and a high-resolution classifier was trained which improved mAP value by 2% and 4%, respectively. In order to detect more than one object by a grid cell, optimal K bounding boxes or anchor boxes were figured out prior to the training using K-means clustering algorithm. We have chosen $k = 2$ prior anchor boxes while training the model.

The Convolutional Block Attention Module (CBAM) [17] is widely used to boost the representation power of the model by recalibrating the feature map through learning weights of each channel. Figure 1 shows the structure of CBAM. This attention module is placed right before classifier, which refines the final feature map (composition of up-sampled global and corresponding local features) before the detection, enforcing the model to consider only meaningful features.

3 Proposed Method

To detect pedestrians effectively in hazy weather conditions, we developed a lightweight network using YOLOv2 + MobileNetv2 + CBAM modules. In the proposed model, the number of network parameters is around nine times fewer than the standard convolution so that computational cost was reduced, which in turn improves the pedestrian detection accuracy. Additionally, to improve detection accuracy further, a weighted normalization module was introduced prior to the attention module. The main function of weight normalization module is to combine multi-scale feature maps and generate a single feature map which is finally fed to the attention module. The generated feature map is then applied to CBAM attention module, which improves the network feature map further by recalibrating the feature map via learning weights.

YOLOv2 [9] is a fast and accurate detector and also detects 9000 classes. The proposed model adopts YOLOv2 as pedestrian detector. Figure 2 shows the structure of the proposed model architecture. We modified the original loss function in YOLOv2 [9]. Since the height of the pedestrian is more compared to the width of the pedestrian, anchor box loss error was reduced by applying normalization on the loss function [9] as shown in Eq. (1).

$$
\lambda_{\text{coord}} \sum_{i=0}^{S^2} \sum_{j=0}^{B} \prod_{ij}^{\text{obj}} \left[\left(x_i - \hat{x}_i \right)^2 + \left(y_i - \hat{y}_i \right)^2 \right]
$$

$$
+ \lambda_{\text{coord}} \sum_{i=0}^{S^2} \sum_{j=0}^{B} \prod_{ij}^{\text{obj}} \left[\left(\frac{w_i - \hat{w}_i}{\hat{w}_i} \right)^2 + \left(\frac{h_i - \hat{h}_i}{\hat{h}_i} \right)^2 \right]
$$

$$
+ \sum_{i=0}^{S^2} \sum_{j=0}^{B} \prod_{ij}^{\text{obj}} \left[\left(c_i - \hat{c}_i \right)^2 + \lambda_{\text{noobj}} \sum_{i=0}^{S^2} \sum_{j=0}^{B} \prod_{ij}^{\text{noobj}} \left(c_i - \hat{c}_i \right)^2 \right]
$$

$$
+ \sum_{i=0}^{S^2} \prod_{i}^{\text{obj}} \sum_{c \in \text{classes}} \left[p_i(c) - \hat{p}_i(c) \right]^2
$$

(1)

In Eq. (1), the first term determines the "localization loss error", the second term determines the "confidence loss error" with and without objects and the third term determines the "classification loss error", where S^2 is number of grid cells, B is number of anchor boxes in each grid cell, (x, y) are the center coordinates of a grid cell; w, h and c refer to width, height and confidence of the anchor box, and p is the confidence of the object, i.e., pedestrian. λ_{coord} corresponds to the weight of the localization loss error, λ_{noobj} corresponds to the weight of the classification loss error and $(\hat{x}, \hat{y}, \hat{w}, \hat{h}, \hat{c}, \hat{p})$ is the ground truth of predicted anchor box value.

Equation (1) in the proposed method is compared with YOLOv2 [9], and $w_i - \hat{w}_i$ and $h_i - \hat{h}_i$ terms are replaced with $\frac{w_i - \hat{w}_i}{\hat{w}_i}$ and $\frac{h_i - \hat{h}_i}{\hat{h}_i}$, to reduce the effect of various sizes of the pedestrians in the captured images. Prior to the training, we applied K-means clustering technique to figure out the optimal number of anchor boxes. Therefore, the proposed model is not only quite suitable for detecting hazy pedestrians, but also helpful while detecting single targets in general.

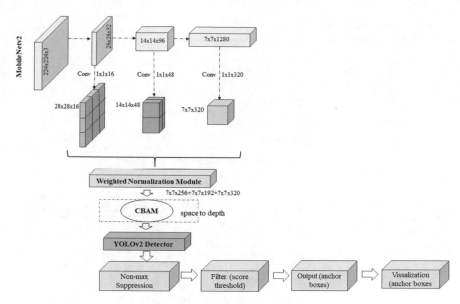

Fig. 2 YOLOv2 + MobileNetv2 + CBAM architecture (proposed method)

4 Experiments and Results

The proposed model carried out training on the standard hazy dataset [18], which consists of 1195 pedestrian images, of which 1052 images are for training and 143 images are for testing. Since the dataset is limited, we applied seven data augmentation techniques such as multiply, contrast, affine, flip, crop and Gaussian noise + blur to enhance the robustness of the proposed model. The experimental setup for processing input images is as follows: Quadro P4000 GPU, CUDA 10.0 and CUDNN 7.4 GPU and TensorFlow 1.13 deep learning framework. Adam [19] is the optimizer solution applied during the model training. The various hyperparameters used while model training are learning rate—0.001, batch size—16 and number of iterations—160 k steps.

To validate the performance of the proposed model with several state-of-the-art (SOTA) algorithms on a testing dataset, we evaluated it in terms of average precision (AP) and frames per second (FPS). We evaluated the model using the criteria which is well-defined in PASCAL-VOC 2012 protocol [5] rules. "Intersection over union" (IoU) measures the accuracy of the model on a test dataset. The performance of the proposed model is compared with HOG + SVM [3], Haar + AdaBoost [4], YOLO [8], Tiny-YOLOv2 [10] and MNPriorBoxes-YOLO [18] methods. Table 1 shows the detection results on hazy person dataset. From the results, it is clear that deep learning-based pedestrian detection methods are superior compared to machine learning-based methods. Of all the methods, the proposed method achieves both highest detection accuracy and testing speed on hazy person dataset.

Table 1 Detected results on hazy person dataset (IoU at 0.5)

Model	Average precision	Speed (FPS)
HOG + SVM [3]	44.8	–
Haar + AdaBoost [4]	34.2	–
YOLO [8]	61.3	78
Tiny-YOLOv3 [10]	80.7	220
MNPriorBoxes-YOLO [18]	86.6	151.9
Proposed	**87.4**	**173.6**

Significance of bold indicates best results

Table 2 Detected results on INRIA pedestrian dataset (IoU at 0.5)

Model	Average precision	Speed (FPS)
HOG + SVM [3]	22.4	–
Haar + AdaBoost [4]	17.2	–
YOLO [8]	38.3	78
Tiny-YOLOv3 [10]	78.9	220
MNPriorBoxes-YOLO [18]	79.2	151.9
Proposed	**82.6**	**173.6**

Significance of bold indicates best results

In order to test the robustness and effectiveness of the proposed model on other datasets, we also carried out training on INRIA pedestrian dataset [3]. Table 2 shows the detection results of the proposed model on INRIA pedestrian dataset. From the quantitative results, it is clear that the proposed model outperforms MNPriorBoxes-YOLO [18], Tiny-YOLOv3 [10], YOLO [8] methods by a reasonable margin. Figure 3 shows the detection results of the proposed model on both Hazy and INRIA pedestrian datasets.

Therefore, the proposed model gives higher detection accuracy on hazy person dataset [18] and does not deliver satisfactory results on INRIA [3] dataset, since there might exist more number of smaller pedestrians in the INRIA dataset.

5 Conclusion

Our proposed lightweight network can effectively detect pedestrians in adverse hazy weather conditions. To improve the detection performance of the proposed model, we applied normalization on the anchor box loss error. Additionally, weighted normalization was applied to improve the model detection accuracy. Compared to the performance of the proposed model with SOTA detection models, it is clear that our model achieved both higher detection accuracy and higher speed. Our model achieves 87.4 and 83.6% average precision, which is +0.8 and +4.4% higher

Fig. 3 Detection results on hazy and INRIA pedestrian dataset. LHS images correspond to detected image and RHS images correspond to ground truth image

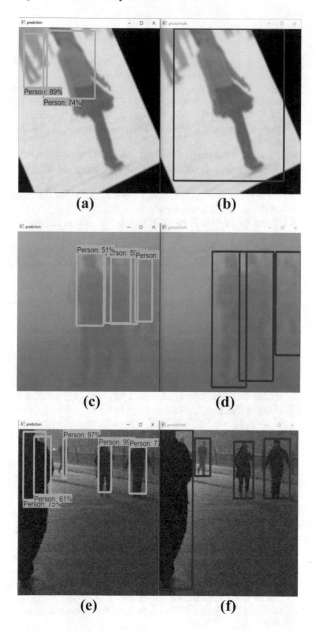

compared to MNPriorBoxes-YOLO on hazy and INRIA pedestrian datasets. Nevertheless, the proposed model detection performance on INRIA pedestrian dataset is not satisfactory and needs to be further improved.

References

1. Global status report on road safety 2018. https://www.who.int/violence_injury_prevention/road_safety_status/2018/en/. Accessed on 1 Sep 2021
2. 2018 Road safety statistics: what is behind the figures? https://ec.europa.eu/commission/presscorner/detail/en/MEMO_19_1990. Accessed on 1 Sep 2021
3. Dalal N, Triggs B (2005) Histograms of oriented gradients for human detection. In: 2005 IEEE computer society conference on computer vision and pattern recognition (CVPR'05), vol 1, pp 886–893
4. Zhang S, Bauckhage C, Cremers AB (2014) Informed haar-like features improve pedestrian detection. In: Proceedings of the IEEE conference on computer vision and pattern recognition, pp 947–954
5. Dollar P, Wojek C, Schiele B, Perona P (2011) Pedestrian detection: an evaluation of the state of the art. IEEE Trans Pattern Anal Mach Intell 34(4):743–761
6. Tuzel O, Porikli F, Meer P (2008) Pedestrian detection via classification on Riemannian manifolds. IEEE Trans Pattern Anal Mach Intell 30(10):1713–1727
7. Murthy CB, Hashmi MF, Bokde ND, Geem ZW (2020) Investigations of object detection in images/videos using various deep learning techniques and embedded platforms—a comprehensive review. Appl Sci 10(9):3280
8. Redmon J, Divvala S, Girshick R, Farhadi A (2016) You only look once: unified, real-time object detection. In: Proceedings of the IEEE conference on computer vision and pattern recognition, pp 779–788
9. Redmon J, Farhadi A (2017) YOLO9000: better, faster, stronger. In: Proceedings of the IEEE conference on computer vision and pattern recognition, pp 7263–7271
10. Redmon J, Farhadi A (2018) Yolov3: an incremental improvement. arXiv preprint arXiv:1804.02767
11. Murthy CB, Hashmi MF, Keskar AG (2021) Optimized MobileNet + SSD: a real-time pedestrian detection on a low-end edge device. Int J Multimedia Inf Retrieval 1–14
12. Murthy CB, Farukh Hashmi M (2020) Real time pedestrian detection using robust enhanced tiny-YOLOv3. In: 2020 IEEE 17th India council international conference (INDICON), pp 1–5
13. He K, Sun J, Tang X (2010) Single image haze removal using dark channel prior. IEEE Trans Pattern Anal Mach Intell 33(12):2341–2353
14. Huang SC, Ye JH, Chen BH (2014) An advanced single-image visibility restoration algorithm for real-world hazy scenes. IEEE Trans Ind Electron 62(5):2962–2972
15. Zhao S, Zhang L, Shen Y, Zhou Y (2021) RefineDNet: a weakly supervised refinement framework for single image dehazing. IEEE Trans Image Process 30:3391–3404
16. Sandler M, Howard A, Zhu M, Zhmoginov A, Chen L (2018) MobileNetV2: inverted residuals and linear bottlenecks. In: 2018 IEEE/CVF conference on computer vision and pattern recognition, pp 4510–4520
17. Woo S, Park J, Lee JY, Kweon IS (2018) CBAM: convolutional block attention module. In: Proceedings of the European conference on computer vision (ECCV), pp 3–19
18. Li G, Yang Y, Qu X (2019) Deep learning approaches on pedestrian detection in hazy weather. IEEE Trans Ind Electron 67(10):8889–8899
19. Kingma DP, Ba JA (2014) A method for stochastic optimization. arXiv preprint arXiv:1412.6980

Hand Gesture-Based Recognition System for Human–Computer Interaction

Rajarshi Das, Roshan Kumar Ojha, Dipam Tamuli, Swapnil Bhattacharjee, and Niranjan Jyoti Borah

1 Introduction

Infiltration of technology in our day-to-day operations is undeniable, thus making human–computer interaction a required field demanding immediate exploration and expansion. Keeping up with the rapid evolution of technology calls for redesigning traditional, fault-ridden modes of interaction, involving the mouse and the keyboard. Presently, technologies such as speech recognition and gesture recognition are taking center stage. But, before diving deep, it is essential to know that gesture is any form of movement in our body to convey a message. Statistically, nonverbal communication conveys around 65% of the message, whereas verbal communication contributes not more than 35% of our interactions [1].

Gesture recognition, specifically, has proven its mettle as a promising principle that has the potential to change human–computer interaction (HCI) by leaps and bounds. Using the hand gesture image as the input and feeding it into the proposed algorithm, many applications such as sign language recognition, augmented reality, sign language interpretation for the disabled, and robotic control can be achieved naturally and non-verbally, opening doors for technological advancement.

The interest in hand gesture recognition and other gesture recognition techniques has led to a large body of research, as has been noted in several review papers [2–7]. Cheok et al. [2] reviewed the modern technique used in recent hand gesture and sign language recognition research in areas such as data acquisition, feature extraction, preprocessing and segmentation. More recently, the review articles highlight the constraints of vision-based gesture recognition for human–computer interaction. In 2020, Aloysius and Geetha [6] reviewed the vision-based continuous sign language recognition (CSLR) system.

R. Das (✉) · R. K. Ojha · D. Tamuli · S. Bhattacharjee · N. J. Borah
Electronics and Telecommunication Department, Assam Engineering College, Guwahati, India
e-mail: rajarshidas24@gmail.com

45
K. Kumar Singh et al. (eds.), *Machine Vision and Augmented Intelligence*, Lecture Notes in Electrical Engineering 1007, https://doi.org/10.1007/978-981-99-0189-0_5

As the world is reeling under the COVID 19 pandemic, gesture recognition has climbed even higher on the importance ladder, owing to hygiene concerns and fear of spreading the disease. One direct effect of that can be seen in the public ATMs. This article dwells on that and attempts to present an effective and efficient method for hand gesture recognition to potentially replace the conventional keypads of ATMs with a touchless system. In this project, the central area of work is on image processing through which few hand gestures have been recognized and in terms are mapped with coordinates on the screen for necessary operations of an ATM keypad. A vision-based approach is adopted for gesture recognition.

The workflow of hand gesture recognition is described as follows. First, the hand region is detected in the original image received from the input device (camera). Then, the skin color range is defined so that the project can be used in any scenario for any human race. After that, mathematical operations like the Cosine rule (1) is used to calculate the angles between the fingers of our hand, Heron's formula (2) to calculate the area of the convex hull, area of contour formed by hand and are then used to calculate the area ratio. These are the parameters, i.e., angle between fingers and the area ratio used to recognize some set of gestures that can be shown by using one hand. Further, these gestures are mapped into specific commands to our computer through various image processing and extraction methods and then maneuvering the ATM interface without touching any buttons or any click to perform a completely touchless process. The detailed methodology will be discussed in later sections.

$$CosA = \frac{b^2 + c^2 - a^2}{2bc} \tag{1}$$

$$Area = \sqrt{s(s-a)(s-b)(s-c)} \tag{2}$$

where a, b, c are the lengths of the sides and A, B, C are the angles of a triangle, respectively. The semi-perimeter of the triangle is denoted by s (3).

$$s = \frac{a+b+c}{3} \tag{3}$$

1.1 Novelty of Work

Much research has already been done on vision-based hand gesture recognition. This includes mapping gestures to numbers as well as other specific commands. In our present work, using a single hand, we have been able to map ten numbers from 0 to 9 and two more specific commands in real time (dynamic hand gesture recognition). We have also used the hand gesture recognition system to implement a touchless ATM keypad which has not been explored so far. This will be useful for society to face further issues in the future, similar to any such possible pandemic situation relating to contagious diseases.

2 Literature Review

Derpanis [8] explained the feature extraction and classification methods of the gesture set of a human hand needed to perform the ultimate goal of human–computer interaction using mean shift clustering. The central principle behind the mean shift is to consider all the points in the d-dimensional feature space as an observed probability density function, in which dense regions in the feature space correlate with the modes or local maxima of the underlying distribution.

Kanniche [9] elaborated that hand gesture recognition schemes are psychological aspects of movements dependent on hand gesture taxonomy and representation. Several gesture recognition taxonomies were suggested in the literature from individual to individual. Some of the taxonomies presented by Kanniche [9] are shown below in Fig. 1.

Bourke et al. [11] proposed recognition systems to detect some specific gestures used in our day-to-day lives using an accelerometer. The HCI model will have to decide on which hand recognition can be done. There are two methods; these methods are 3D model-based detection and appearance-based methods, as shown in Fig. 2.

Chaudhary et al., Moeslund, and Granum [12, 13] gave a detailed explanation about tracking, initialization, pose estimation, and recognition of the motion capture system. Markov models, particle filtering and condensation, optical flow, connection models, and skin color are discussed. They also talked about how dataset size and the required time for gesture detection can dominate the model's efficiency, accuracy, and understandability.

Fang et al. [14] designed a data glove for gesture detection and recognition based on magnetic measurements and inertial units made of three-axis magnetometers, three-axis accelerometers, and three-axis gyroscopes. They obtained data by collecting hand information in a 3D space and fed the data to an artificial neural network model to train the data. They achieved an accuracy of 85.59% for static

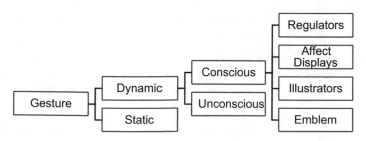

Fig. 1 Vision-based hand gesture taxonomies [10]

Fig. 2 Vision-based hand
gesture representations [10]

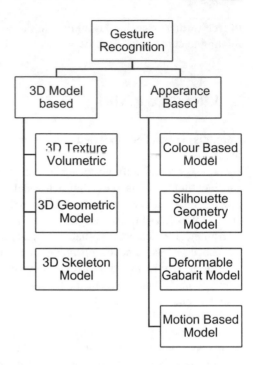

recognition and 82.5% for dynamic gesture recognition and were later applied to robotic arm-hand operation [4].

Shen et al. [15] presented a soft bending sensor. Compared with inertial sensors used earlier, these bending sensors are lighter, are better fitting with gloves, and have a better user experience.

Wu et al. [16] proposed a recognition algorithm based on Kinect sensor which tries to recognize numbers and alphanumeric characters written in the air based on the trajectory followed by the fingertips. He then compared it with the conventional methods and found out that its recognition accuracy had been improved significantly. Murata et al. [17] tested the Kinect sensors' ability to recognize the alphanumeric characters written in space and found that this sensor can work with very high recognition accuracy.

Al-Shamayleh et al. [18] summarized all the challenges of visual gesture recognition from these three features:

- System—response time and cost,
- Environment—background, invariance, and illumination,
- Gesture—feature selection, dynamic gestures, scaling, and rotation.

Shalahudin et al. [19] presented a controller prototype to control the house lamps and other home devices through human gesture recognition. Luo et al. [20] realized the control of a robot using two hand gestures and saw that the system could perform many tasks within time accurately.

Fig. 3 Tracking
sub-divisions [10]

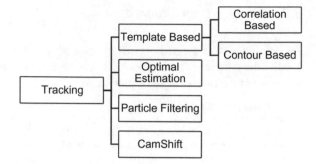

From the above research, it can be concluded that the hand gesture recognition system comprises three fundamental phases—detection, tracking, and recognition. This portion of the survey examines some of the popular strategies for hand gesture identification used by most researchers by grouping the three main phases of detection, tracking, and recognition. The sub-divisions of tracking are shown in Fig. 3.

3 Methodology

Digital image processing is a phenomenon where a digital computer processes digital images through an algorithm. It allows a vast range of algorithms to be used on the input data, avoiding problems such as the building up of noise and distortion during processing.

3.1 Basic Overview

Image processing consists of three steps: importing the image using image acquisition tools; analysis and manipulation of the image to reduce the level of noise; and output based on image analysis: altered image or report. After acquiring the desired results, these results are used to control the keypad interface by noting each coordinate of the interactive buttons and mapping it with the system to work in a user-friendly and interactive way.

3.2 Step-By-Step Process

A click function is defined as performing a click on a particular point of the screen. Firstly, the cursor is set to a position in a screen, and then, an event of clicking is performed by a mouse using Windows API.

```
def performClick(c_x,c_y):
win32api.SetCursorPos((c_x,c_y))
win32api.mouse_event(win32con.MOUSEEVENTF_LEFTDOWN,c_x,c_y,0,0)
win32api.mouse_event(win32con.MOUSEEVENTF_LEFTUP,c_x,c_y,0,0)
```

Terrillon et al. [21] mentioned that skin chrominance could be an essential parameter for detecting human faces in color images. This idea can be used for the detection of human hands from an image [7]. This range of human skin color is defined in hue saturation value using Numpy, a Python Library. This enables the model to identify the hand in the frame, captured through the camera. So whatever comes inside this color range is masked which is used for further detection.

```
hsv_model = cv2.cvtColor(roi, cv2.COLOR_BGR2HSV)
lower_color = np.array([0,20,70], dtype=np.uint8)
upper_color = np.array([150,255,255], dtype=np.uint8)
mask = cv2.inRange(hsv_model, lower_color, upper_color)
```

Dilation and erosion are basic morphological operations which produce contrasting results when applied to binary images or gray scale.

After that, the contour and the convex hull of the hand are determined, and then, the area ratio of the above two is calculated. Figure 4d shows the contour and the convex hull around the hand. The white region shows the contour. The convex hull is formed by joining the extreme points in the contour, which are the fingertips. The outlined region shows the convex hull.

```
areahullvalue = cv2.contourArea(hull)
areacntvalue = cv2.contourArea(cnt)
arearatio = ((areahullvalue - areacntvalue)/areacntvalue) * 100.
```

Then, the model finds the defects of a hand or the space between the two fingers. Geometrically, when two fingers are spilled, a triangle is formed. Using Heron's

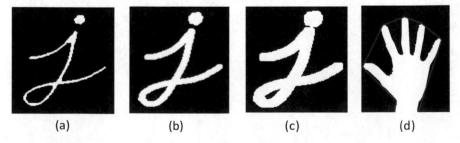

(a)   (b)   (c)   (d)

Fig. 4 **a** Sample image [22], **b** eroded image [22], **c** dilated image [22], **d** contour and convex hull [23]

formula, the area of that triangle is calculated. Using the Cosine rule, the angle is calculated formed between the two adjacent fingers.

```
for k in range(defects.shape[0]):
    s,e,f,d = defects[i,0]
    start = tuple(approx[s][0])
    end = tuple(approx[e][0])
    far = tuple(approx[f][0])
x = math.sqrt((end[0] - start[0])**2 + (end[1] - start[1])**2)
y = math.sqrt((far[0] - start[0])**2 + (far[1] - start[1])**2)
z = math.sqrt((end[0] - far[0])**2 + (end[1] - far[1])**2)
s = (x+y+z)/2
ar = math.sqrt(s*(s - x)*(s - y)*(s - z))          # heron's formula
d=(2*ar)/x
ang = math.acos((y**2 + z**2 - x**2)/(2*y*z)) * 57   #angle defined
```

Comparing these different factors like area ratio and angles, the model determines how many fingers are being shown by the user. Currently, if the area ratio is less than 10 or if the user is showing the 'Clear' gesture, a parameter is manipulated to change its value to 200. Later in the program, a check is done for that parameter, and if it is 200, then a click at the 'Clear' button is executed four times in a row using a *For Loop*.

Similarly, if the ratio is less than 19 and greater than 10, the 'Done' event gets triggered when we show thumbs up. Then, a parameter will be manipulated to change its value to 100. Later, in the program, a check for parameter value will be done, and if it is 100, a click at the 'Done' button is performed.

A 5-s timer will run continuously, i.e., once the timer reaches 0, it will start counting from 5 again. Once the timer reaches 0, at that instance, it captures the current gesture that was being shown and stores the value in a particular variable. In the next session of 5 s, when the timer reaches 0, it will capture the gesture again in the same way and store it in another variable. In this 10-s slot, if the two gestures are numbers, they will be added together and stored in a separate variable. So, in this way, this model can produce outputs ranging from 0 to 9 using one hand, and it also increases the flexibility of the project as a whole.

For example, to get a final term of 7, four different sets of gestures can be shown by the user as follows:

- (Gesture 2, Gesture 5),
- (Gesture 5, Gesture 2),
- (Gesture 4, Gesture 3),
- (Gesture 3, Gesture 4).

In any 5-s slots, if the gesture shown is 'Done' or 'Clear,' a click will be triggered directly to the corresponding buttons.

Once the final term is obtained upon adding the numbers shown by the previous two gestures, a click is performed in a predefined location on the screen. For example, let the two gestures correspond to 2 and 4. Adding them, the final term will be 6. So, a click will be performed above the button corresponding to 6 on the keypad. Using this method, the range of outputs can be increased significantly using one

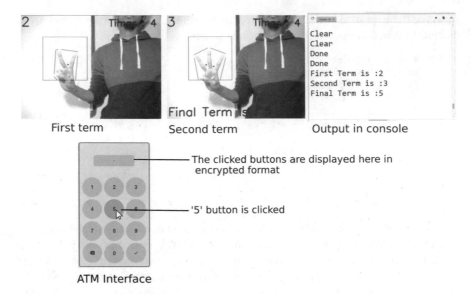

Fig. 5 Addition of 2 and 3 using hand gesture and performing a click in ATM keypad

hand. These gestures are then mapped as per the need; in this model, all the keypad buttons are mapped using eight gestures.

As shown in Fig. 5, we are showing Gesture 2 in the first 5 s, and in the next 5 s, we are showing Gesture 3. After the addition of the two above gestures, we will be getting a final term of 5. Once we get a final term after every 10-s slot, we perform a click in a specific button. The function of click is already discussed in the earlier section. Here, in our case, we performed a click on button '5.'

The eight gestures are as follows:

- 0 Gesture (fist),
- 1 Gesture (raising one finger),
- 2 Gesture (raising two adjacent fingers),
- 3 Gesture (raising three adjacent fingers),
- 4 Gesture (raising four adjacent fingers),
- 5 Gesture (raising five fingers),
- Done Gesture (thumbs up),
- Clear Gesture (upright palm and keeping fingers attached).

3.3 Tools Used

(1) *Anaconda*: Anaconda is a distribution of Python and R languages for scientific computing and is known for efficiently managing the package dependencies. The distribution includes data science packages that can be used for Windows,

Linux, and macOS. It also includes Anaconda Navigator, which can be used as an alternative to the generic Command–Line Interface (CLI).

(2) *Spyder*: Spyder is a cross-platform, open-source Integrated Development Environment (IDE) for scientific programmings, such as machine learning and image processing in Python. Spyder integrates with several prominent packages in the scientific Python stack, including NumPy, SciPy, Matplotlib, IPython, SymPy, Cython, and other open-source software.

(3) *OpenCV*: Open-Source Computer Vision Library (OpenCV) is an open-source machine learning and computer vision software library. OpenCV is used for computer vision applications to accelerate machine perception for easier parameter detection in market-ready products.

(4) *Numpy*: Numpy is the basic package for scientific computing in Python. It is a Python library that provides a multidimensional array object and an assortment of routines for complex and fast operations on arrays. Numpy functions can perform complex mathematical and logical operations. It can also be used for sorting, shape manipulation, selecting I/O, basic linear algebra, random simulation, statistical operations.

(5) *XAMPP*: XAMPP is an open-source and free web server solution stack software developed by Apache Friends, comprising MariaDB, Apache HTTP Server, and interpreters for scripts written in programming languages like Perl and PHP. Using XAMPP, localhost can be made with a fixed IP address where webpages can be hosted without any hassle for testing and development.

4   Result Analysis

This hand gesture recognition system has been proved to work in real time through capturing live hand images. Here, in this project, various output components are observed and identified, which contribute to the final result of this hand gesture recognition system model. After acquiring the result, the hand gestures are mapped into specific commands. Figure 6 shows the critical components in the output of the code.

As seen in the output above, the frame window indicates all the information relevant to the user. The timer can be seen in the top right section, whereas the top left section of the frame shows which gesture is being perceived by the system. The region of interest is where the user needs to put his hand in to detect the gesture. The final term is shown in the bottom section of the frame.

Currently, this system can recognize eight gestures as stated in the methodology. Figures 7 and 8 show the gestures for 'Done' and 'Clear,' respectively.

If this model is implemented in a real-time scenario, the ATM keypad must be replaced with a gesture cavity where users will insert their respective hands and show the gestures as per their requirements (Fig. 9).

In this gesture cavity, three components are a must, and they are as follows:

- LED strips for proper illumination,

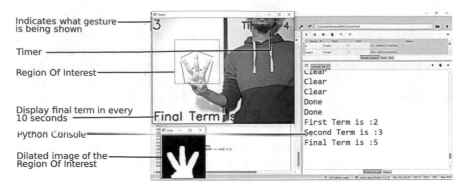

Fig. 6 Key components of output

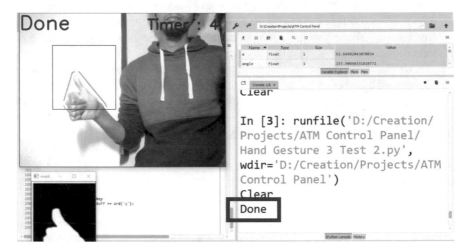

Fig. 7 Gesture 'Done'

- Camera,
- Enough space for maneuvering the hand.

Duan et al. [24] developed a kernel-based tracking system to accomplish hand gesture modeling. The kernel-based design only relied on object tracking techniques and did not consider the issue of gesture recognition of the target. A method for skin detection was also integrated to their method for easier hand detection. Aksac et al. [25] tried to use a convex hull algorithm to extract hand contours. They used a distance classifier to identify and recognize hand gestures with contour distance measurements. Since only a simple skin detection technique was used, it was not able to operate accurately in a complex background. Chiang and Fan [26] removed the background to extract the palm region. They used basic image processing algorithms, like connected-component labeling, hand contour, contour smoothing to extract the

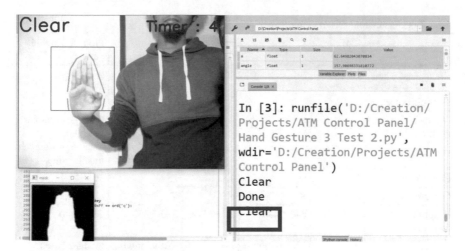

Fig. 8 Gesture 'Clear'

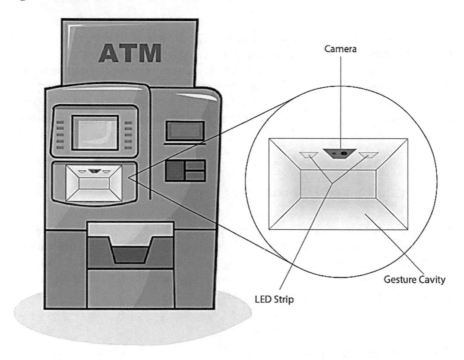

Fig. 9 Pictorial representation of the practical implementation of the project

Table 1 Comparison of hand gesture recognition

Refs.	[24]	[25]	[26]	[27]	Proposed in this project
Robustness when the background is like skin color	✗	✗	✗	✓	✗
Number of gestures	6	6	4	4	Eight gestures can be clubbed together for greater functionality
Frame rate	30	30	15	25	30
Gesture tracking	✓	✗	✓	✓	✓
Resolution of camera	640 * 480	640 * 480	320 * 240	320 * 240	640 * 480
Application	✗	Virtual mouse	✗	Virtual mouse	Gesture-based interface controller

significant features of the hand. Tsai et al. [27] designed a system that achieved to perform mouse functions using simple gestures. For real-time gesture detection, they used skin segmentation and motion detection. They eliminated the objects from the background that did not move for a specific period to get more accuracy and robustness. However, in this paper, we have proposed to club eight gestures for greater functionality. A comparative study of various hand gesture recognition algorithms is shown in Table 1.

5 Conclusion and Future Scope

Human–computer interaction is one of the nascent technologies that can bridge with many other technologies like augmented reality, image processing, machine learning, and Artificial Intelligence. These technologies make our lives much easier, keeping the goal the same as before. We can use such tools to make military, business, and industrial sectors more automated and efficient.

5.1 Summary of Work

The domain of application of vision-based hand gesture recognition systems is essentially huge. But, in this project, due to the ongoing COVID 19 pandemic, the primary focus has been on an application demanding an urgent problem statement that affects the greater masses—demand for a touchless ATM keypad. Thus, the work done for this project is restricted to the single supplication already mentioned. So, the cognitive mapping of the gesture to commands is specific to ATM systems only. A vision-based approach has been adopted for the recognition of hand gestures. At first, the image of the user's hand gesture is analyzed and interpreted to reduce noise. Then, those hand gestures are mapped into specific commands through various image processing and extraction methods.

5.2 Conclusion

The purpose of any hand gesture recognition system is to recognize the hand gestures and use them to convey the intended meaning for computer control or any other device. This vision-based approach works well under several significant situational constraints.

This project outlines a hand gesture recognition system that has been designed to assist the identification of hand gestures in real-time. The highlighted system does not require the user to wear specific equipment or attach any device to the body. A camera reads the hands instead of sensors attached to the device. The natural interaction between the human and the computer has been tapped to a decent extent. This statement is justified as it has been made possible to map hand gestures onto the keypad inputs of the ATM.

5.3 Future Scope

There are some aspects of the project which can be worked upon in the future. For now, all the gestures necessary for an ATM transaction have been mapped. However, this process can be made more seamless and user-friendly by touching upon certain vital areas. For example, currently, in the worst-case scenario, it takes a total of 100 s (20 gestures each of 5 s) for a transaction. Thus, there is scope for improvement in this area to enhance the experience of the system used by inducing less stress and fatigue and ultimately conserving time and energy.

Several real-time challenges may occur during the actual implementation of the hand gesture recognition system in ATMs. Widely, encompassing performance control inspections and surveys must be performed to generate a system that overcomes all these challenges.

Within the scope of this paper, the system has been developed only for use in ATMs. However, it need not be limited and can be expanded for implementation in the industrial machinery sector. The evolution of a hand gesture recognition system capable of switching the cognitive mapping of the same set of gestures to different groups of commands would be game-changing. Using the concept of gesture recognition, it is possible to point the finger at the computer screen, prompting the cursor to follow accordingly. This will help break the two-dimensional constraint associated with the conventional mouse used today and will enable the performing of cursor operations in three dimensions. Click operation of the mouse also seems possible through hand gesture recognition. Thus, such systems can potentially have numerous applications in the industrial, educational, medical, and many other associated fields.

References

1. Pisharady PK, Saerbeck M (2015) Recent methods and databases in vision-based hand gesture recognition: a review. Comput Vis Image Underst 141:152–165
2. Cheok MJ, Omar Z, Jaward MH (2017) A review of hand gesture and sign language recognition techniques. Int J Mach Learn Cybern 10:131–153
3. Chakraborty BK, Sarma D, Bhuyan MK, MacDorman KF (2018) Review of constraints on vision-based gesture recognition for human-computer interaction. IET Comput Vis 12:3–15
4. Rautaray SS, Agrawal A (2012) Vision based hand gesture recognition for human computer interaction: a survey. Artif Intell Rev 43:1–54
5. Moni MA, Ali ABMS (2009) HMM based hand gesture recognition: a review on techniques and approaches. In: 2009 Proceedings of the 2nd IEEE international conference on computer science and information technology, pp 433–437
6. Aloysius N, Geetha M (2020) Understanding vision-based continuous sign language recognition. Multimedia Tools Appl 79:22177–22209
7. Rastgoo R, Kiani K, Escalera S (2021) Sign language recognition: a deep survey. Expert Syst Appl 164:113794
8. Derpanis KG (2005) Mean shift clustering, lecture notes. http://www.cse.yorku.ca/~kosta/CompVis_Notes/mean_shift.pdf
9. Kanniche MB (2009) Gesture recognition from video sequences. Ph.D. Thesis, University of Nice
10. Semantic scholar research paper on hand-gesture-recognition, https://www.semanticscholar.org/paper/Vision-based-hand-gesture-recognition-for-human-a-Rautaray-Agrawal/6e33fca1addd62cc278023cabac60141c4af60ec
11. Bourke AK, O'Brien JV, Lyons GM (2007) Evaluation of a threshold-based tri-axial accelerometer fall detection algorithm. Gait Posture 26:194–199
12. Chaudhary A, Raheja JL, Das K, Raheja S (2011) Intelligent approaches to interact with machines using hand gesture recognition in a natural way: a survey. Int J Comput Sci Eng Surv 2:122–133
13. Moeslund TB, Granum E (2001) A survey of computer vision-based human motion capture. Comput Vis Image Underst 81:231–268
14. Fang B, Sun F, Liu H, Liu C (2018) 3-D human gesture capturing and recognition by the IMMU-based data glove. Neurocomput 277:198–207
15. Shen Z, Yi J, Li X, Lo MHP, Chen MZ, Hu Y, Wang Z (2016) A soft stretchable bending sensor and data glove applications. Robot Biomimetics 3:1–8
16. Wu X, Yang C, Wang Y, Li H, Xu S (2012) An intelligent interactive system based on hand gesture recognition algorithm and Kinect. In: Proceedings of the 5th international symposium on computational intelligence and design, vol 2, pp 294–298
17. Murata T, Shin J (2014) Hand gesture and character recognition based on Kinect sensor. Int J Distrib Sens Netw 2014:1–6
18. Al-Shamayleh AS, Ahmad R, Abushariah MAM, Alam KA, Jomhari N (2018) A systematic literature review on vision based gesture recognition techniques. Multimedia Tools Appl 77:28121–28184
19. Al Ayubi S, Sudiharto DW, Jadied EM, Aryanto E (2019) The prototype of hand gesture recognition for elderly people to control connected home devices. J Phys Conf Ser 1201:012042. IOP Publishing, United Kingdom

20. Luo X, Amighetti A, Zhang D (2019) A human-robot interaction for a Mecanum wheeled mobile robot with real-time 3D two-hand gesture recognition. Abstr J Phys: Conf Ser 1267(1):012056. https://doi.org/10.1088/1742-6596/1267/1/012056

21. Terrillon J, Shirazi M, Fukamachi H, Akamatsu S (2000) Comparative performance of different skin chrominance models and chrominance spaces for the automatic detection of human faces in colour images. In: Proceedings of the fourth IEEE international conference on automatic face and gesture recognition, France, pp 54–61

22. OpenCV24-Python-Tutorials, https://opencv24-python-tutorials.readthedocs.io/en/latest/py_tutorials/py_imgproc/py_morphological_ops/py_morphological_ops.html

23. Intorobotics, https://www.intorobotics.com/9-opencv-tutorials-hand-gesture-detection-recognition/

24. Duan HX, Zhang QY, Ma W (2011) An approach to dynamic hand gesture modeling and real-time extraction. In: IEEE international conference on communication software and networks (ICCSN). IEEE, pp 139–142

25. Aksaç A, Öztürk O, Özyer T (2011) Real-time multi-objective hand posture/gesture recognition by using distance classifiers and finite state machine for virtual mouse operations. In: IEEE international conference on electrical and electronics engineering (ELECO), vol 7, pp 457–461

26. Chiang T, Fan CP (2018) 3D depth information based 2D low-complexity hand posture and gesture recognition design for human computer interactions. In: 3rd International conference on computer and communication systems (ICCCS). IEEE, pp 233–238

27. Tsai TH, Huang CC, Zhang KL (2020) Design of hand gesture recognition system for human-computer interaction. Multimedia Tools Appl 79:5989–6007

28. Wadhawan A, Kumar P (2021) Sign language recognition systems: a decade systematic literature review. Arch Comput Methods Eng 28:785–813

An Overview of Machine Learning Techniques Focusing on the Diagnosis of Endometriosis

Najme Zehra Naqvi, Kritleen Kaur, Shubhi Khanna, and Shivangi Singh

1 Introduction

Endometriosis is a chronic, benign, hereditary, heterogenous, gynecological disease commonly affecting 6–10% of females of reproductive age. In medical terms, endometriosis is known as the growth of endometrial tissue outside the uterus due to estrogen-dependent inflammation. It may cause pelvic pain and health issues like subfertility in the patient, severely decreasing their quality of life [1–4].

Formerly, peritoneal endometriosis was known as "adenomyoma", with descriptions "haematomas of the ovary" or "chocolate cysts" used initially for ovarian endometrioma [5]. Two types of theories have been suggested to explain the cause of the endometrium-like glands and stroma that bring about endometriosis: the transplantation theory, which states that endometriosis is caused by eutopic endometrial tissue being displaced from the uterus, and the in-situ theory, which suggests that endometrial-like tissue is developed from embryonic cells and is displaced along the Müllerian ducts [2].

Endometriosis can be categorized into typical, cystic ovarian, and deep endometriosis lesions. These are benign tumors that develop slowly or not at all after the original burst of growth and do not occur again after they are fully removed.

N. Z. Naqvi · K. Kaur · S. Khanna (✉) · S. Singh
Department of Computer Science and Engineering, Indira Gandhi Delhi Technical University for Women, Kashmere Gate, New Delhi, Delhi 110006, India
e-mail: shubhi150btcse18@igdtuw.ac.in

N. Z. Naqvi
e-mail: najmezehra@igdtuw.ac.in

K. Kaur
e-mail: kritleen094btcse18@igdtuw.ac.in

S. Singh
e-mail: shivangi145btcse18@igdtuw.ac.in

K. Kumar Singh et al. (eds.), *Machine Vision and Augmented Intelligence*, Lecture Notes in Electrical Engineering 1007, https://doi.org/10.1007/978-981-99-0189-0_6

However, new incidents can happen based on genetic and epigenetic conditions passed on while birth or accrued during life [2, 4].

Although endometriosis is predominantly a benign condition, recent epidemiologic research indicates that given the similarity between the two, endometrial lesions might herald development of malignant tumors, possibly leading to ovarian carcinoma. Consequently, women suffering from endometriosis have a higher risk of being susceptible to endometriosis-associated ovarian carcinoma (EAOC) and endometrial cancer [3, 6].

Baranov et al. [1] hypothesize that in order to develop a treatment precisely for endometriosis, the endometriosis development program's (EMDP's) emphasis on prediction as well as prevention of endometriosis might prove to be important. The advantage of EMDP is that it continuously tracks the changes in a female's body to assess the relationship with possible symptoms of endometriosis, thereby customizing the treatment for each individual, offering a pre-emptive solution for endometrial cancer.

Endometriosis cannot be diagnosed solely based on symptoms since these symptoms are shared by multiple other diseases. Depending on the phenotype of endometriosis—endometriomas (ovarian cysts), superficial endometriotic implants (mostly on the peritoneum), and deep infiltrating endometriosis (spreading more than 5 mm below the peritoneum)—different imaging techniques are employed for diagnosis. In addition to transvaginal ultrasonography (TVUS), pelvic ultrasonography, and magnetic resonance imaging (MRI), laparoscopy is an effective method of diagnosis, albeit primarily a surgical one. To improve the results of surgery, approaches have been proposed to improve visualization of endometriosis during surgery [7, 8].

Machine learning techniques are instrumental in prediction of endometriosis based on previous records as well as genetics and epigenetics. Image processing can predict severity and type of endometriosis, and whether the benign lesion could turn malignant, computer vision can identify the location of infected areas. These technologies can be of tremendous aid to medical professionals or radiologists in diagnosis of endometriosis and might even be able to predict survival rates of the affected patients.

2   Image Datasets Used

See Tables 1, 2 and 3 and Figs. 1, 2, 3 and 4.

Table 1 Image modalities

Image modality and format	Description	Position/area covered	Limitations	Cost	Technical difficulties
Laparoscopic images. (format: usually saved in JPEG format)	Laparoscopy is a low-risk, minimally invasive surgical (MIS) procedure that examines the organs inside the abdomen using a laparoscope [9]	Both anterior and posterior positions	High noise. most common infection: internal bleeding, organ damage. Could also sometimes lead to abdominal pain, fever, nausea or vomiting, swelling, etc.	Cost lies between ₹20,000 and ₹50,000	Most technical difficulties are attached to the equipment: scope, camera, insulation tube, and light source [10]
MRI images (format: saved in DICOM format)	MRI, a clinical imaging technique utilized in radiology to deliver photos of the body's physical provisions and physiological cycles, uses magnetic field slopes and radio waves to produce pictures of the body organs	Sagittal T1 weighted for anterior and sagittal T2 weighted for posterior	High noise. Very few to none side effects, usually limited to nausea, headaches, and slight pain. Patients could be allergic to the contrast material leading to itchiness or development of hives	Cost ranges from ₹15,000–₹25,000	Due to its better quality, MRI imaging at 3 T is preferred, which is not always a viable option [11]

(continued)

Table 1 (continued)

Image modality and format	Description	Position/area covered	Limitations	Cost	Technical difficulties
TVUS images (format: saved in DICOM format)	A transvaginal ultrasound, also known as TVUS or TVS, is a type of pelvic ultrasound used to study female conceptive organs. This methodology includes the professional embedding an ultrasound probe into the vaginal canal	Anterior position	Medium noise. No known risk factors aside from slight discomfort. Safe even for pregnant women	Ranges from ₹600–₹800	Easiest to perform. Next to no technical difficulties
Hysteroscopic images (format: usually saved in JPEG format)	Hysteroscopy is a minor surgical method that consists of viewing the interior of the uterus using a tiny fiber optic tube called hysteroscope. Hysteroscopy assists a doctor in treating and diagnosing multiple uterine disorders that may culminate in infertility, recurrent miscarriages, irregular bleeding, pain and is mainly used for diagnosing endometrial lesions	Covers the interior of the vaginal canal	High noise. Even though hysteroscopy is a relatively safer medical treatment, it does have some risk attached to it, some of them being the possibility of infection, heavy internal bleeding, intrauterine scarring, increased possibility of injury to the uterus, cervix, and bowel	Cost lies between ₹15,000 and ₹50,000	Uterine perforation, hemorrhaging, inefficient or wrong cuts, not enough distention of the uterus and difficulty with debris removal [12]

Table 2 Deep infiltrating endometriosis (DIE) diagnosis effectiveness using MRI and TVUS

Location of DIE	Imaging method (current study)	Pooled sensitivity (95% CI) (%)	Pooled specificity (95% CI) (%)
Rectosigmoid	MRI	0.85 (0.78–0.90)	0.95 (0.83–0.99)
Rectosigmoid	TVUS	0.85 (0.68–0.94)	0.96 (0.85–0.99)
Rectovaginal septum	MRI	0.66 (0.51–0.79)	0.97 (0.89–0.99)
Rectovaginal septum	TVUS	0.59 (0.26–0.86)	0.97 (0.94–0.99)
Uterosacral ligaments	MRI	0.70 (0.55–0.82)	0.93 (0.87–0.97)
Uterosacral ligaments	TVUS	0.67 (0.55–0.77)	0.86 (0.73–0.93)

3 Performance Metrics

3.1 Accuracy

Accuracy is the sum of accurate predictions divided by the overall number of samples given as input.

$$\text{Accuracy} = \frac{TP + TN}{TP + TN + FP + FN}. \tag{1}$$

3.2 Sensitivity

Sensitivity is the ratio of true positives to the sum of true positives and false negatives.

$$\text{Sensitivity} = \text{Recall} = \frac{TP}{TP + FN}. \tag{2}$$

3.3 Specificity

Specificity is the ratio of true negatives to the sum of false positives and true negatives.

$$\text{Specificity} = \frac{TN}{FP + TN}. \tag{3}$$

Table 3 Image datasets

Dataset name and description	Size	Specialty	Challenges
Gynecologic laparoscopy endometriosis dataset (GLENDA) [9] contains endometriosis images with regional annotations of single frames, and the frames being related to one of the two: specific video positions or sequences across time are categorized into four subsets based on location, i.e., peritoneum, ovary, uterus, and deep infiltrating endometriosis (DIE). Although key frames are marked for video segments, they were designed with the intention of ensuring that all endometriosis sections on them remain clearly visible [7, 9]	Contains 25 k images, which can be broadly divided into two categories: pathological images (12 k) and non-pathological images (13 k). Here, pathological images are the ones with identified endometriosis present and visible in them and are further divided into four categories based on its location [9]	GLENDA is one of the largest datasets available with over 25 k images, 300+ annotated images, with hand-drawn annotations done by medical professionals. The dataset has minimal smoke and noise with standardized images. The dataset has been updated multiple times, giving the users the opportunity to work on the latest [9]	The huge size of the dataset makes it extremely time consuming to work with. The images are stored in JPEG format which is usually difficult to work with. Moreover, the dataset is not evenly distributed among the four categories, and the results shown may be skewed [7, 9]
A large in-house dataset comprising MRI images is used in [13]	4896 MRI images from 72 patients such that 3456 are T1-weighted and 1440 are T2 weighted	The dataset contains both T1 weighted as well as T2 weighted providing the means to study the aliment in more depth. The images in the dataset are contrast enhanced and contains diverse images covering a number of categories. MR images were obtained using 1.5 T and 3 T superconducting units	Images are of varying formats and resolutions; therefore, the images require a lot of preprocessing. Moreover, the need for data augmentation arises as well

(continued)

Table 3 (continued)

Dataset name and description	Size	Specialty	Challenges
An in-house dataset of hysteroscopic images extracted from "videos of the uterine lumen captured using a hysteroscope" is used in [14]	The input videos were from 177 patients; typical video duration is being between 10.5 s and 395.3 s. The dataset is divided into five categories, normal endometrium (60), endometrial polyp (60), uterine myoma (21), endometrial cancer (21), and AEH (15)	The dataset is recent with data collected from 2011 till 2019. It is categorized into five categories making it easier to work with. There is not much difference between the number of images per category as compared to other datasets	The videos from which the frames have been extracted were recorded using different devices, leading to varying positions, image quality, and image resolution. Therefore, the images require a lot of preprocessing before they can be loaded into a model
An in-house dataset comprising TVUS images is used in [15]	121 patients went for TVUS with 72 abnormal ultrasounds	Dataset are made directly by medical professionals. Images are obtained using the same equipment and techniques	The dataset is really small with only 72 images testing positive for the presence of endometriosis

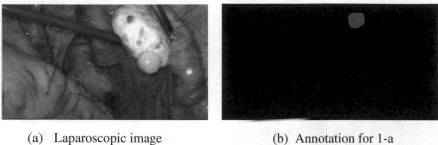

(a) Laparoscopic image   (b) Annotation for 1-a

Fig. 1 Laparoscopic images showing the presences of endometriosis [9]

Fig. 2 Hysteroscopic image
[16]

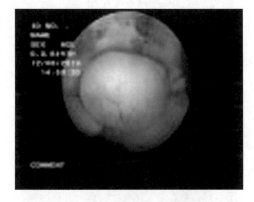

Fig. 3 Transvaginal
ultrasound (TVUS) [15]

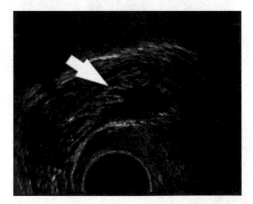

3.4 Precision

Precision is the ratio of true positives to the sum of true positives and false positives.

$$Precision = \frac{TP}{TP + FP}. \qquad (4)$$

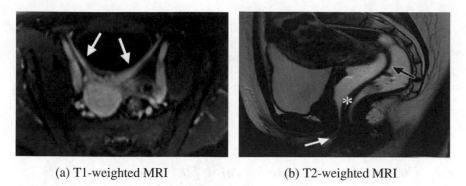

(a) T1-weighted MRI   (b) T2-weighted MRI

Fig. 4 MRI images showing the presences of endometriosis [17]

3.5 *F1-Score*

$F1$-score is the harmonic mean of recall and precision having a range of 0–1.

$$F1\text{-score} = \frac{2 * \text{Precision} * \text{Recall}}{\text{Precision} + \text{Recall}} = \frac{2 * \text{TP}}{2 * \text{TP} + \text{FP} + \text{FN}}. \qquad (5)$$

3.6 *AUC*

Area under curve (AUC) summarizes the Receiver Operator Characteristic (ROC) curve for a classifier. ROC curve maps out sensitivity against 1-specificity.

3.7 *AUROC*

Area under the Receiver Operating Characteristics (AUROCs) are the combination of AUC and ROC, where ROC is a probability curve.

3.8 *P-Value*

Also referred to as observed significance level, it is the likelihood that given that all model assumptions and the test hypothesis is correct, the selected test statistic is at least as big as its observed value.

3.9 C-Index

The concordance index or C-index is the ratio of concordant pairs to the total number of possible evaluation pairs.

4 Techniques

4.1 Unsupervised Machine Learning [18]

Technique. Praiss AM in 2020 built further on the unsupervised machine learning algorithm known as "Ensemble algorithm for clustering cancer data (EACCD)". The parameters used for prediction were "TNM stage, grade, and age". Depending upon these parameters, groups were formed based on survival rates using C-index to cut dendrograms.

Dataset. The dataset used to train EACCD was obtained from the SEER Program with entries ranging from those recorded in 2004 up to and including those recorded in 2015. It had records of 46,773 patients suffering from endometrial cancer or, in other words, endometrioid carcinoma.

Result. Initially, 11 prognostic groups were formed by the algorithm having "a C-index of 0.8380" with the 5 year survival rates ranging from 37.9 to 99.8%. Upon visually reviewing the outcome, further simplification was effected by clubbing the six topmost survival groups into three prognostic groups so that a total of eight updated prognostic groups were created having "a C-index of 0.8313".

Limitations and Scope of Improvement. (a) Adjunct therapy was not given due consideration in the study. Given its importance in the recovery of patients, this can add a holistic approach to the solution. (b) Node analysis was not performed on all patients involved in the study. (c) The EACCD algorithm needs a minimum of 100 patients to fulfill all the combinations and get valid results.

4.2 Logistic Regression [19]

Technique. M Ahmed in 2018 proposed a model to help predict the severity of endometrial cancer using logistic regression. The "Signal Intensity (SI)" of tumors was gauged using the "sagittal T1W1 and sagittal T2W1". Logistic regression was used to evaluate several essential criteria such as grade and subtype of tumor, microsatellite stability status, lymphovascular space invasion, and depth of myometrial invasion, alongside results from magnetic resonance imaging.

Dataset. Data was collected from 71 women suffering from endometrial cancer who underwent MRI for diagnosis of the same. Both types of MRI images, namely T1-weighted and T2-weighted images, were put together to form the dataset used to train this model.

Result. Certain salient points to note were: (a) Tumors most likely to have lympho-vascular invasion were the ones having higher qualitative signal than normal myometrium; (b) higher SI tumor ratio made a tumor 2.36 times more likely to be microsatellite stable; (c) SI ratio of T2 tumor was observed to be $P = 0.006$, whereas the SI ratio of T1 tumor came out to be $P = 0.0014$; (d) tumors showing SI ≤ 209 on delayed T1W1 sequences had lesser recurrence-free survival than the ones showing SI > 209.

Limitations and Scope of Improvement. (a) The subtype and grade of the tumor were not associated with the MRI results. (b) Only the patients who had undergone hysterectomy were a part of the research which indicates a lack of diverse data.

4.3 Logistic Regression + Naive Bayes [20]

Technique. One of the most important diagnosis factors in early-stage endometrial cancer is to detect Lymph Node Involvement (LNI). The study used the Naive Bayes algorithm to do so followed by logistic regression to find the association with the eight independent factors.

Dataset. The dataset used was private and accessible only to the authors and their affiliates. The data was collected from 762 women with symptoms, such as diameter of the tumor, and more, that shed light on the possible existence of endometrial cancer.

Result. Some of the key points were: (a) 59.1 years was the mean age of the patients; (b) LNI was observed in 13.4% (102) of the patients; (c) para-aortic LNI (PaLNI) was observed in 7.1% (54) of the patients; (d) the accuracy was 84.2–88.9% for LNI and 85.0%–97.6% for PaLNI.

Limitations and Scope of Improvement. (a) The design of the model is outdated with newer and better state-of-the-art techniques present. (b) There was no detection of minimum sample size.

4.4 Classification and Regression Trees [21]

Technique. V. Pergialiotis et al. conducted a study in postmenopausal women to forecast endometrial cancer. To do so, classification and regression trees (CARTs) were used, which is a classification algorithm which uses Gini's impurity index to build a decision tree. The same was compared with logistic regression.

Dataset. Data was taken in the form of pathology reports from 178 women of ages 45 and above. Out of those, 106 were women with carcinoma and 72 women had normal histology.

Result. The sensitivity percentages achieved by the CART and regression analyses were 78.3 and 76.4%, respectively, whereas the specificity values were 76.4, and 66.7% for the two methods. The overall accuracy was 77.5 and 72.5% for the two models. Clearly, classification and regression trees performed better than logistic regression analysis.

Limitations and Scope of Improvement. A larger dataset with more variety of data can be used to improve prediction.

4.5   Computer Vision [22]

Technique. To trace the location of endometriosis from a given dataset of images, Sabrina Madad Zadeh employed semantic segmentation using mask R-CNN [23]. In simple words, semantic segmentation is the process in which all the pixels that belong to a given class are labeled the same. This was the first time semantic segmentation based on deep learning which has been employed in gynecology.

Dataset. The data is private and has been obtained from eight laparoscopic hysterectomies performed at CHU Clermont-Ferrand, France. A total of 461 laparoscopic images were annotated with three classes: surgical tools, uterus, and ovaries. Three hundred and sixty-one images were used to train the model, while 100 images were used for validation. This dataset was one of the firsts of its kind.

Result. The training set obtained the accuracies as "84.5% for uterus, 29.6% for ovaries, and 54.5% for surgical tools", while the validation set obtained the accuracies as "97% for uterus, 24% for ovaries, and 86% for surgical tools".

Limitations and Scope of Improvement. (a) A lower accuracy for the detection of ovaries can be attributed to the fact that their appearance differs in various individuals and are often concealed by surrounding organs. (b) The dataset used consisted of 461 laparoscopic images which further identifies a lack of data for better training of the model.

4.6 EXtreme Gradient Boosting (XGB) [24]

Technique. XGB initially forms a simple decision tree and keeps revising the previous tree with weaker learners till the most optimal solution is reached. Ewa J demonstrated the use of XGB to predict the likelihood of developing endometriosis. After feature selection and tuning, it was discovered that the presence of ovarian cysts and genital pain results in a significantly higher possibility of women developing endometriosis sometime in their life.

Dataset. Thirty-six months of medical history were taken for 314,101 female patients of ages 18 and above with pathologically confirmed endometriosis. Top 2300 codes for prescribed medicines, past surgical procedures, and diagnosis were the only ones considered to further analyze the data.

Result. The accuracy, sensitivity, specificity, and precision of the XGB model were 88%, 84%, 93%, and 92%, respectively. Both the $F1$-score and AUC values turned out to be the same at 0.88 each.

Limitations and Scope of Improvement. The model successfully identified features that are very relevant in foreseeing the chances of developing endometriosis. However, models like LightGBM and CatBoost tree may further improve the results. Use of neural networks may also result in a model with a significantly higher prediction rate.

4.7 Natural Language Processing [25]

Technique. While endometriosis has been seen to occur in clusters of families and have a high probability of occurring in close relatives, the genetic theory remains complex to determine. With the aid of text mining, this study retrieved a set of 724 genes which were then scrutinized by a phenotype-based gene analyzer.

Dataset. The authors looked up keywords on the PubMed database that were related to endometriosis and genetics to fetch close to a thousand articles. One of the biggest drawbacks was that genes do not have a well-defined and standardized nomenclature. This makes it difficult for research in the domain to progress.

Result. The study aimed to present genes with the highest association to endometriosis. To do so, two parameters were considered. The first one was how often a particular gene was published with respect to endometriosis. This was achieved via text mining. The second parameter was achieved via the Phenolyzer software which aided in identifying interacting genes to create protein complexes.

Limitations and Scope of Improvement. The study identified nine such genes that were closely associated with endometriosis but had no mention in the title or abstract of the available literature, hence could not be studied further. This study mostly placed importance on genes that were frequently mentioned in the articles. The reason for this is that a certain set of genes have more importance for researchers and doctors. This puts the model at a disadvantage of not getting access to less researched genes.

4.8 Decision Tree [13]

Technique. Dong in 2020 proposed a model to help in-person diagnosis of patients with early-stage endometrial cancer. The study used Convolutional Neural Network along with U-Net for image segmentation. J-48 decision trees were employed to train and test the data. Chi-square test was further used to associate two readings and to check the independence between categorical variables. For continuous variables, Pearson correlation was employed.

Dataset. The dataset consists of 4896 images from 72 patients such that 3456 are T1 weighted and 1440 are T2 weighted. Additionally, clinical reports and geographical information were collected. All the data was ethically made anonymous to conceal the identity of individuals.

Result. The proposed model did not outperform the performance of manual diagnosis by radiologists in most cases except when the myometrial invasion < 50. The accuracy, sensitivity, specificity, and precision are 91%, 0.91, 0.76, and 0.92, respectively.

Limitations and Scope of Improvement. (a) To improve the pre-operative evaluation of patients, a larger dataset with more diverse data can be used. (b) The model failed to diagnose with the same or higher accuracy as radiologists.

4.9 Decision Tree + Generalized Linear Model [26]

Technique. The model used three steps to make an informed decision to predict endometriosis using the DNA and RNA data available. First, normalization was done keeping the type of dataset in mind. Second, GLM was used in combination with decision trees since GLM helps enhance the decision trees. Third, genes were identified that could act as biomarkers.

Dataset. Machine Learning Classifiers for endometriosis using transcriptomics and methylomics data [methylomics] are available on the website of National Center for Biological Information. All the patients were in the age group 18–49. All individuals were in the process of a laparoscopic procedure for other purposes like pain, infertility, or sterilization.

Result. For the transcriptomics data, the best performance was of the model that used TMM for normalization and GLM to classify. It fetched an accuracy of 0.895, sensitivity of 0.813, and specificity of 0.955. For the methylomics data, the best performing model used qNorm/vNorm for normalization and GLM to classify. The accuracy was 0.779, sensitivity was 0.762, and specificity was 0.800.

Limitations and Scope of Improvement. The given models show promising results which are yet to be evaluated on publicly available datasets for a larger variety. Making use of an integrated dataset of transcriptomes and methylomics is likely to give better results.

4.10   Convolutional Neural Network [27]

Technique. Chen X in 2020 used T2-weighted MRI images to detect endometrial cancer with the aid of deep learning. Upon dividing the dataset into two groups on the basis of the pathological diagnosis, the YOLOv3 algorithm [28] was employed to detect the area of the lesion. Then, a deep learning model was fed this data to classify images based on myometrial invasion.

Dataset. Data was obtained in the form of T2-weighted MRI images from 530 patients with pathologically confirmed endometrial cancer. It was a private dataset compiled from 1 January 2013 to 31 December 2017 at the institution where research was conducted.

Result. The hybrid model with the aid of the radiologists performed the best, the following performance matrices: accuracy of 86.2%, specificity of 87.5%, sensitivity of 77.8%, PPV of 48.3%, and NPV of 96.3%.

Limitations and Scope of Improvement. (a) The proposed model has only made use of the T2W1 dataset for training despite the availability of "MRI T1W1, T2W1" and post-contrast MRI. (b) The dataset is skewed with the number of Deep Myometrial Invasion images much lower than the Shallow Myometrial Invasion images. This could further lead to bias.

4.11   ResNet50 Convolutional Neural Network [7]

Technique. Out of other existing methods, ResNet50 stands out for its methodical image classification and recognition. ResNet allows one to go deeper and increase the precision of the detection of the region of interest. Number of deep layers is directly proportional to higher accuracy and throughputs. The number 50 here refers to the number of layers formed by the model.

Dataset. The paper uses 6000 laparoscopic images from GLENDA: Gynecologic Laparoscopy Endometriosis Dataset, which is one of its kind. The dataset itself contains over 25 k images with over 300+ hand annotated images. The dataset can be categorized into two parts: pathological and non-pathological images. The pathological images can then further be categorized into four, namely, peritoneum, ovary, uterus, and deep infiltrating endometriosis (DIE).

Result. The model trained on ResNet50 rendered 91% accuracy on the training dataset but 90% accuracy on the validation dataset. The precision was 83% and recall was 82% with the AUC being 0.78.

Limitations and Scope of Improvement. (a) The black box nature of residual models often puts it at a disadvantage. (b) Batch normalization layers need to be added.

4.12 VGGNet-16 Model [16]

Technique. VGG16 is a convolutional neural network model initially proposed in [29]. VGG16 is one of the most common variants used due to its having less number of layers and parameters and thus lowers the cost as well as the processing time. It is a unique model used for object identification and can support 19 layers.

Dataset. A private dataset was procured from Shengjing Hospital of China Medical University over the course of two years (2017–2019). The researchers took images with an Olympus OTV-S7. A total of 1851 hysteroscopic images were collected from 454 patients. Post preprocessing, a total number of 6478 images were used as input.

Result. In [16] by YunZheng Zhang, the VGGNet-16 model rendered an overall accuracy of 80.8% in the classification task with five categories. The model used was compared with the performance of three gynecologists who manually classified the images. The accuracies of the gynecologists 1, 2, and 3 were 72.8%, 69.2%, and 64.4%, respectively.

Limitations and Scope of Improvement. (a) The dataset being used is obtained from one hospital using the same optical lens, which implies that the dataset does not have diversification. Expanding the dataset can be useful. (b) During the research, past case studies of individual patients were not covered. This could be a key indicator of the underlying condition. (c) There was no process in place for validation of the obtained results by experts.

4.13 Artificial Neural Network [21]

Technique. The study forecasted endometrial cancer in postmenopausal women using ANN. ANNs have the ability to learn and associate complex relationships between variables making it ideal for the study.

Dataset. The dataset was private, compiled in the form of pathology reports from 106 women with carcinoma combined with 72 women exhibiting normal histology, coming out to be 178 women in total. All women were of ages 45 and above.

Result. The ANN model showed better results than regression analysis conducted for comparison. ANN had an overall accuracy of 85.4%, whereas the accuracy of regression was 72.5%, sensitivity of ANN was 86.8%, but sensitivity of classical regression was 76.4%, and specificity of ANN was 83.3%, while specificity for the other model was 66.7%.

Limitations and Scope of Improvement. (a) A larger and more diverse dataset to improve results. (b) Correlation with genetic data.

4.14 Deep Neural Network [14]

Technique. Xception [30], MobileNetV2 [31], and EfficientNetB0 [32] were the three neural networks employed in the model due to their proven record of achieving a high accuracy while not being computationally expensive. This would in turn be economically feasible.

Dataset. The image dataset was extracted from "videos of the uterine lumen captured using a hysteroscope" from 177 patients. The input videos were from 177 patients, and typical video duration is being between 10.5 and 395.3 s. The dataset is divided into categories: normal endometrium (60), endometrial polyp (60), uterine myoma (21), endometrial cancer (21), and AEH (15).

Result. Takahashi Y demonstrated the use of deep neural networks to classify images as "normal endometrium, uterine myoma, endometrial polyp, AEH, and endometrial cancer" with an accuracy of 90.29%.

Limitations and Scope of Improvement. (a) Most of the misclassified images were due to "the flatness of the tumour" and "excessive bleeding". (b) The results can be further improved by training a larger dataset.

Table 4 Results of deep
learning model with
histopathological subtypes

Prediction class	AUROC
Histological subtype	0.969
Copy number high (CNV-H) molecular subtype	0.934–0.958
Microsatellite high (MSI-H) molecular subtype	0.781–0.873

4.15 Deep Learning Along with Histopathological Subtypes [33]

Technique. To aid the process of diagnosis and treatment in patients, molecular subtyping and mutation status enable doctors to deliver customized treatment with better results. Hong devised a custom-made architecture called Panoptes that uses deep CNN models to foresee molecular subtypes. It also predicts 18 recurrent gene mutations along with their histopathological subtypes.

Dataset. Images were taken from two different datasets, namely, Clinical Proteomic Tumor Analysis Consortium (CPTAC) and The Cancer Genome Atlas (TCGA), where 392 and 107 slides were downloaded from respective platforms for the study.

Result. The proposed model outperformed Inception-ResNet by 18% (Table 4).

Limitations and Scope of Improvement. (a) The model is overfitting in some cases, thereby giving non-tumor tissues a vague prediction score. This can be improved by creating a segmentation model that eliminates irrelevant tissues entirely. (b) Integration of clinical results with image will yield a higher accuracy for prediction.

5   Comparison of Several Machine Learning Techniques

See Table 5.

6   Conclusion

Machine learning plays an integral role in diagnosing endometriosis, customizing treatment, and predicting it well in advance. The datasets used in this study are both image-based as well as normal datasets. However, there continues to be a lack of publicly available data that is verified by medical professionals as well as covers all aspects of endometriosis such as images, genetics, and epigenetics.

Various different image modalities exhibit differences in the diagnosis of endometriosis. Out of the four imaging methods mentioned in this review paper, magnetic resonance imaging, transvaginal ultrasound, and hysteroscopy are

Table 5 Comparison of several machine learning techniques

Technique	Data used	Result parameters	Strengths	Weaknesses
Unsupervised machine learning [18]	Details of TNM stage, age group, and grade from 46,773 women were taken (Ordinal Data)	C-index = 0.8313	Use of ensemble algorithm ensures better results in most cases since predictions of various models are combined	1. Secondary treatment statistics not considered 2. Node analysis was not performed 3. The EACCD algorithm needs a minimum of 100 patients
Logistic regression [19]	MRI images (T1W1 and T2W1) from 71 women	SI ratio: P = 0.006 (T2 tumor) P = 0.0014 (T1 tumor) Sensitivity = 40.6% Specificity = 100%	Severity of endometrial cancer was successfully predicted by correlating MRI images with biomarkers	1. Subtype and grade of the tumor was not associated with the MRI results 2. Only hysterectomy data was collected
Logistic regression + Naive Bayes [20]	Dataset of pathological factors like histology, CGSI, and pelvic LNI (ordinal data)	Accuracy: LNI = 84.2%–88.9% PaLNI = 85.0%–97.6%	The most important factor, i.e., lymph nodes was targeted, thereby creating a reliable prediction model for endometrial cancer	1. Models used are outdated 2. There was no power analysis
Classification and regression trees [21]	Ultrasound reports of 178 women with and without carcinoma	Accuracy = 77.5% Sensitivity = 78.3% Specificity = 76.4%	Endometrial cancer remains overlooked in postmenopausal women making this study efficient and relevant	Small dataset with lack of diversity in data
Computer vision [22]	461 laparoscopic images	Accuracy: Uterus = 97% Ovaries = 24% Surgical tools = 86%	The study successfully finds the location of endometriosis, thereby serving as an aid to medical professionals	1. Ovaries vary greatly in individuals and are often concealed by other organs 2. Dataset used is small

(continued)

Table 5 (continued)

Technique	Data used	Result parameters	Strengths	Weaknesses
eXtreme gradient boosting [24]	Medical history of 3,14,101 patients	Accuracy = 88% Sensitivity = 84% Specificity = 93% Precision = 92% F1-score = 0.88 AUC = 0.88	Based on one's medical history, the study aims to predict the likelihood of endometriosis so that appropriate precautions can be taken	Using more advanced models like LightGBM and CatBoost tree is likely to render better results
Natural Language Processing [25]	Text dataset derived from PubMed search results	Successfully identified top six genes linked to endometriosis	The study examines that endometriosis has higher chances of occurring in close relatives and finds the genes most likely to play a role	The study identified nine novel genes with little to no available data; hence, the results could not be verified
Decision Tree [13]	4896 MRI images from 72 patients	Accuracy = 91% Sensitivity = 0.91 Specificity = 0.76 Precision = 0.92	The model helps with the identification of early-stage endometrial cancer	Model failed to outperform manual detection by radiologists in most cases
Decision Tree + Generalized Linear Model [26]	Transcriptomics and methylomics data	Transcriptomics data: Accuracy = 0.895 Sensitivity = 0.813 Specificity = 0.955 Methylomics data: Accuracy = 0.779 Sensitivity = 0.762 Specificity = 0.800	DNA and RNA were used in this study to predict endometriosis which can result in early detection	Model can be used on a geographically diverse population and publicly available datasets to verify efficiency

(continued)

Table 5 (continued)

Technique	Data used	Result parameters	Strengths	Weaknesses
Convolution Neural Network [27]	T2-weighted MRI images from 530 patients	Accuracy = 78.3% Sensitivity = 61.1% Specificity = 80.8% Positive prediction value = 32.4% Negative prediction value = 98.3%	YOLOV3, a CNN based model, was used to classify depth of myometrial invasion	1. Model only made use of the T2W1 dataset for training despite the availability of "MRI T1W1, T2W1" and post-contrast MRI 2. The dataset is skewed with the number of Deep Myometrial Invasion images much lower than the Shallow Myometrial Invasion images
ResNet50 Convolution Neural Network [7]	6000 laparoscopic images from GLENDA: Gynecologic Laparoscopy Endometriosis Dataset	Accuracy = 90% Sensitivity = 82% Specificity = 72% Precision = 83% Recall = 82% AUC = 0.78	The model used ResNet50 to predict the incidence of endometriosis	1. The black box nature of residual models often puts it at a disadvantage 2. Batch normalization layers need to be added
VGGNet-16 model [16]	1851 hysteroscopic images	Accuracy = 80.8%	The type of endometrial lesions are often hard to identify and classify. This model uses VGGNet-16 to classify lesions into five categories and label them as benign or as premalignant/malignant	1. All images in the dataset have been clicked with the same optical lens reducing its diversity 2. Medical history of patients not covered 3. No validation of results by experts

(continued)

Table 5 (continued)

Technique	Data used	Result parameters	Strengths	Weaknesses
Artificial Neural Network [21]	Pathology reports from 178 women	Accuracy = 85.4% Sensitivity = 86.8% Specificity — 83.3%	The study predicts endometrial cancer in postmenopausal women. Using ANN gives it an advantage of being able to link and identify complex relationships in the parameters	1. The model does not account for genetic information of patients 2. Using a larger dataset can yield better results
Deep Neural Network [14]	Images were captured from videos taken using a hysteroscope	Accuracy = 90.29%	The study uses Xception, MobileNetV2, and EfficientNetB0 to facilitate timely detection of endometrial cancer	1. Most of the misclassified images were due to "the flatness of the tumour" and "excessive bleeding" 2. The results can be further improved by training a larger dataset
Deep learning along with histopathological subtypes [33]	Image data from TCGA and CPTAC	AUROC: 0.781–0.873	Molecular subtyping and mutation status enable doctors to deliver customized treatment with better results. The model aims to foresee molecular subtypes and common gene mutations through deep learning	1. The model is overfitting in some cases, thereby giving non-tumor tissues a vague prediction score 2. Integration of clinical results with image will yield a higher accuracy for prediction

primarily focused on diagnosis, whereas laparoscopy is used for both diagnosis as well as surgical excision of endometrial lesion. Not only do the four image extraction techniques have separate requirements during the respective procedures, but also the images obtained from the procedures require preprocessing and machine learning methods specific to each procedure.

The techniques discussed in this review paper use medical history, genetics, family history, age, biomarkers, pathological reports, MRI scans, laparoscopic images, transcriptomics, and methylomics data to feed to models like logistic regression, decision trees, computer vision, NLP, CNN, ANN, and DNN. The potential is promising for further research and enhancement that can lead to revolutionary breakthroughs in the field enabling medical professionals to better predict, prevent, and diagnose endometriosis.

References

1. Baranov V, Malysheva O, Yarmolinskaya M (2018) Pathogenomics of endometriosis development. Int J Mol Sci 19(7):1852
2. Laganà AS, Garzon S, Götte M, Viganò P, Franchi M, Ghezzi F, Martin DC (2019) The pathogenesis of endometriosis: molecular and cell biology insights. Int J Mol Sci 20(22):5615
3. Kajiyama H, Suzuki S, Yoshihara M, Tamauchi S, Yoshikawa N, Niimi K, Shibata K, Kikkawa F (2019) Endometriosis and cancer. Free Radical Biol Med 133:186–192
4. Koninckx PR, Ussia A, Adamyan L, Wattiez A, Gomel V, Martin DC (2019) Pathogenesis of endometriosis: the genetic/epigenetic theory. Fertil Steril 111(2):327–340
5. Benagiano G, Brosens I, Lippi D (2014) The history of endometriosis. Gynecol Obstet Invest 78(1):1–9
6. Yu H-C, Lin C-Y, Chang W-C, Shen B-J, Chang W-P, Chuang C-M (2015) Increased association between endometriosis and endometrial cancer: a nationwide population-based retrospective cohort study. Int J Gynecol Cancer 25(3)
7. Visalaxi S, Muthu TS (2021) Automated prediction of endometriosis using deep learning. Int J Nonlinear Anal Appl 12(2):2403–2416
8. Falcone T, Flyckt R (2018) Clinical management of endometriosis. Obstet Gynecol 131(3):557–571
9. Leibetseder A, Kletz S, Schoeffmann K, Keckstein S, Keckstein J (2020) GLENDA: gynecologic laparoscopy endometriosis dataset. In: International conference on multimedia modeling. Springer, Cham
10. Siddaiah-Subramanya M, Nyandowe M, Tiang KW (2017) Technical problems during laparoscopy: a systematic method of troubleshooting for surgeons. Innov Surg Sci 2(4):233–237
11. Kathiravan S, Kanakaraj J (2013) A review on potential issues and challenges in MR imaging. Sci World J
12. Di Spiezio Sardo A, Calagna G, Santangelo F, Zizolfi B, Tanos V, Perino A, De Wilde RL (2017) The role of hysteroscopy in the diagnosis and treatment of adenomyosis. BioMed Res Int
13. Dong H-C, Dong H-K, Yu M-H, Lin Y-H, Chang C-C (2020) Using deep learning with convolutional neural network approach to identify the invasion depth of endometrial cancer in myometrium using mr images: a pilot study. Int J Environ Res Public Health 17(16):5993
14. Takahashi Y, Sone K, Noda K, Yoshida K, Toyohara Y, Kato K, Inoue F, Kukita A, Taguchi A, Nishida H, Miyamoto Y (2021) Automated system for diagnosing endometrial cancer by adopting deep-learning technology in hysteroscopy. PLoS ONE 16(3):e0248526
15. Saba L, Guerriero S, Sulcis R, Pilloni M, Ajossa S, Melis G, Mallarini G (2012) MRI and "tenderness guided" transvaginal ultrasonography in the diagnosis of recto-sigmoid endometriosis. J Magn Reson Imaging 35(2):352–360
16. Zhang YZ, Zhang Y, Wang Z, Zhang J, Wang C, Wang Y, Chen H, Shan L, Huo J, Gu J, Ma X (2021) Deep learning model for classifying endometrial lesions. J Transl Med 19(1):1–13
17. Visalaxi S, Punnoose D, Muthu TS (2021) Lesion extraction of endometriotic images using open computer vision. In: 2021 international conference on artificial intelligence and smart systems (ICAIS). IEEE

18. Praiss AM, Huang Y, Clair CMS, Tergas AI, Melamed A, Khoury-Collado F, Hou JY, Hu J, Hur C, Hershman DL, Wright JD (2020) Using machine learning to create prognostic systems for endometrial cancer. Gynecol Oncol 159(3):744–750
19. Ahmed M, Al-Khafaji JF, Class CA, Wei W, Ramalingam P, Wakkaa H, Soliman PT, Frumovitz M, Iyer RB, Bhosale PR (2018) Can MRI help assess aggressiveness of endometrial cancer? Clin Radiol 73(9):833-e11
20. Günakan E, Atan S, Haberal AN, Küçükyıldız İA, Gökçe E, Ayhan A (2019) A novel prediction method for lymph node involvement in endometrial cancer: machine learning. Int J Gynecol Cancer 29(2)
21. Pergialiotis V, Pouliakis A, Parthenis C, Damaskou V, Chrelias C, Papantoniou N, Panayiotides I (2018) The utility of artificial neural networks and classification and regression trees for the prediction of endometrial cancer in postmenopausal women. Publ Health 164:1–6
22. Zadeh SM, Francois T, Calvet L, Chauvet P, Canis M, Bartoli A, Bourdel N (2020) SurgAI: deep learning for computerized laparoscopic image understanding in gynaecology. Surg Endosc 34(12):5377–5383
23. He K, Gkioxari G, Dollár P, Girshick R (2017) Mask R-CNN. In: Proceedings of the IEEE international conference on computer vision
24. Kleczyk EJ, Peri A, Yadav T, Komera R, Peri M, Guduru V, Amirtharaj S, Huang M (2020) Predicting endometriosis onset using machine learning algorithms
25. Bouaziz J, Mashiach R, Cohen S, Kedem A, Baron A, Zajicek M, Feldman I, Seidman D, Soriano D (2018) How artificial intelligence can improve our understanding of the genes associated with endometriosis: natural language processing of the PubMed database. BioMed Res Int
26. Akter S, Xu D, Nagel SC, Bromfield JJ, Pelch K, Wilshire GB, Joshi T (2019) Machine learning classifiers for endometriosis using transcriptomics and methylomics data. Front Genet 10:766
27. Chen X, Wang Y, Shen M, Yang B, Zhou Q, Yi Y, Liu W, Zhang G, Yang G, Zhang H (2020) Deep learning for the determination of myometrial invasion depth and automatic lesion identification in endometrial cancer MR imaging: a preliminary study in a single institution. Eur Radiol 30(9):4985–4994
28. Redmon J, Farhadi A (2018) Yolov3: an incremental improvement. arXiv preprint arXiv:1804.02767
29. Simonyan K, Zisserman A (2014) Very deep convolutional networks for large-scale image recognition. arXiv preprint arXiv:1409.1556
30. Chollet F (2017) Xception: deep learning with depthwise separable convolutions. In: Proceedings of the IEEE conference on computer vision and pattern recognition
31. Sandler M, Howard A, Zhu M, Zhmoginov A, Chen LC (2018) Mobilenetv2: inverted residuals and linear bottlenecks. In: Proceedings of the IEEE conference on computer vision and pattern recognition
32. Tan M, Le Q (2019) EfficientNet: rethinking model scaling for convolutional neural networks. In: International conference on machine learning. PMLR
33. Hong R, Liu W, DeLair D, Razavian N, Fenyö D (2021) Predicting endometrial cancer subtypes and molecular features from histopathology images using multi-resolution deep learning models. Cell Rep Med 2(9):100400

A Time-Dependent Mathematical Model for COVID-19 Transmission Dynamics and Analysis of Critical and Hospitalized Cases with Bed Requirements

Avaneesh Singh, Manish Kumar Bajpai, and Shyam Lal Gupta

1 Introduction

Many countries have suffered a lot from this COVID-19. Some countries suffer from loss of beds and ICU beds. Due to triage conditions, doctors have to select critical conditioned people for treatment, and some patients have not been treated due to a lack of hospital beds and ICU beds. It is regrettable to us that someone dies without treatment. Perhaps if they were treated, then save their lives. If the government has prior knowledge of how much beds are needed in a particular time, then the arrangement can be made, and it can save many lives for those who have died of lack of facility. Our proposed model is a new mathematical method that extends the SEIR model by adding death, hospitalized, and critical compartments. The hospitalized compartment and critical compartment are to a new compartment added in this model to enhance the disease transmission visibility. No one has used these two compartments in any model of my knowledge until that time. The model also calculates how many hospital beds and ICU beds are needed in peak time. The proposed model also calculates the case fatality rate and the basic reproduction rate. The calculation process for requiring beds and ICU beds by this method is new. We calculate the basic reproduction number using the logistic regression over time; its unique idea is used in this model. We also consider age groups for case fatality rate analysis; if any country's elderly population is more, then the case fatality rate will be higher in that country.

A. Singh (✉) · M. K. Bajpai
Department of Computer Science and Engineering, PDPM Indian Institute of Information Technology, Design and Manufacturing, Jabalpur, Madhya Pradesh 482005, India
e-mail: avaneesh.singh@iiitdmj.ac.in

S. L. Gupta
Department of Physics, Government College Bassa, Himachal Pradesh University, Gohar, Mandi, Himachal Pradesh 175029, India

© The Author(s), under exclusive license to Springer Nature Singapore Pte Ltd. 2023
K. Kumar Singh et al. (eds.), *Machine Vision and Augmented Intelligence*, Lecture Notes in Electrical Engineering 1007, https://doi.org/10.1007/978-981-99-0189-0_7

The entire world is combating against a new enemy in these days, which is the COVID-19 virus. The virus has spread exponentially around the world since its first appearance in China. Most of the countries are struggling with economic and social fronts due to this virus. Tyrell and Bynoe described the coronavirus for the first time in 1966 [1]. An outbreak of pneumonia was reported in Wuhan, China, in December 2019 [2]. The virus causing that outbreak was provisionally named as 2019-nCoV, which was renames as SARS-CoV-2 by the International Committee on Virus Taxonomy [3–5]. The World Health Organization announced these outbreaks as an international public health emergency on January 30 and a pandemic on March 11, 2020 [6, 7]. COVID-19 caused a global recession and has an impact on social life [8]. More than 22.4 million cases, out of which more than 14.3 million people have recovered and around 788,000 have died, of COVID-19 pandemic have been reported across 188 countries and territories till August 20, 2020 [9]. Worldwide, researchers are working 24 h a day to find the SARS-CoV-2 virus vaccine. There are nearly 231 vaccines reported as potential candidates for the cure of COVID-19 till August 2020; however, none of these have successfully established their safety and efficacy in clinical trials. As per various reports, nearly 25 vaccine candidates are in different stages of clinical trials [10–12].

Asymptomatic cases mean people without symptoms. However, there are reports of loss of sense of smell in people who otherwise have no symptoms. This is now recognized as an official symptom of the virus, and people experiencing it should self-isolate themselves. Reports from many countries suggest that asymptomatic infected individuals are much less likely to transmit the virus than those with symptoms [13]. Most of the symptomatic cases are mild. They do not have to be in the hospital. They can be quarantined at home under the guidance of the doctor. Temperature with minor cough, tiredness, moderate breathlessness, pain in the muscles, headache, sour throat, and diarrhea are the main signs of mild cases. Symptoms of severe cases are more visible in older people. Its symptoms are rarely seen in healthy young people. The main symptoms of severe cases are pneumonia that involves excessive breathlessness, chest pain, high temperature, low oxygen levels, rapid heart rate, and decreased blood pressure. Severe cases need hospital beds for the treatment of patients. Symptoms of critical cases are more visible in older people who have pre-existing diseases such as cardiovascular disease, diabetes, chronic respiratory disease, hypertension, and cancer. Many organs fail to function because of this. Critical cases need ventilators or ICU care for the treatment of patients. COVID-19 shows an increased number of cases and a greater risk of severe disease with increasing age [14, 15].

Mathematical models that forecast the possible effects of various approaches to behavioral changes in the population are an essential source of knowledge for policymakers [16, 17]. Currently, the countries most affected by COVID-19 disease in the world are the United States, Brazil, India, South Africa, Russia, and Mexico. In the present work, we are introducing a new mathematical model for the study of the pandemic transmission and control dynamics of COVID-19 based on the reports of these affected countries. Compartmental models are composed of ordinary differential equations. These models are separated into many compartments. Our proposed SEAIHCRD model has eight compartments: susceptible (*S*), exposed (*E*), asymptomatic infectious (A), symptomatic infectious (I), hospitalized (H), critical (C), recovered (R), and deceased or death (D), collectively termed as SEAIHCRD. The basic rule of the compartmental model is the transition of people from one compartment to another. Models use mathematics to find the different parameters to estimate the effect of various interventions and then to decide which intervention to stop and which to continue. These models are primarily used in epidemiology and many other fields, such as economics, politics, social science, and medicine.

Kermack and McKendrick have introduced the first basic infectious disease compartmental model, SIR [18]. The SEIR model is a commonly used epidemiological model based on the SIR model [19]. The Kermack and McKendrick epidemic model has predicted outbreak behavior very close to the real scenarios seen in many recorded epidemics [19]. Since Kermack and McKendrick's paper, stochastic models, discrete-time models, continuous-time models, and diffusion models have been developed for many diseases. Some manuscripts provide an excellent approach to mathematical models that provide a comprehensive understanding of the disease outbreak scenario [20–34]. The SEIR model has not been able to estimate spread where preventive measures such as social distances, different age groups, number of ICU beds, number of hospital beds, and mortality rates have been adopted. The proposed model in this work is a modification to the SEIR model. The present manuscript includes an updated SEIR model for COVID-19 with all the above parameters. We propose a prediction model that has been constrained by many observed data under uncertainties. The time-dependent SEAIHCRD model estimates the magnitude of peaks for exposed people, the number of asymptomatic infectious people, the number of symptomatic infectious people, the number of people hospitalized, the number of people admitted to ICUs, and the number of deaths of COVID-19 over time. The proposed method includes asymptomatic infectious cases as a separate compartment. Asymptomatic infection cases are either recovered or, if symptoms begin to appear within a few days, enter into the symptomatic infectious compartment.

The time-dependent SEAIHCRD model includes a social distancing parameter, analysis of different age groups, number of ICU beds, number of hospital beds, and lock-down effect, which gives a more accurate estimate of the future requirement of the beds normal as well as the ICU in the hospitals. The proposed model also analyzes the basic reproduction number over time. Early stages of the outbreak, the basic reproductive number (R_0) in January ranged from 1.4 to 2.5, but a subsequent study suggested that it may be around 5.7 [35, 36]. The spread of disease in these areas has been stable or declining since mid-May 2020 [37]. The number of cases doubled in almost seven and a half days in the early stages of the outbreak, but later the rate increased [38]. The proposed model analyzes the case fatality rate over time. The case fatality rate is the ratio of people dying from a specific disease among all individuals suffering from the disease over a certain period [39, 40].

The structure of this paper is as follows; Sect. 1 introduces COVID-19 and explains the significance of this research. A time-dependent SEAIHCRD predictive mathematical model for COVID-19 is presented in Sect. 2. Section 3 discusses the dataset and its analysis used to validate the proposed mathematical models. Results and discussions on the proposed model are discussed in Sect. 4. Finally, the conclusion and some future works are discussed in Sect. 5.

2 Proposed Methodology

Modeling is one of the most powerful tools that give intuitive inferences when multiple factors act together. Compartment models such as SIR and SEIR are mostly used today for the mathematical modeling of infectious diseases. Over the last few weeks, many epidemiologists and data scientists have worked on mathematical modeling of infectious diseases, in particular, coronavirus disease (COVID-19). Coronavirus disease (COVID-19) is an infectious disease that can spread from one member of the population to another. Kermack–McKendrick [18] proposed the basic compartmental SIR model in 1927. Beretta and Takeuchi [41] have developed their theories based on research conducted by Kermack and McKendrick [18] and have proposed a SIR model on time delays. In the spread of infectious diseases, Cooke and Driessche [42] studied the incubation cycle, developed the "Exposed, E" compartment, and suggested a time delay SEIR model.

Singh et al. [27] described the basic compartment model SIR, the SEIR model, and the SEIRD model. Our proposed model, a time-dependent SEAIHCRD model, is a new mathematical method that extends the SEIR model by adding asymptomatic infectious, death, hospitalized, and critical compartments.

COVID-19 infectious disease is essentially categorized as symptomatic infectious and asymptomatic infectious cases. Figure 1 shows the categorization of infectious cases and the flow of infectious cases. There is no need to hospitalize asymptomatic cases and mild cases to reduce the pressure on hospitals. At the same time, it would ensure that serious and urgent patients have access to beds when they are most needed. There may be fear among the positive patients that they are ignored and not provided the necessary treatment. However, there is no need for fear, as mild cases can be cured even if the patients stay at home in isolation with the guidelines as prescribed by health professionals [43].

In Fig. 2, the Actor is a source of infection, and it transfers the infection from one Actor to another. The Actor may be either symptomatic or asymptomatic infected. Most of the cases are mild or asymptomatic. Severe cases are significantly less than mild cases but more than critical cases. Initially, some cases are mild, but with time, it becomes severe or critical; then, they need hospital beds or ICU beds.

Most cases are asymptomatic because many cases are missing from the symptom-based screening test. Children and young adults may become asymptomatic. ICMR has advised asymptomatic and COVID positive cases with mild symptoms like fever and cough to observe self-isolation and put under home quarantine for at least 17 days; hence, the pressure on the designate COVID hospitals is reduced [43, 44].

The non-infected and asymptomatic population is susceptible to COVID-19. There is an incubation period for the susceptible, exposed person (compartment E), which is defined as the duration in which one exposed may become infected

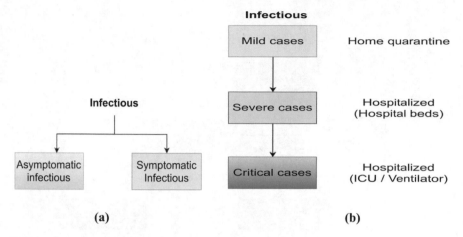

Fig. 1 **a** Infectious categorization. **b** Infectious cases flow

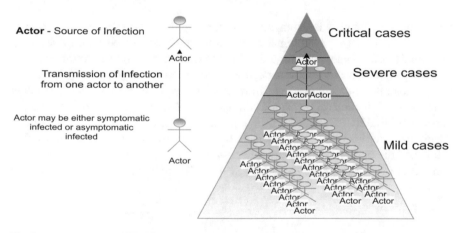

Fig. 2 Hierarchy of COVID-19 cases in numbers

with symptoms or asymptomatic. Asymptomatic infected individuals can enter the symptomatic infected or recover. From symptomatic infected, they can either die or recover shown in Fig. 3.

2.1 A Time-Dependent SEAIHCRD Model

In the present manuscript, the asymptomatic infectious, hospitalized, and critical compartments are three additional compartments for further accurate analysis. This model allows the asymptomatic cases, overflowing hospitals with less number of hospital beds and ICU beds. A time-dependent SEAIHCRD model has been divided

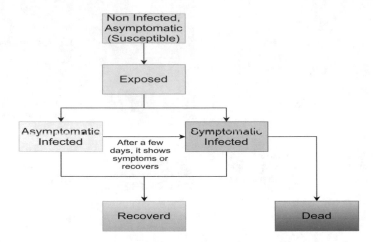

Fig. 3 Flow of asymptomatic infectious cases

into eight population-wise compartments: susceptible (S), exposed (E), asymptomatic infectious (A), symptomatic infectious (I), hospitalized (H), critical (C), recovered (R), and dead (D). A time-dependent SEAIHCRD model describes the transition of people from susceptible to exposed, then exposed to asymptomatic infectious and symptomatic infectious. Then from asymptomatic infectious, they can either symptomatic infectious or recovered compartment. According to the proposed time-dependent SEAIHCRD model, only symptomatic infected individuals can enter the hospitalized compartment and critical compartment. Hospitalized cases may either enter the critical or recover compartment and the critical compartment; they may either die or recover. A time-dependent SEAIHCRD model is shown in Fig. 4.

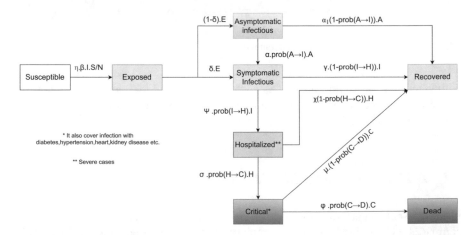

Fig. 4 Time-dependent SEAIHCRD model

Asymptomatic cases and some mild cases, put into a home quarantine that does not require hospitalization, these individuals may recover or, if they show some symptoms, go to the symptomatic infectious compartment in the future. People with a serious infection who have severe pneumonia need hospitalization. These people can either recover or move into the critical compartment. People with critical conditions have multi-organs and multiple disorders and need ICU medication. These people either recover or die of the disease.

Differential Equations for Time-Dependent SEAIHCRD Model

The SEAIHCRD model's ordinary differential equations are as follows:

$$\frac{dS(t)}{dt} = -\eta . \beta(t) . I(t) . \frac{S(t)}{N}, \tag{1}$$

$$\frac{dE(t)}{dt} = \eta . \beta(t) . I(t) . \frac{S(t)}{N} - \delta . E(t) - (1 - \delta) . E(t), \tag{2}$$

$$\frac{dA(t)}{dt} = (1 - \delta) . E(t) - \alpha . \text{prob}(A \rightarrow I) . A(t)$$
$$- \alpha_1 . (1 - \text{prob}(A \rightarrow I)) . A(t), \tag{3}$$

$$\frac{dI(t)}{dt} = \delta . E(t) + \alpha . \text{prob}(A \rightarrow I) . A(t) - \Psi . \text{prob}(I \rightarrow H) . I(t)$$
$$- \gamma(t) . (1 - \text{prob}(I \rightarrow H)) . I(t), \tag{4}$$

$$\frac{dH(t)}{dt} = \Psi . \text{prob}(I \rightarrow H) . I(t) - \sigma . \text{prob}(H \rightarrow C) . H(t)$$
$$- \chi(1 - \text{prob}(H \rightarrow C)) . H(t), \tag{5}$$

$$\frac{dC(t)}{dt} = \sigma . \text{prob}(H \rightarrow C) . H(t) - \varphi . \text{prob}(C \rightarrow D) . C(t)$$
$$- \mu . (1 - \text{prob}(C \rightarrow D)) . C(t), \tag{6}$$

$$\frac{dR(t)}{dt} = \gamma(t) . (1 - \text{prob}(I \rightarrow H)) . I(t) + \mu . (1 - \text{prob}(C \rightarrow D)) . C(t)$$
$$+ \chi(1 - \text{prob}(H \rightarrow C)) . H(t) + \alpha_1 . (1 - \text{prob}(A \rightarrow I)) . A(t), \tag{7}$$

$$\frac{dD(t)}{dt} = \varphi . \text{prob}(C \rightarrow D) . C(t), \tag{8}$$

$$N = S(t) + E(t) + A(t) + I(t) + H(t) + C(t) + R(t) + D(t). \tag{9}$$

The exact value of the initial conditions $(S(0), I(0), R(0))$ is not known. We put the amount of the initial conditions very carefully because these systems of ordinary differential equations are extremely sensitive to the initial parameters.

X   Number of days an infected individual has and may spread the disease $(X = \frac{1}{\gamma})$.

Basic reproduction number $R_0 = \beta \cdot X$.
Therefore, from above, we can write it as $R_0 = \frac{\beta}{\gamma}$.
Let $\beta(t)$ and $\gamma(t)$ be the transmission rate and recovering rate at time t.
Here,

N   Total population,
S   A proportion of the entire population that is healthy and has never been infected,
E   A proportion of the whole population exposed to infection, transmit the infection and become symptomatic or purely asymptomatic without being detected,
A   A proportion of the population that has no symptoms found positive,
I   A proportion of the population with positive symptoms,
H   A portion of the whole population, which is positive in the test and hospital,
C   A proportion of the population is seriously ill and requires ICU,
R   A proportion of the population that has recovered from the infection,
D   A proportion of the whole population who died from the infection.

The description of some of the notations used in the time-dependent SEAIHCRD model's differential equations is

η Social distancing factor,
β Rate of transmission,
γ The recovery rate,
δ The rate of infection transmission from exposed to infectious,
α Median time to develop asymptomatic to symptomatic symptoms,
α_1 Recovery period of asymptomatic cases,
Ψ Median time for developing pneumonia and other hospitalization symptoms,
σ Median time to ICU admission from the hospital,
φ Median intensive care unit (ICU) length of stay,
χ Median hospital stay,
μ The time of recovery for critical people.

We know that there are limited resources of hospital beds and ICUs available in every country. Sometimes the number of critical cases is more than the number of ICUs. In this condition, doctors have to sort and classify the patients to identify priority and place of treatment. All these conditions are considered in this manuscript.

If a B number of ICUs and a C number of critical cases exist, then the following condition occurs:

1.   If there are more ICUs than in severe cases, all patients will be treated.
2.   The number of ICUs is less than the number of critical cases $(C > B)$, and the number of patients treated will be B, and the rest $(C - B)$ dies due to shortages.

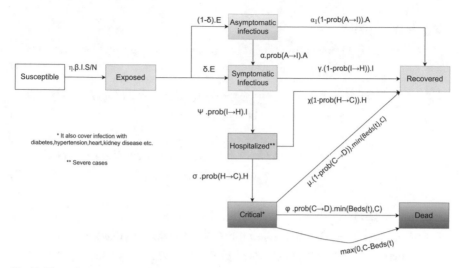

Fig. 5 Time-dependent SEAIHCRD model with critical case analysis

A time-dependent SEAIHCRD model with critical case analysis is shown in Fig. 5. The SEAIHCRD model with critical case analysis will modify the ordinary differential equations (6), (7), and (8). Updated equations are as follows:

$$\frac{dC(t)}{dt} = \sigma \cdot \text{prob}(H \rightarrow C) \cdot H(t) - \varphi \cdot \text{prob}(C \rightarrow D) \cdot \min(\text{Beds}(t), C)$$
$$- \max(0, C - \text{Beds}(t)) - \mu \cdot (1 - \text{prob}(C \rightarrow D)) \cdot \min(\text{Beds}(t), C), \quad (10)$$

$$\frac{dR(t)}{dt} = \gamma(t) \cdot (1 - \text{prob}(I \rightarrow H)) \cdot I(t)$$
$$+ \mu \cdot (1 - \text{prob}(C \rightarrow D)) \cdot \min(\text{Beds}(t), C)$$
$$+ \chi(1 - \text{prob}(H \rightarrow C)) \cdot H(t) + \alpha_1 \cdot (1 - \text{prob}(A \rightarrow I)) \cdot A(t), \quad (11)$$

$$\frac{dD(t)}{dt} = \varphi \cdot \text{prob}(C \rightarrow D) \cdot \min(\text{Beds}(t), C) + \max(0, C - \text{Beds}(t)). \quad (12)$$

We know that COVID-19 data is updated in days [45]. Hence, we update the differential equations (1), (2), (3), (4), (5), (10), (11), and (12) into discrete-time difference equation

$$S(t+1) - S(t) = -\eta \cdot \beta(t) \cdot I(t) \cdot \frac{S(t)}{N}, \quad (13)$$

$$E(t+1) - E(t) = \eta \cdot \beta(t) \cdot I(t) \cdot \frac{S(t)}{N} - \delta \cdot E(t) - (1 - \delta) \cdot E(t), \quad (14)$$

$$A(t + 1) - A(t)$$
$$= (1 - \delta) \, . \, E(t) - \alpha \, . \, \text{prob}(A \rightarrow I) \, . \, A(t) - \alpha_1 \, . \, (1 - \text{prob}(A \rightarrow I)) \, . \, A(t), \tag{15}$$

$$I(t + 1) - I(t) = \delta \, . \, E(t) + \alpha \, . \, \text{prob}(A \rightarrow I) \, . \, A(t) - \Psi \, . \, \text{prob}(I \rightarrow H) \, . \, I(t)$$
$$- \gamma(t) \, . \, (1 - \text{prob}(I \rightarrow H)) \, . \, I(t), \tag{16}$$

$$H(t + 1) - H(t) = \Psi \, . \, \text{prob}(I \rightarrow H) \, . \, I(t) - \sigma \, . \, \text{prob}(H \rightarrow C) \, . \, H(t)$$
$$- \chi(1 - \text{prob}(H \rightarrow C)) \, . \, H(t), \tag{17}$$

$$C(t + 1) - C(t)$$
$$= \sigma \, . \, \text{prob}(H \rightarrow C) \, . \, H(t) - \varphi \, . \, \text{prob}(C \rightarrow D) \, . \, \min(\text{Beds}(t), C)$$
$$- \max(0, C - \text{Beds}(t)) - \mu \, . \, (1 - \text{prob}(C \rightarrow D)) \, . \, \min(\text{Beds}(t), C), \tag{18}$$

$$R(t + 1) - R(t)$$
$$= \gamma(t) \, . \, (1 - \text{prob}(I \rightarrow H)) \, . \, I(t) + \mu \, . \, (1 - \text{prob}(C \rightarrow D)) \, . \, \min(\text{Beds}(t), C)$$
$$+ \chi(1 - \text{prob}(H \rightarrow C)) \, . \, H(t) + \alpha_1 \, . \, (1 - \text{prob}(A \rightarrow I)) \, . \, A(t), \tag{19}$$

$$D(t + 1) - D(t) = \varphi \, . \, \text{prob}(C \rightarrow D) \, . \, \min(\text{Beds}(t), C) + \max(0, C - \text{Beds}(t)). \tag{20}$$

The number of confirmed cases is very low at the very beginning of the spread of the disease, and the majority of the population is susceptible. Hence, for our analysis of COVID-19 in the early stage, we assume that initially, total cases are equal to susceptible cases $\{S(t) \approx n, t \geq 0\}$.

3 Data Analysis and Parameter Estimation

Compartmental models simplify the mathematical modeling of infectious diseases. Compartmental models are based on ordinary differential equations. A compartmental model can also be used with a stochastic framework that is more accurate but much more complex to analyze. Some initial conditions and characteristic parameters are required to solve these ordinary differential equations. These initial parameters are very sensitive. A small change in them may make a significant difference in outcomes, so they must be carefully introduced in the equations. The distribution of COVID-19 is determined by the nature of several variables in the compartment. Preliminary parameter estimation helps to solve essential consequences like the fatality rate and basic reproduction rate, allowing us to understand more deeply the COVID-19 transmission pattern. In this article, we first collect data for a specific period, then estimate the basic reproduction number, the rate of infection, and the rate of recovery of COVID-19. Based on these estimates, we analyze the spread and endpoint of COVID-19.

The social distance parameter means that the transmission of infectious diseases will avoid social interactions and physical interaction. η is the parameter of social distancing. The social distancing factor value lies between zero and one. When a lock is implemented, and all people are put in quarantine, its value is null, and its value is one if they follow unrestricted and the routine.

The Basic Reproduction Number R_0 and Case Fatality Rate Over Time

The basic reproduction number R_0 is the ratio between the transmission rate and the recovery rate. The basic reproduction number is the average number of people who can potentially be infected by an infected person if no intervention measures are in place. The value of the basic reproduction number is significant, which is very useful in the intervention of the disease. The value of basic reproduction number R_0 changes with time; whenever any country adopts lock-downs, the basic reproduction number value decreases, and when that country removes the lock-down, its value begins to increase again. For strict lock-down, the value of R_0 can be reduced to lower than unity.

Transmission Rate $\beta(t)$ and Recovering Rate $\gamma(t)$ by Least Square Method

In this subsection, we track and predict $\beta(t)$ and $\gamma(t)$ by the commonly in linear systems. Denote by $\hat{\beta}(t)$ and $\hat{\gamma}(t)$ the *predicted* transmission rate and recovering rate. From the FIR filters, they are predicted as follows:

$$\hat{\beta}(t) = a_1\beta(t-1) + a_2\beta(t-2) + \cdots + a_j\beta(t-J) + a_0,$$

$$\hat{\beta}(t) = \sum_{j=1}^{J} a_j\beta(t-j) + a_0, \tag{21}$$

$$\hat{\gamma}(t) = b_1\gamma(t-1) + b_2\gamma(t-2) + \cdots + b_j\gamma(t-K) + b_0,$$

$$\hat{\gamma}(t) = \sum_{j=1}^{K} b_j\gamma(t-k) + b_0, \tag{22}$$

where J and K are ($0 < J, K < T-2$), $a_j, j = 0, 1, \ldots, J$ and $b_k, k = 0, 1, \ldots, K$ are the coefficients. There are several widely used machine learning methods for the estimation of these coefficients, e.g., ordinary least squares, regularized least squares (i.e., lasso regression, ridge regression), and partial least squares [46]. We use the least square as our estimation method, which solves the following optimization problem in the present manuscript:

$$\text{Least square for transmission rate} = \min \sum_{t=J}^{T-2} \left(\beta(t) - \hat{\beta}(t)\right)^2, \tag{23}$$

$$\text{Least square for recovering rate} = \min \sum_{t=K}^{T-2} (\gamma(t) - \hat{\gamma}(t))^2. \tag{24}$$

R_0 is the ratio of β and γ in the compartmental models ($R_0 = \beta/\gamma$). Hence, we can say that $\beta = R_0 \cdot \gamma$. In this manuscript, before the lock-down, the value of R_0 is R_0 start, and if the lock-down is imposed on day L, the value of R_0 is reduced to R_0 end, and the value of β will be changed accordingly. In real life, the basic reproduction number R_0 is not constant and changes over time. When social distancing is imposed or removed, its value will change accordingly. The model illustrates the initial impact of social distancing on the basic reproduction number. The time-dependent variation in R_0 can be given as

$$R_0(t) = \frac{R_{0_{\text{Start}}} - R_{0_{\text{End}}}}{1 + e^{-\eta(-t+x_0)}} + R_{0_{\text{End}}}. \tag{25}$$

The description of the parameters is given below:

$R_{0_{\text{Start}}}$ The value of the R_0 for the first day,
$R_{0_{\text{End}}}$ The value of R_0 for the last day.

x_0 is the day when R_0 drastically decreases or inflection point, and

η is the parameter of social distance.

The value of the x_0 should be given very carefully because it makes a big difference to the result and the value of the $R_{0_{\text{End}}}$ must be less than 1.

We know that ($R_0 = \beta/\gamma$) then

$$R_0 = \frac{\beta}{\gamma} = \frac{\beta_1}{\gamma_1} * \delta + \frac{\beta_2}{\gamma_2} * (1 - \delta), \tag{26}$$

where β_1 is the asymptomatic infectious rate, γ_1 is the asymptomatic recovery rate, β_2 is the symptomatic infectious rate, and γ_2 is the symptomatic recovery rate. The combined probability of asymptomatic δ and symptomatic infectious disease $(1 - \delta)$ from the exposed compartment is one $((\delta) + (1 - \delta) = 1)$.

Age-Dependent Fatality Rate
Infection fatality rate is the ratio of the number of deaths to the number of cases. The rate of fatality is not stable and depends on many factors, such as the age factor and fatal diseases. The number of available ICU beds is a common reason, which mostly affects the rate of fatalities. If the majority of people are infected, then the fatality rate is high, and when fewer people are infected, the fatality rate is low. We need more health care if infected people are very high. Sometimes because of the absence of medical facilities, everyone is not treated. Therefore, we need to know what proportion of people are currently infected. Therefore, we describe the fatality rate φ as

$$\varphi(t) = s \cdot \frac{I(t)}{N} + \varphi_{opt}. \tag{27}$$

The description of the parameters is given below:

s It is arbitrary, but the fixed value that controls infection,

φ_{opt} Optimal fatality rate.

The value of parameter s is significant as it controls the above equation; very slight changes in s can make a massive difference in results. Therefore, the value of this parameter should be chosen carefully. $I(t)$ is the infected at time t, and N is the total population.

Case fatality analysis is complex, depending on the age group. Therefore, we divide age into different age groups to better analyze the case fatality (e.g., people aged 0–9, aged 10–19, ..., aged 90–100). Two things are required for the age-group analysis which are the fatality rate by age group and the proportion of the total population in that age group. If the population of older people is higher, then the death rate will be increased, and if the proportion of young people is higher, then the death rate may be low.

Therefore, the death (fatality) rate is calculated as follows:

The rate of fatality (with out comorbidity cases)

$\quad$ = age group fatality rate of all cases $*$ proportion of age group population,

$$\tag{28}$$

The rate of fatality (with comorbidity cases)

$\quad$ = age group fatality rate of all cases $*$ proportion of age group population.

$$\tag{29}$$

The overall death rate is, therefore, a combination of the above two cases

over all fatality rate = with out comorbidity cases + with comorbidty cases. (30)

All the cases of comorbidity are considered critical cases in this manuscript. The death rate is the ratio between the number of deaths and the number of cases. The probability of dying may be described as if infected by a virus (in percentage) and depends on various age groups. Table 1 presents the percentages of deaths if a person is infected with COVID-19 in a given age group [47].

Hospitalized and Critical Cases Analysis
We know there is a limited number of hospital beds and ICU beds in every country. All countries are starting new hospitals, opening rooms, etc., to increase the number of hospital beds and ICU beds when the disease spreads. Hence, the number of hospital beds and ICUs is growing over time. We can model the number of beds as follows:

Table 1 Age-wise death rate and comorbidity in all cases

Age	Death rate of all cases (%)	The death rate of comorbidity cases (%)
80+ years old	14.8	0.98
70–79 years old	8.0	0.86
60–69 years old	3.6	0.57
50–59 years old	1.3	0.26
40–49 years old	0.4	0.10
30–39 years old	0.2	0.06
20–29 years old	0.2	0.05
10–19 years old	0.2	0
0–9 years old	(No fatalities) 0	0

$$\text{Beds}_{\text{hosp}}(t) = \text{Beds}_{\text{hosp0}} + \text{s.t. Beds}_{\text{hosp0}}. \tag{31}$$

Description of the parameters is given below:

$\text{Beds}_{\text{hosp0}}$ Total number of hospital beds available,
s Some scaling factor,

and for ICUs,

$$\text{Beds}(t) = \text{Beds}_0 + \text{s.t. Beds}_0. \tag{32}$$

Description of the parameters is given below:

Beds_0 Total number of ICU beds available,
s Some scaling factor.

As the number of beds shown in the formula increases times per day to determine how many beds are served for the patients in hospitals each day, this is an important factor.

Fitting the Model to Find Some Important Parameters Value

In this manuscript, we focus on fitting a time-dependent SEAIHCRD model with time-dependent basic reproduction number and fatality of age group, hospital beds, and ICUs with actual COVID-19 data, which come close to the real data and find parameters for our model that can be useful in the future discussions.

The Python platform used some important libraries such as pandas, NumPy, LMfit, and ode for all the experimental studies. The processor Intel(R) Core (TM) i7-5500U CPU@2.40 GHz, 2401 MHz, 2 Core(s), and 4 Logical Processor(s), 12 GB RAM hardware configuration is used for simulation work.

The initial assumptions for the parameters are very crucial. First, we need to know what parameters are known and what we need to get out of it. In this proposed model, many parameters have been used. We will calculate some of the parameters and consider some according to the current study and data. There is no need to fit N, just put the population in the place that we need to model. Likewise, one needs not to calculate beds$_0$; simply place the number of ICU beds on the model we have. We value some parameters, i.e., the social distance parameter η, in the range of 0–1, according to the actual data and analysis, where 0 indicates that everyone is locked and quarantined, while one is for a regular lifestyle.

The average incubation period for the virus is 5.2 days but varies between different populations, according to a study by China [48]. For those exposed to infectious agents, the Chinese team study found that 14 days of medical examinations are required. Median hospital stay is around ten days ($\chi = 1/10$), the recovery period is around ten days ($\gamma = 1/10$), the median time to develop asymptomatic to symptomatic symptoms is approximately one week ($\alpha = 1/7$), and the recovery period of asymptomatic cases is around ten days ($\alpha_1 = 1/10$). It takes around five days from the appearance of symptoms to the growth of pneumonia [49, 50], and about severe hypoxemia and ICU admission, the median time between the appearance of symptoms is about five to ten days [50–54]. Therefore, the median time to develop pneumonia and other symptoms of hospitalization ($\Psi = 1/5$) and hospital to ICU admission ($\sigma = 1/7$) are used in this study [55, 56]. Finally, for COVID-19 patients, the length of stay in intensive care units (ICUs) was approximately 8–13 days, and the critical recovery time was eight days in a Chinese report [54, 57]. Therefore, median intensive care unit (ICU) duration of stay $\varphi = 1/8$ and median critical recovery time $\mu = 1/8$ are chosen.

The case fatality rate (CFR) is the proportion of cases that die of the disease [58]. The basic formula for the case fatality rate is CFR $= \frac{\text{Deaths}}{\text{Cases}}$, and this formula is sometimes corrected as CFR $= \frac{\text{Death at day } x}{\text{cases at day } (x-T)}$, where T is the average time from case confirmation to death.

We know that $\beta(t)$ can be calculated by basic reproduction number $R_0(t)$ and γ. Hence, no need to find any separate parameter for β. The beds scaling factor s can be fitted because the number of people being treated due to lack of facility is minimal compared to the number of deaths. Therefore, it does not affect much in the result. The proposed model has four estimates of the probabilities prob($I \to H$), prob($H \to C$), prob($A \to I$) and prob($C \to D$) split by age groups and weighted by age-group proportion. We will try to fit all the above probabilities that are incredibly close to the prediction of a specific risk group, such as diabetics, cancer, heart disease, and high blood pressure, now we have to fit all the probabilities prob($I \to H$), prob($H \to C$), prob($A \to I$) and prob ($C \to D$), and $R_{0_{\text{Start}}}$, $R_{0_{\text{End}}}$, x_0 and η are the parameters of $R_0(t)$.

The Johns Hopkins University Center for Systems Science and Engineering [59] is the principal source of data. We have gathered and cleaned data from UN data [60] for age groups, probabilities, and ICU beds. As the number of reported cases depends on many factors, such as the number of test cases, etc., and hence usually is not very accurate. However, the reported deaths are more accurate. Therefore, we use fatality statistics instead of total or active cases.

Firstly, we have collected all the related available data and parameters available to us from reliable sources and then defined initial guesses and limits for the remaining parameters of this model within certain limits depending on the situation. We have adopted the Levenberg–Marquardt algorithm to extract various parameters from the data fitting as this is the most important and effective reported data-fitting algorithm [61, 62]. For Python, a high-quality interface is provided by the LMfit library for nonlinear optimization and curve-fitting problems [63]. The R-squared value measures the proximity of the data to the fitted line. The R-square value is always between zero and one. In general, higher the R-squared value, better the model a given your data. The curve of death cases in Brazil, India, Mexico, Russia, South Africa, and the United States is shown in Fig. 6 (Table 2).

According to the study, most cases are mild or asymptomatic and can recover at home with proper guidance. Fewer percentages of people are critical, but if the patient is old or has some pre-existing illnesses such as chronic respiratory disease, diabetes, cancer, hypertension, and cardiovascular disease, the risk is very high. We gather and analyze data provided by New York City Health as of June 1, 2020, [63, 64] are shown in Table 3.

We used the publicly available dataset of COVID-19 provided by Johns Hopkins University in this study [83]. This dataset includes the daily count of confirmed cases, recovered cases, and deaths in many countries. The time-series data are available from January 22, 2020, onwards. We also collected and crosschecked data in Worldometer, coronavirus cases [82], a website providing real-time data for COVID-19. These data are gathered through announcements by public health authorities and report public and unidentified patient data immediately; hence, ethical authorization is not necessary.

Distribution of Total cases worldwide: According to WHO, 216 countries are affected by COVID-19. Figure 7 shows that 61% of cases are from six countries only. The United States of America has the highest number of cases, which alone is 27% of the world.

Distribution of Death cases worldwide: As discussed above, death cases are more accurate as there is rarely any chance that death due to COVID-19 is not reported or recorded by the related authorities. Figure 8 shows that 51% of cases are from six countries only. The United States of America has the highest number of cases, which alone is 23% of the world.

Total cases: Fig. 9 shows the country-wise total cases from January 22, 2020, to July 28, 2020, of COVID-19.

Total death: Fig. 10 shows the country-wise total death from January 22, 2020, to July 28, 2020, of COVID-19.

Daily new cases: Fig. 11 shows the country-wise daily new cases from January 22, 2020, to July 28, 2020, of COVID-19.

Daily new death: Fig. 12 shows the country-wise daily new death cases from January 22, 2020, to July 28, 2020, of COVID-19.

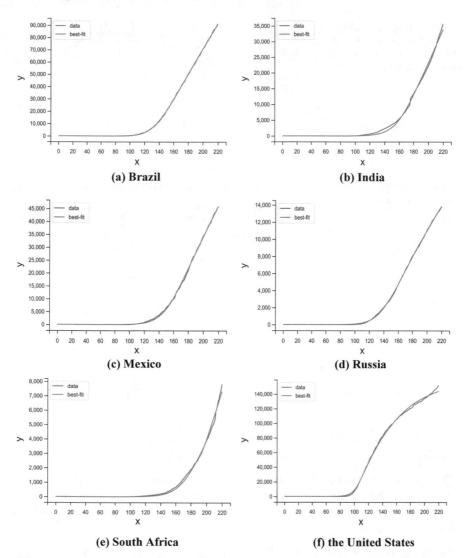

Fig. 6 Curve fitting of death cases in Brazil, India, Mexico, Russia, South Africa, and the United States

Case fatality rate: The overall fatality rate of an ongoing pandemic is difficult to estimate, but the current fatality rate can be calculated. Figure 13 shows the country-wise case fatality rate as of the current date of July 28, 2020.

Age-Wise Population: In terms of the age group, the population of Russia and the United States in 70 years and older is more percentage-sized, according to World Bank data. In the age range of 0–20 years, the population of South Africa, India, and Brazil is higher. In all these countries, the population distribution of Brazil, India,

Table 2 R-squared value of curve fitting for Brazil, India, Mexico, Russia, South Africa, and the United States

Country	R-squared value (death cases)
Brazil	0.992
India	0.962
Mexico	0.985
Russia	0.988
South Africa	0.979
United States	0.968

Table 3 Age-wise rate of hospitalization from infected cases, critical cases from infected cases, and death cases from ICUs

Age	Hospitalization rate from infected cases (%)	Rate of critical cases from infected cases (%)	Rate of dead cases from ICUs (%)
80+ years old	18.4	0.16	0.98
70–79 years old	16.6	0.10	0.86
60–69 years old	11.8	0.07	0.57
50–59 years old	8.2	0.05	0.26
40–49 years old	4.3	0.03	0.10
30–39 years old	3.4	0.025	0.06
20–29 years old	1.0	0.009	0.05
10–19 years old	0.1	0.003	0
0–9 years old	0.01	0.001	0

Mexico, Russia, South Africa, and the United States is nearly equivalent between 20 and 70 years. The population distribution by age group is represented in Fig. 14.

The number of hospital beds per 100 k: Unit beds per 100,000 population or a 100 k population, according to WHO and the OECD. Basic measures focus on all hospital beds that are occupied or empty. The country-wise number of hospital beds is shown in Fig. 15.

The number of ICU beds per 100 k: ICU bed counts are made up of beds per 100,000 population or 100,000 population, according to WHO and OECD. ICU beds are provided for all cases with severe conditions. The country-wise number of ICU beds is shown in Fig. 16.

4   Results and Discussion

We analyze and forecast in this section, using our proposed a time-dependent SEAI-HCRD model, the pattern of COVID-19 among the world's most affected countries. The result of our proposed method shows that Brazil, Russia, South Africa, and the

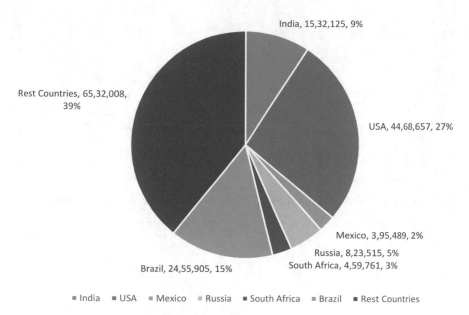

Fig. 7 Distribution of total cases worldwide

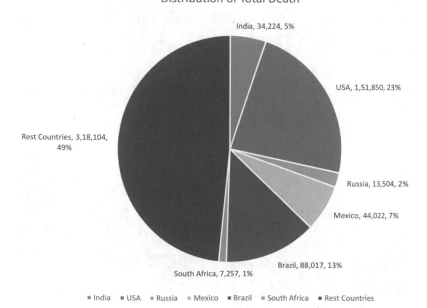

Fig. 8 Distribution of death cases worldwide

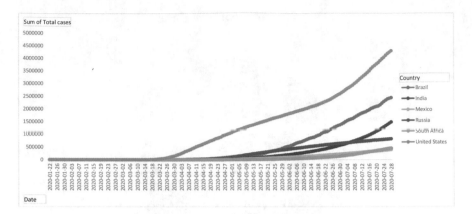

Fig. 9 Day-wise total cases of Brazil, India, Mexico, Russia, South Africa, and the United States

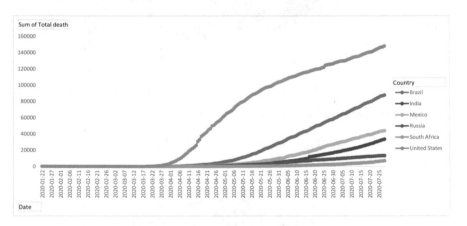

Fig. 10 Day-wise total death of Brazil, India, Mexico, Russia, South Africa, and the United States

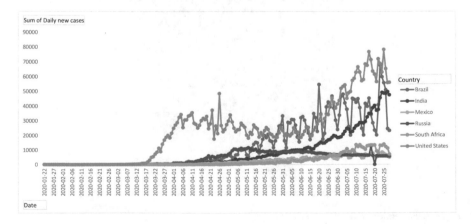

Fig. 11 Daily new cases of Brazil, India, Mexico, Russia, South Africa, and the United States

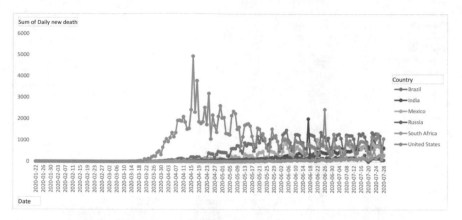

Fig. 12 Daily new death cases of Brazil, India, Mexico, Russia, South Africa, and the United States

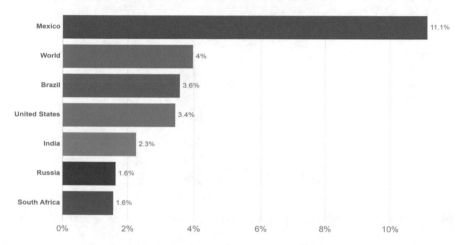

Fig. 13 Case fatality rate as of July 28, 2020, for Brazil, India, Mexico, Russia, South Africa, and the United States

United States have experienced their worst time. India and Mexico have yet to see a peak at the end of August. If the number of cases is very high in the middle and late August, hospital beds and ICU beds will be needed in India and Mexico. Geographical conditions are entirely different in some countries. The distribution of cases in these areas is also very random. In some places, it spreads too much, and in some places, it spreads far less. In India, the distribution of disease is very random, e.g., the number of cases in Maharashtra, Tamil Nadu, Andhra Pradesh, Karnataka, and Delhi is very high as compared to other states. According to the proposed method, cases in India will start to decline continuously in the first week of September, and the cases will end completely in the first week of November. If we compare the results of our proposed method with real-world data, it is mostly the same. In this section, we

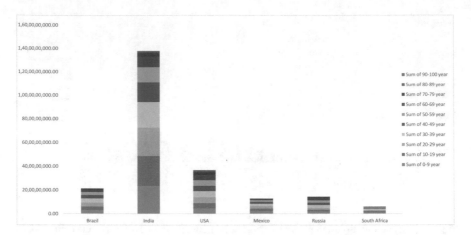

Fig. 14 Distribution of the population according to the age category of Brazil, India, Mexico, Russia, South Africa, and the United States

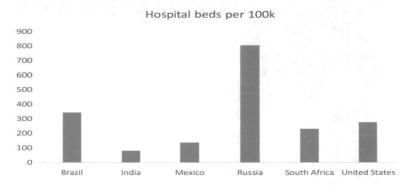

Fig. 15 Country-wise number of hospital beds of Brazil, India, Mexico, Russia, South Africa, and the United States

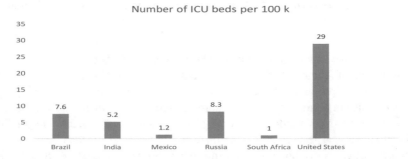

Fig. 16 Country-wise number of ICU beds of Brazil, India, Mexico, Russia, South Africa, and the United States

calculate for each country the basic reproduction number, the case fatality rate, the number of hospital beds required at peak time, and the number of ICU beds required when serious cases are high.

4.1 A Time-Dependent SEAIHCRD Model for Brazil

Brazil is one of the most affected countries by the COVID-19 disease, just behind the United States as of the starting of June 2020. According to the proposed method, cases in Brazil will start to decline continuously in the first week of August, and the cases will end completely in the first week of November. The cases reach a peak in Brazil, according to our proposed method, in July and August. The result of our proposed method shows that Brazil will need some hospital beds and ICU beds in June, July, and August, when the number of cases is at a peak. The result shows the basic reproduction rate which is 4.0 in starting after some time, it starts decreasing visually and goes up to one and even lower. A time-dependent SEAIHCRD model for Brazil shows that the case fatality rate of COVID-19 in Brazil is moderate. There are many ups and downs in the daily case fatality rate, but it goes higher and higher up to 5.5 in our model and then slows down, and total CFR is nearly 3.5 overall. The proposed model for Brazil showing that around 200th day, the number of hospital beds and the number of ICU beds are required. That time the number of death cases is 1800 per day, and daily hospitalized cases are nearly 3100. The proposed method requires approximately 550 hospital beds and 500 ICU beds when the cases are at their peak in Brazil. A time-dependent SEAIHCRD model result for Brazil has shown in Fig. 17.

4.2 A Time-Dependent SEAIHCRD Model for India

India is one of the most affected countries by the COVID-19 disease, just behind the United States and Brazil as of May 2020. According to the proposed method, cases in India will start to decline continuously in the first week of September, and the cases will end completely in the first week of December. The cases reach a peak in India, according to our proposed method in August. The result of our proposed method shows that India will need some hospital beds and ICU beds in July, August, and September, when the number of cases is at a peak. The result shows the basic reproduction rate which is 2.2 in starting after some time, it starts decreasing visually and goes up to one and even lower. A time-dependent SEAIHCRD model for India shows that the case fatality rate of COVID-19 in India is meager. There are many ups and downs in the daily case fatality rate, but it goes higher and higher up to 2.7 in our model and then slows down, and total CFR is nearly 2.2 overall. The proposed model for India shows that around 230th day, maximum number of hospital beds and the number of ICU beds are required. At that time, the number of death cases

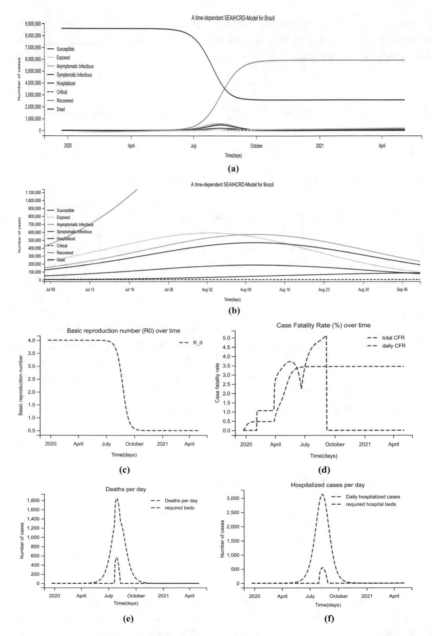

Fig. 17 Time-dependent SEAIHCRD model for Brazil. **a** The spread scenario of a time-dependent SEAIHCRD model for Brazil. A 500-day analysis has been done by the proposed model, which starts from January 22. **b** In this, the peak point of the model has shown by zooming for cases. **c** The basic reproduction number of Brazil over time. **d** The case fatality rate of Brazil over time. **e** Daily death cases in Brazil, where the red line shows the number of deaths per day, and the blue line shows how many ICU beds are required during peak days. **f** Brazil's daily hospital cases, where the red line indicates the number of hospital cases per day, and the blue line shows how many hospital beds are required during peak days

is 1200 per day, and daily hospitalized cases are nearly 2600. As per the proposed method needs approximately 700 hospital beds, and 300 ICU beds will be required during the peak time of COVID-19 in India. A time-dependent SEAIHCRD model result for India has shown in Fig. 18.

4.3 A Time-Dependent SEAIHCRD Model for Mexico

Mexico is the fourth most affected countries by COVID-19 disease. According to the proposed method, cases in Mexico will start to decline continuously in the first week of September, and the cases will end completely in the first week of December. The cases reach a peak in Mexico, according to our proposed method, in August and September. The result of our proposed method shows that Mexico will need some hospital beds and ICU beds in July, August, and September, when the number of cases is at a peak. The result shows the basic reproduction rate which is 2.2 in starting, and then after some time, it starts decreasing visually and goes up to one and even lower. A time-dependent SEAIHCRD model for Mexico shows that the case fatality rate of COVID-19 in Mexico is very high. There are many ups and downs in the daily case fatality rate, but it goes higher and higher up to 11.5 in our model and then slows down, and total CFR is nearly 5.0. The proposed model for Mexico showing that around 240th day, the number of hospital beds and the number of ICU beds are required. That time the number of death cases is 950 per day, and daily hospitalized cases are nearly 650. The proposed method requires approximately 150 hospital beds and 200 ICU beds when the cases are at their peak in Mexico. Mexico's case fatality rate is very high, so the death cases are very high here, and with more critical cases, more ICU beds will be needed. A time-dependent SEAIHCRD model result for Mexico has shown in Fig. 19.

4.4 A Time-Dependent SEAIHCRD Model for Russia

Russia is also one of the most affected countries by COVID-19 disease. According to the proposed method, cases in Russia will start to decline continuously in the first week of June, and the cases will end completely in the last week of October. The cases reach a peak in Russia in May and June, according to our proposed method. The result of our proposed method shows that Russia will need some hospital beds and ICU beds in May, June, and July when the number of cases is at a peak. The result shows the basic reproduction rate which is 3.0 in starting, which starts decreasing visually after some time and goes up to one and even lower. A time-dependent SEAIHCRD model for Russia shows that the case fatality rate of COVID-19 in Russia is very low. There are many ups and downs in the daily case fatality rate with a maximum value of 1.6 in our model and then slows down, and total CFR is nearly 1.4. The proposed model for Russia showing that around 170th day, the number of hospital beds and

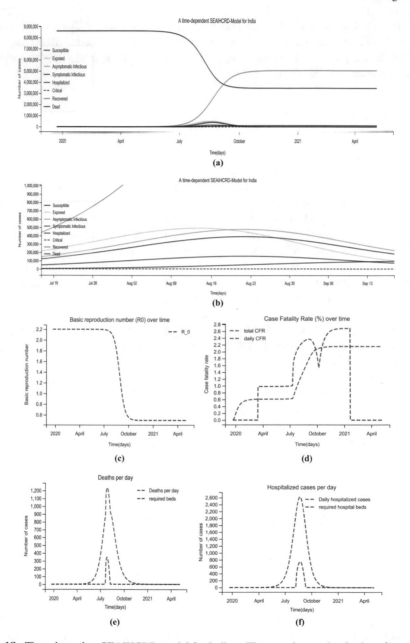

Fig. 18 Time-dependent SEAIHCRD model for India. **a** The spread scenario of a time-dependent SEAIHCRD model for India. A 500-day analysis has been done by the proposed model, which starts from January 22. **b** In this, the peak point of the model has shown by zooming for cases. **c** The basic reproduction number of India over time. **d** The case fatality rate of India over time. **e** Daily death cases in India, where the red line shows the number of deaths per day, and the blue line shows how many ICU beds are required during peak days. **f** India's daily hospital cases, where the red line indicates the number of hospital cases per day, and the blue line shows how many hospital beds are required during peak days

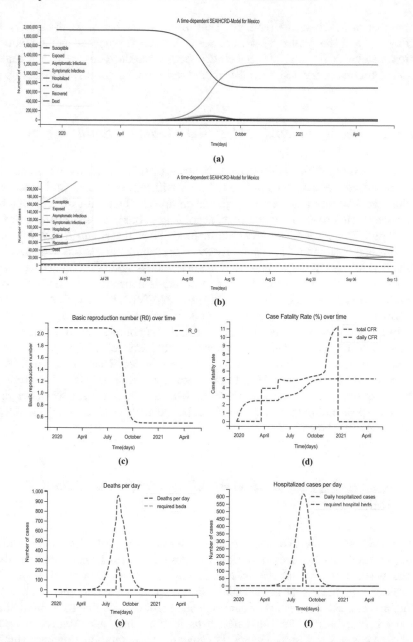

Fig. 19 Time-dependent SEAIHCRD model for Mexico. **a** The spread scenario of a time-dependent SEAIHCRD model for Mexico. A 500-day analysis has been done by the proposed model, which starts from January 22. **b** In this, the peak point of the model has shown by zooming for cases. **c** The basic reproduction number of Mexico over time. **d** The case fatality rate of Mexico over time. **e** Daily death cases in Mexico, where the red line shows the number of deaths per day, and the blue line shows how many ICU beds are required during peak days. **f** Mexico's daily hospital cases, where the red line indicates the number of hospital cases per day, and the blue line shows how many hospital beds are required during peak days

the number of ICU beds are required. That time the number of death cases is 300 per day, and daily hospitalized cases are nearly 2000. The proposed method requires approximately 300 hospital beds and 60 ICU beds when the cases are at their peak in Russia. A time-dependent SEAIHCRD model result for Russia has shown in Fig. 20.

4.5   A Time-Dependent SEAIHCRD Model for South Africa

South Africa is one of the most affected countries by COVID-19 disease. According to the proposed method, cases in South Africa will start to decline continuously in the third week of July, and the cases will end completely in the last week of October. The cases reach a peak in South Africa, according to our proposed method, in July and August. The result of our proposed method shows that South Africa will need some hospital beds and ICU beds in July when the number of cases is at a peak. The result also indicates the basic reproduction rate which is 4.5 in starting that decreases visually to values lower that one at a later time. A time-dependent SEAIHCRD model for South Africa shows that the case fatality rate of COVID-19 in South Africa is very low. The daily case fatality rate attains a maximum of 2.4 with many fluctuations in between and then slows down. The total CFR is coming out to be nearly 1.6. The proposed model for South Africa showing that around 175th day, the number of hospital beds and the number of ICU beds are required. That time the number of death cases is 450 per day, and daily hospitalized cases are nearly 1000. The proposed method requires approximately 150 hospital beds and 60 ICU beds when the cases are at their peak in South Africa. A time-dependent SEAIHCRD model result for South Africa has shown in Fig. 21.

4.6   A Time-Dependent SEAIHCRD Model for the United States

The United States is the most affected country by the COVID-19 disease. According to the proposed method, cases in the United States will start to decline continuously in the first week of July, and the cases will end completely in the last week of November. The cases reach on the peak in the United States, according to our proposed method, in July and August. The results of our proposed method show that the United States will need some hospital beds and ICU beds in June, July, and August, when the number of cases is at a peak. The result shows the basic reproduction rate which is 4.2 in starting, and after some time, it starts decreasing visually and goes up to one and even lower. A time-dependent SEAIHCRD model for the United States shows that the case fatality rate of COVID-19 in the United States is moderate. There are many ups and downs in the daily case fatality rate, but it goes higher and higher up to 5.5 in our model and then slows down, and total CFR is nearly 3.5. The proposed model for

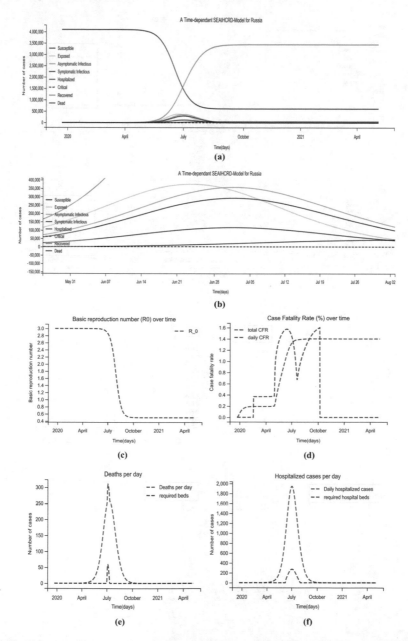

Fig. 20 Time-dependent SEAIHCRD model for Russia. **a** The spread scenario of a time-dependent SEAIHCRD model for Russia. A 500-day analysis has been done by the proposed model, which starts from January 22. **b** In this, the peak point of the model has shown by zooming for cases. **c** The basic reproduction number of Russia over time. **d** The case fatality rate of Russia over time. **e** Daily death cases in Russia, where the red line shows the number of deaths per day, and the blue line shows how many ICU beds are required during peak days. **f** Russia's daily hospital cases, where the red line indicates the number of hospital cases per day, and the blue line shows how many hospital beds are required during peak days

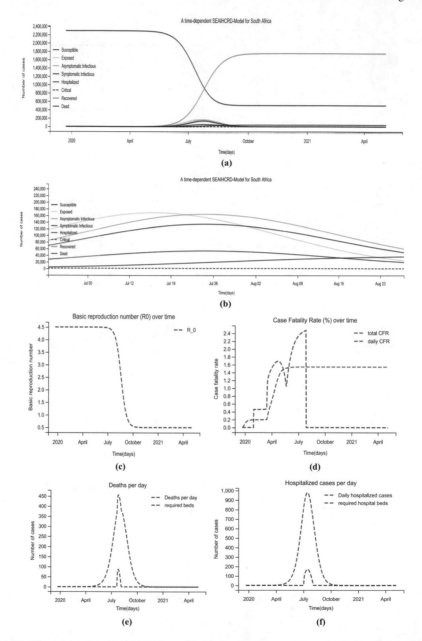

Fig. 21 Time-dependent SEAIHCRD model for South Africa. **a** The spread scenario of a time-dependent SEAIHCRD model for South Africa. A 500-day analysis has been done by the proposed model, which starts from January 22. **b** In this, the peak point of the model has shown by zooming for cases. **c** The basic reproduction number of South Africa over time. **d** The case fatality rate of South Africa over time. **e** Daily death cases in South Africa, where the red line shows the number of deaths per day, and the blue line shows how many ICU beds are required during peak days. **f** South Africa's daily hospital cases, where the red line indicates the number of hospital cases per day, and the blue line shows how many hospital beds are required during peak days

the United States is showing that around the 220th day, the number of hospital beds and the number of ICU beds are required. That time the number of death cases is 3500 per day, and daily hospitalized cases are nearly 14,000. The proposed method requires approximately 1000 hospital beds and 250 ICU beds when the cases are at their peak in the United States. A time-dependent SEAIHCRD model result for the United States has shown in Fig. 22.

Discussion

Results from the time-dependent SEAIHCRD model suggest that this model has excellent potential for predicting the incidence of COVID-19 diseases in time series. The central aspect of our proposed model is the addition of hospitalized, critical and asymptomatic infectious compartment, which improves the basic understanding of disease spread and results. Most of the cases are mild or asymptomatic, and asymptomatic cases do not show any symptoms. Still, after some time, some asymptomatic cases show disease symptoms; all of these scenarios are considered in the proposed model. We have the number of hospital beds and the number of ICU beds of the selected countries; based on that, we have calculated the number of beds required in the peak days of infection. Basic reproduction number and case fatality rate are the basic measures for any epidemic that we have also calculated. Sometimes conditions get worse because of a massive number of infected people at the same time, and the country does not have facilities to treat all critical cases when triage conditions occur. The time-dependent SEAIHCRD model can solve the problem of triage.

The model will propagate and forecast dynamic evolution after estimating the model parameters based on available clinical data. The proposed model is very sensitive to the initial conditions and values of the parameters. We are mainly focused on death cases because death cases hardly go undetected. The proposed model also estimates the approximate date when cases of death are unlikely to occur.

Limitations

Modeling is one of the most powerful tools that give intuitive effects when multiple factors act together. No model is perfect. Like any other mathematical model, our proposed model also has some limitations as following:

Our ordinary differential equations system is very sensitive to initial parameters. Hence, while giving the initial parameters, one should be very careful. Small parameter changes can cause a massive difference in results. We put cases in the death compartment that are serious and not found treatment in ICU care. Our method is focused, in particular, on serious cases and deaths. The proposed model considers that the value of R_0 cannot be increased; either it decreases or remains constant. We have assumed that the cases that have been recovered will be immunized, meaning that they will not be infected again.

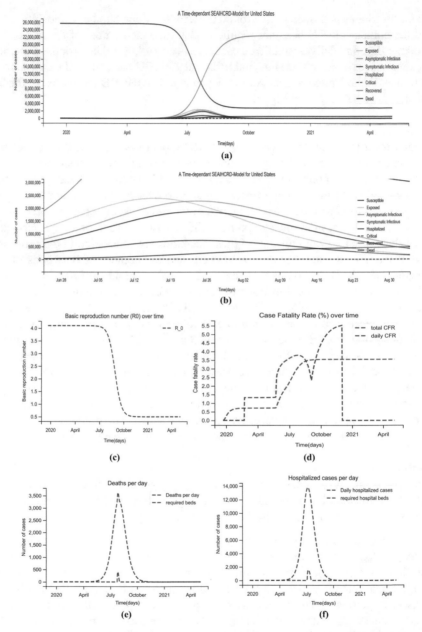

Fig. 22 Time-dependent SEAIHCRD model for the United States. **a** The spread scenario of a time-dependent SEAIHCRD model for the United States. A 500-day analysis has been done by the proposed model, which starts from January 22. **b** In this, the peak point of the model has shown by zooming for cases. **c** The basic reproduction number of the United States over time. **d** The case fatality rate of The United States over time. **e** Daily death cases in the United States, where the red line shows the number of deaths per day, and the blue line shows how many ICU beds are required during peak days. **f** The United States daily hospital cases, where the red line indicates the number of hospital cases per day, and the blue line shows how many hospital beds are required during peak days

5   Conclusion

A mathematical model is a potent tool for the quantitative behavior of any physical phenomenon, including any pandemic like COVID-19. Some mathematical models like the SIR model and SEIR model have been widely used for the prediction of disease outbreak and spread behavior. Our proposed time-dependent SEAIHCRD model is an extension of the SEIR model in which four-compartments are added that are asymptomatic infectious, hospitalized, critical, and death compartment. Some people have not seen any symptoms of the disease. They are going to the asymptomatic infectious compartment. Some people have seen symptoms of the disease. They are going to the symptomatic infectious compartment. People with a serious infection who have severe pneumonia-like symptoms need hospitalization. These individuals may either recover or move to the critical compartment. The study indicates that most cases are mild or asymptomatic and are carefully monitored at home. Less percentage of people are critical, but if the patient is old or has some preexisting disease, such as chronic respiratory disease, diabetes, cancer, hypertension, and cardiovascular disease, they are at high risk and may need treatment in an ICU. They either recover from the disease or die of it.

The proposed model estimates the date and magnitude of peaks of corresponding to exposed people, number of asymptomatic infectious people, symptomatic infectious people, the number of people hospitalized, number of people admitted in ICUs, and the number of death of COVID-19. This proposed model is time-dependent, so we calculate the number of cases asymptomatic infectious cases, symptomatic infectious cases, hospitalized cases, and critical cases with time. We have COVID-19 data on hospital beds and ICU beds of most infected countries after we calculate the hospitalized cases and critical cases using the proposed model. Based on our calculation, we can tell how many beds are required. A time-dependent SEAIHCRD model also calculates the basic reproduction number over time, and its computational results are almost the same as the actual data, but sometimes vary. We also calculate the case fatality rate over time for the countries most affected by COVID-19. The proposed model calculates two types of case fatality rate: one is CFR daily, and the other is total CFR.

According to the present time-dependent SEAIHCRD model, Mexico's case fatality rate is very high, so the death cases are very high there, and with more critical cases, more ICU beds will be needed. The case fatality rate and basic reproduction number of India, South Africa, and Russia are quite low; hence, the number of deaths here is also low. The United States is most affected country by COVID-19 disease. The United States is taking more time to recover because of more number of cases there. The number of cases and death decreased in the country following the lock-down. Cases in India and Mexico will be at the top in August, and the number of hospital beds and ICU beds will be required during this peak period. India cases will almost stop coming in the first week of December. Brazil is one of the most affected countries by the COVID-19 disease just after the United States, and its cases will almost stop coming in the first week of November.

Acknowledgements I would like to express my special thanks of gratitude to our collaborator Harel Dahari of The Program for Experimental and Theoretical Modeling, Division of Hepatology, Department of Medicine, Stritch School of Medicine, Loyola University Medical Center, Maywood IL, United States as well as Jonathan Ozik from Consortium for Advanced Science and Engineering, University of Chicago, Chicago, IL, United States, who gave me the golden opportunity to do work with them on SPARC project that helped us in doing a lot of good research and we came to know about so many new things and I am really thankful to them.

The work has been supported by a grant received from the Ministry of Education, Government of India under the Scheme for the Promotion of Academic and Research Collaboration (SPARC) (ID: SPARC/2019/1396).

Conflicts of Interest The authors have no conflicts of interest to report regarding the present study.

References

1. Novel Coronavirus-China (2020) World Health Organization (WHO), 9 Apr 2020
2. Is the world ready for the coronavirus?—Distrust in science and institutions could be a major problem if the outbreak worsens. The New York Times
3. Laboratory testing of human suspected cases of novel coronavirus (nCoV) infection. Interim guidance, 10 Jan 2020, 20 Jan 2020
4. Error! Hyperlink reference not valid. www.cdc.gov (CDC), 23 Jan 2020
5. 2019 novel coronavirus infection (Wuhan, China): outbreak update. Canada.ca, 21 Jan 2020
6. Statement on the second meeting of the International Health Regulations (2005) Emergency Committee regarding the outbreak of novel coronavirus (2019-nCoV). World Health Organization (WHO), 30 Jan 2020
7. WHO director-general's opening remarks at the media briefing on COVID-19, 11 Mar 2020. World Health Organization, 11 Mar 2020
8. A list of what's been canceled because of the coronavirus. The New York Times, 1 Apr 2020
9. Interim clinical guidance for management of patients with confirmed coronavirus disease (COVID-19), Centers for Disease Control and Prevention (CDC), 6 Apr 2020
10. COVID-19 vaccine development pipeline. Vaccine Centre, London School of Hygiene and Tropical Medicine, 15 July 2020
11. COVID-19 vaccine tracker. Milken Institute, 23 June 2020
12. Draft landscape of COVID 19 candidate vaccines. World Health Organization, 21 July 2020
13. Transmission of COVID-19 by asymptomatic cases, WHO EMRO, 20 Aug 2020
14. Dong Y et al (2020) Epidemiological characteristics of 2,143 pediatric patients with 2019 coronavirus disease in China. Pediatrics 145:e20200702
15. Zhao X et al (2020) Incidence, clinical characteristics and prognostic factor of patients with COVID-19: a systematic review and meta-analysis. Preprint at http://medrxiv.org/lookup/doi/10.1101/2020.03.17.20037572
16. Schifer A.-M.: Controlling COVID-19. Epidemiology Lancet Glob. Health. https://doi.org/10.1016/S2214-109X(20)30074-7, 11 May 2020
17. Bjørnstad ON, Shea K, Krzywinski M, Altman N (2020) Modeling infectious epidemics. Nat Methods 17:453–456
18. Kermack WO, McKendrick AG (1927) A contribution to the mathematical theory of epidemics. In: Proceedings of the royal society of London. Series A, containing papers of a mathematical and physical character, vol 115(772), pp 700–721
19. Brauer F, Chávez C (2001) Mathematical models in population biology and epidemiology. Springer
20. Davies NG, Klepac P, Liu Y et al (2020) Age-dependent effects in the transmission and control of COVID-19 epidemics. Nat Med 26:1205–1211. https://doi.org/10.1038/s41591-020-0962-9

21. Giordano G, Blanchini F, Bruno R et al (2020) Modelling the COVID-19 epidemic and imple-mentation of population-wide interventions in Italy. Nat Med 26:855–860. https://doi.org/10.1038/s41591-020-0883-7
22. Eker S (2020) Validity and usefulness of COVID-19 models. Humanit Soc Sci Commun 7:54. https://doi.org/10.1057/s41599-020-00553-4
23. Vespignani A, Tian H, Dye C et al (2020) Modelling COVID-19. Nat Rev Phys 2:279–281. https://doi.org/10.1038/s42254-020-0178-4
24. Tsay C, Lejarza F, Stadtherr MA et al (2020) Modeling, state estimation, and optimal control for the US COVID-19 outbreak. Sci Rep 10:10711. https://doi.org/10.1038/s41598-020-67459-8
25. Gog JR (2020) How you can help with COVID-19 modelling. Nat Rev Phys 2:274–275. https://doi.org/10.1038/s42254-020-0175-7
26. Xu B, Gutierrez B, Mekaru S et al (2020) Epidemiological data from the COVID-19 outbreak, real-time case information. Sci Data 7:106. https://doi.org/10.1038/s41597-020-0448-0
27. Singh A, Chandra SK, Bajpai MK (2020) Study of non-pharmacological interventions on COVID-19 spread. CMES-Comput Model Eng Sci 125(3):967–990. https://doi.org/10.32604/cmes.2020.011601
28. Singh A, Bajpai MK (2020) SEIHCRD model for COVID-19 spread scenarios, disease predic-tions and estimates the basic reproduction number, case fatality rate, hospital, and ICU beds requirement. CMES-Comput Model Eng Sci 125(3):991–1031. https://doi.org/10.32604/cmes.2020.012503
29. Chandra SK, Singh A, Bajpai MK (2021) Mathematical model with social distancing param-eter for early estimation of COVID-19 spread. In: Bajpai MK, Kumar Singh K, Giakos G (eds) Machine vision and augmented intelligence—theory and applications. Lecture notes in electrical engineering, vol 796. Springer, Singapore. https://doi.org/10.1007/978-981-16-5078-9_3
30. Singh KK, Kumar S, Dixit P et al (2021) Kalman filter based short term prediction model for COVID-19 spread. Appl Intell 51:2714–2726. https://doi.org/10.1007/s10489-020-01948-1
31. Pang L, Liu S, Zhang X, Tian T, Zhao Z (2020) Transmission dynamics and control strategies of COVID-19 in Wuhan, China. J Biol Syst, 1–18. https://doi.org/10.1142/S0218339020500096
32. Dubey B, Patra A, Srivastava PK, Dubey US (2013) Modelling and analysis of a SEIR model with different types of non-linear treatment rates. J Biol Syst 21(3):1350023. https://doi.org/10.1142/S021833901350023X
33. Geisse KV, Ngonghala CN, Feng Z, The impact of vaccination on Malaria prevalence: a vaccine-age-structured modeling approach. https://doi.org/10.1142/S0218339020400094
34. Chen YC, Lu PE, Chang CS, A time-dependent SIR model for COVID-19, arXiv:2003.00122
35. Statement on the meeting of the International Health Regulations (2005) Emergency Committee regarding the outbreak of novel coronavirus 2019 (n-CoV) on 23 Jan 2020. World Health Organization (WHO). Retrieved 9 Apr 2020
36. Sanche S, Lin YT, Xu C, Romero-Severson E, Hengartner N, Ke R (2020) High contagious-ness and rapid spread of severe acute respiratory syndrome coronavirus 2. Emerg Infect Dis 26(7):1470–1477. https://doi.org/10.3201/eid2607.200282. PMC 7323562. PMID 32255761. S2CID 215410037, Apr 2020
37. Roberts L (2020) The importance of the coronavirus R rate in other countries across the globe. Telegraph, 14 May 2020
38. Li Q, Guan X, Wu P, Wang X, Zhou L, Tong Y et al (2020) Early transmission dynamics in Wuhan, China, of novel coronavirus-infected pneumonia. N Engl J Med 382(13):1199–1207. https://doi.org/10.1056/NEJMoa2001316. PMC 7121484. PMID 31995857. Mar 2020
39. Coronavirus Disease 2019 (COVID-19) Centers for Disease Control and Prevention, May 2020
40. Azad A (2020) CDC estimates that 35% of coronavirus patients don't have symptoms. CNN, 22 May 2020
41. Beretta E, Takeuchi Y (1995) Global stability of an SIR epidemic model with time delays. J Math Biol 33:250–260. https://doi.org/10.1007/BF00169563

42. Cooke K, van den Driessche P (1996) Analysis of an SEIRS epidemic model with two delays. J Math Biol 35:240–260. https://doi.org/10.1007/s002850050051
43. Raju A (2020) ICMR advises asymptotic & mild COVID patients to observe home quarantine for 17 days to reduce pressure on hospitals. Pharmabiz.com, 20 June 2020
44. Sharma N (2020) Asymptomatic or mild symptoms Covid-19 patients can home quarantine. Econ Times, 27 Apr 2020
45. COVID-19 dashboard by the center for systems science and engineering (CSSE) at Johns Hopkins University (JHU). Johns Hopkins University
46. Dayal BS, MacGregor JF (1996) Identification of finite impulse response models: methods and robustness issues. Ind Eng Chem Res 35(11):4078–4090
47. The epidemiological characteristics of an outbreak of 2019 novel coronavirus diseases (COVID-19) China. CCDC, 17 Feb 2020
48. Li Q et al (2020) Early transmission dynamics in Wuhan, China, of novel coronavirus–infected pneumonia. N Engl J Med, 29 Jan 2020
49. Guan WJ, Ni ZY, Hu Y (2020) Clinical characteristics of coronavirus disease 2019 in China. N Engl J Med. https://doi.org/10.1056/NEJMoa2002032
50. Yang X, Yu Y, Xu J (2020) Clinical course and outcomes of critically ill patients with SARS-CoV-2 pneumonia in Wuhan, China: a single centered, retrospective, observational study. Lancet Respir Med. https://doi.org/10.1016/S2213-2600(20)30079-5
51. WHO-China Joint Mission (2020) Report of the WHO-China joint mission on coronavirus disease 2019 (COVID-19), 28 Feb 2020. https://www.who.int/docs/default-source/coronavir use/who-chinajoint-mission-oncovid-19-final-report.pdf
52. Huang C, Wang Y, Li X (2020) Clinical features of patients infected with 2019 novel coronavirus in Wuhan, China. Lancet 395:497–506
53. Cao J, Hu X, Cheng W, Yu L, Tu WJ, Liu Q (2020) Clinical features and short-term outcomes of 18 patients with corona virus disease 2019 in intensive care unit. Intensive Care Med. https://doi.org/10.1007/s00134-020-05987-7
54. Zhou F, Yu T, Du R (2020) Clinical course and risk factors for mortality of adult inpatients with COVID-19 in Wuhan, China: a retrospective cohort study. Lancet 395:1054–1062
55. Updated understanding of the outbreak of 2019 novel coronavirus (2019nCoV) in Wuhan, China. J Med Virol, 29 Jan 2020
56. Wang et al (2020) Clinical characteristics of 138 hospitalized patients with 2019 novel coronavirus–infected pneumonia in Wuhan, China. JAMA, 7 Feb 2020
57. Guan WJ (2020) Clinical characteristics of coronavirus disease 2019 in China. N Engl J Med. https://doi.org/10.1056/NEJMoa2002032
58. Ghani, Methods for estimating the case fatality ratio for a novel. Emerg Infect Dis Am J Epidemiol
59. https://data.humdata.org/dataset/novel-coronavirus-2019-ncov-cases
60. https://data.un.org/
61. Levenberg K (1944) A method for the solution of certain non-linear problems in least squares. Quart Appl Math 2(2):164–168. https://doi.org/10.1090/qam/10666
62. Marquardt D (1963) An algorithm for least-squares estimation of nonlinear parameters. SIAM J Appl Math 11(2):431–441. https://doi.org/10.1137/0111030.hdl:10338.dmlcz/104299
63. Non-linear least-square minimization and curve-fitting for python. https://lmfit.github.io/lmfit-py/
64. Coronavirus Update (Live) Worldometer, www.worldometers.info

A Compartmental Mathematical Model of COVID-19 Intervention Scenarios for Mumbai

Avaneesh Singh and Manish Kumar Bajpai

1 Introduction

The whole world is currently facing a novel coronavirus (COVID-19) pandemic that began in December 2019 in Wuhan City of China as an outbreak of pneumonia of unknown cause [1–3]. Many places have been greatly affected by this disease, and Mumbai is one of them. Mumbai is India's financial capital and the capital of the state of Maharashtra. One of the epicenters of COVID-19 in India is Mumbai. As of 2019, Mumbai is the second-most populous city in the country after Delhi, according to the United Nations, and the seventh-most populous city in the world with a population of about 20 million [4]. As per the 2011 Indian Government population census, Mumbai was India's most populous city with an estimated citywide population of 12.5 million living under the Greater Mumbai Municipal Corporation [5]. The model has been parameterized using available mortality data from COVID-19, which is more accurate than case data. In Mumbai, as of November 30, 2020, 280,818 confirmed cases and 11,559 confirmed deaths due to COVID-19 had been reported.

It is an important decision for India to come up with a non-pharmaceutical control strategy such as a 40-day national lockdown to extend the higher phases of COVID-19 and to prevent severe loads on its public health system. On March 11, 2020, the pandemic novel coronavirus 2019 had been first confirmed in Mumbai. The Indian government has introduced a preventive social distance measure in order to avoid large-scale population movements that can accelerate the spread of the disease. On March 22, 2020, India's government introduced a voluntary 14-h public curfew. In addition, on midnight March 24, 2020, India's prime minister also ordered a national lockdown to slow COVID-19 spread.

A. Singh (✉) · M. K. Bajpai
PDPM Indian Institute of Information Technology, Design and Manufacturing, Jabalpur 482005, India
e-mail: avaneesh.singh@iiitdmj.ac.in

Due to absence of specific vaccine, strategies for controlling and mitigating the burden of the pandemic are focused on non-pharmaceutical interventions, such as social distancing, contact tracing, quarantine, isolation, and the use of facemasks in public, tracing, quarantine hospitalized of asymptomatic cases, hospitalization of confirmed cases, etc., are essential to control the spread of COVID-19 [6].

We are proposing a mathematical model that predicts Mumbai's COVID-19 dynamics. The dynamics of diseases transmission can be achieved by mathematical modeling using differential equation system [7]. For the COVID-19 outbreak, several mathematical modeling studies have been done [8–17]. In this study, with epidemic data up to October 30, 2020, we propose a compartmental mathematical model to predict and control the transmission dynamics of the COVID-19 pandemic for Mumbai. We compute the basic reproduction number R_0, which is used to study the predictions and simulations of the model. When epidemiological disease dynamics of transmission are not known, mathematical models play an important role in estimating the worst and best case scenarios. The main objective of the preventive techniques is to preserve the basic reproduction number R_0 below one, in order to control the further development of infection, while the main objective of the mitigation policy is to determine the effect of the outbreak [12]. In order to understand the transmission dynamics of peculiar epidemiological traits of COVID-19, some mathematical models have recently been investigated, and some of these are listed in our Refs. [15, 18–26]. The modeling of COVID-19 pandemics is no new and in the absence of any effective therapeutics and licensed vaccine, most authors have focused on non-pharmaceutical interventions. Within that context, a mathematical model to study the transmission dynamics of the COVID-19 pandemic was studied by Atangana [15], using a system of fractional differential equations using the lockdown effect. In order to obtain epidemiological status from patients, Tang et al. [18] proposed the COVID-19 model, which is very high for infectious diseases and calculated the basic reproduction number 6.47. The new SIDARTHE model for the COVID-19 pandemic has been developed by Giordano and colleagues [20], predicting that restrictive social separation can reduce the prevalence of coronavirus among humans. In order to investigate transmitting dynamics of the COVID-19, the Sarkar and Khajanchi [19, 22] proposed and analyzed a mathematical model with true data, respectively, from India and certain states of India. The authors performed the short-term and long-term predictions based on estimated model parameters. In an extensive version of the classical SEIR model to study infectious diseases intervention strategies that incorporates the fact that asymptomatic and presymptomatic persons infected are believed to be a major role in the dynamics of COVID-19 outbreak transmission [21].

Figure 1 shows the distribution of COVID-19 disease in the Maharashtra state. Case distribution is more in Mumbai, Thane, Nagpur, Nashik, and Pune city.

If we compare Mumbai city with the United States of America, then population wise Mumbai city is nearly same as the New York state. Figure 2 shows the population wise compare of Indian places with the USA states.

The 2019 pandemic novel coronavirus was first confirmed in Mumbai on March 11, 2020. Moreover, Table 1 includes the important events happened in Mumbai city related to COVID-19.

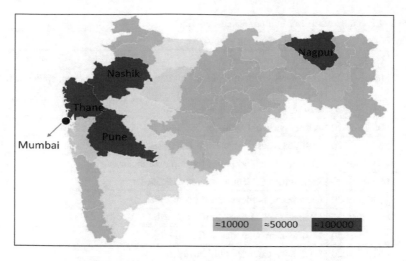

Fig. 1 Geographically COVID-19 case distribution in the state of Maharashtra

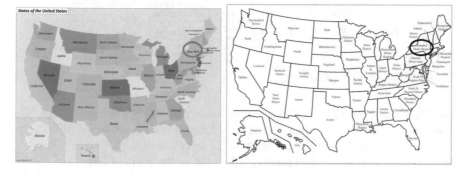

Fig. 2 Population wise comparison of Indian places with USA sates

The organization of this manuscript is as follows: Sect. 1 introduces COVID-19 and explains the importance of this research. The mathematical model and its schematic representation have been proposed in Sect. 2. The qualitative characteristics of the model and data analysis have been discussed in Sect. 3. Numerical simulations and results based on the estimated values of the parameters and the discussion are discussed in Sect. 4. Finally, the conclusion and some future work have been discussed in Sect. 5.

Table 1 Important events in Mumbai related COVID-19

S. No.	Date	Mumbai important events
1	03-11-2020	First positive test result
2	03-13-2020	The Government of Maharashtra declared the outbreak an epidemic in the city of Mumbai
3	03-14-2020	Ban on public gatherings and events
4	03-16 2020	A three-year-old child and her mother were tested positive
5	03-17-2020	First death case because of COVID-19
6	03-20-2020	Closure of all workplaces barring essential services
7	03-22-2020	Imposition of Section 144 and lockdown
8	03-23-2020	Curfew and border seal-off in Mumbai
9	03-25-2020	Nationwide lockdown until 14 April
10	03-26-2020	First woman death due to COVID-19
11	04-11-2020	Lockdown extended until 30 April
12	04-14-2020	Nationwide lockdown until 3 May
13	04-20-2020	53 journalist found positive
14	04-21-2020	Cases surpassed 3000
15	05-01-2020	Nationwide lockdown until 17 May
16	05-07-2020	Total cases in Mumbai crosses 10,000 mark
17	05-16-2020	884 cases were reported in the Mumbai city

2 Proposed Methodology

How the virus spreads from one location to another is called virus transmission. The transmission of infection occurs when an infectious person or source of infection infects susceptible people. There have to be several events that allow viruses to cause infections in susceptible people. This is called the chain of infection.

Two types of transmission mode are

1. Direct transmission and
2. Indirect transmission.

Direct Transmission: In direct transmission, an infectious person, through direct contact or droplet spread, is transmitted from the source of infection to susceptible people.

Indirect Transmission: In indirect transmission, an infectious person, through indirect contact or airborne or vehicle-borne, is transmitted from the source of infection to susceptible people.

Figure 3 shows the chain of infection from an infected person to a susceptible person.

Infection transmission from one infected person to susceptible persons is shown in Fig. 4. The individual may be infected either symptomatically, asymptomatically,

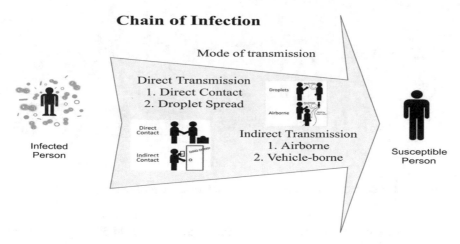

Fig. 3 Chain of infection

or presymptomatically. The lower box suggests that the majority of cases are either moderate or asymptomatic. Severe cases are relatively lesser than mild and asymptomatic cases but more than critical ones. Some cases are initially moderate but with time, severe or critical; they need hospital beds or ICU beds.

The directive issued by the public health department of Brihan Mumbai Municipal Corporation (BMC) [27] says, All public and private hospitals are instructed that no asymptomatic COVID-19 positive patient shall be given admission to ensure prompt availability of beds for the needy and genuinely deserving symptomatic patients. All asymptomatic patients admitted to various public and private hospitals shall be urgently discharged.

COVID-19 infectious disease is classified mainly as symptomatic infectious and asymptomatic or presymptomatic infectious. Figure 5 indicates the categorization

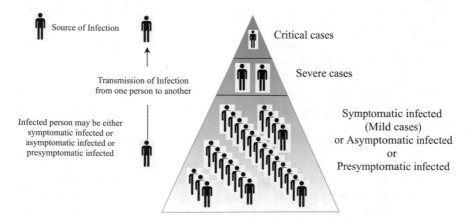

Fig. 4 Hierarchy of infection

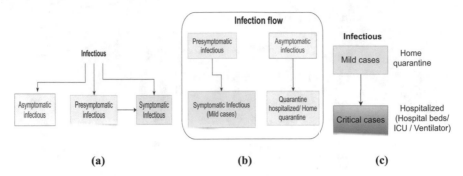

Fig. 5 **a** Infectious cases categorization, **b** infection flow, and **c** mild and severe infection flow

and flow of infectious events and cases and symptoms of mild cases quarantine in the home and severe and critical cases put in the hospital for proper treatment.

Figure 6 shows the flow of the proposed model. Initially, we consider all cases to be susceptible. The overall population is constant throughout the spread of infection. After exposure, some cases are found to be asymptomatic infectious with the help of contact tracing. Some cases are found to be presymptomatic infectious, in which the complete symptoms of the disease begin to appear within a few days. Some of the traced asymptomatic infectious conditions are severe, and then put into quarantine hospitalized after they have recovered. In the case of symptomatic infectious, most cases are mild, and some are severe and critical when taken to the hospital for treatment. After treatment, some cases will be recovered, and some will be dead due to infection.

Compartment models like SIR and SEIR are mostly used today for the mathematical modeling of infectious diseases. The basic compartmental SIR model has been proposed by Kermack-McKendrick [28] in 1927. Cooke and Driessche [29] studied the incubation cycle in the propagation of infectious diseases, developed the 'Exposed, E' compartment, and suggested an SEIR model of time delay. The basic compartment model SIR, the model SEIR, and the model SEIRD have been described by Singh et al. (2020) [8].

In this work, we use a compartmental differential equation model for the propagation of COVID-19 in Mumbai. The model tracks the dynamics of the nine sub-population compartments, which are susceptible ($S(t)$), exposed ($E(t)$), asymptomatic infectious ($A(t)$), presymptomatic infectious ($P(t)$), quarantine hospitalized ($Q(t)$), symptomatic infectious ($I(t)$), hospitalized/ICU ($H(t)$), recovered ($R(t)$), and dead ($D(t)$).

The model simulations will be carried out with the following assumptions:

(a) We are doing an age-wise study of spread scenarios.
(b) The susceptible and infected individuals are homogeneous in the population.
(c) No vaccine has been used with this model to stop the spread of COVID-19.
(d) The population is constant. In our model, no recruiting individuals are permitted.

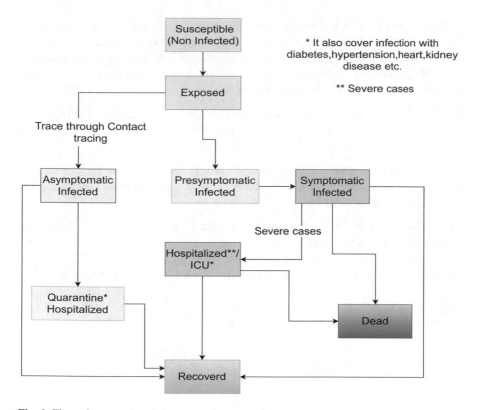

Fig. 6 Flow of proposed model

Susceptible compartment $S(t)$: This compartment's population will remain constant because no recruiting individuals are allowed in our model. This compartment population will decrease after infection due to an interaction with an infected person or an asymptomatic person.

Exposed compartment $E(t)$: This compartment's population consists of infected individuals but cannot infect others, and the population decreases with rate δ to become presymptomatic infectious or asymptomatic infectious.

Asymptomatic infectious compartment $A(t)$: This compartment population is considered infected, but asymptomatic individuals do not develop common symptoms of COVID-19. Asymptomatic individuals are essential to model because they have the ability to spread the virus without knowing it, and with the help of tracing, we find these individuals.

Presymptomatic infectious compartment $P(t)$: The population of this compartment is considered as infected, who have not developed symptoms yet, but who later develop symptoms.

Symptomatic infectious compartment $I(t)$: The population of this compartment is considered as infected. Symptomatic infected individuals exhibit a common symptom of COVID-19. When symptomatic infected individual conditions are critical, they are admitted to the hospital for treatment. Some cases have been recovered, and some cases have been confirmed to be dead.

Quarantine hospitalized compartment $Q(t)$: Older people. Asymptomatic patients who do not have a chronic disease do not need to be hospitalized and may opt for quarantine hospitals if hospitalization is necessary.

Recovered compartment $R(t)$: Recovered cases are referred to as individuals who have gained immunity from COVID-19 disease. We have assumed that the cases which have been recovered will be immunized.

Dead compartment $D(t)$: All infected individuals who died of COVID-19 disease come under this compartment.

We are consider that $N = S + E + A + P + I + Q + H + R + D$ is constant, where N is the size of the population modeled. Figure 7 shows the proposed model.

Differential Equations for Proposed Model
The ordinary differential equations of the proposed model are as follows:

$$\frac{dS(t)}{dt} = -\eta \cdot \beta(t) \cdot I(t) \cdot \frac{S(t)}{N}, \tag{1}$$

$$\frac{dE(t)}{dt} = \eta \cdot \beta(t) \cdot I(t) \cdot \frac{S(t)}{N} - \delta \cdot P(E \rightarrow P) \cdot E(t)$$

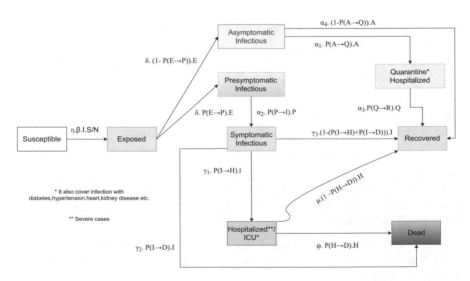

Fig. 7 Proposed model

$$-\delta \cdot (1 - P(E \to P)) \cdot E(t), \tag{2}$$

$$\frac{dA(t)}{dt} = \delta \cdot (1 - P(E \to P)) \cdot E(t) - \alpha_1 \cdot P(A \to Q) \cdot A(t)$$
$$- \alpha_4 \cdot (1 - P(A \to Q)) \cdot A(t), \tag{3}$$

$$\frac{dP(t)}{dt} = \delta \cdot P(E \to P) \cdot E(t) - \alpha_2 \cdot P(P \to I) \cdot P(t), \tag{4}$$

$$\frac{dQ(t)}{dt} = \alpha_1 \cdot P(A \to Q) \cdot A(t) - \alpha_3 \cdot P(Q \to R) \cdot Q(t), \tag{5}$$

$$\frac{dI(t)}{dt} = \alpha_2 \cdot P(P \to I) \cdot P(t) - \gamma_1 \cdot P(I \to H) \cdot I(t) - \gamma_2 \cdot P(I \to D) \cdot I(t)$$
$$- \gamma_3 \cdot (1 - (P(I \to H) + P(I \to D))) \cdot I(t), \tag{6}$$

$$\frac{dH(t)}{dt} = \gamma_1 \cdot P(I \to H) \cdot I(t) - \varphi \cdot P(H \to D) \cdot H(t)$$
$$- \mu \cdot (1 - P(H \to D)) \cdot H(t), \tag{7}$$

$$\frac{dR(t)}{dt} = \alpha_4 \cdot (1 - P(A \to Q)) \cdot A(t) + \alpha_3 \cdot P(Q \to R) \cdot Q(t)$$
$$+ \gamma_3 \cdot (1 - (P(I \to H) + P(I \to D))) \cdot I(t) + \mu \cdot (1 - P(H \to D)) \cdot H(t), \tag{8}$$

$$\frac{dD(t)}{dt} = \varphi \cdot P(H \to D) \cdot H(t) + \gamma_2 \cdot P(I \to D) \cdot I(t), \tag{9}$$

$$N = S(t) + E(t) + A(t) + P(t) + Q(t) + I(t) + H(t) + R(t) + D(t). \tag{10}$$

All parameters with description:

- social distancing factor,
- β— rate of transmission,
- δ—the rate of infection transmission from exposed to presymptomatic infectious or asymptomatic infectious,
- α_1—median time from severe asymptomatic infectious to admission in quarantine hospital,
- α_2—median time from presymptomatic to symptomatic infectious,
- α_3—median time to recover from quarantine hospital,
- α_4—median recovery time of asymptomatic infectious,
- γ_1—median time for developing pneumonia and other hospitalization symptoms,
- γ_2—median time from symptomatic infection (without hospitalization) to death,
- γ_3—median recovery time of symptomatic infectious,
- φ—median time to stay at the hospital/ICU,
- μ—the time of recovery for hospitalized people.

Table 2 Value of parameters from authentic sources

Parameters	Description	Value
η	Stringency index	1
Δ	Exposed to presymptomatic/asymptomatic infectious	1/3.5
α_1	Asymptomatic to quarantine hospitalized	1/2.0
α_2	Presymptomatic to symptomatic infectious	1/2.0
α_3	Quarantine hospitalized to recovered	1/10.0
α_4	Asymptomatic infectious to recovered	1/2.0
γ_1	Symptomatic infectious to hospitalized	1/3.7
γ_2	Symptomatic infectious to dead	1/6.4
γ_3	Symptomatic infectious to recovered	1/10.0
φ	Hospitalized to dead	1/2.4
μ	Hospitalized to recovered	1/10.0

Bold letters in the table shows the better performance among comperative predictive models

There is no known exact value of the initial conditions $(S(0), I(0), R(0))$. We put very carefully the value of the initial conditions, because these ordinary differential equation systems are highly sensitive to initial parameters.

First, we fit the available clinical data, and then, we estimate the model parameters values from it. We used the least square method and the Levenberg–Marquardt model to calculate the parameters R_0_start, R_0_end, k, x_0, s, $P(E \rightarrow P)$, $P(A \rightarrow Q)$, $P(Q \rightarrow R)$, $P(P \rightarrow I)$, $P(I \rightarrow H)$, $P(H \rightarrow D)$, and $P(I \rightarrow D)$ for the proposed model. To estimate the final value of any parameter, we first set the range of the parameter means the maximum value and the minimum value. Then, we have to set the initial value of the parameter to fit the model and get the final fitted value. We do not need to fit some parameter, for example, η, δ, α_1, α_2, α_3, α_4, γ_1, γ_2, γ_3, φ, μ, etc., need not to fit. We have to get these parameter values from the review of research papers and reports of trusted organizations. Tables 2 and 3 show the numerical values of the model parameters for selected countries.

The proposed method mainly focused on death cases because death cases hardly go undetected. The proposed methods result shows the predicted outcome which is very closed to the real scenario.

3 Data Analysis and Parameter Estimation

Mathematical modeling of infectious diseases is simplified by compartmental models. Compartmental models are based on ordinary differential equations. To solve these ordinary differential equations, some initial conditions and characteristic parameters are needed. It is very sensitive to these initial parameters. A minor change in them can make a big difference in results, so in the equations they need to

Table 3 Parameters estimation with fitted value

Parameters	Initial value	Minimum value	Maximum value	Fitted value
$P(E \rightarrow P)$	0.3	0.2	0.5	0.2
$P(A \rightarrow Q)$	0.9	0.85	1.0	0.900438516
$P(Q \rightarrow R)$	0.9	0.8	1.0	0.999642426
$P(P \rightarrow I)$	0.9	0.85	1.0	0.874977863
$P(I \rightarrow H)$	0.1	0.05	0.25	0.239551274
$P(H \rightarrow D)$	0.25	0.20	0.70	0.451287751
$P(I \rightarrow D)$	0.025	0.01	0.10	0.067009916
s	0.003	0.001	0.01	0.003141659
R_0_start	1.5	1	2.2	1.51633527
k	0.2	0.1	0.8	0.2
x_0	180	0	380	180
R_0_end	0.4	0.3	1.0	0.4

Bold letters in the table shows the better performance among comperative predictive models

be carefully implemented. Preliminary parameter estimation helps estimate the case fatality rate and basic reproduction number. The social distance parameter suggests that social contacts and physical contact would be avoided to control the transmission of infectious diseases. The meaning of the social distancing factor lies between zero and one. When a lock is applied, and all individuals are placed in quarantine, its value is zero, and if they obey unregulated and routine, its value is one.

The Basic Reproduction Number R_0 and Case Fatality Rate Over Time
The ratio between the transmission rate and the recovery rate is the basic reproduction number R_0. The basic reproduction number is the average number of people infected by any an infected person, if no intervention measures are in place. The basic reproduction number is important for disease intervention. The value of the basic reproduction number R_0 varies over time; the basic reproduction number value decreases if any country embraces lockdowns, and its value starts to increase again when that country eliminates the lockdown.

R_0 is the ratio of β and γ in the compartmental models ($R_0 = \beta/\gamma$). Hence, we can say that $\beta = R_0 . \gamma$. In this manuscript, before the lockdown, the value of R_0 is R_0 start, and if the lockdown is imposed on day L, the value of R_0 is reduced to R_0 end, and the value of β will be changed accordingly. In real life, the basic reproduction number R_0 is not constant and changes over time. When social distancing is imposed or removed, its value will change accordingly. The model illustrates the initial impact of social distancing on the basic reproduction number. The time-dependent variation in R_0 can be given as

$$R_0(t) = \frac{R_{0_{Start}} - R_{0_{End}}}{1 + e^{-\eta(-t+x_0)}} + R_{0_{End}}. \tag{11}$$

The description of the parameters is given below:

$R_{0_{Start}}$ The value of the R_0 for the first day,
$R_{0_{End}}$ The value of R_0 for the last day.

x_0 is the day when R_0 drastically decreases or inflection point, and

η is the parameter of social distance.

The value of the x_0 should be given very carefully because it makes a big difference to the result and the value of the $R_{0_{End}}$ must be less than one.

Age-Dependent Fatality Rate

The infection mortality rate is the ratio between the number of casualties and the number of cases. The rate of death is not constant and depends on several variables such as age and fatal diseases. If the majority of people are infected, then the fatality rate is high, and the fatality rate is low when fewer people are infected. If infected people are very high, we need more health care. Often, not everyone is treated because of the shortage of medical services. We need, therefore to know what proportions of individuals are currently infected. Therefore, we describe the fatality rate φ as

$$\varphi(t) = s \cdot \frac{I(t)}{N} + \varphi_{opt}. \tag{12}$$

The description of the parameters is given below:

s It is arbitrary, but the fixed value that controls infection,
φ_{opt} Optimal fatality rate.

As it governs the above equation, the value of parameter s is significant; very small changes in s can make a huge difference in performance. The value of this parameter should therefore be carefully chosen. At time t, $I(t)$ is the sick, and N is the total population.

Depending on the age group, case fatality analysis is complex. Therefore, to help assess the case fatality, we classify age into various age classes (e.g., people aged 0–9, aged 10–19, ..., aged 90–100). The fatality rate by age group and the proportion of the total population in that age group are two things that are needed for the age group study. If the elderly population is higher, the death rate will rise, and if the proportion of young people is higher, the death rate will be lower.

Therefore, the death (fatality) rate is calculated as follows:

The rate of fatality = age group fatality rate of all cases
$$* \text{proportion of age group population.} \tag{13}$$

The ratio between the number of deaths and the number of cases is the death rate. The risk of dying can be described as being infected by a virus (in percentage) and depends on different age groups. The following Table 4 presents the percentage of deaths in a given age group if a person is infected with COVID-19 [30].

Table 4 Age-wise death rate in all cases

Age group	Death rate (%)
90+ years old	8.60
80–89 years old	20.89
70–79 years old	20.40
60–69 years old	29.28
50–59 years old	23.75
40–49 years old	11.37
30–39 years old	4.59
20–29 years old	1.56
10–19 years old	0.32
0–9 years old	0.24

Hospitalized Cases Analysis

We know every country has a limited number of hospital beds. In order to raise the number of hospital beds when the disease spreads, all countries are starting new hospitals, opening rooms, etc. The number of hospital beds is, therefore, increasing over time. We can model the number of beds as follows:

$$Beds_{hosp}(t) = Beds_{hosp0} + s.t. \ Beds_{hosp0}. \qquad (14)$$

Description of the parameters is given below:

$Beds_{hosp0}$ Total number of hospital beds available,
s Some scaling factor.

Since the number of beds displayed in the formula varies every day to decide how many beds have been served every day in hospitals for patients, this is a significant factor.

Environment Setting

In this study, Anaconda development platform is considered for running the proposed model. The Python platform used some important libraries such as pandas, NumPy, LMfit, and ode for all the experimental studies. The hardware configuration of the system is reported in Table 5.

Fitting the Model to Find Some Important Parameters Value

In this manuscript, we concentrate on fitting a model with the basic reproduction number and age group fatality, hospital beds with actual COVID-19 data, which are close to the real data and find parameters that can be useful in the future discussions for our model. The initial assumptions of the parameters are extremely important. First, we need to understand what parameters are understood and what we need to get out of them. Many important parameters have been used in this proposed model. Some of the parameters are calculated and considered by the current study and data.

Table 5 Specification of system

Name	Parameter
System RAM	12 GB
The processor	Intel(R) Core (TM) i7-5500U CPU
The processor speed	2.40 GHz
Cores	2 Core(s)
Logical processor	4
GPU RAM	4 GB
Graphics processor	NVIDIA GeForce GTX 950 M
Cuda cores	640
Memory interface 256-bit	128-bit
Memory type	DDR3
Bandwidth 288.5 GB/s	28.80 GB/s
Language	Python

It is not necessary to fit N, put the total population count in place of N. According to the current data and analysis, we value parameters, i.e., social distance parameter β, in the range of 0–1 where 0 shows everyone is in lockdown and quarantined, while one is for a normal way of life.

First from reliable sources, we collected all the related COVID-19 data and parameters available to us and then defined initial guesses and limits within certain limits, depending on the situation, for the remaining parameters of this model. To extract different parameters from the data fitting, we have used the Levenberg–Marquardt algorithm, as this is the most significant and effective data fitting algorithm reported [31, 32]. For Python, the LMfit library provides a high quality interface for nonlinear optimization and curve-fitting issues [33]. The proximity of the data to the fitted line is measured by the R-squared value. The R-square value is between zero and one at all times. Usually, the higher the R-squared value, the better the model that your data is given. Table 6 shows the R-squared value of Mumbai for death cases. The curve of Mumbai death cases is shown in Fig. 8.

The main source of data is www.covidindia.org [34]. For age groups, probability, and hospital beds, we have collected and data from the Indian government data center [35]. From January 30, 2020, onwards, time series data are available. These data are collected through public health authorities with ethical permission.

Distribution of total cases worldwide: According to WHO, 216 countries are affected by COVID-19. Figure 9a shows that 15% of cases come from India. In comparison with the number of global total cases, Mumbai shares one percent.

Table 6 R-squared value of curve fitting for Mumbai

City	R-squared value (death cases)
Mumbai	0.972

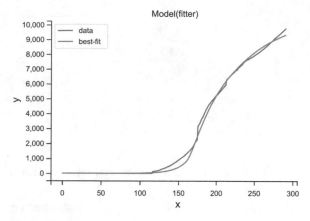

Fig. 8 Curve fitting of death cases in Mumbai

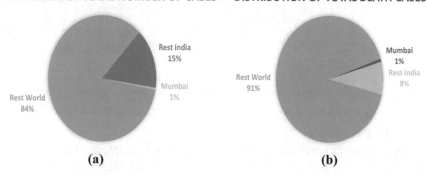

Fig. 9 **a** Distribution of total cases worldwide and **b** distribution of death cases worldwide

Distribution of death cases worldwide: Death cases are more accurate because the associated authorities rarely miss report of death due to COVID-19; hence, death cases are more accurate. Figure 9b shows that 8% of death cases come from India. In comparison with the number of global total death cases, Mumbai shares one percent.

Day-wise total cases and total death cases: Fig. 10a shows the total cases, and Fig. 10b shows the death cases of Mumbai from January 30, 2020, to September 30, 2020, of COVID-19.

Daily new cases and daily death cases: Fig. 11a shows the daily new cases, and Fig. 11b shows daily new death of Mumbai from January 30, 2020, to September 30, 2020, of COVID-19.

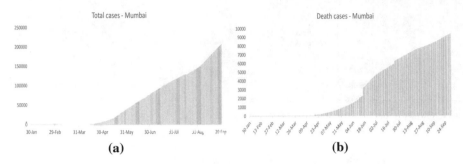

Fig. 10 **a** Day-wise total cases of Mumbai and **b** day-wise total death of Mumbai

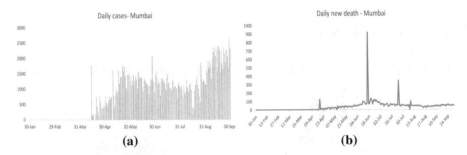

Fig. 11 **a** Daily new cases of Mumbai and **b** daily new death cases of Mumbai

Age-Wise Population

In terms of age, the majority of the population in India is young. The population of old age on this continent is much smaller. The population distribution by age group is represented in Fig. 12 [36].

The number of hospital beds per 100 k: Unit beds per 100,000 population or a 100 k population, according to WHO and the OECD [37]. Basic measures focus on

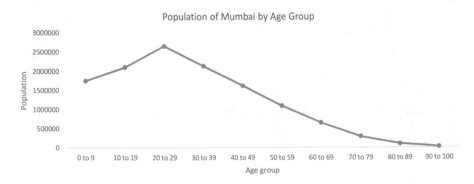

Fig. 12 Distribution of the population according to the age category of Mumbai

Table 7 As of 13 October condition of hospital beds and quarantine beds

Types of bed	Bed capacity	Occupied	Available
DCH and DCHC bed	15,057	9827	5230
ICU bed	1998	1725	273
O$_2$ bed	9145	5869	3256
Ventilator bed	1154	1032	122
CCC1 facilities*	46,677	1047	45,630
CCC2 facilities*	23,806	1150	22,656

* Quarantine hospitalized

all hospital beds that are occupied or empty. Mumbai city number of hospital beds is shown in Table 7.

4 Results and Discussion

We analyze and forecast in this section, using our proposed model, the pattern of COVID-19 of Mumbai. The result of our proposed method shows that Mumbai has experienced their worst time. In Mumbai, the distribution of disease is very random, e.g., the number of cases in Wards RC, RS, KW, PN, KE, KE, GN, S, and Ward *N* is very high as compared to other Wards. If we compare the results of our proposed method with real data, it is approximately close. In this section, we calculate for Mumbai the basic reproduction number, the case fatality rate, and the number of hospital beds required at peak time.

4.1 *Proposed Model for Mumbai*

Mumbai is the most affected country by the COVID-19 disease. According to the proposed method, cases in Mumbai will start to decline continuously after the last week of September, and the cases will end approximately in the last week of March. The cases reach on the peak in Mumbai, according to our proposed method, in September and October. The results of our proposed method show that there will no need of hospital beds in near future. The result shows the basic reproduction rate which is 1.8 in starting, and after some time, it starts decreasing visually and goes up to one and even lower. Proposed model for the Mumbai shows that the case fatality rate of COVID-19 in Mumbai is moderate. There are many ups and downs in the daily case fatality rate, but it goes higher and higher up to 5.5 in our model and then slows down, and total CFR is nearly 4.6. During peak time, the number of death cases is 65 per day, and daily hospitalized cases are nearly 350. Proposed model result for the Mumbai has shown in Fig. 13.

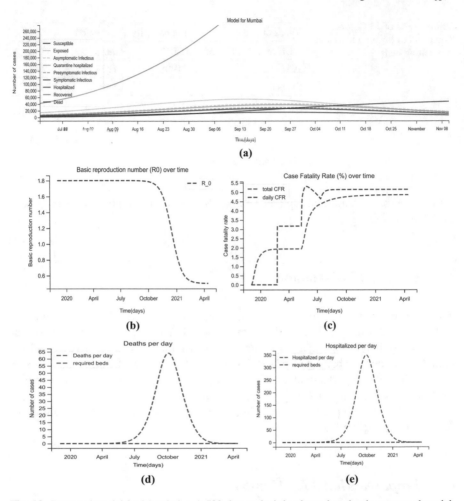

Fig. 13 Proposed model for Mumbai. **a** A 500-day analysis has been done by the proposed model, which starts from January 30. **b** The basic reproduction number of Mumbai over time. **c** The case fatality rate of Mumbai over time. **d** Daily death cases in the Mumbai, where the red line shows the number of deaths per day, and the blue line shows how many hospital beds are required during peak days. **e** Mumbai daily hospitalized cases, where the red line indicates the number of hospitalized cases per day, and the blue line shows how many hospital beds are required during peak days

Figure 14 shows the comparison between actual and forecast data for active cases with 95% interval. Rarely some of the forecast data go beyond the interval decided. For validation purpose, we predict the data for 25 days. Figure 15 shows the comparison between actual and forecast data for daily new cases with an interval of 95%, and Fig. 16 shows the comparison between actual and forecast data for daily death cases with an interval of 95%. Confidence interval is basically the sensitivity analysis

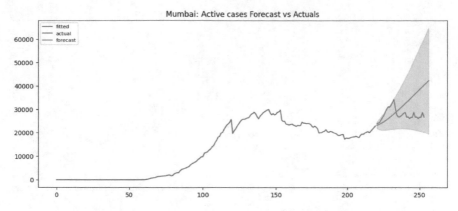

Fig. 14 Compare the actual and forecast active case data with 95% interval

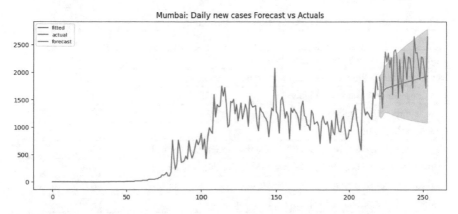

Fig. 15 Compare actual and forecast data for daily new cases with an interval of 95%

to determine the robustness of model predictions to parameter values (reproduction number), and the sensitive parameters are estimated from the real data on the COVID-19 pandemic in Mumbai.

The basic reproduction number for COVID-19 initially is 1.8, but later it goes up to 0.5. After October 2020, the spread of disease is decreasing. The summary of the proposed model results for the selected countries is shown in Table 8.

4.2 Performance Evaluation Criteria

The prediction performance of the proposed system is evaluated using the following metrics.

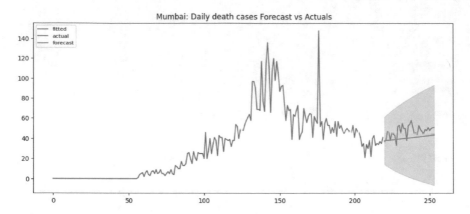

Fig. 16 Compare actual and forecast data for daily death cases with an interval of 95%

Table 8 Summary of infection propagation for Mumbai

Description	Mumbai
Approximate time when the disease is on peak	180–250
The approximate time when cases of death rarely occur	320
Basic reproduction number (highest)	1.8
Case fatality rate (highest)	5.1
Overall case fatality rate	4.6
Approximately needed hospital beds while the disease is at a peak	No
Approximately the needed ICU beds when the disease is at a peak	No
Highest number of people dead in a single day	65
Highest number of people hospitalized in a single day	350

4.2.1 Mean Absolute Percentage Error (MAPE)

Analyze the efficiency of the forecasting model of our method, we use the mean absolute percentage error (MAPE) [38] or mean absolute percentage deviation (MADE) as the criteria standard. Its formula is express as the following equation:

$$\text{MAPE} = \frac{1}{n} \sum_{i=1}^{n} \left| \frac{y_i - x_i}{y_i} \right| \times 100, \tag{15}$$

where y_i denotes the ith actual value and x_i represents the ith predicted value. If the value of MAPE is low, the accuracy of the method is high.

4.2.2   Root Mean Square Error (RMSE)

Root mean square error (RMSE) [39] or root mean square deviation (RMSD) is a measure of the average magnitude of the errors. Specifically, it is the square root of the average squared differences between the prediction and actual observations. Therefore, the RMSE will be more useful when large errors are particularly undesirable. If the value of RMSE is low, the accuracy of the method is high. RMSE formula is express as the following equation:

$$
\text{RMSE} = \sqrt{\frac{1}{n} \sum_{i=1}^{n} \left(y_i^{\text{obs}} - y_i^{\text{pred}} \right)^2}, \tag{16}
$$

where y_i^{obs} and y_i^{pred} are the actual and predicted observations, respectively.

Our basic approach is to predict COVID-19 disease and analyze the spread scenario of COVID-19 disease in India. Data used in the analysis are day wise sequential data. Hence, if we need to compare our proposed work with deep learning models, long short-term memory (LSTM) and sequence-to-sequence deep learning models are well suited for making predictions based on time series data.

The overall performance of deep learning methods is not better because there is less set of training data. If the training data set increases, the performance of the deep learning method will improve. For model validation, we have used precision measures, MAPE and RMSE. The proposed model outperforms the LSTM model and the Seq2Seq model. The result shows that the RMSE and MAPE accuracy of the proposed model better as compared to the LSTM and Seq2Seq models.

The performance evaluation compared with the following state-of-the-art methods:

1. Susceptible infectious recovered model (SIR)
2. Autoregressive integrated moving average model (ARIMA)
3. Seasonal ARIMAX model (SARIMAX).

The proposed model outperforms the state-of-the-art methods such as the SIR model, the ARIMA model, and the SARIMAX model. The proposed model outperforms the LSTM model and the Seq2Seq model. The result shows that the RMSE and MAPE accuracy of the proposed model better as compared to the SIR, ARIMA, and the SARIMAX models.

The results are evaluated using a variety of metrics (RMSE, MAPE) as well as graphically illustrated using Taylor diagrams [44–46]. Taylor diagram (Fig. 17) is used to perform the comparative assessment of several different models and to quantify the degree of correspondence between the modeled and observed behavior in terms of three statistics: Pearson correlation, root mean square deviation (RMSD), and the standard deviation. The model that is located lower on the diagram is considered to represent reality better.

Note that while the proposed model performs better than the ARX model and ARIMA model in terms of RMSD and total RSMD, it has a more considerable bias

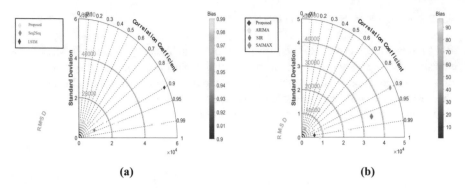

Fig. 17 **a** Taylor diagram and proposed method compare with the deep learning prediction models and **b** Taylor diagram of proposed method compare with the state-of-the-art methods

than the ARX model and ARIMA model. The results are summarized in Table 10. Table 9 summarized the LSTM, Seq2Seq model performances.

Table 9 Proposed method compare with the deep learning prediction models

Prediction models	Root mean square error (RMSE)	Mean absolute percentage error (MAPE)
LSTM[1] [40]	57,752.75	0.9363
Seq2Seq[2] [41]	10,115.92	0.2497
Proposed[3]	**6072.86**	**0.1836**

LSTM[1] Long short-term memory model
Seq2Seq[2] Sequence-to-sequence model
Proposed[3] Proposed method
Bold letters in the table shows the better performance among comparative predictive models

Table 10 Proposed method compare with the state-of-the-art methods

Prediction models	Root mean square error (RMSE)	Mean absolute percentage error (MAPE)
SIR[1] [28]	35,352.16	0.7598
ARIMA[2] [42]	8712.12	0.2968
SARIMAX[3] [43]	48,134.28	0.9412
Proposed[4]	**6072.86**	**0.1836**

SIR[1] Susceptible infectious recovered model
ARIMA[2] Autoregressive integrated moving average model
SARIMAX[3] Seasonal ARIMAX model
Proposed[4] Proposed method
Bold letters in the table shows the better performance among comparative predictive models

Discussion

Results from the proposed model suggest that this model has excellent potential for predicting the incidence of COVID-19 diseases in time series. The central aspect of our proposed model is the addition of hospitalized, quarantine hospitalized, presymptomatic, and asymptomatic infectious compartment, which improves the basic understanding of disease spread and results. Most of the cases are mild or asymptomatic, and asymptomatic cases do not show any symptoms. Still, after some time, presymptomatic cases show disease symptoms; all of these scenarios are considered in the proposed model. We have the number of total hospital beds of Mumbai city; based on that, we have calculated the number of beds required in the peak days of infection. Basic reproduction number and case fatality rate are the basic measures for this epidemic that we have also calculated. Sometimes conditions get worse because of a massive number of infected people at the same time, and the country does not have facilities to treat all critical cases when triage conditions occur. This model can solve the problem of triage. Depending on the current epidemic flow, there will be no need for new hospital beds, but if the next wave comes, this kind of scenario is not covered in this work.

Limitation

Modeling is one of the most powerful tools that give intuitive effects when multiple factors act together. No model is perfect. Models are always simplifications of the real world. No models are perfect; there are some shortcomings in it. Proposed model also has some limitations, which are as follows: Our system of differential equations is very sensitive to initial parameters. We have to very careful while given the initial parameters. Small changes in parameters can cause a massive difference in results. Our present manuscript has especially focused on severe cases and death cases. We have consented the severe cases that do not get treatment in the critical compartment. We have considered recovered cases not infected again in the future. R0 value cannot be increased; it either decreases or remains constant. We have assumed that the cases that have been recovered will be immunized, meaning that they will not be infected again.

5   Summary

In this present manuscript, we have discussed the new model that is an extension of the SEIR model in which four major compartments are added that are asymptomatic infectious, quarantine hospitalized, presymptomatic infectious, and death compartment. Some people have not seen any symptoms of the disease. They are going to the asymptomatic infectious compartment. The proposed model estimates the date and magnitude of peaks of corresponding to exposed people, number of asymptomatic infectious people, presymptomatic infectious people, symptomatic infectious people, the number of people hospitalized, the number of people quarantine hospitalized, and the number of death of COVID-19. A proposed model also calculates the basic reproduction number over time, and its computational results are almost the same as the actual data. According to the proposed model, Mumbai's case fatality rate is very high, so the death cases are very high there, and with cases that are more critical.

For model validation, we have used three precision measures, MAPE, RMSE, and R-squared. The proposed model outperforms the classic ARX model and the ARIMA model. In addition, it outperforms the deep learning model LSTM and Seq2Seq model. To show the performance of the proposed model compared to the ARX and ARIMA models, SARIMAX, LSTM, and Seq2Seq model. To validate the performance of the mode, Taylor diagram is included in the result section.

Acknowledgements I would like to express my special thanks of gratitude to our collaborator Harel Dahari of The Program for Experimental and Theoretical Modeling, Division of Hepatology, Department of Medicine, Stritch School of Medicine, Loyola University Medical Center, Maywood IL, USA as well as Jonathan Ozik from Consortium for Advanced Science and Engineering, University of Chicago, Chicago, IL, USA, who gave me the golden opportunity to do work with them on SPARC project that helped us in doing a lot of good research and we came to know about so many new things I am really thankful to them. We also thank Mrs. Ashwini Bhide, AMC, MCGM for her insights and for her crucial data inputs. We also thank Shri Saurabh Vijay, Secretary, Higher & Technical Education Department, and Government of Maharashtra for his insights and data inputs.

The work has been supported by a grant received from the Ministry of Education, Government of India under the Scheme for the Promotion of Academic and Research Collaboration (SPARC) (ID: SPARC/2019/1396).

Conflicts of Interest The authors have no conflicts of interest to report regarding the present study.

References

1. COVID-19—events as they happen. https://www.who.int/emergencies/diseases/novel-corona virus-2019/events-as-theyhappen
2. Carlos WG, Cruz CSD, Cao B, Pasnick S, Jamil S (2020) Novel Wuhan (2019-ncov) coronavirus. Am J Respir Crit Care Med 201(4):7–8. https://doi.org/10.1164/rccm.2014P7
3. Wang C, Horby PW, Hayden FG, Gao GF (2020) A novel coronavirus outbreak of global health concern. Lancet 395(10223):470–473
4. The World's Cities in 2018 (PDF). United Nations, Oct 2018, p 4. Archived (PDF) from the original on 1 Nov 2018. Retrieved 21 Oct 2019
5. Provisional Population Totals, Census of India 2011; Cities having population 1 lakh and above (PDF). Office of the Registrar General and Census Commissioner, India. Archived from the original (PDF) on 7 May 2012. Retrieved 26 Mar 2012
6. Nikhat S, Fazil M (2020) Overview of Covid-19; its prevention and management in the light of Unani medicine. Science of The Total Environment, 138859
7. Mahajan A, Sivadas NA, Solanki R (2020) An epidemic model SIPHERD and its application for prediction of the spread of COVID-19 infection in India. Chaos Solitons Fractals 140:110156
8. Singh A, Chandra SK, Bajpai MK (2020) Study of non-pharmacological interventions on COVID-19 spread. CMES Comput Model Eng Sci 125(3):967–990. https://doi.org/10.32604/cmes.2020.011601
9. Singh A, Bajpai MK (2020) SEIHCRD model for COVID-19 spread scenarios, disease predictions and estimates the basic reproduction number, case fatality rate, hospital, and ICU beds

requirement. CMES Comput Model Eng Sci 125(3):991–1031. https://doi.org/10.32604/cmes.2020.012503

10. Chandra SK, Singh A, Bajpai MK (2021) Mathematical model with social distancing parameter for early estimation of COVID-19 spread. In: Bajpai MK, Kumar Singh K, Giakos G (eds) Machine vision and augmented intelligence—theory and applications. Lecture notes in electrical engineering, vol 796. Springer, Singapore. https://doi.org/10.1007/978-981-16-5078-9_3

11. Singh KK, Kumar S, Dixit P et al (2021) Kalman filter based short term prediction model for COVID-19 spread. Appl Intell 51:2714–2726. https://doi.org/10.1007/s10489-020-01948-1

12. Ferguson N, Laydon D, Gilani GN, Imai N, Ainslie K, Baguelin M, Bhatia S, Boonyasiri A et al (2020) Report 9: impact of non-pharmaceutical interventions (NPIS) to reduce covid19 mortality and healthcare demand

13. Egger M, Johnson L, Althaus C, Schoni A, Salanti G, Low N et al (2017) Developing WHO guidelines: time to formally include evidence from mathematical modelling studies. F1000 Res 6:1584

14. Khajanchi S, Das DK, Kar TK (2018) Dynamics of tuberculosis transmission with exogenous reinfections and endogenous reactivations. Phys A 497:52–71

15. Atangana A (2020) Modelling the spread of COVID-19 with new fractal-fractional operators: can the lockdown save mankind before vaccination? Chaos Soliton Fract 136:109860

16. Chandra SK, Bajpai MK (2021) Fractional model with social distancing parameter for early estimation of COVID-19 spread. Arab J Sci Eng. https://doi.org/10.1007/s13369-021-05827-w

17. Singh A, Bajpai MK, Gupta SL (2020) A time dependent mathematical model for COVID-19 transmission dynamics and analysis of critical and hospitalized cases with bed requirements. medRxiv 2020.10.28.20221721. https://doi.org/10.1101/2020.10.28.20221721

18. Tang B, Wang X, Li Q, Bragazzi NL, Tang S, Xiao Y, Wu J (2020) Estimation of the transmission risk of the 2019-ncov and its implication for public health interventions. J Clin Med 9(2):462

19. Sarkar K, Khajanchi S, Nieto JJ (2020) Modeling and forecasting of the COVID-19 pandemic in India. Chaos Soliton Fract 139:110049

20. Giordano G, Blanchini F, Bruno R, Colaneri P, Filippo AD, Matteo AD, Colaneri M (2020) Modelling the COVID-19 epidemic and implementation of population-wide interventions in Italy. Nat Med 26:855–860

21. Gatto M, Bertuzzo E, Mari L, Miccoli S, Carraro L, Casagrandi R et al (2020) Spread and dynamics of the COVID-19 epidemic in Italy: effects of emergency containment measures. PNAS 117(19):10484–10491

22. Khajanchi S, Sarkar K (2020) Forecasting the daily and cumulative number of cases for the COVID-19 pandemic in India. Chaos 30:071101

23. Gumel AB, Ruan S, Day T, Watmough J, Brauer F, Driessche PVD, Gabrielson D, Bowman C, Alexander ME, Ardal S, Wu J, Sahai BM (2004) Modelling strategies for controlling SARS outbreaks. Proc R Soc Lond B 271:2223–2232

24. Liu Z, Magal P, Seydi O, Webb GB (2020) A COVID-19 epidemic model with latency period. Infect Dis Model

25. Khajanchi S, Sarkar K, Mondal J, Perc M (2020) Dynamics of the COVID-19 pandemic in India. arXiv: 2005.06286

26. Wu JT, Leung K, Leung GM (2020) Nowcasting and forecasting the potential domestic and international spread of the 2019-ncov outbreak originating in Wuhan, China: a modelling study. Lancet 395:689–697

27. Singh VV (2020) BMC asks hospitals to discharge all asymptomatic patients. Times of India, on TNN, 21 Sept 2020

28. Kermack WO, McKendrick AG (1927) A contribution to the mathematical theory of epidemics. In: Proceedings of the royal society of London.1927. Series A, containing papers of a mathematical and physical character, vol 115(772), pp 700–721

29. Cooke K, van den Driessche P (1996) Analysis of an SEIRS epidemic model with two delays. J Math Biol 35:240–260. https://doi.org/10.1007/s002850050051

30. https://timesofindia.indiatimes.com/city/mumbai/covid-death-rate-drops-across-all-ages-in-city-points-to-better-mgmt/articleshow/78177998.cms
31. Levenberg K (1944) A method for the solution of certain non-linear problems in least squares. Quart Appl Math 2(2):164–168. https://doi.org/10.1090/qam/10666
32. Marquardt D (1963) An algorithm for least-squares estimation of nonlinear parameters. SIAM J Appl Math 11(2):431–441. https://doi.org/10.1137/0111030.hdl:10338.dmlcz/104299
33. Non-linear least-square minimization and curve-fitting for python. https://lmfit.github.io/lmfit-py/
34. https://covidindia.org/open-data/
35. https://www.mohfw.gov.in/
36. http://www.populationu.com/cities/mumbai-population
37. https://twitter.com/ashwinibhide?lang=en
38. Makridakis S (1993) Accuracy measures: theoretical and practical concerns. Int J Forecast 9(4):527–529. https://doi.org/10.1016/0169-2070(93)90079-3
39. Armstrong JS, Collopy F (1992) Error measures for generalizing about forecasting methods: empirical comparisons. Int J Forecast 8(1):69–80. https://doi.org/10.1016/0169-2070(92)90008-w
40. Hochreiter S, Schmidhuber J (1997) Long short-term memory. Neural Comput 9(8):1735–1780
41. Sutskever I, Vinyals O, Le QV (2014) Sequence to sequence learning with neural networks. In: Advances in neural information processing systems, pp 3104–3112
42. Box GE, Jenkins GM, Reinsel GC, Ljung GM (2015) Time series analysis: forecasting and control. Wiley
43. Hyndman RJ, Athanasopoulos G (2015) Seasonal ARIMA models. Forecasting: principles and practice. OTexts. Retrieved 19, 2015
44. Taylor KE (2001) Summarizing multiple aspects of model performance in a single diagram. J Geophys Res 106:7183–7192
45. Jolliff JK, Kindle JC, Shulman I, Penta B, Friedrichs MAM, Helber R, Arnone RA (2009) Summary diagrams for coupled hydrodynamic-ecosystem model skill assessment. J Mar Syst 76:64–82
46. Sidekerskienė T, Woźniak M, Damaševičius R (2017) Nonnegative matrix factorization based decomposition for time series modelling. Lecture notes in computer science, pp 604–613. Available at: https://doi.org/10.1007/978-3-319-59105-6_52

A Mathematical Model for the Effect of Vaccination on COVID-19 Epidemic Spread

Avaneesh Singh, Sawan Rai, and Manish Kumar Bajpai

1 Introduction

Vaccination is one of the most effective public health interventions to prevent, control, and eliminate the disease. Vaccinations are essential to protect individuals because vaccinations can prevent illnesses from developing the disease. Vaccination is most beneficial in preventing epidemics, but it is worried as one of the most negative phenomena in society.

This research aims to identify optimal vaccination incentives, given resource constraints to prevent disease outbreaks in a population. Barriers to high vaccination coverage include vaccine shortages, cost, lack of universal vaccination records, adherence complexity, misinformation, and personal and cultural beliefs. This research will have a broad impact on millions of individuals by providing policymakers with tools to promote vaccination uptake through sequential intervention design and effective healthcare resource utilization to improve population health.

The conditions and scenarios of different countries are different, and the geographical conditions and the spread scenario are different depending on the conditions of each country. In order to stop the spread of the pandemic, we have given priority to some groups, because some groups are highly susceptible to the virus. First, we need to focus on those groups for vaccination. The prime focus of the WHO is that everyone could benefit from the vaccine but start with those who are highly sensitive to the virus.

To highlight the central principle of immunization immunity, we have proposed an epidemic paradigm in which critical people and elderly individuals are first vaccinated and consider all those instances that have been healed, and after some period,

A. Singh (✉) · S. Rai · M. K. Bajpai
PDPM Indian Institute of Information Technology, Design and Manufacturing, Jabalpur 482005, India
e-mail: avaneesh.singh@iiitdmj.ac.in

© The Author(s), under exclusive license to Springer Nature Singapore Pte Ltd. 2023
K. Kumar Singh et al. (eds.), *Machine Vision and Augmented Intelligence*, Lecture Notes in Electrical Engineering 1007, https://doi.org/10.1007/978-981-99-0189-0_9

their immunity has waned. Recovered candidates with waning immunity shall be considered as exposed instances.

Literature Survey: A vaccine, when available, will likely become our best tool to control the current COVID-19 pandemic using age-specific vaccine distribution [1]. Even in the most optimistic scenarios, vaccine shortages will likely occur. Matrait et al. [2] proposed an age-stratified mathematical model, which determines optimal vaccine allocation for four different metrics (deaths, symptomatic infections, and maximum non-ICU and ICU hospitalizations) under a wide variety of assumptions. When minimizing deaths, Bubar et al. [3] found that it is optimal for low vaccine effectiveness to allocate vaccine to high-risk (older) age groups first.

In anticipation of COVID-19 vaccine deployment, Meehan et al. [4] used an age-structured mathematical model to investigate the benefits of optimizing age-specific dose allocation to suppress SARS-CoV-2 transmission.

A genetic algorithm has been proposed by Patel et al. [5] to provide the optimal distribution of vaccines to minimize the number of diseases or deaths in the population. Tuite and his partners [6] explain the spatial spread of illness and identify optimal control interventions used a transmission model. To solve the problem of vaccine distribution optimization, we propose using the algorithm of differential evolution [7, 8] to improve the effectiveness of vaccine protection. DE is a form of evolutionary algorithms [9–15] inspired by the natural development of the best-fit survival. Searching for nonlinear and multimodal space [16] is very suitable for solving continuous optimization problems and has achieved promising performance.

To represent the transmission and development of an epidemic disease, researchers have made various models and simulations. SIR, SIS, and SIRS and their variations in the SEIS, SEIR, MSIR, MSEIR, and MSEIRS models are the most notable models (S: susceptible, I: infected, R: removed, E: latent exposed, and M: passive immune) [17–23]. Table 1 is basically a summary of the proposed work's main findings and motivation.

In the current manuscript, we discuss a multi-parameter mathematical model based on age, co-morbidity, and income to justify a vaccine claim. In this public health crisis, it is essential to develop a regulatory regime to distribute vaccines and allocate scarce healthcare resources. One effective way to protect vulnerable persons from infectious diseases is through vaccination. Our primary drive is to achieve the maximum effects and optimize the distribution of vaccine doses to the individual groups, minimizing the number of infectious people during an epidemic.

2 Proposed Method

Reducing premature death and many other chronic health complications induced by COVID-19, our proposed model includes four key concepts that we have followed during the distribution of the COVID-19 vaccine:

Table 1 Policy summary

Background	Vaccination is one of the most effective public health interventions to prevent, control, and eliminate the disease. When a vaccine for COVID-19 becomes available, it will undoubtedly be in short supply globally, nationally, and locally, raising the question of how that limited vaccine should be prioritized to subpopulations to minimize future cases or deaths. However, numerous factors will be complicated, including the heterogeneity of contact structure, vaccine efficacy and safety, and seroprevalencc
Main findings and limitations	Serological testing is essential to identifying individuals who have been infected and recovered and are again infected due to waning immunity (in the near term) to SARS-CoV-2. Several scenarios have been explored that show substantive decreases in cases, hospitalizations, and deaths compared to baseline given priority wise vaccination that reduce the risk of transmission. As with all modeling studies, our predictions come with reasonable assumptions; nonetheless, controlling the course of the epidemic could benefit from identifying seropositive individuals and integrating their behavior into multifaceted intervention approaches
Policy implications	Our findings reinforce the need for large-scale, serological testing initiatives to identify individuals who are old, are critically ill cases, and find the cases with waning immunity from COVID-19. Although questions remain about the duration and effectiveness identification and deployment of vaccination to reduce transmission for the collective good. Initiating large-scale serological testing initiatives is key to proactive approaches to end the COVID-19 pandemic

1. The vaccine should be given first to those who are in critical condition (ICU/Ventilator).
2. Providing benefits to people who are co-morbid.
3. Giving the vaccine first to the old age patients.
4. Providing equal moral concern to all individuals concerned.

The model focused on reducing the three types of harm that is caused due to COVID-19. These include death and permanent organ damage, strain stress on the healthcare system, and economic destruction.

The rapid spread of the disease may necessitate the swift establishment of multiple stages of the outbreak vaccine research program accompanied by validation of all the previous developments and improvements, culminating in the success of the whole project of reaching the clinical phase more quickly. These vaccine candidates are going to have to be tested using traditional and scientific research methodologies until advancing to the clinical and preclinical stages of progress. A number of strategies are expected to be employed to try to respond to this danger, due to possible sociopolitical and new evidence on the COVID-19 pandemic and the host's possible responses to

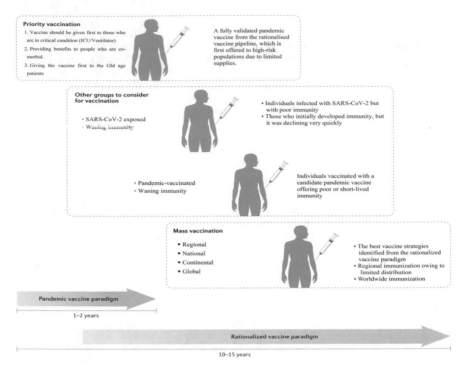

Fig. 1 Current scenarios for global development and demand of COVID-19 vaccines

SARS disease. Figure 1 is divided into three historical parts, with the current work focusing on the first two.

In the present work, we are working on the first and second stage of the vaccine program, the priority vaccination scheme. The first scenario is the high-risk groups, such as healthcare employees, the aged, those with co-morbidities, and ethnic minorities, who were adversely impacted by COVID-19 while the availability of vaccinations was initially restricted. Apart from these priority classes, consideration will need to be given to the prospect of enhanced vaccination of asymptomatic individuals. These patients benefited from COVID-19 but generated low immunity or rapidly decreased immune levels. Those who obtained a fast-growing 'pandemic' vaccine that offered under-optimal defense or quickly decreased immune responses. At the end of the day, local, continuous, and global communities would be exposed to mass vaccine systems depending on the extent of delivery and local intensity of outbreaks.

Interactions between behavior-disease and vaccination have been shown in Fig. 2. The feedback loop encourages vaccination while spreading the disease and increased risk perception. On the other hand, people are returning to abstention if immunization is carried out, and the spread of the disease is efficiently mitigated. However, eventually, this naturally restarts the loop.

Fig. 2 Interactions between behavior-disease and vaccination

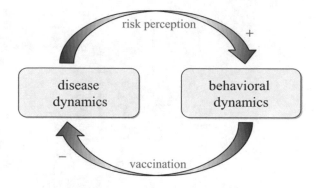

Hence, rather than mixing at random, we consider a relative preference of $1 + \alpha$ that a given person associates with a recovering individual with waning immunity in what may otherwise be a highly contagious interaction. We assume this type of interaction substitution with effective contact rate ratio of $1 + \alpha$ for recovered persons with waning immunity compared to the remaining portion of the population. Differential equation of the susceptible (S), infectious (I), and recovered (R) individuals is given below

$$\frac{dS}{dt} = -\beta \frac{SI}{1 + \alpha R} \tag{1}$$

$$\frac{dI}{dt} = \beta \frac{SI}{1 + \alpha R} - \gamma I \tag{2}$$

$$\frac{dR}{dt} = \gamma I \tag{3}$$

For above equations, when $\alpha = 0$, then it works as the traditional SIR model with transmission rate of β and recovery rate of γ. Here, we consider $1 + \alpha R$ as $S + I + R + \alpha R$, and we know that $S + I + R = 1$ and is equal to $1 + \alpha R$.

Figure 3 illustrates vaccination impacts on a SIR epidemic with different basic reproduction number. After vaccination, the outbreak peak reduces and shortening the time of transmission of the epidemic. We consider a negative feedback loop in cases of waning immunity, and then, the effective reproduction number is given by $\frac{R_{\text{eff}}(t)}{R_0} = S(t)/(1 + \alpha R(t))$. If we increase vaccination, there might be an increase in the number of candidates recovered.

We have studied the long-term vaccine phase in populations with fixed age groups, high-risk persons, and individuals with reduced immunity. Figure 3 shows that all these vaccine schedules are considered.

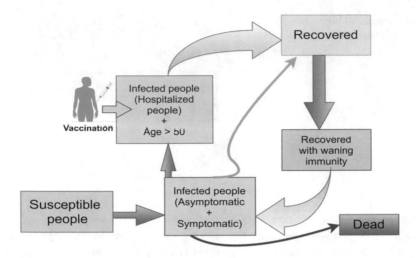

Fig. 3 Simplified schematic of intervention for vaccination to hospitalized infected people and old age people. Some recovered cases waning the immunity after some time then they may again be infected either symptomatic or asymptomatic

3 Mathematical Model

Assumptions for an age-structured model. We have proposed a vaccination model for the dynamics of the COVID-19 pandemic. Here, we consider the different population compartments as susceptible (S), exposed (E), symptomatic infectious (I_s), asymptomatic infectious (I_a), hospitalized $(H_{\text{sub}}$, and $H_{\text{cri}})$, and recovered (R), and the population is free to switch from one compartment to another. A portion of symptomatic patients would need medical attention, which has been divided into sub-acute and acute cases (H_{cri}) which require ICU. It has been predicted that a significant portion of the critical cases will die. For this work, we have considered the population to be constant for the overall scenario. The proposed model is visually illustrated in Fig. 4, and the differential equations of this vaccination model are given below:

$$\frac{dS(a)}{dt} = -\frac{\beta_s S(a) I_{\text{sym,tot}}}{N_{\text{tot}} + \alpha R_{\text{waning}}} - \frac{\beta_s S(a) I_{\text{asym,tot}}}{N_{\text{tot}} + \alpha R_{\text{waning}}} \tag{4}$$

$$\frac{dE(a)}{dt} = \frac{\beta_s S(a) I_{\text{sym,tot}}}{N_{\text{tot}} + \alpha R_{\text{waning}}} - \frac{\beta_s S(a) I_{\text{asym,tot}}}{N_{\text{tot}} + \alpha R_{\text{waning}}} - \gamma_e E(a) \tag{5}$$

$$\frac{dI_a(a)}{dt} = p(a)\gamma_e E(a) - \gamma_a I_{\text{asym}}(a) \tag{6}$$

$$\frac{dI_{\text{sym}}(a)}{dt} = (1 - p(a))\gamma_e E(a) - \gamma_s I_{\text{sym}}(a) \tag{7}$$

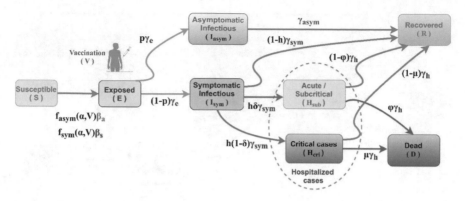

Fig. 4 Mathematical model with vaccination criteria

$$\frac{dH_{sub}(a)}{dt} = h(a)\delta(a)\gamma_s I_{sym}(a) - (1-\varphi(a))\gamma_h H_{sub}(a) - \varphi(a)\gamma_h H_{sub}(a) \quad (8)$$

$$\frac{dH_{cri}(a)}{dt} = h(a)(1-\delta(a))\gamma_s I_{sym}(a) - (1-\mu(a))\gamma_h H_{cri}(a) - \mu(a)\gamma_h H_{cri}(a) \quad (9)$$

$$\frac{dR(a)}{dt} = \gamma_a I_{asym}(a) + (1-h(a))\gamma_s I_{sym}(a) + (1-\varphi(a))\gamma_h H_{sub}(a)$$
$$+ (1-\mu(a))\gamma_h H_{cri}(a) \quad (10)$$

$$\frac{dD(a)}{dt} = \mu(a)\gamma_h H_{cri}(a) + \varphi(a)\gamma_h H_{sub}(a) \quad (11)$$

Here, V_1 and V_2 represent the vaccination to the old age individuals of this compartment, V_3 and V_4 represent the vaccination of all individuals of hospitalized compartment. $I_{sym,tot}$ represents the total number of population of symptomatic infectious individuals of all age groups, $I_{asym,tot}$ the total number of population of Asymptomatic infectious individuals of all age groups, N_{tot} the total population, and R_{waning} the number of individuals recovered who waning their immunity after a period of time.

The mathematical model with waning immunity is illustrated in Fig. 5. The arrow from recovered to exposed compartment indicates that some recovered candidates lose their immunity after a period of time and are then considered exposed candidates. Following the incubation period, we can place them in either the asymptomatic infectious or symptomatic infectious compartment. Infected people who are symptomatic can be acute or critical. Both acute and critical cases are admitted to the hospital for treatment. Vaccination occurs in four compartments in this model, which are listed below:

1. Asymptomatic infectious with old age individuals

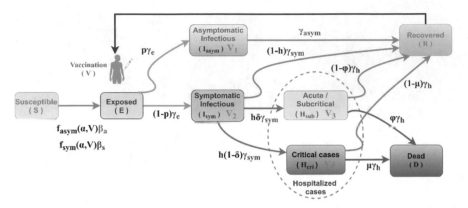

Fig. 5 Mathematical model with waning immunity

2. Symptomatic infectious with old age individuals
3. Acute individuals
4. Critical individuals.

Interactions of emergency patients can be incorporated throughout particular situations with healthcare professionals [24]. We have considered that all healthcare workers are vaccinated first with old age patients and critical patients.

We use certain initial parameters taken directly from authentic sources [24, 25]. Seed and single-exposed human outbreaks before the overall frequency of the epidemic is 0.1%. (10,000 persons infected out of a population of 10,000,000, by which stage the vaccine plan is being implemented). The transmission rates in the low-transmission and high-transmission outbreak cases vary, with basic reproduction number $R_0 = 1.57$ and 2.33, respectively. Basic reproduction number figures from Wuhan have a 95% confidence interval of 2.1–4.5 [26], placing our high-transmission scenario on the optimistic end of the predicted ranges. The basic reproduction number of the high-transmission scenario we are looking at here, on the other hand, is compatible with a range of 2.0–2.6 [27], and a median of basic reproduction number is 2.38 (95% confidence interval, 2.04–2.77) as derived from stochastic model fits to epidemic results in China [28]. Vaccination is determined by a variety of variables, including demographics, the proportion of asymptomatic transmission, and immunity length [24, 28].

Most of the population receive benefits from vaccination. After vaccination, we have found that the number of deaths decreased. Vaccination also increases outcomes in models of varying baseline levels of asymptomatic transmission due to heterogeneity in asymptomatic infection probabilities. Furthermore, our model suggests that immunity develops quickly within two to three weeks and lasts for a long period. Nevertheless, certain cases may experience diminishing immunity over time. According to certain clinical studies, antibodies formed after a total of 28 days after vaccination. If immunity gain period is four months or more, the benefits of vaccination are powerful. Given the variability of immune responses at the person level, different prevention measures that prolong the disease will almost certainly affect the efficacy of vaccination [27, 28]. Furthermore, we consider the implications of serological accuracy rate. If recovered individuals may be re-infected (and with very little risk to themselves) or if these persons are possibly misidentified, which may contribute to contact exchange with others that may infect others, the advantages of vaccination can be harmed. Combining serology and PCR test procedures may eliminate this threat.

In general, several things are used in parallel with the vaccination strategy. We use social distancing and multiple approaches in parallel. Each of these measures reduces the transmission rate. As social distances apply, the contact between people decreases, and then, the transmission decreases. However, the benefits of vaccination are growing at all levels of social distance. Social distancing and vaccination both work together to boost anticipated hospitalization loads, meaning that vaccination can play a role in reducing transmission.

Serological testing is critically necessary in the community. Recognizing both elderly and serious cases in order to produce vaccines to slow transmission. The potential size of the vaccine is determined by the inherent dynamics of the disease, which determine the number of individuals recovered. Priority wise vaccination gives a positive response. For a stronger response, public health authorities should make vaccination a priority. Its necessity for ongoing monitoring could assist intervention efforts while also providing critical information on the risk of re-infection in recovered individuals.

Figure 6 illustrates the relative reduction in total deaths after vaccination for low basic reproduction number (1.55) and high basic reproduction number (2.33). Figure 7 illustrates the peak number of ICU beds required after vaccination for low basic reproduction number (1.55) and high basic reproduction number (2.33).

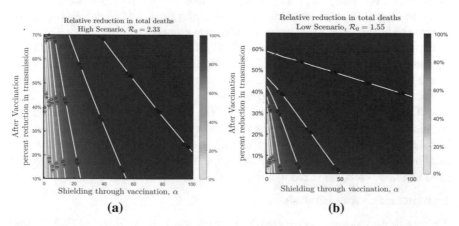

Fig. 6 Effects of vaccination interventions in the high-transmission and low-transmission scenarios. **a** For the high-transmission case, the fractional reduction in deaths relative to baseline (with basic reproduction number 2.33). **b** For the low-transmission case, the fractional reduction in deaths relative to baseline (with basic reproduction number 1.55)

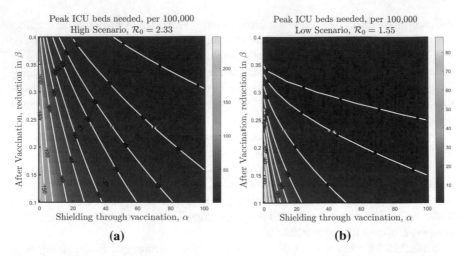

Fig. 7 Peak amount of ICU beds required per 100,000 people on a particular day over the epidemic. The red line represents a demarcation point for surges of 25 ICU beds per 100,000 persons. **a** For the high-transmission scenario (with basic reproduction number 2.33). **b** For the low-transmission scenario (with basic reproduction number 1.55)

4 Result and Discussion

The outcome depicts the behavior of the spread scenario following vaccination. As a result of the vaccination, the number of deaths and the number of ICU beds required will be reduced. The current section also discusses age-related death cases. Because we know that most of the cases are asymptomatic, we will discuss the asymptomatic case analysis separately. This section also includes an analysis of waning immunity cases for people under the age of 60 and people over the age of 60, with a high basic reproduction number and low basic reproduction number.

Figure 8 depicts the spread scenario of COVID-19 dynamics, such as the number of deaths, required ICU beds, and deaths in multiple age classes, without interventions versus baseline and after vaccination.

For analyzing the results, we have used the deaths per day per 100,000, ICU beds per 100,000, and cumulative deaths per 100,000. The number of death cases per day and cumulative deaths decreased after vaccination when compared to the baseline. Furthermore, ICU beds are required less after vaccination when compared to the baseline. When compared to the younger population, people over the age of 60 are more affected. Vaccination reduces deaths in all age groups significantly.

Asymptomatic Cases Analysis

We have looked at how asymptomatic transmission is being affected. We first set the intrinsic asymptomatic fraction p from 0.5 to 0.95. When the simple replication number stays stable, and when vaccination increases, minimizing total deaths

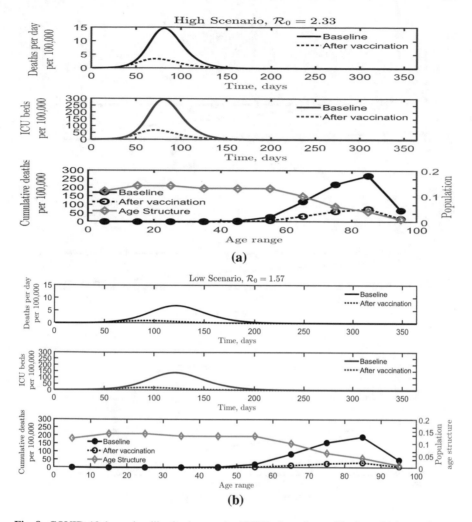

Fig. 8 COVID-19 dynamics, like deaths, required ICU beds, and casualties in multiple age classes, without interventions compared to baseline and after the vaccination scenario. **a** High-transmission scenarios with basic reproduction number 2.33 (**b**) and low-transmission scenarios with basic reproduction number 1.57

and ICU cases by 90%. Second, provided findings of increasing risk based on clinical outcome evidence from Wuhan, China, we have considered the results of age-dependent variance in the inherent asymptomatic proportion, $p(a)$, by setting the average p at 0.5, 0.75, and 0.9 has been shown in Fig. 9.

Figure 9 shown the effect of vaccination on total deaths and peak ICU cases of asymptomatic fraction for low basic reproduction number (1.55), high basic reproductive number (2.33), and a complex scenario of basic reproductive numbers. For both ages, in three cases, the fraction of asymptomatic p is the same.

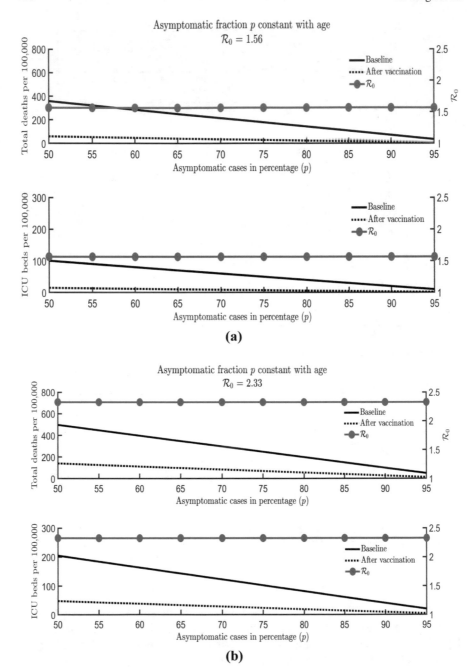

Fig. 9 Effect on total deaths and peak ICU cases of asymptomatic fraction and vaccination. **a** For a constant simple low-scenario reproductive number. **b** For a constant basic high scenario reproductive number, and **c** a complex scenario of basic reproductive numbers. For both ages, in three cases, the fraction of asymptomatic p is the same

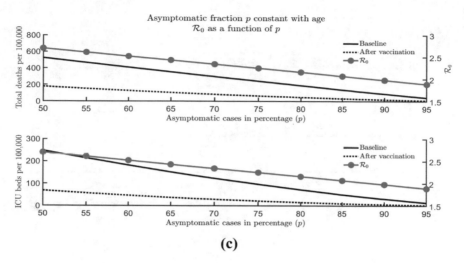

(c)

Fig. 9 (continued)

Analysis of COVID-19 dynamics in a baseline case without interventions compared to baseline with the after vaccination scenarios and three asymptomatic fraction cases ($p = 0.5$, $p = 0.75$, and $p = 0.9$) with high basic reproduction number 2.3 and low basic reproduction number 1.57. Vaccination's effect is resilient to the reported age-specific heterogeneity, resulting in substantial reductions in predicted deaths and ICU admissions as shown in Fig. 10.

Waning Immunity Analysis

Some of the individuals recovered are known to have lost their immunity after some time. This could have an effect on the spread scenario. Given that individuals who lose immunity are more likely to develop a milder disease if re-infected, this is a conservative estimate. The results show that after a period, the down curve rises again due to waning immunity cases. With an average immunity period of two months, Fig. 11 portrays the outbreak dynamics for the high and low reproduction number scenarios. In both cases, vaccination will substantially reduce the number of deaths and the peak number of ICU beds required.

The disease has the greatest impact on elderly patients. People over 60 years of age are more affected in comparison with the younger population. Vaccination significantly reduces mortality in all age ranges. Figure 12 shows that deaths per day, cumulative deaths, and ICU bed requirements are lower for people under the age of 60 than for people over the age of 60. Figure 12 shows how the length of immunity affects the total number of cases, the number of deaths, and the number of ICU beds required for low basic reproduction number (1.55).

After analysis, we have found that vaccination of older people is very important in both asymptomatic and symptomatic cases. As a result, we can conclude that

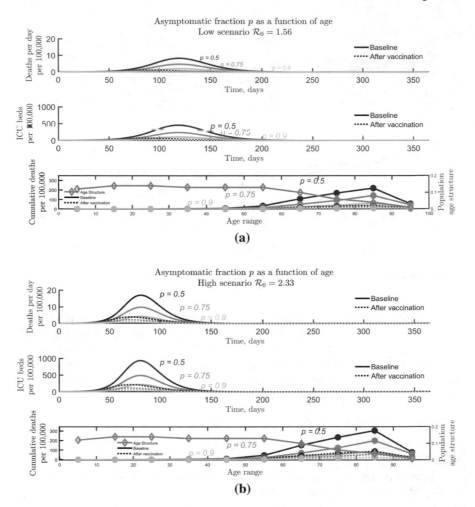

Fig. 10 COVID-19 dynamics in a baseline case without interventions compared to baseline with the after vaccination scenarios and three asymptomatic fraction cases. **a** After vaccination scenarios with three age-distributed asymptomatic fraction values ($p = 0.5$, $p = 0.75$ and $p = 0.9$) are evaluated for both a high scenario (with basic reproduction number 2.3) and **b** low scenario (with basic reproduction number 1.57)

prioritized vaccination can reduce the number of deaths per day, cumulative deaths, and the number of ICUs or ventilator beds.

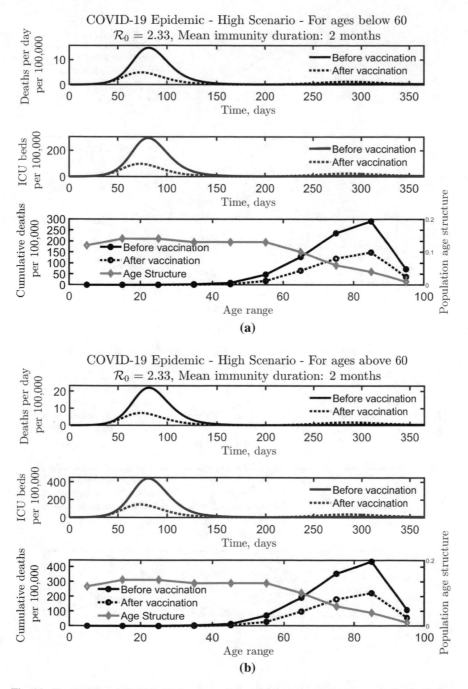

Fig. 11 Simulations of COVID-19 dynamics for **a** high basic reproduction scenarios for below 60 years of age, **b** high basic reproduction scenarios for over 60 years of age

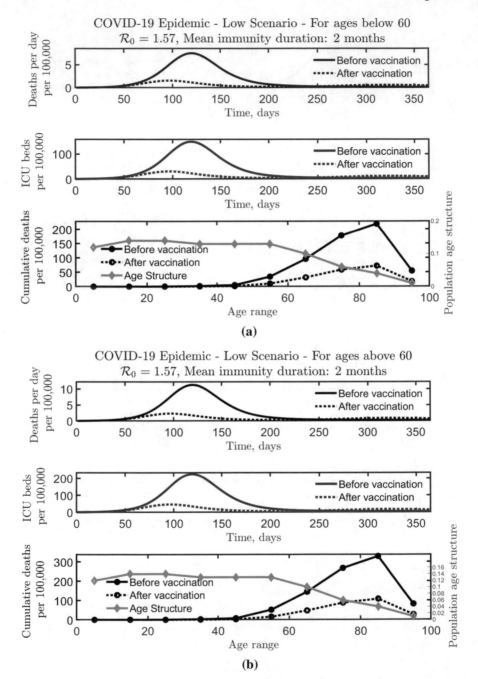

Fig. 12 Simulations of COVID-19 dynamics for **a** low basic reproduction scenarios for below 60 years of age and **b** low basic reproduction scenarios for over 60 years of age

5 Summary

In this manuscript, we have developed and analyzed an epidemiological intervention model that uses serological tests to identify and vaccinate all the elderly and critical people first. Individuals with waning immunity are also covered by this model. Many scenarios have been studied that show significant reductions in cases, hospitalizations, and fatalities when given priority vaccination that lowers the risk of transmission relative to baseline. Our findings emphasize the importance of identifying people who are elderly, chronically ill, or have waning COVID-19 immunity in order to prioritize vaccination.

Acknowledgements I would like to express my special thanks of gratitude to our collaborator Harel Dahari of The Program for Experimental and Theoretical Modeling, Division of Hepatology, Department of Medicine, Stritch School of Medicine, Loyola University Medical Center, Maywood IL, United States and as well as Jonathan Ozik from Consortium for Advanced Science and Engineering, University of Chicago, Chicago, IL, USA, who gave me the golden opportunity to do work with them on SPARC project that helped us in doing a lot of good Research and we came to know about so many new things I am really thankful to them.

The work has been supported by a grant received from the Ministry of Education, Government of India under the Scheme for the Promotion of Academic and Research Collaboration (SPARC) (ID: SPARC/2019/1396).

Conflicts of Interest The authors have no conflicts of interest to report regarding the present study.

References

1. Hu XM, Zhang J, Chen H (2014) Optimal vaccine distribution strategy for different age groups of population: a differential evolution algorithm approach. Math Probl Eng
2. Matrajt L, Eaton J, Leung T, Brown ER (2020) Vaccine optimization for COVID-19, who to vaccinate first? medRxiv
3. Bubar KM, Kissler SM, Lipsitch M, Cobey S, Grad Y, Larremore DB (2020) Model-informed COVID-19 vaccine prioritization strategies by age and serostatus. medRxiv
4. Meehan MT, Cocks DG, Caldwell JM, Trauer JM, Adekunle AI, Ragonnet RR, McBryde ES (2020) Age-targeted dose allocation can halve COVID-19 vaccine requirements. medRxiv
5. Patel R, Longini IM Jr, Halloran ME (2005) Finding optimal vaccination strategies for pandemic influenza using genetic algorithms. J Theor Biol 234(2):201–212
6. Tuite AR, Tien J, Eisenberg M, Earn DJD, Ma J, Fisman DN (2011) Cholera epidemic in Haiti, 2010: using a transmission model to explain spatial spread of disease and identify optimal control interventions. Ann Intern Med 154(9):593–601
7. Storn R Price K (1997) Differential evolution—a simple and efficient heuristic for global optimization over continuous spaces. J Glob Optim 11(4):341–359
8. Price KV, Storn RM, Lampinen JA (2005) Differential evolution—a practical approach to global approach to global optimization. Springer, Berlin
9. Wang Y, Jiao Y, Li H (2005) An evolutionary algorithm for solving nonlinear bilevel programming based on a new constraint-handling scheme. IEEE Trans Syst Man Cybernet Part C 35(2):221–232
10. Wang Y, Dang C (2007) An evolutionary algorithm for global optimization based on level-set evolution and latin squares. IEEE Trans Evol Comput 11(5):579–595

11. Hu X, Zhang J (2013) Minimum cost multicast routing using ant colony optimization algorithm. Math Probl Eng 2013:13. Article ID 432686
12. Hu X, Zhang J, Chung HS, Li Y, Liu O (2010) SamACO: variable sampling ant colony optimization algorithm for continuous optimization. IEEE Trans Syst Man Cybernet Part B 40(6):1555–1566. Hu X, Zhang J, Yu Y et al (2010) Hybrid genetic algorithm using a forward encoding scheme for lifetime maximization of wireless sensor networks. IEEE Trans Evol Comput 14(5):766–781
13. Hu X, Zhang J, Chung HS, Liu O, Xiao J (2009) An intelligent testing system embedded with an ant-colony-optimization based test composition method. IEEE Trans Syst Man Cybernet Part C 39(6):659–669
14. Chen W, Zhang J, Lin Y et al (2013) Particle swarm optimization with an aging leader and challengers. IEEE Trans Evol Comput 17(2):241–258
15. Chen W, Zhang J (2013) Ant colony optimization for software project scheduling and staff with an event-based scheduler. IEEE Trans Softw Eng 39(1):1–17
16. Qin AK, Huang VL, Suganthan PN (2009) Differential evolution algorithm with strategy adaptation for global numerical optimization. IEEE Trans Evol Comput 13(2):398–417
17. Hu X, Zhang J, Chung HS, Li Y, Liu O (2010) SamACO: variable sampling ant colony optimization algorithm for continuous optimization. IEEE Trans Syst Man Cybernet Part B 40(6):1555–1566
18. Singh A, Chandra SK, Bajpai MK (2020) Study of non-pharmacological interventions on COVID-19 spread. CMES Comput Model Eng Sci 125(3):967–990. https://doi.org/10.32604/cmes.2020.011601
19. Singh A, Bajpai MK (2020) SEIHCRD model for COVID-19 spread scenarios, disease predictions and estimates the basic reproduction number, case fatality rate, hospital, and ICU beds requirement. CMES Comput Model Eng Sci 125(3):991–1031. https://doi.org/10.32604/cmes.2020.012503
20. Chandra SK, Singh A, Bajpai MK (2021) Mathematical model with social distancing parameter for early estimation of COVID-19 spread. In: Bajpai MK, Kumar Singh K, Giakos G (eds) Machine vision and augmented intelligence—theory and applications. Lecture notes in electrical engineering, vol 796. Springer, Singapore. https://doi.org/10.1007/978-981-16-5078-9_3
21. Singh KK, Kumar S, Dixit P et al (2021) Kalman filter based short term prediction model for COVID-19 spread. Appl Intell 51:2714–2726. https://doi.org/10.1007/s10489-020-01948-1
22. Chandra SK, Bajpai MK (2021) Fractional model with social distancing parameter for early estimation of COVID-19 spread. Arab J Sci Eng. https://doi.org/10.1007/s13369-021-05827-w
23. Singh A, Bajpai MK, Gupta SL (2020) A time-dependent mathematical model for COVID-19 transmission dynamics and analysis of critical and hospitalized cases with bed requirements. medRxiv 2020.10.28.20221721. https://doi.org/10.1101/2020.10.28.20221721
24. Gonzalez DC, Nassau DE, Khodamoradi K, Ibrahim E, Blachman-Braun R, Ory J, Ramasamy R (2021) Sperm parameters before and after COVID-19 mRNA vaccination. Jama 326(3):273–274
25. Al-Qerem WA, Jarab AS (2021) COVID-19 vaccination acceptance and its associated factors among a middle eastern population. Front Publ Health 9:632914
26. Solís Arce JS, Warren SS, Meriggi NF, Scacco A, McMurry N, Voors M, Syunyaev G, Malik AA, Aboutajdine S, Adeojo O, Anigo D (2021) COVID-19 vaccine acceptance and hesitancy in low-and middle-income countries. Nat Med 27(8):1385–1394
27. Loomba S, de Figueiredo A, Piatek SJ, de Graaf K, Larson HJ (2021) Measuring the impact of COVID-19 vaccine misinformation on vaccination intent in the UK and USA. Nat Human Behav 5(3):337–348
28. Kaur SP, Gupta V (2020) COVID-19 vaccine: A comprehensive status report. Virus Res 288:198114

Text Classification Using Hybridization of Meta-Heuristic Algorithm with Neural Network

Vipin Jain and Kanchan Lata Kashyap

1 Introduction

Opinion mining also known as sentiment classification is a technique that is used to uncover the hidden sentiments in a piece of text. The huge opinion of consumers about online shopping and movie reviews are available in form of comments and tweets on the Internet. Consumer opinion impacts the financial accounts of companies. The problem is that the consumer opinions are expressed in terms of text which is a form of natural language. More than 80% of comments and tweets are saved in unstructured documents such as textual form, document, video, and audio multimedia. Text mining is used for the analysis and classification of the sentiments which are hidden in the text. The sentiment of opinions derived from the unstructured data can be classified as favourable, unfavourable, and neutral. Sentiment analysis and classification include text pre-processing, feature vector extraction, and classification. This work presents a framework for sentiment analysis and classification which includes pre-processing, feature extraction, feature selection, and sentiment classification. The first step includes natural language processing (NLP) for the text pre-processing and feature extraction. After that, the prominent features are selected by the grey wolf optimization technique. Finally, the deep learning technique is applied to classify sentiment as positive or negative. The remaining portions of the paper are organized as follows: The literature review is discussed in Sect. 2. Section 3 introduces the proposed algorithm and methodology. Section 4 contains the results followed by conclusions which is given in Sect. 5.

V. Jain (✉) · K. L. Kashyap
VIT Bhopal University, Sehore, Madhya Pradesh 466114, India
e-mail: vipin.jain2020@vitbhopal.ac.in

K. L. Kashyap
e-mail: kanchan.k@vitbhopal.ac.in

2   Literature Review

Several approaches have already been applied by the various authors for sentiment analysis and classification. Yonghe et al. [18] proposed an enhanced textual feature extraction methodology based on the term frequency–inverse document frequency (TF-IDF) method. Yonghe et al. [17] utilized the improved K-nearest neighbour (KNN) classification method by using a similarity measure and a dimension indexing table. The WordNet and lexical chains are incorporated by Wei et al. [16] to improve the text clustering model. Alsaeedi et al. [1] used support vector machine (SVM), Naive Bayes (NB), max entropy, and multinomial Naive Bayes for sentiment classification on Twitter dataset. The total 80% accuracy has achieved by max entropy and SVM techniques. The sentiment of English-language Hajj tweets has been used by Elgamal et al. [4]. Tweets are analyzed classified by natural language and NB classifier, respectively, as positive or negative. Shoeb et al. [14] examined Twitter posts of people opinion. They developed a variety of machine learning classifiers, namely KNN, NB, and decision tree, using the Rapid Miner software. The highest 84.66% achieved by KNN. Krishnan et al. [6] evaluated English consumer views on Twitter using a vocabulary-based method. Yujie et al. [9] experimented on their media access control service data unit (MSDU) corpus using NLP and SVM model. The highest accuracy of 78.4% and 58% has achieved for binary and three-class classification, respectively. Chaovalit et al. [3] suggested a semantic orientation-based sentiment mining technique in which compound words are applied and subsequently evaluated. The 85.7% accuracy is obtained by machine learning algorithms. Binary grey wolf and moth flame have been utilized by Kumar et al. [7] for feature optimization to increase the accuracy of sentiment classification. Classifiers such as the NB, SVM, KNN, multilayer perceptron, and decision trees have been used. The highest 76.5% accuracy is achieved with SVM with a binary grey wolf optimizer on the SemEval 2016 standard dataset. The SVM and the Firefly algorithm have been used by Kumar et al. [8] to extract features for data classification. To extract features, Shang et al. [13] employed the particle swarm optimization (PSO) technique for the feature extraction procedure.

Contributions
The existing research work is based on traditional text classification methodologies such as bag-of-words (BoW) and part-of-speech (PoS) tagging [2]. The limitation of the conventional bag-of-words technique is the disability to extract proper information from the text document. Machine learning and dictionary approaches have commonly used sentiment classification (SC) techniques. In this work, the selection of text features which is an important and integral step of text categorization is done by grey wolf technique. Finally, the deep learning classifier is used for the sentiment classification.

3 Proposed Model

The block diagram of the proposed framework is shown in Fig. 1. The algorithm of the proposed work is listed in Algorithm 1. The two publicly available datasets [5, 10], namely Imdb and sentiment140, have been used for the experiment. Imdb which is a movie review dataset is used for binary sentiment classification. Whilst the sentiment140 dataset is used to detect the sentiment about any common thing such as product, brand, and reviews. A detailed description of the proposed framework is given in the following subsection.

3.1 Pre-processing

This step is used to remove unwanted data by applying the three sub-steps, namely (a) tokenization, (b) stop word elimination, and (c) stemming. Tokenization partitions the text item into phrases in which each line of text is partitioned into tokens by ignoring the special characters, symbols, or white space. Further, a phrase is divided into words by eliminating the stops word which includes list of widely utilized phrases, namely 'in', 'on', 'at', 'that', 'the', 'of', 'an', 'a', 'she', short words, high-frequency terms, and functional terms. [19]. Stemming process transforms all words which are derived from one common root into a single term by removing its prefixes and suffixes. After that, weight of each simplified word is computed. Feature extraction (vectorization): This step is used to transform the text input into numerical data. The TF-IDF vectorization technique is used in this work. It is a statistical measure that assigns weight to each word based on its importance.

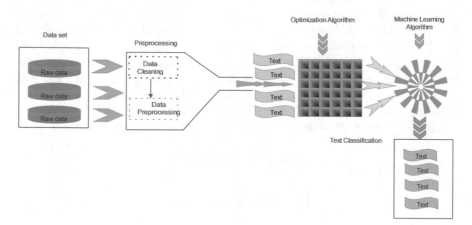

Fig. 1 Flowchart of proposed work

Algorithm 1

Input: Raw dataset.

Output: Classification of text start.

```
1.  Dataset store in a data frame df1
2.  Apply data cleaning and prepossessing in data frame
    df1
3.  df1 ⇐ Delete the null value.
4.  df1 ⇐ Convert df1 text into lower case.
5.  df1 ⇐ Remove stop words, @, and URL from dataset.
6.  df1 ⇐ Remove emoticons and punctuation from df1.
7.  df1 ⇐ Tokenization and lemmatization.
8.  [V_C] ⇐ Vectorization (TF-IDF, n-grams) from df1.
9.  [G_E] ⇐ GWO feature extraction [V_C]
10. Pre mod ⇐ Classification algorithm [G_E]
11. Model (Evaluation)
```

4 Feature Selection

Pre-processed data contain noisy, redundant, and irrelevant features. The feature selection technique deals with dimensionality reduction of feature vectors by selecting the most prominent features only. The computational cost can also be reduced by selecting the important feature. The grey wolf optimization (GWO) method is used in this work for selecting the most important phrases from the pre-processed text. GWO is a meta-heuristic swarm-intelligence algorithm that can quickly identify the ideal point. It is based on the grey wolf social hierarchy and hunting tendencies to identify the prey. Another benefit of the GWO algorithm is that it uses a less number of search parameters for neural network training and performs better as compared to other meta-heuristic algorithms. The entire population is categorized into four distinct categories, namely (α, β, ω, δ) [11]. The grey wolves use three stages (a) tracking, (b) encircling, and (c) attacking for prey hunting [12]. The grey wolves locate their prey by creating encirclement prior to the attack. The mathematical expression of the encircling process is represented as [12].

$$\vec{G} = \left| \vec{F} \cdot \vec{A_s}(w) - \vec{A}(w) \right| \tag{1}$$

$$\vec{A}(w + 1) = \vec{A_s}(w) - \vec{D} \cdot \vec{G} \tag{2}$$

Here, w represents the current iteration. $\vec{G}$ represents the distance between the prey and the wolf $\vec{A}(w + 1)$, $\vec{A}(w)$ denotes the position vector of prey and the wolf, respectively. $\vec{D} = 2\vec{e} \cdot \vec{u} - \vec{a}$, $\vec{F} = 2\vec{u2}$. $\vec{A_s}$ represents the location vector of prey, whereas the grey wolf's position vector is represented by—$\overrightarrow{A_s}$. The parameter value of—$\vec{e}$ is taken between 2 and 0. The $u1$ and $u2$ represent the random vectors, and values are taken in the range [0, 1]. The number of iterations taken by the ω wolf towards the given leader (α, β, and δ) is represented by Eq. (1). Equation (2) denotes end position of omega. The fine tuning of D and F vectors has done. Finally, after achieving the final target, the alpha wolf gains the optimal position.

4.1 Sentiment Classification

The convolution neural network is used in this work for the classification of sentiments as positive or negative. The proposed convolution neural network architecture for sentiment classification is depicted in Fig. 2.

The proposed model consists of a convolution layer, a non-linear layer, and a softmax layer.

Convolution layer The objective of this layer is to extract the patterns. Each component of the layer is computed by the equation which is mathematically represented as follows:

$$Fl = (\mathbf{V} * I)l \tag{3}$$

Here, V and I denote the sentence and filter matrix, respectively. l denotes input of the sentence matrix. Each component of Fl is formed by multiplying V and I.

Pooling The output of the convolution layer becomes the input of the pooling layer. The objective of this layer is to simplify data and minimize dimensionality.

Softmax The outcome of the convolution and pooling is transferred to a softmax layer.

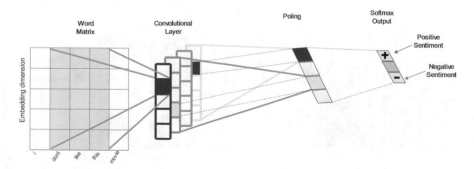

Fig. 2 CNN architecture for text categorization

5   Experiments and Result

The proposed algorithm is implemented in the Python with i8 E-2236 processor, 32 GB RAM, and NVIDIA P2200 display card.

5.1   Dataset Utilized for Experiment

A brief description of the datasets used for the validation of the proposed work is given as follows:

1.   The Imdb dataset contains 50,000 movie which includes 250,000 positive and 250,000 negative reviews [10]. Figure 3a shows the total count of positive and negative reviews in the dataset.
2.   The sentiment140 dataset contains 1.6 million tweets which are annotated as negative and positive [5]. Figure 3b illustrates the data distribution based on the sentiments. Sentiment140 dataset has a total of 119,856 and positive and 120,144 negative tweets. The whole dataset is partitioned into 70% and 30% for training and testing data, respectively.

The parameter value set for the CNN model is shown in Table 1. The width of the convolution filter and number of feature maps is set as 15 and 318, respectively. The $L2$ regularization term and penultimate level are set as 1e$-$4 and 0.5, respectively, with ReLU activation function and max-pooling algorithm. The dimension of word embedding d is set as 100.

The performance of the proposed model is measured by evaluation metrics, namely accuracy, precision, recall, and $F1$ score. The results obtained with all text features and after selecting the text features by applying the GWO method are shown in Table 2. The highest **95.81%** and **93.41%** accuracy is achieved on Imdb and

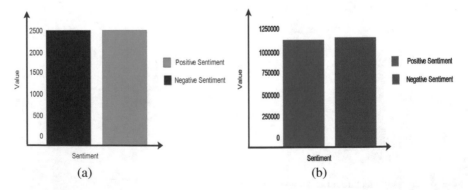

Fig. 3 Number of positive and negative sentiments in **a** Imdb dataset and **b** sentiment140 dataset

Table 1 List of parameters

Parameters name	Value
Convolution filters	16,007
Convolution feature maps	318
Activation function	ReLU
Pooling	Max-pooling
Learning rate	1e−4
Dropout	0.5
Number of epoch	19

Table 2 Result of evaluation metrics

Model	Dataset	Accuracy (%)	Precision (%)	Recall (%)	$F1$ score (%)
Before feature extraction	Imdb	83.61	83.46	80.92	84.74
	Twitter sentiment140	82.29	79.23	78.63	82.33
After feature extraction	Imdb	**95.81**	94.16	94.87	95.22
	Twitter sentiment140	**93.41**	89.43	95.17	92.79

Twitter sentiment140 datasets, respectively. It can be observed that accuracy has been increased with selected feature set.

5.2 Comparative Analysis of the Proposed Algorithm and Existing Research

The comparative analysis of the proposed algorithm with an existing work of Vu et al. [15] is also done. The sentiment analysis had been determined by using the lexicon-based method in their work, and 78.7% accuracy is achieved on Imdb dataset. The comparative result of proposed algorithm with existing work is shown in Fig. 4. It can be observed from Fig. 4 that the proposed algorithm performs better than the existing algorithm.

6 Conclusions

Text categorization sentiment analysis model based on the grey wolf algorithm and deep learning-based convolution neural network is applied in this work. The two publicly available Tweeter and movie review datasets have been used for sentiment

Fig. 4 Suggested method is
compared to Vu [15]

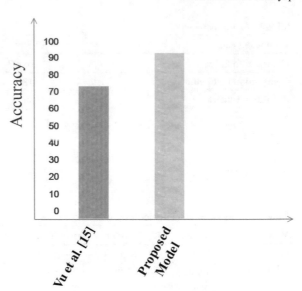

analysis and categorization. The highest 95.81%, 94.16%, 94.87%, 95.22% accuracy, precision, recall, and F-score, respectively, is achieved. On Iamb dataset. The highest 93.41%, 89.43%, 95.17%, and 92.79% accuracy, precision, recall, and F-score, respectively, is achieved on Twitter dataset. Machine learning techniques will be applied for web user behaviour prediction in the future work.

References

1. Alsaeedi A, Khan MZ (2019) A study on sentiment analysis techniques of twitter data. Int J Adv Comput Sci Appl 10(2):361–374
2. Asgarnezhad R, Monadjemi SA, Soltanaghaei M (2021) An application of MOGW optimization for feature selection in text classification. J Supercomput 77(6):5806–5839
3. Chaovalit P, Zhou L (2005) Movie review mining: a comparison between supervised and unsupervised classification approaches. In: Proceedings of the 38th annual Hawaii international conference on system sciences. IEEE, p 112c
4. Elgamal M (2016) Sentiment analysis methodology of twitter data with an application on Hajj season. Int J Eng Res Sci (IJOER) 2(1):82–87
5. Go A, Bhayani R, Huang L (2009) Twitter sentiment classification using distant supervision. CS224N project report. Stanford 1(12)
6. Krishnan H, Pankajkumar G, Poosari A, Jayaraj A, Thomas C, Joy GM (2021) Machine learning based sentiment analysis of coronavirus disease related twitter data. In: 2021 2nd international conference on secure cyber computing and communications (ICSCCC). IEEE, pp 459–464
7. Kumar A, Jaiswal A (2019) Swarm intelligence based optimal feature selection for enhanced predictive sentiment accuracy on twitter. Multimedia Tools Appl 78(20):29529–29553
8. Kumar A, Khorwal R (2017) Firefly algorithm for feature selection in sentiment analysis. In: Computational intelligence in data mining. Springer, pp 693–703

9. Lu Y, Sakamoto K, Shibuki H, Mori T (2017) Are deep learning methods better for twitter sentiment analysis. In: Proceedings of the 23rd annual meeting of natural language processing, Japan, pp 787–90

10. Maas AL, Daly RE, Pham PT, Huang D, Ng AY, Potts C (2011) Learning word vectors for sentiment analysis. In: Proceedings of the 49th annual meeting of the association for computational linguistics: human language technologies. Association for Computational Linguistics, Portland, Oregon, USA, June 2011, pp 142–150. http://www.aclweb.org/anthology/P11-1015

11. Melin P, Castillo O, Kacprzyk J (2017) Nature-inspired design of hybrid intelligent systems. Springer

12. Mirjalili S, Mirjalili SM, Lewis A (2014) Grey wolf optimizer. Adv Eng Softw 69:46–61.https://doi.org/10.1016/j.advengsoft.2013.12.007. https://www.sciencedirect.com/science/article/pii/S0965997813001853

13. Shang L, Zhou Z, Liu X (2016) Particle swarm optimization-based feature selection in sentiment classification. Soft Comput 20(10):3821–3834

14. Shoeb M, Ahmed J (2017) Sentiment analysis and classification of tweets using data mining. Int Res J Eng Technol (IRJET) 4(12)

15. Vu L, Le T (2017) A lexicon-based method for sentiment analysis using social network data. In: Proceedings of the international conference on information and knowledge engineering (IKE). The steering committee of the world congress in computer science, computer engineering and applied computing (WorldComp), pp 10–16

16. Wei T, Lu Y, Chang H, Zhou Q, Bao X (2015) A semantic approach for text clustering using wordnet and lexical chains. Expert Syst Appl 42(4):2264–2275

17. Yonghe L, Xinyu H (2014) Improved KNN classification algorithm based on dimension index table. Inf Stud Theory Appl 5

18. Yonghe L, Yanfeng L (2013) Improvement of text feature weighting method based on TF-IDF algorithm. Libr Inf Serv 57(03):90

19. Zain ZM, Ahmad H, Pebrianti D, Mustafa M, Abdullah NRH, Samad R, Noh MM (2020) Proceedings of the 11th national technical seminar on unmanned system technology 2019: NUSYS'19, vol 666. Springer Nature

GAN-Based Data Generation Technique and its Evaluation for Intrusion Detection Systems

Kundan Kumar Jha, Prabhkirat Singh, Navin Bharti, Ditipriya Sinha, and Vikash Kumar

1 Introduction

The present era has witnessed an extraordinary advancement in communication and information technologies. Many types of neural networks have come into existence to serve people meeting their requirements. We can imagine the emergence of new technologies by this fact that "the number of Internet devices till the end of year 2020 have crossed 50 billion" and still increasing. Developing new Internet functionalities have also given rise to new concerns. Data privacy and vulnerabilities are the one which is mostly targeted these days through different attacks. To avoid these attacks, we need different sophisticated techniques that we have available to us. But, the data on which they run is highly imbalanced, and hence, the performance of the model is not satisfactory.

For balancing the dataset, the part of data which is not balanced can be ignored but ignoring any data means losing data which is not considered a good practice. This paper proposes a model which generates the data instances of the data which have comparatively fewer instances present in the dataset and make the dataset balanced applying generative adversarial networks.

Goodfellow et al. discussed that generative adversarial networks (GANs) are a clever way of training a generative model by framing the problem as a supervised learning problem with two sub-models: the generator model that we train to generate new examples, and the discriminator model that tries to classify examples as either real (from the domain) or fake (generated) [1].

K. K. Jha · P. Singh · N. Bharti · D. Sinha
Department of Computer Science and Engineering, National Institute of Technology,
Patna 800005, India

V. Kumar (✉)
Department of Computer Science and Engineering, ITER, Sikasha 'O' Anusandhan
(Deemed to be University), Bhubaneswar 751030, India
e-mail: vika96snz@gmail.com

The remaining part of the paper is organized in the following sections. Section 2 briefly reviews the recent works in the intrusion detection and cyberattack detection using deep learning models. In Sect. 3, the whole system architecture used for data capturing, pre-processing, training, and testing is defined. Section 4 describes the step-by-step solution proposed in this paper. And the Sect. 5 witnesses all the results obtained. Finally, the Sect. 6 contains the detailed conclusions drawn from this paper and the future scopes.

2 Related Work

2.1 Feature Selection Method

Chandrashekhar et al. proposed filter and wrapper methods to select subset of features based on following factor: simplicity, stability, number of reduced features, classification accuracy, storage, and computational requirements. Overall feature selection provides benefits such as providing insights into the data and better model [2].

Mirsky et al. proposed Kitsune: a plug and play NIDS which can learn to detect attacks on the local network, network, without supervision, and in an efficient online manner. Kitsune's core algorithm (KitNET) uses an ensemble of neural networks called autoencoders to collectively differentiate between normal and abnormal traffic patterns. KitNET is supported by a feature extraction framework which efficiently tracks the patterns of every network channel [3].

Cai et al. [4] defined feature selection as a typical optimization problem in which the optimal solution can only be obtained by an exhaustive search given an evaluation or search criterion. Therefore, researchers still apply the heuristic method with polynomial time complexity for high-dimensional problems.

Davis and Clark [5] reviewed the data pre-processing techniques used by anomaly-based network intrusion detection systems (NIDSs), concentrating on which aspects of the network traffic are analyzed, and what feature construction and selection methods have been used.

Thus, whilst preparing our dataset, we have kept in mind these factors for selecting features for our model, and on the top of it, we used autoencoder differently for dimensionality reduction purpose, so that we end up getting a better model with high efficacy. As data can contain large number of variables of which many of them could be highly correlated with other variables (e.g. when two features are perfectly correlated, only one feature is sufficient to describe the data). The dependant variables provide no extra information about the classes and thus serve as noise for the predictor. This means that the total information content can be obtained from fewer unique features which contain maximum discrimination information about the classes.

2.2 Machine Learning and Deep Learning Methods for Intrusion Detection System:

As a principal component of cyber security, IDs are responsible for monitoring network traffic for suspicious activity and issues alerts when such activity is discovered. As the present era is driven my machine learning and deep learning to solve many complex problems, same is the case with IDs. To solve key IDs issues, several such techniques are proposed.

Mishra et al. performed a compare and contrast between different machine learning technique ability to detect intrusions in the network and briefly discussed the issues which are related to detecting low-frequency attacks using network attack dataset [6]. Sailesh Kumar performed an evaluation of a number of current NIDS systems and the algorithms they employ to detect and combat security threats, both from technical and economical perspective focussing on two important classes of NIDS: signature-based and anomaly-based [7].

Kang and Kang [8] proposed an efficient intrusion detection system (IDS) based on a deep neural network (DNN) for the security of in-vehicular network. We trained the parameters of DNN with probability-based feature vectors extracted from the in-vehicular network packets by using unsupervised pre-training method of deep belief networks, followed by the conventional stochastic gradient descent method. The DNN provides the probability of each class to discriminate normal and hacking packets, and thus, the system can identify any malicious attack to the vehicle as a result.

Ahmed et al. [9] performed a survey of network anomaly detection techniques by mapping different types of anomalies with network attacks, providing an up-to-date taxonomy of network anomaly detection, evaluating the effectiveness of different categories of techniques, and exploring recent research related to publicly available network intrusion evaluation datasets.

Liu et al. proposed an IDS taxonomy that takes data sources as the main thread to present the numerous machine learning algorithms used in this field. Based on this taxonomy, we then analyze and discuss IDSs applied to various data sources, i.e. logs, packets, flow, and sessions study. Deep learning approaches include multiple deep networks which can be used to improve the performance of IDSs. But lack of available datasets are biggest challenges to train the classifier model [10].

Liu et al. took the perspective of imbalance and high dimensionality of datasets in intrusion detection and propose an oversampling intrusion detection technique based on GAN and feature selection. His approach proposes to focus on oversampling the rare classes of attack samples in order to improve the effectiveness of intrusion detection [11].

So, in this paper, we will walk through on the developments on this type of challenges that are faced by our fellow researchers. We use GAN to generate variant of available attack data.

2.3 Classifiers Used for Anomaly Detection

Classifiers are the machine learning algorithms that utilize some training data to understand how given input variables relate to the class and automatically orders or categorizes data into one or more of a set of "classes".

Farnaaz et al. built a model for intrusion detection system using random forest classifier [12]. They have used NSL-KDD dataset for result analysis by making a comparison between random forest modelling with j48 classier in terms of accuracy, DR, FAR, and MCC and shown that the proposed model is efficient with low false alarm rate and high detection rate.

Elbasiony et al. proposed a hybrid framework that the anomaly part is improved by replacing the k-means algorithm with another one called weighted k-means algorithm to detect novel intrusions by clustering the network connections data to collect the most of intrusions together in one or more clusters [13].

Decision trees can perform both classification and regression [14]. They are recursive algorithms, which behave similarly, to the tree data structure, which consists of nodes. The very first node of the tree otherwise known as the root node will be used to split the dataset using the feature that will result in the best possible splitting with the same procedure applied, repetitively, to each consequent node until the end nodes or leaves are reached. The end nodes or leaves represent the final decision or the classification of the particular instance as either vulnerable or non-vulnerable. These intuitive algorithms provide us with a visual representation of the algorithm. Therefore, they have advantages over other algorithms such as in decision trees, it is easy to identify the factors, which contribute to the splitting of the dataset. In the context of our research paper, the decision made at the leaf nodes is regarding whether the network traffic is an anomalous one or not.

Van Efferen et al. in their research paper [15] have clearly mentioned that MLP classifiers show promising result in cyberattack datasets. MLP has an overall higher classification instance.

Following the same trend, we have tested our generated data on all different classifiers like random forest classifier, logistic regression, K-nearest neighbours, MLP classifier, and decision tree classifier to check our model's efficiency.

3 System Architecture

As shown in Fig. 1, intentionally vulnerable Ubuntu Linux virtual machine (Metasploitable v2) is configured as victims whose various open ports are manipulated for capturing the vulnerable network packets for creating dataset. The Metasploitable tool of Kali Linux is used as attacker and Wireshark tool for capturing network packets.

The features of the captured dataset are reduced by passing through autoencoder, and finally, the conditional generative adversarial network (GAN) is trained using

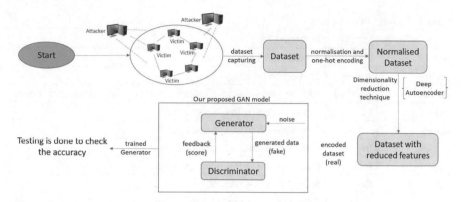

Fig. 1 System architecture

that encoded dataset. After training, the conditional GAN is able to produce a dataset similar to that original dataset.

Then for verification of the generated dataset, properties resemble with the real one various classifiers like random forest classifier, logistic regression, K-nearest neighbours, etc., which are trained using that generated dataset and used to classify the unknown network packets into vulnerable or non-vulnerable.

Finally, a compare and contrast are made between the classification reports from all the mentioned classifiers.

4 Proposed Work

4.1 Dataset Description

Our dataset consists of 11,000 network packets and each having 15 different features. Amongst them, 10,000 packets are used as training dataset, and remaining (11,000 – 10,000=1000) packets are kept separately for the purpose of testing and result analysis. Amongst them, the training dataset consists of 6749 vulnerable network packets and (10,000 – 6749=3251) non-vulnerable network packets, whereas the testing dataset consists of 573 vulnerable network packets and (1000 – 573=427) non-vulnerable network packets.

Features used in our model are mentioned in Table 1 with their respective definitions.

Table 1 Features in our dataset

Features' name	Data type	Definition
dur	Float	Record total duration
proto	Nominal	Transaction protocol
service	Nominal	http, ftp, smtp, ssh, dns, ftp-data, irc and (-) if not much used service
spkts	Integer	Source to destination packet count
dpkts	Integer	Destination to source packet count
sbytes	Integer	Source to destination transaction byte
dbytes	Integer	Destination to source transaction byte
rate	Float	Rate of data transmission
sttl	Integer	Source to destination time to live value
dttl	Integer	Destination to source time to live value
sload	Float	Source bits per second
dload	Float	Destination bits per second
sloss	Integer	Source packets retransmitted or dropped
dloss	Integer	Destination packets retransmitted or dropped
label	Binary	0 for normal records 1 for attacking records

4.2 Dataset Collection

The main task in dataset collection was to find the online hosts and the open ports on which we could perform the attacks. The data used for our study requires dataset (vulnerable and non-vulnerable network packets) captured using Wireshark tool. Amongst them, vulnerable packets are those will be captured by attacking on intentionally vulnerable Ubuntu Linux virtual machine (Metasploitable v2) using Metasploitable tool of Kali Linux, whereas non-vulnerable packets will be through some non-malicious networking like simple browsing. Nmap is a network scanner which we used to discover hosts and services on a computer network by sending packets and analyzing the responses (Figs. 2, 3 and 4).

4.3 Pre-processing Phase

The categorical features **proto** and **service** are one-hot encoded because ML models does not get trained on textual data directly, instead first of all the textual data has to be converted into numerical value using the concept of one- hot encoding. All other features like dur, spkts, dpkts, etc., are normalized manually.

Keras tuner is used here for hyperparameter tuning, so that the hyperparameters in all dimensionality reduction techniques mentioned below are best to the condition.

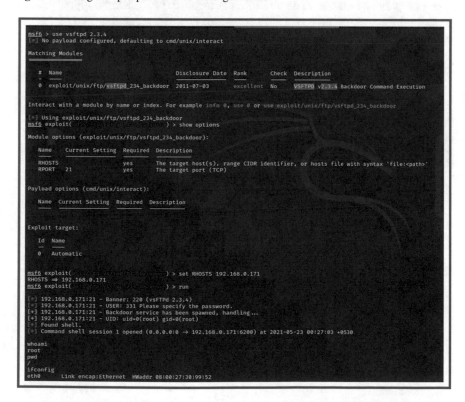

```
┌──(prabhkirat㉿kali)-[~]
└─$ nmap  192.168.0.171
Starting Nmap 7.91 ( https://nmap.org ) at 2021-05-23 00:21 IST
Nmap scan report for 192.168.0.171
Host is up (0.0020s latency).
Nmap done: 1 IP address (1 host up) scanned in 0.10 seconds

┌──(prabhkirat㉿kali)-[~]
└─$ nmap -sV 192.168.0.171
Starting Nmap 7.91 ( https://nmap.org ) at 2021-05-23 00:21 IST
Nmap scan report for 192.168.0.171
Host is up (0.00026s latency).
Not shown: 977 closed ports
PORT     STATE SERVICE     VERSION
21/tcp   open  ftp         vsftpd 2.3.4
22/tcp   open  ssh         OpenSSH 4.7p1 Debian 8ubuntu1 (protocol 2.0)
23/tcp   open  telnet      Linux telnetd
25/tcp   open  smtp        Postfix smtpd
53/tcp   open  domain      ISC BIND 9.4.2
80/tcp   open  http        Apache httpd 2.2.8 ((Ubuntu) DAV/2)
111/tcp  open  rpcbind     2 (RPC #100000)
139/tcp  open  netbios-ssn Samba smbd 3.X - 4.X (workgroup: WORKGROUP)
445/tcp  open  netbios-ssn Samba smbd 3.X - 4.X (workgroup: WORKGROUP)
512/tcp  open  exec        netkit-rsh rexecd
513/tcp  open  login?
514/tcp  open  tcpwrapped
1099/tcp open  java-rmi    GNU Classpath grmiregistry
1524/tcp open  bindshell   Metasploitable root shell
2049/tcp open  nfs         2-4 (RPC #100003)
2121/tcp open  ftp         ProFTPD 1.3.1
3306/tcp open  mysql       MySQL 5.0.51a-3ubuntu5
5432/tcp open  postgresql  PostgreSQL DB 8.3.0 - 8.3.7
5900/tcp open  vnc         VNC (protocol 3.3)
6000/tcp open  X11         (access denied)
6667/tcp open  irc         UnrealIRCd
8009/tcp open  ajp13       Apache Jserv (Protocol v1.3)
8180/tcp open  http        Apache Tomcat/Coyote JSP engine 1.1
Service Info: Hosts:  metasploitable.localdomain, irc.Metasploitable.LAN; OSs: Unix, Linux; CPE: cpe:/o:linux:linux_kernel

Service detection performed. Please report any incorrect results at https://nmap.org/submit/ .
Nmap done: 1 IP address (1 host up) scanned in 17.66 seconds
```

Fig. 2 Scanning for open port/services on target device

```
msf6 > use vsftpd 2.3.4
[*] No payload configured, defaulting to cmd/unix/interact

Matching Modules


   #  Name                                    Disclosure Date  Rank       Check  Description
   -  ----                                    ---------------  ----       -----  -----------
   0  exploit/unix/ftp/vsftpd_234_backdoor    2011-07-03       excellent  No     VSFTPD v2.3.4 Backdoor Command Execution


Interact with a module by name or index. For example info 0, use 0 or use exploit/unix/ftp/vsftpd_234_backdoor

[*] Using exploit/unix/ftp/vsftpd_234_backdoor
msf6 exploit(unix/ftp/vsftpd_234_backdoor) > show options

Module options (exploit/unix/ftp/vsftpd_234_backdoor):

   Name    Current Setting  Required  Description
   ----    ---------------  --------  -----------
   RHOSTS                   yes       The target host(s), range CIDR identifier, or hosts file with syntax 'file:<path>'
   RPORT   21               yes       The target port (TCP)

Payload options (cmd/unix/interact):

   Name   Current Setting  Required  Description
   ----   ---------------  --------  -----------

Exploit target:

   Id  Name
   --  ----
   0   Automatic


msf6 exploit(unix/ftp/vsftpd_234_backdoor) > set RHOSTS 192.168.0.171
RHOSTS => 192.168.0.171
msf6 exploit(unix/ftp/vsftpd_234_backdoor) > run

[*] 192.168.0.171:21 - Banner: 220 (vsFTPd 2.3.4)
[*] 192.168.0.171:21 - USER: 331 Please specify the password.
[+] 192.168.0.171:21 - Backdoor service has been spawned, handling ...
[+] 192.168.0.171:21 - UID: uid=0(root) gid=0(root)
[*] Found shell.
[*] Command shell session 1 opened (0.0.0.0:0 → 192.168.0.171:6200) at 2021-05-23 00:27:03 +0530

whoami
root
pwd
/
ifconfig
eth0      Link encap:Ethernet  HWaddr 08:00:27:30:99:52
```

Fig. 3 Exploiting FTP service running on Port 21

```
msf6 > use auxillary/scanner/http/http_version
   No results from search
   Failed to load module: auxillary/scanner/http/http_version
msf6 > use auxillary/scanner/http/http_version
msf6 auxiliary(                              ) > show options

Module options (auxiliary/scanner/http/http_version):

   Name            Current Setting   Required   Description
   ----            ---------------   --------   -----------
   Proxies                           no         A proxy chain of format type:host:port[,type:host:port][ ... ]
   RHOSTS                            yes        The target host(s), range CIDR identifier, or hosts file with syntax 'file:<path>'
   RPORT           80                yes        The target port (TCP)
   SSL             false             no         Negotiate SSL/TLS for outgoing connections
   THREADS         1                 yes        The number of concurrent threads (max one per host)
   VHOST                             no         HTTP server virtual host

msf6 auxiliary(                              ) > set RHOSTS 192.168.0.171
RHOSTS => 192.168.0.171
msf6 auxiliary(                              ) > run

[+] 192.168.0.171:80 Apache/2.2.8 (Ubuntu) DAV/2 ( Powered by PHP/5.2.4-2ubuntu5.10 )
[*] Scanned 1 of 1 hosts (100% complete)
[*] Auxiliary module execution completed
```

Fig. 4 Exploiting service running on Port no. 80 type

4.3.1   Autoencoders

An autoencoder is a type of artificial neural network used to learn efficient data coding in an unsupervised manner. The aim of an autoencoder is to learn a representation (encoding) for a set of data, typically for dimensionality reduction, by training the network to ignore signal "noise" as shown in Fig. 5.

Basically, we split the network into two segments, such as the encoder and the decoder. The mathematics involved here shown in Eqs. (1), (2), and (3) (Fig. 6).

$$\phi : x \rightarrow F \tag{1}$$

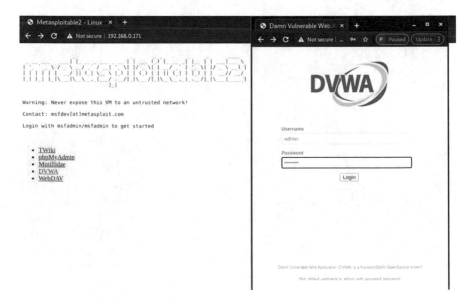

Fig. 5 Wireshark captures data during attack performance

Fig. 6 Working of autoencoder

$$\psi : x \rightarrow F \tag{2}$$

$$\phi, \; \psi = \arg \phi, \; \psi \min |X - (\psi_o \phi)|^2 \tag{3}$$

The encoder function, denoted by ϕ, maps the original data X, to a latent space F, which is present at the bottleneck. The decoder function, denoted by ψ, maps the latent space F at the bottleneck to the output. Basically, we are trying to recreate the original data after some generalized non-linear compression.

Encoding network function shown in Eq. (4):

$$z = \sigma(Wx + b) \tag{4}$$

Decoding network equation shown in Eq. (5):

$$x' = \sigma'\big(W'x + b\big) \tag{5}$$

Loss function shown in Eq. (6).

$$L\big(x, x'\big) = |x - x'|^2 = \big|x - \sigma'\big(W'(\sigma(Wx + b)) + b'\big)\big|^2 \tag{6}$$

where z is the latent dimension

4.4 Model Description

Our model has two main components, such as the generator and the discriminator. Generator generates fake samples using random noise, whilst discriminator discriminates the generated data as real or fake. The generator improves its accuracy on the basis of the score given by the discriminator as shown in Fig. 7.

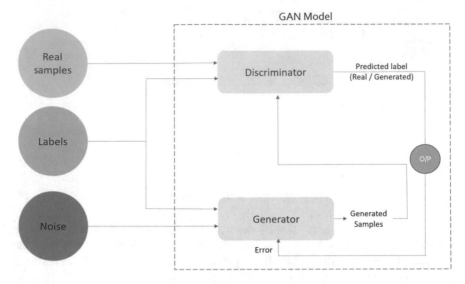

Fig. 7 Working of conditional generative adversarial network

4.4.1   Discriminator

It has only 2 neurons in output layer, and it is nothing but a simple classifier model which gets improved after every epoch and update its weight with real and fake sample with specification of 0 for fake data and 1 for real data so that when it is given with generated data from generator it can classify it as a fake sample. Input to discriminator is any data of either real or fake but with same dimension that of actual data and the output is 0 or 1 according to the input data (0 for fake sample and 1 for real sample). The activation function used in the model is sigmoid. The loss function of the discriminator is binary_crossentropy.

$$\Delta_{\theta d} \frac{1}{m} \sum_{i=1}^{m} \left(\log D(x^{(i)}) + \log\left(1 - D\left(G\left(z^{(i)}\right)\right)\right) \right) \tag{7}$$

The discriminator wants to maximize the stochastic function as shown in Eq. (7).

4.4.2   Generator

In order to generate data of similar dimension as input noise whose properties are the reflection of actual data, the generator has the same input and output dimensions. Between the input and output layer, it has a lot of hidden layers of neurons whose weights get updated during every pass of input from them. It learns from the feedback given by the discriminator and improves itself after every epoch and always strives

Table 2 Result analysis of dimensionality reduction techniques

Autoencoder	ISOMAP	LLE
62.50	52.80	56.70

for fooling the discriminator that the data generated is not fake data, instead it is the actual data. Input to the generator is a random noise, and the output is generated data similar to the original sample. The activation function used in the model is tanh. The loss function of the generator is as follows:

$$\nabla_{\theta_g} \frac{1}{m} \sum_{i=1}^{m} \log\big(1 - D\big(G\big(z^{(i)}\big)\big)\big) \tag{8}$$

The generator wants to minimize the stochastic function shown in Eq. (8).

When the change in this stochastic gradient function becomes negligible, then the generator and discriminator both are trained, so training will be stopped, and now, our generator is ready for production of generated dataset.

5   Result Analysis

In this section, we have first compared the performance of autoencoder with other as dimensionality reduction technique. The performance of proposed GAN-based technique is also evaluated on different ML algorithms.

5.1   Performance Comparison with Other Dimensionality Reduction Techniques

Apart from autoencoders, we also compared our results to other non-linear dimensionality reduction techniques like ISOMAP and LLE. We found that autoencoders performed slightly better than the other two as shown in Table 2.

5.2   Performance of Different ML Techniques on Generated Data Samples

After training the generator, it will be able to generate data samples whose properties resemble with that of real data samples. So, in order to test that the properties of generated and real data samples are similar or not various classifiers like random

Table 3 Accuracy score on different classifiers

Classifier name	Accuracy (%)
Decision tree classifier	69
MLP classifier	58
Random forest classifier	70
Logistic regression	57
K-nearest neighbour	69

Fig. 8 Confusion matrix for random forest classifier

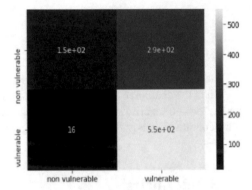

forest classifier, logistic regression, K-nearest neighbours, MLP classifier, and decision tree classifier are trained using that generated dataset. And then, they are used to classify the vulnerable network packets from non-vulnerable ones to make a report on the accuracy of classification of different classifiers trained using generated dataset from our conditional GAN generator (Table 3).

5.2.1 Analysis on Random Forest Classifier

Random forest is on the widely used decision tree-based technique for classification problem. When the data samples generated by the trained generator are applied on the random forest classifier, it gives an accuracy score of 70%. The confusion matrix corresponding to the binary classification is shown in Fig. 8.

5.2.2 Analysis on Logistic Regression

To visualize the performance of generated samples on regression models, we have applied the data on logistic regression. This model gives an accuracy score of 57% for binary classification, and the confusion matrix is shown in Fig. 9.

Fig. 9 Confusion matrix for logistic regression

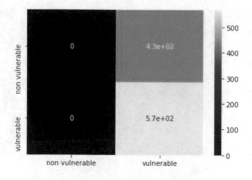

Fig. 10 Confusion matrix for K-nearest neighbours

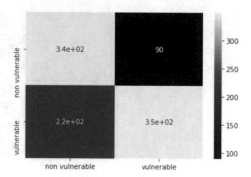

5.2.3 Analysis on K-Nearest Neighbours

We have applied K-nearest neighbours to visualize the performance on generated samples. When classified using K-nearest neighbours, it ended with an accuracy score of 69%, and the confusion matrix is shown in Fig. 10.

5.2.4 Analysis on MLP Classifier

We have applied MLP classifier to visualize the performance on generated samples. When classified using MLP classifier, it ended with an accuracy score of 58%, and the confusion matrix is shown in Fig. 11.

5.2.5 Analysis on Decision Tree Classifier

Finally, we have applied decision tree classifier to visualize the performance on generated samples. When classified using decision tree classifier, it ended with an accuracy score of 69%, and the confusion matrix is shown in Fig. 12.

Fig. 11 Confusion matrix
for MLP classifier

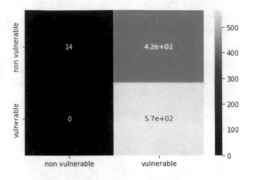

Fig. 12 Confusion matrix
for decision tree classifier

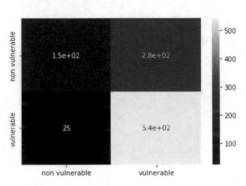

So, by comparing the five models used for evaluation of the proposed scheme to address the problem of data imbalance, it can be observed that random forest gives the highest performance amongst others.

6 Conclusion

In this paper, we have proposed a generative adversarial network-based data generation scheme to generate various attack data that can overcome the problem of data imbalance in various benchmark datasets for intrusion detection system. The feasibility of the generated data is explored using various classifiers like random forest-based classifier, logistic regression, K-nearest neighbour, MLP classifier, and decision tree classifier. In this paper, we have proposed a generative adversarial network-based data generation scheme to generate various attack data that can overcome the problem of data imbalance in various benchmark datasets for intrusion detection system. The feasibility of the generated data is explored using various classifiers like random forest-based classifier, logistic regression, K-nearest neighbour, MLP classifier, and decision tree classifier. And amongst them, random forest classifier has given the best promising accuracy of 70% which proves that the generated dataset from our trained GAN has similar property as that of real data samples and has the capability to overcome the problem of data imbalance by generating data samples for the class which has a smaller number of data samples in comparison with others in the imbalance dataset.

Although the properties of generated dataset very much resemble with that of real ones but in the future, we are aiming to test our model's performance on traditional dataset to detect the zero-day signature attack.

References

1. Goodfellow I, Pouget-Abadie J, Mirza M, Xu B, Warde-Farley D, Ozair S, Courville A, Bengio Y (2014) Generative adversarial nets. In: Advances in neural information processing systems, pp 2672–2680
2. Chandrashekar G, Sahin F (2014) A survey on feature selection methods. Comput Electr Eng 40(1):16–28
3. Mirsky Y, Doitshman T, Elovici Y et al (2018) Kitsune: an ensemble of autoencoders for online network intrusion detection [J]. arXiv preprint arXiv:1802.09089
4. Cai J, Luo J, Wang S, Yang S (2018) Feature selection in machine learning: a new perspective. Neurocomputing 300:70–79
5. Davis JJ, Clark AJ (2011) Data pre-processing for anomaly based network intrusion detection: a review. Comput Secur 30(6–7):353–375
6. Mishra P, Varadharajan V, Tupakula U, Pilli ES (2018) A detailed investigation and analysis of using machine learning techniques for intrusion detection. IEEE Commun Surv Tutorials 21(1):686–728
7. Kumar S (2007) Survey of current network intrusion detection techniques [J]. Washington Univ. in St. Louis, 1–18
8. Kang M-J, Kang J-W (2016) Intrusion detection system using deep neural network for in-vehicle network security. PLoS ONE 11(6):e0155781. https://doi.org/10.1371/journal.pone.0155781
9. Ahmed M, Mahmood AN, Hu J (2016) A survey of network anomaly detection techniques [J]. J Netw Comput Appl 60:19–31
10. Liu H, Lang B (2019) Machine learning and deep learning methods for intrusion detection systems: a survey. Appl Sci 9(20):4396
11. Liu X, Li T, Zhang R, Wu D, Liu Y, Yongheng Z et al (2021) A GAN and feature selection-based oversampling technique for intrusion detection. Secur Commun Netw vol 2021. https://doi.org/10.1155/2021/9947059
12. Farnaaz N, Jabbar MA (2016) Random forest modelling for network intrusion detection system. Procedia Comput Sci 89:213–217
13. Elbasiony RM, Sallam EA, Eltobely TE, Fahmy MM (2013) A hybrid network intrusion detection framework based on random forests and weighted k-means. Ain Shams Eng J 4(4):753–762
14. Raza M, Qayyum U (2019) Classical and deep learning classifiers for anomaly detection. In: 2019 16th international Bhurban conference on applied sciences and technology (IBCAST). IEEE, pp 614–618
15. Van Efferen L, Ali-Eldin AM (2017) A multi-layer perceptron approach for flow-based anomaly detection. In: 2017 international symposium on networks, computers and communications (ISNCC). IEEE, pp 1–6

VSCM: Blockchain-Based COVID-19 Vaccine Supply Chain Management

Sourav Mahapatra, Rakesh Singh Rajput, Manish Kumar, and Ditipriya Sinha

1 Introduction

Animal borne COVID-19 was first spotted in Wuhan, China in December 2019 [1], since then it is exponential spread through community transmission garnered up to November 2021 to around 260 million confirmed cases and more than 5.2 million deaths [2]. All the countries gave their hearts out to restrain the rampant spread of the virus from the ribonucleic acid family. With the development of vaccines, there comes some parallel challenges which are likely to affect the global vaccination program if they will not be properly addressed.

Effective vaccine management (EVM) with advancement of mobile technology improves the cold chain management of Bihar province in India [3]. A detailed study [4] on cold chain management provided by the Ministry of Health, Govt. of India reveals that cold chain management is one of the major challenges in immunization processes for developing countries like India. Table 1 enlisted few available COVID-19 vaccine in India with their temperature constraint in cold chain distribution. Indian government does not have any such system which can deter ill-intended people

S. Mahapatra (✉) · R. Singh Rajput · M. Kumar · D. Sinha
Department of Computer Science and Engineering, National Institute of Technology Patna, Patna, Bihar 800005, India
e-mail: souravm.phd20.cs@nitp.ac.in

R. Singh Rajput
e-mail: rsrajput.cs18@nitp.ac.in

M. Kumar
e-mail: manishkumar.ug18.cs@nitp.ac.in

D. Sinha
e-mail: ditipriya.cse@nitp.ac.in

S. Mahapatra
Department of Information Technology, Techno International New Town, Kolkata, West Bengal 700156, India

K. Kumar Singh et al. (eds.), *Machine Vision and Augmented Intelligence*, Lecture Notes in Electrical Engineering 1007, https://doi.org/10.1007/978-981-99-0189-0_12

Table 1 Temperature
constraints for vaccine
preservation

Vaccine name	Freezer temperatures	Refrigerator temperatures	Max storage duration in days
Covishield	− 5 °C	2–8 °C	45 days
Covaxin	− 4 °C	2–8 °C	6 months
Pfizer	− 70 °C	NA	30 days
Sputnik	− 20 °C	2–8 °C	30 days

from exploiting the gray areas of the traditional system as those people are still making illegal money and creating trouble for the government and citizens. So, the compulsion arises to face these loopholes head-on in safeguard of the people of this country.

Decentralized, distributed, and transparent nature of blockchain technology has proven records on SCM can be used to mitigate our challenges. Therefore, we are proposing a robust system using blockchain technology to cater to the challenges of security, faking/impersonation, data tampering, etc., by designing three separate chains—*Peoples Chain, Vaccine Ledger, and Feedback Chain*. Each chain will take care of all the technical concepts required for safety, security, and immutability of the data.

The flow of the paper is as follows. In Sect. 2, our contribution to the model is expressed. A broad literature review on VSCM and preliminary concept of blockchain is discussed in Sects. 3 and 4, respectively. In Sects. 5 and 6, description of the model and its performance is discussed. At last, but not least, the conclusion is drawn in Sect. 7.

2 Contribution

There are limited suppliers and huge demand in immunization push the system into various challenges from manufacturing to vaccination [20]. Within a short window to make it successful, a transparent, priorities distribution plan is needed which also reduces the shortage and wastage of vaccine. Thus, in this paper to maintaining transparency and efficiency of vaccine registration, demand and supply calculation of vaccine, and self-reporting feedback, we are leveraging on the features of blockchain technology to develop an efficient mechanism for COVID-19 VSCM. The components of the system are as follows:

- A blockchain-based people's chain for beneficiary registration
- A smart contracts-based vaccine ledger for calculating demand of vaccine, registration of vaccine lots, complete traceability of vaccine
- A tamper-proof self-reporting feedback chain for person identification and vaccine association through smart contracts and blockchain.

3 Literature Review

Quality control and tracible distribution of vaccine are the major challenge of any vaccine supply chain management (VSCM), specially for COVID-19 outbreak. Supply chain of vaccine distribution is now open a scope to the researchers to do some contribution. In this respect, researchers enlighten various parts of supply chain management (SCM) which have a crucial role respect to quality, traceability, and security of information. Li et al. [5] and Thakur et al. [6] use blockchain in their model to manage energy treading and land record management, respectively, to explore the scope of traceability and distribution of resources. Adaptation of blockchain architecture in SCM [7] helps to track and monitor the entire supply chain which improve transparency and minimize the transaction error between the stakeholders. Traditional SCM based on centralized control uses various custom algorithm to optimize the distribution and improve the throughput of system [8, 9, 12]. Alkhoori et al. [10] designed an IoT-based "CryptoCargo" smart shipping system which monitors all the required parameters and records them in blockchain to make it trustworthy. Smart container with blockchain is used by Hasan et al. [11] to handle the interaction between sender and receiver. An expert committee highlighted three major interests, namely traceability, stockpiling, and packaging, for improvement of vaccine supply chain management which is discussed by Ghode et al. [12]. In this respect, Marbouh et al. [9] highlighted the different aspects of blockchain to battel the COVID-19 pandemic situation.

In this out break situation, a country like India needs a fast and fair distribution of vaccine where quality of the vaccine will be auditable, and the sensitive information shall be in safe custody. Blockchain with smart contract is a promising technology which leads a safe and automated immunization process with multiparty authentication. An IoT-based [13] real-time information related to vaccine supply chain is kept inside the chain for any time verification.

4 Preliminaries

4.1 Blockchain

Blockchain [14] is typically managed and controlled by a peer-to-peer network for use as a publicly distributed ledger, where nodes collectively adhere to a consensus to communicate and validate new blocks.

It is a collection of several blocks in ordered fashion such that every $block_{i+1}$ is connected to its previous $block_i$ through a backward reference, which is the hash value of its previous block. Each block contains the timestamp, nonce the target hash value of the current block, the root of the Merkle tree, and a root hash of all the contracts. Distributed ledger with immutability and blockchain ensures an authenticated channel for sharing sensitive medical data among the stakeholders.

4.2 Smart Contract

Smart contracts [11] are self-executing contracts or business logics containing the terms and conditions of an agreement among peers. Unlike a traditionally contract, smart contracts need not to rely on third parties to execute. When the smart contract is deployed, the compiler compiles it to bytecode which is later stored in the blockchain which can be referenced by an address for invoking a transaction on it. In a vaccine supply chain, smart contract can improve the overall performance of the system by self-executing business contract.

4.3 Cold Chain Network

A vast network of cold chain [4] stores has been developed at various levels under the Universal Immunization Program, including Government Medical Supply Depots (GMSD), State/Regional/Divisional Vaccine Stores, District, and CHC/PHC vaccine storage points.

  The country's cold chain network has served as the backbone for ensuring vaccine storage and supply between nodes of storage and outreach sites at the recommended temperature for administration to the target population. A transparent monitoring of cold chain with a secure channel is essential for such huge immunization drive.

  In India, vaccine cold chain network contains with 4 GMSDs, 39 state vaccine stores, 123 divisional vaccine stores, 644 district stores, and 22,674 CHC/PHC stores.

5 Proposed Model

To mitigate the emergency of COVID-19 immunization processes, we are going to present our model with a trustworthy distribution, strict monitoring, and real-time feedback control scheme presented in Fig. 1. In this section, first, we introduce proposed blockchain-based vaccine distribution system, and then, step-by-step execution process is also described.

5.1 Proposed Blockchain-Based Vaccine Distribution System

According to Fig. 1 in our proposed model, manufacturers can proactively track for adverse effects and enhance recall control with a vaccine distribution network powered by blockchain. Distributors may gain real-time insight into their supply chains and improve their ability to react to supply chain disruptions. Inventory

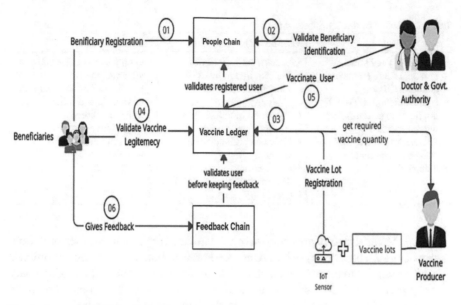

Fig. 1 Proposed VSCM with feedback control

control and safety monitoring also gain benefit from dispensers. Citizens trust the vaccinations and return to society with confidence.

Beneficiary, medical staff, and vaccine manufacturer are the user of this system, who can record their activity in these three blockchain, namely people chain, vaccine ledger, and feedback chain.

5.2 Description of Three Blockchain in Our Proposed Model

Following the steps outlined in Fig. 1, three separate blockchains are created, each with its own set of organization nodes and services to offer. They are, in truth, interdependent but significant. Table 2 represents the activity of three blockchains.

5.3 Step Wise Workflow of Our Proposed Model

From registration to feedback recording, total process is described in 6 steps.

Step 1: Beneficiary may join the network and register themselves for immunization with required data. This data will be checked against the eligibility of registration in smart contract before creating a transaction on *peoples chain*. Registration processes are implemented through *registerBeneficiary()*.

Table 2 Content of three proposed chains

People's chain	Vaccine ledger	Feedback Chain
• Beneficiary registration • Personal detail (ID, name, gender, DOB, etc.) • Age restriction, ID proof, duplicate registration, etc., will be checked • All user's sensitive data are encrypted and secure Public chain	• Vaccine lot registration • Get required number of vaccines need to be produced • Real-time monitoring of vaccines parameters • Checks legitimacy of the vaccine • Records vaccine process data (person, doctor, lot ID) • Consortium chain	• People's direct feedback after vaccination • It helps in further revamping of vaccine and other research studies • Helps citizens to get unmanipulated true feedback • Public chain

Step 2: Medical staff or government official initiates a verification process without prevailing the beneficiary detail. A smart contract initiated by government officials sends a request to the central database where all the credentials of the beneficiary are preserved and ask for its hash value only. Now, it will be compared with the hash value $H(PI_{bnf})$ available in people chain to authenticate the user.

Step 3: Manufacturer can enroll themselves with their vaccine lot in vaccine ledger for its distribution. Vaccine lots are allotted through *registerVaccineLot()*. After taking details of total people registered for vaccination and the people who got vaccinated, based on these two and already registered vaccine lots, the number of vaccines required for further vaccination can be calculated. In this way, we can efficiently calculate the required number of vaccines, reducing vaccine wastage by overproduction or under production, since blockchain will ensure no tampering with data would happen.

Step 4: Before vaccination, beneficiary can inspect and trace the vaccine transportation. Beneficiary can check the legitimacy and venue of the vaccination from the vaccine ledger and generate a hash as a proof of authentication which will be shown to officials at the vaccination center.

Step 5: The authority appointed at each immunization center validates the beneficiary against a hash value obtained in Step 4 and execute *vaccinate()* to complete the vaccination. All inventory updates are followed in this step.

Step 6: After immunization, feedback report is most important for further improvement of the vaccine and rapid control of disease spreading. Only the vaccinated beneficiary can fill up the feedback for reporting any complicacy if arise and stored it into *feedback chain*. In Eq. (3), with the help of $H(Tx_{reg})$ and $H(Tx_{lot})$, we can validate a vaccinated beneficiary.

5.4 Security Analysis

All the transactions that take place in three chains are cryptographically secure and validated by automated contract rule imposed in smart contract. To hide the details of beneficiary and feedback from beneficiary, we use SHA-256 hashing technique. At the time of vaccination, government official verifies the beneficiary by this hash value without revealing the identity of beneficiary. All the transactions take place in different chains which are digitally signed and encrypted by owner's private key as a proof of ownership.

Equations (1), (2), and (3) represent the cryptographic transaction details of *people's chain, vaccine ledger, and feedback chain,* respectively.

Beneficiary can register himself through a transaction Tx_{reg}

$$Tx_{reg} = \{ID_{bnf}, Ts1, H(PI_{bnf}), S_{bnf}, H(Tx_{reg})\} \qquad (1)$$

where

ID_{bnf}	*Beneficiary ID*
$Ts1$	*Time stamp for Tx_{reg}*
S_{bnf}	$Sig(Sk_{bnf}, H(ID_{bnf}, Ts1$
$H(PI_{bnf}))$	$H(Tx_{reg}) = $ Hash of whole Txreg
PI_{bnf}	*Personal details of beneficiary.*

According to Eq. (1) to verify Tx_{reg}, smart contract requests central database to get a hash of the beneficiary details linked with ID_{bnf} and compare it with the $H(PI_{bnf})$ as mentioned in Step 2. After this successful verification, Tx_{reg} can be added to the people's chain.

Vaccine lots are enrolled in the vaccine ledger chain for distribution through a transaction Tx_{lot}, as described in Step 3. Equation (2) represents the component of Tx_{lot}, which used for vaccine lot registration and distribution.

$$Tx_{lot} = \{ID_{pro}, Ts2, H(V_{info}), S_{pro}, H(Tx_{lot})\} \qquad (2)$$

where

ID_{pro}	*ID of vaccine producer*
$Ts2$	*Time stamp for Tx_{lot}*
S_{pro}	*Signature of vaccine producer* $= Sig(Sk_{pro}, H(ID_{pro}, Ts2, H(V_{info})))$
$H(Tx_{lot})$	*Hash of whole Tx_{lot}.*

Now, smart contract for vaccine ledger allots vaccine to the beneficiary and continuously monitor all the parameters like temperature, date of expiry, etc. After vaccination, beneficiary can add a transaction Tx_{feed} to the feedback chain which is defined in Eq. (3).

$$Tx_{feed} = \{ID_{bnf}, Ts3, \text{Feedback}, H(Tx_{reg}), H(Tx_{lot})\} \qquad (3)$$

where

Ts3   Time stamp
Feedback   post vaccination report
$H(Tx_{reg})$ and $H(Tx_{lot})$ Link with people chain and vaccine ledger chain.

6 Performance Evaluation

We implement our framework in Ethereum platform and a contract-oriented language. Solidity is used to design smart contract. To evaluate the performance of our scheme, supporting infrastructures are listed in Table 2.

Overall performance of our model is highly impacted by the blockchain performances. So, it is important to emphasize up on the transaction cost and execution cost.

Transaction costs (Tc) are based on the cost of sending the data to the blockchain. Four items make up the full transaction cost.

1. Base cost (B_c)
2. Contract deployment cost (C_c)
3. Zero code cost (Z_c)
4. Non-zero code cost (NZ_c).

$$\text{So, transaction cost}(T_c) = B_c + C_c + Z_c + NZ_c \tag{4}$$

Transaction costs are calculated for the three different chains respected to their gas amount following Eq. (4) which are compared in Fig. (2).

Execution costs are based on the cost of computational operations which are executed because of the transaction. A comparative study of proposed 3 chains on gas expenditure respect to their execution cost is plotted in Fig. (3).

Fig. 2 Transaction cost

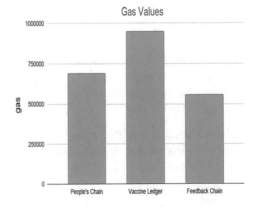

Fig.3 Execution cost

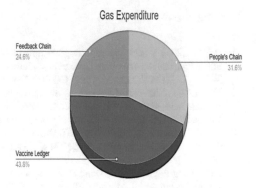

The blockchain with its integrated security can resist our framework from the very common traditional attacks like-

DDoS. In distributed denial-of-service (DDoS) attack, malicious nodes are easily identified and eliminated from the peer-to-peer network by its transaction fees which is linked with the consensus protocol used.

Sybil Attack. This type of attack can manipulate the peer-to-peer network by adding malicious node. By increasing the cost to create an identity may control the malicious node. To select a node as miner, a huge computational task and resource are needed, which eliminate malicious nodes as fake miner.

Selfish Mining. Malicious miners, hiding their new block for long time, and release them at once to increase their share on the chain. This type of activity can be restricted by applying fine to the late miner.

7 Conclusion

COVID-19 pandemic has triggered an ongoing crisis, but recent technological advancements have also provided opportunities to combat the crisis. The blockchain's secure features will significantly improve the security of health data and traceability of vaccines as compared to existing systems. As a result, this system examines and verifies all the relevant information transparently, securely, and immutably in blockchain and provides us most reliable system in the context of the COVID-19 crisis. In addition, we look at the advantages of blockchain-enabled solutions for COVID-19 from three angles: patient information, vaccine supply chain management, and non-alterable patient feedback. It is expected that, with the help of blockchain-enabled solutions and other innovations, we can smoothen the immunization process.

References

1. WHO (2021) Weekly epidemiological update—5 January 2021. https://www.who.int/public ations/m/item/weekly-epidemiological-update---5-january-2021
2. WHO (2021) WHO Coronavirus (COVID-19) Dashboard. https://covid19.who.int/
3. Negandhi P, Chauhan M, Das AM, Neogi SB, Sharma J, Sethy G (2016) Mobile-based effective vaccine management tool: an m-health initiative implemented by UNICEF in Bihar. Indian J Public Health 60(4):334–335. https://doi.org/10.4103/0019-557X.195869. PMID: 27976659
4. Dai H-N, Imran M, Haider N (2020) Blockchain-enabled internet of medical things to combat COVID-19. IEEE Internet Things Mag 3(3):52–57. https://doi.org/10.1109/IOTM.0001.200 0087
5. Li Z, Kang J, Yu R, Ye D, Deng Q, Zhang Y (2018) Consortium blockchain for secure energy trading in industrial internet of things. IEEE Trans Industr Inf 14(8):3690–3700. https://doi. org/10.1109/TII.2017.2786307
6. Thakur V, Doja MN, Dwivedi YK, Ahmad T, Khadanga G (2019) Land records on blockchain for implementation of land titling in India. Int J Inf Manage 52:101940. https://doi.org/10. 1016/j.ijinfomgt.2019.04.013
7. Keeling MJ, Shattock A (2012) Optimal but unequitable prophylactic distribution of vaccine. Epidemics 4(2):78–85. https://doi.org/10.1016/j.epidem.2012.03.001
8. Ignaciuk P, Wieczorek Ł (2020) Continuous genetic algorithms in the optimization of logistic networks: applicability assessment and tuning. Appl Sci 10(21):7851. https://doi.org/10.3390/ app10217851
9. Marbouh D, Abbasi T, Maasmi F et al (2020) Blockchain for COVID-19: review, opportunities, and a trusted tracking system. Arab J Sci Eng 45:9895–9911. https://doi.org/10.1007/s13369-020-04950-4
10. Alkhoori O et al (2021) Design and implementation of cryptocargo: a blockchain-powered smart shipping container for vaccine distribution. IEEE Access 9:53786–53803. https://doi. org/10.1109/ACCESS.2021.3070911
11. Hasan H, AlHadhrami E, AlDhaheri A, Salah K, Jayaraman R (2019) Smart contract-based approach for efficient shipment management. Comput Ind Eng 136:149–159. ISSN 0360-8352. https://doi.org/10.1016/j.cie.2019.07.022
12. Ghode D, Jain R, Soni G, Singh S, Yadav V (2021) Architecture to enhance transparency in supply chain management using blockchain technology. Procedia Manufact 51:1614–1620. https://doi.org/10.1016/j.promfg.2020.10.225.
13. Musamih A, Jayaraman R, Salah K, Hasan HR, Yaqoob I, Al-Hammadi Y (2021) Blockchain-based solution for distribution and delivery of COVID-19 vaccines. In: IEEE Access 9:71372–71387. https://doi.org/10.1109/ACCESS.2021.3079197
14. Yong B, Shen J, Liu X, Li F, Chen H, Zhou Q (2020) An intelligent blockchain-based system for safe vaccine supply and supervision. Int J Inf Manage 52(C):102024. https://doi.org/10. 1016/j.ijinfomgt.2019.10.009.
15. Antal C, Cioara T, Antal M, Anghel I (2021) Blockchain platform for COVID-19 vaccine supply management. IEEE Open J Comput Soc 2:164–178. https://doi.org/10.1109/OJCS.2021.306 7450.
16. Riewpaiboon A, Sooksriwong C, Chaiyakunapruk N, Tharmaphornpilas P, Techathawat S, Rookkapan K, Rasdjarmrearnsook A, Suraratdecha C (2015) Optimizing national immunization program supply chain management in Thailand: an economic analysis. Public Health 129(7):899–906. https://doi.org/10.1016/j.puhe.2015.04.016
17. WHO (2019) Rolling updates on coronavirus disease (COVID-19). World Health Organization. https://www.who.int/emergencies/diseases/ novel-coronavirus-2019/events-as-they-happen. Accessed 25 May 2020
18. Handbook for Vaccine & Cold Chain Handlers 2nd edition, https://immu.mizoram.gov.in/sto rage/download_document/5diY39THY1dfdlRun2D28na7enOmmQKc3yy 38FkY.pdf, Last accessed 23/3/21.

19. Wang S, Zhang D, Zhang Y (2019) Blockchain-based personal health records sharing scheme with data integrity verifiable. IEEE Access 7:102887–102901
20. Sharma A, Gupta P, Jha R (2020) COVID-19: impact on health supply chain and lessons to be learnt. J Health Manage IIHMR
21. Mills MC, Salisbury D (2021) The challenges of distributing COVID-19 vaccinations. EClinicalMedicine. 31:100674. https://doi.org/10.1016/j.eclinm.2020.100674.Epub

Polyp Segmentation Using Efficient Multi-supervision Net: A Deep Learning Technique Uses Attention Unit and EfficientNet Model

Sabarinathan, R. Suganya, and R. S. Rampriya

1 Introduction

A colorectal cancer starts from the growth of polyps mainly in the inner linings of colon. This has risen to become one of the world's major causes of death. Utmost colorectal cancers are due to old age and life factors, with only a small number of cases due to underpinning inheritable diseases. Detecting this kind of cancer is a challenging task. There are various computerized image analysis and medical methodologies carried out for diagnosis. Colonoscopy [15] is one such favored approach for finding and eliminating colorectal polyps (predecessors of colorectal cancers—CRCs).

Most colorectal cancers start as benign polyps, and removal of these polyps can reduce the risk of developing cancer. Survival is directly related to discovery and the type of cancer involved, but overall is poor for characteristic cancers, as they are generally relatively advanced. Survival rates for early stage discovery are about five times that of late stage cancers. Polyps appear as a protrusion of the mucosa that resembles a rough shape. However, the form, size, and strength of polyps vary widely, and diffuse reflection in colonoscopy pictures makes it difficult to identify. This can have a significant influence on CRC patients, leading to a greater mortality rate. Deep learning being the successor of machine learning is an AI function that mimics the workings of the human brain in processing data. The main idea behind this technology is about the network of structures. It builds more networks in order to train the model with the unstructured or unlabeled data. This is also called deep

Sabarinathan
Couger Inc, Tokyo, Japan

R. Suganya (✉)
Vellore Institute of Technology, Chennai, Tamilnadu, India
e-mail: suganya.ramamoorthy@vit.ac.in

R. S. Rampriya
Anna University (MIT Campus), Chennai, Tamilnadu, India

© The Author(s), under exclusive license to Springer Nature Singapore Pte Ltd. 2023
K. Kumar Singh et al. (eds.), *Machine Vision and Augmented Intelligence*, Lecture Notes in Electrical Engineering 1007, https://doi.org/10.1007/978-981-99-0189-0_13

neural networks. This kind of framework apparently requires a large amount of data to fetch greater accuracy. Hence, inputs were given in the form of huge datasets to the model. One of the most important features of the deep neural networks is to process large numbers of features, so that it becomes powerful when dealing with unstructured data.

In some cases, deep learning-based techniques were also chosen to build the model that is capable of detecting the specimen from the polyps and it also improved the detection rate, despite the complexity of case during colonoscopy, where screening and analysis of polyps are dependent on experienced endoscopists. The nature of specimen will decide whether there is a need for treatment or not. But this kind of accurate classification is highly pertinent. Medico polyp segmentation [4] intention is to implement automatic polyp segmentation through testing various polyp segmentation techniques on different training images, which provides accurate detection as well as mask out polyps (such as flat, tiny, or irregular polyps). This paper portrayed the deep learning neural network model competences for achieving polyp segmentation especially in medico automatic polyp segmentation challenges and issues. In addition, automatic polyp segmentation results of proposed model are compared with state-of-the-art approaches and proved that the deep neural learning techniques can precisely segmented the polyps even at flat, tiny, or irregular in shape. The major contributions involved in this paper are as follows:

- Proposed a novel efficient multi-supervision net architecture that contains model training using numerous output layers
- Evaluated the proposed design on a complex and comprehensive colorectal dataset with the help of EfficientNet B4 and attention unit used as backbone and significant features extraction, respectively. Experimental outcomes provide better accuracy in terms of precision, F1-score, recall, and loss.

2   Related Work

Most of the polyp segmentation methods use convolutional neural network (CNN). In the work mentioned in [1], a novel image patch selection method is performed in the training phase, and in the test phase, an effective post processing is done on the probability map that is produced by the network. Sabarinathan et al. [2] used coordinate convolutional layer and attention unit for kidney tumor segmentation where supervision layers were introduced in the decoder part that refines minimal regions in the output. A deeper convolutional neural network called DenseNet [3] can be used as they are more accurate and has high performance. Despite numerous breakthroughs in polyp identification and treatment, one of the feasible remedies for neglected polyps is detected by automatic polyp segmentation system developed in [4].

Polyp segmentation is a challenging task. These challenges are addressed and implemented with the parallel reverse attention network [12]. ResUNet++, an improvised ResUNet architecture, was introduced [17] for colonoscopy image segmentation and it achieved a high evaluation scores compared to other deep learning architectures. Kvasir-SEG: New polyp segmentation developed dataset to prop multimedia experimenters in carrying out expansive and reproducible exploration [5]. Kajal et al. [11] proposed an android application that uses image processing techniques and is capable of detecting blood related diseases through patient's blood samples.

The squeeze excitation (SE) blocks updation within fully convolution neural networks (F-CNNs) for image segmentation is introduced in [6] which outperforms the channel-wise squeeze and excitation process. They demonstrated that SE blocks yield a harmonious enhancement for three different F-CNN infrastructures and for two different segmentation operations. Hence, recalibration with SE blocks seems to be a fairly general conception to boost performance in CNNs. Strikingly, the substantial increase in segmentation delicacy comes with a negligible increase in model complexity. ResUNet++ is an architecture addresses for the more accurate segmentation of colorectal polyps found in colonoscopy examinations [18]. Evaluation using different available datasets demonstrates that the ResUNet++ model outperforms the state-of-the-art U-Net and ResUNet architectures in terms of producing semantically accurate predictions. Updation of post processing techniques can potentially be applied to ResUNet++ to achieve even better segmentation results. Apart from the convolutional model, to have better accuracy, the EfficientNet was also considered to achieve top 1 accuracy in the imaging field. EfficientNet is mainly contributed for scaling the dimensions uniformly [9]. In order to make the representation power of convolutional neural network more efficient, CBAM can be used. It can be easily fit into the layers of CNN, as they are lightweight module. They are used for identifying the intermediate features of the image [8].

Deep convolutional neural network techniques are used in the proposed polyp segmentation model for learning an association between polyp images which are provided as inputs. Figure 1 illustrates the general block diagram of the proposed design that majorly comprises of five layers like:

Layer 1: Convolutional blocks
Layer 2: Layer that is efficient [6]
Layer 3: EfficientNet B4 resides at encoder part
Layer 4: Integration of DenseNet [2] and concurrent spatial and channel attention (CSCA) [5] layers at the decoder part
Layer 5: Convolution block attention module (CBAM) [7], which extracts significant features.

In this system design, the convolutional layer obtains the input size as 332 × 487 that is contracted to 384 × 256 pixels which is further divided by 255. The proposed network was inspired by multilevel hyper vision net [1] which comprises of encoder block, supervision block in the form of topology, and decoder block. The encoder block was constructed using EfficientNet B4 which acted as a backbone

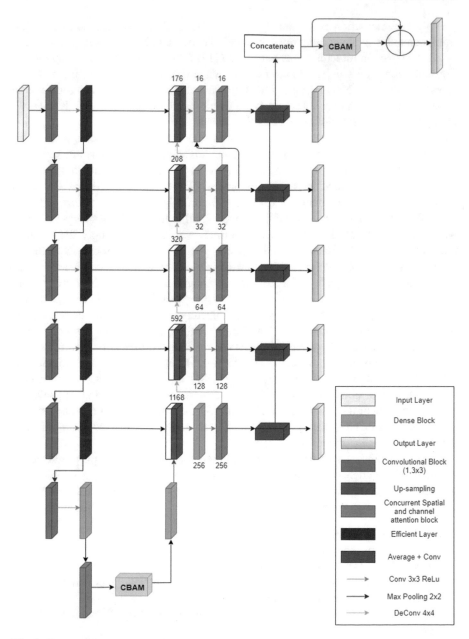

Fig. 1 Proposed system design for polyp segmentation

of the proposed model. The integration of dense block and CSCA block created the decoder module. CBAM extracts significant features and associates both the encoder and decoder.

All outcomes of encoder block are supervised that means each outcome of decoder is up sampled with all the output blocks and supervised through loss function. After that, all the up sampled outcomes are concatenated together and passed to CBAM attention unit. The proposed architecture produces an aggregate of six outcomes in which convolution transpose layer is utilized for upsampling process. The intention of CBAM is to oblige CNN to learn and lay emphasis on the significant information. It aids to create bond between encoder module and decoder module. The proposed neural network model maintains two robust and sequential functions such as channel and spatial. The channel function utilizes outcome of max-pooling and outcome of average pooling with multi-layer perceptron network. The spatial utilizes outcomes of two pooling layers with axis of channel.

The processing outcomes of CSCA layer outcomes are passed in to CBAM. Similarly, outcomes produced by CBAM are received by the dense blocks. During this process, a bottom up approach is followed by the proposed method, which continuously advancing to the subsequent dense layer and CSCA layer along with 5th efficient blocks estimated outcomes. CSCA block coupled average pooling layer and convolutional layer for receiving the outcomes of pooling and convolution by output layers. Consequently, CSCA block outcomes are up sampled and concatenated with 4th efficient blocks estimated outcomes. This process is maintaining by the remaining blocks which is similar to the previous stages. Every outcome of average pooling and convolution layer is received by CBAM and concatenation process once the procedures are completed up to 5 times. At last, concatenation process produces outcome at the output layer where the polyp segmentation is obtained through combination of canonical categorical with dice loss operation.

3 Experimental Results and Discussion

3.1 Dataset

As shown in Fig. 2, the Kvaris-SEG [4], a polyp segmentation dataset, has nearly 1000 polyp images with ground truth mask. Gastroenterologist experts in Baerum Hospital, Norway collected data in real-time regular clinical checkup. The resolution of picture varies from 332×487 to 1920×1072 pixels. ScopeGuide (Olympus), a scope location markings, can be founded in the lower-left corner of images in Fig. 3 which is represented as green color thumbnails. For testing the proposed model, another benchmark dataset is considered in this study which is developed by medico team in 2020.

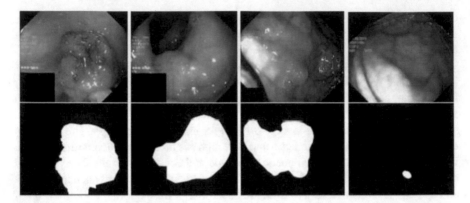

Fig. 2 Polyps images and its respective ground truth masks in Kvasir-SEG

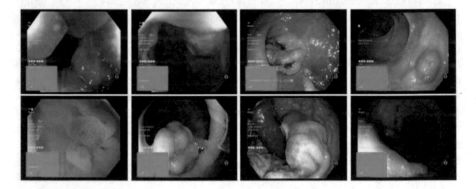

Fig. 3 Sample polyp images collected from test dataset

3.2 Training

The proposed architecture was trained and validated using medico automatic polyp segmentation challenges task: a polyp segmentation dataset.

The proposed efficient multi-supervision net model was inspired from the hyper vision net [4]. Shared dataset was created by a total of 1000 polyp segmented images gathered from gastrointestinal system. The whole dataset is randomly divided into 70 percent and 30 percent for training and validation, respectively. Adam optimizer is employed with a learning rate 0.001; subsequently, the learning rate is reduced into 0.00001 and used 500 epochs for training the proposed model. The IntelCore i7 processor, GeForce GTX 1070 GPU, 8 GB RAM, and platform Keras were used to train the suggested network.

Table 1 Quantitative outcomes of the proposed model on medico 2020 test dataset

Model name	mIoU	Dice	Precision	Recall	Accuracy	F1-score
Efficient multi-supervision net	0.77	0.85	0.916	0.83	0.95	0.87
ResUNet++	0.67	0.81	0.82	0.81	0.93	0.85
KD-ResUNet++	0.7	0.83	0.84	0.82	0.94	0.84
UNet	0.59	0.71	0.75	0.84	0.93	0.83

Bold values represents quantitative outcomes

3.3 Data Augmentation

To normalize the image between 0 and 1, we divided it by 255. To enhance the image count, we used data mining algorithms such as vertical flip, horizontal flip, rotate at $(-10, 10)$, and blur operation with limit which is assigned as 3. The network model outcomes are supervised by integrating two separate loss functions like categorical cross-entropy and dice loss. Consideration of 500 epochs and an Adam optimizer with a learning rate 0.001 to 0.00001 is utilized for training the proposed model. For evaluating the proposed model, recall, dice coefficient, precision, mean intersection over union (mIoU), and F1-score are considered.

For the proposed model using the above evaluation metrics, the Jaccard value is 0.777, and the accuracy of the model is 0.957. Precision and recall values are 0.839 and 0.916, respectively. All the above furnished details are shown in Table 1.

Endoscopists are increasingly interested in developing computer-aided diagnosis (CAD) systems which can be utilized as digital helper and second operator. Benchmarking of algorithm is one of the suitable approaches for comparing the outcomes of various procedures. As an evaluation metric, the model will employ mIoU, also called as Jaccard index, a typical metric used especially for medical segmentation tasks. In both runs 1 and 2 of our proposed approach, the mIoU value is 0.777. The effectiveness is also demonstrated by various evaluation criteria such as precision, dice, recall, and F1-score for evaluation. In addition, examples of segmentation images generated by ResUNet++ , KD-ResUNet++ , and efficient supervision net are illustrated in Fig. 4. Figure 4 depicts that the outcomes of efficient multi-supervision net are almost looks like ground truth masks compared with the outcomes of ResUNet++ and KD-ResUNet++ .

4 Conclusion

To increase picture segmentation accuracy under various variables, the proposed model has been presented with an innovative and distinctive efficient multi-supervision net model engaging EfficientNet B4 as the proposed model backbone. We did this by using pictures from the medico polyp segmentation challenge task dataset 2020 for training the multi-layer attention network. This dataset has aided

| Image | Ground Truth | ResUNet++ | KD-ResUNet++ | EffSupNet (Proposed) |

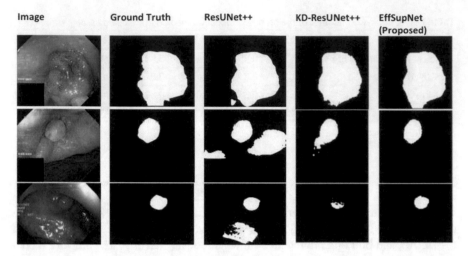

Fig. 4 Examples of segmentation images generated by ResUNet++, KD-ResUNet++, and efficient supervision net

the model's efficiency in learning. In addition to increase image quality, we include a CSCA block in the decoder. CBAM makes a big contribution by enhancing the quality mechanism and incorporating characteristics from the encoder block. Through series of comparison and evaluation of the new model with the previous works show that, the EfficientNet B4 served as a best fit for the quantitative and qualitative performances. Hence, the optimized model for the detection of polyps is developed.

References

1. Akbari M, Mohrekesh M, Nasr-Esfahani E, RezaSoroush-mehr SM, Karimi N, Samavi S, Najarian K (2018) Polyp segmentation in colonoscopy images using fullyconvolutional network
2. Sabarinathan D, Parisa Beham M, Md.Mansoor Roomi SM (2019) Hyper vision net: kidney tumor segmentation using coordinate convolutional layer and attention unit. arXiv preprint arXiv:1908.03339
3. Huang G, Liu Z, van der Maaten L, Weinberger KQ (2017) Densely connected convolutional networks. arXiv:1608.06993
4. Jha D, Hicks SA, Emanuelsen K, Johansen H, Johansen D de Lange T, Riegler MA, Halvorsen P (2020) Medico multimedia task at mediaeval 2020: automatic polyp segmentation. In: Proc. of the MediaEval 2020 Workshop
5. Jha D, Smedsrud PH, Riegler MA, Halvorsen P, de Lange T, Johansen D, Johansen HD (2020)Kvasir-SEG: A segmented polyp dataset. In: Proceedings of international conference on multimedia modeling, 451–462
6. Roy AG, Navab N, Wachinger C (2018) Concurrent spatial and channel squeeze excitation in fully convolutional networks. arXiv:1803.02579
7. Dabass M, Vashisth S, Vig R (2019) Review of classification techniques using Deep learning for colorectal cancer imaging modalities
8. Woo, Sanghyun (2018) CBAM: convolutional block attention module. In: Proceedings of the european conference on computer vision (ECCV)

9. Tan M, Quoc V (2019) EfficientNet: rethinking model scaling for con volutional neural networks. arXiv:1905.11946
10. Liu Y, Zhang Q, Zhao G, Qu Z, Liu G, Liu Z, An Y (2019) Detecting diseases by Human-Physiological-Parameter based Deep Learn ing
11. Jewani K, Boddu K, Gumani P, Solapure K (2018) Detection of diseases via blood analysis using image processing techniques
12. Fan DP, Ji GP, Zhou T, Chen G, Fu H, Shen J, Shao L (2020) Pranet: parallel reverse attention network for polyp segmentation. arXiv preprint arXiv:2006.11392
13. Guo Y, Bernal J, J. Matuszewski B (2020) Polyp segmentation with fully convolutional deep neural networks—extended evaluation study
14. Guo YB, Matuszewski B (2019) GIANA polyp segmentation with fully convolutional dilation neural networks. In: Proceedings of international joint conference on computer vision, imaging and computer graphics theory and applications
15. Jha D, Ali S, Tomar NK, Johansen HD, Johansen D, Rittscher J, Riegler MA, Halvorsen P (2020) Real-time polyp detection, localisation and segmentation in colonoscopy using deep learning. arXiv preprint arXiv:2006.11392
16. Jha D, Riegler MA, Johansen D, Halvorsen P, Johansen HD (2020) DoubleU-Net: a deep convolutional neural network for medical image segmentation. In: Proceedings of international symposium on computer-based medical systems
17. Jha D, Smedsrud PH, Riegler MA, Johansen D, De Lange T, Halvorsen P, Johansen HD (2019) ResUNet++: an advanced architecture for medical image segmentation. In: Procedings of international symposium on multimedia
18. Mahmud T, Paul B, Fattah SA (2020) PolypSeg- Net: A modified encoder-decoder architecture for automated polyp segmentation from colonoscopy images. Comput Biol Med (2020)
19. Wang P, Xiao X, Brown JRG, Berzin TM, Tu M, Xiong F, Hu X, Liu P, Song Y, Zhang D et al (2018) Development and validation of a deep-learning algorithm for the detection of polyps during colonoscopy

Traffic Analysis on Videos Using Deep Learning Techniques

Srihasa Telanakula and Hemantha Kumar Kalluri

1 Introduction

In today's world, people always want to make their works need to be done easily and quickly. But with the increase in the number of vehicles every day, the rate of traffic congestion is also being increased simultaneously. Due to this problem, people are unable to reach their destinations on time. As a result, it leads to several disciplinary issues, various pressures at work that may impose an adverse effect on their work. Also, being in traffic for a longer duration will lead to wear and tear of vehicles. In addition to that, it may also lead to wastage of non-renewable resources, i.e., fuel. To solve these issues to some extent in this paper, we are proposing an automated system that will make use of traffic videos, which were being recorded continuously by static cameras deployed at various locations in the road to monitor the traffic. From these videos, the proposed system will detect and classify different vehicles and obtain a count under each category. With this analysis, it is possible to regulate the traffic toward less congested routes. Thus, this system will be beneficial for self-driving cars as well as for the drivers of emergency vehicles such as ambulances, fire extinguishing vehicles, and even for normal vehicle users. It is essential to understand that the possibility of traffic congestion will not only depend upon the number of vehicles but also on the size of vehicles. With this intention, the proposed approach counts the vehicles under each category separately.

The research paper is further organized as related work is described in Sect. 2. The explanation of the proposed system is given in Sect. 3. Section 4 describes the obtained results. Future scope and conclusions are presented in Sects. 5 and 6, respectively.

S. Telanakula
VFSTR Deemed to be University, Guntur, Andhra Pradesh, India

H. K. Kalluri (✉)
SRM University AP, Guntur, Andhra Pradesh, India
e-mail: hemanth_mtech2003@yahoo.com

2 Related Work

When compared to the usage of sensors and inductive loops, videos will provide the
overall information about the traffic scenario, and it is also very easy and cheap to
obtain as well as maintain. Liu et al. [1] used an automatic real-time background
update algorithm for vehicle detection, and virtual loop and virtual line detection techniques were deployed for counting the vehicles based upon the situation.
Researchers proposed separate algorithms for daytime, nighttime, during free, and
congested traffic flows to improve the robustness. Zhu et al. [2] compared their deep
vehicle counting framework (DVCF) with existing detection-based, motion-based,
deep learning-based approaches for vehicle detection and explained that DVCF has
two phases. For vehicle detection with type identification, they used enhanced SSD.
They performed vehicle tracking and counting, where they compared the effectiveness of features obtained from AlexNet, VGGNet, ResNet with features obtained by
HOG, SIFT, and SURF.

Chen et al. [3] proposed a vehicle detection method based on CNN that uses
VGG16 as a base model, and this model had combined both high-level and low-level
features upon which they applied the inception module to represent the features in a
better way. They applied data augmentation and hard negative mining to reduce the
class imbalance. It uses K-means clustering on the dataset to generate the bounding
boxes. This model can classify vehicles into four larger vehicles, and it achieved a
6.5% mAP improvement than faster RCNN. Arinaldi et al. [4] proposed a system
where the key functionality of the system is vehicle detection and vehicle classification from the videos. The researchers had compared the MOG + SVM system with
faster RCNN and exhibited that faster RCNN was far better than MOG to detect the
static vehicles and to detect the vehicles even at night times. Also, faster RCNN was
better than SVM to classify vehicles based upon their appearances in a more accurate
manner.

Memon et al. [5] proposed a system that will classify the vehicles into LTV,
MTV, and HTV. The tasks such as vehicle detection and vehicle counting were
performed using GMM background subtraction, and vehicle classification was done
by comparing contour areas with assumed values. The researchers compared the
classification done using contour comparison (CC) and BOF + SVM methods. They
concluded that the classification error for CC was lesser than BOF + SVM in most
of the videos. Saran et al. [6] extracted histograms of oriented gradients (HOG) and
geometric measures as features, and ANN was used for the classification of vehicles.
Krishna et al. [7] explained the benefits of deep learning over machine learning.
They also explained about different layers we make use of in CNN architectures for
image classification. The researchers had given a brief idea about different pre-trained
models and explained how the number of epochs and the dataset size will have their
impact on the performance of those models using the popular datasets that are easily
available over the Internet. Zhang et al. [8] proposed vehicle classification based
on an unmanned aerial vehicle (UAV)-based videos using deep learning techniques.
Byun et al. [9] proposed vehicle speed identification based on UAV videos using deep

learning techniques. Mandal et al. [10] used mask RCNN, faster RCNN, YOLO, and CenterNet for vehicle detection.

The literature survey shows that there is a need to develop an efficient traffic analysis system using deep learning techniques.

3 Proposed System

In most cases to solve many of the real-world problems need to make use of more than one algorithm to get a robust solution for our problems. We can observe only a few problems that can be solved by deploying a single algorithm. In the same way, this paper discussed the various techniques deployed at various stages to obtain better results. The proposed system architecture is shown in Fig. 1.

3.1 Background Subtraction

Background subtraction is very useful for identifying the moving objects in a video. In the proposed approach, it uses the following technique for detecting moving vehicles.

The MoG2 is a parametric method, which is shown in Fig. 2, that will estimate the mean and standard deviation. To separate the background from the foreground, create a histogram of the RGB values over the specified number of frames. The resultant histogram is a probability distribution that is usually a normal distribution. Then, we estimate the mean at every intensity and make use of this mean at the intensity to calculate an average image that represents a background. By keeping track of mean and variance, we can determine foreground pixels by seeing how far away the intensity value is from the distribution. To compute this distance, adopted Mahalanobis distance scaled across three channels. Mahalanobis distance is calculated by using Eq. (1).

$$D = \sqrt{\frac{(x_B - \mu_B)^2}{\sigma_B^2} + \frac{(x_G - \mu_G)^2}{\sigma_G^2} + \frac{(x_R - \mu_R)^2}{\sigma_R^2}} \tag{1}$$

```
cv2.createBackgroundSubtractorMOG2
(
history=200, varThreshold=16, detectShadows=True
)
```

Fig. 2 MoG2 constructor with default values

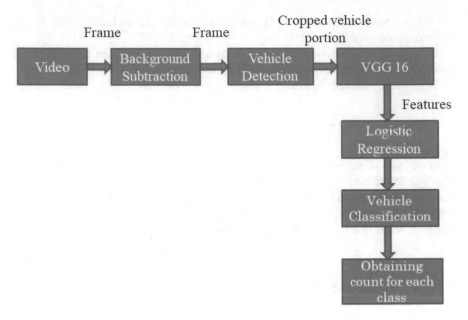

Fig. 1 Proposed system architecture

After getting the background, take the frames of the video. In this frame, calculate the Mahalanobis distance across each channel, and if the distance is greater than the threshold given a parameter, then we can determine that pixel as a foreground pixel.

Thus at first, created a background subtractor, i.e., background subtractor MOG2, and then trained it. Later, applied the trained background subtractor on every frame of the input video to obtain a foreground mask. This foreground mask needs to be filtered to remove noises such as shadow, and then, we will get the contours.

3.2 Detection and Classification of Vehicles

The vehicles will be detected by drawing a bounding box around the contours. Then, this contour will be given to the classifier to classify it into one of the vehicle categories. To make the classifier work properly, need a dataset to train the classifier.

3.3 Pre-Trained Models

Experiments were conducted with various pre-trained models such as MobileNetV2, ResNet50, VGG16, and VGG19 to classify the vehicles more accurately. These pre-trained models were trained over a large dataset, i.e., ImageNet (Fig. 3).

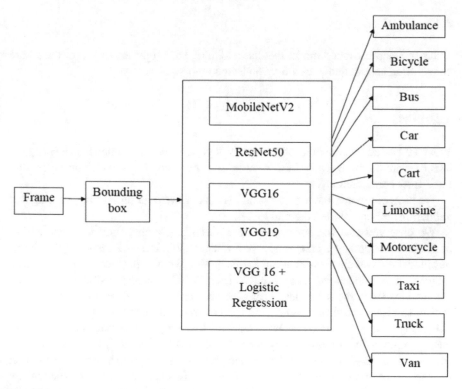

Fig. 3 System with a pre-trained model

The input image size for any of these pre-trained models is 224 × 224.

3.3.1 MobileNetV2

MobileNetV2 has mainly two kinds of blocks, namely residual block with stride one and residual block with stride two that is helpful for downsizing. This model can be deployed in several applications such as image classification, object detection, and semantic segmentation.

3.3.2 ResNet50

ResNet50 is one of the pre-trained models whose architecture has 50 layers. The key feature of ResNet50 is a skip connection.

3.3.3 VGG 16

VGG 16 is a pre-trained model that has a total of 16 weight layers out of the 13 are convolution layers, and 3 are fully connected layers.

3.3.4 VGG 19

VGG 19 has an architecture of 19 weight layers, which is somewhat deeper than VGG 16 architecture. Out of those 19 layers, there are 16 convolution layers and three fully connected layers.

We have compared the accuracy and loss that were obtained during training and validation and had plotted them in Fig. 4.

We observed that for our approach, VGG16 is giving better accuracy. So, to improve the accuracy furthermore, we are using VGG16 + logistic regression as our model for vehicle classification. In this model, we will provide the total training images, i.e., 17,667 as input for VGG16. Then, VGG16 is responsible for obtaining the features from those images. These features are then divided into training and testing features, and these features are used to train and test the logistic regression (LR). Logistic regression is one of the machine learning models that can be useful for classification problems. It is mainly useful for binary classification. It can be deployed in multi-class classification problems where the LR will perform binary classification for each and every class. Logistic regression transforms its output using the logistic sigmoid function to return a probability value. We can term the logistic regression as a linear regression model but the logistic regression uses a more complex cost function, and this cost function can be defined as the "sigmoid function" instead of a linear function. The sigmoid function equation is as follows:

$$S(x) = \frac{1}{1 + e^{-x}} \tag{2}$$

The function maps any real value into another value between 0 and 1 because the numerator is always smaller than the denominator by 1.

$$S(x) = \frac{1}{1 + e^{-x}} = \frac{e^x}{e^x + 1} \tag{3}$$

The basic idea of logistic regression is to cast the problem into a generalized linear regression model. The equation is as follows:

$$\hat{y} = \beta_0 + \beta_1 x_1 + \cdots + \beta_n x_n \tag{4}$$

Where $\hat{y}$ = predicted value, x = independent variables, and the β is coefficients to be learned.

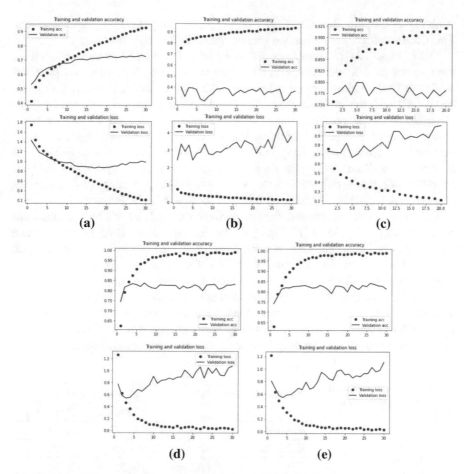

Fig. 4 Comparison of accuracy and loss during training and validation **a** CNN model, **b** MobileNetV2, **c** ResNet50, **d** VGG19, **e** VGG16

After classifying, we will obtain the count of vehicles for every category in that particular route. The results obtained with those pre-trained models, VGG16 + LR, and CNN model from scratch will be described in the later section.

4 Results

Dataset

Experiments were conducted using several traffic videos [10]. A vehicle dataset was taken from Kaggle [11]. This dataset consists of 10 vehicle classes such as

Ambulance, Bicycle, Bus, Car, Cart, Limousine, Motorcycle, Taxi, Truck, and Van. This dataset has 17,667 images for training and 5,879 images for testing.

Out of these 17,667 images, we are using 80%, i.e., 14,133 images are used for training the model, and 20%, i.e., 3534 images are used for validation purposes while working with the pre-trained models like MobileNetV2, ResNet50, VGG16, and VGG19. Using the MobileNetV2 with Adam optimizer, it obtained 36.56%. Using ResNet50 with Adam, it obtained 78.18% accuracy. Using VGG19 with Adam optimizer, it obtained 81.35% accuracy. Using VGG16 with an RMSprop optimizer, it obtained 82.74% accuracy. Using VGG16 with Adam optimizer, it obtained 84.32% accuracy. The discussed results are about Top-1 accuracies, depicted in Table 1. MobileNetV2, ResNet50, VGG19, and VGG16 (RMSProp, Adam) Top-5 accuracies are obtained as 54.34%, 82.01%, 85.67%, 91.78%, and 99.77%, respectively.

Once our model was trained, then to perform the analysis, we have applied our model to the traffic videos [8]. Using the background subtraction technique once the vehicles are detected, that detected region will be cropped, and that cropped portion will be supplied as an input for VGG16. Then, it will detect the features from those images, and those features are supplied as an input for logistic regression to perform classification. After vehicle classification is done, vehicle counting will be done under each category. Based upon that vehicle count traffic analysis will be done which will tell whether that road has heavy traffic or moderate traffic or low traffic. Figure 5 will provide an idea about the analysis done and their outcomes.

Table 1 Accuracy obtained with different pre-trained models

Pre-trained model	Optimizer	Obtained accuracy	
		Top-1 (%)	Top-5 (%)
MobileNetV2	Adam	36.56	54.34
ResNet50	Adam	78.18	82.01
VGG19	Adam	81.35	85.67
VGG16	RMSProp	82.74	91.78
VGG16	Adam	84.32	99.77

Fig. 5 Vehicle detection and classification in videos and the analysis results; **a** represents road with low traffic and **b** represents road with heavy traffic

5 Future Scope

This work obtained the count of vehicles of each category that are passing through the particular route. In future, it is possible to suggest the best route out of all available routes to reach the destination by obtaining the vehicle category count of all routes between the source and the destination, analyzing the traffic rate at each route, and based on such analysis.

6 Conclusion

From these results, we can conclude that VGG16 + logistic regression is well suited for our project when compared to other models as it has given top-1 accuracy of 84.32% and top-5 accuracy of 99.77% which is far better than other pre-trained models. Our system had performed well even it has to classify across such a large number of classes, i.e., 10. The future scope of this work is to improve the accuracy even when the real-time traffic videos were given as input.

References

1. Liu F, Zeng Z, Jiang R (2017) A video-based real-time adaptive vehicle-counting system for urban roads. PLoS ONE 12(11):e0186098
2. Zhu J, Sun K, Jia S, Li Q, Hou X, Lin W, Liu B, Qiu G (21018) Urban traffic density estimation based on ultrahigh-resolution UAV video and deep neural network. IEEE J Sel Topics Appl Earth Observations Remote Sensing, 11(12):4968–4981
3. Chen L, Ye F, Ruan Y, Fan H, Chen Q (2018) An algorithm for highway vehicle detection based on convolutional neural network. Eurasip J Image Video Process 2018(1):1–7
4. Arinaldi A, Pradana JA, Gurusinga AA (2018) Detection and classification of vehicles for traffic video analytics. Procedia Comput Sci 144:259–268
5. Memon S, Bhatti S, Thebo LA, Talpur MMB, Memon MA (2018) A video based vehicle detection, counting and classification system. Int J Image Graphics Signal Process 10(9):34
6. Saran KB, Sreelekha G (2015) Traffic video surveillance: vehicle detection and classification. In: 2015 international conference on control communication and computing India (ICCC). IEEE, pp 516–521
7. Krishna ST, Kalluri HK (2019) Deep learning and transfer learning approaches for image classification. Int J Recent Technol Eng (IJRTE), 7(5S4):427–432
8. Zhang H, Liptrott M, Bessis N, Cheng J (2019) Real-time traffic analysis using deep learning techniques and uav based video. In: 2019 16th IEEE international conference on advanced video and signal based surveillance (AVSS). IEEE, pp 1–5
9. Byun S, Shin IK, Moon J, Kang J, Choi SI (2021) Road traffic monitoring from UAV images using deep learning networks. Remote Sensing 13(20):4027
10. Mandal V, Mussah AR, Jin P, Adu-Gyamfi Y (2020) Artificial intelligence-enabled traffic monitoring system. Sustainability 12(21):9177
11. https://medusa.fit.vutbr.cz/traffic/data/2016-ITS-BrnoCompSpeed-video-previews/

Computer Vision with the Internet of Things (IoT)

Reeya Agrawal and Sangeeta Singh

1 Introduction

The Internet of things necessitates creating and exchanging data from an endless number of devices [1]. This is why the IoT software platform is complicated and made up of many different things that depend on each other to connect the real world of objects to the virtual world and store and analyze data from sensors to monitor and control connected objects or create a history that allows predictions. Traditional architecture is not the same for every project. Even if there are numerous weak dependencies, it is feasible to draw out a perfect design and employ computer vision technology every day [2]. Many aspects of our lives have been affected by this issue. Computer vision has been around for a long time and is widely employed in both the private and public sectors. There are several more uses for optical sensors that can detect light waves in different spectrum ranges: quality assurance in manufacturing; environmental management; and high-resolution cameras that gather information across battlefields [3]. These instruments are used to keep track of items. A handful of the sensors is fixed, while others are connected to a moving object. Among these are satellites, uncrewed aircraft, and automobiles.

Before, just a select, few of these apps could be used on various sorts of mobile devices [4]. IoT will be increasingly fascinating and lucrative when new technologies like computer vision, IP connection, powerful data analytics, and artificial intelligence come together. Our sense of touch is the most developed of the five senses [5].

R. Agrawal (✉)
GLA University, Mathura, India
e-mail: Agrawalreeya0304@gmail.com

R. Agrawal · S. Singh
Microelectronics and VLSI Lab, National Institute of Technology, Patna 800005, India
e-mail: sangeeta.singh@nitp.ac.in

2 What is Computer Vision?

A picture or set of thoughts may be taken, stored, then turned into information that can be utilized to perform other tasks. This is the beginning of computer vision. Various technologies function together in this system [6]. People who work in computer vision engineering must be familiar with multiple technologies, and how they interact to succeed. Real-time motion capture and 3D settings may be combined in games because of this technology. Robotics, virtual reality (VR), augmented reality (AR) applications, and gaming can benefit from this technology [7]. Figure 1 shows computer vision driven by advancements.

Sensor technology is also getting better at many levels, not just camera sensors. There have been some recent examples, as shown in Fig. 2.

Fig. 1 Advancements drive computer vision. *Image credit* IFA

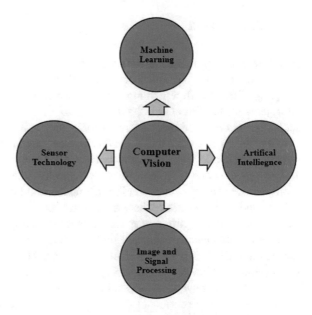

Fig. 2 Sensor technology

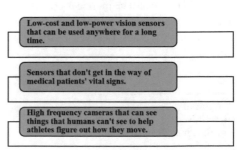

3 Computer Vision Gets Smart

3.1 Early Applications

Surveillance is among the first industries to employ image processing and video analytics to make sense of what they are seeing. Video analytics is a form of computer vision that tries to identify patterns in hours of video. The ability to automatically recognize and identify predetermined patterns in real-world circumstances might assist several enterprises [8]. Algorithms built by humans are the first type of video analytics technology. They search photos and videos for particular items. They performed exceptionally well in laboratory and simulation tests. Lighting conditions and camera perspectives impact performance; however, the design was not matched by input data such as these. Working on algorithms and creating new ones that might be used differently took a long time for scientists and engineers. Meanwhile, cameras and video recorders that employ these algorithms still are not powerful enough. Despite modest development over the years, poor performance in the actual world has hampered the usability and acceptance of the technology in the real world [9].

3.2 Deep Learning Breakthrough

In recent years, the emergence of deep learning algorithms has brought new life to computer vision. A method termed an "artificial neural network" (ANN) is used in "deep learning" to mimic sections of the human brain [10]. Research into artificial neural networks (ANNs) became possible in the early 2010s because of graphics processing units (GPUs). Researchers can train their neural networks on a wide variety of video and picture data thanks to video sites and IoT devices. It was found in 2012 that CNN, a kind of deep neural network (DNN), was far more accurate than DNN had previously been. Computer vision engineering became more exciting and popular. Classifying photos and identifying faces have become easier for deep learning algorithms than for people. Also crucial to note is that these algorithms can learn and adapt to diverse conditions, much like people [11]. Computer vision and deep learning can now work together to tackle high-level, complicated issues that were formerly exclusively for the human brain with the assistance of deep understanding. Faster CPUs, better machine learning algorithms, and deeper integration with edge devices will only improve these systems in future [12]. Figure 3 shows IoT architecture with computer vision.

Many things need to be done to make technology more practical and affordable for everyone (Fig. 4).

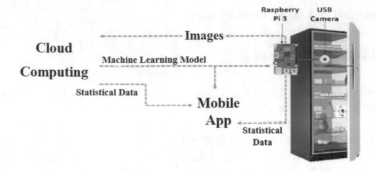

Fig. 3 IoT architecture with computer vision [13]

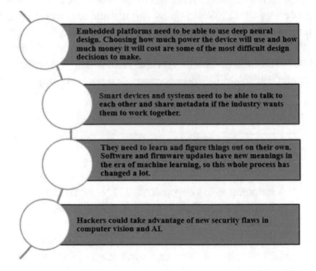

Fig. 4 Challenges in computer vision of IoT

4 Artificial Intelligence, Computer Vision, and Technologies Can be Used to Make Internet of Things

Weld quality inspection demands the capacity to verify each weld every 17 ms, which is hard for an individual to do on their own while inspecting five million car welds daily [14]. The physical and digital worlds are becoming increasingly intertwined thanks to the proliferation of IoT sensors like cameras, microphones, and other high-tech devices. These AI-powered gadgets can instantly analyze medical imaging for worrisome abnormalities, listen to equipment noises for maintenance concerns, or provide more extensive remote monitoring in a wide range of locations. IoT technologies and services like deep learning, computer vision, and audio or voice capabilities may be used by enterprises with Intel and Microsoft Azure [15].

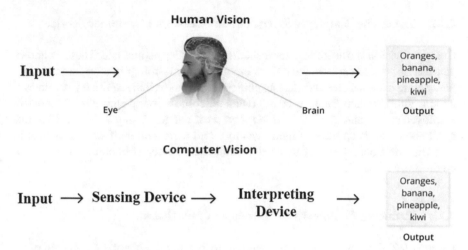

Fig. 5 AI visual inspection for defect detection in manufacturing

Adding computer vision and AI to IoT solutions, for example, enhances their business value by enabling them to address additional challenges. Figure 5 shows AI visual inspection for defect detection in manufacturing.

4.1 Four Ways Enterprises are Benefitting from AI and Computer Vision

In their field, artificial intelligence (AI) and machine learning (ML) algorithms excel due to their ability to process large amounts of data far quicker than humans can and make choices in real-time. Here are four examples of how Intel and Azure IoT solutions are being put to use in a variety of different contexts [16, 17].

4.1.1 Improving Typical IoT-Enabled Applications

These technologies may be used to improve daily IoT-enabled operations, including monitoring devices from afar and foreseeing maintenance needs. Video feeds may be automatically analyzed to detect movement or abnormal activity and deliver alerts immediately. Telemedicine's computer vision enables remote monitoring of patients' health status from afar.

4.1.2   Enhancing Employee Safety, Patient Care, and Customer Service

Computer vision and artificial intelligence can help keep people safe. These technologies can assist medical technicians in scanning medical photographs by automatically identifying irregularities and alerting clinicians to photos that require further investigation. Video streams can be used by AI and machine learning algorithms to monitor employee safety and alert them when there is a danger. Using a system like this, retail shops can keep track of their inventory and alert their staff when it is time to reorder. Additionally, it may be used to limit the number of clients in a congested environment.

4.1.3   Reducing Complexity for Developers and Users

Even as IoT devices and services continue to improve, technology companies are making them easier to set up. To produce IoT devices that are plug-and-play compatible, Intel and Azure encourage developers to create toolkits that connect rapidly and speed up the process of getting them up and running quickly [18]. People that utilize technology and systems daily benefit from this type of attentiveness.

4.1.4   Accelerating Potential Return on Investment

Increasing the IoT solutions' return on investment (ROI) through the use of more advanced technologies is another possibility. Companies using AI are more satisfied with IoT than those using IoT technology are, with 96% saying they are. Because they regard IoT as vital to their business's success, they are more inclined to invest in and use IoT. The technology itself can save companies a significant amount of money and time.

4.2   Advanced Technologies in IoT Solutions

As IoT technology improves, so does its capacity to solve business challenges [19]. As part of their collaboration, Intel and Azure are making it more straightforward for companies of all sizes and across a wide range of sectors to learn about and select the appropriate IoT devices and services to assist them in achieving their objectives. The two firms provide the hardware, software, edge and cloud services, and support. Our technology has been utilized to create ready-to-sell solutions in various industries, including manufacturing, retail, transportation, intelligent spaces, and more.

4.3   Evolving Toward IoT and AI

Machine vision might benefit significantly from the Internet of things. For example, it might save money and speed up the process. Lightweight communication technologies like Bluetooth, MQTT, and Zigbee have contributed to the proliferation of consumer IoT devices. Low-bandwidth messages or beacon data can be exchanged using these protocols. The real-time decision-making capability of imaging is dependent on uncompressed, low-latency data sources. A camera or sensor sends data back to a central processor for processing in the past [20]. Using various pictures and data from many sources, such as hyperspectral and 3D sensors, might be an issue for future IoT applications. Designers are researching intelligent gadgets at the network's edge. As a result, the bandwidth issue may soon be solved. Tiny sensors and embedded processing boards that do not require a camera are examples of devices that may be used in conjunction with an existing inspection network.

When a gadget is considered "intelligent," it gathers and processes data, makes a choice, and then transmits that decision or data to another device or the cloud. The quantity of data sent back to a central computer is significantly reduced when decisions are made locally. More processing power may be employed for more difficult analysis jobs because less bandwidth is required. With the help of these little devices, network intelligence may be dispersed throughout the system. Using an existing camera to feed data into an intelligent frame grabber in a quality inspection line is possible. Other system components will not have to deal with raw video data because of it [21]. It also converts the sensors into GigE Vision devices so that the program has one set of data to work with throughout its many components. As a result, current inspection systems can benefit from new inspection techniques like hyperspectral imaging and 3D scanning. Using an intelligent frame grabber to perform edge processing is more cost-effective than replacing expensive cameras and processing equipment. With this method, it is possible to add additional AI capability to an existing inspection line quickly.

It is particularly good at spotting defects or matching patterns when customized to a known data set. On the other hand, AI can be taught and can detect, identify, and differentiate more items or issues as more information is obtained [22]. Adding an intelligent frame grabber allows for more advanced AI algorithms. The camera and AI-processed video stream may be delivered to machine vision software already compatible with the technology. At the sensor level, embedded intelligent devices allow for more complicated processing. Low-cost and tiny embedded circuits with the computational capacity needed to analyze photos in real-time have been developed. Robotic procedures that require a lot of repetition, like edge detection in a pick-and-place system, benefit significantly from embedded intelligent devices. AI may be used in vision applications more quickly with embedded intelligent devices, just as the intelligent frame grabber. Artificial intelligence (AI) help train computer models to recognize objects and errors and advance robotics systems toward self-learning capabilities [23]. There are several advantages to using AI on both local and cloud-based computers and various smart devices.

4.4 Solving the Connectivity Challenge

The GigE Vision standard in 2006 was a significant change for machine vision system designers. It made it easier for products to work together and connect to the Internet. Today's designers thinking about IoT and AI face the same problems, but they also have to deal with more imaging and non-imaging sensors and new ways to use data that are not just for inspection [24]. This is not the first time that GigE Vision has helped us get to a more sophisticated level of analysis. Industrial IoT promises to use a variety of sensors and edge processing to speed up and improve the quality of inspections. Even though high-definition inspection could use 3D, hyperspectral and infrared (IR) capabilities, each tool has a different interface and data format that would need to be used. High-bandwidth sensors and more data sources make it hard to have enough capacity [25]. This makes it easy for devices to communicate and back to local or cloud processing. Edge processing also significantly reduces the amount of data that needs to be sent, making wireless transmission for real-time vision applications possible. These 3D sensors are small and do not use a lot of power. They are often part of a mobile inspection system without room for more hardware. With software, these devices can be made to look like "virtual GigE sensors" and work together to create a network that's easy to use [26]. GigE Vision is a machine vision processing that can look at images from these sensors. In future, there will be a lot of value in fully integrating the output from all of the sensors in an application so that a complete data set can be used for analysis and AI.

5 Machine Vision and the Cloud

The cloud and access to a larger data set are needed to introduce IoT to the vision market. Historically, production data has been restricted to a single plant. AI and machine learning processing algorithms may be constantly updated and enhanced with a cloud-based method to learn from fresh data sets. Initial AI capabilities can be integrated into vision systems using smart frame grabbers and embedded image sensors [27].

Cloud-based machine learning security is shown in Fig. 6. Rules-based inspection is excellent at detecting faults based on known factors, such as whether a part is present or is too far away from the next part. While a human inspector may struggle to locate and categorize scratches of varying sizes and locations on examined equipment, a computer-based system using machine learning is better equipped to handle these kinds of inspection issues [29]. Because of this, the system can be trained to recognize scratches on various devices or pass/fail tolerances for different clients with a new reference data set. It is possible to utilize a proven data set to configure a robotic vision system for parts assembly to recognize things and determine what action to do next, and then take that action. High-bandwidth sensor data transfer and sharing to the cloud would necessitate new developments in vision industry

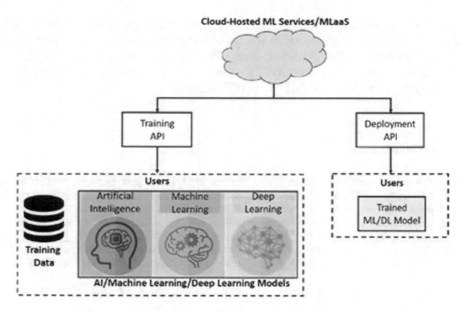

Fig. 6 Shows securing machine learning in the cloud [28]. They are reproduced from Qayyum [28] under the terms of the Creative Attribution Commons License 4.0 (CC-By 4.0). http://creati vecommons.org/licenses/by/4.0/

technologies, such as lossless compression, encryption, and security, in addition to higher-bandwidth wireless sensor interfaces [30].

6 Conclusion

They claim that forecasts and analyst papers on how AI would be employed with the Internet of things (IoT) abound. Currently, they are working on how they function together and why "IoT requires AI" and occasionally "IoT needs AI." Even though IoT and AI have been utilized together in many enterprises for a long time, this is a bit surprising. Even yet, it is becoming increasingly difficult to keep up with the fast emergence of various forms of AI throughout the entire IoT equation. Machine learning, big data, and the shift to the edge were previously included on the list of IoT predictions for 2017 as critical stages "to feed machine learning engines and additional AI applications." There were also mentions of moving to the edge and the coming of new data analytics streaming technologies. As Ovum stated, IoT and linked systems also boost AI since intelligent automation is required to make sense of the massive volumes of data that sensors generate. Perhaps it would be helpful to look at examples of this already occurring. Information and enjoyment are displayed on computer and television displays. The rise of IoT technologies has been helped by better main technologies and a lot of different things. There are new sensors, more computing power, and reliable mobile connectivity that can help make things even better in the next few years, which will make things even better. When existing IT devices need to be linked to the IoT, the market for the IoT will grow. As a result of this, there is a lot of demand for integrating devices. There are more than five billion smart phones, two billion PCs, and one billion tablets.

References

1. Rohith M, Sunil A (2021) Comparative analysis of edge computing and edge devices: key technology in IoT and computer vision applications. In: 2021 international conference on recent trends on electronics, information, communication & technology (RTEICT). IEEE
2. Liu F, Chen Z, Wang J (2021) Intelligent medical IoT system based on WSN with computer vision platforms. Concurrency Comput Pract Experience 33(12):e5036
3. Rohith BN (2021) Computer vision and IoT enabled bot for surveillance and monitoring of forest and large farms. In: 2021 2nd international conference for emerging technology (INCET). IEEE
4. Raj A, Raj A, Ahmad I (2021) Smart attendance monitoring system with computer vision using IOT. J Mobile Multimedia, 115–126.
5. Ye Z, Lei S (2021) The use of data mining and artificial intelligence technology in art colors and graph and images of computer vision under 6G internet of things communication. Int J Syst Assur Eng Manage 12(4):689–695
6. Taylor O, Ezekiel PS, Emmah VT (2021) Smart Vehicle Parking System Using Computer Vision and Internet of Things (IoT). European J Inf Technol Comput Sci 1.2:11–16
7. Qureshi KN et al (2021) A secure data parallel processing based embedded system for internet of things computer vision using field programmable gate array devices. Int J Circuit Theory Appl 49(5), 1450–1469
8. Rong F, Juan Z, ShuoFeng Z (2021) Surgical navigation technology based on computer vision and vr towards iot. Int J Comput Appl 43(2):142–146
9. Sahitya G, et al (2021) IOT-based domestic aid using computer vision for especially abled persons. In: Advances in communications, signal processing, and VLSI. Springer, Singapore, pp 91–102
10. Shuzan, NI et al (2021) IoT and computer vision-based electronic voting system. In: Advances in computer, communication and computational sciences. Springer, Singapore, pp 625–638
11. Tetiana M et al (2021) Computer vision mobile system for education using augmented reality technology. J Mob Multimedia, pp 555–576
12. Liu S et al (2021) Fuzzy-aided solution for out-of-view challenge in visual tracking under IoT-assisted complex environment. Neural Comput Appl 33(4):1055–1065
13. Lopez-Castaño C, Ferrin-Bolaños C, Castillo-Ossa L (2018) Computer vision and the internet of things ecosystem in the connected home. In: International symposium on distributed computing and artificial intelligence. Springer, Cham
14. Sood S et al (2021) Significance and Limitations of Deep Neural Networks for Image Classification and Object Detection. In: 2021 2nd international conference on smart electronics and communication (ICOSEC). IEEE
15. Shreyas E, Sheth MH (2021) 3D object detection and tracking methods using deep learning for computer vision applications. In: 2021 international conference on recent trends on electronics, information, communication & technology (RTEICT). IEEE
16. Kamal R et al (2021) A design approach for identifying, diagnosing and controlling soybean diseases using CNN based computer vision of the leaves for optimizing the production. In: IOP conference series: materials science and engineering. 1099(1). IOP Publishing

17. Chand AA et al (2021) Design and analysis of photovoltaic powered battery-operated computer vision-based multi-purpose smart farming robot. Agronomy 11(3):530
18. Sophokleous A et al (2021) Computer vision meets educational robotics. Electronics 10(6): 730
19. Yang L et al (2021) Computer vision models in intelligent aquaculture with emphasis on fish detection and behavior analysis: a review. Arch Comput Meth Eng 28(4):2785–2816
20. Hu X et al (2020) The 2020 Low-Power Computer Vision Challenge. In: 2021 IEEE 3rd international conference on artificial intelligence circuits and systems (AICAS). IEEE
21. Podder AK et al (2021) IoT based smart agrotech system for verification of Urban farming parameters. Microprocess Microsyst 82:104025
22. Kumer, SV Aswin et al (2021) Controlling the autonomous vehicle using computer vision and cloud server. Mater Today Proc 37:2982–2985
23. Paissan F, Massimo G, Elisabetta F (2021) Enabling energy efficient machine learning on a ultra-low-power vision sensor for IoT. arXiv preprint arXiv:2102.01340
24. Iqbal U et al (2021) How computer vision can facilitate flood management: a systematic review. Int J Disaster Risk Reduction 53:102030
25. Oliveira-Jr A et al (2020) IoT Sensing Box to Support Small-Scale Farming in Africa. In: International conference on e-infrastructure and e-services for developing countries. Springer, Cham
26. Chaudhary R, Kumar M (2021) Computer vision-based framework for anomaly detection. In: Next generation of internet of things. Springer, Singapore, 549–556
27. Manjunathan A et al Design of autonomous vehicle control using IoT. In: IOP conference series: materials science and engineering. 1055(1). IOP Publishing
28. Qayyum A et al (2020) Securing machine learning in the cloud: a systematic review of cloud machine learning security. Front Big Data 43
29. Tabeidi RA et al (2021) Smart computer laboratory: IoT based smartphone application. In: The international conference on artificial intelligence and computer vision. Springer, Cham
30. Ghazal TM, Alshurideh MT, Alzoubi HM (2021) Blockchain-enabled internet of things (IoT) platforms for pharmaceutical and biomedical research. In: The international conference on artificial intelligence and computer vision. Springer, Cham

Single Under-Water Image Enhancement Using the Modified Transmission Map and Background Light Estimation

Gunjan Verma, Manoj Kumar, and Suresh Raikwar

1 1. Introduction

During the last few years, the importance of image processing for under-water robots has received a lot of attention. Under-water robots (such as automated under-water vehicle and remotely operated vehicle) mainly depend on vision sensors to gather data about the under-water environment and marine life. Under-water robots face challenges in obtaining data due to its physical properties such as non-uniform lightning, color cast, and limited range of visibility [1]. Due to the complex under-water properties the existing under-water image enhancement (UIE) methods does not perform well [2]. As the captured under-water images usually appear blue, green, and blue-green with an increase in depth. Moreover, the captured under-water image usually suffers from faded color, limited visibility, uneven lightning, and poor contrast. Due to under-water medium change from air to water the light intensity decreases. The decrease in intensity 2 Gunjan et al. depends on the color wavelength [3]. The reduction of light intensity is known as light attenuation. The light attenuation occurs because of scattering and absorption phenomenon. The level of under-water visibility decreases around 20m in clean water and less than 5m in turbid water [4]. The light traveling through the water loses its intensity depending on the wavelength of color. The longest wavelengths, with the lowest frequency, are absorbed first, i.e., red color. The red color starts losing the intensity just after 1m and disappears at about 4−5m distance [5] as shown in Fig. 1a. Therefore, images captured under-water seem to be blue (shortest wavelength).

G. Verma (✉) · M. Kumar
Department of Computer Engineering and Applications, GLA University, Mathura, Uttar Pradesh 281406, India
e-mail: vgunjan1102@gmail.com

S. Raikwar
Department of Computer Engineering and Applications, Thappar University, Patiala, Punjab 147004, India

© The Author(s), under exclusive license to Springer Nature Singapore Pte Ltd. 2023   235
K. Kumar Singh et al. (eds.), *Machine Vision and Augmented Intelligence*, Lecture Notes in Electrical Engineering 1007, https://doi.org/10.1007/978-981-99-0189-0_16

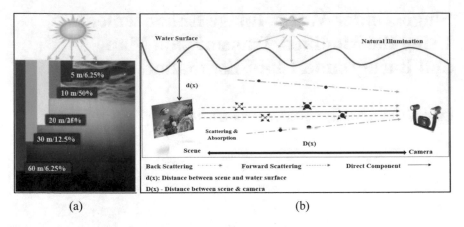

(a)   (b)

Fig. 1 **a** The visual illustration of the diminishing of color in under-water environment. **b** The pictorial representation of under-water image formation model

The images obtained under-water suffer from distorted color and contrast. Hence, the crucial information of the under-water image is lost. As a result, under-water image processing approaches are required to enhance the image contrast and color to extract the lost information. To improve the contrast of the degraded image usually contrast-based enhancement methods are applied on the image [6]. The existing UIE methods focus on contrast enhancement [5], but does not consider the important parameters of the under-water image. In order to resolve issues, a modified transmission light estimation method is proposed. In the past few years, deep neural-based techniques have advanced rapidly, and they are now widely used in image processing tasks [7–9]. The deep neural based approaches show enhanced performance in the object tracking, detection [10], and recognition tasks [11]. Deep learning approaches show improved performance in terms of low vision and high vision task [12]. Moreover, image super resolution [13], image de-blurring and image de-noising tasks are also performed using deep learning-based approaches. Despite the fact that deep learning-based approaches give appealing results but depend on several parameters (epoch, training size, and hyper-parameters). However, the deep neural based techniques highly rely on the large number of datasets. But due to the complex under-water environment, it is difficult to obtain the degraded image and ground truth, respectively.

The major highlights of the paper are mentioned below:

(i)   The U-TMBL is used to compute the modified transmission map based on exponential attenuation coefficient that estimates the direct light that reaches the camera without scattering

(ii) The U-TMBL is used to compute the attenuated light using the proposed attenuation coefficient

(iii) The U-TMBL uses the wavelength information to estimate the attenuation coefficient that helps in regaining the attenuated color

(iv)   The U-TMBL is used to estimate the background light of the degraded imaged using an optimal approach.

The paper consists of five sections. Section 1 discusses need of UIE process and challenges behind it. Section 2 discusses the background study of UIQM and existing methods to estimate the transmission map. Section 3 presents the proposed U-TMBL method. Section 4 analyzes results based on qualitatively and quantitative results. Section 5 gives the conclusion of the paper.

2   Background Study

The existing literature survey is discussed based on the under-water image formation model (UIFM) and the state-of-the-art methods to estimate the transmission map.

2.1   The UIFM

The UIFM is same as Jaffe McGlamery [14] air-borne hazy image formation model, where total radiance obtained at the camera includes three components as shown in Fig. 1b. The 3 components are (i) Backscattering, the light received after scattering due to under-water particles, (ii) Forward scattering, the light received after scattering at a small angle due to under-water particles, and (iii) Direct attenuation, the light received from the object to the camera without reflection. Usually, forward scattering is neglected in under-water image processing approaches. The Eq. (1) shows the under-water image formation.

$$I^C(u, v) = J^C(u, v)t^C(u, v) + B^C\left(1 - t^C(u, v)\right) \tag{1}$$

where B^c is the background light, J^c (x, y) is the clear image, I^c (x, y) is the degraded under-water image at (x, y), c belongs to the color channel, and t^c (x, y) is the estimated transmission light map. It is the remaining light that is obtained at the camera after the scattering and absorption of the light. The t^c (x, y) is computed using Eq. (2)

$$t^c(x, y) = e^{\beta^c d(x)} \tag{2}$$

where β^c is the total attenuation coefficient at color channel c that is considered as constant value for each c and $d(x)$ is the estimated scene depth. That implies that t^c (x, y) can be obtain, if the scene depth $d(x)$ is known.

Note Eq. (2) is considered when haze is homogeneous. The $J^c(x, y)$ can be enhanced by removing haze from $I^c(x, y)$. The $J^c(x, y)$ is the portion of incident light that is reflected through reflectivity. Moreover, the incident light includes artificial light and the environmental illumination. Therefore, the degraded color and veiling light may occur in $J^c(x, y)$, due to the impact of the artificial light source and natural illumination along the path.

2.2 Transmission Map Estimation

To computer the transmission maps, several methods have been proposed among which the dark channel prior (DCP) [15] is most used. The DCP assumes that at least one pixel of three RGB channels will have low intensity value in non-sky patch. Also, due to the strong attenuation of the red channel, the DCP considers only green–blue channel. This is described in Eq. (3).

$$J_{\text{dark}}^{\text{rgb}}(x) = \min_{y \in \Omega} \left\{ \min_c J^c(y) \right\} = 0 \tag{3}$$

After that minimum filter is applied on Eq. 3 and then divided by background light B^c. The resultant is given by Eq. (4).

$$\min_{y \in \Omega} \{ \min_c \frac{I^c(y)}{B^c} \} = \min_{y \in \Omega} \left\{ \min_c J^c(y) \right\} + 1 - t_{DCP}(x) \tag{4}$$

The transmission map is estimated using Eq. (5)

$$t_{DCP}(x) = 1 - \min_{y \in \Omega} \left\{ \min_c \frac{I^c(y)}{B^c} \right\} \tag{5}$$

Furthermore, Drews [16] introduced $t_{DCP}(x)$ in which $I^c(y)$ is replaced by $I^{c'}(y)$. To estimate the transmission map, the maximum intensity prior method is used as shown in Eq. (6).

$$\begin{cases} D_{mip}(x) = \max y \in \Omega - I^r(y) - y \in \Omega \max(I^{c'}(y)) \\ t_{MIP}(x) = D_{mip}(x) + 1 - \max(D_{mip}(x)) \end{cases} \tag{6}$$

To estimate the scene depth of the under-water image, the stretching is performed on *three* depth maps consisting of the maximum intensity d_D, the image blurriness d_B and the red channel d_R, maximum filter as shown in Eq. 7

$$d_n = \theta_b[\theta_a d_D + (1 - \theta_a)d_R] + (1 - \theta_b)d_B \tag{7}$$

where θ_b and θ_a are based on same sigmoid function. Then, the depth map is further enhanced using the guided filter. At last, the relative distance is transformed as per the actual distance to obtain the final depth d_f of the image. Equation (8) presents the transmission map estimation of the attenuated red channel.

$$t^r(x) = e^{-\beta^r d_f} \tag{8}$$

where $\beta^r \in \left(\frac{1}{8}, \frac{1}{5}\right)$ as per [17, 18]. Furthermore, the transmission map of the green and blue channels is calculated using their attenuation ratios with respect to the red channel [19].

3 The proposed U-TMBL

A novel U-TMBL method is proposed to enhance the under-water images for resolving color cast issue. The U-TMBL method includes three steps: (i) Scene depth estimation $(D(x))$- uses inverse red-channel attenuation inverse red-channel attenuation [20] (ii) Background light estimation B^c, improves the color and contrast of the image (iii) Modified Transmission estimation t^c, uses novel attenuation coefficient that uses scene depth and further refined by guided filter and box filter. Finally, the enhanced image is obtained using the mentioned steps. The proposed algorithm is shown in 1.

Algorithm 1 Algorithm of proposed U-TMBL

Input: Batch of images n
Output: Enhanced image J_c
for i = 1 to n **do**
      read the image I^c
      calculate the $D^{'}(x)$ via Eq. (11)
      calculate the B^c via Eq. (14)
      calculate the T^c via Eq. (15)
      apply guided filter and box filter on T^c
end for

---

i. Scene depth estimation $(D(x))$-The traditional DCP does not perform well on complex under-water images due to under-water small particles (such as phytoplankton) and uneven lightning which impacts the transmission map of the image. The normal light attenuations of red are 18%, green is 5%, and blue channel is 2.5% traveling under the water. After considering the strong relation of the scene depth (the distance between the object and the camera) with the wavelength, the scene is estimated considering the limited lightning case.

Whenever the under-water image is captured in low-light conditions, the following condition is observed where the ratio of the mean intensity of the red channel and the maximum intensity between blue and green channels should be small. The ratio is presented in Eq (9).

$$R = \frac{\text{mean}\left(I^{\text{red}}\right)}{\max\left(\text{mean}(I^{\text{green}}), \text{mean}\left(I^{\text{blue}}\right)\right)} \tag{9}$$

This shows the foreground area is bright, whereas the background area is dark of the image. In these instances, inverse red channel attenuation, which is described in [20], reflects the unique properties of an under-water image. The scene points that obtain small values in Eq. (10) are presumed to be near to the camera.

$$A^{\text{invred}}(x) = \min_{x' \in \Omega(x)} \left(1 - I^{\text{red}}(x')\right) \tag{10}$$

The Eq. (11) is used to estimate the final scene that is obtained with the computation of the original distance between the object and the camera.

$$D'(x) = (D(x) + \alpha) \tag{11}$$

where $\alpha = 0.2$ is the closet point near the camera. The α is the distance between the closest estimated scene point, and camera and $D(x)$ is the scene depth.

ii. BL Estimation (B^c)- The B^c estimation is the main factor that can improve the color and contrast of the image. However, the smaller value of B^c leads to more degraded image, whereas the higher value of the B^c. To estimate the background light, a modified optimal approach is proposed that includes three steps to estimate the B^c-

(a) The minimum channel map D is attained from red, blue, and green channels using the Eq. (12)

$$D = \min_c (J^c(x)) \tag{12}$$

$$B_\Omega^C = x_{\in\phi(z)}^{\max}(D) \tag{13}$$

(b) The maximum patch is applied on the Eq. (8) as shown in Eq. (1)
(c) The optimal value of B^c is computed using the Eq. (14). Firstly, a large area 15% is selected of the degraded under-water image to understand the light present. After that, a small nearby area of 5% is selected to avoid incorrect estimation due to incomplete prior knowledge. At last, an optimal background light can be obtained based on two patches of ω as shown in Eq. (14)

$$B^C = \sum_{i=1} B_{\Omega_i}^C / T_\Omega \tag{14}$$

where $B_{\Omega_i}^C$ is the estimation of both the ω patches and T_Ω is the total number of operations performed.

iii. Transmission map (t^c)-The UIFM requires the estimation of the background light and transmission light. Usually, the t^c is estimated with [21, 22]. But, due to color degradation the DCP sometimes do not perform well on complex underwater environment. In U-TMBL, a modified transmission map is proposed that is further refined using the guided filter and box filter. The t^c is transparent layer that includes the depth information. The propose U-TMBL is shown in Eq. (15) where transmission is estimated using weights of single exponential method and the color information of all three channels based on wavelengths.

$$tc = me - \alpha D'(x) + ne - \gamma D'(x) \tag{15}$$

where m and n are weights of the exponential function. The value of m = 0.6 and n = 0.4. The Eq. (16) and (17) is used to compute the value of attenuation coefficients including α and γ.

$$\alpha = \int_{400}^{600} \beta^c s(\lambda) d\lambda \tag{16}$$

$$\gamma = \int_{600}^{750} \beta^c s(\lambda) d\lambda \tag{17}$$

where β^c is the adaptive attenuation coefficient depending on each wavelength, and the $s(\lambda)$ is the spectral sensitivity of each wavelength based on the camera response function of CMV12000 camera [23]. Finally, the t_c and β^c are estimated using Eq. (14) and (15), respectively. If t_c obtains zero that means the image contains unwanted noise. So, we considered a bound t_0. The proposed method shows superior performance with the modified transmission map estimation and background light estimation. Finally, clear under-water image is obtained using the Eq. (18).

$$J^c(x) = \frac{I^c(x) - B^c}{\max(t_c(x), t_0)} + B^C \tag{18}$$

4 Evaluation and Analysis

The effectiveness of the proposed U-TMBL is analyzed using the real-world image enhancement (RUIE) dataset on existing HE [24], CLAHE [25], ICM [26], UCM [27], RGHS [28], and UWCNN [29] methods. The experiments are implemented on i7 processor and Windows 10 operating system using the MATLAB. The proposed U-TMBL method is analyzed using the natural image quality evaluator (NIQE) [30],

UIQM [31], and blind/reference-less image spatial quality evaluator (BRISQUE) [32] evaluation metric.

4.1 Evaluation Metric

The proposed U-TMBL method has been analyzed using the non-reference evaluation metric. As ground truth information is not available in RUIE dataset. The input of the non-reference evaluation metric is the enhanced image that estimates the quality of the input image. In this paper, three evaluation metrics are used: NIQE, UIQM, and BRISQUE.

The NIQE is based on human vision perception [30]. The lower the NIQE value, better is the image quality. The NIQE is estimated using Eq. (19).

$$D(v_1, v_2, \Sigma_1, \Sigma_2) = \sqrt{(v_1 - v_2)^T \left(\frac{\Sigma_1 + \Sigma_2}{2} \right)^{-1} (v_1 - v_2)} \qquad (19)$$

where v_1, v_2 are mean vectors, Σ_1, Σ_2 are co-variance matrices and the degraded image of the multi-variance Gaussian model.

BRISQUE [32]: It is based on the amount of distortion. It computes the loss of naturalness of the input image. The lower the BRISQUE value better is the image quality. The BRISQUE is computed using Eq. (20).

$$\hat{I}(i, j) = \frac{I(1, j) - \mu(i, j)}{\sigma(i, j) + C} \qquad (20)$$

where $I(i, j)$ is the intensity of the input image, $\mu(i, j)$ is the mean, $\sigma(i, j)$ is the standard deviation and C is constant.

UIQM [33]: It is based on the human vision system perceptiveness. The UIQM is estimated based on three parameters: under-water image colorfulness, sharpness, and contrast measure. The higher the UIQM value better is the image quality. The UIQM is estimated using the Eq. (21).

$$UIQM = c1 \times UICM + c2 \times UISM + c3 \times UIConM \qquad (21)$$

where, c_1, c_2 and c_3 are the weights.

4.2 Testing Dataset

The proposed U-TMBL method is compared and analyzed on real-world under-water dataset (RUIE) [33]. The RUIE is collected from real-world under-water environment

Fig. 2 The sample images of RUIE dataset

that shows properties of complex under-water environment. The RUIE consists of 4, 230 images. The dataset includes marine animals (such as urchins and scallops) and shows issues (such as color cast, haze, and limited lightning). The sample images of the dataset are shown in Fig. 2.

4.3 Visual Analysis

In visual analysis, five real under-water images are used to compare the performance of HE [24], CLAHE [25], ICM [26], UCM [27], RGHS [28], UWCNN [29], and U-TMBL. The five images are selected based on the degradation level and issues such as color cast, lightning, and haze.

Figure 3 shows the comparison of the HE, CLAHE, ICM, UCM, RGHS, UWCNN, and U-TMBL methods. It can be observed that HE removes the color cast but introduces unwanted noise and artifacts. The enhanced images are over-amplified and over-enhanced. As, HE is based on the equalization of the pixel value. CLAHE is unable to remove the color cast as it is dependent on the clip limit. ICM improves the visibility of the degraded image but is unable to completely remove the color cast issue. Moreover, some colors are restored as ICM uses contrast stretching issue.

On the other hand, UCM improves the quality of the degraded image but partially remove the color cast. Also, real colors of the images are not recovered as it focuses on the saturation and intensity stretching in HSI model. RGHS method works well for nearby objects but is unable to completely remove the color cast from the input image. Also, noise is introduced. UWCNN method is able to remove the color cast but introduces yellow color in the enhanced images. The UWCNN is unable to regain the true color of the image. The proposed U-TMBL method is able to remove the color cast from all the input five images. It can be observed that brightness is improved and the colors are restored. Therefore, the proposed U-TMBL method works well for color cast and limited lightning issue.

4.4 Quantitative Analysis

The quantitative analysis is conducted on first 200 images of the RUIE dataset to analyze the performance of the proposed U-TMBL.

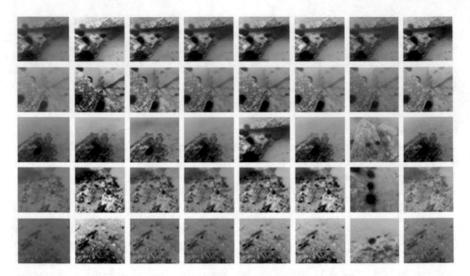

Fig. 3 The qualitative comparison of existing HE, CLAHE, ICM, UCM, RGHS, UWCNN, and the proposed U-TMBL

Figure 4 shows the comparison of the HE [24], CLAHE [25], ICM [26], UCM [27], RGHS [28], UWCNN [29], and U-TMBL methods. The U-TMBL outperforms all the existing methods in terms of NIQE, BRISQUE, and UIQM.

Figure 4 shows that the proposed U-TMBL obtained the minimum value in terms of NIQE. That implies that the U-TMBL is able to recover the naturalness of the degraded image. However, HE obtains the highest value because noise is introduced in the enhanced image due to pixel equalization.

Figure 5 shows that the proposed U-TMBL obtained the lowest value in terms of BRISQUE. That proves that the U-TMBL is able to recover the image as per human

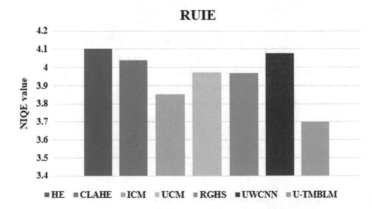

Fig. 4 Comparison of HE, CLAHE, ICM, UCM, RGHS, UWCNN, and UIETM on 200 images of RUIE dataset in terms of NIQE

visual system. Also, real color is recovered. However, HE obtains the highest value because it equalizes the intensity value.

Figure 6 shows that the U-TMBL method obtained highest value. This implies that the proposed method is able to enhance image in terms of color, contrast and sharpness. Whereas, UWCNN obtained minimum value as the training of the network does not considers real underwater images. Moreover, the deep neural networks highly rely on the training dataset and the hyper-parameters.

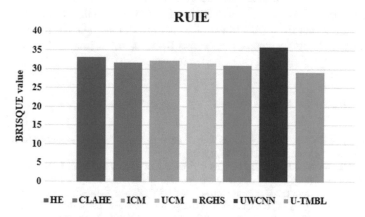

Fig. 5 Comparison of HE, CLAHE, ICM, UCM, RGHS, UWCNN, and UIETM on 200 images of RUIE dataset in terms of BRISQUE

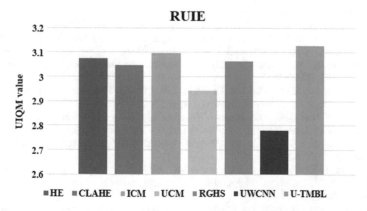

Fig. 6 Quantitative comparison of U-TMBL with HE, CLHAE, ICM, UCM and RGHS

5 Conclusion

In the paper, U-TMBL is presented based on modified transmission estimation. The qualitative and quantitative results show that the U-TMBL method overcomes the issues of color cast and low-lightning. Furthermore, the existing HE, CLAHE, ICM, UCM, RGHS, and UWCNN are compared with U-TMBL method. The results prove that the U-TMBL can successfully remove color cast and show more appealing qualitative results. The quantitative results demonstrate that the U-TMBL works well in terms of UIQM, NIQE, and BRISQUE. However, in the qualitative results, it can be observed that the partial blue color cast is still observed. In future, the focus will be on completely removal of color cast from the input image.

References

1. Anwar S, Li C (2020) Diving deeper into underwater image enhancement: A survey. Signal Process Image Commun 89:115978–115978
2. bt Shamsuddin N, b Baharudin B, Kushairi M, Rajuddin M, bt Mohd F, et al (2012) Significance level of image enhancement techniques for underwater images. In: 2012 international conference on computer & information science (ICCIS), vol 1. IEEE, pp 490–494
3. Schettini R, Corchs S (2010) Underwater image processing: state of the art of restoration and image enhancement methods. EURASIP J Adv Signal Process 1–14:2010
4. Muhammad Suzuri Hitam, Ezmahamrul Afreen Awalludin, Wan Nural Jawahir Hj Wan Yussof, and Zainuddin Bachok. Mixture contrast limited adaptive histogram equalization for underwater image enhancement. In 2013 International conference on computer applications technology (ICCAT), pages 1–5. IEEE, 2013.
5. Yoav Y Schechner and Nir Karpel. Recovery of underwater visibility and structure by polarization analysis. IEEE Journal of oceanic engineering, 30(3):570–587, July 2005.
6. CL Philip Chen, Hong Li, Yantao Wei, Tian Xia, and Yuan Yan Tang. A local contrast method for small infrared target detection. IEEE Transactions on Geoscience and Remote Sensing, 52(1):574–581, March 2013.
7. Jiang Q, Zhang Y, Bao F, Zhao X, Zhang C, Liu P (2022) Two-step domain adaptation for underwater image enhancement. Pattern Recogn 122:108324
8. Hua Yang, Fei Tian, Qi Qi, QM Jonathan Wu, and Kunqian Li. Underwater image enhancement with latent consistency learning-based color transfer. IET Image Processing, 2022.
9. Zheng M, Luo W (2022) Underwater image enhancement using improved cnn based defogging. Electronics 11(1):150
10. Ling J, Tan X, Yardibi T, Li J, Nordenvaad ML, He H, Zhao K (2014) On bayesian channel estimation and fft-based symbol detection in mimo underwater acoustic communications. IEEE J Oceanic Eng 39(1):59–73
11. Kumar M, Bhatnagar C (2017) Crowd behavior recognition using hybrid tracking model and genetic algorithm enabled neural network. Int J Comput Intell Syst 10(1):234–246
12. Zhang J, Pan J, Ren J, Song Y, Bao L, Lau RW, Yang MH (2018) Dynamic scene deblurring using spatially variant recurrent neural networks. In: IEEE conference on computer vision and pattern recognition, pp 2521–2529
13. Huimin L, Li Y, Uemura T, Kim H, Serikawa S (2018) Low illumination underwater light field images reconstruction using deep convolutional neural networks. Futur Gener Comput Syst 82:142–148
14. McGlamery BL (1980) A computer model for underwater camera systems. In: Ocean optics VI, international society for optics and photonics vol 208, pp 221–231

15. He K, Sun J, Tang X (2010) Single image haze removal using dark channel prior. IEEE Trans Pattern Anal Mach Intell 33(12):2341–2353
16. Drews P, Nascimento E, Moraes F, Botelho S, Campos M (2013) Transmission estimation in underwater single images. In: Proceedings of the IEEE international conference on computer vision workshops, pp 825–830
17. Chiang JY, Chen YC (2011) Underwater image enhancement by wavelength compensation and dehazing. IEEE Trans Image Process 21(4):1756–1769
18. Duntley SQ (1963) Light in the sea. JOSA 53(2):214–233
19. Zhao X, Jin T, Song Q (2015) Deriving inherent optical properties from background color and underwater image enhancement. Ocean Eng 94:163–172
20. Peng YT, Cosman PC (2017) Underwater image restoration based on image blurriness and light absorption. IEEE Trans Image Process 26(4):1579–1594
21. Yang HY, Chen PY, Huang CC, Zhuang YZ, Shiau YH (2011) Low complexity underwater image enhancement based on dark channel prior. In: 2011 second international conference on innovations in bio-inspired computing and applications. IEEE, pp 17–20
22. Wen H, Tian Y, Huang T, Gao W (2013) Single underwater image enhancement with a new optical model. In: 2013 IEEE international symposium on circuits and systems (ISCAS). IEEE, pp 753–756
23. CMV12000. Cmv12000 camera sensor response graph. https://ams.com/en/cmv12000/. Accessed 02 November 2021
24. Hummel R (1975) Image enhancement by histogram transformation. Comput Graphics Image Process 6(2):184–195
25. Reza AM (2004) Realization of the contrast limited adaptive histogram equalization (clahe) for real-time image enhancement. J VLSI Signal Process Syst Signal Image Video Technol 38(1):35–44
26. Iqbal K, Salam RA, Osman A, Talib AZ (2007) Underwater image enhancement using an integrated colour model. IAENG Int J Comput Sci 34(2)
27. Iqbal K, Odetayo M, James A, Salam RA, Talib AZ (2010) Enhancing the low-quality images using unsupervised colour correction method. In: IEEE international conference on systems, man and cybernetics. IEEE, pp 1703–1709
28. Huang D, Wang Y, Song W, Sequeira J, Mavromatis S (2018) Shallow-water image enhancement using relative global histogram stretchingbased on adaptive parameter acquisition. In: international conference on multimedia modeling, pp 453–465. Springer
29. Li C, Anwar S, Porikli F (2020) Underwater scene prior inspired deep underwater image and video enhancement. Pattern Recogn 98:107038
30. Mittal A, Soundararajan R, Bovik AC (2012) Making a "completely blind" image quality analyzer. IEEE Signal Process Lett 20(3):209–212
31. Panetta K, Gao C, Agaian S (2016) Human-visual-system-inspired underwater image quality measures. IEEE J Oceanic Eng 41(3):541–551
32. Mittal A, Soundararajan R, Bovik AC (2012) Making a "completely blind" image quality analyzer. IEEE Signal Process Lett 20(3):209–212
33. Liu R, Fan X, Zhu M, Hou M, Luo Z (2020) Real-world underwater enhancement: challenges, benchmarks, and solutions under natural light. IEEE Trans Circuits Syst Video Technol 30(12):4861–4875

Quality Assessment of the Experimental Data of Wood Structure Using Kanpur Theorem

Anand Shukla, Manabendra Saha, and Richa Dixit

1 Introduction

Computerized tomography (CT) has turned out to be a standard method for examination in the fields of material sciences and medicine. The principal advantage of CT imaging over conventional technique is that it permits detection and quantification of heterogeneities and internal defects for material density determination.

As CBP algorithm is the foundation of CT scanners used in NDE for computerized tomography, convolution backprojection (CBP), a reconstruction algorithm, is used to reconstruct the object cross section. This algorithm makes use of filter functions, which are user-dependent. For the same dataset, different filter functions lead to different reconstruction. This is followed from the mathematical formulation of the CBP algorithm, and it can be demonstrated that for a reconstruction process, the reconstruction with any given filter will lead to a theoretical error. In the initials days of CT imaging, Natterer [1] gave an account of a mathematical study, which showed the probable use of Sobolev-space techniques for inferring the errors involved in the tomographic reconstruction process, which resulted the final CT images from the gamma-ray (X-ray) projection data. Munshi et al. [2, 3] carried out the further work on error theorems.

First Kanpur theorem gives the user with a quantitative estimate of the local error in the CT image, and second Kanpur theorem informs about global error obtained by most engineering/medical scanners. Second level of reconstructions (acquired by original CT images) gives an error estimate that is not achievable otherwise. This approach results in very useful tools for quantification of nature of internal defects in the engineering materials as well as in human tissues.

A. Shukla (✉) · M. Saha
ABES Engineering College, Dr. A.P.J. Abdul Kalam Technical University, Ghaziabad, India
e-mail: anand.srcem@gmail.com

R. Dixit
St. Aloysius College, Rani Durgawati University, Jabalpur, India

1.1 Theoretical Background of CT

The ray travels from source to detector through object in X-ray tomography. When these rays passes through a part of an object, it gets the information of it. To scan whole object, the source and detector are rotated around it for large number of views. From these projection data stored in detector, distribution of few properties like attenuation coefficients within the object is reconstructed making use of the reconstruction techniques.

The objective of CT is to get information regarding the nature of the material occupying exact positions inside the component or body. To obtain information, every point inside the body is allotted a number which is particular to the material occupying that part. A fit candidate for this number is the material's X-ray attenuation coefficient (Fig. 1).

The relation between intensities I_{in} and I_{out} shown in Fig. 1 is given according to *Lambert–Beer* law as

$$I_{out} = I_{in} \exp\left(-\int_L f(x, y)dl\right) \tag{1}$$

Application of natural log both sides gives

$$\ln\left[\frac{I_{in}}{I_{out}}\right] = \int (f(x, y))dl \tag{2}$$

This implies that the detector detects line integral of the object function along a particular line and for a specific view. To get the full extent of the whole object function, the line integral is collected for many numbers of rays at different angles. In case of X-ray CT, the attenuation coefficient, $\mu(x, y)$, which is the characteristics of the object is represented by the object function, $f(x, y)$.

The attenuation of X-ray beam primarily occur either because of scattering from their original direction of travel or due to absorption by the atoms of material. The accountable mechanisms for this attenuation are Compton effect and photoelectric effect, respectively. Munshi [2] has made an effort to estimate errors occurring

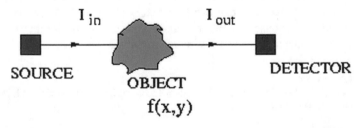

Fig. 1 X-ray attenuation through the object

in different tomographic algorithms under the supposition that the object cross-section posses band-limited projection data. In the study, he evolved a simplified two-dimensional Cartesian formula (KT-1) for predicting the comparative performance of the Fourier filters used in the convolution back projection algorithm. This approach involves the Laplacian of the object function and the second-order derivatives of the filter functions. The norms are local in character rather than the global norms in this study.

Herman [4] has categorized and explored the computational and mathematical procedures underlying the data collection, image reconstruction, and image display in practice of computerized tomography. He also described the reconstruction algorithms and presented the treatment of the computational problems linked with the display of the results. The methods for estimation of error incurred in reconstruction method are explained in details too.

Radon [5] has given a radon inversion formula derived in 1971 which helped to solve the problem of image reconstruction from the projection data. In an experiment, the datasets gathered by detectors are the set of line integrals along a particular line passing through the object cross section. Radon also proved that any arbitrary function could be retrieved from its set of line integrals taken along various chords and various directions.

All the studies mentioned above make use of the methods to estimate the inherent error incurred in the reconstruction of images. The theorems by Munshi et al. [6, 7] are known as Kanpur Error Theorem that gives the formula to estimate the inherent error. The present study aims at detection and quantification of internal disease of the body parts by applying Kanpur Error Theorems on scanned images.

2 Material and Methods

Projection data is required for the reconstruction of object function $\mu(x, y)$. There are two modes mainly used for projection data collection, called parallel beam geometry (PBG) and fan beam geometry (FBG).

(a) Parallel beam geometry

PBG mode of data collection comprises several pairs of radiation source and detector system, using which the object can be scanned completely. The object to be scanned is placed on a table, which can be rotated for giving different views, and the source-detector pairs are spaced uniformly. The SD (source detector) line represents the data ray path. The angle of the source position (or object rotation) is denoted by θ and the perpendicular distance of the ray from the origin is denoted by 's'. PBG setup is represented in Fig. 2.

(b) Fan beam geometry

All medical and industrial scanners incorporate the FBG mode collection mechanism, which involves a rotating module including a source and array of detectors placed in

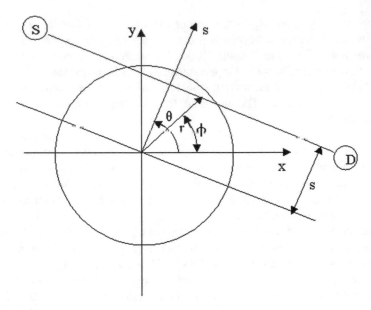

Fig. 2 Parallel beam geometry

an arc around the object. FBG configuration is shown in Fig. 3. For computational feasibility of reconstruction algorithms, the projection data collected in FBG, i.e., $g(\rho, \beta)$, must be converted into PBG '$p(s, \theta)$.

Projection data collected from the detectors '$p(s, \theta)$, of an object $f(x, y)$, is actually the radon transform $R\ f(s, \theta)$, and is equivalent to line integrals through the object in all possible directions. That is, a single radon value is the integral of all points along a line with angle θ and perpendicular distance 's' from the origin, as shown in Fig. 4.

The radon transform can be written as:

$$p(s, \theta) = R\ f(s,\ \theta) = \int \int f(x, y)\, \delta\, (x\, \cos\, \theta + y \sin \theta - s) \mathrm{d}x\, \mathrm{d}y \qquad (3)$$

The correlation between the Fourier transform and the radon transform is given by the Fourier slice theorem. This theorem states "one dimensional Fourier transform of the Radon transform along a radial line is identical to the same line in the two dimensional Fourier transforms of the object." The theorem, illustrated in Fig. 5, mathematically, is written as:

$$F_1 R\ f(R, \theta) = F_2 R\ f(R \cos \theta,\ R \sin \theta) \qquad (4)$$

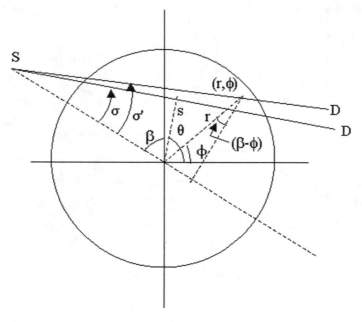

Fig. 3 Fan beam geometry

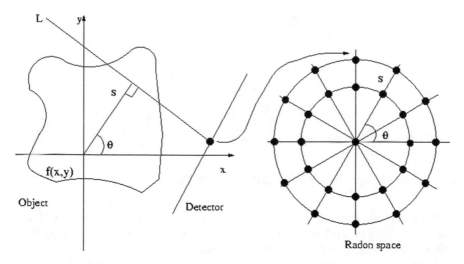

Fig. 4 Radon value is the line integral along the line *L*

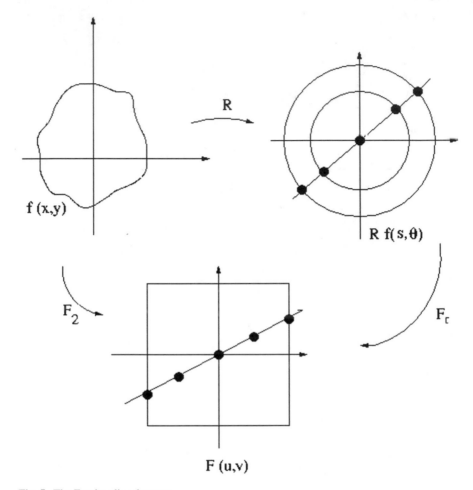

Fig. 5 The Fourier slice theorem

2.1 Image Reconstruction from Projections

The application range of image reconstruction is very wide. Shown in Fig. 6 is the computation of the inverse radon transform. Object function is evaluated using inverse radon transform from the given projection data.

Image reconstruction is very appropriately defined in words of Herman [4] as: "Image reconstruction from projections is the process of producing an image of a two dimensional distribution (usually of some physical property) from estimates of its line integrals along a finite number of lines of known locations".

CT numbers from the projection data is obtained using this method. A mathematical formula for image reconstruction was given by radon. For its evaluation, an efficient algorithm is needed. There has been a lot of activity in the past years to

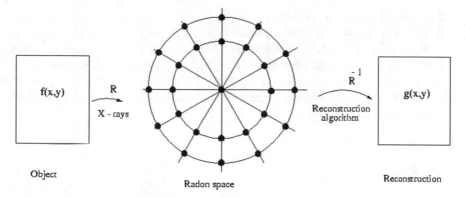

Fig. 6 Computing inverse of the Radon transform

find algorithms that are fast when implemented on a computer and which produce acceptable reconstructions despite the finite and inaccurate nature of the projection data. Reconstruction algorithms are chiefly categorized into two basic groups:

(a)   Transform methods and
(b)   Series expansion methods.

Convolution back projection (CBP) is one such algorithm coming under former category and is used most of the times for medical and NDT applications. Filtering of projection data is incorporated in CBP. There are many filter functions and the choice of which is dependent on user. Different filter functions result in different reconstructions for the same set of projection data.

3   Results and Discussions

3.1   First Kanpur Error Theorem (KT-1)

The projection data is not band-limited because the objects being reconstructed usually have a finite support. However, the reconstruction approximation obtained is band-limited due to a finite Fourier cut-off frequency, incorporated for computational feasibility. Hence, the inherent error arises from this band-limiting aspect. This error can be predicted with the help of First Kanpur theorem. It is local by nature and is an excellent tool for quantification of reconstruction. It shows point-wise error. Shown in Maisl et al. [8] is that if N_{max} represents the maximum value of grey level in reconstruction then the overall error is directly proportional to $1/N_{max}$. In the simplified form, this theorem says that the overall error ($1/N_{max}$) in reconstruction is directly proportional to the second order partial derivative of filter function at Fourier space origin $W''(0)$, The KT-I theorem is local in nature, hence, deals with every pixel to pixel error. *This theorem provides a very good idea of overall error incurred even if original cross section is not known, which is also the case in all real-life situations.*

Two samples of Palash and Rosewood of 1 cm × 1 cm × 1 cm are scanned using CT-Mini micro-CT scanner. Further, two slices both of Palash and Rosewood are selected randomly for validation of experiment. For each slice, the image reconstruction is done with the help of five filters, namely, Hann, Hamming, Cosine, Shepp-Logan, and Ram-Lac.

3.2   *Palash*

(1)   **Slice 692**

Figure 7a–f shows original and reconstructed images using Hann, Hamming, Cosine, Shepp-Logan, and Ram-Lac filters, respectively. Others parameters used are same for all reconstructed images, e.g., dimensions of mesh, interpolation, span, etc. It can be seen that, for Palash, a bigger central hole is present and fibers are distributed about it unsymmetrically. Further, it can be observed that gray level of reconstructed images changes with different filters.

Table 1 shows N_{max}, i.e., maximum value of gray level for the reconstructed images using different filters. For Hann, it is 260.9750, for Hamming it is 263.2942, for Cosine it is 276.2953, for Shepp-Logan it is 285.4775, and Ram-Lac it is 292.9257.

Table 2 gives values of $W''(0)$ for different filters used in image reconstruction. The window function $W(\alpha)$ is related to filter parameter α as

$$W(\alpha) = \alpha + (1 - \alpha) \sin c(\alpha/1 - \alpha) \tag{1}$$

Hence, $W''(0)$ can be found for each filter used.

Figure 8 shows the KT plot of $1/N_{max}$ versus $W''(0)$. The x axis represents $W''(0)$ and y axis represents $1/N_{max}$. The plotted points are very close to fitted straight line. Table 3 provides the slope and intercept of the fitted straight line which are equal to 0.00082 and 0.0034, respectively. The resultant "Goodness of Fit" comes out to be 99.18.

For Palash slice 692, slope = 0.00082.

Hence, its Goodness of Fit = 100 * (1 − 0.00082) = 99.18.

(2)   **Slice 912**

Figure 9a–f shows original and reconstructed images using Hann, Hamming, Cosine, Shepp-Logan, and Ram-Lac filters, respectively. Others parameters used are same for all reconstructed images, e.g., dimensions of mesh, interpolation, span, etc. Again for this slice of Palash also, it can be seen that a bigger central hole is present and fibers are distributed about it unsymmetrically. Further, it can be observed that gray level of reconstructed images changes with different filters.

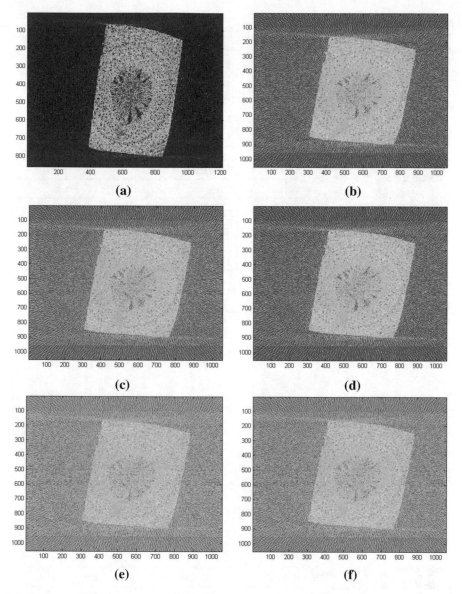

Fig. 7 Original and reconstructed images of Palash slice 692 **a** Original **b** Hann **c** Hamming **d** Cosine **e** Shepp-Logan **f** Ram-Lak

Table 4 shows N_{max}, i.e., maximum value of gray level for the reconstructed images using different filters. For Hann, it is 268.2430, for Hamming it is 270.3833, for Cosine it is 282.5012, for Shepp-Logan it is 298.7857, and Ram-Lac it is 310.1384. Table 5 gives values of $W''(0)$ for different filters used in image reconstruction. It remains same as that of Table 2.

Table 1 $1/N_{max}$ values for reconstructed images using different filters

S. No.	Filter used	N_{max}	$1/N_{max}$
1	Hann	260.9750	0.0038
2	Hamming	263.2942	0.0038
3	Cosine	276.2953	0.0036
4	Shepp-Logan	285.4775	0.0035
5	Ram Lak	292.9257	0.0034

Table 2 Values of $W''(0)$ for different filters

S. No.	Filter used	α	$W''(0)$
1	Hann	0.50	0.50
2	Hamming	0.54	0.46
3	Cosine	0.75	0.25
4	Shepp-Logan	0.91	0.09
5	Ram-Lak	0.99	0.01

Fig. 8 KT plot for Palash slice 692

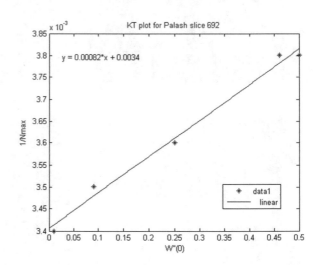

Table 3 Slope and intercept of the KT1 plot for Palash slice 692

S. No.	Slope	Intercept
1	0.00082	0.0034

Figure 10 shows the KT plot of $1/N_{max}$ versus $W''(0)$. The x axis represents $W''(0)$, and y axis represents $1/N_{max}$. The plotted points are very close to fitted straight line. Table 6 provides the slope and intercept of the fitted straight line which are equal to 0.001 and 0.0032, respectively. The resultant "Goodness of Fit" comes out to be 99.9.

For Palash slice 912, slope = 0.001.

Fig. 9 Original and reconstructed images of Palash slice 912 **a** Original **b** Hann **c** Hamming **d** Cosine **e** Shepp-Logan **f** Ram-Lak

Hence, its Goodness of Fit $= 100*(1 - 0.001) = 99.9$.

Table 4 $1/N_{max}$ values for reconstructed images using different filters

S. No.	Filter used	N_{max}	$1/N_{max}$
1	Hann	268.2430	0.0037
2	Hamming	270.3833	0.0037
3	Cosine	282.5012	0.0035
4	Shepp-Logan	298.7857	0.0033
5	Ram Lak	310.1384	0.0032

Table 5 Values of $W''(0)$ for different filters

S. No.	Filter used	α	$W''(0)$
1	Hann	0.50	0.50
2	Hamming	0.54	0.46
3	Cosine	0.75	0.25
4	Shepp-Logan	0.91	0.09
5	Ram-Lak	0.99	0.01

Fig. 10 KT plot for Palash slice 912

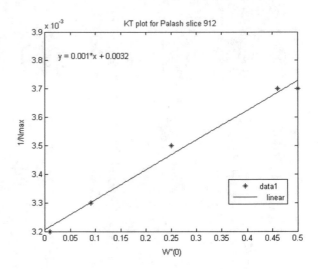

Table 6 Slope and intercept of the KT1 plot for Palash slice 912

S. No.	Slope	Intercept
1	0.001	0.0032

3.3 Rosewood

(1) Slice 448

Figure 11a–f shows original and reconstructed images using Hann, Hamming, Cosine, Shepp-Logan, and Ram-Lac filters, respectively. Others parameters used are same for all reconstructed images, e.g., dimensions of mesh, interpolation, span, etc. For Rosewood, it can be seen that a small central hole is present and fibers are distributed about it symmetrically. Further, it can be observed that gray level of reconstructed images changes with different filters.

Fig. 11 Original and reconstructed images of Rosewood slice 448 **a** Original **b** Hann **c** Hamming **d** Cosine **e** Shepp-Logan **f** Ram-Lak

Table 7 $1/N_{max}$ values for reconstructed images using different filters

S. No.	Filter used	N_{max}	$1/N_{max}$
1	Hann	206.4679	0.0048
2	Hamming	209.9287	0.0048
3	Cosine	223.1424	0.0045
4	Shepp-Logan	240.6033	0.0042
5	Ram-Lak	249.7281	0.0040

Table 8 Values of $W''(0)$ for different filters

S. No.	Filter used	α	$W''(0)$
1	Hann	0.50	0.50
2	Hamming	0.54	0.46
3	Cosine	0.75	0.25
4	Shepp-Logan	0.91	0.09
5	Ram-Lak	0.99	0.01

Table 7 shows N_{max}, i.e., maximum value of gray level for the reconstructed images using different filters. For Hann, it is 268.2430, for Hamming it is 270.3833, for Cosine it is 282.5012, for Shepp-Logan it is 298.7857 and Ram-Lac it is 310.1384. Table 8 gives values of $W''(0)$ for different filters used in image reconstruction. It remains same as that of Table 2.

Figure 12 shows the KT plot of $1/N_{max}$ versus $W''(0)$. The x axis represents $W''(0)$, and y axis represents $1/N_{max}$. The plotted points are very close to fitted straight line. Table 9 provides the slope and intercept of the fitted straight line which are equal to 0.001 and 0.0032, respectively. The resultant "Goodness of Fit" comes out to be 99.9.

Fig. 12 KT plot for Rosewood slice 448

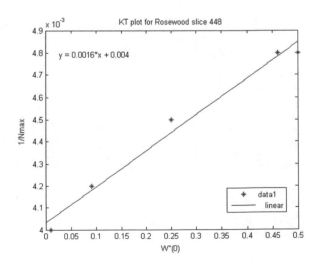

Table 9 Slope and intercept of the KT1 plot for Rosewood slice 448	S. No.	Slope	Intercept
	1	0.0016	0.004

For Rosewood slice 448, slope $= 0.0016$.

Hence, its Goodness of Fit $= 100 * (1 - 0.0016) = 99.84$.

(2) Slice 591

Figure 13a–f shows original and reconstructed images using Hann, Hamming, Cosine, Shepp-Logan, and Ram-Lac filters, respectively. Others parameters used are same for all reconstructed images, e.g., dimensions of mesh, interpolation, span, etc. Again, for this Rosewood also, it can be seen that a small central hole is present and fibers are distributed about it symmetrically. Further, it can be observed that gray level of reconstructed images changes with different filters.

Table 10 shows N_{max}, i.e., maximum value of gray level for the reconstructed images using different filters. For Hann, it is 207.4564, for Hamming it is 209.7615, for Cosine it is 222.0279, for Shepp-Logan it is 231.5470, and Ram-Lac it is 236.3579. Table 11 gives values of $W''(0)$ for different filters used in image reconstruction. It remains same as that of Table 2.

Figure 14 shows the KT plot of $1/N_{max}$ versus $W''(0)$. The x axis represents $W''(0)$, and y axis represents $1/N_{max}$. The plotted points are very close to fitted straight line. Table 12 provides the slope and intercept of the fitted straight line which are equal to 0.0013 and 0.0042, respectively. The resultant "Goodness of Fit" comes out to be 99.87.

For Rosewood slice 591, slope $= 0.0013$.

Hence, its Goodness of Fit $= 100 * (1 - 0.0013) = 99.87$.

4 Conclusion

A scanning experiment is performed on samples of Palash and Rosewood of 1 cm $\times$ 1 cm $\times$ 1 cm each using CT-Mini micro-CT scanner, and a corresponding dataset is obtained. The dataset, also called the projection data, comprises 180 scans corresponding to 180° rotation of the object (i.e., 1 scan per degree of rotation) within the 'Field of View' of Source-detector system. It is actually $\ln[I_{in}/I_{out}]$, which theoretically should be equal to radon transform of object function 'f', i.e., $\int f(x, y) \mathrm{d}l$.

This dataset is used in a program of image reconstruction, and an image is reconstructed. We call this as 'original-image'. This 'original image' has been used as the object itself. *Kanpur theorem*-1 could not be applied on experimental dataset itself, and $1/N_{max}$ versus $W''(0)$ could not be plotted because it was not known if the dataset is the outcome of an experiment complying a scientific law (here *Lambert–Beer* law) or not. It might have been corrupted by an experimental error, or some

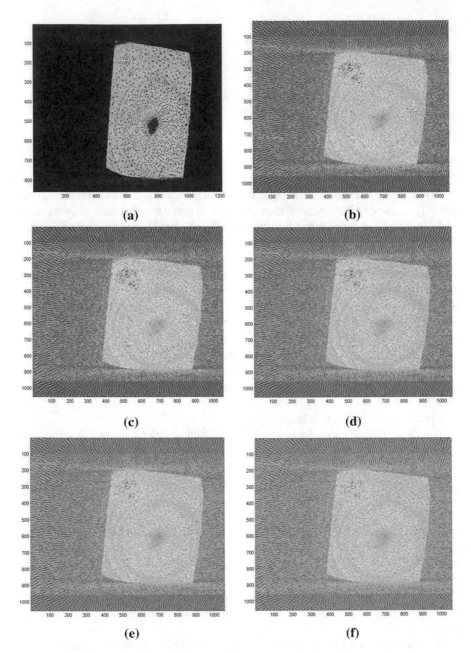

Fig. 13 Original and reconstructed images of Rosewood slice 591 **a** Original **b** Hann **c** Hamming **d** Cosine **e** Shepp-Logan **f** Ram-Lak

Table 10 $1/N_{max}$ values for reconstructed images using different filters

S. No.	Filter used	N_{max}	$1/N_{max}$
1	Hann	207.4564	0.0048
2	Hamming	209.7615	0.0048
3	Cosine	222.0279	0.0045
4	Shepp-Logan	231.5470	0.0043
5	Ram-Lak	236.3579	0.0042

Table 11 Values of $W''(0)$ for different filters

S. No.	Filter used	α	$W''(0)$
1	Hann	0.50	0.50
2	Hamming	0.54	0.46
3	Cosine	0.75	0.25
4	Shepp-Logan	0.91	0.09
5	Ram-Lak	0.99	0.01

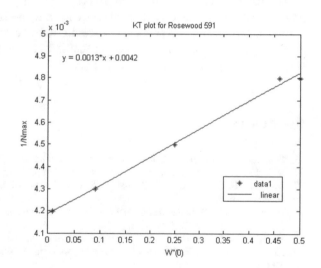

Fig. 14 KT plot for Rosewood slice 591

Table 12 Slope and intercept of the KT1 plot for Rosewood slice 591

S. No.	Slope	Intercept
1	0.0013	0.0042

intentional/unintentional modification had affected it. The scanner had just given $\ln[I_{in}/I_{out}]$, which we could not assume to be equal to $\int f(x, y)dl$ without validating the experiment.

On considering the 'original image' as an object itself, hardly an error of 3% could be introduced. Hence, it could be safely considered to be an object with a small inherent error. Now, using MATLAB, the radon transform of this original image, i.e., $\int f(x, y)\mathrm{d}l$ is done, and hence a new dataset gets generated. If there is no experimental error, then this new dataset would be approximately equal to the dataset obtained via experiment.

Now, the Fourier transform of the new dataset is taken, five filters are applied one by one, and two-dimensional inverse Fourier transform is taken to generate five reconstructed images finally. For each image, N_{max} is calculated, and a plot of $1/N_{max}$ (which is proportional to error) versus second derivative of filter function at origin, i.e., $W''(0)$ is drawn with the help of MATLAB. If the reconstructed image only has inherent errors (propagated by considering original image as an object and arising due to use of filters), then the plots should have points very close to the fitted line and occurring at fixed spacing from it. But if there are experimental errors, then the filters can behave arbitrarily on their edges, and the plots will have points that are randomly spaced from the line. Hence, with this process, one can judge the quality of image and conclude if the experiment performed is free of errors or not. It should also be noted that in entire process, we are assuming discretization error to be almost negligible.

The most important benefit of this work is that it provides a precise method of predicting the quality of reconstructed image in computerized tomography, and hence one can determine if the experiment is required to be performed again or not. Further on an application note, this method can facilitate comparison of inner structure of two objects very easily and accurately.

References

1. Natterer F (1986) The mathematics of computerized tomography. Wiley, New York
2. Munshi P (1992) Error analysis of tomographic filters I: theory. NDT&E Int 25(4/5):191
3. Munshi P, Rathore RKS, Ram KS, Kalra MS (1991) Error estimates for Tomographic inversion. Inverse Prob 7:399
4. Herman GT (1980) Image reconstruction from projections: the fundamentals of computerized tomography. Academic, New York
5. Radon J (1971) Uber die Bestimmung von Funktionen durch ihre Integralwerte langs gewisser Maanigfaltigkeiten. Berichte Sachsische Akademie der Wissenschaften Leipzig, Math-Phys Kl 69:262
6. Munshi P, Rathore RKS, Vijay S (1994) A numerical investigation of an inverse theorem for computerized tomography. Eur J Non-destr Test 3:104
7. Razdan M, Kumar A, Munshi P (2006) Second level KT-1 signature of CT scanned medical images. Int J Tomogr Stat 4:20
8. Munshi P, Maisel M, Reiter H (1997) Experimental aspects of the approximate error formulae for tomographic reconstruction. Mater Eval 55(2):188
9. Munshi P (1988) Error estimates for the convolution back projection algorithm in computerized tomography. PhD Thesis, IIT Kanpur
10. Munshi P, Maisl M, Reter H (1995) Experimental study of tomographic contrast resolution. Nucl Instrum Methods Phys Res B95:402
11. Munshi P, Singh SP (1998) Hamming signature of three composite specimens. Res Nondestr Eval 10:109
12. Razdan M, Jauhari RK, Munshi P (2007) Analysis of pre and post-treatment CT images using KT-1 and fractal dimension. Trans Am Nucl Soc 346

Software Fault Prediction Using Deep Neural Networks

Y. Mohana Ramya, K. Deepthi, A. Vamsai, A. Juhi Sai, Neeraj Sharma, and B. Ramachandra Reddy

1 Introduction

In the software engineering discipline, many prediction methods are employed including predictive cost prediction, prediction of consistency, provision of safety, predictions of reuse, predictions of faults, and prevention of effort. Dealing with this type of fault is a significant problem in the software development process. However, the aforementioned approaches are still at the beginning of the project, and more analysis needs to be conducted to achieve robustness [1].

Software fault prediction is by far the most common area of study in these prediction methods with several research centres launching new ventures [2]. To identify which models are defective, software metrics and defect data are used. To report the error binary form is used, if the module is faulty that it is marked as 0 else 1. Software faults are programming errors that cause your system to function differently from your intended conduct. In any stage of software, development, defects may be introduced [3]. They can also be programmed or coded or from outside environments. Some software defects can cause anything, from a simple miscalculation to a whole device failure according to the nature of the defects. According to the study survey and the elimination of software faults, this is around 50% of the overall project budget. So it will save a great deal of software development expense to identify and repair faults as soon as possible [4]. It helps to define the susceptibility of fault in software modules for the previous test process using some of the underlying software device properties. It, therefore, assists in the effective and cautious allocation of test resources.

Y. Mohana Ramya · K. Deepthi · A. Vamsai · A. Juhi Sai · N. Sharma · B. Ramachandra Reddy (✉)
Department of Computer Science and Engineering, SRM University, Amaravati, Andhra Pradesh, India
e-mail: brreddy@iiitdmj.ac.in

© The Author(s), under exclusive license to Springer Nature Singapore Pte Ltd. 2023
K. Kumar Singh et al. (eds.), *Machine Vision and Augmented Intelligence*, Lecture Notes in Electrical Engineering 1007, https://doi.org/10.1007/978-981-99-0189-0_18

Abundant research has been done in the past to construct and detect the problematic modules in software systems assess fault prediction models. To detect software system defects, many statistical and machine learning techniques have been developed and studied [5, 6]. These techniques include logistic regression, decision tree, random forest, KNN algorithm, and SVM [1–3, 7]. Despite their contributions, there are still problems preventing their widespread application in practice. Most of the past software fault prediction researches predict the failure susceptibility of software sub-modules from two aspects: defect and non-defect [8]. There are numerous disagreements over this binary class classification. Even though the projected models performed well, the interpretation of the findings, as well as the idea and identification of the number of defects per module, are difficult to put into the right usability perspective.

As today's software development is so complex and has such a large dataset, early fault prediction is essential. One-third of software development flaws should be recognised early to reduce rework. It is vital to correct the similarities between the flaws of newly developed software and those of previously established software. There are numerous software development approaches available. Problem descriptions, requirements, data collecting, and development are all steps in the software process. Testing is used to check and validate the developed software once it has been developed. Manual and automated testing are also possible. This paper includes the analysis of various defect prediction methods. The study is to give a process for locating flaws early on in order to reduce rework from the users perspective.

Software fault forecasting attempts to predict fault-prone programming modules by utilising certain hidden aspects of the product structure. It is intended to help them streamline their product quality assurance efforts, as well as advance their product fault detection, proofing, and expulsion efforts and costs. Programming problem forecasting is performed by constructing expectation models for a known mission utilising venture attributes filled with faulty data and created model to predict faults for an unknown initiative. We conducted a thorough examination of the existing machine fault prediction techniques and found the best accuracy based on our findings.

The tech industry is growing rapidly, and software is becoming more and more complex. These sophisticated software systems are not only impossible to debug, but they also leave people scratching their heads when it comes to modules classified as faulty or non-faulty. The classification method was used early on in the software development process. Instead of classifying errors as types, we try to use error estimates in the module. To estimate the number of faults in a dataset, we used a variety of algorithms like linear regression, random forest, SVM, DNN, etc., and other fault prediction techniques. The key aim is to find the faults in specific modules with a high degree of prediction such that possible debugging can be simplified in future.

The rest of the work is structured as follows. Section 2 summarises some related work on software failure prediction using different machine learning models. Section 3 briefly describes the proposed deep neural network model for predicting software failures. Section 4 presents the experimental data and conclusions in Sect. 5.

2 Related Work

In recent years, there has been an emotional uptick in interest in search-based software engineering, a method of dealing with software engineering (SE) that employs search-based optimization equations to solve SE problems. SBSE has been linked to problems in the SE life cycle, from requirements and mission requirements to maintenance and reengineering. The solution is attractive because it provides a variety of flexible mechanised and semi-robotised arrangements in situations encapsulated by large dynamic problem spaces with many competing and conflicting goals. This thesis examines and categorises writing on SBSE. This research project identifies similarities and relations between the approaches and the implementations of which they are linked, as well as gaps in the writing and roads for further investigation. Defect assumption on new projects or activities with little authentic data is an intriguing topic in programming development. This is large because gathering surrender data to mark a dataset for planning an expectation illustrates is difficult. Cross-venture imperfection forecasting (CPDP) has attempted to solve this problem by reusing expectation models established by various undertakings with sufficient reported data. However, because of the different conveyances among datasets, CPDP does not always produce a solid forecast display. Methodologies for imperfection assumption on unlabelled datasets have also sought to resolve the problem by receiving unsupervised adapting, but this has one significant drawback: it requires manual effort. In this study, they propose two new methodologies, CLA and CLAMI, that show the ability to predict deformity on unlabelled datasets in a robotised manner without the need for manual labour. The CLA and CLAMI methods are based on the idea of labelling an unlabelled dataset using the size of metric qualities. The CLAMI method generated positive forecast exhibitions of 0.636 and 0.723 in normal and AUC and f-measures that are equivalent to those of deformity expectation in light of administered learning in this exact investigation on seven open-source extensions. According to the National Institute of Standards and Technology, goods fraud charges the US economy $60 billion per year. It's worth noting that identifying and following these deformities has a measurable impact on programming dependability.

SQA is a method of tracking and optimising the process of software development in order to produce the best software at the lowest possible price. Examples include formal security visual inspection, code overviews, software monitoring, and software error prediction. By predicting the failure of software components in advance, software fault prediction aims to make the most efficient and effective use of available SQA resources. The ability of software fault prediction (SFP) to detect flawed software components early in the deployment entire lifecycle has received over most recent twenty years. Previous predictive model experiments used a variety of prediction methods to estimate the SFP units. These studies' findings revealed that the algorithm's potentials are limited, its reliability in predicting programme errors. The fault-prediction accuracy of strategies was noticed to be marginally lower, varying from 70 to 85%, with such a significant level of misclassification. A major issue in the context of SFP is the lack of appropriate performance tools to assess the capability of SFP models. Another source of worry is the disproportionate distribution of faults in machine error datasets, which could result in learning disruption. Furthermore, a few other issues, like the programme parameters being used in fault/defect prediction models. The software project dataset repositories, including NASA Metrics Data Program1 and PROMISE Data Repository2, have recently become public [9]. The creation of these libraries has stimulated further research and the creation of new applications.

In this paper, we investigate various aspects of the SFP models and evaluate their impact on model performance. Kamei and Shihab [10] published recent research on SFP, provided a brief description of SFP, its components, and addressed some of the field's achievements. In contrast, the authors focuses on the various aspects of the software fault prediction mechanism. We describe and evaluate the various events that occur during the software fault prediction process, as well as their impact on the fault prediction accuracy. The authors look at the recorded works that are relevant to these operations, such as software measurements, fault prediction methods, data quality issues, and assessment measures. There has been statistical analysis presented.

Early detection of flaws could end in timely correction and delivery of maintainable software. Within the literature, there are various computer code metrics. These software metrics and fault knowledge are accustomed build models for classifying faulty modules early within the software process. SFP is accomplished by categorising modules/classes as fault prone or not fault prone. Within the early stages of software development, software practitioners will then focus out there testing resources on the fault-prone areas of the software. For example, if only 30% of the evaluation resources are available, knowing the weak areas will help the tester focus the remaining resources on fixing classes/modules that are more prone to bugs. As a result, cost-effective, high-quality, and maintainable software can be produced within time and budget constraints. Soft computing techniques are well suited for practical problems that require the extraction of useful information from complex and difficult-to-solve problems in a short period of time. You can tolerate inaccurate, partially incorrect, or uncertain data. Machine learning technology is an important part of soft computing technology.

3   Proposed Method

Previous software metrics and failure data are used in software fault prediction methods to forecast fault-prone modules for the next release of the software. If an error is detected during machine or field testing, the fault data for that module is set to 1, otherwise, it is set to 0. The aim of software fault prediction is to predict fault-prone software modules based on the software project's underpinning properties. It's usually done by creating a prediction model. Detection of defective modules at an early stage can be beneficial in streamlining efforts implemented in later stages of software process.

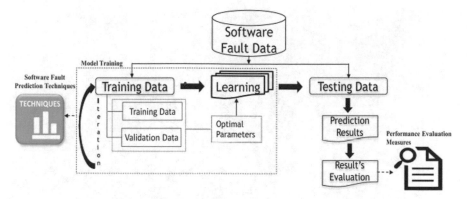

Fig. 1 Software fault prediction process [3]

The software fault prediction mechanism is depicted in the diagram. Software fault dataset, prediction methods, and performance assessment steps are three essential components of the SFP process, as shown in Fig. 1.

3.1 Deep Neural Networks (DNN)

Deep learning is a subfield of machine learning that deals with artificial neural networks, which are algorithms inspired by the structure and operation of the brain. Deep neural networks have recently emerged as the go-to solution for a wide range of computer vision issues.

Information processing and remote networking nodes in biological systems inspired artificial neural networks (ANNs) [8]. ANNs vary from biological brains in a number of ways. In particular, neural networks are static and abstract, while most living organisms' biological brains are complex (plastic) and analogue.

Following that, values of various software metrics are extracted as independent variables, with the necessary fault information in relation to fault prediction acting as the dependent variable.

Fault prediction models are typically construct using statistical and ML techniques. Finally, different performance assessment metrics are accuracy, precision, recall, and AUC are used to assess model's performance.

Furthermore, to a brief discussion of the four components of software fault prediction listed above, the following sections include comprehensive reviews of the various published works on each of these components. Here in our case, input is based on different datasets, there are three hidden layers and two outputs (Fig. 2).

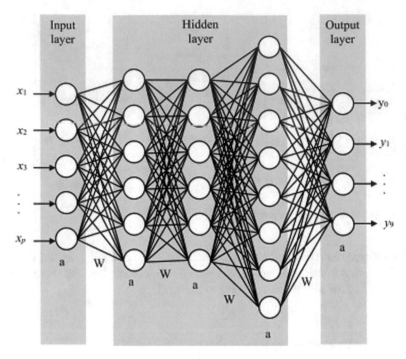

Fig. 2 Architecture of deep neural networks

3.2 Dataset

The software fault dataset description is presented in Table 1 [9]. We have used the following software fault data to test the proposed model.

Table 1 Data set

S. No.	Dataset	Classes	Fault classes	Percentage of faulty classes (%)
1	Tomcat	858	77	9
2	prop-6	660	66	10
3	Xerces	588	437	74
4	Xalan	909	898	98
5	Jedit	492	11	2.5

Table 2 Accuracy of different datasets using different ML algorithms

S. No.	Dataset	LR	SVM	DT	RF	DNN
1	Tomcat	89.093	89.922	86.046	89.922	91.03
2	prop-6	89.09	92.424	83.636	87.373	90.00
3	Xerces	91.156	88.135	85.714	93.22	92.86
4	Xalan	98.245	98.901	97.807	99.633	99.67
5	Jedit	97.18	97.9729	95.121	97.9729	97.76

3.3 Performance Measures

To compare software defect prediction, we need some meaningful performance measurements. The proposed model is trained with 90% of the data, with the remaining data being used for testing. We employed accuracy in performance measurement in this approach.

$$\text{Accuracy} = \text{Number of correction predictions/Total number of predictions} \quad (1)$$

4 Experimental Setup and Result Analysis

The proposed model is trained and evaluated for software fault prediction using three benchmark datasets: Tomcat, Prop, Xerces, Xalan, and Jedit [9]. Our suggested DNN is compared to logistic regression [11], decision tree, SVM [12], and random forest [3].

We chose three hidden layers for the DNN model, each of which contains 15 neurons. Table 2 and Fig. 3 demonstrate the results of the DNN model and machine learning models prediction for Tomcat, Prop, Xerces, Xalan, and Jedit. It has been determined that deep neural network modelling outperforms logistic regression, decision tree, SVM, and random forest approaches. For all datasets, linear regression performs worse than other methods. The DNN model outperforms alternative classical growth models, as evidenced by the preceding results and discussion.

5 Conclusion

A deep neural networks model technique with a hidden layer of artificial neural networks for software defect prediction is proposed in this paper. From the above analysis, accuracy is higher in the deep neural networks than the basic machine learning algorithms. We used generative deep learning models in the defect prediction process. These models achieve higher accuracy than the others, as shown by our

Fig. 3 Performance of
machine learning models and
deep neural network models

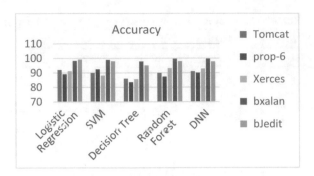

experimental findings. Although the results obtained for some datasets are remarkable. DNN is more accurate than others because it has layer architecture and connects input variable and output variables.

References

1. Catal C, Diri B (2009) A systematic review of software fault prediction studies. Expert Syst Appl 36(4):7346–7354
2. Malhotra R (2015) A systematic review of machine learning techniques for software fault prediction. Appl Soft Comput 27:504–518
3. Rathore SS, Kumar S (2019) A study on software fault prediction techniques. Artif Intell Rev 51(2):255–327
4. Song Q, Jia Z, Shepperd M, Ying S, Liu J (2010) A general software defect-proneness prediction framework. IEEE Trans Softw Eng 37(3):356–370
5. Pandey SK, Mishra RB, Tripathi AK (2021) Machine learning based methods for software fault prediction: a survey. Expert Syst Appl 172:114595
6. Sharma D, Chandra P (2019) Software fault prediction using machine-learning techniques. In: Proceedings of smart computing and informatics. Springer, Singapore, pp 541–549
7. Elish KO, Elish MO (2008) Predicting defect-prone software modules using support vector machines. J Syst Softw 81(5):649–660
8. Xiao H, Cao M, Peng R (2020) Artificial neural network based software fault detection and correction prediction models considering testing effort. Appl Soft Comput 94:106491
9. Ferenc R, Tóth Z, Ladányi G, Siket I, Gyimóthy T (2018) A public unified bug dataset for java. In: proceedings of the 14th international conference on predictive models and data analytics in software engineering, pp 12–21
10. Kamei Y, Shihab E (2016) Defect prediction: accomplishments and future challenges. In: 2016 IEEE 23rd international conference on software analysis, evolution, and reengineering (SANER), vol 5, pp 33–45
11. Gao K, Khoshgoftaar TM, Wang H, Seliya N (2011) Choosing software metrics for defect prediction: an investigation on feature selection techniques. Softw: Pract Exp 41(5):579–606
12. Erturk E, Sezer EA (2015) A comparison of some soft computing methods for software fault prediction. Expert Syst Appl 42(4):1872–1879

A Hybrid and Multi-objective Approach for Data Leak and Tamper Detection in Healthcare Cloud Data

Saptarshi Roychowdhury and Binod Kumar Singh

1 Introduction

In this modern digitization era, cloud computing is becoming one of the trusted and commonly used computing technology as it provides the availability of in-demand resources as and when they are required [1]. A huge shift can be observed in terms of usage techniques opted by the users in the different sectors of our daily life. This shift will become more prominent if we compare the previous and post COVID-19 era in context of our daily lifestyle. The changes are becoming the new part of our daily life accompanied with modern digital world aids. Education, research, IT infrastructure, healthcare, agriculture, and all other inevitable areas are continuously importing the trending computing techniques like cloud computing, IoT, blockchain, etc. Among these areas healthcare is one of the most vital parts of our daily life that too in a current worldwide pandemic crisis. It has been proven that the deployment of the cloud infrastructure has been time and cost effective with the maximum utilization of the available resources [2]. Cloud computing is the technology which has hugely transformed the healthcare sector and helped it to become the e-healthcare by providing centralized and distributed access spaces for all the parties involved in a healthcare system [3]. In the context of the e-healthcare, the electronic health record EHR) is considered as the main property of the e-healthcare system. The EHR is mostly related with the patients' information and thus required to be secured. The integrity, authenticity and non-repudiation should be maintained for all the EHRs in an e-healthcare system [4]. Because misplacement of the patients' digital records can let to

S. Roychowdhury (✉) · B. K. Singh
Department of Computer Science and Engineering, National Institute of Technology, Jamshedpur, Jharkhand, India
e-mail: sap.ratul@gmail.com

B. K. Singh
e-mail: bksingh.cse@nitjsr.ac.in

© The Author(s), under exclusive license to Springer Nature Singapore Pte Ltd. 2023
K. Kumar Singh et al. (eds.), *Machine Vision and Augmented Intelligence*, Lecture Notes in Electrical Engineering 1007, https://doi.org/10.1007/978-981-99-0189-0_19

(i)   Harm the social reputation of the patient.
(ii)   Wrong diagnosis of the disease.
(iii) Affect the healthcare organizations in business perspective.

Any presence of the possibility of confidentiality violation is a major area of concern for the e-healthcare systems [5]. The researchers have taken this issue seriously and proposed a lot of good viable solutions to encounter the security issues of the EHR. Those solutions are mostly proposing different encryption techniques [6] and privacy preservation techniques like LSB-based watermarking. But, it is observed that the security professionals feel helpless if the attack comes from a malicious insider in the cloud-based e-healthcare system.

In this research work, we have examined the existing methods to identify the malicious insider and checked the shortcomings of those methods. We have also observed that the LSB-based watermarking method is one of the most popular techniques among them for identity preservation of the hostile insider. It is also observed that these techniques alone are not performing as efficiently as required but can be more beneficial if combined with any of the effective encryption techniques. While making combination of any two or more techniques, it will obviously increase the complexity of the system. We have also taken care of that in this proposed method by keeping the system energy efficient as possible.

2 Related Works

There are wide range of research works have been done to strengthen the security of data in cloud environment. Some of them fully concentrate on the security of EHRs in the cloud-based healthcare systems. We mention some of those relevant research works here.

The authors in [7] have done a detailed description on every component of a cloud environment. They have identified the possible area of vulnerability in the cloud architecture by examining the possible attacks and threats for the components of cloud environment. This work gives us a robust idea on the possible security threats in any cloud environment, which is very helpful in building a secure cloud-based environment. They have also listed the modern set of solutions for the traditional attacks from the inside and outside of the cloud environment. While concluding, they have also defined the area of concern for security as the open research area.

The transformation of healthcare into e-healthcare is discussed by the authors of [8]. They have shown how the latest technologies like cloud computing, Internet of Things and fog computing are developing the traditional healthcare system into an e-healthcare system. The authors have examined the different ways to implement the e-healthcare system using those modern technologies. They have categorized the wide range of benefits of the e-healthcare systems and some possible area of concerns. They have identified the attacks and security threats as the biggest area of concern in implementing the e-healthcare system. A detailed discussion on the possible security threats has been done with the state-of-the art solutions have also examined by the authors. They have identified the open issues of attacks and threats which require some more robust solutions to make the e-healthcare system more secure.

In the survey work done in [9], the authors have examined how cloud computing has emerged as a beneficial technology for e-healthcare system. They have discussed the operational advancements done by adopting the cloud architecture concept in e-healthcare system. The challenges in implementing the e-healthcare system have also been categorized in this work. While they have identified the security concern as the prime challenge of the e-healthcare systems. A categorical discussion on the security threats of e-healthcare system can be found in this work and the present viable solutions have also been mentioned. This work helps to identify the advancement in the security of cloud-based e-healthcare system.

The authors in [10] have identified the possible insider attack in cloud environment. They have categorically presented a threat model and the possible insider attacks. Their proposed solution detects the insider attack in a multi-tenant cloud environment and can also locate the threat in the system.

In the detailed study [11], the authors have demonstrated the possible data leak problems due to insider attacks in cloud computing. A malicious insider can cause a large-scale damage to the cloud data, that has been discussed in this work. To categorize the possible solution to deal with malicious insider, they have done a case study on the 79 different cloud service providers of Australia and New Zealand.

In [12], the authors have identified the insider attack in the cloud-based e-healthcare system as the area of concern. To solve the issues, they have proposed a key-sharing encryption technique combined with LSB watermarking for protecting the medical images from insider attacks. In this work, the LSB watermarking has been done in the boundary region of the medical image data.

The authors in [13] have proposed an approach of data leakage detection in cloud computing environment. In their approach, they have combined the concept of encryption and LSB watermarking to identify the data leak. Here, the user details are being encrypted into a QR code and then watermarked into the original image. This watermarked information helps to identify the user who is responsible for the leak of the data.

In the work [14], the authors have provided a comparison between different encryption algorithms while considering the various metrices of comparison. They have identified the AES 128-bit encryption as the fastest and energy-efficient algorithm among them.

In [15], the authors have discussed the different characteristics of digital watermarking. They have identified the possible implementations of the digital watermarking approach. While discussing the characteristics, they have examined the watermark embedding and the extraction approaches carefully. The issues of digital watermarking techniques and their available standard solutions have also been categorized in this work.

The authors of [16] have identified the insider attack in healthcare cloud as the vital issue, as this can lead the false examination of the patients' health through the tampering of the medical reports. They have identified that neither encryption techniques nor the watermarking approach alone is sufficient to protect the healthcare cloud data from insider attack. Thus, they have proposed a hybrid approach to defend the insider attack by combining the cryptographic technique and the watermarking approach.

The authors in [17] have increased the probability of detecting the malicious client by allocation of data objects. To achieve their goal, they have distributed several data objects among the clients. They have shown that the fake objects have been useful to identify the malicious client by performing the similarity check between the clients' data and the leaked data.

3 Problem Definition

Our problem statement is to design and implement a system to identify the insider data leak source and to detect tampering in medical image data in cloud-based e-healthcare systems.

Our proposed model is hybrid in nature and multi-objective in outcome. We have made a fusion of AES 128-bit [18] encryption with Iterative Least Significant Bit (ILSB) watermarking to first encrypt and then embed the user's details into medical images while providing the access to those files to the authorized user. We have ensured that, in the proposed model, no user will be able to avoid these steps before accessing the medical images from healthcare cloud.

4 Proposed Methodology

In context with the observations from the previous work, we have developed a multi-objective and multi-layered mechanism for detecting the insider attack and to identify the tamper done in the medical images in healthcare cloud. If we consider any modern e-healthcare system, all the patients' EHRs are stored in a private cloud environment. Those EHRs include the medical images of various kind of tests and inspections. In this modern healthcare era, the medical images can be both in grayscale or in color format. While developing our system, we have considered that the medical images can both be in color or grayscale format, so that our system can identify all the insider attacks on different types of medical images in a healthcare cloud.

In any cloud-based e-healthcare environment, the medical images which are stored in a private cloud are only allowed to be accessed by the authorized users belongs to that organization. Several access control techniques have been proposed already by the researchers for secured access control in any private cloud. After getting the access to the private cloud, any authorized person will then be able to access the medical images which can simply be downloaded in the local system. Here arises the issue of a malicious insider, who can share that data to the outside of the organization. We can identify this data leak by watermarking any employee's ID in the accessed medical image data. As, we are working with the medical images, we have to make least possible pixel value modification as all the possible medical information should be kept unchanged in those medical images. Thus, LSB-based watermarking technique is used to embed the employee ID of the user with the accessed medical image. This will not make any visual changes in the medical image, and no problem will occur for further diagnosis.

We have examined that only using the LSB-based watermarking technique to embed the user's ID with the medical image will not be strong enough to identify any data leak. When the watermarked medical image is shared outside the organization, any watermark extractor program can be used to identify and tamper the watermarked information by LSB bit alteration which lead to non-identifying or miss-identifying the malicious intruder or insider. This issue is also taken into consideration in our proposed approach so that no meaningful information can be retrieved by using any watermark extractor program used by the attacker.

To nullify the issues discussed above, we have proposed a malicious insider detection model for healthcare cloud medical image data by combining the encryption technique with the LSB-based watermarking. In this approach, AES encryption algorithm is used to encrypt the employee ID of the logged-in user. That encrypted cipher is watermarked in the accessed medical image by using an Iterative LSB (ILSB) watermarking technique, where the cipher will be embedded iteratively and separated by a delimiter bit string. If any watermark extractor function is used on this watermarked medical image, a combination of cipher and the delimiter bit string can be extracted which is not a meaningful data for the attacker and will not resolute to the attacker that any watermarking has been done on the image.

Our proposed encrypted watermarking procedure (Fig. 1)

(i) *Read employee_id of the user from login details.*
(ii) *employee_id is encrypted using AES 128-bit encryption and generate emp_en_id as cypher.*

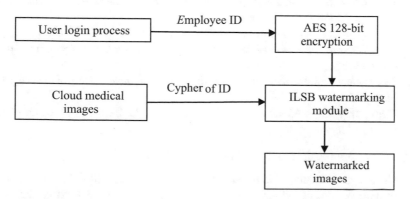

Fig. 1 Watermarking module

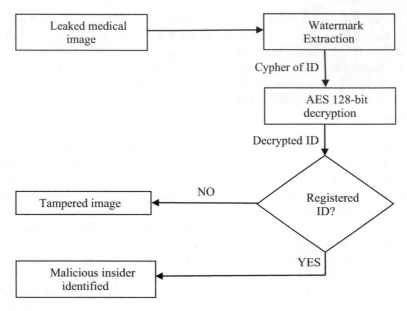

Fig. 2 Insider attack and tampering detection module

(iii) *Watermark information (water_string) is generated by concatenating emp_en_id and delimiter string.*
(iv) *The user accesses any medical image and initiates the process to store it in the local system.*
(v) *The binary converted water_string is watermarked using ILSB watermarking and the watermarked image (wat_image) is now stored in the user's local system.*

Our proposed insider attack and tampering detection procedure (Fig. 2)

(i) *The healthcare cloud admin receives the leaked medical image (wat_image) for identification of malicious insider.*
(ii) *Admin tracks down the LSB sequence from the watermarked image.*
(iii) *Admin uses the delimiter bit string to separate two or more consecutive cyphers (emp_en_id).*
(iv) *The cypher is then decrypted, and the malicious user's ID (employee_id) is identified.*
(v) *If no consecutive identical cyphers are found, the image is considered as a tampered image.*

Our proposed approach is divided into six separate modules

(i) User-Login module: This module is secured by the use of unique user ID and password, without which every login attempt would be denied to access the private cloud data.

(ii) AES 128-bit encryption module: Here, we have used the Electronic Code Book (ECB) of AES algorithm with 128-bit-sized encryption key. We have chosen ECB mode for having faster processing and ignored the shortcomings because that hasn't made any negative impact on our proposed methodology. As no key sharing is needed during any transmission, symmetric encryption algorithm like AES performs very fast and serves the purpose.

(iii) Watermarking module: This is considered as the central module of our proposed methodology. In this step the encrypted user id is watermarked in the least significant of each and every pixel of the medical image repeatedly.

(iv) Admin-login module: This module is also secured by the standard user id and password mechanism.

(v) Watermark extraction module: This module comes active if any data leak is occurred. The leaked medical image is given as the input into this module and the encrypted watermark is regained by processing the LSB bits of each and every pixel of the leaked image.

(vi) Insider attack or tampering detection module: This module either identifies the inside attacker or it can confirm tampering of the leaked medical image. If a correct employee id can be fetched by this module after watermark extraction, it identifies the malicious insider; otherwise, it will indicate as the image tampering.

From the literature review, it can be observed from the above set of modules that no one alone can fully identify the insider attack or medical image tampering. Thus, we propose the above combined approach to achieve our targeted objectives.

5 Experimental Results and Discussion

We have implemented our proposed ISLB watermarking to watermark color medical images mainly acquired from [19, 20] databases. Images with various resolutions, types, and sizes have been used to examine the accurate working of the algorithms. In our implementation using Python, we have taken a 12-character long employee ID and 4-character long delimiter, by concatenating which we got 128 bit of bit string which have been watermarked in the images of variety. As in the case of medical image, a small amount of distortion can result false diagnosis after human or machine inspection of those medical images, and we have checked for any visible distortion have been done in the images or not. The resulted watermarked images have showed no any distortion in it. As the part of preprocessing, the input medical images have been resized into 5 resolution categories as 2000×1000, 1000×800, 800×600, 500×300 and 500×200. We have also converted the JPEG image into PNG format to avoid any lossy compression-related unwanted effect which can remodify the LSB bits. Figure 3 demonstrates three sets of original and watermarked images belongs to three different classes of resolutions.

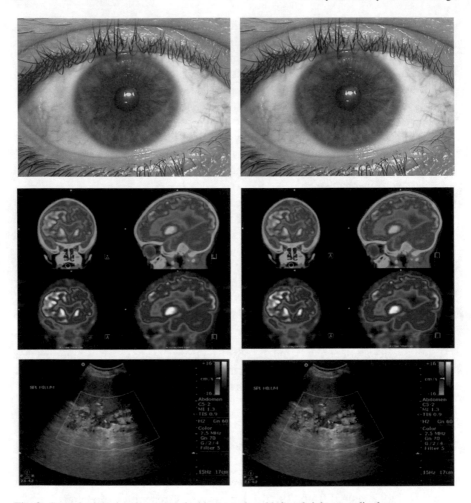

Fig. 3 Sets of original and watermarked images placed left and right accordingly

5.1 Objective I

We have examined all the watermarked images to extract the watermarked bit string and converted those into characters. Those character strings have been decrypted using AES 128-bit decryption algorithm, and the respective employee IDs have been accurately fetched. In this examination we have assumed the input watermarked images as the leaked medical images, and the results have been accurate to fetch the employee IDs watermarked into those images, which successfully have satisfied our first objective.

5.2   Objective II

The second objective of our proposed algorithm is to detect the tamper in the leaked medical images, if there is any. To examine the accurate working of our proposed algorithm in this respect, we have forcefully embedded some noise elements into our watermarked medical images. As the result of which the LSB bits have been modified, and our algorithm hasn't found any employee ID from the bit string, and thus, it has successfully identified that image as the tampered medical image. By implementing the algorithm in this way, we have seen that out proposed algorithm has also satisfied our second objective.

5.3   Watermarked Image Quality

Peak signal-to-noise ratio (PSNR) is the one of the largely accepted procedure to examine the quality of any processed image with respect to the original image. We have examined the quality of our watermarked image by finding out the PSNR value for every class of images. The PSNR is being defined by the Mean Square Error MSE for the two matrices. The following equation number 1 defines the MSE and equation number 2 defines the PSNR.

$$\text{MSE} = \frac{1}{rc} \sum_{i=0}^{r-1} \sum_{j=0}^{c-1} (I(i, j) - W(i, j)) \tag{1}$$

Here r is the number of rows, and i refers to index of rows of the image. c represents the number of columns, and j refers to index of columns of the image. I and W are representing the input image and watermarked image, respectively.

$$\text{PSNR} = 20 \log_{10}\left(\frac{\text{MIL}}{\sqrt{\text{MSE}}}\right) \tag{2}$$

Here, MIL represents the maximum intensity level for a pixel of the image.

We have calculated the PSNR using Python code, and the result shows that PSNR values lies over 80 dB. We have observed that the PSNR value has increased for the better resolution images. As a whole, we can confirm that our proposed ILSB algorithm hasn't done any visible distortion in the medical images and quality of those images has been maintained properly without any compromise. Table 1 shows the result of the PSNR calculation for all five separate class of images.

Table 1 PSNR calculation
results

Image resolution	PSNR for ILSB watermarking
2000 × 1000	94.52
1100 × 800	89.11
800 × 600	85.32
500 × 300	82.11
500 × 200	81.68

6   Conclusion and Recommendation

Our proposed hybrid and multi-objective approach by combining encryption and ILSB watermarking has performed accurately and achieved the given two objectives. As the watermarking is done in the spatial domain of a digital images, we have to perform a check for any possible quality degradation in the output image, and our proposed method has shown no visible deformation in the output watermarked images. This resolute the integrity of our proposed hybrid approach. Though we have used simplest version of the AES encryption and decryption algorithms, the shortcomings of the AES algorithm haven't put any effect in this approach as no key sharing has been done in the proposed method. In recent times the LSB watermarking remover methods have emerged as the limitation of the LSB based data hiding approaches. But, we have converted that shortcoming into a new way of identifying the tamper detection in the medical images stored in private cloud-based healthcare environment. This proposed approach has successfully watermarked the users ID into medical images stored in healthcare cloud and identifies the user who has leaked the information to the outside of the private cloud environment. It has also successfully identified the medical image as tampered if it has been. The experimental results show a strong support to the above verdicts.

If we consider the possible advancements in the proposed approach, we have some strong areas to examine and decide. Any machine learning-based classification of the region of interest and region of non-interest in the medical images will be helpful for the researchers to localize the best possible area of watermarking in the medical image. If we consider the modern-day medical images, they contain some texts in it and those texts are not the part of the diagnosis. The identifying of text area in the medical images and to use them as the area of watermarking can be a viable solution. We have implemented our approach by using the 1st LSB bits, but implementing the same methodology by hiding data in the 2nd or 3rd LSB bits can also be possible area of enhancement, but with the possible check for amount of degradation in the watermarked image.

References

1. Duipmans E, Pires DLF (2012) Business process management in the cloud: business process as a service (BPaaS). University of Twente
2. Mustapha AM, Arogundade OT, Vincent OR, Adeniran OJ, Chen X (2017) A model-based business process compliance management architecture for SMSE towards effective adoption of cloud computing. In: 2017 international conference on computing networking and informatics (ICCNI). IEEE, pp 1–6
3. Senft N, Everson J (2018) eHealth engagement as a response to negative healthcare experiences: cross-sectional survey analysis. J Med Internet Res 20(12):e11034
4. Ismail K, Ammar O (2021) Security and privacy of electronic health records: concerns and challenges. Egypt Inform J 22(2):177–183. ISSN: 1110-8665
5. Santos N, Gummadi KP, Rodrigues R (2009) Towards trusted cloud computing. HotCloud 9(9):3
6. Zhou Y, Li N, Tian Y, An D, Wang L (2020) Public key encryption with keyword search in cloud: a survey. Entropy 22:421
7. Tabrizchi H, Kuchaki Rafsanjani M (2020) A survey on security challenges in cloud computing: issues, threats, and solutions. J Supercomput 76:9493–9532
8. Dang LM, Piran MJ, Han D, Min K, Moon H (2019) A survey on internet of things and cloud computing for healthcare. Electronics 8:768
9. Yazan AI, Mohammad AO, Ahmed T (2019) eHealth cloud security challenges: a survey. J Healthc Eng 2019(article id 7516035):15 pp
10. Jing Z, Xudong F, Jin H, Yaqi G, Xiaoqing X, Qian Z (2020) CIADL: cloud insider attack detector and locator on multi-tenant network isolation: an OpenStack case study. J Ambient Intell Hum Comput 11:3473–3495
11. Edson MDS, Abid S (2021) Data loss prevention from a malicious insider. J Comput Inf Syst
12. Okikiola FM, Mustapha AM, Akinsola AF, Sokunbi MA (2020) A new framework for detecting insider attacks in cloud-based e-health care system. In: International conference in mathematics, computer engineering and computer science (ICMCECS), pp 1–6
13. Naik R, Gaonkar MN (2019) Data leakage detection in cloud using watermarking technique. In: International conference on computer communication and informatics (ICCCI), pp 1–6
14. Jeeva AL, Palanisamy V, Kanagaram K (2012) Comparative analysis of performance and security measures of some encryption algorithm. Int J Eng Res Appl 2(3):3033–3037
15. Kumar C, Singh AK, Kumar P (2018) A recent survey on image watermarking techniques and its application in e-governance. Multimed Tools Appl 77:3597–3622
16. Garkoti G, Peddoju SK, Balasubramanian R (2014) Detection of insider attacks in cloud based e-healthcare environment. In: International conference on information technology, pp 195–200
17. Mishra R, Chitre DK (2012) Data leakage and detection of guilty agent. Int J Sci Eng Res 3(6)
18. Fathy A, Tarrad IF, Hamed HF, Awad AI (2012) Advanced encryption standard algorithm: issues and implementation aspects. In: International conference on advanced machine learning technologies and applications. Springer, Berlin, Heidelberg, pp 516–523
19. Proença H, Alexandre LA (2005) UBIRIS: a noisy iris image database. In: Roli F, Vitulano S (eds) Image analysis and processing—ICIAP 2005. ICIAP 2005. Lecture notes in computer science, vol 3617. Springer, Berlin, Heidelberg
20. MedPix: open access online database for medical images. https://medpix.nlm.nih.gov

Information Retrieval Using Data Mining

Archika Jain, Harshita Virwani, Neha Shrotriya, and Devendra Somwanshi

1 Introduction

It is necessary to collect a large amount of data in order to develop information. Simple numerical numbers and text documents can be used, as well as more complicated information including spatial data, multimedia data, and hypertext pages. It is difficult to keep track of the large volume of data saved in files, databases, and other repositories.

It's becoming increasingly vital to provide sophisticated tools for analyzing and interpreting such data, as well as for extracting useful knowledge that might aid decision-making. Data mining is a collection of techniques for analyzing large amounts of data and discovering new, hidden, or unexpected patterns in data, as well as uncommon patterns in data. Data mining software forecasts future trends and behaviors, allowing firms to make informed, proactive decisions. Data mining's automated, future analyzes go beyond the analysis of previous occurrences provided by decision support systems' retrospective capabilities. Data mining tools can provide answers to business questions that were previously too time-consuming to answer. They scour databases for hidden patterns, uncovering predicting data that specialists may overlook because it falls beyond their realm of experience. There are many different types of data mining tools on the market, each with its own set of advantages and disadvantages. Internal auditors must be informed of the various types of data mining technologies available and advocate the acquisition of one that best suits

A. Jain (✉) · H. Virwani · N. Shrotriya
Department of CSE, Poornima College of Engineering, Jaipur, India
e-mail: archika.jain@poornima.org

H. Virwani
e-mail: harshita.virwani@poornima.org

D. Somwanshi
Department of EC, Poornima College of Engineering, Jaipur, India

the organization's present investigation requirements. There are four types of data mining tasks that are often used [1].

Classification: Data is organized into predetermined groups by classification. An email programmer, for example, might try to determine whether an email is genuine or spam common algorithms include decision tree learning, naive Bayesian classification, and neural networks [2].

Clustering: It's similar to classification, except the groups aren't predefined, thus the algorithm will try to group elements that are related [2].

Regression: Attempts to discover the least error-prone function for modeling the data [2].

Learning association rules: Correlations between variables are sought. A supermarket, for example, might keep track on its customers' shopping habits. The store can use association rule learning to figure out which issues are routinely purchased jointly and use that data for vending. On occasion, this is mentioned to as "market basket analysis" [2].

2 Approved Assessment Procedure

A writing study is required to learn about the research topic and what problems have been solved and what problems still need to be solved in the future. To keep the procedure simple and customizable, the review process was broken down into five steps. The stages were as follows (Fig. 1):

Stage 0: Get a "feel" for the situation

This step gives the details that will be checked before using a broader domain, conduct a literature review, and categories the results as reported to the specification.

Stage 1: Acquire a sense of the "big picture"

The research articles are organized into groups based on common topics and application subcategories. It is vital to read the section and subsection headings, as well as the title, abstract, introduction, and conclusion, in order to grasp the work and to find the answers to particular queries.

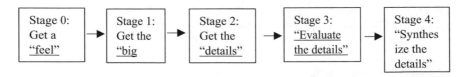

Fig. 1 Review process adopted

Stage 2: Find out the "details"

Stage 2 entails delving deeper into each research study to comprehend the technique used to account for the complication, the relevance and creativity of the infusion salute, the specific topic label, the significant benefaction, opportunity, and restrictions of the projects given.

Stage 3: "Evaluate the details"

This is evaluates the specifics, such as the seriousness of the problem, novelty, relevance of the solution, uniqueness of approach, veracity of statements, and so on.

Stage 4: "Synthesize the details"

It is concerned with evaluating the information provided, as well as, to some extent, generality the writers' synthesis of the data, concept, and outcomes takes place at this stage.

3   A Range of Problems in the Area

After reading 40 research papers on information retrieval, I came to the conclusion that using data mining, we uncovered the following concerns, which are detailed below.

The problems are as follows:

(1)   Information retrieval.
(2)   Similarities and differences in spatial data mining techniques.
(3)   The problem of data cluster mining.
(4)   Problem of changing in land price.
(5)   Data load balance issue.
(6)   Problem of privacy protection.
(7)   Problem of gap between academia and business tools.

4   Issue-Wise Discussion

Issue 1: Information retrieval

Most of the perspectives were used for information retrieval which are SD-miner, spatial priory algorithm, knowledge discovery in database, spatial clustering, and Bayesian network. Ant colony optimizer and genetic algorithm has also been proposed. ACO handles uncertainty property of customer data and GA overcome the sensitivity to the initial election data. Information retrieval may be correctly managed and mined using these solution ways.

Issue 2: Similarities and differences in spatial data mining techniques

Four tier of J2EE architecture, hair data model, cross thermometric, and visualization technique are the approaches that have been given. J2EE architecture provides data sharing, fast, easy access to spatial knowledge, and treatment to mass data. When problem occur then hair data model frequently change the data. Cross thermometric provide higher accuracy and reliability of temporal data and also improved the speed.

Issue 3: The problem of data cluster mining

The technique of "density based sampling algorithm" for solves the problem of mining of data clusters. It provides scalability to large datasets effectively and efficiently. BIRCH, a data clustering algorithm that is highly efficient for clustering big databases, has been proven.

Issue 4: Problem of changing in land price

Integrated techniques between geographic information system and spatial data mining solve the problem of changing in land price. The idea is to combine the spatial data mining with geographic information system is to establish an intelligent land grading information system. It is helpful in route design, route guide and route display.

Issue 5: Data load balance issue

Grid-based parallel data mining and MapND strategy have been solved the data load balancing problem. MapND strategy divided the datasets into data blocks than combined every data chunk to communicate mining node according to less time. Author use the parallel data mining for data mapping.

Issue 6: Problem of privacy protection

Bottom-up generalization method has been given for solving the problem of privacy protection. Once the data has been masked, typical data mining techniques can be used without any changes.

Issue 7: Gap between academia and business tools

Actionable knowledge discovery system has been analyzing the gap between academia and business tools. AKD system used the flexible framework for the hidden patterns.

5 Issue-Wise Solution Assessment Used

The infusion assessments below the different matter have been pictured in Table 1. The comparative examination of alternative solution approaches is also described in the same table.

Table 1 Solution approaches and outcomes by issue

Issue name	Solution approach	Results	References
Information retrieval	SD-miner technique	Handle both spatial and non-spatial data easily, and automatically detect what kind of data is used	[3]
	Bayesian network	It combines qualitative and quantitative analysis and has a great aptitude for reasoning and semantic representation	[4]
Similarities and differences in spatial data mining techniques	Four tier of J2EE architecture	It provides data sharing, fast, easy access to spatial knowledge, and treatment to mass data	[5]
	Hair data model	When problem occur then hair data model frequently change the data	[3]
The problem of data cluster mining	Density based sampling algorithm	It provides scalability to large data sets effectively and efficiently	[4]
Problem of changing in land price	GIS and SDM techniques	They dynamically explore the land data and deal with wide range of application	[6]
Data load balance issue	Grid based parallel data mining MapND strategy	Dynamic flexibility is poor and hardware demand is high	[7]
Problem of privacy protection	Bottom-up generalization method	Once the data has been masked, standard DM technique can be applied without modification	[8]
Gap between academia and business tools	Actionable knowledge discovery (AKD) system	AKD system use flexible framework for hidden patterns	[9]

6 Solution Approaches for the Specific Issues

6.1 Common Findings

Issue 1: Information retrieval

- The SD-miner technique has been enhanced to readily support both geographical and non-spatial data. And, it can provide techniques for geographical data mining that are more successful and efficient in real-world applications.

- CD-TIN technique is considered worst approach because in this implicit and obscure knowledge in spatial database cannot be discovered. And, second data mining approach does not paid much attention in real-world application like finance and business field.

Issue 2: Similarities and differences in spatial data mining techniques

- Four tier of J2EE architecture has been considered as the best approach because it provides data sharing, fast, easy access to spatial knowledge, and many treatments to mass data.
- Because it cannot execute on a data warehouse, the spatial data cube's spatial data mining technique is regarded as the worst approach. Complex spatial data is not supported by this data model.

Issue 3: The problem of data cluster mining

- Density-based sampling algorithm has been considered as the best approach because it not only solves the dual clustering problem but it also scales effectively and efficiently to big datasets.
- ICC algorithm has been considered as the worst approach because it has not solved the dual clustering problem effectively.

Issue 4: Problem of changing in land price

- Geographic information system and spatial data mining techniques dynamically explore the land data.

Issue 5: Data load balance issue

- Map ND strategy can solve the problem of data load balancing for data mining nodes and also improve the performance of parallel data mining in grid.

Issue 6: Problem of privacy protection

- After the data has been masked, typical data mining techniques can be used without any changes. But, it has some quality and scalability issues.

Issue 7: Gap between academia and business tools

- Actionable knowledge discovery is used for hidden patterns. It is a flexible framework.

7 Conclusion

In order to examine and discover current difficulties and scope of work, a study of 40 research articles in the domain of Information Retrieval Using Data Mining was conducted. Following the review, I discovered a number of issues that should be addressed when data mining is done properly. These papers are contemplate of different mining matters that have an impact on related data mining work. The motive of these methodologies and strategies is to decrease data mining inefficiencies and improve system reliability. I found seven separate issues that were handled using different strategies and techniques.

8   Future Work

SPMML will be extended to describe the spatio-temporal data models. The spatial data types and spatial data transformation in SPMML will be redesigned too. Due to the distributed nature of biodatabases security issue is very important. So, privacy mechanism and security issues should be taking into future work. For that developed a new data mining algorithm that is capable in extracting frequent, sequential and structured patterns, as well as classifying and clustering bio data analyzed some other trajectory datasets like vehicle and animal movement and include temporal information during clustering.

References

1. Xingxing J, Yingkun C, Kunqing X (2005) A novel method to integrate spatial data mining and geographic information system. Major Project of National Natural Science Foundation, IEEE
2. Smith GB, Bridges SM (2002) Fuzzy spatial data mining. IEEE
3. Bae D-H, Baek J-H, Oh H-K, Song J-W, Kim S-W (2009) SD-Miner: a spatial data mining system. IEEE
4. Huang J, Yuan Y (2007) Construction and application of Bayesian network model for spatial data mining. In: 2007 IEEE international conference on control and automation, FrC7-5, Guangzhou, China, 30 May to 1 June 2007
5. YueShun H, Wei X (2006) A study of spatial data mining architecture and technology. IEEE
6. Maddox J, Shin D-G (2009) Applying relational dependency discovery framework to geo-spatial data mining. In: International conference on information and multimedia technology. IEEE
7. Shamim A, Shaikh MU, Malik SU (2010) Intelligent data mining in autonomous heterogeneous distributed bio databases. In: Second international conference on computer engineering and applications. IEEE
8. Wang K, Yu PS, Chakraborty S (2004) Bottom-up generalization: a data mining solution to privacy protection. In: Fourth IEEE international conference on data mining
9. Zhow J, Guan J, Zhany M (2007) Fast implementation of dual clustering algorithm for spatial data mining. In: Fourth international conference on fuzzy systems and knowledge discovery (FSKD 2007). IEEE
10. Wu HC, Lu CN (2001) A spatial modeling technique for small area load forecast. IEEE

A Novel Approach Toward Detection of Glaucoma Using Machine Learning Techniques

Addepalli Venkatanand ram and Benjoshuva Methari

1 Introduction

Age-related chronic illness described as a disorder of the eye around a group of progressive optic neuropathies. Optic neuropathy associated with increased glaucomatous damage is defined as the progression of glaucoma as loss of RGC during the early and undiagnosed stages of the disease, followed by narrowing of the retinal nerve fiber layer (RNFL) thinning, and ultimately damage to the visual acuity (VF). According to a previous study, the chances of developing from ocular hypertension to one-dimensional vision loss (i.e., formal blindness) are 1.5–10.5% [1] in patients who could not be treated due to missed diagnosis. As a result, early detection is essential to prevent further progression of the disease and loss of vision.

- Age-related chronic illness described as a disorder of the eye around a group of progressive optic neuropathies. Optic neuropathy associated with increased glaucomatous damage is defined as the progression of glaucoma as loss of RGC during the early and undiagnosed stages of the disease, followed by narrowing of the retinal nerve fiber layer (RNFL) thinning, and ultimately damage to the visual acuity (VF). According to a previous study, the chances of developing from ocular hypertension to one-dimensional vision loss (i.e., formal blindness) are 1.5–10.5% in patients who could not be treated due to missed diagnosis. As a result, early detection is essential to prevent further progression of the disease and loss of vision.
- Computer-assisted diagnostic (CAD) [2] tools are critical in determining an accurate, reliable, and timely diagnosis of glaucoma13. Convolutional neural networks

A. Venkatanand ram (✉)
University College of Engineering, Osmania University, Amberpet, Hyderabad 500007, India
e-mail: venkatananda.be21@uceou.edu

B. Methari
Swansea University, Singleton Park, Sketty, Swansea SA2 8PP, UK

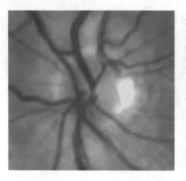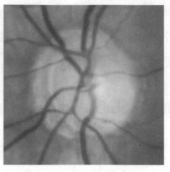

Fig. 1 Eye images that are affected by glaucoma (left) and not affected (right)

(CNN) have been implemented as a result of recent developments in processing power capabilities, allowing for autonomous glaucoma classification based on complicated features extracted from thousands of available fundus pictures. fastai uses minor components of academics that be combined and matched to create novel techniques. It also uses major components that can provide avant-garde results in the convolutional neural networks by which the libraries that are used by practitioners can get access to deep learning libraries. It strives to achieve both goals without sacrificing usability, flexibility, or performance. The architecture has been designed such that it expresses most the common basic deep learning and data processing techniques ready and easy for use.

- The dataset consists of images in JPEG format consisting of fundus images and normal images that have been divided to half each of them summing to 2230. Each class of images consists of 1115 images. Figure 1 shows a healthy image according to the dataset.

2 Literature Review

Christopher et al. [3] proposed method that compares and contrasts deep learning algorithms to detect glaucoma in fundus images and to explore strategies for introducing new data into models. Two datasets consisting of fundus datasets have been taken from the Diagnostic Innovations in Glaucoma Study/African Descent and Glaucoma Evaluation Study and Matsue Red Cross Hospital. Both the datasets have been independently used for detecting glaucoma at the University of California, San Diego, and University of Tokyo. They have concluded that deep learning glaucoma detection can achieve a high level of accuracy with appropriate strategies. A high range of sensitivity and specificity of the deep learning algorithms suggest that role of AI in detection of glaucoma in primary detection that range from moderate-to-severe for a wider population [4].

Chen et al. [5] proposed a deep learning method that uses the automatic feature learning called ALLADIN in which the method adopts micro neural networks (multi-layer perceptron). Unlike the traditional CNNs that uses linear filters firstly and then nonlinear activation function that scans the input. To extract the information from the receptive field that has got high complex structures, the network uses the concept of micro neural networks. Furthermore, in order to differentiate between glaucoma and the healthy images the network uses the outputs of other pre-trained CNNs as themes to improve the performance of the model and is also used to represent the images as a hierarchical way.

Howard et al. [6] proposed a new deep learning tool-fastai, that grades the tensors in a semantic way as well as includes a novel Python dispatch system. For implementing the code in few lines, the optimizer of the GPU-optimized computer library refactors the common functionality into two pieces. This is not only a new way of two-way callback system that can access any data points but also can change the optimizer or model at any point of time. We were able to use this package to successfully develop a whole deep learning course in less time than we could with previous approaches.

3 Methodology

We used the CNN ResNet34 integrated with fastai. We could use the trainable parameters from the database of the fastai that provides other models as well. A series of the steps were followed while writing the code that have been depicted in Fig. 2.

Rolling back torch to 1.4 is not a necessary step. One can even work on the latest torch, but as and when we import libraries, we get messages saying, "The default behaviour for interpolate/upsample with float scale_factor will change in 1.6.0 to align with other frameworks/libraries.". The best way that we found to handle such situations is that scaling it back to 1.4. Although this does not affect the overall functioning of the algorithm, but gives a sense that we are working in an older environment.

Importing the necessary libraries for the further steps is an essential step in the beginning. Initially, we have to ensure that fastai is installed on our Python hosts. If not, we have install using the command pip install fastai. Once this is installed, we import necessary libraries from fastai libraries and metrics.

Image transformation is essential in our case. Because the dataset consists of limited images viewing each of them from different angles becomes needy when we want accuracy to be high. In all such cases fastai provides us with full image transformation that is created from scratch in Pytorch. Although the library's primary goal is data augmentation for use in computer vision model training, it can also be used for more general picture manipulation. We'll look at a fast overview of the data augmentation parts that you'll almost surely need to use before we go into the details of the entire API.

Fig. 2 Flowchart
representing the series of
steps involved while building
the model

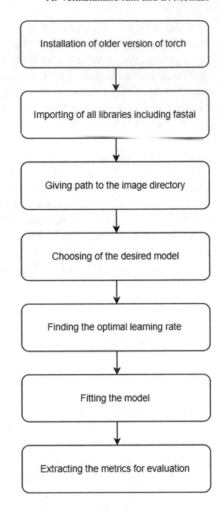

We can change the pixel values but cannot change what is there in the human eye, i.e., properties of the image. For these, we have to do minor changes in the transformations of the image that include rotation, zoom translation, etc. This avoids the regular feeding of the images every time and instead does the actual data augmentation which is one of the important regularization techniques. Models that have been trained using data augmentation will then generalize more effectively. Image augmentation is a technique by which artificial expansion of the training dataset changes the versions of images in the given dataset. It uses techniques such as padding, flipping, zooming, and cropping. It helps the model from getting overfitted and makes the model more robust even for slight variations.

Splitting the data: For training and testing purposes for our model, we split our data into three distinct datasets. Splitting the dataset is essential for an unbiased evaluation of prediction performance. The actual dataset where the model is trained after each epoch again and again till it finishes learning the features. Once the model is trained on the training dataset and validation dataset it is trained on the test dataset, which is a set of observations used to evaluate the performance of the model with some specific parameter.

After setting all the initial parameters, our next is to see all the models in the directory. ResNet34 is the model we have selected because by default, it downloads the pre-trained weights from ImageNet. If we wish to build a CNN by using the cnn_learner can be used to build a convnet style model. We chose ResNet34 as it optimizes the deterioration of the accuracy to a great extent.

Fitting the model to our set parameters to train our model we use the trainable parameters and then evaluate the metrics for the analysis of the working of our model.

4   Experimental Results

We have experimented with all the ResNet models namely ResNet18, ResNet34, and ResNet50. Figures 3 and 4 depict the loss versus the learning rate. Although variations can be seen for the following graphs ResNet50 outperforms the other two.

From the above three graphs, it is clear that min loss attained by the ResNet50 is least, and thus, it is clear enough that the model works best for the dataset.

4.1   Confusion Matrices and Metrics

Figure 5 depicts the confusion matrix obtained for the two models that we have used to train the dataset. Here, the X-axis represents the predicted obtained from the system, and Y-axis represents the actual data output.

Metric specifications like the accuracy, specificity, precision, and sensitivity, have been calculated by the given formulas in the equations below.

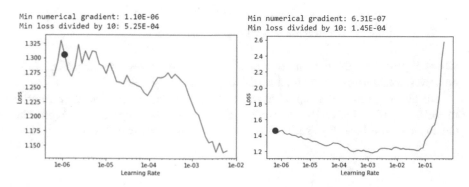

Fig. 3 Represents ResNet18, ResNet34 loss versus learning rate graphs

Min numerical gradient: 2.29E-04
Min loss divided by 10: 1.20E-04

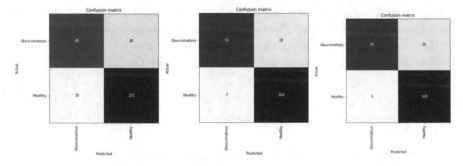

Fig. 4 Represents ResNet50 loss versus learning rate

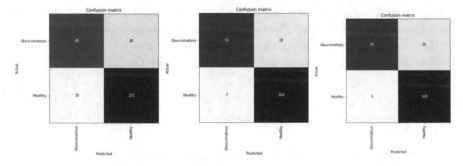

Fig. 5 Represents confusion matrices for the three models of ResNet architecture

$$\text{Precision} = \text{TP}/(\text{TP} + \text{FP})$$
$$\text{Sensitivity} = \text{TP}/(\text{TP} + \text{FN})$$
$$\text{Specificity} = \text{TN}/(\text{TN} + \text{FN})$$
$$\text{Accuracy} = (\text{TP} + \text{TN})/(\text{P} + \text{N})$$

where TP, FP, TN, FN, P, N are true positives, false positives, true negatives, false negatives, total positives, and total negatives, respectively (Table 1).

The above given tables represent the metrics calculations for the three ResNet models, namely, ResNet18, ResNet34, and ResNet50, respectively. From the calculations, it is clear that ResNet50 outperforms the other two ResNet models.

Table 1 Metrics table calculation

Resnet18	Accuracy	Specificity	Sensitivity	Precision
Glautomas	83.78	90.99	76.57	89.47
Healthy	83.78	89.47	79.53	90.99
Resnet34	Accuracy	Specificity	Sensitivity	Precision
Glautomas	88.74	93.69	83.78	93.00
Healthy	88.74	83.78	93.69	85.25
Resnet50	Accuracy	Specificity	Sensitivity	Precision
Glautomas	91.44	97.30	85.59	96.94
Healthy	91.44	85.59	97.30	87.10

5 Future Scope

The detection of the glaucoma has been done the dataset of retinal images. We have used the ResNet model of various versions, namely, ResNet18, ResNet34, and ResNet50 and utilized their performance on the given dataset. As the number of the images of the dataset are small ResNet performed less accurately. Performance of the model has been discussed in the metrics table and each model's accuracy, sensitivity, specificity, and precision has been calculated and analyzed [7]. If we try to consider the overall performance of the three models and thus take into account average accuracy it is clear that ResNet50 performed better than the other two model.

6 Conclusion

Detection and classification of the fundus images have been performed using three deep learning models ResNet18, ResNet34, and ResNet50. The performances of the models have been evaluated in terms of accuracy, sensitivity, specificity, and precision. The results of them have been analyzed and can be concluded that ResNet50 performs better than the other two. Although number of images are less, we can still with try ResNet50 and further improvements can be made by taking a large dataset.

References

1. https://www.nature.com
2. Gheisari S, Shariflou S, Phu J et al (2021) A combined convolutional and recurrent neural network for enhanced glaucoma detection. Sci Rep 11:1945. https://doi.org/10.1038/s41598-021-81554-4

3. Christopher M, Nakahara K, Bowd C, Proudfoot JA, Belghith A, Goldbaum MH, Rezapour J, Weinreb RN, Fazio MA, Girkin CA, Liebmann JM, De Moraes G, Murata H, Tokumo K, Shibata N, Fujino Y, Matsuura M, Kiuchi Y, Tanito M, Asaoka R, Zangwill LM. Effects of study population, labeling and training on glaucoma detection using deep learning algorithms. Transl Vis Sci Technol 9(2):27
4. http://tvst.arvojournals.org/
5. Chen X, Xu Y, Yan S, Wong DWK, Wong TY, Liu J (2015) Automatic feature learning for glaucoma detection based on deep learning. In: Navab N, Hornegger J, Wells W, Frangi A (eds) Medical image computing and computer-assisted intervention   MICCAI 2015, MICCAI 2015. Lecture notes in computer science, vol 9351. Springer, Cham
6. Howard J, Gugger S (2020) fastai: a layered API for deep learning, computer vision and pattern recognition (cs.CV); neural and evolutionary computing (cs.NE); machine learning (stat.ML), arXiv:2002.04688
7. Serener A, Serte S (2019) Transfer learning for early and advanced glaucoma detection with convolutional neural networks. In: 2019 Medical technologies congress (TIPTEKNO), pp 1–4. https://doi.org/10.1109/TIPTEKNO.2019.8894965

Corn Leaf Disease Detection Using ResNext50, ResNext101, and Inception V3 Deep Neural Networks

Neeraj Kumar Sharma, Bhargavi Kalyani Immadisetty, Aishwarya Govina, Ram Chandra Reddy, and Priyanka Choubey

1 Introduction

Corn, also known as maize, is one of the most widely grown crops in India and worldwide. It is a flexible crop that can thrive in a variety of climates [1]. Among all grains, maize produces the largest yield [2]. Crop diseases pose a significant risk to food security. Early detection of crop diseases is a difficult task. However, precise disease identification is still critical. The illnesses can be seen with the naked eye in various parts of the plant, such as the leaves and stems. The most frequent diseases that influence maize farming are common rust, northern leaf gray spot, and blight [3]. Identifying these disorders by visual inspection is extremely difficult, and the results may not be reliable. As a result, pesticides are used in an excessive amount. Furthermore, the illness of the maze crop influences crops quality and quantity. Therefore, maize disease identification is a critical problem for ensuring high-quality and large-scale maize production.

The traditional method for identifying the illness of maize is by visual inspection [4]. But the key limitation of the traditional method is low accuracy in identifying the disease in the maize leaf because different leaf diseases look similar in their

N. Kumar Sharma (✉) · B. Kalyani Immadisetty · A. Govina · R. Chandra Reddy · P. Choubey
Department of Computer Science and Engineering, SRM University, Amaravati, AP, India
e-mail: neeraj16ks@gmail.com

B. Kalyani Immadisetty
e-mail: bhargavikalyani_i@srmap.edu.in

A. Govina
e-mail: aishwarya_govina@srmap.edu.in

R. Chandra Reddy
e-mail: brreddy@iiitdmj.ac.in

P. Choubey
e-mail: priyankajit1@gmail.com

© The Author(s), under exclusive license to Springer Nature Singapore Pte Ltd. 2023
K. Kumar Singh et al. (eds.), *Machine Vision and Augmented Intelligence*, Lecture Notes in Electrical Engineering 1007, https://doi.org/10.1007/978-981-99-0189-0_22

early stages. Therefore, it is difficult to tell the difference between healthy and sick leaves with the naked eye. The other drawback of the traditional visual inspection method is that the required regular crop monitoring as well as also requires agriculture professionals to keep the crop disease-free. The above-mentioned limitations of the traditional visual inspection method led to a lot of time consumption, cost, and unreliability to maintain the crop healthy. Therefore, farmers are unable to take preventative actions on those plants at the appropriate time.

Hence, there is a need to design and develop a cost effective, reliable, and fast automated system to early detect maize crop disease. Many researchers have employed different machine learning (ML) and deep learning (DL) methods to identify crop diseases automatically. The key limitations of the ML model are that it requires huge effort to pre-process data and extract key feature vectors from the dataset to train the model. The accuracy of the ML algorithm is also low in the case of high-volume multi-dimensional datasets. On the other hand, DL is more suitable for high-volume multi-dimensional datasets, and DL automatically extracts the key feature vectors to train the model. But the key limitation of DL is, it requires lots of memory and computational power to train the model over many epochs. To overcome all these challenges, in this paper, we applied a transfer learning technique to classify maize diseases. Transfer learning is one of the methods of machine learning/deep learning, where an already trained model for different problems on a high volume of data with huge computational power and memory [5]. In transfer learning, a developed model is used to solve a problem with high accuracy. The key motivation to use transfer learning is, we can get high accuracy of the classification problem with less volume of data and computational resources. At present, there are different CNN architectures such as LeNet, AlexNet, VGGNet, and InceptionV1-V3, exist for different DL problems. These architectures act as rich feature extractors, which are critical for image categorization, object detection, and other applications [5].

This paper deals with the type of three CNN architectures known as ResNext101, ResNext50, and Inception V3 for corn disease classification problems. The overall idea of the proposed work in this paper is described as follows. First, we acquired the corn dataset from the Kaggle website of 4187 images [6]. The acquired dataset consists of four different types of images such as healthy, cercosporin, common rust, and northern leaf blight. To drop blur images from the data, pre-processing is performed on the dataset. Then, after the acquired dataset is divided into three parts such as training, validation, and testing parts. To generate a greater number of images, data augmentation is performed on the dataset. The greater number of images train the models in a more accurate way. Further, all three models were trained by applying training datasets over several epochs. At the end, testing is performed by applying a testing dataset on the trained models. The performance of the three models is observed by calculating different performance metrics. The key contributions of the proposed work in this paper are described as follows:

1. To convert the dataset for training the models by performing different operations such as data pre-processing and data augmentation.

2. To train three CNN models such as ResNext101, ResNext50, and Inception V3 by using a training dataset.
3. To test the model and calculate different performance metrics by testing and validation dataset.

The rest of the paper is organized as follows. Section 2 deals with the background and detailed literature survey. Section 3 deals with the proposed work w.r.t. corn disease classification problem. Section 4 highlights the results and discussion part. At the end Sect. 5 deals with the conclusion and future direction of work.

2   Background and Literature Survey

Yu et al. [7] proposed a K-mean clustering and ResNet- and VGG16-based corn disease prediction, in their proposed work, the authors divided the different corn diseases into a number of clusters and then applied different cluster images into ResNet, and VGG16 model for corn disease prediction. In their experimental work, ResNet18 and VGG16 achieved 90% and 89% average accuracy, respectively. Saleem et al. [8] presented different deep learning and machine learning architectures for crop disease prediction, and in their research work, they also explained the different deep learning models used to visualize the data. The key limitation of their proposed work is they did not mention how to predict and classify the disease in the early stage.

Wu et al. [9] proposed tomato leaf disease detection using Deep Convolutional Generative Adversarial Networks (DCGAN). In their proposed work, they classified five different tomato plant diseases with 94.33% accuracy. The DCGAN not only increased the size of the dataset but has the characteristics of diversity. Hence, by this way, they make their DCGAN-based tomato disease classification model more robust in nature. Further, they used GoogLeNet to train the model. The key limitation of their work was that they used only one transfer learning CNN architecture.

Das and Lee [10] designed and developed a two-stage few-shot learning approach to recognize the image. In their research work, the author proposed a multi-layer network architecture that encodes the feature vectors from the annotated images. Then after they implemented two training stages, in the first stage, they obtained a low-dimensional discriminative space, and in the second stage, they calculated the variance of each class. The proposed work does not deal with the corn dataset.

Rangarajan et al. [11] proposed a tomato plant disease prediction using a transfer learning approach. In their proposed methodology, they applied input images to two pre-trained deep neural networks such as AlexNet and VGG16 net. Further, they calculated different performance matrices by tugging different hyperparameters such as batch size, weight, and bias values. In their experimental work, 97.29% of accuracy was achieved by VGG16 and 97.49% of accuracy was achieved by AlexNet models. Xian and Ngadiran [12] presented a plant disease classification model using machine learning approach . In their proposed work they pre-processed an image via HSV color space and feature extraction via Haralick textures. After that, they applied extracted feature vectors to their proposed model for plan disease classification. Author in their proposed work used tomato plant disease dataset t. The image pre-processing, feature extraction, and machine learning based proposed tomato disease classification model achieved 84.94% accuracy. The key limitation of the proposed work is the accuracy of the proposed model is less as compared to the existing transfer learning techniques.

3 Proposed Work

(A) The flowchart of the proposed work for corn disease classification is illustrated in Fig. 1. First, the input dataset of maize leaf was collected by the Kaggle website. Then, data augmentation operations such as flip, rotation, increasing brightness, and increasing contrast are performed on the corn image dataset. Further, the corn image dataset is divided into three parts such as training data, validation data, and testing data. The training dataset was used to train three different CNN architectures such as ResNext101, ResNet50, and Inception V3. A detailed explanation of all the components is described as follows.

(B) **Corn Dataset**: A maize dataset contained 4187 images, which correspond to four different classes like healthy (1162 images), cercospora (574 images), common rust (1306 images), and northern blight (1145 images). These three common diseases of maize leaves were chosen because these three styles of diseases may be visually identified from leaves, which is important to train a CNN. The gray leaf spot (GLS) is a foliar fungal disease caused by the pathogen cercospora zeae maydis in corn. The first symptoms could appear in the form of small, necrotic spots with halos and on corn including leaf lesions, discoloration

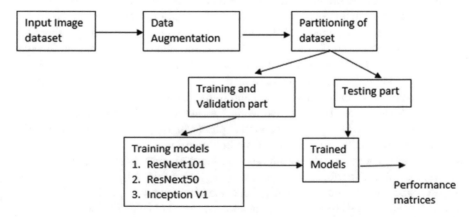

Fig. 1 Flowchart of maize leaf disease classification model

1.Cercospora Common   **2. common rust**   **3. Northern Leaf Blight**

Fig. 2 Images of different types of diseases in the maize leaf

(chlorosis), and foliar blight. Environmental conditions like high humidity and warmth are most responsible for this disease in the maize leaf.

The common rust is caused by the fungus *Puccinia sorghi* and occurs every season. It's seldom a priority in hybrid corn. Rust pustules usually first appear in late June. Early symptoms of common rust begin as flecks and then expand into tiny tan spots. These soon elongated to be powdery, brick-red pustules because the spores break through the leaf surface. Pustules are oval, about 1/8 in. long, and scattered sparsely or grouped together. The leaf tissue around the pustules may turn yellow or die, leaving lesions of dead tissue. The lesions sometimes form a band across the leaf and whole leaves will die if severely infected. Because the pustules age, the red spores turn black; therefore, the pustules appear black and still erupt through the leaf surface. The northern blight is one of the earliest diseases to be recorded on maize crops. This disease is caused by E. Turucicum fungi; it occurs in the early stages, oval-shaped, water-soaked small spots appearing on the leaf. Three common maize diseases are illustrated in Fig. 2.

(C) **Data augmentation**: The over-fitting problem of the CNN model can be resolved by data augmentation. In this process, we can create different kinds of images by transforming an image such as horizontal flip, vertical flip, horizontal shifting, vertical shifting, zooming, adding noise, and so on. The main purpose of data augmentation is if we have a smaller number of images in the dataset and we require a greater number of images to classify the images. Then, by data augmentation, we can create different kinds of images. Figure 3 shows the six different images after performing a sequence of transformation operations by the data augmentation.

(D) **Partition of maize dataset**: The maize dataset is divided into two parts as the 80% training part and 20% testing part. Further, the training part is divided into two parts such as 60% training part and 20% validation part. The training dataset is used to train three models, and the validation part is used to tune the model hyperparameters such as weight and bias values.

(E) **CNN Architectures**: The different CNN architectures used in the paper are described as follows.

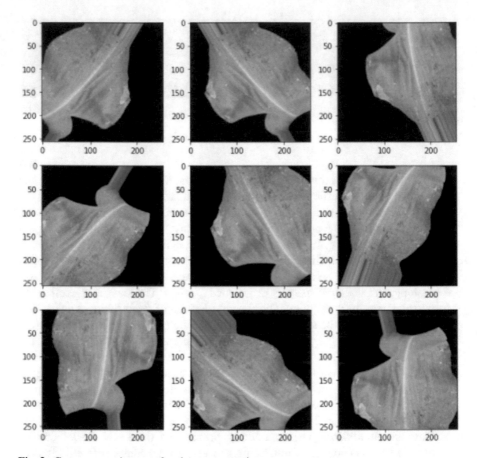

Fig. 3 Common rust images after data augmentation

ResNeXt50 and ResNext101: It is the extension of deep residual networks. It is a homogeneous neural network that reduces the number of hyperparameters by conventional ResNet. This can be achieved by using a new dimension cardinality on the top of width and height. Cardinality defines the size of the set of transformations. To classify the images a split-transform merge strategy is applied in the ResNeXt. In other words, a network block splits the input, transforms it into a required format, and merges it to get the output where each block follows the same strategy. Instead of high depth and width, having high cardinality helps in decreasing validation errors. The architecture of ResNxt50, ResNxt101 [13], and different types of filters, and operations is described in Fig. 4.

InceptionV3: It is a module of the GoogLeNet architecture. This network belongs to the Inception family network and makes more improvements such

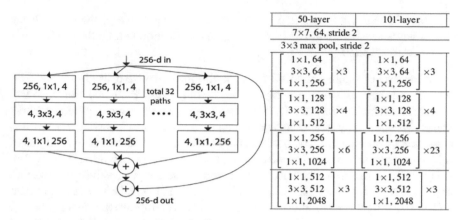

Fig. 4 ResNext architecture and its operations [13]

as label smoothing. It is a model which is 48 layers deep. It uses 7×7 factorized convolution. It uses batch normalization to label the information down the network. Figure 5 shows the architecture diagram and different operations performed on Inception V3 [14].

Steps to train and test the pre-trained CNN architectures such as ResNext101, ResNext50, and Inception V3 are described as follows.

(F) **Training and Testing**: First, we pre-processed the corn dataset by applying the filter function of TensorFlow. In this way, we removed all the blur images from the dataset. Then, we performed data augmentation to generate a greater number of images in the dataset by applying the Image Data Generator function in Keras. All the images generated after data augmentation are divided into a fixed size of batches. Further, data is divided into two categories, such as training and testing by using the take and skip functions in TensorFlow. Since ResNext101

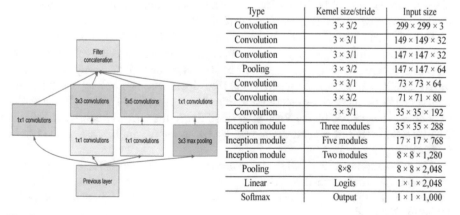

Fig. 5 Inception V3 architecture and its operations [14]

and ResNext50 accept 256 * 256 size of the input image, therefore all the images are resized to 256 * 256 using resize function to train the ResNext101 and ResNext50.

In the case of the Inception V3 network, the images were resized to 299 * 299. Further, all three networks are implemented using TensorFlow and Keras. In this process, we removed the last fully connected layer from the pre-connected networks and added a new fully connected layer which consists of four classes such as healthy, cercospora, common rust, and northern blight. Then, we randomized the weights of fully connected layers and froze all the weights of pre-trained networks. Training data was applied to the pre-trained networks to update the weights. Validation data was applied to tune the hyperparameters of the pre-trained networks. The Adam optimizer and Xavier weight initialization techniques were used to improve the model accuracy. The fine-tuning of the models is performed by applying several epochs. In the end testing, the dataset is used to test all the models.

4 Experimental Setup and Results Discussion

To check the performance of all the CNN architectures for maize disease prediction experiment carried out on Intel core i5 processor. Further, we used Google Colab notebook to implement, train, test, and store the dataset on Google Drive. Since, Google Colab provides built-in Python libraries such as NumPy, Matplotlib, Seaborn, TensorFlow, and Keras to implement and visualize the performance of the CNN. It also provides CPU, GPU, and TPU free of cost to train and test CNN models up to a certain limit. Hence, all these factors motivated us to deploy our model on Google Colab. To visualize the accuracy of a classifier confusion matrix can be used. Figures 6a and 6b show the confusion matrix and ROC curve of the ResNext101 classifier respectively. The highest amount of accuracy performed by the ResNxt101 classifier in the case of health leaf is 96%. The lowest amount of accuracy achieved by the ResNxt101 in the case of blight leaf is 37%.

Figures 7a and 7b show the confusion matrix and ROC curve of the ResNext50 classifier respectively. The highest amount of accuracy performed by the ResNxt50 classifier in cases of health leaf is 91%. The lowest amount of accuracy achieved by the ResNxt50 in the case of bright leaves is 1%. Figures 8a and 8b show the confusion matrix and ROC curve of the Inception V3 classifier respectively. The highest amount of accuracy performed by the ResNxt50 classifier in the case of health leaf is 92%. The lowest amount of accuracy achieved by Inception V3 in the case of the bright leaf is 8%.

The evaluation metrics of all the three models such as ResNxt101, ResNxt50, and Inception V3 are described in Table 1. The highest amount of accuracy, 91.59%, achieved by ResNext101 models, and the lowest accuracy, 78.12%, achieved by the Inception V3 model.

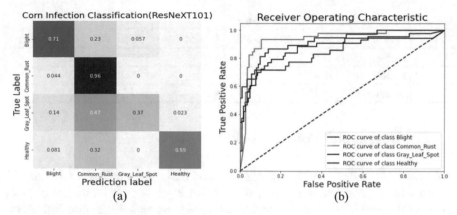

Fig. 6 Confusion matrix and ROC of ResNeXt101 model

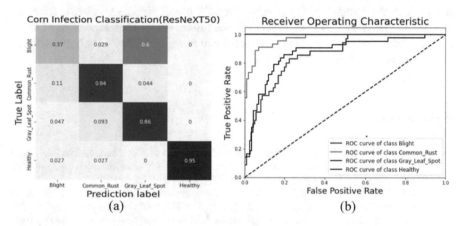

Fig. 7 Confusion matrix and ROC curve of ResNeXt50 model

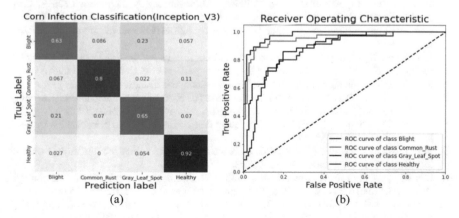

Fig. 8 Confusion matrix and ROC curve of Inception V3 model

Table 1 Evaluation metrics of different models

S. No.	Model	Average accuracy (%)	Precision (%)	Recall (%)	$F1$-score (%)
1	ResNext101	91.59	92	97	95
2	ResNext50	88.43	97	89	93
3	Inception V3	78.5	85	89	87

5 Conclusion and Future Work

This paper highlights corn disease classification using three different CNN architectures. In the proposed work, we classified four labels for 4187 corn leaf disease images. The ResNeXt101 model predicted crop disease with the highest amount of 91.59% accuracy as compared to the other two models. The lowest 78.1% accuracy achieved by the Inception V3 network. But still, blight disease prediction accuracy was low in the case of all three models. In the future, we will implement more state-of-the-art architectures or design a new architecture which will achieve high accuracy in the case of blight disease prediction.

References

1. De Chant C, Wiesner-Hanks T, Chen S, Stewart EL, Yosinski J, Gore MA, Nelson RJ, Lipson H (2017) Automated identification of northern leaf blight-infected maize plants from field imagery using deep learning. Phytopathology 107(11):1426–1432
2. Xu J-H, Shao M-Y, Wang Y-C, Han W-T (2020) Recognition of corn leaf spot and rust based on transfer learning with convolutional neural network. Trans Chin Soc Agric Mach 51(2):230–236
3. Fan X-P, Zhou J-P, Xu Y (2020) Recognition of field maize leaf diseases based on improved regional convolutional neural network. J South China Agric Univ 41(6):82–91
4. Picon A, Seitz M, Alvarez-Gila A, Mohnke P, Ortiz-Barredo A, Echazarra J (2019) Crop conditional convolutional neural networks for massive multi-crop plant disease classification over cell phone acquired images taken on real field conditions. Comput Electron Agric 167:Art. no. 105093
5. Li L, Zhang S, Wang B (2021) Plant disease detection and classification by deep learning—a review. IEEE Access 9:56683–56698. https://doi.org/10.1109/ACCESS.2021.3069646
6. https://www.kaggle.com/smaranjitghose/corn-or-maize-leaf-disease-dataset
7. Yu H et al (2021) Corn leaf diseases diagnosis based on K-means clustering and deep learning. IEEE Access 9:143824–143835. https://doi.org/10.1109/ACCESS.2021.3120379
8. Saleem MH, Potgieter J, Arif KM (2019) Plant disease detection and classification by deep learning. Plants 8(11):468489
9. Wu Q, Chen Y, Meng J (2020) DCGAN-based data augmentation for tomato leaf disease identification. IEEE Access 8:98716–98728
10. Das D, Lee CSG (2020) A two-stage approach to few-shot learning for image recognition. IEEE Trans Image Process 29:3336–3350. https://doi.org/10.1109/TIP.2019.2959254
11. Rangarajan AK, Purushothaman R, Ramesh A (2018) Tomato crop disease classification using pre-trained deep learning algorithm. Procedia Comput Sci 133:1040–1047
12. Xian TS, Ngadiran R (1962) Plant diseases classification using machine learning. J Phys: Conf Ser

13. https://medium.com/@14prakash/understanding-and-implementing-architectures-of-resnet-and-resnext-for-state-of-the-art-image-cc5d0adf648e
14. https://www.researchgate.net/figure/Detailed-Specification-of-Inception-v3-Network_tbl2_335442913

SPEG—Semiotics-Based Panel Extraction from Graphic Novel

D. M. Divya, M. S. Karthika Devi⓪, and B Ramachandran⓪

1 Introduction

Graphic novels got a lot of interest as individuals recognize it as an unpredictable type of realistic articulation that can pass on profound thoughts and significant feelings. Comic research includes information retrieval, extraction of components, and other analysis. Among the graphic novel analysis tasks, the character detection task is the most difficult part due to their variant shape and appearance and also as they are hand drawn. As the conventional detection methods cannot be applied directly, it is understood that there are only very few works on character detection and retrieval tasks.

The visual dialects of the graphic novels emerge in numerous sociocultural methods, for example, the guidance manuals, sand drawing, emoticon, and so on. The combinatorial characteristics of morphology reach out past notable portrayals, and the compositional visual morphology utilizes different semiotic references to communicate meaning. And the combinatorial characteristics are the vocabularies of visual dialects between structures that can remain solitary (like an individual's picture) and those that can't (like a movement line or way line). These components must connect to another component and must be connected to be bound morphemes

D. M. Divya
Department of Artificial Intelligence and Data Science, R.M.K Engineering College,
Kavaraipettai, Chennai, Tamil Nadu, India
e-mail: dad.ad@rmkec.ac.in

M. S. Karthika Devi (✉) · B. Ramachandran
Department of Computer Science and Engineering, College of Engineering, Guindy, Anna
University, Chennai, Tamil Nadu, India
e-mail: mskarthikadevi2014@annauniv.edu

B. Ramachandran
e-mail: baaski@annauniv.edu

© The Author(s), under exclusive license to Springer Nature Singapore Pte Ltd. 2023   315
K. Kumar Singh et al. (eds.), *Machine Vision and Augmented Intelligence*, Lecture Notes
in Electrical Engineering 1007, https://doi.org/10.1007/978-981-99-0189-0_23

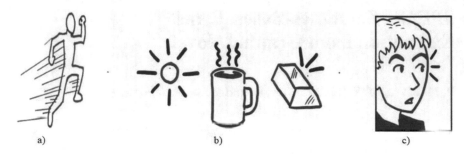

Fig. 1 Semiotics of movement lines, radial lines, and focal lines

as they can't exist free of the root object of what they need to adjust as shown in Fig. 1.

The visual dialects utilize fundamental systems to join morphemes as verbal dialects. The visual components append in "up fixes" which indicates joins that are "up," for example, lights, hearts, and stars, and so forth which show up over a character's head, the stars as up fixes implies confusion. This up fix likewise incorporates attaches which are the gathering of stars and bended movement lines. Stars alone have no inborn significance other than being a shape. Along with the face, these morphemes imply that the individual is dazed. Inside replacement is demonstrated when the eyes of a character are supplanted by hearts to reflect want felt for the item in vision, stars (want for distinction), dollar signs (want for cash). The motion lines are utilized to signify ways. These ways can likewise happen in scopic lines utilizing specked lines to portray the character's eyes to show what they are looking at. In spiral lines, it is similar to the straight lines that originate from sparkling items, for example, sun. The wavy lines are utilized to portray warmth or scents from the garbage or espresso and the central lines portray causing to notice something from the eyes. The spiral lines appear from the gold and central lines appear from the eyes. SPEGYOLO is proposed to distinguish these conventions. The realistic novel image of the custom dataset is annotated by utilizing VOTT which is the visual object tagging tool. Then the annotated files are converted into the YOLO format files for the model training. YOLOv3 utilizes darknet, which has 53 layer networks. The YOLOv3 detector model is trained on our custom dataset which successfully detected the characters and semiotics placed at different orientations, and the output is shown through the bounding boxes. Using a contour detection algorithm, the panels containing the semiotics of interest are extracted from the given graphic novel strips. The model performance is evaluated using intersection over union (IOU) and mean average precision (mAP) is **75.8%** which is the accuracy of the model. The results show that the SPEGYOLO identifies the semiotics such as movement lines and path lines associated with the objects when they are placed at different directions and orientation with good accuracy.

2 Related Work

This section reviews the most relevant work on visual semiotics, graphic novel analysis, and panel extraction. The empirical examinations were centered on the uncertainty of the visualization. The tests were carried out with two calculated viewpoints. Combined results provide initial guidelines to represent uncertainty proposed by Ref. [1].

Reference [2] proposed methods to determine sentiment scores associated with the semiotics in a sentence. Sentiment analysis [3] on a multilingual dataset with Japanese version [4] is done. Visual language theory proposes that the successive significant sounds establish spoken dialects, while shared organized deliberate consecutive pictures are characterized by visual dialects.

Reference [5] proposed a method to combine the semiotics vocabulary and class hypothesis to perform investigation of representation. It shows how cycles of representation fit the semiotic structures.

Human decision making includes psychological processes to solve decision issues. The ordinary support systems don't facilitate the automatic interpretation that leads to undesired solutions. Ref. [6] proposed a method to overcome this limitation; a hybrid decision support method is developed. It joins case-based thinking cycles, semiotic ideas [7], and association of self-guides.

2.1 Character Detection

Reference [8] proposed techniques that give various calculations and models to different undertakings like panels and character detection balloon segmentation, text recognition, and so forth. Detection of objects was implemented by incorporating deep learning techniques [9].

2.2 Graphic Novel Analysis

Reference [10] proposed a novel sparse self-attention LSTM model for the automatic construction of the sentiment lexicons. Challenges and opportunities for conceiving the graphic novels are outlined [11]. Graphic novels are intricate as they incorporate components like content, drawings, balloons, panels, sound to word imitation, and so on. The reviews are based on the previous research about graphic novels related to what has been done so far and the knowledge about the significant viewpoints [12].

Reference [13] proposed a method to generate a precise, concise story that best depicts a series of images. A convolutional neural network is used to extract features from the image [14]. [15] concentrated on recognition of text using OCR and also used distance based methods for speech balloon associations. Ref. [16] proposed a deep neural network model to solve this issue. Finding the texture and basic lines is a significant analysis for producing colorized graphic novels. Ref. [17] proposed an improved method that outperforms the original YOLOv3 method in detection tasks. The automatic generation of a storyboard [15] containing panels with the constituents of a graphic novel conveys the moral behind a Thirukkural.

2.3 Panel Extraction

Reference [8] proposed a different graphic novel panel extraction from the traditional approach which is the three class segmentation model based on the UNet architecture. The frame and text were automatically extracted from graphic novels by the connected component method [18].

A strategy dependent on deep learning accomplishes better exploratory outcomes, but its architecture is repetitive and the time productivity isn't acceptable. To defeat these issues, Ref. [19] have proposed a start to finish, two-stage quadrilateral network architecture for graphic novel panel detection that acquires the faster R-CNN architecture. Various methodologies are utilized to recognize and extract panels [20] from the graphic novels. Recursive cut algorithm with the multi-layer perceptron [21] are utilized to recognize and extract panels from the graphic novels and improve the precision of graphic novel component extraction.

Reference [22] utilized watershed segmentation technique to recognize panels. Ref. [23] had built up a recursive technique to divide the graphic novel pages in panels by using the density gradient.

3   Proposed Architecture—SPEGYOLO

The architecture of SPEGYOLO is divided into two stages which includes training the character and semiotic recognition model and then the semiotic constraint-based panel extraction.

The input to the model is a set of graphic novel strips from a tinkle graphic novel dataset that are annotated before training. At the first stage, the dataset annotation is done using the VOTT tool to label the characters and semiotics of our interest. The annotated files are converted to the YOLO format files for the training process. The model is pre-trained using the YOLOv3 algorithm on our custom tinkle graphic novel dataset. The YOLO format files along with the training images are given as an input to the model for training. Once the model is trained, it is used to detect the semiotics from the test images. The final stage of the process is to identify the semiotics from the individual panels of the graphic novel strips and extract them. The panels are extracted using a contour detection algorithm, and the extraction is done for the panels containing semiotics of interest. The SPEGYOLO method identifies the semiotics such as motion lines, path lines associated with objects/characters at different orientations and locations which helps to apprehend the meaning behind these graphic novel images. When compared with other object detection methods, SPEGYOLO gave better results in identifying the semiotics.

The architecture of SPEGYOLO is shown in Fig. 2, and the various algorithms used are discussed.

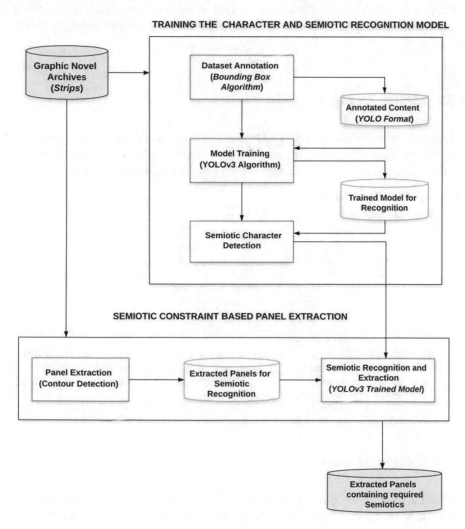

Fig. 2 SPEGYOLO architecture

3.1 Dataset Annotation

Dataset annotation is done by the process of labeling the images with the characters and semiotics of interest. Before training a model, the images have to be annotated. The tinkle dataset (a set of graphic novel images) is created which is further annotated with the characters and semiotics. The output of annotating a graphic novel strip is a csv file that consists of the depth, width, and position of the particular object that is annotated.

3.2 Model Training

Training the model is based on YOLOv3, which detects the characters and semiotics of interest from the graphic novel strips. The model is trained by providing the training images along with data train.txt and data classes.txt files as an input.

INPUT: YOLO format file
OUTPUT: Trained model

```
1. FLAGS ← parser.parse_args()
2. if not FLAGS.warnings:
3. tf.logging.set_verbosity(tf.logging.ERROR)
4. os.environ["TF_CPP_MIN_LOG_LEVEL"] = "3"
5.     warnings.filterwarnings("ignore")
6. anchors ← get_anchors(anchors_path)
7. num_val ← int(len(lines) * val_split)
8. num_train = len(lines) − num_val
9. batch_size = 32
10. print("Train on{}samples,val on{}samples, with batch-
size{}.".format(num_train,num_val, batch_size))
11.     file      ←      open(os.path.join(log_dir_time,
"step1_loss.npy"), "w")
12. file.close()
```

3.3 Semiotic Character Detection

After the training process, the model is used to detect the characters and semiotics associated with it in a given graphic novel strip. The output is a bounding box of the characters with the identified label and the score that the model justifies the semiotics.

INPUT: Trained model, Test images
OUTPUT: Detected panels containing characters with required semiotics

```
1. Input Image Path
2. img_endings = (".jpg", ".jpeg", ".png")
3. for item in input_paths:
4. if item.endswith(img_endings):
```

```
5.       input_image_paths.append(item)
6. else:
7.       output_path ← FLAGS.output
8. Yolo detector open_session()
9. classfile = open(FLAGS.classes_path, "r")
10. Print(Input Lables)
11. for i and img_path in enumerate:
12.      print(img_path)
13. start = timer()
14. end = timer()
15. yolo.close_session()
```

3.4   Panel Extraction

Panel extraction is important as each panel contains a vital snapshot of a specific story. The panels are divided by frames with space in between known as the gutters. The panels are usually rectangular in shape, but it may vary to artists. The contour detection algorithm is applied to get panels out of contours in pixels.

INPUT: Graphic novel strips
OUTPUT: Extracted panels

```
1. Input ← File_name Parse_image
2. contours ← cv.findContours()
3. for contour in contours:
4.      arclength = cv.arcLength(contour,True)
5.      epsilon = 0.01 * arclength
6.      approx = cv.approxPolyDP(contour,epsilon,True)
7. for panel in infos['panels']:
8.      n += 1
9. return infos
10.   if p2y >= p1b − self.gutterThreshold and
p2y >= p1y − self.gutterThreshold:
11.      return −1
12.   if p1y >= p2b − self.gutterThreshold and
p1y >= p2y − self.gutterThreshold:
13.      return 1
14.   if p2x >= p1r − self.gutterThreshold and
p2x >= p1x − self.gutterThreshold:
15.      return −1
16.   if p1x >= p2r − self.gutterThreshold and
p1x >= p2x − self.gutterThreshold:
17.      return 1
18. return 0
```

3.5   Constraint-Based Extracted Panels

The panels are given as an input to the trained model where the panels containing the required semiotics are identified and extracted.

4   Implementation Results

4.1   Experimentation

The dataset is a collection of tinkle graphic novel books from the Internet. The pages of the books are cropped, and graphic novel strips are created which are then annotated for model training. The individual strips are provided as an input for panel extraction to obtain constraint-based panels.

4.2   Experimental Results

Given a graphic novel, every strip is annotated. The annotated files are converted into YOLO format files. These files along with the training images are given as an input to the model for training. The model is trained using the YOLOv3 algorithm for semiotic character detection. The training process is continued if the results are unsatisfactory, and a trained model weight for initial and final stages is saved. The panel extraction is done using contour analysis where the algorithm scans for edges and returns the coordinate points. The panels containing the required semiotics are extracted and saved in the database. Thus, the custom trained proposed method identifies the metadata (semiotics) associated with the object. It identifies that the object is moving which is represented by movement lines and path lines as shown in Figs. 3 and 4, whereas the baseline model could track these objects and by using a machine learning algorithm, and it can only say that the objects are moving. Similarly, the ground truth proposals can provide insights that a bird is moving fast on seeing the other animal. From the results obtained by the SPEGYOLO method, it is evident that the objects/characters can be identified at different orientation and locations which aids in apprehending the actual meaning conveyed through the images.

5   Evaluation Metric and Performance Analysis

SPEG was evaluated through intersection over union (IOU) and mean average precision (mAP). The confidence score is the likelihood that an anchor box contains the object.

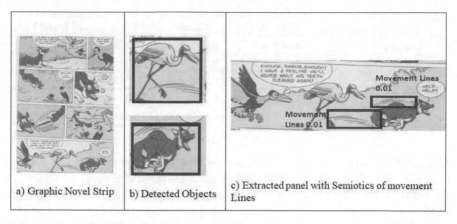

| a) Graphic Novel Strip | b) Detected Objects | c) Extracted panel with Semiotics of movement Lines |

Fig. 3 Detected panels with movement lines

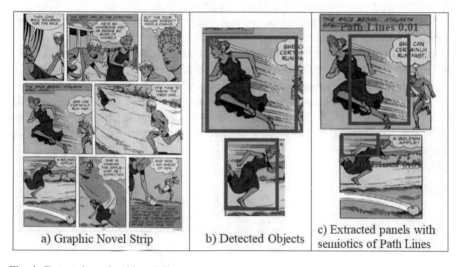

| a) Graphic Novel Strip | b) Detected Objects | c) Extracted panels with semiotics of Path Lines |

Fig. 4 Detected panels with path lines

Intersection over union (IOU) is characterized as the region of the convergence isolated by the territory of the association of an anticipated bouncing box (Bp) and a ground truth box (Bgt). IOU is given by Eq. 1

$$IOU = area(Bp \cap Bgt)/area(Bp \cup Bgt). \tag{1}$$

Average precision (AP) is a mainstream metric in estimating the exactness of object detectors like faster R-CNN and SSD. The value is computed in the range of 0–1. It measures how precise the predictions are.

Table 1
Evaluation—precision, recall, and $F1$-score

Iteration	Precision	Recall	$F1$-score
Iteration 1	0.694	0.708	0.701
Iteration 2	0.738	0.75	0.744
Iteration 3	0.757	0.763	0.760
Iteration 4	0.798	0.792	0.795
Iteration 5	0.803	0.843	0.822

Mean Average precision (mAP) is an enhancement of average precision. In average precision, we only calculate individual objects, but in mAP, it gives the precision for the entire model. To find the percentage of correct predictions in the model, mAP is used.

Table 1 gives the computed results of the images. The graphical representation of Table 1 is shown in Fig. 5. The mean average precision (mAP) is calculated to be **75.8%** which is the total accuracy of the entire model.

Generally, in graphic novel component analysis, character detection is a very difficult task as it is of free form, and the author may have their own style of presentation. Many researches have been carried out in detecting those objects using R-CNN and Single Shot Detector (SSD) and shown impressive results, whereas SPEGYOLO aimed to apprehend the meaning of semiotics associated with the character of interest. From Table 2, it can be observed that SPEGYOLO has given successive results with the average precision of **0.823** for detection of characters when analyzed with fast R-CNN and SSD. Also SPEGYOLO yields an average precision of 0.758 for identifying semiotics.

Fig. 5 IOU graph analysis

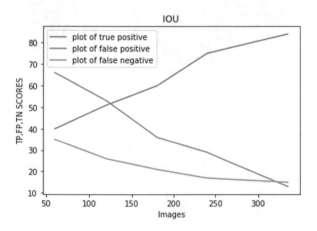

Table 2 Comparison on character detection and semiotic identification with different methods

Methods	Object											
	Character and object detection						Semiotic identification					
	Ground truth proposals			Learnt proposals			Ground truth proposals			Learnt proposals		
	Precision	Recall	F1-score	Precision	Recall	F1-score	Precision	Recall	F1-score	Precision	Recall	F1-score
SSD	0.781	0.86	0.810	0.765	0.841	0.801	–	–	–	–	–	–
FAST R-CNN	0.823	0.90	0.858	0.810	0.892	0.848	–	–	–	–	–	–
SPEG YOLO	0.847	0.91	0.879	0.823	0.903	0.861	0.823	0.85	0.835	0.758	0.771	0.766

6 Conclusion and Future Work

The visual morphology uses semiotic references such as motion lines, scopic lines, radial lines, and focal lines to convey the meaning but depending on the location they are placed, the meaning varies. These conventions have been analyzed from the panels of the graphic novel strip, and the constraint-based panel extraction from the graphic novels has been implemented. The custom trained model has shown better performance in identifying various semiotics present at different orientation and locations. The extracted semiotics help to perform further analysis to infer the meaning associated with it.

References

1. MacEachren AM, Roth RE, O'Brien J, Li B, Swingley D, Gahegan M (2012) Visual semiotics and uncertainty visualization: an empirical study. IEEE Trans Vis Comput Graph 18(12):2496–2505
2. Chauhan D, Sutaria K, Doshi R (2018) Impact of semiotics on multidimensional sentiment analysis on Twitter: a survey. In: 2018 second international conference on computing methodologies and communication (ICCMC). IEEE, pp 671–674
3. Huang M, Xie H, Rao Y, Liu Y, Poon LK, Wang FL (2020) Lexicon-based sentiment convolutional neural networks for online review analysis. IEEE Trans Affect Comput 13(3):1337–1348
4. Chen J, Iwasaki R, Mori N, Okada M, Ueno M (2019) Understanding multilingual four-scene comics with deep learning methods. In: International conference on document analysis and recognition workshops (ICDARW), vol 1, pp 32–37
5. Vickers P, Faith J, Rossiter N (2012) Understanding visualization: a formal approach using category theory and semiotics. IEEE Trans Vis Comput Graph 19(6):1048–1061
6. Martins DML, de Lima Neto FB (2017) Hybrid intelligent decision support using a semiotic case-based reasoning and self-organizing maps. IEEE Trans Syst Man Cybern Syst 50(3):863–870
7. Weber W (2019) Towards a semiotics of data visualization—an inventory of graphic resources. In: 2019 23rd international conference information visualisation (IV). IEEE, pp 323–328
8. Rigaud C, Burie JC et al (2019) What do we expect from comic panel extraction? In: 2019 international conference on document analysis and recognition workshops (ICDARW). IEEE, vol 1, pp 44–49
9. Karthika Devi MS, Fathima S, Baskaran R (2020) CBCS-comic book cover synopsis: generating synopsis of a comic book with unsupervised abstractive dialogue. Procedia Comput Sci 172:701–708
10. Deng D, Jing L, Yu J, Sun S (2019) Sparse self-attention LSTM for sentiment lexicon construction. IEEE/ACM Trans Audio Speech Lang Process 27(11):1777–1790
11. Rayar F (2017) Accessible comics for visually impaired people: challenges and opportunities. In: 2017 14th IAPR international conference on document analysis and recognition (ICDAR). IEEE, vol 3, pp 9–14
12. Augereau O, Iwata M, Kise K (2018) A survey of comics research in computer science. J Imaging 4(7):87
13. Karthika Devi MS, Fathima S, Baskaran R (2020) SYNC—short, yet novel concise natural language description: generating a short story sequence of album images using multimodal network. In: ICT analysis and applications. Springer, Berlin, pp 235–245

14. Xie X, Cai X, Zhou J, Cao N, Wu Y (2018) A semantic-based method for visualizing large image collections. IEEE Trans Vis Comput Graph 25(7):2362–2377
15. Karthika Devi MS, UmaaMahesswari G, Baskaran R (2022) Dialogue extraction and translation from stories on thirukural using verb cue quote content source identifiers. In: Senjyu T, Mahalle PN, Perumal T, Joshi A (eds) ICT with intelligent applications. Smart innovation, systems and technologies, vol 248. Springer, Berlin, pp 525-537
16. Zhou L, Li W, Ogunbona P, Zhang Z (2020) Jointly learning visual poses and pose lexicon for semantic action recognition. IEEE Trans Circuits Syst Video Technol 30(2):457–467
17. Zhao L, Li S (2020) Object detection algorithm based on improved yolov3. Electronics 9(3):537
18. Rigaud C, Tsopze N, Burie JC, Ogier JM (2011) Robust frame and text extraction from comic books. In: International workshop on graphics recognition. Springer, Berlin, pp 129–138
19. Qin X, Zhou Y, He Z, Wang Y, Tang Z (2017) A faster r-cnn based method for comic characters face detection. In: 2017 14th IAPR international conference on document analysis and recognition (ICDAR). IEEE, vol 1, pp 1074–1080
20. Pang X, Cao Y, Lau RW, Chan AB (2014) A robust panel extraction method for manga. In: Proceedings of the 22nd ACM international conference on multimedia, pp 1125–1128
21. Chan CH, Leung H, Komura T (2007) Automatic panel extraction of color comic images. In: Pacific-Rim conference on multimedia. Springer, Berlin, pp 775–778
22. Ponsard C, Fries V (2008) An accessible viewer for digital comic books. In: International conference on computers for handicapped persons. Springer, Berlin, pp 569–577
23. Tanaka T, Shoji K, Toyama F, Miyamichi J (2007) Layout analysis of tree-structured scene frames in comic images. In: IJCAI, vol 7, pp 2885–2890

Study of Various Word Vectors
for Sentiment Analysis

**S. Madhusudhanan, N. M. Jyothi, A. Vishnukumar, S. Sathya,
and N. Arun Vignesh**

1   Introduction

Natural Language Processing (NLP) is concerns with understanding of the language
to perform certain tasks such as:

- Sentiment analysis: the process of finding the opinion from the piece of text.
- Machine translation: To translate the sentence or paragraph into other language
  (e.g., Google Translation).
- Speech recognition: Machine can understand the voice.
- Image-to-text representation: creating a Captcha for an image as input.

Sentiment analysis is the recognition and categorization of concepts presented in
text form to determine whether an author expressed his view on an object, product,
or other as positive, negative, or neutral. Sentiment analysis covers a wide range of
applications, including contextual semantic search, brand value recognition, stock
price prediction, and customer service [1–4]. In today's marketing world, sentiment
analysis is very popular, and companies like Google, Microsoft, IBM, Amazon, and

S. Madhusudhanan (✉) · N. M. Jyothi
Department of Artificial Intelligence and Data Science, Prathyusha Engineering College,
Thiruvallur, Chennai, Tamilnadu, India
e-mail: ssmadhu80@gmail.com

A. Vishnukumar
Department of Information Technology, Vel Tech High Tech Dr. Rangarajan Dr. Sakunthala
Engineering College, Vel Nagar, Avadi, Chennai, Tamil Nadu, India

S. Sathya
Department of Electronics and Communication Engineering, Gojan School of Business and
Technology, Edapalayam, Red Hills, Chennai, Tamil Nadu, India

N. Arun Vignesh
Department of Electronics and Communication Engineering, Gokaraju Rangaraju Institute of
Engineering and Technology, Hyderabad, India

© The Author(s), under exclusive license to Springer Nature Singapore Pte Ltd. 2023   329
K. Kumar Singh et al. (eds.), *Machine Vision and Augmented Intelligence*, Lecture Notes
in Electrical Engineering 1007, https://doi.org/10.1007/978-981-99-0189-0_24

Facebook have their own sentiment detection services, such as Google NLP API, Microsoft Azure, IBM Tone Analyzer, and AWS Comprehend [5].

In recent years, various research works are supported to analyze this massive amount of data to extract the sentiment on a specific topic. Deep learning is the process of analyzing large amounts of data, such as text, to extract the points of view stated on a specific topic [6]. Deep learning can be applied to all aspects of computerized word prediction, text classification and summarization. Word embedding is a task for the automatic processing of natural language. It operates by projecting a collection of k words onto a vector space of dimension M, where M is the size of a word-rich dataset. The main contribution of this is to study the various word embedding feature representations and compare its performance in deep learning algorithm.

The following sections are: "Related work" section discussed about the existing work. Then, "Methodology" contains the methods used in this work, Implementation of the proposed methods and Results discussion. Finally, the concluding section discusses the potential approaches and future ideas.

2 Related Work

To build the subvector model, the author offered two approaches: global matrix factorization and local context window methods, both of which rely on non-zero components in word–word representation [7]. They were able to get a model performance of 75%. The author's proposed model might include non-sentiment annotations as well as continuous and multi-dimensional sentiment information. The proposed method, which made use of document-level sentiment polarity annotations accessible in many online publications [8], outperformed the previous model. For text classification, the author combined the convolutional neural networks (CNN) and bidirectional long short-term memory (BiLSTM) models with Doc2Vec embedding [9]. They have achieved 90.66% accuracy. The Doc2Vec paradigm was proposed by the author [4]. Each document is created as a dense vector to train and predict terms in the document. The proposed method corrects the flaws of bag-of-words models.

The author employed deep learning techniques such as the convolutional neural network model and long short-term memory [10] to train the IMDB dataset, which contains 50,000 movie reviews. The emotional tweets were then predicted in the Twitter dataset for categorization.

To determine mood polarity, researchers [11] suggested the use of a hybrid heterogeneous support vector machine (HSVM). They also compared the performance of the proposed strategy with the performance of recurrent neural networks (RNNs) and support vector machines (SVMs). The author has developed the RGWE methodology based on the idea of sentiments [12].

The author proposed to solve the problem that modern word expression algorithms cannot fully integrate sentiment information into classification problems. An IMDB dataset containing 50,000 movie reviews using deep learning techniques such as convolutional neural network models and long short-term memory are utilized to solve the above problem [10]. Emotional tweets were also predicted in the Twitter dataset for classification.

The author [13] proposes a deep learning model incorporating sentiment-based text classification. In sentiment classification, the model's accuracy outperformed the basic deep learning strategy.

3 Proposed Approach

Previous research has concentrated on machine learning models for sentiment analysis [1], which use a bag of words, term frequency, and inverse document frequency (TF-IDF) to extract the best features from a dataset. Word embeddings, on the other hand, are utilized in deep learning for word representation. The proposed study focuses on the development of numerous word embedding models (word2vec, Doc2Vec, FastText, Glove) in combination with the DL approach.

3.1 Methodology

In artificial neural network, a word vector is a two-layer artificial neural network architecture that can learn to represent each word with a real number vector with its own semantic properties, allowing related words to be joined into a single vector.

3.1.1 Word2Vector

Word2vec may train using one of the two models: continuous bundle of words (CBOW) and skip-gram model.

(i) CBOW is based on context-based word prediction.
    Because it may be a single word or a sequence of words, this method has a big benefit in that it does not require a great amount of resources [14]. The negative logarithmic word probability (wt) with respect to the context ($\hat{r}$) is calculated in this model.
(ii) Skip-gram is much like CBOW aside from that, this version accepts a phrase as input and outputs all viable words.

3.1.2 Global Vectors (GloVe)

Rather than a term co-occurrence matrix, the GloVe model learns word embeddings from a term co-occurrence matrix [7]. The co-occurrence matrix is a $V \times V$ matrix, where V is the size of the vocabulary. Each component of the matrix represents how often vocabulary items provided within a given context framework, including the entire corpus, are displayed together. GloVe uses vector embedding to reduce reconstruction errors between the predicted co-occurrence statistics of the model and the global co-occurrence statistics of the training corpus [15]. Vector-embedded dimensions and matrix-embedded dimensions are two hyperparameters that need to be properly specified in the model. GloVe calculates measurements in a larger window, so it can capture longer-term situations than word2vec, but queries for those conditions are lost. Neither word2vec nor GloVe seem to have a significant advantage when it comes to accurate detection, as overall performance is affected by a variety of factors.

3.1.3 FastText

The FastText model exploits flaws in approaches such as word2vec and GloVe. It can accommodate new out-of-vocabulary words by adding internal subword data [8] as the character n-gram (that is, grouping of adjacent characters) to the word2vec skip-gram (SG) model. Based on the placement of these subword components, this approach provides a vector representation of words, allowing the model to reflect word morphology and vocabulary comparability and build ambiguous word vectors.

3.1.4 Doc2Vec

Because it is a word2vec extension, it is known as Doc2Vec [9]. The purpose of Doc2Vec is to generate numerical representations of phrases, paragraphs, and texts. Unlike word2vec, Doc2Vec computes a feature vector for each document in the corpus. It may be used to compare sentences, paragraphs, and papers, among other things.

3.1.5 Distributed Memory—DM

This version is just like the CBOW version in word2vec [6]. Paragraph vectors are generated by training a neural network to infer the central word based on the context word and the context paragraph. Mikolove et al. applied the DM model in two ways: using the average calculation process or the concatenating calculation approach.

4 Deep Learning Algorithm

4.1 Long Short-Term Memory (LSTM) Network

Long short-term memory (LSTM) network is a kind of RNN capable of learning long-term dependencies [16]. RNNs are all made up of a series of repeating modules. In typical RNNs, this repeating module has a simple structure. The LSTM repeating module, on the other hand, is more advanced. Instead of a single neural network layer, there are four that interact in different ways. It also has two states: hidden and cell state. Recurrent Neural Networks (RNNs) are made up of LSTM units. RNN have a number of limitations, including the inability to recall the context of a statement for an extended period of time and the inability to selectively forget. These issues do not exist with LSTMs because they can remember for a long time and selectively forget [10].

LSTMs are made up of three gates: Input Gate: This gate keeps the input as a vector while discarding irrelevant information. The sigmoid function is in charge of forgetting information. It generates values ranging from 0 to 1. If the value is 1, it remembers; if it is 0, it forgets. Tanh is a tool for creating input vectors.

Forgot Gate: This gate is used to selectively forget information. This is accomplished through the application of the sigmoid function.

Output Gate: This gate generates the LSTM network's output. The operation of an output gate can be separated into three steps: (1) generate a vector by scaling the cell state values from -1 to $+1$ with the tanh function; (2) making a vector with the $ht - 1$ and Xt values to control the values that must be produced from the previously built vector. In this filter, a sigmoid function is utilized once again; and (3) as the output, multiply the value of this normative filter by the vector created in step 1.

5 Experiment and Result

The Amazon dataset [17] is used as input for LSTM algorithm. The performance of word embedding algorithms is shown in Table 1.

Table 1 Base classifiers' accuracy LSTM

Word embedding	LSTM algorithm Accuracy in %
Word2Vec	79.29
FastText	81.23
Glove	82.41
DBoW (Doc2Vec)	68.34
DMC	82.55
DMM	**83.67**

From the result, the word embedding DMM provides better result compared with other.

6 Conclusion

The different word embeddings' techniques are implemented in this work. The performance of LSTM is better on DMM embedding and achieved better result. The main aim of this study focused on performance of various word embeddings in sentiment analysis. The expansion of Doc2Vec embedding techniques in text representation is more suited for sentiment categorization. In the future, we want to test these word embedding approaches on a variety of domains with the help of other deep learning techniques.

References

1. Pang B, Lee L (2008) Opinion mining and sentiment analysis. In: Foundations and trends in information retrieval, vol 2, no 1–2, pp 1–135
2. Sajana T, Narasingarao MR (2018) Classification of imbalanced malaria disease using Naïve Bayesian algorithm. Int J Eng Technol 7(2.7):786–790
3. Sanjay Bhargav P, Nagarjuna Reddy G, Ravi Chand RV, Pujitha K, Mathur A (2019) Sentiment analysis for hotel rating using machine learning algorithms. Int J Innov Technol Exploring Eng 8(6):1225–1228
4. Srinivas PVVS, Pavan Sai Sujith LVN, Sarvani PM, Kumar DS, Parasa D (2019) Prediction of hospital admission using machine learning. Int J Sci Technol Res 8(112)
5. Kaur H, Ahsaan SU, Alankar B et al (2021) A proposed sentiment analysis deep learning algorithm for analyzing COVID-19 tweets. Inf Syst Front. https://doi.org/10.1007/s10796-021-10135-7
6. Ian Goodfellow AC, Bengio Y (2015) Deep learning book. Deep Learn. http://doi.org/10.1016/B978-0-12-391420-0.09987-X
7. Pennington J, Socher R, Manning CD (2014) GloVe: global vectors for word representation. In: Proceedings of the 2014 conference on empirical methods in natural language processing (EMNLP 2014), pp 1532–1543
8. Le Q, Mikolov T (2014) Distributed representations of sentences and documents. In: Proceedings of the 31th international conference on machine learning, Beijing, China, 21–26 June 2014, pp 1188–1196
9. Rhanoui M, Mikram M, Yousfi S, Barzali S (2019) A CNN-BiLSTM model for document-level sentiment analysis. Mach Learn Knowl Extr 1:832–847. http://doi.org/10.3390/make1030048
10. Gandhi UD, Malarvizhi Kumar P, Chandra Babu G et al (2021) Sentiment analysis on Twitter data by using convolutional neural network (CNN) and long short term memory (LSTM). Wireless Pers Commun. https://doi.org/10.1007/s11277-021-08580-3
11. Salur MU, Aydin I (2020) A novel hybrid deep learning model for sentiment classification. IEEE Access 8:58080–58093. https://doi.org/10.1109/ACCESS.2020.2982538
12. Yin W, Kann K, Yu M, Schütze H (2017) Comparative study of CNN and RNN for natural language processing. Computing Research Repository (CoRR). arXiv:1702.01923
13. Maas L, Daly RE, Pham PT, Huang D, Ng AY, Potts C (2011) Learning word vectors for sentiment analysis. In: Proceedings of the 49th annual meeting of the association for computational linguistics: human language technologies (HLT 2011), pp 142–150

14. Tang D, Wei F, Yang N, Zhou M, Liu T, Qin B (2014) Learning sentiment-specific word embedding. ACL. https://doi.org/10.3115/1220575.1220648
15. Wang Y, Huang G, Li J, Li H, Zhou Y, Jiang H (2021) Refined global word embeddings based on sentiment concept for sentiment analysis. IEEE Access 9:37075–37085. https://doi.org/10.1109/ACCESS.2021.3062654
16. Olah C (2015) Understanding LSTM networks [Blog]. http://doi.org/10.1007/s13398-014-0173-7.2
17. Nafis NSM, Awang S (2021) Enhanced hybrid feature selection technique using term frequency-inverse document frequency and support vector machine-recursive feature elimination for sentiment classification. IEEE Access 9:52171–52192

A Comparative Analysis of 2D Ear Recognition for Constrained and Unconstrained Dataset Using Deep Learning Approach

Ravishankar Mehta and Koushlendra Kumar Singh

1 Introduction

Convolutional neural network has tremendous impact on ear recognition technologies in the field of person identification. Recent work has shown that its performance on different computer vision task like image classification [1–5], object detection [6–9], segmentation [10], and image recognitions [11–13] and alike has great impact. Many researchers confirmed that for person identification in biometric community, ears are one of the unique traits [14]. Deep learning-based ear recognition system has been under rigorous research in the last few years. There exist two phases in this module: First is ear detection and the second is ear recognition. Many journal and research paper has been explored in this field from more than twenty years but still we cannot say that ear recognition system based on deep CNN approaches gives tremendous result in presence of variation in rotation, occlusion, environmental factor, sensing device, and poor illumination factors [15, 16]. Under this circumstances, an accurate ear recognition can be a challenging task specially when sample of ear images is taken under unconstrained environment. The previous work of ear recognition performed well under controlled environment. But these techniques require manual feature engineering for feature that are used to discriminate the individual based on specific patterns. Its performance is mainly depends on effectiveness of classifier and the feature extraction methods. Manual extraction of these features from ear image is cumbersome task and also time-consuming. Therefore, failing to these short coming results in degradation of recognition accuracy. These short comings are overcome through deep learning approaches specially through deep CNN [10]. It improves the

R. Mehta (✉) · K. K. Singh
Machine Vision and Intelligence Lab, Department of Computer Science and Engineering,
National Institute of Technology Jamshedpur, Jamshedpur, Jharkhand, India
e-mail: rmehta.online@gmail.com

K. K. Singh
e-mail: koushlendra.cse@nitjsr.ac.in

K. Kumar Singh et al. (eds.), *Machine Vision and Augmented Intelligence*, Lecture Notes
in Electrical Engineering 1007, https://doi.org/10.1007/978-981-99-0189-0_25

337

results of several factors like availability of large amount of training data with label, high speed computation (i.e., GPU's), efficient network architecture, and specific optimization techniques. Unlike traditional ear recognition techniques where a deep CNN perform does the task of feature extraction and classification in end to end manner with the help of training data. Though it requires large amount (millions) of training data with proper label. Also acquiring of these data is quite expensive. In this paper, we focused to develop an effective CNN model for ear recognition with minimum number of layers (convolution and MaxPooling) and limited amount of training data. Different activity has been opted to develop this effective CNN. In brief, we contributed following activity as listed below:

- We developed a CNN model which consists of only six layers for ear recognitions tasks.
- We have considered limited dataset of constrained and unconstrained environment.
- We tune the network parameter to see how it affects the accuracy on constrained and unconstrained dataset.
- Finally, we perform comparative analysis of our model by performing experiment on different datasets.

The paper is organized as follows: Sect. 2 describes the proposed CNN architecture. Section 2.1 describes the database description and experimental setup. Experimental Result and Analysis are discussed in Sect. 3, and finally, we concluded our work in Sect. 4, respectively.

2 Methodology

In this article, we put our interest to develop the CNN-based model for ear recognition task. First, we do some amount of preprocessing task in which we resize all image to 180×50. These input images are fed into the first convolutional network of model. Next kernel is applied on it which convolved on to the entire image to produce the filtered image. The number of filtered image will be same as the number of kernel. We have kept stride value as one. WE also used same padding, so that size of filtered image and input image will remain same. After this convolution operation, ReLU activation function is applied that maps all the negative value of filtered image to zero. Next MaxPooling operation with filter size 2×2 is applied that reduces the size of filtered image to half. This reduced filtered image is again fed into second convolutional operation, and this process continues till six convolutional layer. At the last layer of convolution, output of filtered image is flattened to get one dimensional feature vector. In our case, we get 1280 feature vector. At fully connected layer, we apply 100 neuron, since we have total 100 subjects. Finally, softmax function is used at fully connected layer which gives probability based output to determine that which image belongs to which particular class. Here, the task of feature extraction is performed by convolution and MaxPooling layers, whereas the fully connected layer

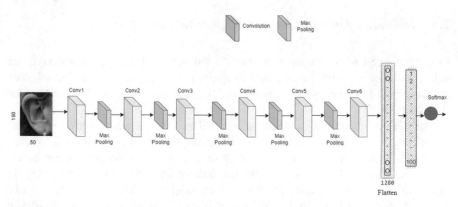

Fig. 1 Network architecture of the proposed CNN for constrained and unconstrained datasets

at the end does the task of classification. The network architecture of the developed CNN model is shown in Fig. 1.

The network consists of six convolutional layers. A sub-sampling layer is introduced after ear convolution layer to reduce the dimensionality of the input image. Each stages produces large number of abstract features. Finally, these features are used by fully connected layer to classify the input image. To enhance the training of CNN model and network stability, a batch normalization is introduced. In our work, we have used batch size of 512 which reduces the sensitivity of network initialization. It is found that the proposed architecture of CNN gives total of 522,324 trainable parameters.

Since, it is a multiclass classification problem, we have used categorical cross-entropy as a loss function which is illustrated in Eq. (1).

$$E(\varphi) = -\frac{1}{C} \sum \sum_{i=0}^{C} \log p_j^m + (1 - y_j) \log(1 - p_j^m) \tag{1}$$

where p_j and y_j are the actual and predicted labels, respectively, C is the number of class and m represents the corresponding layers. To minimize the problem of overfitting, we drop a set of nodes for every iteration of gradient descent. Here, we have used RMSProp optimizers to update the weight and the weight update rule is given by formulae in Eq. (2).

$$\varphi_{I+1} = \varphi_i - \frac{\eta}{\sqrt{(1 - \lambda)\nabla_{\varphi_i}^2 J(\varphi_i) + \lambda \nabla_{\varphi_i} J(\varphi_i) + \varepsilon}} \tag{2}$$

where η is learning rate, λ is the decay term whose values range from 0 to 1, and ∇_{φ_i} is moving average of squared gradients.

2.1 Database Description and Experimental Setup

In the proposed work, we have used AWE ear dataset for experiment. AWE ear dataset contains total 1000 images of 100 distinct subjects. All images of this dataset are taken under unconstrained environment. Some sample images of this dataset are shown in Fig. 2.

For comparison purpose, we have also tested our experiment on two other dataset of ear images, namely AMI and IITD-II. The description of these datasets is illustrated in Table 1. Table shows that the images of these datasets have different characteristics.

To train our CNN model, we split the dataset into 70% for training purpose and 30% for testing purpose. We tested our model with different optimizers like Adam, Adagrad, and RMSProp, It is found that the model works fine with RMSProp optimizers. We set the learning rate with two different value, i.e., $\eta = 0.001$ and $\eta = 0.0001$. With learning rate $\eta = 0.0001$, our model gives better result. We tune the parameter of proposed CNN model for higher classification result.

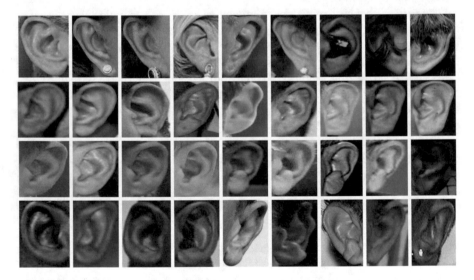

Fig. 2 Sample images of ear from AWE dataset

Table 1 Description of different dataset used in the proposed work

Datasets	Country	No. of subjects	Number of images	Image size
AWE	Slovenia	100	1000	Varied
AMI	Spain	10	700	492×702
IITD-II	India	221	793	50×180

Table 2 Performance measurement of the proposed model on different dataset of ear images by varying different parameters

Dataset	Rotation	Kernel size	Optimizers	Learning rate (η)	No. of epochs	Recognition rate (%)
IITD-II	15°	3×3	RMSProp	0.001	100	82.13
	30°	3×3	RMSProp	0.0001	1000	83.61
AWE	15°	3×3	Adagrad	0.0001	100	80.11
	30°	3×3	RMSProp	0.001	1000	81.58
AMI	15°	3×3	RMSProp	0.001	100	68.31
	30°	5×5	Adam	0.0001	1000	69.54

3 Result and Performance Evaluation

This section contains the experimental result and its comparison with different datasets. The proposed work is evaluated on three datasets. In the first step of experiment, we trained the model with varying parameters like optimizers, rotations, learning rate, and number of epochs. Table 2 illustrates the list of parameter used to train the proposed model.

From the experiment, it is observed that the proposed model gives accuracy 83.61% for 1000 epochs with IITD-II dataset when RMSProp optimizers, and learning rate is set to 0.0001. The performance of trained model on different dataset of ear image is shown in Fig. 3a–c.

4 Conclusion

In this work, we explored a comparative analysis of constrained and unconstrained dataset for ear recognition system using CNN-based model. We have tuned the different network parameters like activation function, kernel size, optimizers, and value of learning rate to check whether our model is improving its performance or not. This task is obviously more difficult as there is no predetermined rule to decide the number of layers required to build CNN model that will give satisfactory result. In terms of future work, we are planning to perform better sampling techniques and mechanism that allow a model to learn more robust and distinct features for the classification task. As a future work, we will explore different CNN architectures which can be applied to solve the problem of constrained and unconstrained dataset for ear recognition system.

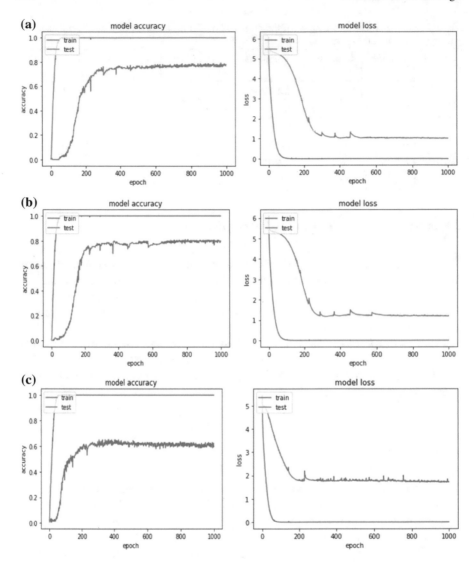

Fig. 3 **a** Accuracy and loss for AWE dataset using *RMSProp* in 1000 epochs. **b** Accuracy and loss for IITD-II dataset using *RMSProp* in 1000 epochs. **c** Accuracy and loss for AMI dataset using *RMSProp* in 1000 epochs

References

1. Saikia T, Kumar R, Kumar D, Singh KK (2022) An automatic lung nodule classification system based on hybrid transfer learning approach. SN Comput Sci 3(4):272
2. Mehta R, Singh KK (2023) Ear recognition system using averaging ensemble technique. In Machine Learning, Image Processing, Network Security and Data Sciences. In: Proceedings 4th International Conference, MIND 2022, Virtual Event, January 19–20, 2023, Part II, pp 220–229
3. He K, Zhang X, Ren S, Sun J (2016) Deep residual learning for image recognition. In: Proceedings of IEEE conference on computer vision and pattern recognition (CVPR), June 2016, pp 770–778
4. Szegedy C, Vanhoucke V, Ioffe S, Shlens J, Wojna Z (2016) Rethinking the inception architecture for computer vision. In: Proceedings of IEEE conference on computer vision and pattern recognition (CVPR), June 2016, pp 2818–2826
5. Huang G, Liu Z, Van Der Maaten L, Weinberger KQ (2017) Densely connected convolutional networks. In: Proceedings of IEEE conference on computer vision and pattern recognition (CVPR), July 2017, pp 4700–4708
6. Saikia T, Hansdah M, Singh KK, Bajpai MK (2022) Classification of lung nodules based on transfer learning with K-Nearest Neighbor (KNN). In 2022 IEEE international conference on imaging systems and techniques (IST), June 2022, pp. 1–6. IEEE
7. Girshick R, Donahue J, Darrell T, Malik J (2014) Rich feature hierarchies for accurate object detection and semantic segmentation. In: Proceedings of IEEE conference on computer vision and pattern recognition, June 2014, pp 580–587
8. Redmon J, Divvala S, Girshick R, Farhadi A (2016) You only look once: unified, real-time object detection. In: Proceedings of IEEE conference on computer vision and pattern recognition (CVPR), June 2016, pp 779–788
9. Lin T-Y, Dollár P, Girshick R, He K, Hariharan B, Belongie S (2017) Feature pyramid networks for object detection. In: Proceedings of IEEE conference on computer vision and pattern recognition (CVPR), July 2017, pp 2117–2125
10. Kumar Singh K, Kumar S, Antonakakis M, Moirogiorgou K, Deep A, Kashyap KL, Bajpai MK, Zervakis M (2022) Deep learning capabilities for the categorization of microcalcification. Int J Environ Res Public Health 19(4):2159
11. Mehta R, Garain J, Singh KK (2022) Cohort selection using mini-batch k-means clustering for ear recognition. In: Advances in Intelligent Computing and Communication, pp. 273–279
12. Redmon J, Divvala S, Girshick R, Farhadi A (2016) You only look once: unified, real-time object detection. In: Proceedings of the IEEE conference on computer vision and pattern recognition, pp 779–788
13. Erhan D, Szegedy C, Toshev A, Anguelov D (2014) Scalable object detection using deep neural networks. In: Proceedings of the IEEE conference on computer vision and pattern recognition, pp 2147–2154
14. Singh O, Kashyap KL, Singh KK (2023) Mesh-free technique for enhancement of the lung CT image. Biomedical Signal Processing and Control, vol 81, pp 104452
15. Tian L, Mu Z (2016) Ear recognition based on deep convolutional network. In: Proceedings of 9th international congress on image and signal processing, BioMedical engineering and informatics (CISP-BMEI), Oct 2016, pp 437–441
16. Rastogi A, Bhoumik U, Choudhary C, Akbari AS, Kumar Singh K (2021) Ear localization and validation using ear candidate set. In Machine Vision and Augmented Intelligence—Theory and Applications: Select Proceedings of MAI 2021, pp 109–120. Springer Singapore

Robust Sliding Mode Controller and Shunt Active Power Filter for Improvement of Power Quality Indices of an Autonomous Microgrid

Subhashree Choudhury, Devi Prasad Acharya, Sambeet Kumar Sahu, Azizuddin Khan, and Taraprasanna Dash

1 Introduction

The traditional power system primarily depends on nonrenewable energy-based fuel sources such as coal and other fossil fuels. These resources are gradually depleting and are not eco-friendly as they release hazardous chemicals into the atmosphere hence are not dependable. So the use of renewable energy-based energy resources is necessary. The microgrid (MG) is a small electrical energy generating unit with less production capacity and local loads and can be connected to the utility grid. In this scenario, the MG can function in both islanded and grid-tied operations, respectively. The evolution of the microgrid has led to the use of multiple remote Distributed Energy Resources (DER) in conventional grid systems. This approach requires the utilization of inverters and FACT devices. Again, rapid industrialization and exploding population have given rise to more complex delicate nonlinear loads. All these above phenomena introduce disturbances associated with the power system, also referred to as power quality issues such as Total Harmonic Distortion (THD), frequency deviation, poor power factor, voltage sag, and voltage swell. These power quality issues must be adequately eradicated for the healthy and reliable operation of the power system network. These issues can cause maloperation and overheating delicate and complex equipment associated with the generation, transmission, and distribution systems. Moreover, the power distribution should be performed with

S. Choudhury (✉) · D. P. Acharya · S. K. Sahu · A. Khan
Department of Electrical and Electronics Engineering, Siksha 'O' Anusandhan (Deemed to be University), Bhubaneswar 751030, India
e-mail: subhashreechoudhury@soa.ac.in

T. Dash
Department of Electronics and Communication Engineering, Siksha 'O' Anusandhan (Deemed to be University), Bhubaneswar 751030, India
e-mail: taradash@soa.ac.in

© The Author(s), under exclusive license to Springer Nature Singapore Pte Ltd. 2023
K. Kumar Singh et al. (eds.), *Machine Vision and Augmented Intelligence*, Lecture Notes in Electrical Engineering 1007, https://doi.org/10.1007/978-981-99-0189-0_26

an acceptable power quality range for customer satisfaction. Hence, the filtering of electrical power is of prime importance in the power distribution network.

The entire research article has been organized into six sections. Section 2 discusses about the review of literature. In Sect. 3, entire system modeling has been detailed. The traditional and the proposed controller has been elaborated in Sect. 4. In Sect. 5, the MATLAB/Simulink model has been illustrated and the results obtained are analyzed. Finally, in Sect. 6, the conclusion from the whole study has been highlighted.

2 Literature Review

The literature review suggests many methods to improve power quality issues associated with the Microgrid. For instance, in [1], a Shunt Active Power Filter (SAPF) is proposed containing H-bridge for the supervision of energy mandate and improvement of power quality issues, where the SAPF is tuned with the help of a Sliding Mode Controller (SMC). Using the Fuzzy Logic Control (FLC) technique is suggested for multilevel converter-based SAPF to reduce the THD of the current associated with the source in [2] under nonlinear loading conditions. The authors in [3] have suggested a unique approach for incorporating a PV array with a storage unit along with a SAPF for electric vehicle applications. The PV-Battery-integrated SAPF achieves the purpose of THD reduction, production of clean energy, storage of electric power, etc. The power quality issues associated with an off-grid MG system consisting of a PV array, wind energy, and the fuel cell are scrutinized along with a SAPF. The SAPF is controlled using the synchronous and modified reference frame reference methods for generating the reference current, the conventional PI controller and FLC for controlling DC side capacitor voltage, and a hysteresis-based current regulator for the generation of gate pulses [4]. The reduction of THD in a solar power-based microgrid system incorporated with a SAPF and a three-phase nonlinear rectifier load is proposed in [5]. The power quality improvement of a fuel cell-centered MG with a SAPF is suggested in [6]. The improvised hybrid particle swarm optimization-gravitational search algorithm (PSO-GSA) technique is used to optimize SAPF, thereby improving the power quality of the microgrid. The utilization of the soft computing method for compensating the reactive power associated with the harmonic current is proposed in [7], which utilizes the Adaptive Neuro-Fuzzy Inference System (ANFIS). The popular ANFIS manages the PID controller to provide proper gate pulse to the SAPF with the help of hysteresis current regulation method. Several optimization methods are used for tuning the SAPF parameters for improving the power quality issues associated with the microgrid system. These algorithms optimize the microgrid functioning by tuning the SAPF parameters such as DC capacitance, filter inductance, and PI controller gains Kp and Ki. The use of enhanced current control method with the help of particle Swarm optimization (PSO) is suggested in [8] for meeting the two optimization goals such as the reduction of harmonics associated with the source current and the increased application ratio for the capability of SAPF.

3   System Modeling

The proposed microgrid model consists of a PV array a fuel cell as the distributed energy resources connected to the utility grid at the PCC. The SAPF is also connected at the PCC parallel to the load. The line impedance block is attached to the utility grid, whose magnitude can be altered with need. The two control techniques, such as Sliding Mode Control and PI control, can regulate the SAPF controller action. The model of the proposed system is denoted in Fig. 1. The DERs are connected with the grid with the help of a DC/AC inverter and a universal bridge. The specifications associated with the DERs are given in Table 2.

3.1   PV Panel

The PV array is a DER that uses solar irradiance to convert solar energy to electrical energy [9]. The PV array combines PV cells, which trap the solar insolation on its surface by generating photoelectric current by the excited electrons. The PV panel acts as a current source in the electric circuit, which produces photoelectric current mathematically denoted as [10]

$$I = I_{\mathrm{Ph}} - I_0 \left[\exp\left(\frac{q V_{\mathrm{D}}}{n K T} \right) - 1 \right] - \frac{V_{\mathrm{D}}}{R_{\mathrm{Sh}}} \tag{1}$$

where 'I' denotes PV output current, 'I_{ph}' denotes photoelectric current, 'I_0' represents reverse saturation current, 'q' is the charge of an electron, 'V_{D}' denotes voltage across the diode, 'n' is the diode ideality factor, 'K' is the Boltzmann constant, 'T'

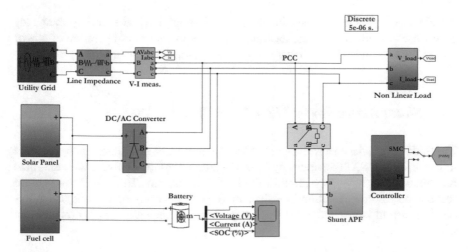

Fig. 1 System model

is the operating temperature, 'R_{Sh}' is the shunt resistance, 'V_D' is the voltage across the diode, and 'R_S' is the series resistance.

3.2 Fuel Cell

A fuel cell is a DER where the electrochemical reaction of the electrolyte generates electrical energy. The fuel cell comprises two electrodes such as anode and cathode, surrounded by electrolytic material. The electrochemical reactions which produce current at the electrodes are given below [11]:

At cathode:

$$H_2 + \frac{1}{2}O_2{}^{2-} + 2e^- \rightarrow H_2O+ \tag{2}$$

At anode:

$$H_2 \rightarrow 2H^+ + 2e^- \tag{3}$$

The overall reaction inside fuel cell:

$$\frac{1}{2}O_2 + H_2 = H_2O \tag{4}$$

3.3 Battery

A battery storage system is taken in this model for supplying power during emergency power backup situations to the local loads in case of failure of operation of one or more DERs taken [12]. The battery considered in this study is of lithium-ion type.

3.4 Shunt Active Power Filter (SAPF)

The SAPF is a device that is always connected to the system in a shunt manner parallel to the load. The SAPF operates by injecting a compensating current with the same magnitude and phase opposition to the harmonic current. The SAPF can achieve reactive power compensation by balancing the unbalanced load current. The reimbursing current is inserted at the PCC to perform the reactive power compensation [3].

4   Controller

4.1   PI Controller

The PI controller is a simple control technique used to control the SAPF. It is a combination of proportional and integral controllers where the proportional control can improve the rise time, and the integral controller can reduce the steady-state error. The overall mathematical representation of a PI controller is given by Mohanty et al. [13]

$$x(t) = K_p e(t) + K_i \int e(t).dt \tag{5}$$

'$x(t)$' is the control variable, 'K_p' is the proportional gain, 'K_i' denotes the integral gain parameter, and '$e(t)$' represents the error signal. The traditional PI controller can control a linear system with a finite set of variables.

4.2   Sliding Mode Controller (SMC)

The SMC is a control technique for nonlinear systems that change a complex system's functioning by using an intermittent control signal by compelling the plant to move within the system's normal behavior [14]. The SMC construction comprises of two phases. In the first phase, a sliding surface is appropriately considered, which determines the performance of the proposed plant during sliding [15]. In the second phase, a controller action is considered, which steers all the state trajectories toward the sliding surface in a limited time and then enforces them to remain on the sliding surface. The sliding establishment ensures that the system becomes unchanged due to modeling imprecisions and external turbulences [16].

In the proposed model, a hysteresis-based SMC is used to improve the error signal of the dc voltage associated with the SAPF. The error signal is generated by comparing the dc voltage obtained, and the reference dc voltage is taken. The hysteresis band is taken as 0.2, and the upper and lower limit of the control action are taken as 2.5 and -2.5, respectively. The basic block diagram of SMC is given in Fig. 2. The sliding window architecture is depicted in Fig. 3. For a better dynamic response at the output, a sliding surface equation in the state space can be denoted as a linear combination of state variable error given as

$$S = (V_{dc}) = K\varepsilon \tag{6}$$

where 'S' is the sliding surface, 'K' is the gain factor, and 'ε' is the DC voltage error function.

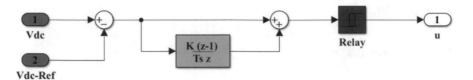

Fig. 2 Sliding mode control functioning

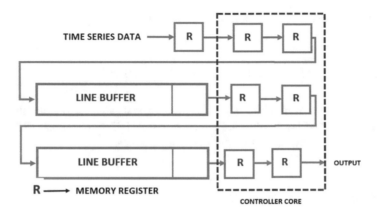

Fig. 3 Sliding window architecture

$$\varepsilon = V_{dc} - V_{dc\text{-}ref} \qquad (7)$$

$$S = K(V_{dc} - V_{dc\text{-}ref}) \qquad (8)$$

5 Results and Discussion

The proposed microgrid model is simulated for two cases. In the first case, the active power associated with the three-phase load is increased to 1.5 times for a specific time, and in the second case, the line impedance associated with the transmission line is increased to 2 times. The results obtained with the proposed SMC controller-based SAPF are compared with the PI controller-based SAPF. The power quality issues considered in this study are active power (P), reactive power (Q), voltage deviation, and Total Harmonic Distortion.

Case-1: Change in active power

The proposed model is simulated for 0–1 s. Then, the active power associated with the load is increased to 1.5 times for the duration of 0.4–0.6 s, and the active power, reactive power, voltage deviation, and THD are observed at the PCC. The real and unreal power plots are shown in Figs. 4 and 6. From the results, it can be perceived that the SMC-based SAPF can control the variation of both active and reactive power more efficiently than PI controller-based SAPF. The voltage deviation and THD curves are given in Figs. 5 and 7, respectively. The SMC-based SAPF can minimize the voltage deviation to 7%, while the PI-based SAPF can control the voltage deviation above 9%. Also it can be observed that with the PI controller-based SAPF, the THD is as high as 10%, but the SMC-based SAPF can minimize the THD to below 4%.

Case-2: Change in Line Impedance

The proposed model is also simulated for 0–1 s in the second case. The line impedance associated with the transmission line is increased to 1.5 times for 0.4–0.6 s, and the active power, reactive power, voltage deviation, and THD are observed at the PCC. The plots shown in Figs. 8 and 10 denote active and reactive power variation. The

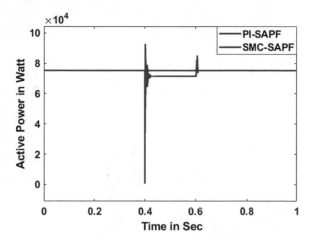

Fig. 4 Active power at the PCC for change in active power

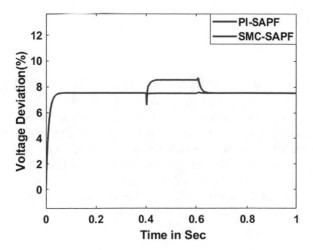

Fig. 5 Voltage deviation at the PCC

Fig. 6 Reactive power at the PCC for change in active power

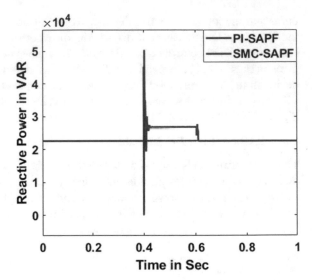

Fig. 7 THD at the PCC

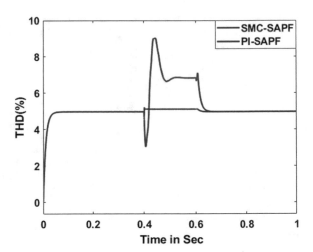

figures show that the SMC-controlled SAPF can efficiently control the fluctuation of both active and reactive power more efficiently than the PI controller-based SAPF. The THD variation and voltage deviation curves are denoted in Figs. 9 and 11. By comparing the results, it can be observed that with the PI controller-based SAPF, the THD is as high as 8.3%, but the SMC-based SAPF can minimize the THD to below 5%. The voltage deviation with the PI-SAPF is more than 15%, while the SMC-SAPF can limit the voltage deviation to 8%. The result analysis of THD and voltage deviation for SMC and PI has been presented in Table1.

Fig. 8 Active power at the PCC for change in line impedance

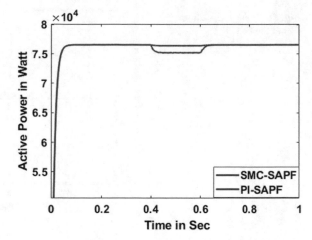

Fig. 9 THD (%) at the PCC

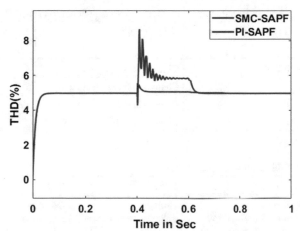

Fig. 10 Reactive power at the PCC for change in line impedance

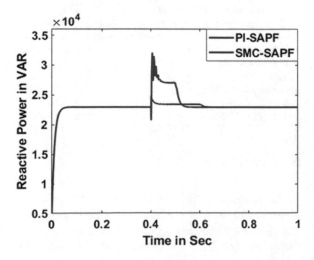

Fig. 11 Voltage deviation
(%) at the PCC

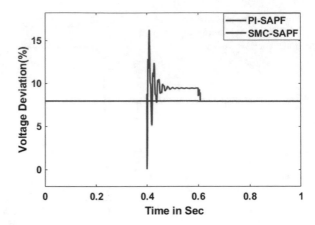

Table 1 Result analysis of THD and voltage deviation for SMC and PI

Type of controller	Type of fault	Parameters	
		THD in %	Voltage deviation
SMC	Change in active power	4	7
	Change in line impedance	5	8
PI	Change in active power	10	9
	Change in line impedance	8.3	15

Table 2 System parameters

PV array	Battery (Li-ion type)	SAPF	Fuel cell (PEMFC)
Max. power—213.15 W, Parallel strings—40, Cells per module—10, OC voltage—36.3 V, SC current—7.84 A, Light generated current—7.86 A, Shunt resistance—313.05 Ω, Series resistance—0.3938 Ω	Nominal voltage—400 V, Rated capacity—20,000 Ah, Initial state of charge—40%, Battery response time—0.03 s	DC side capacitance—43 μF, Filter coupling inductance—1.34 mH, Proportional gain K_p—0.1, Integral gain K_i—0.0015, V_{dc-ref}—450 V	Nominal stack power—50,000 W, Resistance of fuel cell—0.66404 Ω, Nernst voltage of cell—1.1342 V, System temperature—338 K, Air supply pressure—1 bar

6 Conclusion

In this research work, a fuel cell stack PV array is used as DER, and a SAPF is connected to the MG model and simulated successfully using MATLAB/Simulink. The detailed values of all system parameters are given in the Table 2. The conventional PI-based SAPF and proposed SMC-based SAPF are assumed for the controller operation. The comparison of the results unquestionably shows the efficiency of the proposed MNC-based SAPF controller by refining the power quality issues such as active power, reactive power, THD (%), and voltage deviation (%) at the PCC compared to the PI-controlled SAPF. The efficiency of the proposed controller is tested with the increase of active power of the load to 1.5 times and increasing the line impedance of the transmission line to 2 times for the duration of 0.4–0.6 s. The proposed model is simulated for 0–1 s, and the results obtained are denoted and discussed systematically. Hence, from the proposed research study, it can be resolved that the SMC-controlled SAPF-based MG system has improved action in terms of enhanced active power, reactive power, lower THD, and minimized voltage deviation at the PCC, which authenticates its performance.

References

1. Muneer V, Bhattacharya A (2020) Peak power demand management by using SMC-controlled three-level CHB-based three-wire and four-wire SAPF. IEEE Trans Ind Inform 17(8):5270–5281
2. Narasimhulu V, Ashok Kumar DV, Sai Babu Ch (2020) Fuzzy logic control of SLMMC-based SAPF under nonlinear loads. Int J Fuzzy Syst 22(2):428–437
3. Kumar R, Bansal HO, Kumar D (2020) Improving power quality and load profile using PV-battery-SAPF system with metaheuristic tuning and its HIL validation. Int Trans Electr Energy Syst 30(5):e12335
4. Barik PK, Shankar G, Sahoo PK (2020) Power quality assessment of microgrid using fuzzy controller aided modified SRF based designed SAPF. Int Trans Electr Energy Syst 30(4):e12289
5. Acharya DP, Nayak N, Choudhury S (2019) Power quality enhancement of a photovoltaic based micro grid system using optimized fuzzy controller with SAPF. In: 2019 international conference on smart systems and inventive technology (ICSSIT). IEEE
6. Acharya DP et al (2020) Power quality improvement in a fuel-cell based micro-grid with shunt active power filter. Int J Renew Energy Res (IJRER) 10(3):1071–1082
7. Goswami G, Goswami PK (2020) ANFIS supervised PID controlled SAPF for harmonic current compensation at nonlinear loads. IETE J Res 1–12
8. Nayak AS, Acharya DP, Choudhury S (2020) Photovoltaic cell with shunt active power filter for harmonic cancelation using modified PSO-based PI controller. In: Advances in electrical control and signal systems. Springer, Singapore, pp 455–467
9. Choudhury S, Rout PK (2019) Modelling and simulation of fuzzy-based MPPT control of grid connected PV system under variable load and irradiance. Int J Intell Syst Technol Appl 18(6):531–559
10. Choudhury S et al (2020) A novel control approach based on hybrid fuzzy logic and seeker optimization for optimal energy management between micro-sources and supercapacitor in an islanded microgrid. J King Saud Univ Eng Sci 32(1):27–41
11. Choudhury S et al (2021) Harmonic profile enhancement of grid connected fuel cell through cascaded H-bridge multi-level inverter and improved squirrel search optimization technique. Energies 14(23):7947
12. Choudhury S, Khandelwal N (2020) A novel weighted superposition attraction algorithm-based optimization approach for state of charge and power management of an islanded system with battery and supercapacitor-based hybrid energy storage system. IETE J Res 1–14
13. Mohanty M et al (2020) Application of salp swarm optimization for pi controller to mitigate transients in a three-phase soft starter-based induction motor. In: Advances in electrical control and signal systems. Springer, Singapore, pp 619–631

14. Riaz U, Tayyeb M, Amin AA (2021) A review of sliding mode control with the perspective of utilization in fault tolerant control. Recent Adv Electr Electron Eng (Formerly Recent Pat Electr Electron Eng) 14(3):312–324
15. Gambhire SJ et al (2021) Review of sliding mode based control techniques for control system applications. Int J Dyn Control 9:363–378
16. Chincholkar SH, Jiang W, Chan C-Y (2017) A modified hysteresis-modulation-based sliding mode control for improved performance in hybrid DC-DC boost converter. IEEE Trans Circ Syst II Express Briefs 65(11):1683–1687

An Approach for Waste Classification Using Data Augmentation and Transfer Learning Models

Nikhil Venkat Kumsetty⬵, Amith Bhat Nekkare, S. Sowmya Kamath⬵, and M. Anand Kumar

1 Introduction

Effective management of waste is an arduous and challenging undertaking anywhere in the world, with severe negative consequences for human health and well-being, the balance of the ecosystem and wildlife habitat, and the economy, if not tended to correctly. Even though campaigns to segregate waste at source have gained momentum in recent years, it is still extremely common to see different types of garbage mixed up and thrown in the trash. This severely impacts effective recycling programs aimed at improving sustainable management of reusable resources like glass, metal, cardboard, etc. Additionally, carelessly discarded bio-hazardous items like medical waste, used syringes, etc., can result in irreversible contamination of landfills and water bodies, making correct waste segregation and management a crucial requirement.

There are mainly two methods of waste management that have been widely adopted in several countries—burning of the waste (called incineration) and burial of the waste in designated areas (called landfills). However, neither method is particularly optimal with respect to the environment—incineration causes air pollution even in the most controlled of circumstances, and land filling causes land pollution due to leaching of heavy elements into the underground water table. In fact, it is

N. V. Kumsetty (⬵) · A. B. Nekkare · S. Sowmya Kamath · M. Anand Kumar
Department of Information Technology, National Institute of Technology Karnataka, Surathkal, Mangalore 575025, India
e-mail: nikhilvenkat26@gmail.com

A. B. Nekkare
e-mail: amithbhat01@gmail.com

S. Sowmya Kamath
e-mail: sowmyakamath@nitk.edu.in

M. Anand Kumar
e-mail: m_anandkumar@nitk.edu.in

© The Author(s), under exclusive license to Springer Nature Singapore Pte Ltd. 2023
K. Kumar Singh et al. (eds.), *Machine Vision and Augmented Intelligence*, Lecture Notes in Electrical Engineering 1007, https://doi.org/10.1007/978-981-99-0189-0_27

also common for fires to occur in landfill sites as flammable objects come in contact with electricity or fire. Moreover, these sites are health hazards for humans and animals living in the area, with noxious smells emanating from them. Furthermore, such methods of waste disposal completely forgo the economic and environmental impact of failing to recover reusable and recyclable materials such as plastic, metal, paper, and cardboard, or of separating the biodegradable organic materials to be composted for use as fertilizer. Finally, landfills take up a lot of space, due to the sheer volume of trash generated per day in cities; land is a finite resource, and hence for that reason alone we must segregate and dispose off waste correctly.

To manage these problems, city municipal corporations often look for solutions to decrease the amount of trash going into the landfills/incineration sites. Manual sorting is not an option at the scale of a city waste management plant even though it is very effective; the cost becomes prohibitively expensive. However, due to the highly variable kinds of trash present (which could be literally any object under the sun) and the different types of trash encountered, it is extremely difficult to create an automated system which can detect the category of trash and segregate it accordingly, without the use of machine learning. If the system does exist, it will take more amount of time to run, as the types of trash objects increases.

Existing waste sorting machines rely completely on non-computerized methods to segregate trash. Rather, they use physical phenomena such as ballistic separators and rotating trommel screens to do the segregation. The disadvantage of such methods is that it takes up too much energy per trash object and is definitely less time-effective than a computerized automated system. Also, such systems have many moving parts, which requires more maintenance. However, since deep learning by its nature improves its understanding of the type of trash object with each given input, any proposed deep learning solution will be time-efficient. Hence, deep learning-based solutions offer higher accuracy than a normal computerized system and can help improve the accuracy of the underlying mechanical system.

Most existing works on waste management thus far have focused on comparison of existing deep learning frameworks on a particular dataset. Not much attention was paid to optimizing the model, or on improving the quality of the dataset used. A major challenge of trash classification task is the lack of quality datasets. The standard dataset used by most researchers, TrashNet [1] provides only 2527 images. The authors of this dataset themselves cite the low number of data points in their dataset as a point of concern. We attempt to resolve this issue by increasing the number of images in the existing datasets, either by applying conventional data augmentation techniques, or by generating synthetic trash images using GANs. The focus is on improving the quality of existing datasets using data augmentation and various other image processing techniques in addition to transfer learning model optimizations to improve performance.

The rest of this paper is organized as below: Sect. 2 presents a discussion on recent and notable work carried out in the field of trash classification. Section 3 discusses the detailed methodology, especially with respect to the data augmentation, image generation areas, and transfer learning model. In Sect. 4, the specifics of the experiments performed and the results obtained are discussed in detail, followed by conclusion and scope for future work.

2 Related Work

Waste classification using machine learning concepts has garnered active research interest in the past decade. Thung and Yang [1] created the benchmark TrashNet dataset, which contains 2527 images of six different classes. It was used to train a SVM model and a CNN model; the SVM model outperformed the CNN, giving 63% accuracy during testing. However, the number of data points in the dataset is limited, and also, both the CNN and SVM models gave very low accuracy. Proença and Simões [2] created TACO, an open-source image dataset for litter detection and segmentation. These images are manually labeled and segmented according to a hierarchical taxonomy to train and evaluate object detection algorithms. Currently, there are 1500 images in the dataset divided into 59 classes with 4784 annotations, and annotations are provided in the COCO format.

Majchrowska et al. [3] proposed a two-stage deep learning framework that initially localizes the trash objects in an input image and then classifies the trash object using two separate neural networks. The authors tried out various existing deep learning frameworks and implemented these models on publically available benchmark datasets and observed that the EfficientDet-D2 model gave best results for trash object localization with an AP@50 at 66.4%. Similarly, for the task of classification, the EfficientNet-B2 model gave the best results with an accuracy of 75%. Azis et al. [4] proposed to use a simple CNN model to classify the trash objects. For the implementation, they used the Inception-v3 model and trained it with 2400 images from the Plastic Model Detection dataset on GitHub. To simulate practical conditions, they used Raspberry Pi as their processor and changed the input size of the Inception model to 299×299 since that is the default image dimension of the Raspberry Pi camera. During testing, they got an accuracy of 92.5%.

Adedeji and Wang [5] used the ResNet-50 CNN model to create a waste classification system. The TrashNet dataset used was augmented by using techniques such as image shearing and image scaling. After getting the features from the ResNet model, it was passed onto a multi-class SVM model where the actual classification takes place. It gave an accuracy of 87%. However, no reason is provided as to why the SVM model was used for classification. Also, no other preprocessing step was done apart from the data augmentation. Mao et al. [6] used a genetic algorithm-optimized DenseNet-121 model, which gave an accuracy of 99.6% when run on TrashNet. A grad-CAM model was used to interpret the results of the optimized DenseNet model. They also established that data augmentation of the existing dataset gives better results than optimizing the fully connected layer of the DenseNet-121 model. However, even with the extremely high accuracy achieved, this model is highly computationally expensive. Such computational resources may not be available in every computer, especially to do it within reasonable amount of time.

Meng and Chu [7] performed a survey of existing machine learning and deep learning methods to classify and segregate waste objects. In addition, a new approach using a histogram of oriented gradients (HOG) was proposed. Data augmentation on the images in the TrashNet dataset was also performed. While the best results were achieved with the DenseNet model (95% accuracy), the proposed HOG + CNN model performed well, with 93.56% accuracy. However, we note that the authors don't seem to have performed any preprocessing on the input data apart from the data augmentation. Ozkaya and Seyfi [8] developed a deep learning application which detects types of garbage into trash in order to provide recyclability with vision system. Training and testing were performed on the TrashNet dataset, with image data consisting of several classes on different garbage types. Also, transfer learning was used to obtain shorter training and test procedures with and higher accuracy. As fine-tuned models, AlexNet, VGG-16, GoogleNet, and ResNet structures were carried. In order to test performance of classifiers, two different classifiers—softmax and support vector machines, were used. Six different type of trash images were correctly classified with GoogleNet + SVM which achieved the highest accuracy of 97.86%.

Masand et al. [9] developed a deep learning model based on the EfficientNet architecture. They also developed ScrapNet, a new dataset created by combining several other pre-existing datasets and standardizing the images in them. They achieved an accuracy of 98% on the TrashNet dataset and 92.87% on the ScrapNet dataset using the EfficientNet B3 model. Rishma and Aarthi [10] proposed a waste classification model using a convolution neural network model. They used the TrashNet dataset developed by [1] and augmented the images therein by performing various operations such as rotations, translation, and flipping. On testing, they obtained 87% accuracy. Yadav et al. [11] proposed an IOT-based automated trash management system. They compare the performance of several transfer learning models, such as ResNet-34, ResNet-50, ResNet-101, and AlexNet to decide the core deep learning algorithm of the system. Their experimental evaluation found that ResNet-34 model performed best, with 91.8% accuracy.

Based on the detailed review, several issues and gaps were identified. The standard datasets used do not have sufficient frequency and variety of trash object images in certain classes, leading to poor model training, thus affecting prediction results. We observed that the TACO [4] dataset has not been utilized much in the trash classification task, possibly due to the recency of the dataset. As mentioned above, existing works do not attempt to improve the quality of the datasets used. Rather, they focus on comparing the performance of pre-existing deep learning frameworks. In view of these issues, we focus on improving the image processing and prediction capabilities of multiple models for the task of waste classification. We also propose an improved and efficient model for waste object detection and classification using the concept of transfer learning. In this paper, we attempt to resolve the dataset issue by increasing the number of images in the existing datasets, either by applying conventional data augmentation techniques, or by generating synthetic trash images using GANs. We also experiment with transfer learning-based models such as ResNet and VGG for fast and accurate detection and classification of waste.

3 Methodology

The processes defined as part of the proposed approaches are illustrated in Fig. 1. The concept of transfer learning is leveraged to improve the model's object detection and feature extraction capabilities. We describe each of these processes in detail in the subsequent sections.

3.1 Datasets

In our work, we consider two popular waste classification datasets—TrashNet [1] and TACO [2] to detect and classify the trash objects in an input image. TrashNet is a balanced dataset and has approximately 400 images after balancing in each of six different labeled classes (glass, paper, cardboard, plastic, metal, and trash). We divide the dataset into train, validation, and test in the ratio 80:10:10. The resolution of the input data is $512 \times 384 \times 3$. Each images consists of a single trash object. We also used the Trash Annotations in Context for Litter Detection (TACO) dataset in

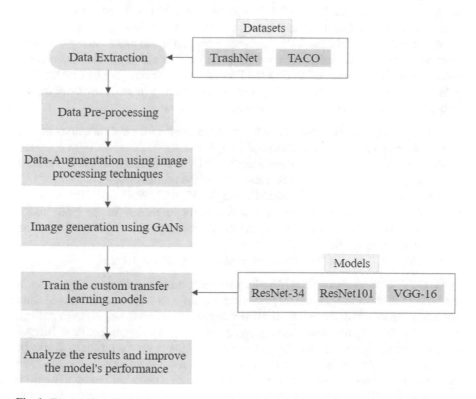

Fig. 1 Proposed methodology

this analysis. TACO is a growing image dataset of "waste in the wild," i.e., images of trash in the environment, as opposed to TrashNet whose trash objects are on a plain background. It contains around 1500 annotated images of litter taken under diverse environments: woods, roads, and beaches. These images are manually labeled and segmented according to a hierarchical taxonomy to train and evaluate object detection algorithms. In this dataset, an image can have one or more trash objects. While the original dataset consists of various classes, we have considered only the plastic, paper, glass, and drink can classes for this analysis.

3.2 Data Preprocessing and Augmentation

The TrashNet and TACO datasets exhibit data imbalance, which hinders an effective classification model. Hence, preprocessing and augmentation techniques were applied to improve the quality of the datasets. We preprocessed TrashNet by performing operations like flipping, rotations, shearing, etc., to augment the dataset. This helps in creating new images with different feature characteristics for the same input image, thereby helping to improve the frequency of the dataset. The images in dataset are initially resized to the dimension $512 \times 384 \times 3$ and split into train, test, and validation directories in the ratio of 80:10:10 for the respective classes of TrashNet and TACO datasets. The images are then shuffled to make the input images from train, test, and validation set random. Once, the dataset is split into the intended ratio, a label file is generated to map the images to the classes they belong to. This helps in evaluating the model during training and testing phase. Furthermore, we also implemented data augmentation techniques such as

- *Center Cropping*: The input image is center cropped with the dimensions of 256 × 256 and then resized to the original image size.
- *Flipping*: The input image is flipped horizontally and vertically so as to rearrange the pixels, thereby creating different copies of the original image.
- *Rotation*: The input image is rotated through 45°, 135°, 225°, and 315° angle.
- *Brightness adjustment*: Increase and decrease the brightness of the input image in order to factor in various lighting effects on the trash object. We have used the brightness range of 0.25–1.75.
- *Translation*: The input image is translated along x-axis and y-axis.

In addition, we augment TrashNet by preparing a collage of trash objects from the individual trash images, thereby creating a collage of four trash objects in each images. In order to simulate real-world conditions, we generate two types of collage images: overlapping and non-overlapping images. The overlapping collage images contain four random trash objects that overlap randomly on each other. Similarly, the non-overlapping collage images contain four random trash objects that are each placed on a quadrant. In each collage image, four trash objects belonging to random classes of TrashNet dataset were merged and simultaneously bounding boxes were used to label the object to which class it belongs. This is possible due to the fact that each image in the original dataset has only one trash object. This is done with the help of Gaussian-Poisson Generative Adversarial Networks (GP-GANs) [12]. We chose GP-GANs in particular, to leverage their unique classical gradient-based approach, as well as those of GANs. Following these processes, the augmented TrashNet dataset has 10,108 images.

With regard to the TACO dataset, we found that it was initially heavily imbalanced with more than 50% of images were of the cigarette butts class. This was dealt with by the removal of this class. We also combined several sub-classes of the TACO dataset to create a dataset containing paper, glass, metal, and plastic classes. However, after all these steps we were left with around 150 images per class. To remedy this issue, we applied the same techniques as we did to the TrashNet dataset, i.e., operations like flipping, rotations, cropping, etc. We also applied various image filters like blurring, noise filters, etc. This helped us to boost the frequency of images in the dataset to 2642, with each class having around 450 images.

3.3   Synthetic Image Generation Using GANs

As mentioned above, we observed that the existing datasets have low frequency of images. Therefore, we investigated this issue by creating synthetic images of trash objects. Generic Generative Adversarial Networks [13] (GANs) were used to generate synthetic data points so as to increase the number of images to better train the models. The constructed GAN model consists of two neural network components—a generator model and a discriminator model. The generator model that generates new images by mapping the noise variables to the generated data space. The discriminator model helps to measure the probability of the image generated by the generator is in fact having features related to the original dataset. The proposed model consists of fully connected layers and convolutional neural networks which act as the main computational layers of our model. To this model, we input the TrashNet dataset to generate synthetic images of trash objects. The main aim of the GAN model is to learn to minimize the following minmax equation (Eq. 1) to maximize the chance of discriminator D effectively classifying the generated image by the generator G if it consists of similar features.

$$\min \max(G, D) = E_{x-p_{\text{data}}(x)}\left[\log D(x)\right] + E_{x-p_z}[\log(1 - D(G(z)))] \quad (1)$$

3.4   Custom Transfer Learning Models

For the purpose of this study, we have mainly used transfer learning models rather than any other machine or deep learning model. Transfer learning involves the use of models pre-trained on a very large dataset such as ImageNet [14], and COCO, and using these models to solve a particular problem with a new dataset. This means that the model is not initialized with random weights, instead using the weights inherited from the previously trained dataset. This helps to increase the training accuracy, reduce the amount of computations performed and increase the overall performance of the model. ImageNet pre-weights were used in the proposed model as it contains a specific class of images on trash objects, which helps the transfer learning models to extract features and process the data much effectively.

We initially start constructing the custom transfer learning models by importing pre-trained ResNet-34, ResNet-101, and VGG-16 models and inheriting weights of the ImageNet dataset into these models. We further customize the imported models architecture by adding Batch Normalization layers, rectified linear units (ReLU) activation layers, Eq. 2, in each convolutional block with a kernel size of 3×3 and stride as 2. A dropout layer with rate as 0.5 is added on the fully connected layers to avoid overfitting. Finally, adding a Global Average Pooling layer, four dense layers, and a softmax layer, Eq. 3, to generate the out are added to complete the model. The loss was calculated with the help of categorical-cross entropy loss function Eq. 4, where, $CE(y, \hat{y})$ is the categorical-cross entropy loss of the model. The main objective of adding the Global Average Pooling layer is to eliminate the need to fine-tune the hyper-parameters of the custom transfer learning model.

$$Relu(x) = \max(0, x) \tag{2}$$

$$Softmax(x_i) = \frac{\exp(x_i)}{\sum_j \exp(x_j)} \tag{3}$$

$$CE(y, \hat{y}) = -\sum_{i=1}^{N_c} y_i \log(\hat{y}_i) \tag{4}$$

The model is trained on each dataset with the dimensions of input image as $512 \times 384 \times 3$, by freezing all base layers and training the output layer by a large learning rate, then after a few epochs, we reduce the learning rate. The advantage of this approach is that it does not change the weights of the base layers drastically in the first few epochs when the last few layers have not yet stabilized. We ran this setup for three different transfer learning models, namely ResNet-34 [15], ResNet-101, and VGG-16 [16]. The model training was done over 100 epochs.

4 Experimental Results and Discussion

The experimental validation of the proposed model was performed on two standard benchmark datasets—TrashNet and TACO. The models presented were constructed using Python 3.8.5 and we used the PyTorch open-source library to develop our deep learning models. All the models were run for 100 epochs during this analysis.

(a) Overlapping trash objects   (b) Non-overlapping trash objects

Fig. 2 Collage images generated using GP-GANs

The models thus developed were then trained on Nvidia P100 and T4 GPUs with a minimum of 8 GB RAM.

During data augmentation experiments using GP-GANs, we observed that the model successfully created both overlapping and non-overlapping collage images with four trash objects in each image of the TrashNet dataset. The generator was able to recognize the most significant object from the given trash image and was able to identify the similarity of the generated image from the actual input image. Figure 2a shows an example of overlapping trash object collage image and Fig. 2b shows an example of non-overlapping trash object collage image.

During synthetic image generation using GANs, we also experimented with GANs to check if the generated data of trash images can be viable for extended experiments. However, the results were not of sufficient quality to move forward with this approach. Figure 3 shows the sample of generated synthetic images by the GAN model. It is clear from the samples that the synthetic images generated by the GAN model were lacking in details about the features of various input trash object images and having poor quality. Hence, we choose to discard this approach and adopted transfer learning based models for the classification task.

For validating the transfer learning based models, the TrashNet and TACO datasets were again used. We created a train, test, validation split for building ResNet-34, ResNet-101, VGG-16 transfer learning model. Table 1 shows the results obtained by the transfer learning models run on the augmented TrashNet dataset, while Table 2 shows the results obtained by the transfer learning models for the augmented TACO dataset. It can be observed that the ResNet-34 and ResNet-101 models achieved better results than the VGG-16 model. We hypothesize this to be due to the nature of the ResNet model, which results in the building of a lighter but deeper network in each layer. This in turn helps reduce the number of computation operations performed in each layer and preserves the weights of the inherited ImageNet dataset for a longer period.

To evaluate and compare the proposed model with existing works, we performed further benchmarking experiments. The TrashNet dataset has been utilized by many researchers, while the TACO dataset is relatively new, and fewer works are available for comparison. In case of TrashNet dataset, we achieved an accuracy of 93.13% which is comparable to the latest state-of-the-art models developed on this dataset as given in Table 3. While we have slightly lower accuracy than some existing models, we believe this is due to differences in their approach and model architectures. In the case of TACO, we achieved exceptional results with our custom-built ResNet-based model with an accuracy of 91.34%, which is an improvement of over 16% over the existing work as given in Table 4.

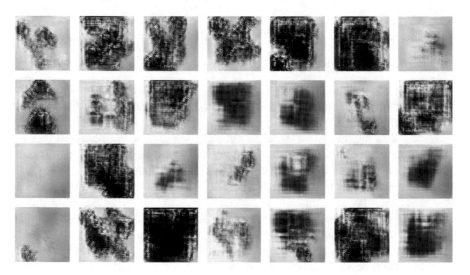

Fig. 3 Synthetic images generated by GANs

Table 1 Observed results for transfer learning models trained on TrashNet

Model	Training (%)	Validation (%)	Testing (%)
ResNet-34	95.64	91.67	**93.13**
ResNet-101	96.82	**92.61**	91.67
VGG-16	92.25	88.84	91.67

Table 2 Observed results for transfer learning models trained on TACO dataset

Model	Training (%)	Validation (%)	Testing (%)
ResNet-34	95.47	88.4	89.13
ResNet-101	96.87	**89.78**	**91.34**
VGG-16	89.29	88.75	87.5

Table 3 Results on benchmarking experiments on TrashNet dataset

Works	Classification model	Accuracy (%)
Thung and Yang [1]	SVM	63
Adedeji and Wang [5]	ResNet-50 + SVM	87
Azis et al. [4]	Inception-v3	92.5
Meng and Chu [7]	ResNet-50	95.35
Ozkaya and Seyfi [8]	GoogleNet + SVM	97.86
Masand et al. [9]	ScrapNet	98
Proposed model	Custom ResNet-34	**93.13**

Table 4 Results on benchmarking experiments on TACO dataset

Authors	Model	Accuracy (%)
Majchrowska et al. [3]	EfficientNet-B2	75
Proposed model	Custom ResNet	**91.34**

5　Conclusion and Future Work

In this paper, an attempt to develop waste detection and classification models built on enhanced datasets was presented. We undertook a thorough analysis of different techniques applicable to transfer learning models in the field of trash detection and classification. To address the weaknesses of existing datasets, we investigated the possibility of using synthetic datasets generated using GANs, which did not yield any significant results. Further, we experimented with two standard datasets, TrashNet and TACO. Both datasets required augmentation, due to insufficient number of images in them. The augmented dataset was then run on three different transfer learning models, namely ResNet-34, ResNet-101, and VGG-16. Out of this, the best results were obtained in the ResNet-101 model. In the future, we intend to create a custom dataset with greater variety and number of images. We also plan to include medical waste and e-waste classes, which have not been considered in other trash datasets.

References

1. Thung G, Yang M (2016) Classification of trash for recyclability status [Online]. Available: https://github.com/garythung/trashnet
2. Proença PF, Simões P (2020) Taco: trash annotations in context for litter detection. arXiv preprint arXiv:2003.06975
3. Majchrowska S, Mikolajczyk A, Ferlin M, Klawikowska Z, Plantykow MA, Kwasigroch A, Majek K (2021) Waste detection in Pomerania: non-profit project for detecting waste in environment. arXiv:2105.06808
4. Azis FA, Suhaimi H, Abas E (2020) Waste classification using convolutional neural network. In: Proceedings of the 2020 2nd international conference on information technology and computer

communications, ITCC 2020. Association for Computing Machinery, New York, NY, USA, pp 9–13

5. Adedeji O, Wang Z (2019) Intelligent waste classification system using deep learning convolutional neural network. Procedia Manuf 35:607–612. In: The 2nd international conference on sustainable materials processing and manufacturing, SMPM 2019, 8–10 Mar 2019, Sun City, South Africa

6. Mao W-L, Chen W-C, Wang C-T, Lin Y-H (2021) Recycling waste classification using optimized convolutional neural network. Resour Conserv Recycl 164:105132

7. Meng S, Chu W-T (2020) A study of garbage classification with convolutional neural networks. In: 2020 Indo–Taiwan 2nd international conference on computing, analytics and networks (Indo-Taiwan ICAN), pp 152–157

8. Ozkaya U, Seyfi L (2019) Fine-tuning models comparisons on garbage classification for recyclability. arXiv preprint arXiv:1908.04393

9. Masand A, Chauhan S, Jangid M, Kumar R, Roy S (2021) Scrapnet: an efficient approach to trash classification. IEEE Access 9:130947–130958

10. Rishma G, Aarthi R (2022) Classification of waste objects using deep convolutional neural networks. In: Kumar A, Senatore S, Gunjan VK (eds) ICDSMLA 2020. Springer, Singapore, pp 533–542

11. Yadav S, Shanmugam A, Hima V, Suresh N (2021) Wasteclassification and segregation: machine learning and IoT approach. In: 2021 2nd international conference on intelligent engineering and management (ICIEM), pp 233–238

12. Wu H, Zheng S, Zhang J, Huang K (2017) GP-GAN: towards realistic high-resolution image blending. arXiv:1703.07195

13. Goodfellow IJ, Pouget-Abadie J, Mirza M, Xu B, Warde-Farley D, Ozair S, Courville, Bengio Y (2014) Generative adversarial networks

14. Deng J, Dong W, Socher R, Li L-J, Li K, Fei-Fei L (2009) Imagenet: a large-scale hierarchical image database. In: 2009 IEEE conference on computer vision and pattern recognition, pp 248–255

15. He K, Zhang X, Ren S, Sun J (2015) Deep residual learning for image recognition. arXiv:1512.03385

16. Simonyan K, Zisserman A (2014) Very deep convolutional networks for large-scale image recognition. arXiv preprint arXiv:1409.1556

Adaptive Ridge Edge Detection in Multitemporal Satellite Images

Hemlata Dakhore and Kanchan Lata Kashyap

1 Introduction

The image enhancement and segmentation are very important image preprocessing operation. The objective of image preprocessing operation is to increase the analysis and usefulness of images which provide its subjective analysis in terms of human prospective. The image enhancement can be used in order to interpret the images and to obtain the certain conclusions on the computer vision based algorithm. Therefore, the enhancement is the primary preprocessing stage of image processing techniques [1]. It contains the gray level pixels, contrast stretching, remove the noise, edge detection, segmentation, filtering, interpolation, and color orientation. The image enhancement methods are categories into two different methods frequency domain method and spatial domain method. In the frequency domain method, the image enhanced is based on the two dimensional Fourier transformation process which can be improved through the Fast Fourier transformation. In spatial domain, many images features are emphasized based on filtering, edge detection, segmentation, interpolation, and color orientation. Thresholding is desirable for remote sensing applications to select a particular region from an image. The threshold values are considered as those pixels values which lie between the specified values in multispectral image. Edges are typically on the boundary between two regions indicates significant local changes of intensity in an image. The second-order-based edge detection methods include Sobel operator, Prewitt operator, and Roberts operator. The Canny Edge detection algorithm determines the image Laplacian operator which smooths the image and remove the noise with respective pixels values in the given image. The

H. Dakhore (✉) · K. L. Kashyap
School of Computing Science and Engineering, VIT University, Bhopal, Madhya Pradesh 466114, India
e-mail: hemlatadakhore2020@vitbhopal.ac.in

K. L. Kashyap
e-mail: kanchan.k@vitbhopal.ac.in

algorithm suppresses the pixel to detect optimal edge detector to perform the in X-direction with differential and in Y-direction smoothing took place. This is an efficient convolution in recursive manner. Ridge edge detection algorithm detects ridge edges by magnitude and direction in third coordinate and fourth coordinates of image respective of sub-pixels point in specific location. Each pixel of the 3rd band magnitude and 4th band orientation of the gradient [Ridge Valley] [2]. The present work focuses on the comparative studies of edge detection (boundaries) of the crop area using canny edge detection and the ridge edge detection algorithms. The main aim of this proposed work is to select the area of interest (AOI) for determining healthy crop area. This work also determines the month in which the healthier development of the crop is started in its life cycle.

2 Related Work

Tony Lindeberg has introduced novel approach of scale space [3] edges in gradient direction with corresponding gradient magnitude over local maximum values. Strength of the edges has been measured local maximum scales and it scales up very along edges of the images with two specific parameters gradient magnitude and differential in segmentation. This approach was used to determine the closed curves of the edges by integrating to the strength of edges. Scale information of the edges provides the physical structure of edges. Similar concepts can be used to formulate the automatic ridge edge detection. The approach is validated and supported by mathematical theoretical analysis.

Different edge detection method such Canny, Roberts, Prewitt, Sobel was applied on 3D images and observational results indicates Canny edge detection [2] was efficient to detect the boundaries and extract the features from medical images. Further improvement in edge detection took place using bilateral filter [4] which increased the edge of line thicker than Gaussian filter; it was not detected in canny edge detection. Edges are localized and identified a low level task evaluation metric which provides the structural and visual information fidelity area [5] to measure the quality of hyper spectral images and to detect the edges of hyper-spectral images.

Joshua Abraham and Calden Wlokay have focused on preprocessing methods to detect the semantic edges detection in satellite imagery with deep learning technique. Semantic edges detection method was used to determine boundaries of area whether natural or man-made boundaries of roads, buildings, and coast lines.

3 Proposed System and Implementation

The proposed work consists of various steps as shown in Fig. 1. In the first step, the satellite multispectral images of size 3610×3200 are taken as input images. Multispectral images are taken to identify the three color composition such as red, green, and NIR which are useful for the human visual interpretation. The varying multispectral images show NIR (red color) to the healthy vegetation which reflects the vegetation to the highest hues of red color. The geometric arrangement of pixel represents in terms of shape and size. The shape of the objects are distinguished into different object image and size of the object that depends on the scale [6]. In the next step, the contrast stretching method is applied in which the bright portion become brighter and dark portion become darker. The transformation function produces the modified gray levels images (I_g) of size 512×512 [7]. The threshold levels of an image are determined by pixel intensity values. The intermediate threshold divides the range into equal intervals of intensity levels. The referred interval values are used to modify the individual pixels values step by step to produce the two threshold levels such as low and high, respectively [8]. Automatic scale up represents L values of a pixels $P(x, y)$ that is obtained by convolving pixels P to represents Gaussian kernels ($G(x, y)$) of different widths. The output of Laplace operators are used to represent large number of basic operation such as segmentation, feature detection, template matching, and computation of curvature shapes. This curve represents the edges (boundaries) of healthy crop. This is a most appropriate system to represent partial differential multiscale invariants.

Fig. 1 Proposed system for edge detection

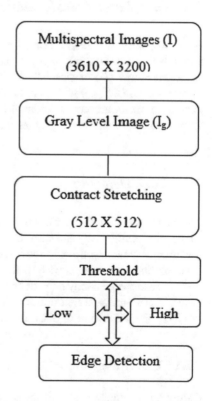

Fig. 2 Difference between **a** canny edge detector and **b** ridge edge detector

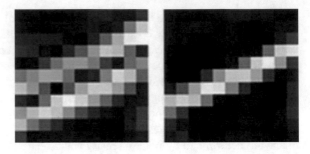

3.1 Data Acquisition

Multitemporal images are captured by the satellite from the month of October 2019 to March 2020 of same agricultural area. All set of multispectral images of average size 3610 × 3200 are collected from Maharashtra Remote Sensing Center, Nagpur.

3.2 Gray Level Transformation

First, originally the satellite images are converted into gray scale images (I_g). After that, the contrast starching of gray scale images is done which resized it into contract stretched image (I_s) of size 512 × 512. The output of image transformation into gray is shown in Fig. 4 in which the relative pixel value ranges from 0 to 255. The expensive pixels are not considered for conversion into gray. The important pixel values are converted into a gray level image.

3.3 Edge Detection

The edges are initial and essential characteristics of an image [9]. Edge content shape, size may convey the texture of the image. Edge detection is useful to detect meaningful discontinuities in the intensity values. These ridge edges are boundary between different regions with distinct gray level intensity values. Figure 2 shows difference between canny edge detector and ridge edge detector with different properties. It can analyzed that both the first and second order derivative edge detector produces the some kind of discontinuities.

3.3.1 Canny Edge Detection

Canny edge detection algorithm is generally acknowledged as reliable and most powerful algorithm. This technique is used to find the edges by separating the noise from the image. It does not affect the any properties of the image. The basic procedure of canny can be summarized as [7].

Step 1. Smoothed Gaussian Kernel

This is the primary step to reduce the noise by selecting larger width of the Gaussian kernel, will remove the noise gives best smoothing effect in the image.

Step 2. Local Gradient

Strength of edge can be determined by taking Sobel operators in horizontal position and vertical position then magnitude will be added in direction.

$$E(x, y) = |G_x(x, y)| + |G_y(x, y)| \tag{1}$$

Step 3. Edge Direction

To calculate the edge direction,

$$\theta = \tan^{-1} \frac{G_y(x, y)}{G_x(x, y)} \tag{2}$$

Step 4. Digitized the Edge Direction

In the digital image approximate the edge direction with four possible angle in the quadrant 0 direction, 90 direction, 45 direction and 135, respectively, then approximation u is calculated by 2 which is closest to four angles.

Step 5. Suppression of Pixel with No Maximum Value

After knowing the edge directions, non-maximum suppression is used to trace digitized edge direction and suppressing pixel value set to zero that is not considered as the edge. This leads to thin line in the output image.

Step 6. Hysteresis Threshold

To track the remaining edge pixels which is not suppressed by edge value and threshold of the image. The threshold values are higher value T_2 and lower value T_1. The each pixel is then determined according to the following conditions:

(a) If $|E(x, y)| < T_1$, then rejected if non-edge pixel
(b) If $|E(x, y)| > T_2$, then accepted if an edge pixel
(c) If $T_1 < |E(x, y)| < T_2$ then edge pixel is connected to an unconditional edge pixel where a consist path with $|E(x, y)| > T_2$, other pixels are rejected.

Canny method is used to smooth the image using Gaussian kernel [10]. Then, it finds gradient in both vertical and horizontal direction [9]. Gaussian kernel applied before masking therefore canny edge detection can detect the weak edges [11].

3.3.2 Ridge Edge Detection Algorithm

The ridge edge detection computes the gradient of spatial domain on the given image. It highlights high spatial frequency component of the region which leads a curvature surface of edges with help of partial derivative. Ridge edge detection algorithm is differential geometric approach, a bright pixel (dark) referred as ridge values for the bright assumes a maximum pixels or minimum pixels curvature direction. Then a local maxima (p, q) system.

$$\begin{cases} L_p = 0 \\ L_{pp} < 0 \\ |L_{pp}| \geq |L_{qq}| \end{cases} \tag{3}$$

Normalized ridge edge detection algorithm implements as follows:

Step 1. Smoothed Gaussian Filter

Apply the Gaussian kernel with

$$L(x, y, t_0) = g(x, y, t_0 + t) \tag{4}$$

Step 2. Gradient Magnitude

Normalized gradient is a vector which has certain magnitude and direction.

$$\text{magnitude}(f) = \begin{pmatrix} \frac{\partial f}{\partial x} \\ \frac{\partial f}{\partial y} \end{pmatrix} \tag{5}$$

$$\sqrt{\left(\frac{\partial f}{\partial x}\right)^2 + \left(\frac{\partial f}{\partial y}\right)^2} \tag{6}$$

$$|M_x| + |M_y| \tag{7}$$

Step 3. Edge Direction

To calculate the edge direction,

$$\theta = \tan^{-1} \frac{M_y(x, y)}{M_x(x, y)} \tag{8}$$

The magnitude of gradient provides the strength of the edge.

Step 4. Digitized the Edge Direction

The direction of gradient is 90°, and edge direction is perpendicular to the gradient of the edge.

Step 5. Suppression of Pixel with No Maximum Value

After finding the edge point, along the edge direction all values of gradient non-maximum suppression as a ridge point.

Step 6. Hysteresis Threshold

To track the remain pixels which is not suppressed to edge value as ridge point. For each pixel (x, y) do:

if Gradient Magnitude $(i, j) < M_x (i_1, j_1)$ or Gradient magnitude $(i, j) < M_y (i_2, j_2)$

then TN $(i, j) = 0$

else TN $(i, j) = $ Gradient Magnitude (i, j)

The Adaptive ridge edge detection algorithm [3] detects the edges with curvature corner of multispectral images.

4 Experimental Results

Experiment is conducted on multitemporal images datasets provided by MRSC. All the set of image are multispectral satellite images of size average 3610×3200 of crop area grown up in winter season from October to March month. These multitemporal images as shown in Fig. 3 are multispectral images of same area acquired from the October to March month to detect the changes in crop development cycle. The experiment has been carried out MATLAB and QGIS. The multispectral images are transformed into gray level transformation then threshold values for canny edge detection algorithm and ridge edge detection algorithm are taken as $T_1 = 0.05$, $T_2 = 0.50$ and $M_x = 0.15$ and $M_y = 0.37$, respectively, as shown in Fig. 4. After deciding threshold and sigma values, the canny edge detection algorithm and ridge edge detection algorithm are applied which show results of edges detection and ridge edge with curvature surface it include the healthy crop area. The output after applying canny and ridge edge detection algorithm is showing the boundaries of healthy crop are in Figs. 5 and 6, respectively. The detail statistics analysis of mean, standard deviations, and SNR are given in Table 1.

Canny edge detection algorithm shown in Fig. 5 firstly removes the noise and determines image gradient. It suppresses the any pixel values of multispectral image not a maximum pixel value. To detect the optimal edge in filter performs the differentiation and smoothing in X and Y direction respectively in recursive manner.

Ridge edge detection algorithm shown in Fig. 6 detects the adaptive ridge edges for an image using magnitude and direction. Adaptive ridge edges are detected with

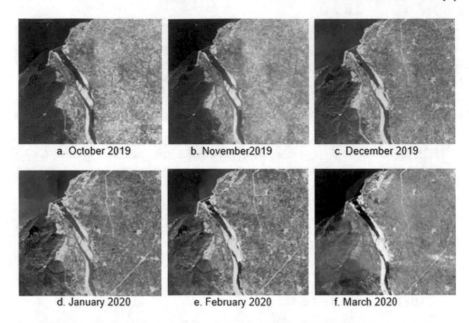

Fig. 3 Multitemporal satellite images of agriculture area indicate the false color composite images from October 2019 to March 2020

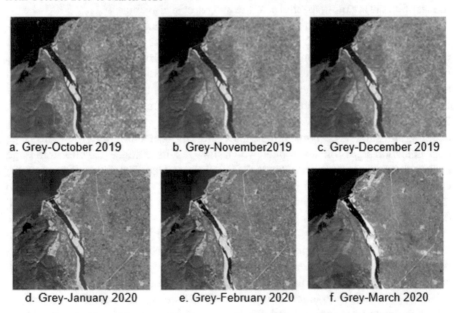

Fig. 4 Converted gray images of agriculture area from October 2019 to March 2020

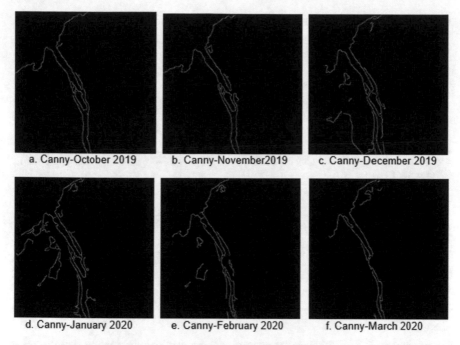

Fig. 5 Canny edge detection algorithm from October 2019 to March

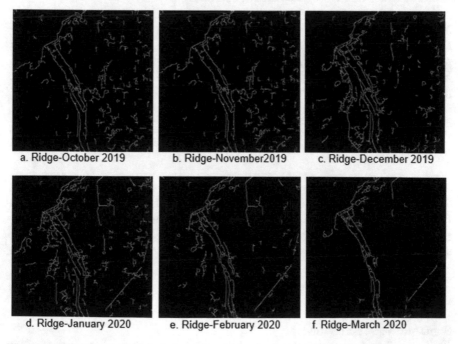

Fig. 6 Adaptive ridge edge detection algorithm from October 2019 to March 2020

Table 1 Statistics analysis of various parameter of canny edge detection and ridge edge detection algorithm

Image I	Gray image I_g	Canny edge I_{gc}				Ridge edge I_{gr}		
		Threshold = 0.05 (low) *Threshold = 0.50 (high)* *Sigma = 3*				*Threshold = 0.15 (low)* *Threshold = 0.37 (high)* *Sigma = 2*		
		Mean	**Standard deviation**	**SNR**		**Mean**	**Standard deviation**	**SNR**
Oct 2019 3609 × 3201	Oct 2019 512 × 512	1.75	21.08	0.14		6.34	39.72	0.051
Nov 2019 3610 × 3201	Nov 2019 512 × 512	1.87	21.74	0.15		4.17	32.35	0.033
Dec 2019 3609 × 3200	Dec 2019 512 × 512	2.24	24.89	0.20		7.03	41.76	0.057
Jan 2020 3610 × 3200	Jan 2020 512 × 512	3.06	27.78	0.25		7.28	42.46	0.060
Feb 2020 3610 × 3201	Feb 2020 512 × 512	2.24	23.79	0.18		5.05	35.54	0.041

the parameter high negative curvature and local maximum height in the axes direction which indicates the healthy crop area in data sets.

Mean

Mean is the sum of all pixel values in the image sample divided by the total number of pixels in the image sample. Each pixels represents the brightness of the pixel. Mean (average) is the basic statistical measure classified as spatial filtering to reduce the noise in the image.

$$\text{Mean} = \frac{\text{Sum of pixel values}}{\text{Total no. of pixel values}} \quad (9)$$

Standard Deviation

Standard deviation is descriptive statistical measures that conveys the deviated values from the average value in the image to quantify the contract of image. If the gray level image pixels are distributed equally, then that image is called as contract image with high levels.

$$\text{Standard Deviation} = \text{root mean square} \quad (10)$$

Signal-to-Noise Ratio (SNR)

SNR is ratio of mean value and standard deviation value of the noise in the image. Maximum intensity within image is useful to determine random and uniform distributed noise that will characterize the quality of the image.

$$\text{Signal to Noise Ratio (SNR)} = \frac{\text{Mean } (M)}{\text{Standard Deviation (SD)}} \qquad (11)$$

Sigma

Sigma is the probability function of the Gaussian distribution operator which smooths the noisy image with by average of neighborhood pixels values which is the intensity within center of pixel with fixed sigma range. Sigma is variance of standard deviation.

$$\text{Sigma} = (\text{Standard Deviation})^2 \qquad (12)$$

5 Conclusion

Proposed method represents the image enhancement technique for a preprocessing, performed intensity level correction, contrast adjustment, edge enhancement, and remove noise. The ridge edge detection algorithm can be used to enhance the satellite image boundaries segmentation and detect the curve shape boundaries of crop area in multispectral images. The following conclusion can be obtained from the experimental results:

- Preprocessing of the images gives the lowest SNR and sigma values which leads to improved image enhancement.
- Accuracy of contract enhancement with lowest threshold 0.15 and highest threshold 0.37 concluded as best.
- Edge detection algorithm objective to extract and enhanced the boundaries of a desired area contained in the image with high intensity.
- Ridge edge detection algorithm decreases the noise and detects the more continue edges.

This work represents a comparison of thresholding, different edge detection techniques for multitemporal/multispectral satellite images. The efficiency of canny edge detection and ridge edge detection is tested individually to achieve with improved results successfully. The detail analysis of canny edge detection and adaptive ridge edge detection algorithms are represented in Table 1, and it concluded that best and enhanced results are obtained for adaptive ridge edge detection. After applying this ridge edge detection algorithm, it gives output as uniform contrast image to produce intensity values to contribute and detect most of continue edges in the multispectral. In the future work, the comparative study of image segmentation will be done with different clustering techniques.

References

1. Kashyap KL, Bajpai MK, Khanna P (2015) Breast cancer detection in digital mammograms. In: International conference on imaging techniques
2. Hemalatha R, Rasu R, Santhiyakumari N, Madheswaran M (2018) Comparative analysis of edge detection methods for 3D-common carotid artery image using LabVIEW. In: IEEE conference on emerging devices and smart systems, pp 106–109
3. Lindeberg T (1998) Edge detection and ridge detection with automatic scale selection. Int J Comput Vis 117–154
4. Fawwaz I, Zarlis M, Suherman, Rahmat RF (2018) The edge detection enhancement on satellite image using bilateral filter. In: 10th international conference numerical analysis in engineering
5. Sasikala N, Shruthi Ch, Mohana A, Harika M, Supriya S (2020) An adaptive edge detecting method for satellite imagery based on canny edge algorithm. Int J Adv Eng Res Sci 7(4):293–298
6. Kar SA, Kelkar VV (2013) Classification of multispectral satellite images. In: International conference in advanced technology
7. Pugazhenthi A, Kumar LS (2017) Image contrast enhancement by automatic multi-histogram equalization for satellite images. In: International conference on signal processing, communications and networking
8. Enyedi B, Konyha L, Fazekas K (2005) Threshold procedures and image segmentation. In: 47th international symposium ELMAR
9. Solomon C, Breckon T (2011) Fundamentals of digital image processing: a practical approach with examples in Matlab
10. Pandey P, Dewangan KK, Dewangan DK (2017) Satellite image enhancement techniques. In: International conference on energy, communication, data analytics and soft computing
11. Bidwai P, Tuptewar DJ (2015) Resolution and contrast enhancement techniques for grey level, color image and satellite image. In: International conference on information processing

FCM-RGM: Segmentation of Nuclei via Exact Contour Enhancement in Pap Smear Images

J. Jeyshri and M. Kowsigan

1 Introduction

Cervical cancer is the fourth highest frequently diagnosed type of cancer in women worldwide and the fourth major cause of cancer death in women. GLOBOCAN projected that 604,000 women would be diagnosed with cervical cancer, and 342,000 would die of the disease by 2020 [1]. Cervical cancer incidence and mortality rates have decreased significantly in the majority of the world during the last decades [2]. With better screening methods, the number of women who get cervical cancer has dropped dramatically over the years. There will still be 14,480 new cases of ovarian cancer in the USA in 2021, though. A human papillomavirus (HPV) infection is thought to be the cause of more than 90% of all cervical cancers. A cervical tumor doesn't happen to every woman who has HPV, but getting a vaccine to protect against the virus is known to help. In contrast to most other types of cancer, cervical cancer is usually found in young or middle-aged women.

As the National Cancer Institute (NCI) says, the average age of a woman who has cervix cancer is 50 years old. In women between the ages of 20 and 44, more than one-third of new cervical cancer diagnoses are caused by a virus called HPV. In women who are younger than 65, about 80% of cervical cancer cases are caused by the virus. It is the most common type of cervical cancer, which is squamous cell carcinoma. Cervical intraepithelial neoplasia (CIN) and squamous intraepithelial lesions are two types of precancerous cervical squamous epithelium that don't spread to the outside of the body: (SIL) Some cases of CIN/SIL don't become cancerous, and some cases may go away on their own. Cases of high-grade CIN/SIL are linked to high-risk HPV

J. Jeyshri (✉) · M. Kowsigan
Department of Computing technologies, College of Engineering and Technology, SRM Institute of Science and Technology, Chengalpattu, Kattankulathur, Tamil Nadu, India
e-mail: jj1483@srmist.edu.in

M. Kowsigan
e-mail: kowsigam@srmist.edu.in

© The Author(s), under exclusive license to Springer Nature Singapore Pte Ltd. 2023   381
K. Kumar Singh et al. (eds.), *Machine Vision and Augmented Intelligence*, Lecture Notes in Electrical Engineering 1007, https://doi.org/10.1007/978-981-99-0189-0_29

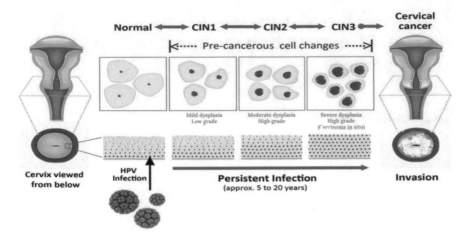

Fig. 1 Procedure for classifying cervical cancer

serotypes and a greater risk of cancer. Early detection and diagnosis of CIN/SIL are important in preventing invasive Carcinoma.

It's important to know how much cervical cancer you have, where it is in your body, and if it has spread. Cervical cancer has four stages. Treatments vary based on the stages of cancer. As soon as it is found that you have cancer of the cervix, your doctor will figure out what stage it is in before you start treatment. The cervix is the lower, narrow part of your uterus that connects to your vagina. Cervical cancer stages can include a lot of different tests, like imaging studies, to figure out how much cancer you have and where it is in your body. The stages of cervical cancer are named from the earliest stage 0, which is almost always curable, to stage IV, which means that cancer has spread. It's just that there are different sub-categories in each stage, depending on how much evidence was found about a malignancy during the cervical cancer staging process (Fig. 1).

Squamous intraepithelial lesions are the term for these types of things (SIL). In a report on cytology smears, these are some of the things that could happen: In the body, there are normal cells. No, the squamous intraepithelial lesion isn't there. CIN 1: Low-Grade SIL (mild dysplasia on histology). It has CIN 2 and CIN 3 in it. This is called High-Grade SIL1 (HSIL) (moderate to severe dysplasia on histology). The squamous cell carcinomas that form from Low-Grade SIL can spread to other parts of the body. A high grade of SIL can become cancerous, but only about 6–74% of them become cancerous. In higher-grade lesions, there is less cytoplasm and more of a ratio between the nucleus and the cytoplasm.

2   Related Works

To begin, nucleus/cell segmentation algorithms identify each pixel in an image using a region-based approach. Threshold techniques are common ways for nucleus segmentation [3], a technique of region growth algorithms [4], clustering algorithms [5], and watershed algorithms [6]. Second, there is a differential operator, and an active contour approach is two segmentation algorithms that employ the irregularity of gray information to segment the image [7, 8]. Thirdly, techniques for segmenting cells or nuclei are primarily based on research hypotheses [9], such as wavelet analysis, mathematical morphology, evolutionary algorithms, and neural networks. Additionally, many existing or nuclei segmentation methods are built on a combination of algorithms, named fusion algorithms that compensate for the lack of a single methodology by generating higher segmentation results. Due to variations in slice preparation and staining processes, the appearance of cervical smears varies (for better or worse), as seen by uneven dyeing and a complicated backdrop to the smear pictures.

1. Additionally, the uneven form of cervical cells and the overlap of cells complicate the straightforward segmentation of complete cervical cells. Only segmenting and then analyzing cervix nuclei in considerably overlapping cell clusters may be applied for cervical cancer testing. Here, the bulk of pathogenic features is found in the nuclei of cancer cells. Thus, quantitative measurement of nucleus shape is accurate while having no effect on the screening findings for cervical cancer cells. On the other hand, it helps to reduce segmentation trouble and improves the operation process.

2. Image segmentation is an essential step in the image recognition process. The objective of this phase is to modify the illustration of a picture into something more coherent and simpler to understand. The techniques are classified into two groups based on two factors: irregularity and similarity. This attribute divides image segmentation into two types: edge- and region-based segmentation. These methods that rely on the irregularity feature of pixels are known as edge-based approaches. A region-based segmentation separates a picture into related pixels in comparable locations. Region-based techniques include edge detection, region expansion, and region splitting and merging [10–15]. In image segmentation, thresholding is a frequent approach. To distinguish items of interest from the background, the main principle is to find an appropriate gray-level limit value based on the objects of interest in a picture.

3. In this manuscript, contrast enhancement and preprocessing are used to improve the internal areas of the cervical image in order to achieve high segmentation of the abnormal area. The cervical picture is an RGB file that is changed to a grayscale file for more processing. Low-contrast cervical images also need to be improved, which makes the image's edges look better. The oriented local histogram equalization (OLHE) enhancement technique is used in this manuscript which is tried to achieve in low-resolution cervical images [16–18]. This method is similar to local histogram equalization (LHE), except it captures edge orientation, which LHE does not. OLHE is recalculated for each pixel on a

cervical picture on the local $W * H$ (Width and Height) window centered on this pixel.

4. The following findings are revealed by traditional cervical cancer detection methods. Only high-resolution cervical pictures are suitable for conventional procedures. The external boundary zone of the cancer regions was the only one identified. For further cervical cancer diagnosis, the accuracy and sensitivity rate was not ideal. By presenting a computer-aided fully automatic strategy for screening the cervical cancer area using a Neural Network classifier, the limitations of existing methods are removed.

3 Motivations and Contributions

We present an automated approach for cervical nuclei that can be separated from cell clusters directly-based on learning and combining the findings of previous investigations. Its goal is to enhance cell nuclei segmentation accuracy and also ease the developing procedure.

The following are the paper's major points:

1. FCM-RGM uses a specific hybrid search method to automatically divide a large number of small cervical cell picture ROIs. Besides not having to cut large files, this also makes it easier to break up multiple objects into single objects, which makes it easier to do fine segmentation.
2. FCM-RGM is the best proposal to avoid repeating segmentation and enhance the performance of segmentation.
3. FCM-RGM improved the quality of cell image segmentation when there's not a low contrast between the cells.
4. We have experimented with Herlev public dataset, with detailed ground truth labeling.

3.1 Cervical Cancer Dataset Description

The input data for the proposed cervical cancer detection model were gathered from a single database called "http://mde-lab.aegean.gr/index.php/download" This is a collection of six datasets for the diagnosis of cervical cancer. The images for the input are taken from Part I of the "Old Pap smear database." There are 13 classes in this collection, and there are several cervical pictures. There are a total of 1062 cervical pictures in the collection.

4 Preprocessing

This is a generic term for actions on photos where the input and output are both intensity images. These enduring images are identical to the sensor's original data, with an intensity image often represented by a matrix of image brightness values. The purpose of this article is to enhance the internal regions of the cervical picture in order to achieve a high level of abnormal area segmentation. The ovarian picture is in RGB format and is transformed to grayscale for further processing. Additionally, for low-brightness cervical pictures, enhancing is required, which improves the image's edges [19, 20]. Although geometric transformations of images are classified as preprocessing methods here due to the similar techniques used, the purpose of preprocessing is to improve the image data by suppressing undesirable distortions or enhancing certain image features critical for subsequent processing.

5 Median Filtering

Median filtering is a nonlinear procedure that can be used to reduce impulsive noise or salt-and-pepper noise. Additionally, the median filter is utilized to maintain edge qualities while lowering noise. Additionally, smoothing techniques such as Gaussian blur are employed to minimize noise, but they do not retain edge features. Because it preserves edge features, the median filter is commonly employed in digital image processing.

5.1 Algorithm

Input: Image I of size $P * Q$, filter size S
Output: Image J of similar size as I

Initialize histogram H and starting point k
for $K = 1$ to P **do**

  for $L = 1$ to Q **do**

    for $M = -n/2$ to $n/2$ **do**

      Remove $I_{k+l, 1-s/2}$ from H
      Add $I_{k+m,l+n/2}$ to H
      Update k

    end for

    $J_{k, 1---}$ median (H, k)

  end for

end for

6 Image Enhancement

The contrast enhancement is to improve an image's global or local contrast. Histogram equalization, Genetic algorithms, and fuzzy set algorithms are some of the enhancing strategies. To raise the contrast of the photographs, many changes are made to the normal approaches.

As demonstrated in Fig. 2a, the majority of Pap smear images were noisy and low contrast. To remove the disturbances and Fig. 2b raise the contrast, picture enhancement was required. Figure 2c shows how a median filter was used to remove noises, and Fig. 2d shows how image enhancement (histogram equalization) was utilized to increase contrast. Cell segmentation was easier and more exact in high contrast photos than in low contrast ones.

There have been numerous image-enhancing techniques proposed and developed. Histogram equalization is one of the most widely used image improvement techniques (HE). Because HE is computationally fast and simple to implement, it is often employed for image contrast enhancement. HE works by remapping the image's gray levels according to the probability distribution of the input gray levels. It's a contrast-adjustment method in image processing that makes use of the image's histogram. From Fig. 3, the histogram's intensities can be more evenly distributed. This enables locations with low local contrast to obtaining a boost in contrast. This is done by the application of histogram equalization, which effectively spreads out the most common intensity value.

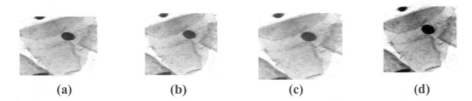

    (a)   (b)   (c)   (d)

Fig. 2 **a** Input pap smear image, **b** gray scale image, **c** noise removal by median filter technique, and **d** image contrast enhancement

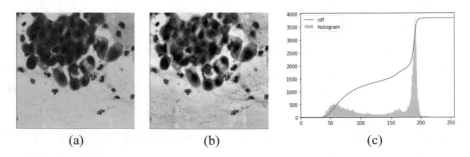

    (a)   (b)   (c)

Fig. 3 **a** Original image, **b** image enhancement, and **c** histogram equalization

$$H(v) = \text{round}\left\{ \frac{\text{cdf}(v) - \text{cdf}_{\min}}{(m * n) - \text{cdf}_{\min}} * (L - 1) \right\} \tag{1}$$

Here, $\text{cdf}_{\text{mi}} \rightarrow$ minimum nonzero value of the cumulative distribution function, $M \times N$ gives the number of image pixels, where M is width and N the height and L is the number of used gray levels.

7 Fuzzy Growing Model

FCM is a useful categorization technique that allows for the assignment of a piece of data to more clustering centers, each with its own membership value. The following objective function is attempted to be minimized using FCM:

$$J_{\text{fcm}(p,q,r)} = \sum_{i=1}^{N} \sum_{j=1}^{C} p_{i,j}^{m} d^2(r_i, q_j) \quad 1 < m < \infty \tag{2}$$

The vector $R = \{r_1, r_2, r_3, \ldots, r_N\}$ consists of N number of pixels, the vector $Q = \{q_1, q_2, q_3, \ldots, q_C\}$ is the center of the cluster, $d^2(r_i, q_j)$ is termed as the distance metric of object of the object r_i from the center point of jth cluster. This conventional algorithm uses fuzzy memberships to allocate pixels to each cluster, where $P_{i,j}$ is the degree of memberships.

The following three requirements are met by the degree of membership:

$$\sum_{j=1}^{C} P_{i,j} = 1 \sum_{i=1}^{N} P_{i,j} \leq N, \quad i = 1, 2, \ldots, N \quad j = 1, 2, 3 \ldots c \tag{3}$$

In the iterative process, the clustering centers and membership degrees are constantly updated, while the objective function value approaches the minimal value. The membership matrix and cluster center point are updated using the following formula:

$$P_{i,j} = \frac{1}{\sum_{k=1}^{c} \left(\frac{d_{i,j}}{d_{i,k}} \right)^{\frac{2}{m-i}}}, \quad q_j = \frac{\sum_{i=1}^{N} P_{i,j}^{m} r_i}{\sum_{i=1}^{N} P_{i,j}^{m}} \tag{4}$$

To address FCM's imperfection, we could use the data's local information instead of the data to mitigate the algorithm's negative effects. The membership calculation is influenced by noise. The membership matrix and clustering calculations. Multiple items in the pixel's local area are used to optimize the center.

7.1 Region Growing Method

The proposed cervical cancer diagnosis method establishes a different segmentation method called FCM-RGM by integrating Fuzzy clustering and region growing approach to attain better segmentation results. The region-growing algorithm has been successfully utilized to segment image data. The current study took it a step further by examining the possibility of using a thresholded region expanding algorithm as a tool for extracting characteristics. The research framework is termed as region growing model (RGM). Four features or parameters of cervical cells were extracted using this methodology: nucleus size, cytoplasm size, nuclei gray level, and cytoplasmic gray level.

A correlation test was applied between data extracted using the proposed RGM algorithm with the data extracted manually by cytotechnologists. The RGM algorithm is appropriate and capable of being utilized as an image extraction tool to extract critical properties of cervical cells, as indicated by the strong correlation value obtained in the correlation test. This would assist cytotechnologists in cervical cancer screening by providing accurate values of size and gray level of nuclear and cytoplasmic features.

The exact segmentation of the abnormal Pap cell nucleus is critical for the early detection of cervical cancer. This challenge is especially difficult due to cell overlapping, irregular staining, contrast adjustment, and other imaging objects. A novel method for segmenting cell nuclei from overlapping cervical smear cell images is proposed in this study. Using Fuzzy c-means grouping, the proposed technique employs a circular shape function to improve the robustness of the smear test understanding the molecular basis segmentation.

This imposes a shape restriction on the formed clusters while improving the nucleus boundary. The shape function enables distinguishing pixels with similar pixel intensities but located in different spatial units.

8 Proposed FCM-RGM-Based Abnormality Segmentation

See Fig. 4.

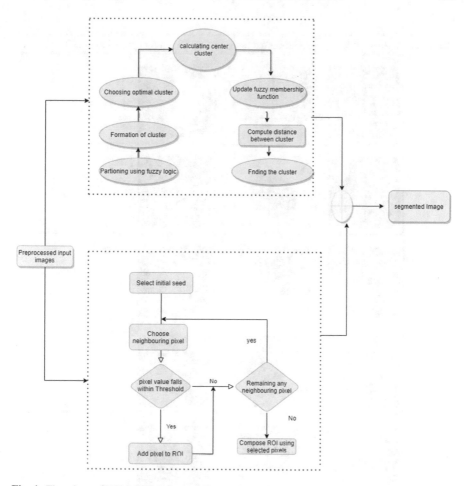

Fig. 4 Flowchart of FCM-RGM abnormality segmentation

9 Results

Datasets	Actual image	Preprocessed image	Segmented image (FCM-RGM) technique
Pap smear images			

(continued)

(continued)

Datasets	Actual image	Preprocessed image	Segmented image (FCM-RGM) technique

10   Segmentation, Review, and Discussion

We describe an approach for segmentation that is not based on learning that does not require user interaction or personal annotation for model learning. The methodology achieves satisfactory outcomes when segmenting cell nuclei from entire smear images. We evaluate our method strategy to current segmentation methods such as computer vision (CV) model with improvement, like Automatic Fuzzy Clustering Framework (AFCF) [21] and Adaptive Morphological Reconstruction (AMR) [22]. We analyze the segmentation outcomes using the Dice, Jaccard, Precision, and Recall measures. These parameters are defined as follows:

$$\text{Dice}(F, G) = 2 * \frac{F \cap G}{F + G} = 2 * \frac{\text{TP}}{\text{TP} + \text{FP} + \text{TP} + \text{FN}} \tag{5}$$

$$\text{Jaccard} = \frac{F \cap G}{FUG} = \frac{\text{TP}}{\text{TP} + \text{FP} + \text{FN}} \tag{6}$$

$$\text{Precision} = \frac{\text{TP}}{\text{TP} + \text{FP}} \tag{7}$$

$$\text{Recall} = \frac{\text{TP}}{\text{TP} + \text{FN}}, \tag{8}$$

where F denotes the ground truth picture and G denotes the final outcome image. In Table 1, we can see the results of the comparison, in which FCM-RGM has the best results in all four coefficients for low resolution nuclei, whereas FCM-RGM has the best results in Dice, Jaccard, and Recall for high resolution nuclei behaves effectively in terms of precision since it typically segments greater regions than the ground truth. Experiments show that FCM-RGM is better at imaging nuclei than AFCF and AMR, with a 10% and 22% increase in the Dice, respectively. Moreover, the Recall increases by 13.4% and 14.4%, respectively. FCM-RGM outperforms the non-enhanced technique in low-contrast pictures, with the Dice increasing by 4% and the Recall increasing by 5%, respectively.

Table 1 Comparison of the segmentation performance analysis with exiting methodology

Group	Methods	Dice	Jaccard	Precision	Recall
Low intensity	RGM-FCM	**0.9132**	**0.881**	**0.95**	**0.8813**
	Without enhancement	0.8215	0.8215	0.9713	0.8511
	AFCF	0.6978	0.6978	0.8721	0.7832
	AMR	No result	No result	No result	No result
High contrast	RGM-FCM	**0.9321**	**0.8910**	**0.9417**	**0.9411**
	Without enhancement	0.9502	0.8817	0.9513	0.9510
	AFCF	0.8312	0.7413	0.9624	0.7681
	AMR	0.7211	0.6412	0.7515	0.7314
Mean	RGM-FCM	**0.9214**	**0.8312**	**0.9612**	**0.9111**
	Without enhancement	0.9236	0.8760	0.9513	0.8512
	AFCF	0.8406	0.7124	0.9178	0.7765
	AMR	0.7340	0.6412	0.7512	0.7651

11   Conclusion

The research proposes a non-learning-based model—FCM-RGM—for accurately segmenting cell nuclei from entire slide Pap smear pictures. Most significantly, as compared to the CV model, AFCF, and AMR, the proposed technique improves the segmentation accuracy of nuclei with low contrast and unclear edges. The experimental results illustrate the resilience and performance of the method when it comes to region extraction and nucleus segmentation. Thus, the suggested technique is exceedingly promising for computer-assisted medical diagnosis as a fundamental but important stage in quantitative nuclear morphology analysis. Future research will focus on increasing the accuracy of region extraction and on implementing FCM-RGM as a final solution. Additionally, we are evaluating a variety of deep neural networks for use in our application.

References

1. Zhao M, Wang H, Han Y, Wang X, Dai H-N, Sun X, Zhang J, Pedersen M (2021) SEENS: nuclei segmentation in pap smear images with selective edge enhancement. Future Gener Comput Syst 114:185–194. Krishnapuram R, Keller JM (1993) A possibilistic approach to clustering. IEEE Trans Fuzzy Syst 1(2):98–110
2. Wilailak S, Kengsakul M, Kehoe S (2021) Worldwide initiatives to eliminate cervical cancer. First published: 20 Oct 2021. http://doi.org/10.1002/ijgo.13879
3. Wang Z (2019) Cell segmentation for image cytometry: advances, insufficiencies, and challenges. Cytometry A 95(7):708–711
4. Wang P, Hu X, Li Y, Liu Q, Zhu X (2016) Automatic cell nuclei segmentation and classification of breast cancer histopathology images. Signal Process 122:1–13
5. Song Y, Tan E-L, Jiang X, Cheng J-Z, Ni D, Chen S, Lei B, Wang T (2016) Accurate cervical cell segmentation from overlapping clumps in pap smear images. IEEE Trans Med Imaging 36(1):288–300
6. Gamarra M, Zurek E, Escalante HJ, Hurtado L, San-Juan-Vergara H (2019) Split and merge watershed: a two-step method for cell segmentation in fluorescence microscopy images. Biomed Signal Process Control 53:101575
7. Molnar C, Jermyn IH, Kato Z, Rahkama V, Östling P, Mikkonen P, Pietiäinen V, Horvath P (2016) Accurate morphology preserving segmentation of overlapping cells based on active contours. Sci Rep 6:32412
8. Song T-H, Sanchez V, ElDaly H, Rajpoot NM (2017) Dual-channel active contour model for megakaryocytic cell segmentation in bone marrow trephine histology images. IEEE Trans Biomed Eng 64(12):2913–2923. Dasari S, Wudayagiri R, Valluru L (2015) Cervical cancer: biomarkers for diagnosis and treatment. Clin Chim Acta 445:7–11
9. Reljin N, Slavkovic-Ilic M, Tapia C, Cihoric N, Stankovic S (2017) Multifractalbased nuclei segmentation in fish images. Biomed Microdev 19(3):67
10. Xue JH, Pizurica A, Philips W, Kerre E, Van de Walle R, Lemahieu I (2003) An integrated method of adaptive enhancement for unsupervised segmentation of MRI brain images. Pattern Recogn Lett 24(15):2549–2560
11. Liew AW, Leung SH, Lau WH (2000) Fuzzy image clustering incorporating spatial continuity. IEEE Proc Vis Image Signal Process 147(2):452–455
12. Pham DL, Prince JL (1999) Adaptive fuzzy segmentation of magnetic resonance images. IEEE Trans Med Imaging 18(9):737–752

13. Szilágyi L, Szilágyi SM, Benyó Z (2007) A modified FCM algorithm for fast segmentation of brain MR images. In: Analysis and design of intelligent systems using soft computing techniques, pp 119–127
14. Chen L, Zou J, Chen CP (2014) Kernel spatial shadowed C-means for image segmentation. Int J Fuzzy Syst 16(1):46–56
15. Saha I, Maulik U, Plewczynski D (2011) A new multi-objective technique for differential fuzzy clustering. Appl Soft Comput 11:2765–2776. Li C, Chen H, Zhang L, Xu N, Xue D, Hu Z, Ma H, Sun H (2019) Cervical histopathology image classification using multilayer hidden conditional random fields and weakly supervised learning. IEEE Access 7:90378–90397
16. Kurnianingsih KHSA, Nugroho LE, Widyawan LL, Prabuwono AS, Mantoro T (2019) Segmentation and classification of cervical cells using deep learning. IEEE Access 7:116925–116941
17. Luo YM, Zhang T, Li P, Liu PZ, Sun P, Dong B, Ruan G (2020) MDFI: multi-CNN decision feature integration for diagnosis of cervical precancerous lesions. IEEE Access 8:29616–29626
18. Hayakawa T, Prasath VS, Kawanaka H, Aronow BJ, Tsuruoka S (2021) Computational nuclei segmentation methods in digital pathology: a survey. Arch Comput Methods Eng 28:1–3
19. Diniz DN, Rezende MT, Bianchi AG, Carneiro CM, Ushizima DM, de Medeiros FN, Souza MJ (2021) A hierarchical feature-based methodology to perform cervical cancer classification. Appl Sci 11(9):4091
20. Nucleus segmentation of cervical cytology images based on multi-scale fuzzy clustering algorithm. Bioengineered 11(1):484–501. http://doi.org/10.1080/21655979.2020.1747834
21. Lei T, Jia X, Liu T, Liu S, Meng H, Nandi AK (2019) Adaptive morphological reconstruction for seeded image segmentation. IEEE Trans Image Process 28(11):5510–5523
22. Lei T, Liu P, Jia X, Zhang X, Meng H, Nandi AK (2019) Automatic fuzzy clustering framework for image segmentation. IEEE Trans Fuzzy Syst 28(9):2078–2092. Hayakawa1 T et al (2021) Computational nuclei segmentation methods in digital pathology: a survey. Arch Comput Methods Eng 28:1–13

Pulmonary Lung Cancer Classification Using Deep Neural Networks

Jagriti Goswami and Koushlendra Kumar Singh

1 Introduction

Lung cancer is a major threat to human life with its high rate of occurrence and death rate. As of 2020, it accounts for 11.4% of the total new cases and 18% of total deaths due to cancer [1]. Because of insufficient screening programs and the late emergence of clinical symptoms, majority of patients are diagnosed with advanced-stage disease. To enhance patient survival chances, lung cancer must be discovered early. Low-dose computed tomography is one technology that can help with this. Lung nodules are little abnormal growths in the lungs. There may be one or several nodules found in a lung, and they can be cancerous or non-cancerous. The size and shape of the nodules as well as their location and relationship to neighboring structures can be determined via a chest CT scan [2].

The goal of computer-assisted detection and diagnosis (CAD) software is to help radiologists quickly and accurately analyze various radiography images and decrease the cost incurred due to manual reading of scans. Studies show that despite advancement in CAD systems over the past decade, there has been no clear proof of improvement in performance over time [3]. Existing CAD systems can benefit from machine learning approaches to improve their capabilities. Machine learning analyzes complex patterns and supports radiologists in making rational choices using radiological data such as conventional radiography, CT, MRI and PET images, as well as radiology reports [4].

Deep learning, a branch of machine learning, has lately shown to be extremely successful in the field of medical imaging. Thus, there is a scope of devising a new

J. Goswami (✉) · K. K. Singh
Machine Vision and Intelligence Lab, Department of Computer Science and Engineering,
National Institute of Technology Jamshedpur, Jamshedpur, Jharkhand 831014, India
e-mail: jagriti.goswami10@gmail.com

K. K. Singh
e-mail: koushlendra.cse@nitjsr.ac.in

© The Author(s), under exclusive license to Springer Nature Singapore Pte Ltd. 2023   395
K. Kumar Singh et al. (eds.), *Machine Vision and Augmented Intelligence*, Lecture Notes
in Electrical Engineering 1007, https://doi.org/10.1007/978-981-99-0189-0_30

set of tools to help assist radiologists and improve the prediction accuracy of lung cancer. Convolutional neural networks (CNNs), the most dominant among various deep learning models, are being widely employed in the disciplines of computer vision and medical image analysis and have been used to solve problems ranging from classification, segmentation, face recognition [5], to super-resolution and image enhancement [6]. Recently, a deep learning approach called transfer learning has gained much attention where an already existing pre-trained model can be used for developing a model for a related task. VGG16, VGG19, InceptionV3, MobileNet-V2, ResNet-50 and DenseNet-121 are some of these state-of-the-art pre-trained CNNs which have shown promising results in the field of image analysis [7, 8]. In this paper:

1. Given a set of raw chest CT scans, we extracted the nodule patches and classified them into Adenocarcinoma, Small Cell Carcinoma and Squamous Cell Carcinoma.
2. We trained four state-of-the-art deep learning models VGG16, VGG19, InceptionV3 and MobileNetV2 by fine-tuning the last layers of the pre-trained models on ImageNet.
3. We then compared the results by using evaluation metrics: Accuracy, Precision, F1-score, Cohen's Kappa score and AUC score.

2 Related Work

The computer-aided detection (CAD) technology was initially utilized to detect lung nodules, but the results were not appealing due to a lack of computational resources for advanced image processing techniques at the time. The performance of CAD systems improved dramatically with the advent of the graphical processing unit (GPU) and convolutional neural networks (CNNs). A great majority of research on lung cancer detection has typically focused on image segmentation. Shen et al. in [9, 10] removed the need for nodule segmentation and hand-crafted feature engineering work by directly feeding raw patches of images to the model without any prior definition of nodule morphology and achieved good results compared to the previous works. Kang et al. proposed a 3D multi-view convolutional neural network (MV-CNN) to capture the 3D context of the CT scan. Both 3D CNN with chain architecture (such as LeNet and AlexNet) and with DAG architecture (such as residual network and GoogLeNet) are explored [11]. To efficiently learn nodule features, Zhu et al. developed a 3D faster regions with convolutional neural network (R-CNN) for nodule detection with 3D dual path blocks and a U-net like encoder–decoder structure and a gradient boosting machine (GBM) with 3D dual-path network features for nodule classification [12]. While a lot of the previous works have utilized a 3D model to capture the multi-view perspective of the CT scans, T. Fang combined multi-view of the CT scans into an image using median intensity projection to preserve the integrity of a 3D image and trained it on a GoogLeNet-based CNN [13]. Zhao et al. proposed an agile CNN architecture with only two convolutional layers and a small number of kernels. It was a hybrid LeNet–AlexNet structure that integrated the layer settings of LeNet with the parameter settings of AlexNet. This model provided good results even for small datasets [14]. Shao et al. devised an algorithm which used adaptive iterative threshold twice for pulmonary parenchyma segmentation. It further applied histogram analysis with compactness features to identify candidate nodules and then achieve features extracted from the ROI [15]. Not only 3D models, even 2D models achieved good results in case of lung nodule classification [16]. Transfer learning is being used widely in different domains. Training machine learning models for medical image analysis is particularly hard due to the lack of good amount of labeled medical image data, and hence, there have been several works involving application of transfer learning in CNN models. Nóbrega et al. analyzed the accuracy of 11 different state-of-the-art pre-trained models and five classification methods to achieve a highest accuracy of 89.91% using Xception model as feature extractor and MLP as classifier [17]. S. Guan and M. Loew used VGG16 as a feature extractor as well as by fine-tuning some of the convolutional layers for breast cancer detection [18]. R. Palaskar took a similar approach using MobileNet, ResNet and InceptionV3 for oral cancer detection [19]. K. George et al. extracted nuclei features from biopsy images using pre-trained networks AlexNet, ResNet-18, ResNet-50, ResNet-101 and GoogleNet which were then combined to get image level features [20]. Transfer learning has also been used to develop various fast and accurate models for the detection of the disease which caused the recent pandemic worldwide, i.e., COVID-19 [21, 22].

3   Methodology

3.1   Dataset

The dataset used in this study has been taken from a Large-Scale CT and PET/CT Dataset for Lung Cancer Diagnosis (Lung-PET-CT-Dx) with XML annotation files that provide tumor locations using bounding boxes' coordinates. It consists of CT and PET-CT DICOM images of lung cancer patients diagnosed with Adenocarcinoma (A), Small Cell Carcinoma (B), Large Cell Carcinoma (E) and Squamous Cell Carcinoma (G). We ignored the class Large Cell Carcinoma as there are very little data available to even perform data augmentation and get reliable results. The slice interval of the CT scans varies from 0.625 mm to 5 mm and includes scanning modes-plain, contrast and 3D reconstruction [23]. Nodule patches are extracted from the CT slices using the bounding box coordinates and resized to a size of 128 * 128 before feeding to the network. Due to system limitations, a subset of the data containing 4557, 4667 and 4630 patches of classes A, B and G, respectively, has been used for the experiment.

In order to remove the imbalance in the dataset, we applied common data augmentations on some of the images of class B such as rotate 90°, 180°, 270°, zoom out, zoom in, flip respect to x-axis and y-axis (Figs. 1 and 2).

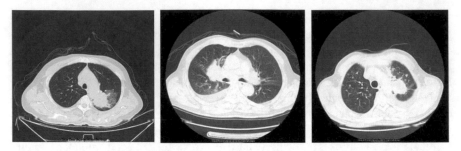

Fig. 1 CT scan slices with Adenocarcinoma, Small Cell Carcinoma and Squamous Cell Carcinoma taken from Lung-PET-CT-Dx dataset [23]

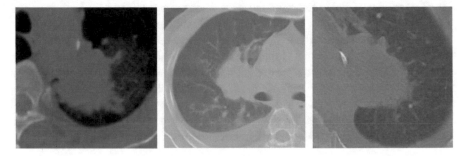

Fig. 2 Nodule patches extracted from CT slices with Adenocarcinoma, Small Cell Carcinoma and Squamous Cell Carcinoma taken from Lung-PET-CT-Dx dataset [23]

3.2 Transfer Learning

Transfer learning refers to situations, in which one tries to apply what has been learnt in one task to improve generalization in another. To train deep learning models from start, a vast amount of data is necessary. We can design a relatively well-performing model with minimal training data using transfer learning. This is of major benefit while training models with medical imaging data as there are very less labeled data available in this domain.

Transfer learning can be applied in two ways. In the first method, the pre-trained model can be used as a feature extractor, and a task-specific classifier is trained on top of it. This is based on the concept that neural networks are used in computer vision to detect edges in the first layer, shapes in the intermediate layer and task-specific properties in the latter layers. In the second method, the architecture of the pre-trained model is used, and we fine-tune the whole network for our specific task [24, 25]. In the proposed approach, we have used the pre-trained models as feature extractor and fine-tuned the fully connected layers for the task. Following are some transfer learning models which have proved to show good results with medical imaging data over the years.

VGG16 and VGG19

VGG is a very large network with approximately 138–144 million parameters and 16–19 weight layers of depth. It uses convolutional layers of 3 * 3 filter size with a stride of 1px and a spatial padding of 1px to preserve the spatial resolution after convolution. Max-pooling layers of size 2 * 2 with stride of 2 follow some of the convolutional layers [26]. Although the network is slow to train and takes up quite a lot of memory and bandwidth, it has shown some great results over the years on medical imaging datasets.

InceptionV3

The main idea behind the inception network was to use kernels of varying size and operate on the same level [27]. InceptionV1 uses a rudimentary inception module, as seen in the diagram below. Convolution is performed on the input using kernels of three different sizes (3×3, 5×5 and 7×7). The output is then concatenated and passed along to the following inception module. Several such inception modules are stacked together. Also, due to the high depth of the network, auxiliary classifiers were implemented to prevent the middle half of the network from dying out, basically applying softmax activation to the output of the inception modules. The weighted sum of the auxiliary and real losses was used to calculate the total loss function.

Enhanced editions of the Inception network have been released over time. In this paper, we will be using InceptionV3 as shown in Fig. 3. The key feature of InceptionV3 are [28]:

- It combines 1xn and nx1 convolutions to factorize convolutions of filter size n * n.
- It uses the RMSProp optimizer.

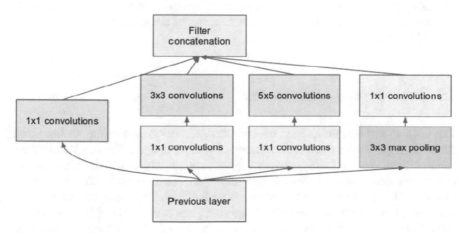

Fig. 3 Inception module with dimension reduction [27]

Fig. 4 Convolutional blocks for MobileNetV2 [29]

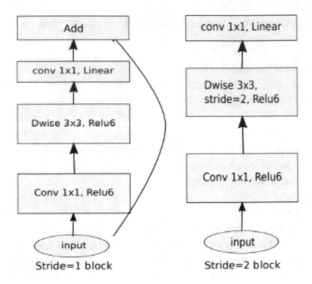

Stride=1 block   Stride=2 block

- It uses BatchNorm on auxiliary classifiers.
- It carries out label smoothing. Label smoothing is a regularizing component that stops the network from overfitting by stopping it from being overly confident about a class.

MobileNetV2

A new layer was developed in this model, which is an inverted residual structure with shortcut connections between narrow bottleneck layers. A low-dimensional condensed representation is expanded to high dimension by this module before filtering it with a lightweight depth-wise convolution by applying a single convolutional filter per input channel. By computing linear combinations of input channels, a pointwise convolution of 1 * 1 is used to construct additional features. In order to maintain the representational power, nonlinearities are removed from the narrow layers [29] (Fig. 4).

3.3 Training and Classification

The CNN model is a pre-trained network that was developed using the ImageNet dataset, a huge publicly accessible dataset of natural images. The top layers of the network were removed and fine-tuned for our unique objective. To determine the relative predicted probabilities for each class, alternate dropout and dense layers with the ReLU activation function are employed, followed by a final dense layer with the softmax activation function. The suggested class is the one that has the highest probability. The gap between predicted probability and ground truth is minimized using the cross-entropy loss function and the Adam optimizer (Fig. 5).

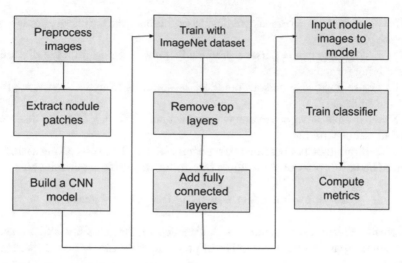

Fig. 5 Flow diagram for the proposed approach

4 Experimental Results

This section presents experimental results achieved by training VGG16, VGG19, InceptionV3 and MobileNetV2 with Lung-PET-CT-Dx dataset for lung cancer classification with a learning rate of 0.0001 over 30 epochs. We have used a batch size of 32 and Adam optimizer to optimize the loss function. Before being fed to the network, the images are scaled to 128 * 128 pixels. The proposed method is tested on Google Colab's GPU. The CNN models are imported from the Keras library and run on top of TensorFlow. The models were assessed using the indicators listed below. The equations below are summarized and cited from [30] and [31].

Accuracy is the percentage of right predictions made by our model.

$$Accuracy = (TP + TN) / (TP + TN + FP + FN). \qquad (1)$$

Precision is a measure of the number of correct positive predictions provided by our model.

$$Precision = TP / (TP + FP). \qquad (2)$$

Recall measures the number of positive predictions our model correctly made out of all the possible positive predictions that could have been made.

$$Recall = TP / (TP + FN), \qquad (3)$$

where

TP = True Positive = persons predicted as suffering from the disease are suffering from the disease.

TN = True Negative = persons predicted as not suffering from the disease are not suffering from the disease.

FP = False Positive = persons predicted as suffering from the disease are found to be not suffering.

FN = False Negative = persons who are actually suffering from the disease are found to be not suffering.

F1-score provides the combined effect of precision and recall by taking a harmonic mean of both. It is particularly useful while comparing different classifiers.

$$F1 = 2 * (\text{precision} * \text{recall}) / (\text{precision} + \text{recall}). \tag{4}$$

Cohen's Kappa score eliminates the chance of the classifier and a random guess agreeing and counts the number of predictions the model makes that are not explainable.

$$\kappa = (p_0 - p_e)/(1 - p_e), \tag{5}$$

where p_0 denotes the overall accuracy of the model and p_e denotes the degree of agreement between the model predictions and the actual class values as they happened by chance (Table 1).

Receiver operating characteristics' (ROC's) curve is a plot of False-Positive rate versus True-Positive rate for a variety of different classification threshold values ranging from 0 to 1. Classifiers with curves that are closer to the top-left corner of the plot indicate a better performance. Because changing classification objectives may make one point on the curve more suited for one task and another more suited for a different task, so looking at the ROC curve is a technique to evaluate the model irrespective of the threshold chosen (Fig. 6).

Area Under Curve (AUC) is a measure of performance that encompasses all possible classification thresholds. AUC is the likelihood that a random positive example will be ranked higher than a random negative example by the model. The AUC value

Table 1 Comparison of accuracy, precision, recall, F1-score and Cohen's Kappa score for lung cancer classification

Model	Accuracy (%)	Precision (%)	Recall (%)	F1-score (%)	Cohen's Kappa score (%)
VGG16	82.28	82.73	82.28	82.46	73.42
VGG19	84.28	84.30	84.28	84.09	76.42
InceptionV3	81.48	82.89	81.48	81.67	72.23
MobileNetV2	87.61	87.78	87.61	87.61	81.43

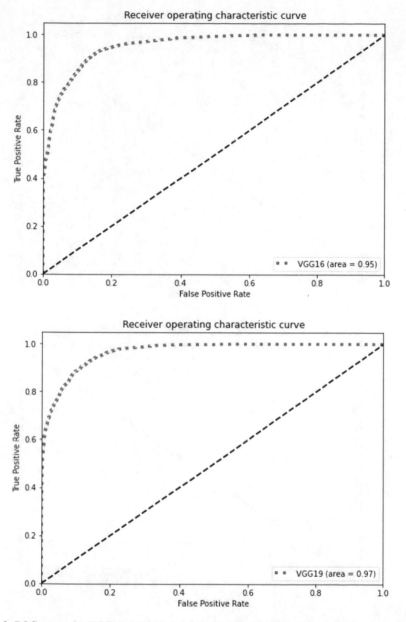

Fig. 6 ROC curves for VGG16, VGG19, InceptionNetV3, MobileNetV2 are shown, respectively, from top to bottom

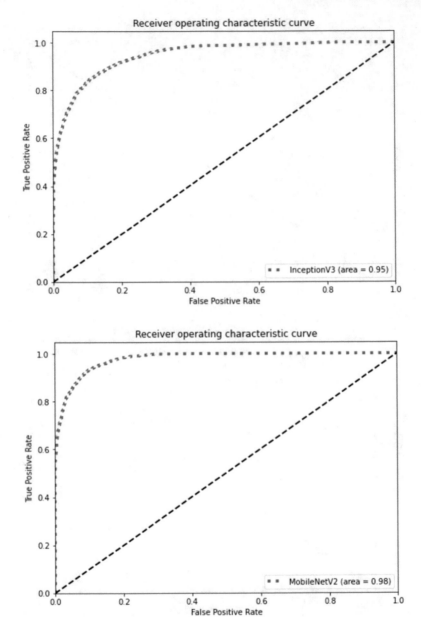

Fig. 6 (continued)

Table 2 Comparison of area under curve (AUC) for lung cancer classification

Model	VGG16	VGG19	InceptionNetV3	MobileNetV2
AUC (%)	95.37	96.67	94.58	97.73

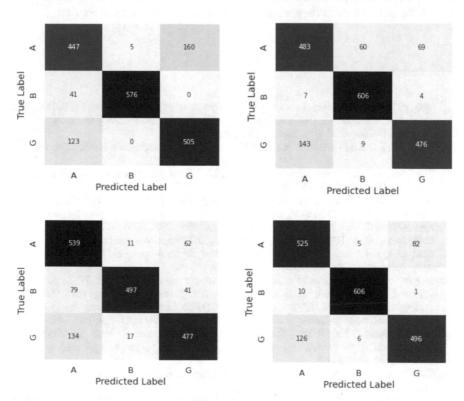

Fig. 7 Confusion matrix for VGG16 (top left), VGG19 (top right), InceptionNetV3 (bottom left), MobileNetV2 (bottom right)

varies from 0 to 1. The AUC of a model whose predictions are 100% incorrect is 0.0, whereas the AUC of a model whose predictions are 100% correct is 1.0 (Table 2).

Confusion Matrix is presented to show the distribution of actual samples versus predicted samples (Fig. 7).

5 Conclusion

In this paper, we performed transfer learning using four state-of-the-art deep learning models as feature extractor to classify between three types of lung cancer from the CT and PET-CT images provided by publicly available Lung-PET-CT-Dx dataset.

It was shown that machine learning can be used as an effective technique for lung cancer diagnosis. The best performing model for lung cancer classification achieved an accuracy of 87.61% and AUC of 97.73%. Due to limitation of system resources, the training could be performed only on a subset of the original data that was available. The model performance is expected to improve using the complete dataset.

References

1. Sung H, Ferlay J, Siegel RL, Laversanne M, Soerjomataram I, Jemal A, Bray F (2021) Global cancer statistics 2020: GLOBOCAN estimates of incidence and mortality worldwide for 36 cancers in 185 countries. CA Cancer J Clin 71:209–249
2. Gridelli C, Rossi A, Carbone D et al (2015) Non-small-cell lung cancer. Nat Rev Dis Primers 1:15009
3. Elter M, Horsch A (2009) CADx of mammographic masses and clustered microcalcifications: a review. Med Phys 36(6):2052–2068
4. Wang S, Summers RM (2012) Machine learning and radiology. Med Image Anal 16(5):933–951
5. Fuad MTH et al (2021) Recent advances in deep learning techniques for face recognition. IEEE Access 9:99112–99142. https://doi.org/10.1109/ACCESS.2021.3096136
6. Kashyap KL, Singh KK, Bajpai MK, Khanna PS (2017) Fractional order filter based enhancement of digital mammograms. In: Proceedings of the world congress on engineering and computer science 2017, vol 1. San Francisco, USA
7. Minaee S, Kafieh R, Sonka M, Yazdani S, Jamalipour SG (2020) Deep-COVID: predicting COVID-19 from chest X-ray images using deep transfer learning. Med Image Anal 65:101794
8. Sekeroglu B, Ozsahin I (2020) Detection of COVID-19 from chest X-ray images using convolutional neural networks. SLAS Technol: Translat Life Sci Innov 25(6):553–565
9. Shen W, Zhou M, Yang F, Yang C, Tian J (2015) Multi-scale convolutional neural networks for lung nodule classification. Information processing in medical imaging: proceedings of the ... conference, 24:588–599
10. Shen W et al (2016) Multi-crop convolutional neural networks for lung nodule malignancy suspiciousness classification. Pattern Recogn
11. Kang G, Liu K, Hou B, Zhang N (2017) 3D multi-view convolutional neural networks for lung nodule classification. PLoS ONE 12(11):e0188290
12. Zhu W, Liu C, Fan W, Xie X (2018) DeepLung: deep 3D dual path nets for automated pulmonary nodule detection and classification. IEEE winter conference on applications of computer vision (WACV) 2018:673–681. https://doi.org/10.1109/WACV.2018.00079
13. Fang T (2018) A novel computer-aided lung cancer detection method based on transfer learning from GoogLeNet and median intensity projections. IEEE international conference on computer and communication engineering technology (CCET) 2018:286–290. https://doi.org/10.1109/CCET.2018.8542189
14. Zhao X, Liu L, Qi S, Teng Y, Li J, Qian W (2018) Agile convolutional neural network for pulmonary nodule classification using CT images. Int J Comput Assist Radiol Surg 13(4):585–595
15. Shao H Cao L Liu Y (2012). A detection approach for solitary pulmonary nodules based on CT images. In: Proceedings of 2nd international conference on computer science and network technology, ICCSNT 2012. pp 1253–1257. https://doi.org/10.1109/ICCSNT.2012.6526151
16. Tran GS, Nghiem TP, Nguyen VT, Luong CM, Burie J-C (2019) Improving accuracy of lung nodule classification using deep learning with focal loss. J Healthc Eng 2019, Article ID 5156416, 9p
17. d. Nóbrega RVM, Peixoto SA, da Silva SPP, Filho PPR (2018) Lung nodule classification via deep transfer learning in CT lung images. In: 2018 IEEE 31st international symposium on

computer-based medical systems (CBMS), 2018, pp 244–249, https://doi.org/10.1109/CBMS.2018.00050

18. Kumar Singh K, Kumar S, Antonakakis M, Moirogiorgou K, Deep A, Kashyap KL, Bajpai MK, Zervakis M (2022) Deep learning capabilities for the categorization of microcalcification. Int J Environ Res Public Health 19:2159. https://doi.org/10.3390/ijerph19042159

19. Palaskar R, Vyas R, Khedekar V, Palaskar S, Sahu P (2021) Transfer learning for oral cancer detection using microscopic images. arXiv

20. George K, Faziludeen S, Sankaran P, Joseph KP (2020) Breast cancer detection from biopsy images using nucleus guided transfer learning and belief based fusion. Comput Biol Med 124:103954. https://doi.org/10.1016/j.compbiomed.2020.103954. Epub 2020 Aug 4 PMID: 32777599

21. Taresh MM, Zhu N, Ali TAA, Hameed AS, Mutar ML (2020). Transfer learning to detect COVID-19 automatically from X-ray images using convolutional neural networks. Int J Biomed Imaging, 2021

22. Arora V, Ng EY-K, Leekha M, Darshan A (2021) Singh Transfer learning-based approach for detecting COVID-19 ailment in lung CT scan, Computers in Biology and Medicine, p 104575

23. Li P, Wang S, Li T, Lu J, HuangFu Y, Wang D (2020) A large-scale CT and PET/CT dataset for lung cancer diagnosis. The Cancer Imaging Archive

24. Marcelino P Transfer learning from pre-trained models. https://towardsdatascience.com/transfer-learning-from-pre-trained-models-f2393f124751

25. Brownlee J, Transfer learning in Keras with computer vision models. https://machinelearningmastery.com/how-to-use-transfer-learning-when-developing-convolutional-neural-network-models

26. Simonyan K, Zisserman A (2014) Very deep convolutional networks for large-scale image recognition. arXiv

27. Saikia T, Kumar R, Kumar D et al (2022) An automatic lung nodule classification system based on hybrid transfer learning Approach. SN Comput Sci 3:272. https://doi.org/10.1007/s42979-022-01167-0

28. Szegedy C, Vanhoucke V, Ioffe S, Shlens J, Wojna Z (2016) Rethinking the inception architecture for computer vision. In: 2016 IEEE conference on computer vision and pattern recognition (CVPR), Las Vegas, NV, USA, 2016, pp 2818–2826

29. Sandler M, Howard A, Zhu M, Zhmoginov A, Chen L-C (2018) MobileNetV2: inverted residuals and linear bottlenecks. 4510–4520. https://doi.org/10.1109/CVPR.2018.00474

30. Wu P, Sun X, Zhao Z, Wang H, Pan S, Schuller B (2020) Classification of lung nodules based on deep residual networks and migration learning. Comput Intell Neurosci 2020:8975078. Published 2020 Mar 30. https://doi.org/10.1155/2020/8975078

31. Bland, Martin. Cohen's kappa. University of York Department of Health Sciences. https://www-users.york.ac.uk/~mb55/msc/clinimet/week4/kappa_text.pdf

Radar Signal Processing for Shaft Rotation Monitoring

Denis Valuyskiy, Sergey Vityazev, and Vladimir Vityazev

1 Introduction

Radar technology has been used for defense and security applications for a long time and is now strongly developed and formalized. At the same time, a new trend in this field can be seen recently. With radar technology, miniaturization and wavelength decrease to millimeters and less radars actively go to civilian, commercial and even household applications [1]. Autonomous driving stimulates this trend strongly [2], but other applications also have significant impact. Industrial equipment monitoring is one of the fields where radar sensors are promising approach. Rotating shafts are often the main parts of many industrial machines. Continuous motion reasons shafts or bearings wear and tear. Evenness of rotation, however, can be very important to provide high quality of equipment operation. This is why continuous shaft rotation monitoring is an important task to be solved.

Traditional shaft fault detection is based on vibration signal analysis. Usually, fast Fourier transform (FFT) is used, and spectrum components are analyzed. Shaft faults produce an increase of additional components at Fourier spectrum. A number of works are devoted to Fourier components analysis for different situations [3]. In [3], the method of shaft condition monitoring based on autocorrelation and power spectral density function is offered. All approaches described in [3] do not deal with radar sensors.

Reference [4] is one of the first papers devoted to radar condition monitoring systems for shaft fault detection. It uses 24-GHz radar setup to investigate feasibility of helicopter drivetrain monitoring. Signal spectrums are obtained and analyzed. An efficient metric of drivetrain condition is not offered, however.

D. Valuyskiy · S. Vityazev (✉) · V. Vityazev
Ryazan State Radio Engineering University, Gagarina, 59/1, 390005 Ryazan, Russian Federation
e-mail: vityazev.s.v@tor.rsreu.ru

D. Valuyskiy
e-mail: valuyskiy.d.v@tor.rsreu.ru

In [5], 77-GHz AWR1642BOOST [6] automotive radar evaluation board is used to detect target vibrations in laboratory environment and to compare it with laser vibrometer. The obtainable performance of radar system is evaluated in terms of frequency and displacement estimation precision. Rotation is not considered. Also, target condition is not estimated.

Industrial fan wear and tear detection with radar is investigated in [7]. Experimental results are given, which show Doppler spectrograms of radar reflections from new and damaged fan blades. It is stated that reflections from blades are much weaker for the case of damaged fan. It is offered to use this fact as a way of fan crack detection. Reflection intensity becomes less because the effective area of the blades is reduced. This approach, however, does not work for a rotating shaft, because there are no blades and no area reduction in this case.

Reference [8] offers the method of signal processing with quadrature signal transformation to separate phase change. The method is dedicated to precise vibration estimation in industrial environment. Operation quality is high, and displacement estimation precision achieves units of wavelength. However, practical results in real-life environment remain the subject of future work.

This paper considers the problem of shaft rotation monitoring with radar. Experimental data for the shafts of electric power steering are registered and analyzed. A criterion for shaft damage detection is formulated, and a signal processing approach for automatic rotation evenness estimation is offered.

In Sect. 2, radar theory basics and evaluation board description are given. In Sect. 3, the experimental testbed and the results of the experiments are described. In Sect. 4, the real-life signals are analyzed and the signal processing algorithm is proposed. Final remarks and future work are formulated in the conclusion.

2 Theoretical Background

2.1 Radar Basics

According to [9], basic radar operation involves three main tasks: target range detection, velocity estimation and direction of arrival definition. The range to target is determined by round-trip time delay of transmitted signal. In other words, this is the time it takes for the transmitted pulse to propagate to and from the detected target. The signal reflected from the target can be described in digital form as follows:

$$s(n) = \alpha \cdot s(n - N) + \omega(n) \tag{1}$$

where α represents attenuation, N is the round-trip time and $\omega(n)$ represents additive white noise.

Target velocity estimation is based on the Doppler effect. The radar transmits periodic wideband frequency-modulated pulses, whose frequency increases linearly during the pulse. Reflected waveform, received by the radar, can be considered as a two-dimensional signal with slow time indices p corresponding to the pulse number and the fast time indices n corresponding to the number of sample within each pulse. This two-dimensional signal can be described as follows:

$$s(n, p) = \exp\left(j2\pi \cdot \left(\left(\frac{2KR}{c} + f_d \right) \cdot \frac{n}{f_s} + f_d p T_0 + \frac{2f_c R}{c} \right) \right) + \omega(n, p) \quad (2)$$

where K is a modulation constant, f_c is a carrier frequency, f_d is a Doppler frequency, f_s is sampling frequency, T_0 is pulse duration and c is the speed of light.

For the direction of arrival estimation, the radar should collect reflected signals across multiple receive antennas. Then, the signal can be described in three-dimensional form as follows:

$$s(l, n, p) = \alpha \cdot \exp\left(j2\pi \cdot \left(\left(\frac{2KR}{c} + f_d \right) \cdot \frac{n}{f_s} + \frac{f_c l d \sin\theta}{c} + f_d p T_0 + \frac{2f_c R}{c} \right) \right)$$
$$+ \omega(n, p) \quad (3)$$

where d is the distance between the receiving antennas and θ is the azimuth angle.

From (3), it can be concluded that target range, velocity and azimuth information can be extracted from the signal with three FFTs. The first FFT is performed in fast time and gives range resolution. The second FFT is accomplished in slow time and provides frequency or velocity resolution. Finally, the third FFT goes across receiving antennas and provides azimuth resolution. This typical signal processing is used as a basis during the experiments carried out in our research.

2.2 AWR1642BOOST Evaluation Board

Texas Instruments AWR1642BOOST is a frequency-modulated continuous wave (FMCW) radar-on-chip evaluation module with an operating frequency of 77 GHz, combining an analog radar subsystem and a digital signal processing system on a single chip. This radar device consists of the three main parts. Analog part includes two transmit and four receive antennas and analog processing module. Digital signal processor TMS320C674x with 600-MHz clock frequency performs main signal processing and target detection. ARM Cortex-R4F microcontroller controls the interaction between analog and digital parts of radar chip.

The appearance of AWR1642BOOST radar-on-chip evaluation board is shown in Fig. 1.

The best range resolution of AWR1642BOOST is 4 cm. Velocity resolution is up to 0.01 m per second. And, azimuth resolution reaches 15 degrees with two transmit and four receive antennas multiple-input and multiple-output (MIMO) technology [6].

Fig. 1 AWR1642BOOST
radar-on-chip evaluation
board

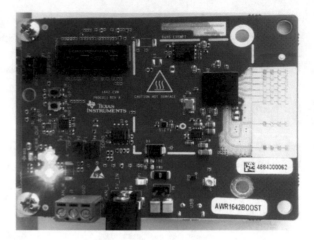

In our research work, we use this evaluation board to monitor the rotating shaft of an industrial machine and perform Doppler frequency analysis.

3 Experiment

The experiments carried out during our research work consist of recording and analyzing signals reflected from rotating metal shafts. Two shafts from car electric power steering are investigated. The first one is not damaged, and the second one has some defects, which was determined by the practical use of these two electric power steering devices.

The testbed consisting of the following components is constructed in our work (Fig. 2). Texas Instruments AWR1642BOOST evaluation board is used as a sensor. MmWave software development kit, which is a collection of software packages, is used to provide communication between laptop and TI's radar evaluation module. Texas Instruments Demo Visualizer browser application gives control over TI's radar evaluation module. Two car electric power steering devices are the targets to be investigated. Registered signals are recorded and then processed at laptop.

During the experiments, the radar evaluation module was configured with the following parameters. The speed resolution is 0.01 m per second which is the best resolution AWR1642BOOST provides. The duration of the recorded signal is 1 ms as it is the longest time of signal registration limited by the board internal memory.

By changing the voltage applied to the electric motor, the speed of rotation of the shaft can be adjusted. Thereby, reflected signals for three different shaft rotation speeds were recorded: low speed corresponds to 2 Hz frequency of shaft rotation, middle speed—3 Hz and high speed—5 Hz. Range-Doppler heatmaps and Doppler spectra for damaged and undamaged shafts are shown in Figs. 3 and 4, respectively.

Fig. 2 Testbed

4 Approach to Signal Processing

4.1 Experiment Result Analysis

Based on the analysis of the recorded spectra and heatmaps shown in Figs. 3 and 4, some conclusions can be made.

An increase in the shaft rotation frequency leads to the gaining and widening of Doppler spectrum components. As different points of a shaft move simultaneously with different radial velocities, they produce wide Doppler spectrum occupying frequency band between 0 Hz and $F_{dmax} = 2V_{max}/\lambda$. In our experiments, $F_{dmax} = 25$ Hz for the low-speed case and $F_{dmax} = 63$ Hz for the high-speed experiment.

In the case of low rotation frequency, the full Doppler frequency band can be seen at a heatmap, because the maximum Doppler frequency is less than the sampling frequency (equal to pulse repetition frequency). The points with the maximum backscattering intensity which are assumed to be close to the points of the maximum Doppler frequency form the spectrum, so there are two wide peaks on the Doppler-range heatmaps for low rotation speed.

With an increase of shaft rotation frequency, Doppler band becomes wider and may go beyond the range of analysis. Doppler spectrum takes a discrete form as it can be seen in Fig. 4b, c.

Indeed, by the analysis of Fig. 4b, c, it can be seen that signal, reflected from undamaged shaft, has a strictly periodical narrow peaks in its spectrum. So, it can

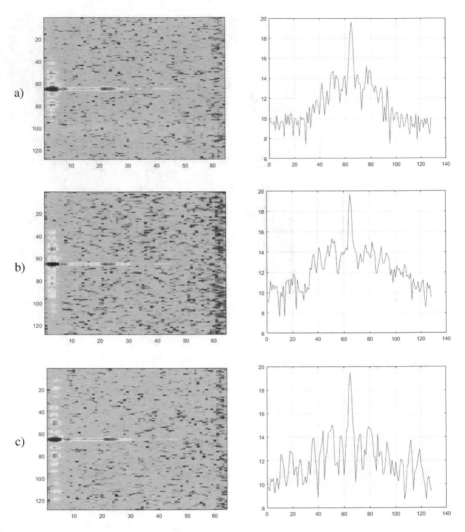

Fig. 3 Damaged shaft. Range-Doppler heatmaps and Doppler spectra: **a** low speed; **b** middle speed; **c** high speed

be considered as the discrete spectrum. It is well-known [10] that discrete form of spectrum is reasoned by the periodicity in time domain. This periodicity can be explained by the strict periodical repetition of shaft teeth during rotation. At the same time, damaged shaft teeth move unevenly due to beatings in shaft movement. For this reason, the spectrum of the reflected signal is blurred for the damaged shaft.

Thus, the degree of severity of spectral lines may serve as a measure of the evenness of the shaft rotation.

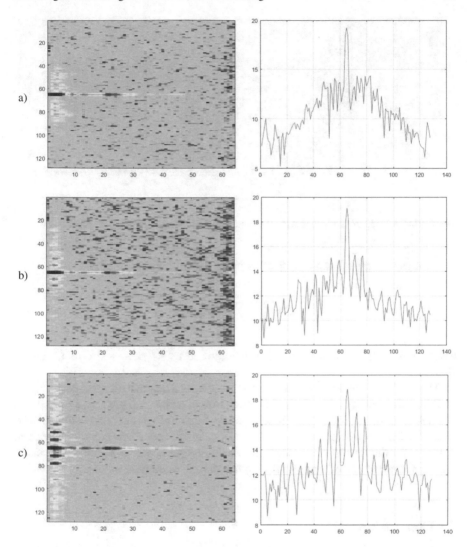

Fig. 4 Undamaged shaft. Range-Doppler heatmaps and Doppler spectra: **a** low speed; **b** middle speed; **c** high speed

4.2 The Proposed Approach for Shaft Rotation Evenness Estimation

The proposed approach is based on the evaluation of spectrum lines' severity. The signal processing algorithm assumes Doppler spectrum estimation and Range-Doppler heatmap formation which are performed in usual way. Then, spectrum lines' severity is estimated through the heatmap sharpness calculation. One of image sharpness metrics can be used as a measure of the evenness of shaft rotation.

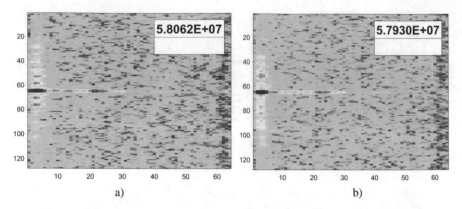

Fig. 5 Range-Doppler heatmap sharpness estimation: **a** undamaged shaft; **b** damaged shaft

Heatmap sharpness can be estimated using the following formula [11]:

$$C = \sum_{i=0}^{K} \sum_{j=0}^{M} X(i, j)^4,$$ (4)

where X depicts the source heatmap points of K by M size, and C is an image sharpness.

The results of sharpness estimation for the obtained heatmaps are shown in Fig. 5.

As we can see in Fig. 5, sharpness estimation of a heatmap gives us a measure to evaluate shaft rotation stability. The sharpness estimation is higher for the undamaged shaft than for the damaged shaft. Heatmaps for middle-speed shaft rotation are given in Fig. 5. Similar results are obtained for the high-speed case. In future research, the proposed method can be evolved using other sharpness metrics and neural networks.

5 Conclusion

A testbed for shaft rotation monitoring with radar sensor was built. Reflections from damaged and undamaged shafts were registered and analyzed. It was noticed that undamaged shaft gives a signal with a strictly discrete spectrum, while damaged shaft spectrum has blurred peaks in its spectrum. It was offered to use this fact as a basis for signal processing algorithm in a shaft testing device. The degree of severity of spectral lines may be estimated through the heatmap sharpness calculation. Experimental results prove the feasibility of shaft rotation monitoring with radar but require additional investigation to improve algorithm performance.

References

1. Radar systems for modern civilian applications: part 1. IEEE Signal Process Mag 36(4) (2019)
2. Radar systems for modern civilian applications: part 2. IEEE Signal Process Mag 36(5) (2019)
3. Gradzki R, Kulesza Z, Bartoszewiczoster B (2019) Method of shaft crack detection based on squared gain of vibration amplitude. Nonlinear Dyn 98:671–690
4. Bharadwaj R et al (2013) Condition monitoring using standoff vibration sensing radar. In: AHS airworthiness, CBM, and HUMS specialists' Meeting, Huntsville, AL
5. Ciattaglia G et al (2021) Performance evaluation of vibrational measurements through mmWave automotive radars. Remote Sens 13(1)
6. AWR1642 Evaluation Module (AWR1642BOOST) Single-Chip mmWave sensing solution user's guide. Texas Instruments (2020)
7. Zeintl C, Eibensteiner F, Langer J (2019) Evaluation of FMCW radar for vibration sensing in industrial environments. In: 29th International conference Radioelektronika (RADIOELEK-TRONIKA). IEEE
8. Khablov D (2021) Signal processing of Doppler microwave vibration sensors with quadrature transformation. In: 23rd International conference on digital signal processing and its applications (DSPA). IEEE
9. Patole SM, Torlak M, Wang D, Ali M (2017) Automotive radars: a review of signal processing techniques. Signal Process Mag 34(2):22–35
10. Skolnik M (2008) Radar handbook, 3rd edn. McGraw Hill Companies
11. Hayes MP, Fortune SA (2005) Recursive phase estimation for image sharpening. In: Image and vision computing New Zealand

Machine Learning Assisted MPU6050-Based Road Anomaly Detection

Jyoti Tripathi and Bijendra Kumar

1 Introduction

The condition of roadways has a significant role in our daily lives. Road anomalies such as potholes, sunk-in manhole covers, or missing pavements can cause damage to vehicles or it may lead to accidents. Also, we can't deny that roads in poor conditions badly affect the comfort of drivers and passengers. Finally, government spend lots of money for maintenance of road and keeping them in good condition, but that itself become a cause for traffic jams, stress during driving, extra fuel consumption and cause delays in our daily routine lives. However, this detection of road anomalies requires expensive and specially designed equipment and vehicles that cost considerable amounts of money, and trained people to monitor and drive the instruments and vehicles, respectively. Nowadays, almost everybody has smartphone, which generally have sensing systems, namely accelerometers deployed within it. Moreover, now a days almost everyone carries a smartphone. Thus, we can use mobiles as road anomaly detectors, which will convert every vehicle into a specialized road-monitoring vehicle. This novel application of smartphone as an effective road anomaly detection system will greatly improve the viability of autonomous vehicles as well as non-autonomous vehicles, with reduced related road accidents.

In 2014, the total cost of motor vehicle crashes in the United States was 871 billion. In order to avoid problems that are related to road anomalies, a system has been proposed that can figure out road anomalies by means of smartphone sensors.

Road anomalies cause the abnormal vibration to the vehicle. By installing acceleration data collection systems within these vehicles, the vibration data induced by

J. Tripathi (✉)
Department of CSE, Netaji Subhas University of Technology and Assistant Professor at G B Pant
DSEU, Okhla-1 Campus, New Delhi, India
e-mail: loginjyoti@gmail.com

B. Kumar
Department of CSE, Netaji Subhas University of Technology, New Delhi, India

© The Author(s), under exclusive license to Springer Nature Singapore Pte Ltd. 2023   419
K. Kumar Singh et al. (eds.), *Machine Vision and Augmented Intelligence*, Lecture Notes
in Electrical Engineering 1007, https://doi.org/10.1007/978-981-99-0189-0_32

road conditions can be collected as the vehicle move through the road. The vibration data can be further given to the detection system, which analyzes the vertical acceleration. This process can be distributed in two stages. In the initial phase, the focus is on the issue of locating road anomalies by analyzing acceleration data. In the later stage, we performed different calculations with the help of the statistics generated from the acceleration data or the results derived in the initial stage to detect the conditions of each road section.

This work addresses the following issues

(1) Classification of road surface and evaluation of road condition.
(2) Design and development of road anomalies monitoring system.
(3) Communication of the data to centralized server.

A concise literature review has been presented in Table 1 for reference.

This work detailed in three sections. Section 2 explores the methodology. Result and Implementation addressed in Sect. 3, followed by conclusion and future scope discussion in Sect. 4.

2 Methodology

As this work intend to monitor and record the acceleration value of the vehicle, to record the data and based on the recorded data we process. We design the novel hardware to record the acceleration values. The hardware constitutes of Raspberry Pi and MPU 6050 and used to monitor the acceleration value. The flowchart of proposed methodology is shown in Fig. 1 and further explained below.

2.1 Flowchart Explanation

The working of hardware system which will be embedded in a vehicle moving on road is as follows:

1. Start the Raspberry PI module and whole hardware system by turning on the power supply from the battery module.
2. As the vehicle will be on move, the Raspberry Pi will keep reading the acceleration values for entire trip.
3. Check the variation in accelerometer's values which hardware system is recording.
4. If values are changing then we will store them in memory, i.e., SD card embedded inside our hardware system, else check if the vehicle is stopped, in that case we will stop the power of hardware system by turning off the battery module.
5. In case the vehicle is not stopped then we will keep collecting the data values (acceleration values) and keep storing the values in memory.

Table 1 Brief summary of related work

S. No.	Title of paper	Authors	Problem addressed	Future scope
1	Automatic road anomaly detection using smart mobile device [1]	Yu-chin Tai, Cheng-wei Chan	The paper focuses on the issues of the road safety and to make the transportation more safer by considering real-time information related to road quality through mobile sensor computing systems	More accurate dataset related to road surface anomalies is needed that may help to find out the issues
2	A Survey of accelerometer-based Techniques for Road Anomalies Detection and Characterization [2]	A. M. Aibinu, Liz Onwuka	Irregularity in the measured signals from an accelerometer has been used by the author to classify the anomaly as speed bumps or potholes	More accurate techniques is required for classifying the anomaly into potholes based on the irregularly measured acceleration signals
3	Driver behavior profiling: An investigation with different smartphone sensors and machine learning [3]	Yoshihiko Suhara, Alex Pentland	The behavior of driver is considered as on the main parameter and profiling is the process of automatically collecting driving data (e.g., speed, acceleration, breaking, steering, location) and using a computational model on them with an aim to generate a safety score for the driver	More data is expected to be collected from a greater number of driving events samples using different vehicles Android smartphone models, road conditions, and temperature
4	Anomaly Detection in Road Traffic Using Visual Surveillance: A Survey [4]	Santhosh Kelathodi Kumaran, Debi Prosad Dogra	Different analysis techniques has been explored for road anomaly detection that can applied on road environment which includes vehicles, people using visual surveillance	To fulfill the gap in our outcomes different computer vision techniques can be explored

(continued)

Table 1 (continued)

S. No.	Title of paper	Authors	Problem addressed	Future scope
5	Evaluation of Detection Approaches for Road Anomalies Based on Accelerometer Readings [5]	Fernando Martínez, Luis C. González	Outcomes of this work has indicated a linear relationship between the acceleration impulse and the potholes dimensions in terms of their mean depth	Deeper analysis is required for the circumstances under which STDEV(Z) showed their lowest performance

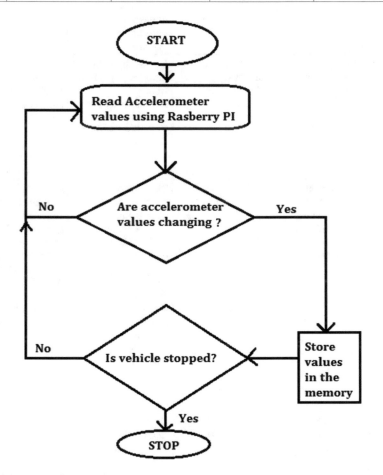

Fig. 1 Flowchart of proposed methodology

The data was collected using three separate automobiles on three different days. To avoid external interference, the majority of the data was collected late at night or early in the morning in low-traffic areas. As a result, the process is safe, and we avoid other issues like traffic bottlenecks and pedestrians crossing roads, which could impair data quality.

2.2 Requirement Specification:

Raspberry PI 4

In this work, Raspberry pi 4 is used as the personal computer due to its high Random Access Memory (RAM) and powerful processor. It can run both Linux and Windows10. It requires power supply of 5 V, 3 A powered by Universal Serial Bus (USB) C adapter as depicted in Fig. 2. It also has 2 micro High Definition Multimedia Interface (HDMI) ports that can support up to 4 K resolution at 60frame per second (FPS) high video quality worked upon.

Raspberry pi 4b has an on-board boot controller that boots the operating system (OS) from SD card mount on the Raspberry pi. SanDisk EVO PLUS 64 GB SD card has been used to store the data on run that gives 100 MB/s of read & write speed. It ensures efficient working of the system with high data I/O speed. SD card is used to keep the operating system that needs to be run on Raspberry pi. The read and write speed of the SD card determines the read and write speed in Raspberry pi.

MPU6050

It is an Inertial Measurement Unit (IMU) sensor module shown in Fig. 3. The main function of this unit is generate gyroscopic angles and acceleration values in X, Y and Z-axis. This device works in 6-axis related with the motion tracking. The six axis includes 3-axis Gyroscope, 3-axis Accelerometer as well as Digital Motion

Fig. 2 Raspberry PI [6]

Processor in a single small package as shown in Fig. 4. It also has an additional feature that is an on-chip sensor to measure the temperature. In order to communicate with the microcontrollers, it uses I2C bus interface. It consists of an Auxiliary I2C bus to communicate with different sensor devices like Pressure sensor, 3-axis Magnetometer, etc. The MPU6050 uses a 3-axis Gyroscope along with Micro Electro Mechanical System (MEMS) technology. It helps in detecting rotational velocity along three different axes.

Fig. 3 MPU 6050 [7]

Fig. 4 Polarity and rotation of MPU 6050

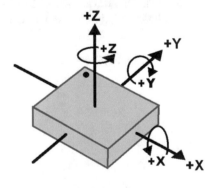

2.3   Data Collection

We have collected road data (i.e., accelerometer values) using our hardware system on moving vehicle. We have kept some sample data in the road_data.txt file. Then we separated out X, Y and Z components of acceleration to study them separately. On all X, Y and Z acceleration components we calculated deviation using the Eq. (1), as mentioned below.

$$\text{Deviation}(i) = \text{acceleration of } (i+2)\text{th second} - \text{acceleration of } i\text{th second} \quad (1)$$

According to above we prepared three files

1 X-deviations—all X deviations in sorted order—range $\rightarrow$ $-$ 14 to 13
2 Y-deviations—all Y deviations in sorted order—range $\rightarrow$ $-$ 31 to 23
3 Z-deviations—all Z deviations in sorted order—range $\rightarrow$ $-$ 17 to 15.

Then we grouped these values in increasing numerical values of 2. For ex–1–3, 4–6, 7–9, etc.

And we prepared three more files

1 X-deviation-grouping-data
2 Y-deviation-grouping-data
3 Z-deviation-grouping-data.

In these files we kept frequency of acceleration deviations in groups of two and we can pick values with least frequency values as anomaly values.

In X-deviation-grouping-data $\rightarrow$ Acceleration deviation values $-$ **11 to** $-$ **15 and 11 to 13** can be taken as anomaly values as they are least in frequency.

In Y-deviation-grouping-data $\rightarrow$ Acceleration deviation values $-$ **20 to** $-$ **32 and 18 to 22** can be taken as anomaly values as they are least in frequency.

In Z-deviation-grouping-data $\rightarrow$ Acceleration deviation values $-$ **10 to** $-$ **18 and 8 to 16** can be taken as anomaly values as they are least in frequency.

The 3-axial accelerometer piggybacked on mobile devices can capture the data with different frequencies such as fastest—100 Hz, game—50 Hz, normal—5 Hz and UI—16 Hz.

Analysis of vertical acceleration impulse is as follows:

The temporal derivative of the acceleration absolute maximum amplitude per second is given as $d(Az\text{-max}—Az\text{-min})$, which is basically representing the difference between the maximum and minimum value of the vertical acceleration in the well-defined unit of time. This value will be used to evaluate the quality of road surface taking into consideration the safety parameter. The vertical acceleration correlates to high-energy events on the road surface, which are labeled as "anomalies." To detect potholes and bumps on road an algorithm is used that is based on the value of the vertical acceleration impulse: the temporal derivative of the acceleration absolute amplitude per second, basically calculated as the difference between the highest and the lowest value in the prescribed unit of time. High-energy occurrence, i.e., the

Fig. 5 Data acquisition
through hardware system

vertical acceleration impulse (DVA) on the road surface is labeled as an abnormality
or anomaly.

Figures 5, 6 and 7 demonstrate the data collection method using three different
vehicles on three separate days. To avoid external interference, the majority of the
data was collected late at night or early in the morning in low-traffic areas. As a result,
the method is safe, and we prevent additional issues that could lead to erroneous data,
such as traffic congestion and pedestrians crossing the road.

3   Results and Implementation

Figure 8 is depicting the image of data collected by our hardware system fitted on
moving vehicle, data comprises of three values for each reading

1   X component of Acceleration
2   Y component of Acceleration
3   Z component of Acceleration.

Figure 9 is depicting the X, Y and Z deviations that are calculated from above
acceleration readings shown in Fig. 8 by using Eq. (1) as discussed in the Sect. 2.

X-deviation-grouping-data → Acceleration deviation values $-$ **11 to** $-$ **15 and
11 to 13** can be taken as anomaly values as they are least in frequency.

In Y-deviation-grouping-data → Acceleration deviation values $-$ **20 to** $-$ **32 and
18 to 22** can be taken as anomaly values as they are least in frequency.

Fig. 6 Data acquisition through hardware system

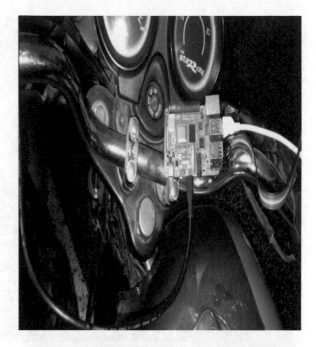

Fig. 7 Data acquisition through hardware system

1	6.73728347168,	6.9767036377,	−0.435744702148
2	6.65348641357,	6.96712683105,	−0.409408483887
3	6.71334145508,	6.90966599121,	−0.418985290527
4	6.61996759033,	6.99825145264,	−0.361524450684
5	6.65827481689,	7.02219346924,	−0.316034619141
6	6.60320817871,	7.16345136719,	−0.335188232422
7	6.6702458252, ,	6.96712683105,	−0.29927520752
8	6.65109221191,	6.988674646,	−0.387860668945
9	6.73249506836,	7.0006456543,	−0.414196887207
10	6.73249506836,	7.10359632568,	−0.325611425781
11	6.63193859863,	6.92403120117,	−0.332794030762
12	6.07648381348,	7.28076724854,	0.0550666381836
13	8.06845959473,	5.70538255615,	−1.25695587158
14	9.98142672119,	6.76361968994,	−1.76452662354
15	8.48265648193,	6.75643708496,	−3.37821854248
16	8.48744488525,	5.08528432617,	−3.13400997314
17	8.09479581299,	5.33906970215,	−4.04141240234
18	6.40209523926,	5.88015927734,	−3.72777198486
19	6.77080229492,	6.75883128662,	−4.18745870361
20	6.31590397949,	7.65665690918,	−4.80516273193
21	5.65031591797,	7.80270321045,	−5.70059415283
22	5.28879146729,	7.67581052246,	−5.52581743164

Fig. 8 Reading of acceleration

X-Deviations grouping

X-Deviation groups		Frequency
−15 <–> −13	–>	2
−13 <–> −11	–>	3
−11 <–> −9	–>	14
−9 <–> −7	–>	33
−7 <–> −5	–>	64
−5 <–> −3	–>	150
−3 <–> −1	–>	305
−1 <–> 1	–>	659
1 <–> 3	–>	293
3 <–> 5	–>	159
5 <–> 7	–>	61
7 <–> 9	–>	33
9 <–> 11	–>	11
11 <–> 13	–>	4

Y-Deviations grouping

Y-Deviation groups		Frequency
−32 <–> −30	–>	1
−30 <–> −28	–>	0
−28 <–> −26	–>	0
−26 <–> −24	–>	0
−24 <–> −22	–>	1
−22 <–> −20	–>	0
−20 <–> −18	–>	10
−18 <–> −16	–>	12
−16 <–> −14	–>	22
−14 <–> −12	–>	36
−12 <–> −10	–>	42
−10 <–> −8	–>	80
−8 <–> −6	–>	77
−6 <–> −4	–>	115
−4 <–> −2	–>	151
−2 <–> 0	–>	331
0 <–> 2	–>	367
2 <–> 4	–>	171
4 <–> 6	–>	109
6 <–> 8	–>	81
8 <–> 10	–>	50
10 <–> 12	–>	43
12 <–> 14	–>	37
14 <–> 16	–>	22
16 <–> 18	–>	21
18 <–> 20	–>	7
20 <–> 22	–>	5

Z-Deviations grouping

Z-Deviation groups		Frequency
−18 <–> −16	–>	1
−16 <–> −14	–>	0
−14 <–> −12	–>	1
−12 <–> −10	–>	5
−10 <–> −8	–>	12
−8 <–> −6	–>	25
−6 <–> −4	–>	101
−4 <–> −2	–>	237
−2 <–> 0	–>	517
0 <–> 2	–>	505
2 <–> 4	–>	244
4 <–> 6	–>	101
6 <–> 8	|–>	28
8 <–> 10	–>	7
10 <–> 12	–>	7
12 <–> 14	–>	0
14 <–> 16	–>	1

Fig. 9 X, Y and Z deviations

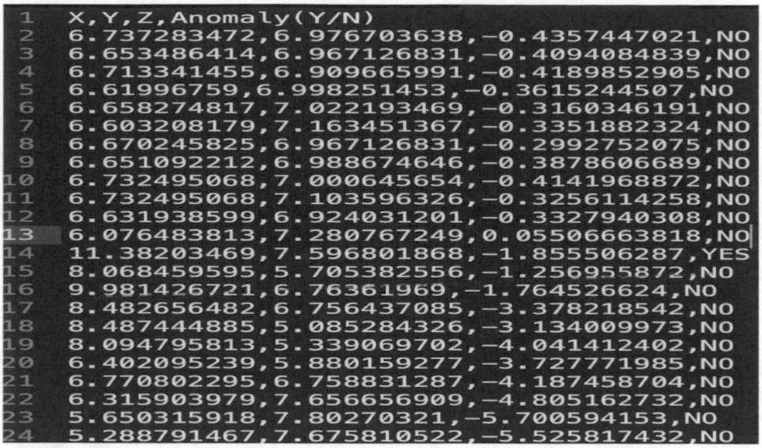

```
 1   X,Y,Z,Anomaly(Y/N)
 2   6.737283472,6.976703638,-0.4357447021,NO
 3   6.653486414,6.967126831,-0.4094084839,NO
 4   6.713341455,6.909665991,-0.4189852905,NO
 5   6.61996759,6.998251453,-0.3615244507,NO
 6   6.658274817,7.022193469,-0.3160346191,NO
 7   6.603208179,7.163451367,-0.3351882324,NO
 8   6.670245825,6.967126831,-0.2992752075,NO
 9   6.651092212,6.988674646,-0.3878606689,NO
10   6.732495068,7.000645654,-0.4141968872,NO
11   6.732495068,7.103596326,-0.3256114258,NO
12   6.631938599,6.924031201,-0.3327940308,NO
13   6.076483813,7.280767249,0.05506663818,NO
14   11.38203469,7.596801868,-1.855506287,YES
15   8.068459595,5.705382556,-1.256955872,NO
16   9.981426721,6.76361969,-1.764526624,NO
17   8.482656482,6.756437085,-3.378218542,NO
18   8.487444885,5.085284326,-3.134009973,NO
19   8.094795813,5.339069702,-4.041412402,NO
20   6.402095293,5.880159277,-3.727771985,NO
21   6.770802295,6.758831287,-4.187458704,NO
22   6.315903979,7.656656909,-4.805162732,NO
23   5.650315918,7.80270321,-5.700594153,NO
24   5.288791467,7.675810522,-5.525817432,NO
```

Fig. 10 Test data

In Z-deviation-grouping-data → Acceleration deviation values − **10 to − 18 and 8 to 16** can be taken as anomaly values as they are least in frequency.

Further, we prepared our test data using above findings and adding one more column in collected data that is weather this record can be assumed as an anomaly or not in the form of YES or NO as depicted in Fig. 10.

3.1 Training the ML Model

We trained our model using above discussed training dataset. We have used supervised machine leaning approach for our model. Support vector machine (SVM) algorithm in machine learning comes under the category of supervised machine learning algorithm and SVM can easily generalize betwcen two different classes if the set of labeled data is provided as input at the time of training the model. SVM checks that hyperplane that can easily and clearly distinguishes between the two classes. SVM is able to create best decision boundary that can even separate n-dimensional space into classes. In case of SVM, the best line or decision boundary has given a special name that is hyperplane.

Support vectors are used by SVM to select the extreme points/vectors that are mainly helpful in creating the hyperplane. Consider the Fig. 11, given below in which there are two different categories that are classified using a clear decision boundary or hyperplane:

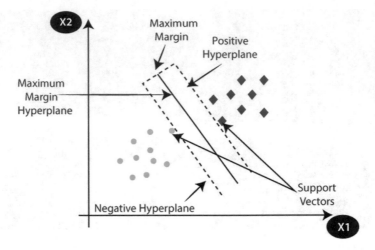

Fig. 11 SVM-based classification

3.2 Graphical Representation

The acceleration values obtained further plotted in Figs. 12, 13 and 14 for X, Y and Z-axis, respectively.

Further Fig. 15, depicts the SVM Decision Region Boundary graph. SVM tries to decide boundary in such a way that the separation between the two classes (that street) is as wide as possible. Here blue squares (□) depict non-anomaly values and orange triangles (▲) depict the probable anomaly values in given data set.

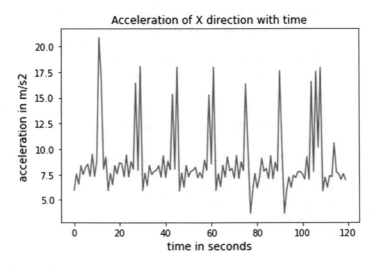

Fig. 12 Acceleration in X-axis

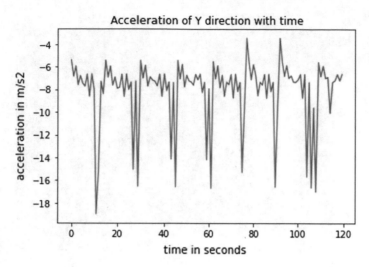

Fig. 13 Acceleration in *Y*-axis

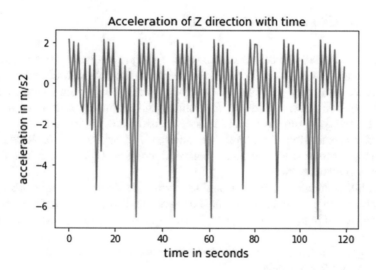

Fig. 14 Acceleration in Z-axis

The model generated using SVM has been trained and tested on the dataset collected using MPU sensor. The proposed system has shown an accuracy of 95.2%.

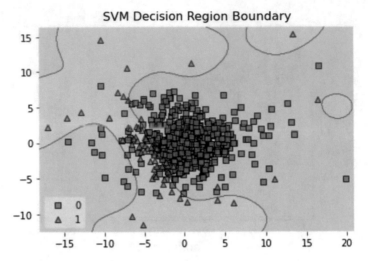

Fig. 15 SVM graph

4 Conclusion and Future Scope

To calculate and store acceleration readings, a unique hardware system is created using Arduino Nano and MPU 6050. Furthermore, the data was trifurcated across the three axes and then evaluated in the testing dataset by grouping them according to frequency and result. In addition, the training and testing datasets are used to train the model using the support vector machine classification algorithm.

In a future extension of this work, we can use GPS position while collecting data, allowing any motorist to report an anomaly to a central server, which can then be broadcast to other users.

A mobile application can be created to record data from a smartphone's sensors and analyze it to provide better results. Furthermore, broad use of the created application can result in more samples, which can improve the result in terms of anomaly detection.

This type of research could pave the way for safer roads, with improved driving conditions and fewer accidents.

Acknowledgements Being an assistant professor at G B Pant.

References

1. Tai Y, Chan C, Hsu JY (2010) Automatic_road_anomaly_detection_using_smart_mobile_device Conference: 2010 15th Conference on Artificial Intelligence and Applications (TAAI)
2. Salau HB, Onumanyi AJ, Aibinu AM (2019) A survey of accelerometer-based techniques for road anomalies detection and characterization. March 2019; project: development of a vehicle ad-hoc network communication system for road defects monitoring
3. Ferreira J, Carvalho E, Ferreira BV, de Souza C, Suhara Y, Pentland A (2017) Driver behavior profiling: an investigation with different smartphone sensors and machine learning. Published: April 10, 2017. https://doi.org/10.1371/journal.pone.0174959
4. Kumaran SK, Dogra DP, Roy PP (2019) "Anomaly detection in road traffic using visual surveillance: a survey"; subjects: computer vision and pattern recognition (cs.CV) Cite as: arXiv:1901.08292 [cs.CV]
5. Carlos MR, Aragón ME, González LC, Escalante HJ, Martínez F (2018) Evaluation of detection approaches for road anomalies based on accelerometer readings. 18 January 2018
6. Rasberry Pi—Retrieved from Wikipedia https://en.wikipedia.org/wiki/Raspberry_Pi
7. ElectronicWings (2018) Sensors Module MPU 6050. Retrieved from ElectronicWings: https://www.electronicwings.com/sensors-modules/mpu6050-gyroscope-accelerometertemperature-sensor-module

Computer-Aided Leaf Disease Classification Based on Logistic Regression and Transfer Learning Approach

Trishna Saikia, Malho Hansdah, and Koushlendra Kumar Singh

1 Introduction

India is a one of those countries where more than half of the total population's living hood depends on agricultural fields. The quality and quantity of agricultural farms have been decreased with time. This is mostly due to some environmental factors as a result of which diseases of plant leaf increase day by day. Currently, farmers are adopting a new idea of doing smart farming to get rid of all these problems [1]. Therefore, a computer-aided system to detect and classify plant leaf diseases becomes most essential as it helps to identify and classify diseases at the initial stage so that it cannot spread to the whole farm. This study has proposed three different machine learning-based techniques with Adam optimizer to classify plant leaf diseases. Initial technique that we have used is Logistic Regression, and later, we have tried to build two models based on transfer learning and SVM. We are combining VGGNet with SVM in the last two models. Here, particularly, we are adopting VGG16 and VGG19 architectures. We have used augmented PlantVillage dataset for implementing our models. The dataset contains 61,486 images of 39 categories. We have used only 4000 of images belonging to ten different categories, namely, Apple_scab, Apple_black_rot, Apple_cedar_apple_rust, Apple_healthy, Corn_Cercospora_leaf_spot Gray_leaf_spot, Corn_Common_rust, Corn_healthy, Corn_Northern_Leaf_Blight, Potato_Early_blight, Potato_Late_blight in our research study [2]. VGG16 and VGG19 with SVM gave highest training accuracy which is 89.25% among all the proposed methods with PlantVillage dataset for plant leaf diseases classification. The comparison of each technique is listed in the result section. The sections of this paper are ordered as follows. Section 2 describes a brief description of related work. Section 3.1 is a short note on the dataset. Section 3.2 is a

T. Saikia (✉) · M. Hansdah · K. K. Singh
Machine Vision and Intelligence Lab, Department of Computer Science and Engineering,
National Institute of Technology Jamshedpur, Jamshedpur, India
e-mail: tinasaaikiaa1997@gmail.com; phd2201101014@iiti.ac.in

© The Author(s), under exclusive license to Springer Nature Singapore Pte Ltd. 2023   435
K. Kumar Singh et al. (eds.), *Machine Vision and Augmented Intelligence*, Lecture Notes
in Electrical Engineering 1007, https://doi.org/10.1007/978-981-99-0189-0_33

brief description of Adam optimizer. Section 3.3 is all about methodology. Section 3.4 explains the performance evaluation. Section 4 and Sect. 5 contain the result and conclusion, respectively.

2 Related Work

There are variety of researchers around the world who have proposed several methods for the detection and classification of plant leaf diseases. Vijay et al. have put forward a technique which is based on genetic algorithm for image segmentation. Their aim is to build an automated system for detection and classification of plant leaf diseases. They used a self-prepare dataset for their experiment where images were taken from digital camera or similar kind of tools. MATLAB platform was used by them to implement their research work [3].

Yin et al. have also proposed a method for plant leaf diseases detection and classification. They have adopted image processing techniques for their research work. Histogram equalization was used for image enhancement, and k-means clustering is also used by them for image segmentation. The classification has been done by them with the help of three techniques, those are SVM classification, ensemble classification and K-NN classification. Their research study puts forward an automated system which can detect and classify four different plant leaf diseases. They are, namely, Cercospora leaf spot, Bacterial blight, Rust and Powdery Mildew [4].

Sushil et al. have proposed a method which can identify and classify the plant leaf diseases accurately. Their proposed method contains three major steps. The very beginning step is carried out resizing of all the images and transforms each image to HIS format with the help of segmentation technique. The second step accomplished features' extraction in terms of eccentricity, minor and major axis. These extracted features were used by the classifier to classify the plant leaf diseases accurately in the last stage. They adopted Artificial Neural Network for the classification purpose. They considered a dataset which contains two different classes of images which are Powdery Mildew and Downy Mildew for their research study [1].

Melike et al. have incorporated a hybrid method which combines two different algorithms for the detection and classification of tomato leaf diseases. One is convolutional neural network and another one is learning vector quantization. They used a dataset which contains tomato leaves' images of four different symptoms of diseases for their experiment. They used a total of 500 images from their dataset [5].

Umit et al. presented a model which did not use any preprocessing of images for the classification of plant leaf diseases. They used EfficientNet deep learning method for their research work to perform the classification. They compared the above-mentioned method result with other deep learning methods. They used original PlantVillage datasets which contains a total of 55,448 images to train their models [6].

Chaitali et al. have discussed about the phases of detection and classification of plant leaves. They primarily focused on image preprocessing, acquisition of images, segmentation of images and they also focused their studies on feature extraction and classification. They also reviewed different image processing and segmentation techniques which are basically used for automated system of plant leaf diseases detection and classification [7].

Hussain et al. have recommended K-nearest neighbor classifier for the classification of plant leaf disease. They have applied their proposed techniques to classify diseases, namely, anthracnose, Alternaria alternata, leaf spot, Bacterial blight and canker of various plants [8]. G. Geetha et al. have also used K-nearest neighbors technique to find the solution for the classification and detection of plant leaf diseases [9].

Chaowalit et al. have presented a technique which is based on unsupervised neural network for the extraction of plant leaf diseases' features and classification of plant leaves' diseases. They have categorized types of diseases with the help of simplified fuzzy ARTMAP neural network [10]. K. Deeba and B. Amutha have proposed a deep neural network-based architecture for the classification and prediction of vegetable leaf diseases [11]. Jagadeesh et al. have presented different feature extraction techniques for tomato leaf disease classification. They have extracted features like Haralick, Local Binary Pattern and Hu moments. They have adopted Decision tree and Random Forest classifier for the classification purpose [12].

Tian et al. have used Support Vector Machine (SVM) with optimized genetic algorithm for the recognition of apple leaf diseases [13]. Ramar et al. have incorporated a deep convolutional-based neural network for the classification of maize leaf diseases [14]. Pranjit B. Padol et al. have used SVM classification technique for the detection and classification of grape leaf diseases [15]. Monu et al. have proposed an optimized Support Vector Machine technique to classify plant leaf into two categories: healthy and unhealthy, and furthermore, they have detected the type of leaf disease in case it is classified as unhealthy [16].

Yin Min Oo and Nay Chi Htun have suggested a technique which is based on digital image processing for the detection and analysis of plant leaf diseases. They have performed their research work mainly by using four major plant leaves' diseases: Cercospora leaf spot, Rust, Powdery Mildew and Bactcrial blight [4]. Anusha Rao and S. B. Kulkarni have presented a hybrid techniques accomplished with three phases. First phase consisted image enhancement and image conversion scheme. Second phase consisted a combine feature extraction techniques which was consisted of GLCM, complex Gabor filter, Curvelet and Image moments. At the last phase, extracted features were used to train a Neuro-Fuzzy Logic classifier. They used MATLAB for their research work [17]. Hiteshwari Sabrol and Satish Kumar have proposed a technique for plant leaf disease detection and classification. They also used GLCM matrix for feature extraction, and for disease recognition, they have adopted the ANFIS-based classification model [18].

Rizqi et al. have used VGG16 and VGG19 convolutional neural network architecture to classify four types of potato plant diseases [19]. Rajasekaran et al. have adopted transfer learning-based deep convolutional neural network for the detection of tomato leaf diseases. They have used rcal-time images for their research work [20].

Sujatha et al. have compared different deep learning techniques with machine learning techniques that have been used for the detection and classification of plant leaf diseases. They have compared three machine learning techniques: Support Vector Machine, Random Forest and Stochastic Gradient Descent with three deep learning techniques: Inception-V3, VGG19 and VGG16 [21]. Sherly et al. have also reviewed different machine learning techniques that have been used for the classification of various types of plant diseases [22].

3   Materials and Methods

3.1   Dataset Description

The dataset we have used for our models is PlantVillage dataset which originally contains a total pf 39 different categories of plant leaf diseases along with background images. The total number of images that are belonging from these 39 classes is 61,486. The dataset contains two different forms of images. First one is images with augmentation and the second one is images without augmentation. We have used images with augmentation for our research work. They used a total of six different augmentation techniques. The augmentation techniques that they used are image flipping, Gamma correction, noise injection, PCA Color Augmentation, rotation and scaling. The dataset is in the zip format which size is 905 MB [2]. Figure 1 shows some images from our dataset.

3.2   Adaptive Moment Estimation

Adam combines the merit of the two previously existing methods: Adaptive Gradient Algorithm (AdaGrad) and Root Mean Square Propagation (RMSProp) [23]. It has calculated a moving average of the first and second moments of the gradient for updating parameters instead of calculating the gradient itself. In this context, moving average is initialized to zero, and hence, they are biased toward zero. So, a bias correction term is used which would make the parameters' estimates more accurate during the initial steps. It requires less memory and is very efficient when working with large datasets with noisy and/or sparse gradients. Further research revealed that Adam does not converge to the optimal solutions for non-convex settings. These convergence issues can be resolved by providing such algorithms with memory of gradients far in the past. AMSGrad is one such variant of Adam algorithm which fixes the convergence issues and often leads to improve empirical performance [24].

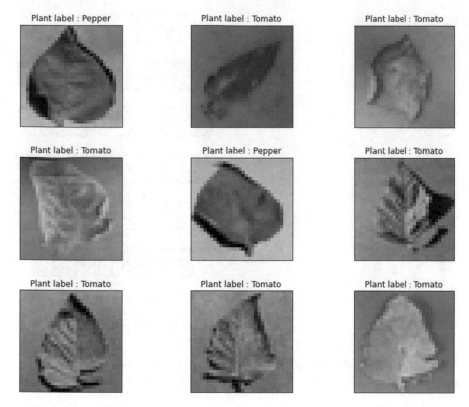

Fig. 1 Some images from the dataset

3.3 Methodology

The methodology acquired primarily four steps as shown in Fig. 2. Each image has been resized and also labeled with an appropriate class label. Normalization is performed for all images. We have used Logistic Regression, VGG16 and VGG19 architecture for feature extraction. SVM is combined with VGG16 and VGG19 to train the classification layers. We have used Adam optimizer to optimize the model. We have divided the total data into training and testing sets. Different data splitting methods have been used by different researchers till now. In our study, we have divided the whole dataset into two sets, training set and testing set with the help of train–test split method. We have utilized a total pf 4000 images of ten different categories, namely, Apple_scab, Apple_black_rot, Apple_cedar_apple_rust, Apple_healthy, Corn_Cercospora_leaf_spot Gray_leaf_spot, Corn_Common_rust, Corn_healthy, Corn_Northern_Leaf_Blight, Potato_Early_blight, Potato_Late_blight. Each category contains 400 images. Training set contains 80% of the total data, and testing set contains 20% of total data.

Fig. 2 System flow chart

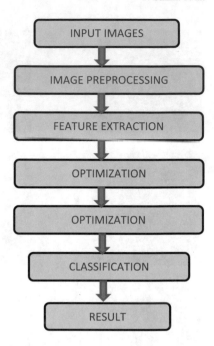

The architecture of VGGNET which we have adapted for our experiment is shown in Table 1, where 256 × 256 images were used as the input.

3.4 Performance Evaluation

All the methods have been implemented by using TensorFlow machine learning technique. We have used transfer learning with the pre-trained VGG16 and VGG19 model and also SVM classifier for feature extraction and further train the classification layer. The list of parameters that we have used for measuring the achievement of our models is precision, recall, accuracy and F-score. Following are the formula for calculating those parameters.

(a) $\text{Precision} = \dfrac{\text{True Positive}}{(\text{True Positive} + \text{False Positive})}$,

(b) $\text{Recall} = \dfrac{(\text{Total true classified samples})}{\text{Total supplied samples}}$,

(c) $\text{Accuracy} = \dfrac{\text{Total True classified samples}}{\text{Total no of supplied samples for classification}} \times 100$,

(d) $F - \text{score} = 2\dfrac{\text{Precision} * \text{Recall}}{\text{Precision} + \text{Recall}}$.

Table 1 VGG16 and VGG19 architectures

VGG16			VGG19		
Layer	Output	Parameter	Layer	Output	Parameter
Input	$256 \times 256 \times 3$	0	Input	$256 \times 256 \times 3$	0
Conv-1	$256 \times 256 \times 64$	1792	Conv-1	$256 \times 256 \times 64$	1792
Conv-2	$256 \times 256 \times 64$	36,928	Conv-2	$256 \times 256 \times 64$	36,928
Max pooling	$128 \times 128 \times 64$	0	Max pooling	$128 \times 128 \times 64$	0
Conv-1	$128 \times 128 \times 128$	73,856	Conv-1	$128 \times 128 \times 128$	73,856
Conv-2	$128 \times 128 \times 128$	147,584	Conv-2	$128 \times 128 \times 128$	147,584
Max pooling	$64 \times 64 \times 128$	0	Max pooling	$64 \times 64 \times 128$	0
Conv-1	$64 \times 64 \times 256$	295,168	Conv-1	$64 \times 64 \times 256$	295,168
Conv-2	$64 \times 64 \times 256$	590,080	Conv-2	$64 \times 64 \times 256$	590,080
Conv-3	$64 \times 64 \times 256$	590,080	Conv-3	$64 \times 64 \times 256$	590,080
Max Pooling	$32 \times 32 \times 256$	0	Conv-4	$64 \times 64 \times 256$	590,080
Conv-1	$32 \times 32 \times 512$	1,180,160	Max pooling	$32 \times 32 \times 256$	0
Conv-2	$32 \times 32 \times 512$	2,359,808	Conv-1	$32 \times 32 \times 512$	1,180,160
Conv-3	$32 \times 32 \times 512$	2,359,808	Conv-2	$32 \times 32 \times 512$	2,359,808
Max pooling	$16 \times 16 \times 512$	0	Conv-3	$32 \times 32 \times 512$	2,359,808
Conv-1	$16 \times 16 \times 512$	2,359,808	Conv-4	$32 \times 32 \times 512$	2,359,808
Conv-2	$16 \times 16 \times 512$	2,359,808	Max pooling	$16 \times 16 \times 512$	0
Conv-3	$16 \times 16 \times 512$	2,359,808	Conv-1	$16 \times 16 \times 512$	2,359,808
Max pooling	$8 \times 8 \times 512$	0	Conv-2	$16 \times 16 \times 512$	2,359,808
			Conv-3	$16 \times 16 \times 512$	2,359,808
			Conv-4	$16 \times 16 \times 512$	2,359,808
			Max pooling	$8 \times 8 \times 512$	0
Total parameters		14,714,688	Total parameters		20,024,384

4 Result

The performance of all the models is quite satisfactory. We have considered images of both healthy leaves and infected leaves with some disease, and the most challenging thing is that leaves belonging to different categories do not have much difference. So, it is difficult to categories them properly. Both VGG16 and VGG19 with SVM give the highest training accuracy in our experiment. The performance measurement of all the models is mentioned in Table 2. The accuracy and loss curve of Logistic

Table 2 Efficiency of the proposed method

Model Name	Accuracy (%)	Precision (%)	Recall (%)	F1-score (%)
VGG16 with SVM	89.25	95.24	91.75	93.42
VGG19 with SVM	89.25	94.89	91.87	93.29
Logistic Regression	75.87	78.19	75.87	75.14

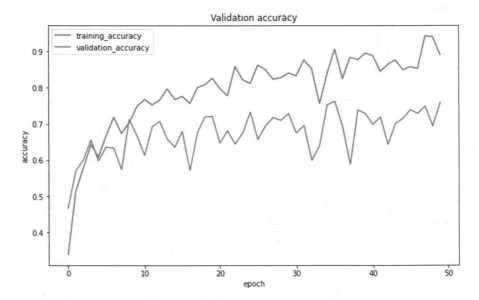

Fig. 3 Accuracy curve for logistic regression

Regression for 50 epochs are shown in Figs. 3 and 4. Similarly, Figs. 5 and 6 show the confusion matrix of VGG16 and VGG19 models with SVM classifier.

5 Conclusion

The main motive of this research is to find out the efficient techniques which can classify plant leaf diseases accurately. All the presented methods have used a subset of PlantVillage dataset. The performance of all the methods is above average. The combination of VGG16 and VGG19 architectures with SVM gives highest training accuracy among all the proposed techniques which is 89.25% for the classification of ten different classes of plant leaf diseases which contains both healthy and diseases infected leaves. The future aspect of this study is to see the performance of mentioned models with high scale data and also with other categories of plant leaf diseases which we do not use in this research study.

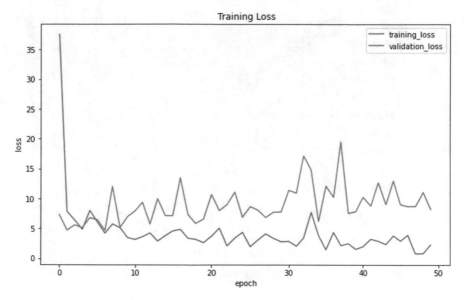

Fig. 4 Loss curve for logistic regression

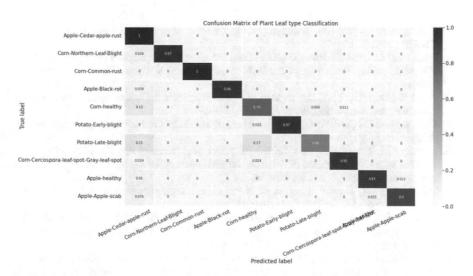

Fig. 5 Confusion matrix of VGG16 with SVM model

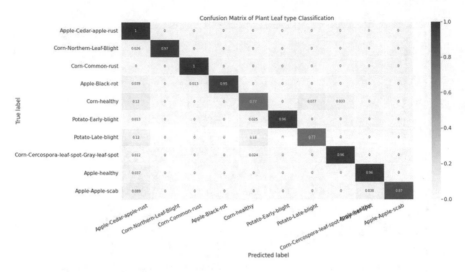

Fig. 6 Confusion matrix of VGG19 with SVM model

References

1. Kamlapurkar SR (2016) Detection of plant leaf disease using image processing approach. Int J Sci Res Publ 6(2):73–76
2. Arun Pandian J, Geetharamani G (2019) Data for: identification of plant leaf diseases using a 9-layer deep convolutional neural network. Mendeley Data, V1. https://doi.org/10.17632/tyw btsjrjv.1
3. Singh V, Misra AK (2017) Detection of plant leaf diseases using image segmentation and soft computing techniques. Inf Process Agric 4(1):41–49
4. Oo YM, Htun NC (2018) Plant leaf disease detection and classification using image processing. Int J Res Eng 5(9):516–523
5. Sardogan M, Tuncer A, Ozen Y (2018) Plant leaf disease detection and classification based on CNN with LVQ algorithm. In: 2018 3rd International conference on computer science and engineering (UBMK). IEEE, pp 382–385
6. Atila Ü, Uçar M, Akyol K, Uçar E (2021) Plant leaf disease classification using EfficientNet deep learning model. Eco Inform 61:101182
7. Dhaware CG, Wanjale KH (2017) A modern approach for plant leaf disease classification which depends on leaf image processing. In: 2017 International conference on computer communication and informatics (ICCCI). IEEE, pp 1–4
8. Hossain E, Farhad Hossain Md, Rahaman MA (2019) A color and texture based approach for the detection and classification of plant leaf disease using KNN classifier. In: 2019 International conference on electrical, computer and communication engineering (ECCE). IEEE, pp 1–6
9. Geetha G, Samundeswari S, Saranya G, Meenakshi K, Nithya M (2020) Plant leaf disease classification and detection system using machine learning. J Phys: Conf Ser 1712(1):012012
10. Khitthuk C, Srikaew A, Attakitmongcol K, Kumsawat P (2018) Plant leaf disease diagnosis from color imagery using co-occurrence matrix and artificial intelligence system. In: 2018 International electrical engineering congress (iEECON). IEEE, pp 1–4
11. Deeba K, Amutha B (2020) ResNet-deep neural network architecture for leaf disease classification. Microprocess Microsyst (2020):103364
12. Basavaiah J, Anthony AA (2020) Tomato leaf disease classification using multiple feature extraction techniques. Wirel Pers Commun 115(1):633–651

13. Tian J, Hu Q, Ma X, Han M (2012) An improved KPCA/GA-SVM classification model for plant leaf disease recognition. J Comput Inf Syst 8(18):7737–7745
14. Priyadharshini A, Ramar, Arivazhagan S, Arun M, Mirnalini A (2019) Maize leaf disease classification using deep convolutional neural networks. Neural Comput Appl 31(12):8887–8895
15. Padol PB, Yadav AA (2016) SVM classifier based grape leaf disease detection. In: 2016 Conference on advances in signal processing (CASP). IEEE, pp 175–179
16. Bhagat M, Kumar D, Haque I, Munda HS, Bhagat R (2020) Plant leaf disease classification using grid search based SVM. In: 2nd International conference on data, engineering and applications (IDEA). IEEE, pp 1–6
17. Rao A, Kulkarni SB (2020) A hybrid approach for plant leaf disease detection and classification using digital image processing methods. Int J Electr Eng Educ:0020720920953126
18. Sabrol H, Kumar S (2019) Plant leaf disease detection using adaptive neuro-fuzzy classification. In: Science and information conference. Springer, Cham, pp 434–443
19. Sholihati RA, Sulistijono IA, Risnumawan A, Kusumawati E (2020) Potato leaf disease classification using deep learning approach. In: 2020 International electronics symposium (IES). IEEE, pp 392–397
20. Thangaraj R, Anandamurugan S, Kaliappan VK (2021) Automated tomato leaf disease classification using transfer learning-based deep convolution neural network. J Plant Dis Prot 128(1):73–86
21. Sujatha R, Chatterjee JM, Jhanjhi NZ, Brohi SN (2021) Performance of deep learning vs machine learning in plant leaf disease detection. Microprocess Microsyst 80:103615
22. Annabel LSP, Annapoorani T, Deepalakshmi P (2019) Machine learning for plant leaf disease detection and classification–a review. In: 2019 International conference on communication and signal processing (ICCSP). IEEE, pp 0538–0542
23. Saikia T, Kumar R, Kumar D, Singh KK (2022) An automatic lung nodule classification system based on hybrid transfer learning approach. SN Comput. Sci. 3:272. https://doi.org/10.1007/s42979-022-01167-0
24. Reddi S, Kale S, Kumar S (2018) On the convergence of Adam and beyond. In: 6th International conference on learning representations, 2018

Heart Disease Prediction and Classification Using Machine Learning Models

Sourabh Kumar and Saroj Kumar Chandra

1 Introduction

Heart is one of the most important muscular organ of the human body [1]. It circulates food, oxygen, water, minerals, and many more substances in the form of blood to other parts of the body. Abnormal blood circulation leads to serious health issues including death. Heart disease arises due to abnormal function of heart. It can lead to permanent heart failure and death. It happens due to decrease of blood flow in heart muscle. In the last decade, many incidence taken place due to heart attack in early age of between 30 and 48 year [2]. This is usually caused by a blockage in the arteries. This heart attack is one of the big medical emergency and needs to given higher attention. Heart disease symptom's include chest pain, neck pain, abnormal heart beats and anxiety. It is found that 70% deaths are because of artery disease and cerebral stroke. Personal habits such as using tobacco and drinks and high stress level leads to cause the heart attack [2]. The medical diagnosis of heart disease plays a important role in tacking perfect action to prevent death of a person. Several different symptoms are associated with heart disease, which make it difficult to diagnose it quicker and better. Heart attack symptoms comprises neck, arms, back, dizziness, tiredness, abnormal heartbeat, consternation and tightfistedness or affliction majorly in the chest. Risk factors comprises both changeable and unchangeable. The changeable factors covers age, sex, and family background. The changeable factors covers smoking, high cholesterol, high blood pressure, fatness, deficiency of proper diet as well as exercise, and a huge amount of stress. Bypass surgery is one of the most used treatment method in case of heart attacks [3, 4]. The present work is about to predict heart disease early so that appropriate action can be taken to prevent permanent heart failure or death using machine learning models.

S. Kumar (✉) · S. K. Chandra
Computer Science and Engineering, OP Jindal University, Raigarh, India
e-mail: satishsaurabh.kumar@gmail.com

S. K. Chandra
e-mail: saroj.chandra@opju.ac.in

© The Author(s), under exclusive license to Springer Nature Singapore Pte Ltd. 2023   447
K. Kumar Singh et al. (eds.), *Machine Vision and Augmented Intelligence*, Lecture Notes in Electrical Engineering 1007, https://doi.org/10.1007/978-981-99-0189-0_34

In the literature, many machine learning models namely Naive Bayes classifier, KNN, support vector machine, logistic regression, decision tree, and random forest models have been used to predict and classify heart disease [5–10]. Archana et al. and Devansh et al. have used machine learning models for the prediction of a heart disease. In the manuscript, the authors have reported that KNN gives higher accuracy in predicating heart disease on the dataset by using different features. Comparative study with confusion matrix has been done with Support Vector Machine, decision tree and linear regression [5, 6]. Hidayet et al. have used an Support Vector Machine (SVM) supervised machine learning model with a feature engineering approach for predicting heart disease. In the comparative study they have shown maximum 84% accuracy with optimal feature selection [7]. Asha et al. used Naïve Bayes classifier for prediction and classification of heart disease. In the comparative study ,they have reported 52% accuracy [8]. R. Chitra et al. have used Fuzzy C-Means classifier in the prediction model with 13 features and 270 records [9]. Farman et al. proposed a deep learning and feature fusion model in the heart attack disease prediction. In the model, they have used information gain and conditional probability to select key features from the dataset [10].

The present work is articulated as follows. The Flow chart of the proposed model is presented in Sect. 2. In this section, brief description of each of the modules have been presented along with brief description of machine learning models used. Algorithm design of the presented model is presented in Sect. 2.1. Section 3 discusses the results obtained by the proposed model.

2 Proposed Methodology and Algorithm Design

Flowchart of the present work is shown in Fig. 1. The work has been divided mainly into loading the dataset, preprocessing of data, division of the dataset into training and testing set and then applying machine learning models to the divided dataset and evaluations. The brief description of each of the step is presented in the following section.

Data Set: Heart dataset has been downloaded form kaggle and has been used in the present work [11]. It contains 14 features and 303 records. The some of the records with features are shown in Table 1.

Pre-processing and Division the Dataset: In preprocessing step, data normalization and standardization has been used to optimize the performance of classifiers used. In the division of dataset, 70% data has been used to train the model and rest 30% data has been used to test the model. In the random state 42 has been chosen to select the same data values and same result in the subsequent simulation of the models.

Machine Learning Models

1. Logistic Regression: Logistic Regression is type of regression in which outcome variable is categorical instead of continuous [12]. It is a special case of linear regression. It uses sigmoid function to map the independent variables into probabilistic

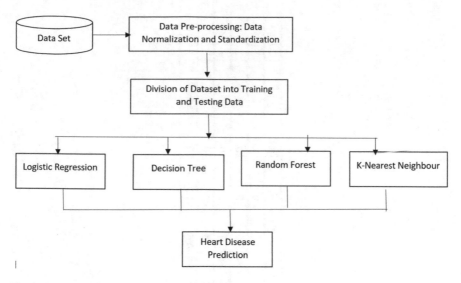

Fig. 1 Proposed system for heart attack disease prediction

model. It is used to predict a binary outcome (1 / 0, Yes / No, True / False) given a set of independent variables. It predicts the probability of occurrence of an event by fitting data to a logit function which is defined as

$$Y = \log\left(\frac{p}{1-p}\right) \tag{1}$$

$\log\left(\frac{p}{1-p}\right)$ is the link function. Logarithmic transformation on the outcome variable allows us to model a non-linear association in a linear way. Here (p/1-p) is the odd ratio.

2. K-Nearest Neighbor: K-Nearest Neighbor is one of most popular and simplest supervised machine learning Algorithm [12]. It is used in both classification and regression. it is widely used for handling missing value problem in the dataset. It assigns class to new data points based on majority class of nearest data points. It uses distance metric to compute the closeness to data points. The most popular distance metric used is euclidean distance which is calculated by using following formula:

$$D(x, y) = \sqrt{(x_1 - y_1)^2 + (x_2 - y_2)^2 + (x_1 - y_1)^2 \dots (x_n - y_n)^2} \tag{2}$$

where x and y are location of data points in R^2 space.

3. Decision Tree: Decision tree is supervised machine learning model [12]. It is used for classification as well as regression problems. it uses tree structure to classify the data points. In the tree, root node contains all the data in the dataset. Splitting of the dataset is performed on internal nodes. Leaf nodes gives final classification of the

Table 1 Sample records of heart dataset

	Age	Sex	cp	trtbps	Chol	fbs	restecg	thalachh	exng	Oldpeak	slp	caa	thall	Output
0	63	1	3	145	233	1	0	150	0	2.3	0	0	1	1
1	37	1	2	130	250	0	1	187	0	3.5	0	0	2	1
2	41	0	1	130	204	0	0	172	0	1.4	2	0	2	1
3	56	1	1	120	236	0	1	178	0	0.8	2	0	2	1
4	57	0	0	120	354	0	1	163	1	0.6	2	0	2	1

data in the dataset. The internal node uses the entropy function to split the internal node. Entropy measures randomness in the data points in dataset. Hence, the internal node with higher entropy values are chosen for splitting the dataset. The goal is to reduce randomness. The entropy function is defined as

$$\text{entropy} = -\sum_{i=1}^{c} -p_i \log (p_i) \tag{3}$$

where p_i is probability of an element/class i in our data.

4. Random Forest: Random forest is one of the widely used supervised machine learning model to solve over fitting problem in decision tree [12]. It falls in the category of ensemble learning where bootstrap and data aggregation method are used. In the bootstrap process the dataset are divided into subsets based on row and column sampling. The sampled data are given to the model. In this way multiple machine learning models are created for the same dataset. Bootstrapping process confirms that each randomly selected data gives unique decision tree in the random forest. Hence, It actually consists of many decision trees that form random forest. In the classification of new data point, each decision tree provides a response as class. The random forest aggregates all the responses from each of the decision trees and assigns class label to new data point based on majority of the class responses obtained.

Machine Learning Model Evaluation: Logistic regression, K-NN, Decision and Random forest machine learning models have been used for heart attack disease prediction. Precision, Recall, F1-score and accuracy score have been used for quantitative comparative study. AROC AROC (Area under Receiver Operating Characteristic curve) has been used to visually inspect the performance of each of the machine learning model used.

2.1 Algorithm Design for Proposed Model

An Algorithm 1 is presented to predict and classify the heart disease. The Algorithm 1 is self explanatory in the nature. The first step is to load the dataset. In the second step normalization has been perform. In the third step data standardization has been performed. In the next step, dataset has been divided in to training and testing then machine learning models have been used to predict and classify the heart disease. In the final step, confusion matrix, accuracy score, precision, recall and F1-score have been calculated.

Algorithm 1 Tumor Extraction(*Image*, Tumor)

Require: *HeartDataset*
Ensure: Class labels
  begin
  DF:Loading of dataset
  Normalized DF= normalize(DF)
  Standardized DF= normalize(Normalized DF)
  x=features(1:13)
  y=feature(14)
  x train, x test, y train, y test = train test split (x, y, test size= 0.3, random state= 42)
  training machine learning models
  testing machine learning models
  Compute Confusion Matrix for each of the model
  Compute Accuracy score for each of the model
  Compute Precision, Recall and F1-Score for each of the model **end**

---

3 Results and Discussion

Python programming language has been used to carry out experimental work. The hardware used simulation work is tabulated in Table 2. The dataset used for the experimental purpose has 14 features. Correlation analysis has been done on all the 14 features. The heat map of the correlation is shown in Fig. 2. Heatmap represents correlation among different features in the dataset. Correlation value lies between 0 and 1. Increases/decreases in one feature value leads to an increase/decrease in another feature value those features are said to be positively correlated to each other [13]. If increment in one feature value decreases another feature value then they are said to be negatively correlated. If an increase/decrease in one feature does not affect another feather then they are said to be uncorrelated to each other. The presence of correlated features leads to complexity and hence should be removed. From Fig. 2, it can be analyzed that all the features taken into consideration are independent to each other.

Precision, Recall and F1-score have been considered for quantitative evaluation of proposed model [14]. The results obtained have been tabulated in Table 3. The confusion matrix for different machine learning models is shown in Fig. 3. It is 2×2 matrix which tabulates predicated class labels versus actual class labels. The column number (1, 1) and (2, 2) represent the values of TP and TN. TP and TN are true positive and true negative rates respectively which gives exact match between

Table 2 Hardware configuration used

Hardware	Capacity
CPU clock speed	1.60 Ghz
RAM	8 GB
L1 Cache Memory	256 KB
L2 Cache Memory	1 MB
L3 Cache Memory	6 MB

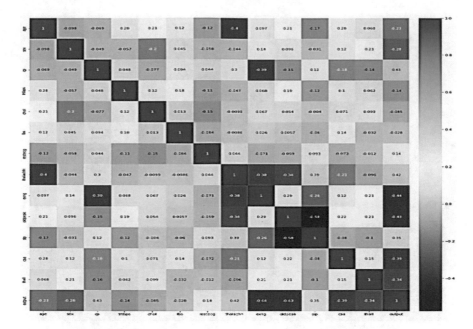

Fig. 2 Correlation among different features in the heart dataset

predicted and actual classes. The column (1, 2) represents False positive (FP) rate which is type 1 error in the classification. FP gives percentage of negative data points which are predicated as positive class. Column (2, 1) represents FN which is type 2 error in the classification. It is opposite to the FP where positive class data points are predicated as negative class. The confusion matrix for different models logistic regression, KNN, Decision tree and Random forest are shown in Fig. 3. It can be analyzed from Fig. 3 that logistic repression and random forest gives same classification accuracy as compared to the other models considered for comparative study. Also, their accuracy score are high as compared to other models. However, random forest is more complex as compared to logistic regression model. Hence, logistic regression is superior than that if random forest. The precision is ratio of true positives and total positive calculated positives. Recall is ratio of true positives and total actual positives in the dataset. Their values lies between 0 and 1. The values closer to 1 gives higher performance while values closer to 0 represent lower performance in both precision and recall. Its values are tabulated in Table 3. It can be analyzed from Table 3 that logistic regression and random forest gives same and higher performance measurement in heart attack disease prediction as compared to other models such as KNN and Decision matrix. Sometimes both precision and recall play an important role in model selection. In such cases, F1-scores are being calculated which is the harmonic mean of precision and recall. Its value lies between 0 and 1. The values closer to 1 represent a better model as compared to models which have values near to 0. As, it can be analyzed from Table 3 that on an average logistic regression and random forest gives higher F1-score.

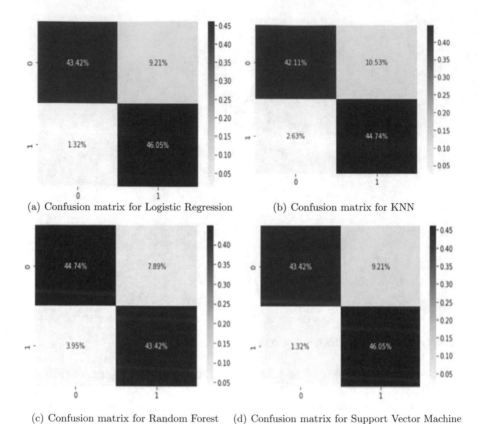

(a) Confusion matrix for Logistic Regression   (b) Confusion matrix for KNN

(c) Confusion matrix for Random Forest   (d) Confusion matrix for Support Vector Machine

Fig. 3 Confusion matrix of different machine learning models

Table 3 Quantitative analysis of different machine learning models

M/L models	Accuracy	Precision	Recall	F1-score
Logistic regression	0.8947	0.8333	0.9722	0.8974
K-nearest neighbor	0.8684	0.8095	0.9444	0.8710
Decision tree	0.8815	0.8461	0.9166	0.8800
Random forest	0.8947	0.8333	0.9722	0.8974

4 Conclusion

Heart disease prediction and classification model has been presented in the present work. Logistic regression, Decision Tree, K-Nearest Neighbor and Random Forest machine learning models have been used in the heart disease prediction. The models have been evaluated with confusion matrix, accuracy score, precision, recall, and F1-score. It has been found that logistic regression and random forest shows equal performance in predicting and classifying heart disease. However, complexity is high in the random forest due to random sampling and multiple decision trees. Hence, it is concluded that logistic regression is better one. In the future, more datasets can be used to analyze the performance of the presented work.

References

1. T. E. o. E. Britannica, Heart. www.britannica.com/science/heart
2. Heart Attack. www.mayoclinic.org/diseases-conditions/heart-attack
3. Yasue HE, Harada E, Mizuno Y (2019) Coronary artery spasm—clinical features, pathogenesis and treatment. Proc Jpn Acad Ser B Phys Biol Sci 95(2):53–66
4. Fass R, Achem S (2011) Noncardiac chest pain: epidemiology, natural course and pathogenesis. J Neurogastroenterol Motil 17:110–123. https://doi.org/10.5056/jnm.2011.17.2.110
5. Singh A, Kumar R (2020) Heart disease prediction using machine learning algorithms, pp 452–457. https://doi.org/10.1109/ICE348803.2020.9122958
6. Shah D, Patel SB, Bharti SK (2020) Heart disease prediction using machine learning techniques. SN Comput Sci 1:345
7. Takci H (2018) Improvement of heart attack prediction by the feature selection methods. Turk J Elec Eng Comp Sci 26:1–10. https://doi.org/10.3906/elk-1611-235
8. Rajkumar A, Reena M, Diagnosis of heart disease using datamining algorithm, Global J Comput Sci Technol 10
9. Jegan C (2013) Heart attack prediction system using fuzzy c means classifier. IOSR J Comput Eng 14:23–31. https://doi.org/10.9790/0661-1422331
10. Ali F, El-Sappagh S, Islam SMR, Kwak D, Ali A, Imran M, Kwak KS (2020) A smart healthcare monitoring system for heart disease prediction based on ensemble deep learning and feature fusion. Inf Fusion 63:208–222
11. Heart Attack Analysis & Prediction Dataset. https://www.kaggle.com/rashikrahmanpritom/heart-attack-analysis-prediction-dataset
12. Belyadi H, Haghighat A (2021) Chapter 5—Supervised learning. In: Belyadi H, Haghighat A (eds) Machine learning guide for oil and gas using Python. Gulf Professional Publishing, pp 169–295. https://doi.org/10.1016/B978-0-12-821929-4.00004-4. https://www.sciencedirect.com/science/article/pii/B9780128219294000044
13. Akoglu H (2018) User's guide to correlation coefficients. Turk J Emerg Med 18(3):91–93. https://doi.org/10.1016/j.tjem.2018.08.001. https://www.sciencedirect.com/science/article/pii/S2452247318302164
14. Chandra SK, Bajpai MK, Fractional mesh-free linear diffusion method for image enhancement and segmentation for automatic tumor classification. Biomed Signal Process Control 58. https://doi.org/10.1016/j.bspc.2019.101841

Artificial Intelligence and Machine Learning Techniques for Analysis of Yoga Pose

Siddharth Gupta and Avnish Panwar

1 Introduction

These days, the issue is fragile and extensive spectrum of health conditions, of which musculoskeletal disorders may be a critical field that requires immediate attention. Every year, a large number of people are impacted by numerous musculoskeletal illnesses as a result of accidents or ageing. Yoga is being practised these days to overcome the aforementioned condition and to gain good health [1]. Yoga is a series of activities that originated in ancient India and is concerned with a person's physiological, intellectual, and spiritual well-being. In the medical sector, yoga has gained a lot of traction. Yoga has numerous advantages, including improved health, mental power, and weight loss [2]. Yoga should be done under the direction of an expert trainer because poor posture may lead to many health issues like ankle injuries, stiff necks, muscular pulls, and so on. During training, the yoga instructor must adjust the individual postures. Yoga may only be practised on one's own after sufficient training. However, in today's circumstances, individuals are more at ease in their own homes, and nearly, everything is done online. People are now using their cell phones to learn how to execute yoga positions and begin practising them, but they have no means of knowing whether or not the yoga stance they are performing is correct. Many efforts have been made to alleviate these constraints. AI software that acts as a trainer was created using computer vision and data science methodologies. This programme explains the benefits of that posture. It also reveals the precision with which the act was delivered [3].

S. Gupta (✉)
Graphic Era Deemed to Be University, Dehradun, India
e-mail: sidgupta307@gmail.com

A. Panwar
Graphic Era Hill University, Dehradun, India

© The Author(s), under exclusive license to Springer Nature Singapore Pte Ltd. 2023   457
K. Kumar Singh et al. (eds.), *Machine Vision and Augmented Intelligence*, Lecture Notes in Electrical Engineering 1007, https://doi.org/10.1007/978-981-99-0189-0_35

These days, DL models and ML algorithms are utilised to classify images. Machine learning is a technology that has seen a rapid increase in popularity and utilisation over the last several years. The algorithms are thought to have a high degree of accuracy in classifying images into appropriate categories. Machine learning's capacity to automate numerous decision-making activities is a very useful feature [4]. In the present work, we have taken the large dataset that comprises different yoga poses and these images were pre-processed. The features were collected from these scans by using computer vision techniques and tf-pose algorithm. This model creates a skeleton of a human body by marking and connecting all of the body's joints, resulting in a stick diagram known as a skeleton as shown in Fig. 1. This approach extracts coordinates and angles created by joints, which may subsequently be utilised as features in machine learning models. Finally, the machine learning algorithms classify the images into the relevant class.

The second half of the report outlines the investigations conducted by various researchers. Section 3 contains a discussion of the material and techniques employed, as well as the dataset gathering, architecture, and evolution criteria. The next part Sect. 4 provides the findings and discussion, which demonstrates the result produced utilising various architectures, and the last Sect. 5 concludes the work.

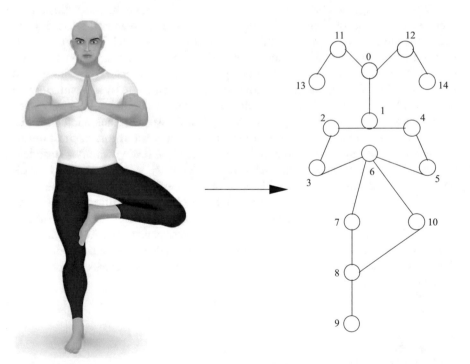

Fig. 1 Dataset image of tree yoga pose converted to stick diagram

2 Literature Work

Pullen et al. [5] created a project that aims to create laboratory measurements of yoga as an useful strength training exercise and to see if yoga skill acquisition can be quantified in a contributed to higher style and used as a method to encourage physical activities. The author intends to use yoga training to examine the effects of body mass and age on posture alignment and limb stretch in specific groups. The detailed work can be extracted from [5]. Adhikari et al. [6] used a 640 480 Kinect camera to create a human posture detection system. They identified six postures done by five participants (sitting, standing, bending, reclining, crawling, and others). Using the background removal approach, they were able to recover a total of 21 499 still human silhouettes from the original Kinect data. The detection rate of the system was 74%. Yadav et al. [7] employed deep learning methods as well as the Open-Pose approach with CNN and LSTM in [7]. These strategies were used to process temporal information. At a conventional taught position, a sample yoga stance is also used. The identification of key points is displayed after 45 frames predicted by CNN and LSTM, based on the results. This is to ensure that the key points are in synchronisation. The accuracy results are shown as a percentage of the total posture. Huang et al. [8] present an OpenPose-based yoga assistance mobile application that gives users oral directions and feedback to help them fix non-standard Yoga postures based on pose skeleton scores. One of the enhancements to study more humanised activities and services is to investigate a more sophisticated model that can have three characteristics: first, it can reliably detect key points in complicated sceneries; second, it can be installed on any device; and third, it can be used by anybody. Finally, it can do calculations in less than a second. Thibhodee et al. in [9] this study use the OpenPose library, a way to detect 18 key points on a human structure, to evaluate full-body drawings and the idea of human pose estimation. Drawing sketches of 22 first-year students, each of whom made three drawings of three models, were used in this study. The angle and distance between key points are determined from detected key points, yielding 26 characteristics. These characteristics were modelled using artificial neural networks (ANNs) to predict the grades of drawings labelled as good, middling, or bad. The resultant key points are then used to calculate the skeleton's angles and distances, extracting 26 features, and employing these features to build an ANN classification model. The model's performance was assessed with a 56%.

3 Methodology

The several steps involved in the methodology include the dataset description, preprocessing of the dataset images, description of deep learning models for feature extractor, and machine learning algorithms for classification of yoga poses.

Table 1 Yoga poses' dataset description

Dataset/classes	Training	Testing	Total
Downdog	223	97	320
Goddess	180	80	260
Plank	266	115	381
Tree	160	69	229
Warrior	252	109	361
Total	1081	470	**1551**

(a)   (b)   (c)

Fig. 2 Dataset images after pre-processing

3.1 Dataset Description and Pre-processing

Yoga is a well-known technique for reducing anxiety and tension. The downward dog stance, goddess pose, tree pose, plank pose, and warrior pose are some of the most well-known yoga poses. To distinguish between them, different AI techniques were imposed. In the current work, to detect the correct yoga pose using deep and machine learning algorithms, the yoga poses' dataset was used which was publically available at Kaggle [10]. The dataset is separated into train and test subdirectories, with five subdirectories in each directory corresponding to the five yoga posture classes. The training and testing datasets have a 70:30 ratio. Table 1 shows the dataset description.

Figure 2 shows the dataset images after pre-processing for the different yoga poses.

3.2 Convolutional Neural Network

CNN is a well-known deep neural network for visual image processing. The CNN model is depicted in Fig. 3 below. Convolutional layer, activation layer, pooling layer, and fully linked layer are the four main architectural elements of CNN [11].

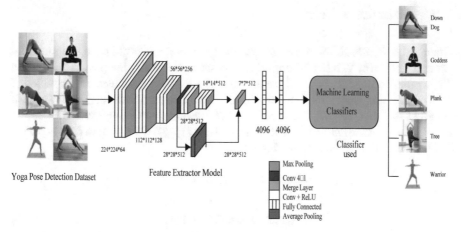

Fig. 3 Deep and machine learning architectures for classifying yoga pose

The convolutional layer is a filter that runs through an image, each time controlling a matrix of pixels. This layer's output will be a layer that contains information about all of the pixels that the channel detected. The activation layer is a grid created by the convolutional layer with a lower estimation than the initial image. This framework is activated by a nonlinear actuation layer, which allows the arrangement to self-organise through backpropagation. The pooling layer employs the "pooling" strategy to encourage downsampling and reduce the framework's size. A channel is handed across from the previous layer, which selects one number from each group of values (max pooling) by selecting the most maximum value. The classic multi-layer perception structure is made up of fully linked layers. The output is represented as a one-dimensional vector as its input. The categorization choice is based on the label with the highest chance of acceptance [12].

3.3 Machine Learning Classifier

Following feature extraction, a variety of ML classifiers, such as SVM, LR, KNN, decision tree, Naive Bayes, and RF, were used to assess the approaches' performance. The predictions of ML classifiers (LR [13], RF [14], KNN [15], Naive Bayes [16], and tree [17]) are utilised as input to CNN in this study. The architecture of the suggested hybrid of ML and DL for posture detection is shown in Fig. 3.

3.4 Parameters Used

Standard (LR, RF, KNN, Naive Bayes, decision tree, and SVM) and deep learning models (VGG16, VGG19, Inception v3) are used to identify the posture prediction. Skew, percentile, SR, SD, and mean were amongst the variables we extracted. It is worth noting that a total of three trials have been carried out. Precision [18], recall [18], F1-score [19], and accuracy [19] measures were employed to assess the effectiveness of the applied technique. Equations (1)–(4) were used to find the values for various DL models and ML classifiers.

$$\text{Accuracy} = (TN + TP)/(TN + TP + FN + FP), \tag{1}$$

$$\text{Recall} = TP/(TP + FN), \tag{2}$$

$$\text{Precision} = TP/(TP + FP), \tag{3}$$

$$F1\text{-score} = 2 * (\text{Recall} * \text{Precision}) / \text{Recall} + \text{Precision}, \tag{4}$$

where TP is True Positive, TN is True Negative, FP is False Positive, and FN is False Negative.

4   Experiments Conducted and Results

Once the dataset images are gathered, the following steps are applied as shown in Fig. 4 below. In the first step, the gathering and collection of dataset images are done. After this, the tf-pose estimation algorithm is applied to the dataset images followed by the extraction of features from the images. Once the pre-trained CNN models extract all the feature, then in the next step, all the images were transferred to distinct ML classifiers for the classification of images into different poses.

4.1 Dataset Images

All of the dataset images have had their brightness boosted, and the parameters have been improved. In order to correct the dataset images in the tf-pose estimation technique, the image resolution was increased to 500 × 500 pixels. These changes were done in order to obtain a precise and accurate result.

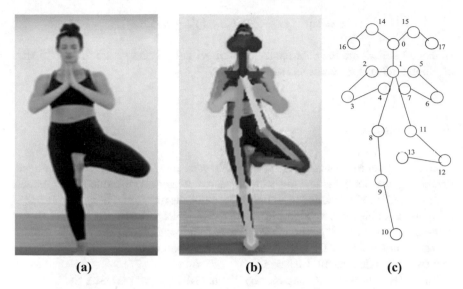

Fig. 4 Dataset image of tree yoga pose (**a**) normal tree pose (**b**) skeleton made by using tf-pose algorithm (**c**) stick diagram made by using tf-pose algorithm

4.2　*Creating Skeleton (Tf-Pose Estimation)*

The tf-pose estimation method [9] is used to generate a skeleton of the individual executing yoga poses. The methodology labels each joint of the body and links it to a skeleton/stick diagram, as illustrated in Fig. 4 (C). The algorithm is also quite accurate in real time.

4.3　*Feature Extraction*

The coordinates of the joints are recovered in the following stage using the tf-pose estimation technique; the number of joints are displayed in Fig. 4. The coordinates are utilised to calculate 12 distinct angles that will be used to identify and correct yoga positions. Below is the formula for determining the angle [20]:

$$x^2 = y^2 + z^2 - 2yz \cos X, \tag{5}$$

where
　　$x =$ from point p1 to point p2 distance,
　　$y =$ from point p2 to point p3 distance,
　　$z =$ from point p1 to point p3 distance,
　　$X =$ angle made by point p2.
　　To find the distance between two points [21],

$$a = \text{sqrt}((x1 - x2) * 2 + (y2 - y1) * 2), \tag{6}$$

where $x1$ and $x2$ are the coordinates of point $p1$ and $y1$ and $y2$ are the coordinates of point 2. Also, sqrt represents square root.

4.4 Classification

Once the dataset images are formed, then they were pre-processed. After image pre-processing was done, the features were extracted using the pre-trained CNN models such as VGG16, VGG19, and Inception v3. Finally, the image classification is applied using the machine learning algorithms like SVM, KNN, LR, RF, NN, and AdaBoost that classifies the new input image as of one of the yoga poses [7].

The results stated in Tables 2, 3, and 4 show the values of different classifiers for accuracy, precision, recall, F1-score.

Table 2 shows the values obtained by distinct ML algorithms and VGG16 model.

Table 3 reflects the values obtained by distinct machine learning algorithms and VGG19 model.

Table 4 shows the values gained by training the Inception v3 model and different machine learning algorithms on dataset images. The maximum value is obtained by Inception v3 model and LR algorithm.

Table 2 Obtained values for VGG16 model and distinct ML algorithms

Method	AUC	Accuracy	F1-score	Precision	Recall
KNN	0.942	0.933	0.931	0.934	0.933
SVM	0.898	0.925	0.928	0.949	0.925
RF	0.949	0.935	0.952	0.960	0.955
NN	0.968	0.945	0.944	0.954	0.955
LR	0.970	0.952	0.962	0.972	0.962
AdaBoost	0.871	0.838	0.836	0.838	0.838

Table 3 Extracted values for VGG19 model and distinct ML algorithms

Method	AUC	Accuracy	F1-score	Precision	Recall
KNN	0.942	0.933	0.931	0.934	0.933
SVM	0.898	0.925	0.928	0.949	0.925
RF	0.949	0.935	0.922	0.930	0.945
NN	0.968	0.945	0.934	0.944	0.935
LR	0.970	0.922	0.932	0.942	0.932
AdaBoost	0.871	0.838	0.836	0.838	0.838

Table 4 Obtained values for Inception v3 model and distinct ML algorithms

Method	AUC	Accuracy	F1-score	Precision	Recall
KNN	0.942	0.923	0.911	0.914	0.923
SVM	0.898	0.825	0.828	0.849	0.825
RF	0.949	0.905	0.902	0.900	0.925
NN	0.968	0.925	0.924	0.934	0.944
LR	0.970	**0.962**	0.962	0.932	0.922
AdaBoost	0.871	0.878	0.876	0.878	0.868

We are considering KNN, SVM, RF, NN, LR, and AdaBoost classifier on different parameters. The bold represent LR classifier obtained the highest accuracy comparing to the other classifiers

5 Conclusion

Using pre-trained CNN models and machine learning approaches, this paper demonstrated yoga posture identification for detecting the appropriateness of postures during yoga workouts. The various yoga posture images were gathered in the dataset and pre-processed to bring all of the images in the dataset to the same scale. Relevant characteristics were collected from the dataset scans, which were then forwarded to machine learning algorithms for accurate yoga posture categorization. The findings reveal that combining the Inception v3 pre-trained architecture with the LR algorithm yields a maximum cumulative accuracy of 96.2%. The findings suggest that by incorporating deep and machine learning techniques into yoga practise, the odds of making a mistake is much reduced.

References

1. Nagalakshmi Vallabhaneni DPP (2021) The analysis of the impact of Yoga on healthcare and conventional strategies for human pose recognition. Turk J Comput Math Educ (TURCOMAT) 12(6):1772–1783
2. Ding W, Hu B, Liu H, Wang X, Huang X (2020) Human posture recognition based on multiple features and rule learning. Int J Mach Learn Cybern 11:2529–2540
3. Babu A, Dube K, Mukhopadhyay S, Ghayvat H, Jithin Kumar MV (2016) Accelerometer based human activities and posture recognition. In: 2016 International conference on data mining and advanced computing (SAPIENCE), 2016, pp 367–373. https://doi.org/10.1109/SAPIENCE.2016.7684120
4. Verma M, Kumawat S, Nakashima Y, Raman S (2020) Yoga-82: a new dataset for fine-grained classification of human poses. In: Proceedings of the IEEE/CVF conference on computer vision and pattern recognition workshops, pp 1038–1039
5. Pullen P, Seffens W (2018) Machine learning gesture analysis of yoga for exergame development. IET Cyber-Phys Syst: Theory Appl 3(2):106–110
6. Adhikari K, Bouchachia H, Nait-Charif H (2017) Activity recognition for indoor fall detection using convolutional neural network. In: 2017 Fifteenth IAPR international conference on machine vision applications (MVA). IEEE, pp 81–84

7. Yadav SK, Singh A, Gupta A, Raheja JL (2019) Real-time Yoga recognition using deep learning. Neural Comput Appl 31(12):9349–9361
8. Huang R, Wang J, Lou H, Lu H, Wang B (2020) Miss Yoga: a Yoga assistant mobile application based on keypoint detection. In: 2020 Digital image computing: techniques and applications (DICTA). IEEE, pp 1–3
9. Thibhodee, S. and Viyanon, W (2021) An application of evaluation of human sketches using deep learning technique. In: The 12th International conference on advances in information technology, pp 1–7
10. Dataset Description: https://www.kaggle.com/niharika41298/yoga-poses-dataset
11. Gupta S, Panwar A, Gupta S, Manwal M, Aeri M (2022) Transfer learning based convolutional neural network (CNN) for early diagnosis of Covid19 disease using chest radiographs. In: Misra R, Shyamasundar RK, Chaturvedi A, Omer R (eds) Machine learning and big data analytics (Proceedings of international conference on machine learning and Big Data analytics (ICMLBDA) 2021). ICMLBDA 2021. Lecture Notes in Networks and Systems, vol 256. Springer, Cham. https://doi.org/10.1007/978-3-030-82469-3_22
12. Panwar A, Semwal G, Goel S, Gupta S (2020) Stratification of the lesions in color fundus images of diabetic retinopathy patients using deep learning models and machine learning classifiers. In: 26th Annual international conference on advanced computing and communications (ADCOM 2020)
13. Hosmer DW (2000) Assessing the fit of the model. Appl Logistic Regression pp 143–202
14. Gupta S, Panwar A, Goel S, Mittal A, Nijhawan R, Singh AK (2019) Classification of lesions in retinal fundus images for diabetic retinopathy using transfer learning. Int Conf Inf Technol (ICIT) 2019:342–347. https://doi.org/10.1109/ICIT48102.2019.00067
15. Panwar A, Yadav R, Mishra K, Gupta S (2021) Deep learning techniques for the real time detection of Covid19 and pneumonia using chest radiographs. In: IEEE EUROCON 2021—19th International conference on smart technologies, 2021, pp 250–253. https://doi.org/10.1109/EUROCON52738.2021.9535604
16. Gupta S, Panwar A, Mishra K (2021) Skin disease classification using dermoscopy images through deep feature learning models and machine learning classifiers. In: IEEE EUROCON 2021—19th International conference on smart technologies, 2021, pp 170–174. https://doi.org/10.1109/EUROCON52738.2021.9535552
17. Kulikajevas A, Maskeliunas R, Damaševičius R (2021) Detection of sitting posture using hierarchical image composition and deep learning. PeerJ Comput Sci 7:e442
18. Gupta S, Aggarwal P, Chaubey N, Panwar A (2021) Accurate prognosis of Covid-19 using CT scan images with deep learning model and machine learning classifiers. Indian J Radio Space Phys 50:19–24
19. Panwar A, Gupta S (2022) Deep learning models for early detection of pneumonia using chest X-ray images. In: Dua M, Jain AK, Yadav A, Kumar N, Siarry P (eds) Proceedings of the international conference on paradigms of communication, computing and data sciences. Algorithms for Intelligent Systems. Springer, Singapore. https://doi.org/10.1007/978-981-16-5747-4_60
20. Liaqat S, Dashtipour K, Arshad K, Assaleh K, Ramzan N (2021) A hybrid posture detection framework: integrating machine learning and deep neural networks. IEEE Sens J 21(7):9515–9522. https://doi.org/10.1109/JSEN.2021.3055898
21. Saroja MN, Baskaran KR, Priyanka P (2021) Human pose estimation approaches for human activity recognition. In: 2021 International conference on advancements in electrical, electronics, communication, computing and automation (ICAECA), 2021, pp 1–4. https://doi.org/10.1109/ICAECA52838.2021.9675787.

2D Ear Recognition Using Data Augmentation and Deep CNN

Ravishankar Mehta and Koushlendra Kumar Singh

1 Introduction

In the field of biometric community, a lot of work has been done by considering the ear as a modality. In biometric system, a person is identified with the help of his/her measurable and physiological characteristics. These characteristics are extracted from the sample images which are taken either in controlled or uncontrolled environment. Ear is considered as a passive, inexpensive, non-intrusive and socially accepted modalities which gives almost accurate results. Finally, the ear-based recognition system is enough hard to circumvent. Convolutional neural network (CNN) comes with state-of-the-art solution for many images' classification problem. The primary role of convolutional layer of CNN is to extract the feature with the help of trainable filters from every part of the image. An effective deep CNN-based model that extracts robust feature to identify a person uses such distinctive features [1]. Many research work confirmed that ear contains enough distinctive features to identify a person through biometric system [2]. In this paper, we discussed about this limitation and introduced an idea to overcome this problem. In this regard, CNN-based model comes with a general solution to the image classification when there exist a variety of input data [3]. Most of the researcher discussed on the fact that how CNN-based method is influenced by the input data size [4, 5]. We have incorporated this problem in our work. Here, we have transformed the original image to the synthetic image from the available dataset through augmentation technique. It produces large variety of image from input data. Hence, our model will get large

R. Mehta (✉) · K. K. Singh
Machine Vision and Intelligence Lab, Department of Computer Science and Engineering,
National Institute of Technology Jamshedpur, Jamshedpur, India, Jharkhand
e-mail: rmehta.online@gmail.com

K. K. Singh
e-mail: koushledra.cse@nitjsr.ac.in

© The Author(s), under exclusive license to Springer Nature Singapore Pte Ltd. 2023   467
K. Kumar Singh et al. (eds.), *Machine Vision and Augmented Intelligence*, Lecture Notes
in Electrical Engineering 1007, https://doi.org/10.1007/978-981-99-0189-0_36

variation of input data and get more robust feature. As a result, it increases the recognition accuracy. Experiments will show how the augmentation technique influences the performance of the model.

2 Related Work

Person recognition based on ear as modality has put a rising interest in recent years and attained acceptable recognition accuracy under controlled environments [6–9]. In our proposed work, we evaluated our experiments using small ear datasets where all the images are taken under laboratory-like environments which include occlusion, variation in head position and lighting conditions. The performance of the recognition system degrades when there occur such types of variations like occlusion, illuminations, blurring or head positions and other factors [10–12]. In conventional method of ear detection, Viola–Jones which is based on cascaded AdaBoost classifiers contributed good detection performance for ear detection [13]. Here, a strong classifier is formed by combining a set of weakly effective classifiers. By doing this approach, most of the irrelevant features can be rejected at early stages. Abaza et al. in his work, reduce the training time by modifying the AdaBoost algorithm and obtained recognition rate about 95% [14]. Yuan and Mu achieve high detection rate by enhancing the original cascaded AdaBoost classifier by taking the input image taken under unconstrained environments [15]. In CNN, same filters are applied to extract distinct features from different locations of the images [16]. The pooling operation of CNN incorporates the rotation invariance features to the translations. But still, there exists some problem with the input rotations. In comparison to conventional machine learning algorithms, deep CNN appears as a better solution for computer vision tasks. Dieleman et al. used combined augmentation with varying rotations together with flipping, cropping and other transformations [17]. It results in 12 variants of input images. A little different approach was given by Laptev et al. They have used transformation invariant pooling technique where feature map is produced by taking element-wise maximum [18].

3 Material and Methodology

3.1 Dataset Descriptions

We have used AMI and AWE ear datasets for evaluating the experiments. AWE dataset contains 1000 images of 100 distinct subjects. The images of this dataset are taken under varied conditioned. The resolution of each image in this dataset is varying in nature. These datasets are very challenging one. As it includes variations across pose, ethnicity, occlusions, gender and alike are common in these environments.

Table 1 Brief summary of available ear dataset used in this work

Datasets	Country	No. of subjects	Number of images	Image size
AWE	Slovenia	100	1000	Varied
AMI	Spain	100	700	492 × 702

Table 2 Number of images in the training and testing set for the proposed model in different dataset

Dataset	Input shape	No. of images in dataset	No. of images in training set	No. of image in the testing set	Train-test split ratio
AMI	100 × 150	700	560	140	0.2
AWE	50 × 120	1000	700	300	0.3

The AMI dataset contains 100 distinct subjects with total 700 images. It contains one image of left ear and six images of right ear. All the images are taken under same lightning condition and hence taken constrained conditioned. Each image of AMI dataset has resolution of 492 × 702 pixels and is available in jpeg format. Description of these dataset is listed in Table 1. For evaluating our experiments, each of this dataset is split into training set and test set with different ratios. From AMI dataset, 490 images are used for training purpose and 210 images are used for testing purpose. Similarly, from total 1000 images of AWE dataset, 700 images are used for training set and 300 images are used for test. The number of training image and test image from each of these datasets used in our experiments are illustrated in Table 2.

3.2 Data Augmentation

In last few years, many researchers have explored different techniques for generating the new sample images. These techniques include algorithm like Generative Adversarial Networks (GANs), Deep Belief Network (DBN), Variational Autoencoders (VAEs) and flow-based generative models. But, for deep learning context, there must be a need of diversity of data available so that network learning capability can be increased for training and testing purpose.

There exist various parameters to increase these diversity of training data as shown in Fig. 1. So, to achieve this capability and overcome the problem of narrow diversity and limited data, we have opted data augmentation technique. In the proposed work, we have opted following parameters of augmentation for AMI and AWE datasets which are listed in Tables 3 and 4.

Some sample images generated through the augmentation effect on AMI datasets are shown in Fig. 2.

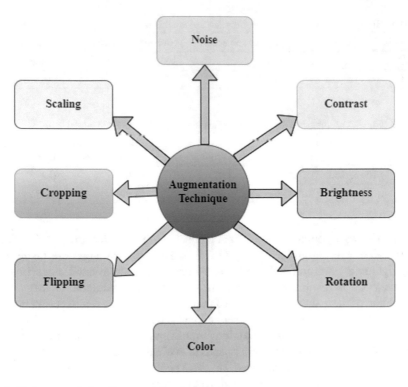

Fig. 1 Various parameter of augmentation technique

Table 3
Following parameters of
augmentation used to increase
the training data for AMI
dataset

	Parameters	Values
AMI dataset	Rotation range	15–45°
	Flipping	Horizontal
	Zoom range	0.2–0.8
	Fill mode	Nearest

Table 4 Following
parameters of augmentation
used to increase the training
data for AWE dataset

	Parameters	Values
AWE dataset	Rotation range	7–30°
	Flipping	Horizontal
	Zoom range	0.3–0.7
	Fill mode	Nearest

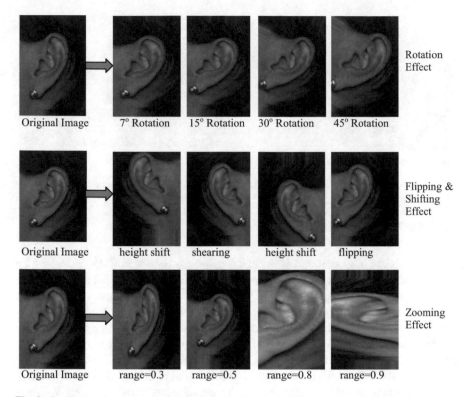

Fig. 2 Synthetic image generated after applying the augmentation transformation

3.3 The Proposed ER System

The framework of the proposed ear recognition system is shown in Fig. 3. First, the sample image from ear dataset is randomly shuffled and split into training set and testing set. Then, augmentation technique is applied to the training set to generate the new artificial (synthetic) sample image. The number of images produced by the augmentation techniques depends on the number of parameters used. Some sample of the produced images corresponding to the different parameters of augmentation techniques has been illustrated in Fig. 2.

Since these generated images are of different perspectives, it makes the model to learn more generalize and robust feature from these produced images. Once the CNN model is trained with augmented training set, the model will be tested with the test set. We also tune the hyperparameter of the network for better optimization. For the classification task, a number of fully connected layers are used at the last layer of network. In our experiments, we have used 100 fully connected layers, since the number of subject in both the datasets is 100. Note that augmentation technique is applied only to training data and not to test data. Reason is that the model capability is evaluated with the testing data, so there is no need to augment the test data.

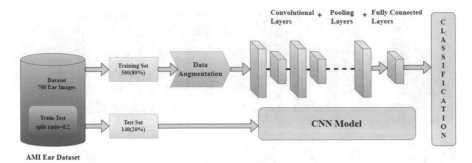

Fig. 3 Proposed frameworks of ear recognition system with augmentation transformation

4   Experimental Result and Analysis

The role of data augmentation is analyzed using the proposed CNN model which is illustrated in Fig. 3. It is implemented using Python version 3.7.8 and 3.40 GHz processor with 4 GB Memory (RAM). We have tested our experiments using various optimizers like RMSprop, Adagrad, Adam. We kept the kernel size 3×3 and learning rate $\eta = 0.0001$. The data augmentation transformation is applied on these datasets resulting in total ten sets. Each image from this set was separately used for training purpose. Accuracy from the proposed CNN for different training sets has been illustrated in Table 5. From the experiments, we found that after applying the augmentation transformation, an accuracy about more than 5% has been increased. We have done some analysis on the parameter of augmentation transformation that has more impact on the system performance. Each type of data augmentation contributes some amount of accuracy to the model which are illustrated in Table 6. It has been observed that a combined transformation of rotation, flipping and zooming contributes more than the single transformation.

Influence of augmentation transformation on AMI ear dataset has been shown in Fig. 4 through model accuracy and model loss.

It can also be observed from the graph that the application of data augmentation also reduces the overfitting problem.

Table 5 Accuracy for each transformation derived from the original dataset

Training dataset	Accuracy (%)
Original	43.57
Rotation	64.40
Zooming	64.87
Flipping	65.37
Rotation + shifting	79.24
Rotation + flipping	82.11

Table 6 Percentage of contribution of augmentation transformation on original dataset

Training dataset	Accuracy (%)
Rotation	25
Zooming	30
Flipping	40
Shifting	25

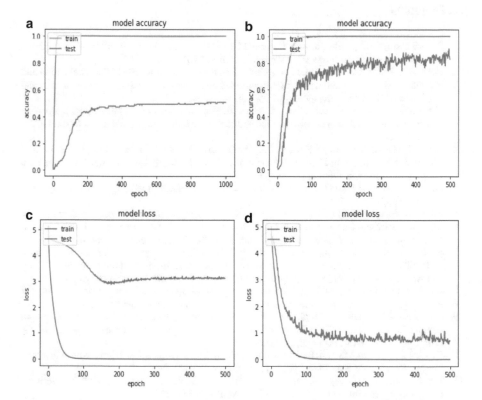

Fig. 4 **a** Model accuracy without augmentation. **b** Model accuracy with augmentation. **c** Model loss versus epochs without augmentation. **d** Model loss versus epochs with augmentation

5 Conclusion

This work presents the role of data augmentation for ear recognition problem with limited data. For this, we considered a simple CNN model and trained this model with augmented data and analyzed its effects. Generally, a CNN model requires diversity of data for training purpose which is not an easy task. For limited data, it is not possible to obtain the distinct features from the available data. To overcome this limitation, augmentation transformation is applied to generate new synthetic data and trained our ear recognition model with newly generated data. It has been observed that application of augmentation approaches improves the accuracy of model. Each transformation of augmentation technique provides certain percentage of improvements in its accuracy. Further research can also be done to apply more complex augmentation approach to improve the accuracy of the system.

References

1. Priyadharshini RA, Arivazhagan S, Arun M (2021) A deep learning approach for person identification using ear biometrics. Appl Intell 51(4):2161–2172
2. Rastogi A, Bhoumik U, Choudhary C, Akbari AS, Kumar Singh K (2021) Ear localization and validation using ear candidate set. In: Machine vision and augmented intelligence—theory and applications. Springer, Singapore, pp 109–120
3. Ciresan DC, Meier U, Masci J, Gambardella LM, Schmidhuber J (2011) Flexible, high performance convolutional neural networks for image classification. In: Proceedings of the IJCAI, pp 1237–1242
4. Saikia T, Hansdah M, Singh KK and Bajpai MK (2022) Classification of lung nodules based on transfer learning with K-Nearest Neighbor (KNN). In: IEEE International Conference on Imaging Systems and Techniques (IST) pp 1–6. IEEE
5. Schroff F, Kalenichenko D, Philbin J (2015) FaceNet: a unified embedding for face recognition and clustering. In: CVPR
6. Mehta R, Singh KK (2023) Ear recognition system using averaging ensemble technique. In Machine Learning, Image Processing, Network Security and Data Sciences: 4th International Conference, MIND 2022, Virtual Event, January 19–20, 2023, Proceedings, Part II, pp 220–229
7. Rastogi A, Bhoumik U, Choudhary C, Akbari AS and Kumar Singh K (2021) Ear localization and validation using ear candidate set. In Machine Vision and Augmented Intelligence—Theory and Applications: Select Proceedings of MAI 2021, pp 109–120. Springer Singapore
8. Mehta R, Garain J, Singh KK (2022) Cohort selection using mini-batch k-means clustering for ear recognition. In: Advances in Intelligent Computing and Communication, pp 273–279
9. Srivastava AK, Sneha H, Singh KK (2020) Pose invariant face recognition using principal component analysis. In Soft Computing: Theories and Applications: Proceedings of SoCTA 2019 (pp. 1029–1043). Springer, Singapore
10. Bustard JD, Nixon MS (2010) Toward unconstrained ear recognition from two-dimensional images. IEEE Trans Syst Man Cybern A Syst Hum 40(3):486–494
11. Hassaballah M, Alshazly HA, Ali AA (2019) Ear recognition using local binary patterns: a comparative experimental study. Expert Syst Appl 118:182–200
12. Emeršič Ž, Štruc V, Peer P (2017) Ear recognition: more than a survey. Neurocomputing 255:26–39
13. Viola PA, Jones MJ (2004) Robust real-time face detection. Int J Comput Vis 57(2):137–154
14. Abaza A, Hebert C, Harrison M (2010) Fast learning ear detection for real-time surveillance. In: Proceedings of the fourth IEEE international conference on biometrics: theory applications and systems (BTAS), p 16
15. Yuan L, Mu Z (2014) Ear recognition based on Gabor features and KFDA. Sci World J 2014
16. Kumar Singh K, Kumar S, Antonakakis M, Moirogiorgou K, Deep A, Kashyap KL, Bajpai MK, Zervakis M (2022) Deep learning capabilities for the categorization of microcalcification. Int J Environ Res Public Health 19(4):2159
17. Dieleman S, Willett KW, Dambre J (2015) Rotation-invariant convolutional neural networks for galaxy morphology prediction. Mon Not R Astron Soc 450:1441–1459
18. Laptev D, Savinov N, Buhmann JM, Pollefeys M (2016) TI-POOLING: transformation-invariant pooling for feature learning in convolutional neural networks. arXiv:1604.06318

Binary Pattern for Copy-Move Image Forgery Detection

Neeraj Rathore, Neelesh Jain, and Pawan Singh

1 Introduction

Due to the rapid development of technology the Image Forgery or modification of digital images is challenging task in the digital world. In Today's time, we cannot envision the correct utilization of digital images each day for different purposes [1]. It is a fact that an image tells a thousand words. Images are utilized to clarify extreme ideas and inspire us effortlessly in every field. With the easy availability of the Internet, digital cameras, and editing software's anything but difficult to make a fake image without any training or extra knowledge. The pattern of alteration in digital images is increasing day by day. Images can be a source of evidence in various areas of our day to day life applications.

N. Rathore (✉) · P. Singh
Indira Gandhi National Tribal University, Amarkantak, Madhya Pradesh, India
e-mail: neerajrathore37@gmail.com; neeraj.rathore@igntu.ac.in

P. Singh
e-mail: Pawan.singh@igntu.ac.in

N. Jain
Jaypee University of Engineering and Technology, Guna, Madhya Pradesh, India
e-mail: neelesh.dei@gmail.com

P. Singh
Central University Rajasthan, Ajmer, India

© The Author(s), under exclusive license to Springer Nature Singapore Pte Ltd. 2023
K. Kumar Singh et al. (eds.), *Machine Vision and Augmented Intelligence*, Lecture Notes
in Electrical Engineering 1007, https://doi.org/10.1007/978-981-99-0189-0_37

Images and videos are ubiquitous in today's society, and they're becoming increasingly crucial in forensics, and most of the evidence in the trial is based on visual data collected on digital devices. Images are prominent methods for communication and numerous individuals depend on them, so it is important that their genuineness ought to be demonstrated. As the field of image processing and its applications has developed and stretched out to the vast territory, there is an increase in the accessibility of image editing software. Because of the simple accessibility of digital editing tools, alteration, and manipulation turned out to be simple and as a result forgery detection becomes a complex and threatening issue [2].

There are three types of image forgery: copy-move (cloning), retouching, and splicing. Copy-move forgery is performed by changing a segment of a given image with another section from the same image. The copied and pasted regions in picture splicing are from separate photos. The goal of image forgery is to copy or cover a specific object in a picture, or to create a counterfeit image. Image retouching is a less harmful type of digital image counterfeiting in which particular characteristics of the original image are boosted or diminished. Preprocessing methods such as JPEG compression, noise addition, and image blurring, as well as geometric operations such as scaling, shifting, and rotation, are commonly used to make detection assignments more difficult. Based on many advanced approaches, a forgery detection method detects and reports an image as counterfeit or authentic.

Many writers have proposed various ways for detecting digital image counterfeiting using various algorithms. However, when compared to previous digital picture forgery detection methods, this study, a new feature for detection of copy-move image fraud employing Gabor filter and Center Symmetric Local Binary Pattern, has numerous advantages.

In this work, feature extraction technique is developed for copy-move forgery detection for classifying the input image as forged or authenticate. The proposed method can detect the presence of any forgery depend on integration of feature extraction techniques such as Gabor filter and Center Symmetric Local Binary Pattern. The Gabor filter is applied to the input image at various scales and orientations in this method. For each Gabor image (sub-band) [3], values for the Center Symmetric Local Binary Pattern are obtained. CSLBP values from various sub-bands are concatenated to create a single feature vector, which is used as input for classification.

Section 2 surveys image forgery detection based on several methodologies and their limitations, Sect. 3 gives the implementation of proposed methodology, Sect. 4 illustrates the experimental findings, and Sect. 5 closes this study with future enhancements.

2   Related Works

Many researchers done research in image forgery-based various algorithms but they facing certain limitations. Kashyap et al. [4] proposed meta-heuristic search algorithm for the copy-move image forgery detection. A new framework for detecting copy-move forging utilizing the CMFD-CS is developed, which includes the CS method into SVD. CMFD is used within a block-based framework that subdivides into distinct processes for detection, and it uses CS methods to calculate the Customized parameter values for images. This technique distinguishes the matched point which generally increases the truly matched blocks to detect the duplicate block more susceptible.

Kaur and Walia [5] presents the forgery detection strategies-based noise estimation by using feature extraction methods. The image is first converted to YIQ colorspace and after that, the block segmentation is applied on Y part of the YIQ image. Principal Component Analysis (PCA) and HOG features used for noise estimation to extract the features from every block of the image. An unsupervised clustering method is utilized to cluster the image block by SVM classifier. The performance results are carried out on CASIA database v1.0 and v2.0 individually demonstrates that the proposed method efficiently detects the forged image-based noise variance as an increase of 4.8 and 5.79% in the accuracy than the other methods.

Singh et al. [6] proposed Ant Colony Optimization for image forgery detection to enhance the low detection rate of the forged regions in the computerized photo image. ACO is implemented to recognize the copy-move forgery detection by finding portion which is manipulated with some software and also cause change it to original pixel values. In the experimental results the proposed method shows the excellent detection of the tampered regions and mainly it is implemented to find the manipulated areas present within the input image precisely.

Ujjainiya and Chugh [7] presented image forgery detection based on texture and clustering techniques. The detection of image forgery is performed by different pixel and transform-based texture strategy are applied to detect the image forgery. This strategy based on two algorithms includes discrete wavelet transform function is employed to obtain texture features of original image and clustering technique to match the block for detection. The performance results are carried out on standard forgery image dataset MFICC2000 and simulated by MATLAB which achieves the efficient reduction in false negative and improve the value of detection.

Swetha and Kishore [8] discuss the image forgery detection-based machine learning algorithms. Illuminati map is distinguished from the given input image from which the face part is detected by viola john method. The recognized face part includes certain features such as energy, entropy, and correlation are extracted by Gray Level Co-Occurrence Matrix (GLCM) and fed to machine learning classifier support vector machine (SVM) to classify the forgery images. The performance results are carried out by publicly available dataset and it achieves efficient classification accuracy.

Kaur and Babbar [9] proposed copy-move forgery detection-based Discrete Cosine Transform and Bacterial Foraging Optimization. Numerous methods have been proposed to distinguish the image forger but time complexity is one of the major challenges is needed to overcome by the optimization algorithm. Discrete Cosine Transform (DCT) is used to partition the input grayscale images into blocks and are processed to produce the quantization matrix of original and forged images and Bacterial Foraging Optimization (BFO) algorithm is then used to identify the forged region based on the classification of weights. The experimental results show that the proposed method is proficient and robust to multiple copy-move forgeries.

Cozzolino et al. [10] presents an image forgery detection-based machine learning and block matching methods. Dense local descriptors for splicing detection and machine learning for classification are generally utilized as a part of forgery detection due to efficient result. The traditional methods are accomplished good performance but they contribute less to the forgery descriptors. So copy-move detection based on machine learning and fuse detections are applied to decrease the missing detection rate and to identify the forgery image and it accomplishes efficient result in classification accuracy and specificity.

Kumar et al. [11] suggested a quick copy-move forgery detection approach based on DCT. The input image is divided into overlapping blocks to detect copy-move fraud in digital photos. To represent block features, which are expressed as row vectors, the DCT transform is used, followed by sorting. Blocks that do not belong to a possible cluster are sometimes left over. The shift values are calculated, and then compared to the threshold value. When compared to other methodologies, the performance results are efficient. The region is detected as forged if the shift value is bigger than the threshold value, although it suffers from temporal complexity.

Xu et al. [12] analysis of the phase correlation to detect the image forgeries. This proposed method depends on non-block matching and if the image is forged then to get a sharp peak in the phase correlation showing the proof of tampering.

Pan et al. [13] proposed a forgery detection technique depend upon the clustering blocks on the basis of noise variances. Initially, blocks are classified based on the initial noise estimation and separated into original and forged blocks.

The detected region was additionally partitioned into segments and refined noise estimation for the following steps then the proposed method achieves the improved detection results.

Peng and Wang [14] proposed image forgery detection-based blur estimation and abnormal hue detection. Blurring is performed to traces of forgery however it crushes the joint consistency of color channels in the image. Based on this principle, blur estimation is done to the image and obtain the blur region, and precisely locate the artificial blur region by distinguishing the abnormal hue in the blur region.

Problem definition

At the moment, numerous multi-media authoring tools are causing copy paste and tampering in digital multi-media. In the contemporary multi-media situation, the tampered and copy paste image changes the actual state of the original image and its illegal procedure. Although the existing method performs better in several detection and estimation tasks, it has a flaw in the procedure for feature selection and coefficient block region selection. The main issue is determining the degree of similarity between the forgery and the original image. For the purpose of detection, optimal feature selection is used when the picture noise value equals the higher intensity value of the actual image, causing the forged image's region to be inaccurate. This method is enhanced to overcome these types of limitation in the proposed algorithm.

3   Proposed Methodology

In this section a novel integration of feature extraction algorithm is presented for copy-move image forgery is considered to detect the image as forgery or authenticate. The detailed description of the proposed methodology is discussed below.

Initially, the resized input image is taken and pre-processed by Wiener filter and the image features are extracted by integration of Gabor filter and Center Symmetric Local Binary Pattern to achieve efficient extraction. The steps for image forgery detection are given in Fig. 1.

The extracted features are matched by Manhattan distance to identify the exact match of the authenticated image. Finally, the matched image is classified by fed into a hybrid combination of neural network and decision tree to detect and classify the forgery image. This proposed method is compared with the feature extraction of the existing SURF and PCA. The limitation of SURF and PCA can be overcome by Gabor filter and CSLBP and classified by HNN-DT.

3.1   Preprocessing by Wiener Filter

Prior to computational processing, preprocessing is required to minimize noise, remove low-frequency background noise, normalize the intensity of individual particle images, and remove enhancing data images. Preprocessing with a Wiener filter is used to minimize noise, blurring, and improve the image's visual quality (Fig. 2).

The assessment of Wiener filter requires the assumption that the signal and noise processes are second-order stationary.

The Wiener filter is a linear restoration mapping such that the original image f and the restoration f_i satisfy [14]

$$E\|f - f_1\|^2 = \text{Minimum} \tag{1}$$

Step 1. The input image resized with 256 x256 is taken. The input image is read and transformed to a grayscale image.

Step 2. The wiener filter is used to reduce noise from the input images.

Step 3. Using the Gabor filter and the feature extraction procedure, the appropriate features from the images are extracted. Centre Symmetric Local Binary Pattern.

Step 4. The similarity matching by Manhattan distance.

Step 5. The image is classified by HNN-DT to classify the image as forgery and authenticate.

Step 6. The Performance evaluations of proposed method are estimated by certain performance metrics such as measure of accuracy, Sensitivity and Specificity.

Fig. 1   Image forgery detection algorithm

Fig. 2 Flowchart for
HNN-DT

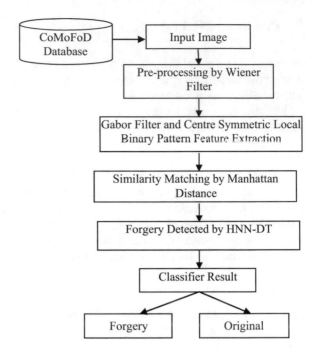

Wiener filter [15] is utilized to solve the extraction of the signal from the noise of a filtering method. Wiener filter is essentially utilized for the medical image noise spots and uneven brightness, and its linear system. If it is the unit sample response to $h(n)$, when the input of a random signal $r(n)$ is denoted as

$$r(n) = u(n) + v(n), \tag{2}$$

where $r(n)$ signal, $v(n)$ to express the noise, the output $O(n)$ is expressed as [15]

$$O(n) = \sum_m h(m)r(n-m)$$
$$O(n) = S(n),$$

where $s(n)$ denotes the estimated value of the output.

3.2 Feature Extraction by Gabor Filter and CSLBP

In general, image fraud detection is based on the digital image's lower content feature. Color, texture, and shape size are three sorts of elements that are typically included in a digital image. The sampling of the original image and the fabricated image is described in this article.

The texture feature is an important element for image counterfeit detection analysis. Feature extractor was used to extract texture features. The required features for categorization are extracted using the feature extractor.

3.3 Gabor Filter

The Gabor filter is a popular feature extraction method for core point detection. Because of their invariance to rotation, scaling, and translation, as well as their robustness in the face of photometric conflicts, the Gabor filters are ideal for dealing with illumination variations and picture noise [16].

In the spatial domain, a two-dimensional Gabor filter as a Gaussian kernel function is modulated by a complex sinusoidal plane wave and

the optimized Gabor filter kernels are sinusoids modulated which are denoted below [8]

$$\sigma_u = k \tag{3}$$

$$\sigma_v = \frac{\sigma_u}{\Upsilon} \tag{4}$$

$$u_0 = u \cos \theta + v \sin \theta$$

$$v_0 = -u \sin \theta + v \cos \theta$$

$$\text{GF}_0 = \exp\left\{-\frac{1}{2}\left(\frac{u_\theta^2}{\sigma_u} + \frac{(\Upsilon v)_\theta^2}{\sigma_v}\right)\right\} \cos\left(2\pi \frac{u_\theta}{\lambda}\right) \tag{5}$$

where σ_u = Standard deviation of filter.

σ_v = Standard deviation of filter that control the orientation selectivity.

θ = Angle of represents the filter orientation.

λ = Wavelength of the Gabor filter.

Υ = Spatial aspect ratio.

Ψ = Phase offset.

σ_u signifies that the filter's forms are independent of the image pixels.

λ and γ values are utilized to maintain false positive rate and ψ represents (2π) rotation phase.

As the combination of the frequency and the orientation is applied to build the Gabor filter bank, the highest frequency f^m signifies the total number of frequencies n_f and the total number of orientations n_o of the Gabor filters. The relationship between f^m and n_o is shown as [17].

$$f_l = a - {}^1 f^m, \quad l = 0, 1 \ldots n_f - 1 \tag{6}$$

$$\theta_k = k \frac{2\pi}{n_o}, \quad k = 0, 1, \ldots n_o - 1, \tag{7}$$

where f_l and θ_k are the lth frequency and kth orientation. The magnitude of every response is reserved and integrates to generate the resulting image.

3.4 Classification by HNN-DT

The classification accuracy rate can be improved by training classification algorithms with these features. To categories the forgeries photographs, the classification procedure is carried out in which extracted features are given as input to the classification. To categories the counterfeit and original images, a blend of neural network and decision tree was used. In a decision tree, the best tree is chosen and trained using a neural network to classify images (forgery).

3.5 Decision Tree

A decision tree is a classification method for existing data that is adaptable and does not require any space learning [16]. It can handle high-dimensional data since it is versatile and does not require any space learning. A decision tree is the visual representation of a scientific and quantitative categorization and theory technique for a dataset. A decision tree is a tree-shaped diagram that has been altered to apply the action strategy or statistical probability. Each branch of the decision tree represents a possible decision that could lead to another trademark until it reaches a leaf node. Each branch of the decision tree indicates the objective value, which is marked by a leaf, with input components supplied at each branch.

The tree learning method of the decision tree specifies that the source is split into subsets iteratively until leaf level is achieved. A decision tree classifier iteratively splits the training set into sections, with the goal of ensuring that the vast majority of the records are of relative class. The algorithm starts at the root node with the complete dataset. The dataset is divided into subgroups using splitting criteria that leverage legitimate systems like as entropy, Gini index, and gain ratio, among others. The dataset's splitting is completed by selecting the property that best separates the remaining nodes into the various classes.

3.6 Neural Network

The selected input image (best tree) from the decision tree is forwarded to the NN [18–35] for classifying the forgery image. A neural network is a biological approach depends on the progression of the biological nervous system and it be similar to the human mind function. These frameworks are data allowance method and are propelled coincidentally as the human intelligence process. The essential managing components of neural networks are denoted as artificial neurons and it comprises of certain possessions of neural networks. It is a versatile framework that progressions its design depends on internal or external information that streams from end to end through the framework. Learning in the hereditary or biological system includes a shift in synaptic relations that exists among neurons in neural systems. They are prevailing devices for displaying especially when the original data relationship isn't perceived. After training, they can be utilized to estimate the outcome of new independent input data. Figure 3 denotes the neural network model which comprises of N inputs to the system and linked weights up to W_N. According to the mathematical approach of the neural network, the synapses effect are denoted by connection weights that adapt the related input signals and the nonlinear characteristics demonstrate by the neurons which are denoted by transfer function [12]. In this approach, the weights are related to the learning ability of the system [26–36].

The two types of feature vectors are gathered for training the neural network which includes that one from original images database and another one from the forged images database. ANN consists of 20 input neurons and 1 output neuron with 8 hidden neurons and remaining 300 are used to test the ANN.

4 Experimental Results

The performance of the proposed method hybrid neural network with decision tress based on feature extraction Gabor filter with Center Symmetric Local Binary Pattern is simulated by MATLAB Tool under windows environment. In this research work, feature extraction process is compared and fed to the classification process to classify

Fig. 3 Neural network model

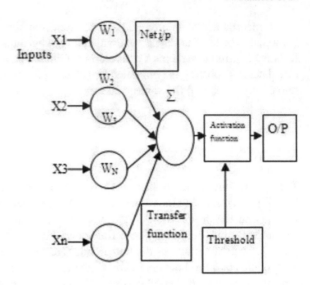

the forgery image. The feature extraction of Gabor filter with Center Symmetric Local Binary Pattern is compared with the existing SURF with Principal Component Analysis to evaluate the classification accuracy. Randomly input image is selected and the proposed method techniques such as preprocessing, feature extraction, similarity matching, and HNN-DT classification techniques are implemented. The results are compared with certain performance metrics to evaluate the performance of proposed method.

4.1 Description of Dataset

The CoMoFoD database is collected from the publicly available dataset, resized and forwarded to the process of the proposed method. The input images are selected randomly by proposed HNN-DT and images has been trained and tested. Each dataset are split into five sets. In each set contains 300 images, in that, 150 original images and 150 forgery images.

4.2   Performance Evaluation

The performance of proposed HNN-DT with feature extraction GF-CSLBP is evaluated and compared with HNN-DT with SURF and PCA by certain performance metrics such as accuracy, sensitivity, specificity, F-measure, and G-mean. The CoMoFoD database is split into five sets for each image on each set performance metrics is applied and evaluated. Figures 4 and 6 show the process of a simulation result of forgery and authenticate image which undergoes a process of proposed method as preprocessing and feature extraction image (Figs. 5, 6, 7, 8, 9 and 10).

Input Image   Forgery Image

Pre-processed Image   Feature Extraction Image

Fig. 4 Simulation result for the detection of forgery image

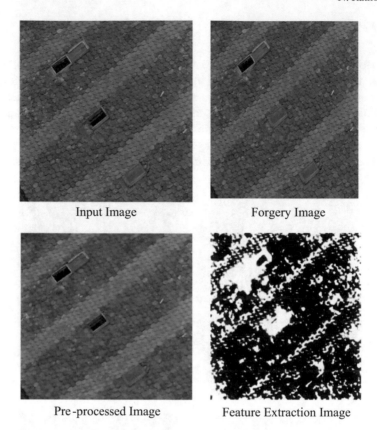

Input Image   Forgery Image

Pre-processed Image   Feature Extraction Image

Fig. 5 Detection of original image

Table 1 shows the comparison of proposed method HNN-DT with feature extraction of Gabor filter and Center Symmetric Local Binary Pattern for each input set. The proposed method is evaluated in terms of certain performance metrics such as true positive, true negative, false positive, false negative for estimation of accuracy, sensitivity, specificity, F-measure, and G-mean for each set of CoMoFoD database [25, 26, 28, 32–39].

Figures 11, 12 and 13 shows the performance comparison of proposed HNN-DT (GF-CSLBP) with existing HNN-DT (SURF-PCA), HELM-FSK, IRVM and HMM-SVM in terms of performance metrics such as accuracy, sensitivity, specificity, F-measure, and G-mean. It is clear that the proposed method obtains better result when compared to other existing methods [18–55].

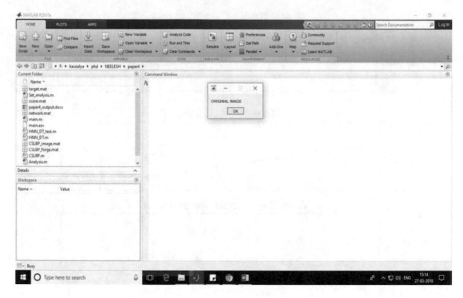

Fig. 6 Simulation result for the detection of authentic image

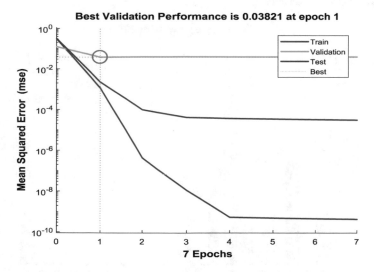

Fig. 7 Simulation result of performance of proposed method

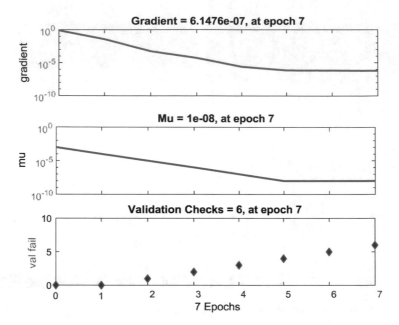

Fig. 8 Training state of input image

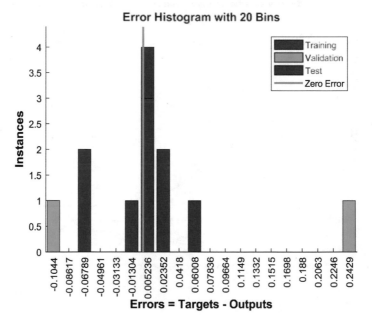

Fig. 9 Histogram estimation of input image

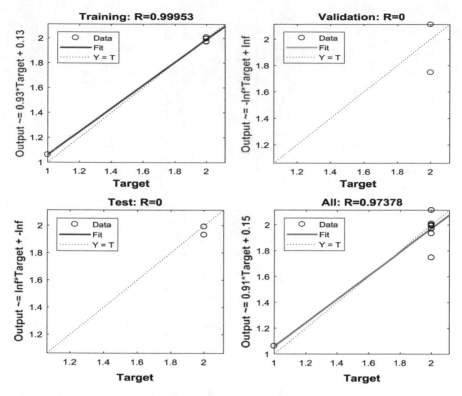

Fig. 10 Regression result of input image

5 Conclusion

Due to rising development of image processing tools image forgery can be performed very easily. Copy-move forgery is the highly popular tampering method. The implemented proposed method reduces the computational complexity and improves the high classification accuracy. In this work, feature extraction process is compared to evaluate the classification accuracy. The preprocessing by the weighted median filter to reduce noise and feature extraction by Gabor filter with Center Symmetric Local Binary Pattern. The extracted feature vector is matched by Manhattan distance and fed tot eh HNN-DT classifier to classify the forgery and authenticate image. The resultant image is evaluated and compared with the existing methods in terms of performance metrics and the proposed method shows the efficient result in forgery image classification. In this work proposed HNN-DT feature extraction of GF-CSLBP is compared with HNN-DT with SURF-PCA and it achieves the efficient classification results

Table 1 HNN-DT with GF-CFS performance comparison for each set

Input set	Number of authentic images	Number of forged images	T_p	T_n	F_p	F_n	Accuracy (%)	Sensitivity (%)	Specificity (%)	F-measure (%)	G-mean (%)
Set-1	150	150	132	137	18	11	92	87.3	98.3	95.5	93.6
Set-2	150	150	139	141	19	12	93.6	89.5	95.2	96.3	94.4
Set-3	150	150	141	145	21	13	94	95.22	93.2	97.4	95.4
Set-4	150	150	145	145	25	15	96	96.8	92.8	97.8	95.4
Set-5	150	150	148	141	23	18	98.9	97.4	91.8	98.3	96.1

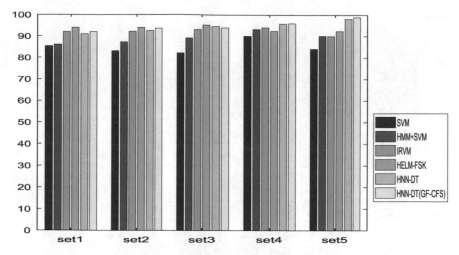

Fig. 11 Accuracy comparison of proposed method

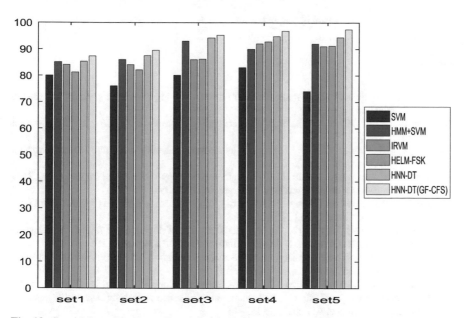

Fig. 12 Sensitivity comparison of proposed method

with highly robust and less computational complexity. In future, such methods can be developed which are robust to post processing operations applied to images with less complexity.

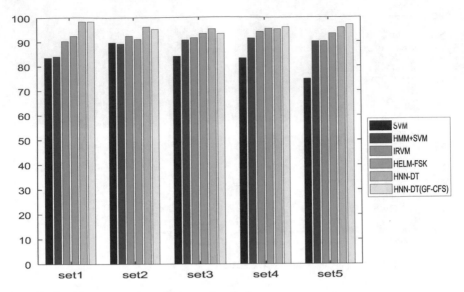

Fig. 13 Specificity comparison of proposed method

References

1. Ganesan C, Bhuma VR. Digital image forgery detection using color illumination and decision tree classification
2. Kurmi M (2017) New copy-move image forgery detection based on DCT. Int J Adv Res Comput Sci 8(5)
3. Birajdar GK, Mankar VH (2013) Digital image forgery detection using passive techniques: a survey. Digit Investig 10(3):226–245
4. Kashyap A, Agarwal M, Gupta H (2017) Detection of copy-move image forgery using SVD and cuckoo search algorithm. arXiv preprint arXiv:1704.00631
5. Kaur M, Walia S (2016) Forgery detection using noise estimation and hog feature extraction. Int J Multimed Ubiquitous Eng 11(4):37–48
6. Singh S, Agrawal S, Singh G (2016) Accuracy detection of digital image forgery by using ant colony optimization technique. MATEC Web Conf 57. EDP Sciences
7. Ujjainiya U, Chugh S (2016) Digital image forgery detection based on texture feature and clustering technique. Int J Comput Appl 147(11)
8. Swetha GR, Kishore MR (2015) Machine-learning algorithm for digital image forgeries by illumination color classification. In: International conference on industrial scientific research engineering conference, Apr 2015, pp 149–152
9. Kaur H, Babbar G. Copy move forgery detection using discrete cosine transform and bacterial foraging optimization
10. Cozzolino D, Gragnaniello D, Verdoliva L (2013) Image forgery detection based on the fusion of machine learning and block-matching methods. arXiv preprint arXiv:1311.6934
11. Kumar S, Desai J, Mukherjee S (2013) A fast DCT based method for copy move forgery detection. In: 2013 IEEE second international conference on image information processing (ICIIP), Dec 2013. IEEE, pp 649–654
12. Xu B, Liu G, Dai Y (2012) A fast image copy-move forgery detection method using phase correlation. In: 2012 fourth international conference on multimedia information networking and security (MINES), Nov 2012. IEEE, pp 319–322

13. Pan X, Zhang X, Lyu S (2011) Exposing image forgery with blind noise estimation. In: Proceedings of the thirteenth ACM multimedia workshop on multimedia and security, Sept 2011. ACM, pp 15–20
14. Peng F, Wang XL (2010) Digital image forgery forensics by using blur estimation and abnormal hue detection. In: 2010 symposium on photonics and optoelectronic (SOPO), June 2010. IEEE, pp 1–4
15. Chen J, Kang X, Liu Y, Wang ZJ (2015) Median filtering forensics based on convolutional neural networks. IEEE Signal Process Lett 22(11):1849–1853
16. Xu Q, Yang J, Ding S (2005) Texture segmentation using LBP embedded region competition. Electron Lett Comput Vis Image Anal (ELCVIA) 5(1):41–47
17. Vinod Kumar RS. A comparative analysis of histogram of gradient (HOG), Gabor filter bank and DCT based feature extraction methods used for fingerprint recognition
18. Rathore NK (2016) Faults in grid. Int J Softw Comput Sci Eng 1(1):1–19
19. Rathore NK (2016) Installation of Alchemi.NET in computational grid. J Comput Sci (JCOM) 4(2):1–5
20. Rathore NK (2016) Ethical hacking & security against cyber crime. J Inf Technol (JIT) 5(1):7–11
21. Rathore NK (2015) Efficient agent based priority scheduling and load balancing using fuzzy logic in grid computing. J Comput Sci (JCOM) 3(3):11–22
22. Rathore NK (2015) Map reduce architecture for grid. J Softw Eng (JSE) 10(1):21–30
23. Rathore NK (2015) GridSim installation and implementation process. J Cloud Comput (JCC) 2(4):29–40
24. Rathore NK, Chana I (2013) Report on hierarchal load balancing technique in grid environment. J Inf Technol (JIT) 2(4):21–35. ISSN Print: 2277-5110
25. Rathore NK, Chana I (2010) Checkpointing algorithm in Alchemi.NET. Pragyaan J Inf Technol 8(1):32–38. ISSN: 0974-5513. In: IEEE, CSI and MPCET, Dehradun, June 2010. IMS Dehradun
26. Jain N, Rathore NK, Mishra A (2017) An efficient image forgery detection using biorthogonal wavelet transform and singular value decomposition. In: 5th international conference on advance research applied science, environment, agriculture & entrepreneurship development (ARASEAED), Bhopal, Janparishad, 04–06 Dec 2017. JMBVSS & International Council of People, Bhopal, pp 274–281
27. Rathore NK, Chana I (2013) A sender initiate based hierarchical load balancing technique for grid using variable threshold value. In: International conference on IEEE-ISPC, 26–28 Sept 2013, pp 1–6. ISBN: 978-1-4673-6188-0
28. Rathore NK, Chana I (2011) A cognitive analysis of load balancing technique with job migration in grid environment. In: World congress on information and communication technology (WICT), IEEE proceedings paper, Dec 2011. IEEE, Mumbai, pp 77–82. ISBN: 978-1-4673-0127-5, e-book 978-1-4673-0125-1. https://doi.org/10.1109/WICT.2011.6141221
29. Rathore N (2015) Efficient load balancing algorithm in grid. In: 30th M.P. Young scientist congress, Bhopal, 28 Feb 2015, p 56
30. Rathore NK (2014) Efficient hierarchical load balancing technique based on grid. In: 29th M.P. Young scientist congress, Bhopal, 28 Feb 2014, p 55
31. Chouhan R, Rathore NK (2012) Comparison of load balancing technique in grid. In: 17th annual conference of Gwalior academy of mathematical science and national symposium on computational mathematics & information technology, JUET, Guna, 7–9 Dec 2012
32. Rathore NK, Chana I (2010) Fault tolerance algorithm in Alchemi.NET middleware. In: National conference on education & research (ConFR10), third CSI national conference of CSI division V, Bhopal chapter, 6–7 Mar 2010, JUIT, India. IEEE Bombay, MPCST, Bhopal
33. Rathore NK, Chana I (2009) Checkpointing algorithm in Alchemi.NET. In: Annual conference of Vijnana Parishad of India and national symposium recent development in applied mathematics & information technology, Dec 2009. JUET, Guna
34. Rathore NK, Chana I (2008) Comparative analysis of checkpointing. In: PIMR third national IT conference, IT enabled practices and emerging management paradigm book and category

is communication technologies and security issues, pp 32–35, topic no/name 46. Prestige Management & Research, Indore

35. Rathore NK, Chana I (2018) An efficient load balancing technique for grid. Scholar's Press, Mauritius. Project id: 6621. ISBN: 978-3-330-65134-0

36. Rathore NK, Singh P (2016) An efficient load balancing algorithm in distributed networks. Lambert Academic Publication House (LBA), Germany. ISBN: 978-3-659-78892-5

37. Rathore NK, Chohan R (2016) An enhancement of GridSim architecture with load balancing. Scholar's Press. Project id: 4900. ISBN: 978-3-639-76989-0

38. Rathore NK, Sharma A (2015) Efficient dynamic distributed load balancing technique. Lambert Academic Publication House, Germany. Project ID: 127478. ISBN: 978-3-659-78288-6

39. Rathore NK, Chana I (2010) Checkpointing algorithm in Alchemi.NET. Lambert Academic Publication House (LBA), Germany. ISBN-10: 3843361371

40. Rathore N (2018) Performance of hybrid load balancing algorithm in distributed web server system. Wireless Pers Commun 101(4):1233–1246

41. Jain N, Rathore N, Mishra A (2017) An efficient image forgery detection using biorthogonal wavelet transform and improved relevance vector machine with some attacks. Interciencia J 42(11):95–120

42. Rathore N (2016) Dynamic threshold based load balancing algorithms. Wireless Pers Commun 91(1):151–185

43. Rathore N, Chana I (2016) Job migration policies for grid environment. Wireless Pers Commun 89(1):241–269

44. Rathore N, Chana I (2015) Variable threshold-based hierarchical load balancing technique in grid. Eng Comput 31(3):597–615

45. Sharma V, Kumar R, Rathore NK (2015) Topological broadcasting using parameter sensitivity based logical proximity graphs in coordinated ground-flying ad hoc networks. J Wireless Mob Netw Ubiquitous Comput Depend Appl (JoWUA) 6(3):54–72

46. Rathore N, Chana I (2014) Load balancing and job migration techniques in grid: a survey of recent trends. Wireless Pers Commun 79(3):2089–2125

47. Rathore N, Chana I (2014) Job migration with fault tolerance based QoS scheduling using hash table functionality in social grid computing. J Intell Fuzzy Syst 27(6):2821–2833

48. Rathore NK, Khan F (2018) Internet of things: a review. J Cloud Comput (JCC) 5(1):20–25. ISSN Print: 2349-6835, ISSN Online: 2350-1308

49. Rathore NK, Khan F (2018) Survey of IoT. J Cloud Comput (JCC) 1(1):1–13

50. Rathore NK, Singh PK (2017) A comparative analysis of fuzzy based load balancing algorithm. J Comput Sci (JCS) 5(2):23–33

51. Rathore NK, Singh H (2017) Analysis of grid simulators architecture. J Mob Appl Technol (JMT) 4(2):32–41

52. Rathore NK (2016) Checkpointing: fault tolerance mechanism. J Cloud Comput (JCC) 3(4):27–34

53. Rathore NK (2017) A review towards: load balancing techniques. J Power Syst Eng (JPS) 4(4):47–60

54. Gugulothu VK, Mohan Rao SK (2020) Classification of IRS LISS-III images by using artificial neural networks. Int J Emerg Technol Adv Eng 10(4):24–31. ISSN: 2250-2459

55. Hamid MS, Manap NA, Hamzah RA, Kadmin AF (2021) Stereo matching algorithm based on hybrid convolutional neural network and directional intensity difference. Int J Emerg Technol Adv Eng 11(6):87–97. ISSN: 2250-2459

56. Gomathi R (2017) Forged image detection by analyzing edge, visual saliency and textural features using SVM classifier

57. Marra F, Poggi G, Roli F, Sansone C, Verdoliva L (2015) Counter-forensics in machine learning based forgery detection. In: Media watermarking, security, and forensics 2015, Mar 2015, vol 9409. International Society for Optics and Photonics, p 94090L

58. Sokolova M, Japkowicz N, Szpakowicz S (2006) Beyond accuracy, F-score and ROC: a family of discriminant measures for performance evaluation. In: Australasian joint conference on artificial intelligence. Springer, Berlin, Heidelberg, pp 1015–1021

59. Hsu Y-F, Chang S-F (2006) Detecting image splicing using geometry invariants and camera characteristics consistency. In: 2006 IEEE international conference on multimedia and expo. IEEE, pp 549–552
60. Shi YQ, Chen C, Chen W (2007) A natural image model approach to splicing detection. In: Proceedings of the 9th workshop on multimedia & security. ACM, pp 51–62
61. Fridrich J, Soukal BD, Lukas AJ (2003) Detection of copy move forgery in digital images. In: Proceedings of the digital forensic research workshop, Cleveland, OH, Aug 2003
62. Muhammad G, Hussain M, Bebis G (2012) Passive copy move image forgery detection using undecimated dyadic wavelet transform. Digit Investig 9(1):49–57
63. Zheng N, Wang Y, Xu M (2013) A LBP based method for detecting copy-move forgery with rotation. Springer Science, pp 261–267
64. Zhang Y, Zhao C, Pi Y, Li S (2012) Revealing image splicing forgery using local binary patterns of DCT coefficients. In: Communications, signal processing, and systems. Springer, New York, pp 181–189

Dynamic Deployment Approach to Maximizing Probabilistic Area Coverage in Randomly Scattered WSNs

Mrutyunjay Rout

1 Introduction

Wireless sensor networks (WSNs) have recently come into prominence due to their numerous exciting features such as scalability, self-organization, easy deployment, multicast routing, self-healing, low-complexity, and energy efficiency. For these reasons, they are well suited for many applications such as monitoring of movement of wild animal, target tracking, disaster management, precision agriculture, military surveillance, intrusion detection, manufacturing and business asset management. A WSN is formed by a large number of inexpensive, compact size, low-power, and multifunctional wireless sensor nodes. Usually, the wireless sensor nodes are scattered in the area of interest to collect and process some useful data about the physical world and transmit these data to the nearby base stations through single-hop or multi-hop communications. The performance of a sensor network mainly depends on the sensor deployment in the field of interest [1–6]. The selection of deployment strategy mainly depends on the type of application, the environment, and the sensors. For instance, the applications such as forest fire detection, disaster management, border protection, and battlefield surveillance, the sensor nodes are dropped from aircraft. This random deployment may not good enough to ensure the network coverage and connectivity. Therefore, it is necessary that the sensor nodes have locomotion capability, and with some energy efficient self-adjustment algorithms, which results the nodes in the network can self-adjust, starting from the initial random state to the optimal state. In this paper, an energy efficient auto-adjustment and obstacle avoidance distributed algorithm is proposed to enhance the probabilistic area coverage while maintaining. Simulation results carried out with the proposed algorithm not only improves the probabilistic area coverage but also ensures the network connectivity.

M. Rout (✉)
National Institute of Technology Jamshedpur, Jamshedpur, India
e-mail: mrutyunjay.ece@nitjsr.ac.in

© The Author(s), under exclusive license to Springer Nature Singapore Pte Ltd. 2023   497
K. Kumar Singh et al. (eds.), *Machine Vision and Augmented Intelligence*, Lecture Notes
in Electrical Engineering 1007, https://doi.org/10.1007/978-981-99-0189-0_38

The proposed algorithm is localized and executed at each sensor node. In the proposed scheme, each sensor node act as a virtual charge particle and considers all attractive and repulsive virtual forces due to its connected neighbors, obstacles, and the sensing field boundary to compute its location for improvement of probabilistic area coverage while maintaining connectivity with less power consumption.

In the next section, concept of probabilistic area coverage is outlined. Our proposed deployment algorithm, Probabilistic Coverage Virtual Force Algorithm (PCVFA) has been described in Sect. 3. In Sect. 4, simulation results and performance analysis are presented followed by conclusions in Sect. 5.

2 Probabilistic Area Coverage

Network coverage is one of the important aspects to evaluate the performance of the sensor networks. Coverage problem in WSNs is caused mainly due to shortage of sensor nodes to cover the whole region of interest (ROI), limited sensing range, and random deployment of sensor nodes. As reported in various literatures [1–4], coverage can broadly be categorized as blanket or area coverage, point or target coverage, and barrier coverage. Area coverage or blanket coverage ensure that each and every single point within the field of interest must be monitored by at least one sensor node or by the joint detection of several sensor nodes, whereas point coverage or target coverage monitors fixed number of targets in the field of interest. Usually, point coverage is used to monitoring of enemy troops and bases. The purpose of barrier coverage is to detecting intrusion on a given area. In barrier coverage, sensor nodes have to form a dense barrier in order to detect each event that crosses the barrier such as detection of illegal intrusion across the international borders. Most of the researchers [1, 4, 7–20], used the notion of area coverage for solving the coverage problem in WSNs.

Definition 1 (*Coverage ratio*) It is the ratio of the sensible area by the sensor nodes to the entire area of ROI.

To a large extent, the area coverage of WSNs depends on the sensing model of sensor nodes. There are various sensing models are reported in literature [6–9, 12, 21]. In most of the previous works [3, 4, 6], binary or disk sensing model is used for coverage calculation for its simplicity. According to this model, an event is detected by a sensor node if it occurs within its sensing range. But this model is not suitable in real world applications because it does not consider the uncertainty in the sensing process. To overcome this problems, probabilistic sensing model [7, 8, 12, 21] is used. According to this model, the probability of detection of an event follows an exponential function of distance from the sensor as expressed in (1).

$$C_{xy}(p, s_i) = \begin{cases} 0 & \text{if } d(s_i, p) \geq (R_s + R_e) \\ e^{-\lambda \alpha^\beta} & \text{if } (R_s - R_e) < d(s_i, p) < (R_s + R_e) \\ 1 & \text{if } d(s_i, p) \leq (R_s - R_e) \end{cases} \tag{1}$$

Fig. 1 Relationship between the parameters, λ and β

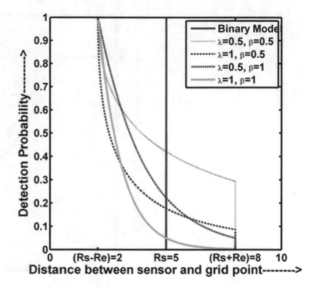

where $C_{xy}(p, s_i)$ represent the detection probability of a point $p(x, y)$ covered by the sensor node s_i, $d(s_i, p)$ is the distance between the point p and the sensor node s_i, R_s is the sensing range of the sensor node s_i, $R_e (R_e < R_s)$ defines the uncertain range in sensor detection, $\alpha = d(s_i, P) - (R_s - R_e)$, λ, and β are the parameters related to the sensors' hardware properties. The relationship between the parameters, λ and β is shown in Fig. 1.

From Fig. 1 it is cleared that, different values of λ and β yield different translations reflected by different detection probabilities. It is also observed that there is a jump transition of detection probability in the end, which is not practical. To overcome this, a modified probabilistic sensing model is used which is expressed in (2). This model [7, 21] provides smooth continuity of detection probability as shown in Fig. 2.

$$C_{xy}(p, s_i) = \begin{cases} 0 & \text{if } d(s_i, P) \geq (R_s + R_e) \\ e^{\left((-\alpha\lambda_1^{\beta_1}/\lambda_2^{\beta_2})\right)} & \text{if } (R_s - R_e) < d(s_i, P) < (R_s + R_e) \\ 1 & \text{if } d(s_i, P) \leq (R_s - R_e) \end{cases} \tag{2}$$

In the above equation $\lambda_1 = d(s_i, P) - (R_s - R_e)$ and $\lambda_2 = (R_s + R_e) - d(s_i, P)$; α, β_1, and β_2 are the parameters that measure the detection probability when a target is at a distance greater than $(R_s - R_e)$, but within a distance $(R_s + R_e)$ from the sensor and their values are set according to the physical properties of the sensor. The detection probabilities for various values of α, β_1, and β_2 are shown in Fig. 2.

Suppose N sensor nodes $s_1, s_2, s_3, \ldots, s_N$ are deployed randomly over an A_x by A_y sensing field and probabilistic sensor model given in (2) is used for coverage calculation. It is observed that, the grid points within ROI are not uniformly covered with the same probability due to the uncertainty in sensor detection responses. Since a point might be covered by multiple sensors at the same time, each contributing

Fig. 2 Relationship between the parameters, α, β_1, and β_2

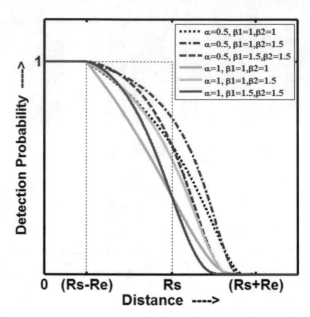

a certain value of coverage. Thus, for coverage calculation we considered joint detection probability as expressed in (3).

$$C_{xy}(p, S_N) = 1 - \prod_{i=1}^{N}\big(1 - \big(C_{xy}(p, s_i)\big)\big) \tag{3}$$

The term $\big(1 - \big(C_{xy}(p, s_i)\big)\big)$ is the probability that the point $P(x_i, y_i)$ is not covered by the node s_i. Since the detection probability of a point by any node is independent of other then the joint probability of the point not being covered by N nodes is $\prod_{i=1}^{N}\big(1 - \big(C_{xy}(p, s_i)\big)\big)$. Hence, one minus this product gives the probability that point p is covered by at least one of the neighboring nodes and is defined as its total coverage.

Definition 2 (*Probabilistic point coverage*) A point $p(x, y)$ is said to be probabilistically covered by N sensors if the joint detection probability is larger than a predefined threshold C_{th} ($0 < C_{th} \leq 1$), i.e.,

$$C_{xy}(p, S_N) = 1 - \prod_{i=1}^{N}\big(1 - \big(C_{xy}(p, s_i)\big)\big) \geq C_{th}. \tag{4}$$

Definition 3 (*Probabilistic area coverage*) An area A is probabilistically covered by N sensors if $C_{xy}(p, S_N) = 1 - \prod_{i=1}^{N}\big(1 - \big(C_{xy}(p, s_i)\big)\big) \geq C_{th}$ for every point $P(x, y)$ in A.

3 Proposed Scheme

The proposed Probabilistic Coverage Virtual Force Algorithm (PCVFA) is based on the following assumptions. They are: (i) All the sensor nodes have locomotion capability and can move effectively to any direction and any distance within the sensing boundary, (ii) Each sensor node has one unique ID, (iii) All sensors are equipped with localization system (i.e., GPS) to know their location, (iv) Every sensor node is able to acquire the relative position of their connected neighbors, (v) The sensing field is a square sized area demarcated with a clear boundary, (vi) The sensing field contains obstacles of different shapes and sizes, and (vii) Every sensor node is able to detect the shape and position of any obstacles in its sensing range and can calculate the nearest distance from the obstacle by using the time-of-flight method.

The main objective of our proposed PCVFA is to improve the probabilistic area coverage while maintaining connectivity but also to reduce the moving energy requirement in the presence of various obstacles in ROI. In this work, each sensor node s_i is subjected to an attractive or repulsive force ($\overrightarrow{F_{ij}}$) by its connected neighbor sensor node s_j, a repulsive force $\overrightarrow{F_{iO_m}}$ by an obstacle O_m, and a repulsive force $\overrightarrow{F_{ib}}$ by sensing field boundaries. Thus, the net force acting on the sensor node s_i is calculated as in (5).

$$\overrightarrow{F_i} = \sum_{j=1, j \neq i}^{K} \overrightarrow{F_{ij}} + \sum_{m=1}^{N_0} \overrightarrow{F_{iO_m}} + \overrightarrow{F_{ib}} \tag{5}$$

where K is the number of connected neighbor sensor nodes of s_i and N_0 is the number of obstacles that are within the sensing range of s_i in the ROI. The position of each sensor nodes s_i is updated by considering the total force $\overrightarrow{F_i}$ as in (6).

$$x_{iN} = x_{iP} + F_{ix}; \quad y_{iN} = y_{iP} + F_{iy} \tag{6}$$

where (x_{iP}, y_{iP}) and (x_{iN}, y_{iN}) represent the coordinates of the current location and updated location of sensor node s_i respectively; F_{ix} and F_{iy} denote the x and y directional components, respectively, of the displacement of sensor node s_i goes through as it is subjected to the force $\overrightarrow{F_i}$. The maximum distance traveled by a sensor node in each step is decided by its speed. The proposed algorithm is given in Algorithm 1. The proposed algorithm is localized and is executed at each sensor node s_i. Each sensor node ceases its movement if it oscillates within a predefined threshold distance for a specific duration of time.

Algorithm 1 Probabilistic coverage virtual force algorithm (PCVFA)

Notation
N_i = No. of connected neighbors of s_i
P_i = Position vector of sensor node s_i
P_j = Position vector of connected neighbor s_j
d_{th} = Optimal threshold distance between any two active nodes ($< R_c$)
$d_{th\,obs}$ = Optimal threshold distance between sensor node and obstacle ($< R_s$)
$d_{th\,b}$ = Optimal threshold distance between sensor node and boundary of ROI ($< R_s$)
F_A = Attractive force coefficient
F_R = Repulsive force coefficient
Input
F_A
F_R
$d_{th\,obs}$
$d_{th\,b}$
d_{th} (Decided by probabilistic sensing model and R_c)
Process
1. Each sensor node s_i collect its position P_i through GPS or any localization method
2. List the connected neighbor N_i of s_i by sending HELLO message
3. Calculate Euclidean distance between s_i with each of its connected neighbors s_j, i.e., d_{ij}
4. **For** each connected neighbor j **do**
5. **if** $d_{ij} > d_{th}$ **then**
6. Calculate attractive force $\overrightarrow{F_{ij}} = \left(F_A\left(d_{ij} - d_{th}\right)\right)\left(\frac{P_j - P_i}{d_{ij}}\right)$
7. **else if** $d_{ij} < d_{th}$ **then**
8. Calculate repulsive force $\overrightarrow{F_{ij}} = \left(F_R\left(d_{th} - d_{ij}\right)\right)\left(\frac{P_i - P_j}{d_{ij}}\right)$
9. **else**
10. $\overrightarrow{F_{ij}} = 0$
11. **end if**
12. Calculate repulsive force due to boundary of ROI $\overrightarrow{F_{ib}} = (F_R(d_{th\,b} - d_{ib}), \alpha_{ib} + \pi)$
13. Calculate repulsive force $\overrightarrow{F_{iO_j}} = \left(F_R(d_{th\,obs} - d_{iO_j}), \alpha_{iO_j} + \pi\right)$ due to all obstacles that are within the sensing rage of s_i
14. Calculate total force $\overrightarrow{F_i} = \overrightarrow{F_{ij}} + \overrightarrow{F_{iO_j}} + \overrightarrow{F_{ib}}$
15. **end for**
16. Sensor s_i move to its new location depends of $\overrightarrow{F_i}$ and speed

4 Simulation Results and Discussion

The proposed algorithm is implemented in MATLAB platform. At beginning, all mobile sensor nodes are split into four groups and randomly deployed at the four corners of a 50 m × 50 m square shape sensing field with and without any obstacle as shown in Figs. 3 and 4. The final sensor positions after execution of PCVFA are presented in Figs. 5 and 6. The parameters used for simulation are given in Table 1.

From the above results, it is observed that at the end of the final deployment, no mobile sensor node remains outside the ROI and these nodes never stray beyond

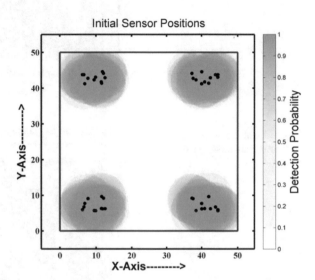

Fig. 3 Initial sensors' positions, with coverage rate 36.69%

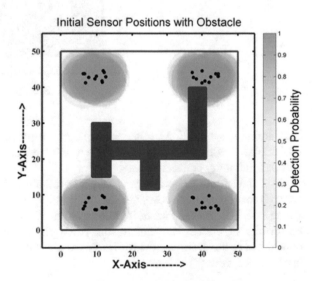

Fig. 4 Initial sensors' positions, with coverage rate 41.09%

Fig. 5 Final sensors' positions, with coverage rate 96.86%

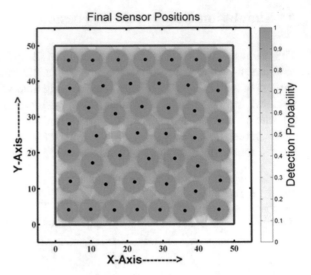

Final Sensor Positions

Fig. 6 Final sensors' positions, with coverage rate 96.73%

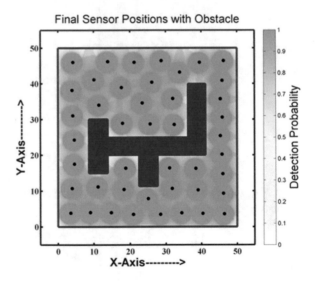

Final Sensor Positions with Obstacle

ROI during the execution of the self-deployment procedure. The sensor nodes are self-deployed with avoidance of obstacle to improve the probabilistic area coverage while maintaining connectivity.

To demonstrate the performance of proposed algorithm four aspects are considered: (i) coverage ratio or coverage rate, (ii) moving energy consumption, (iii) convergence rate, i.e., the number of iterations required to achieve steady state, and (iv) uniformity of the deployment. In this work, the moving energy consumption is considered as the average moving distance of all of the sensor nodes in each step and is calculated as in (7).

Table 1 Simulation parameters for homogeneous mobile sensor network

Parameter	Value
Field size	50 m × 50 m
Grid size	0.25 m × 0.25 m
Number of mobile sensor nodes	44
Max. speed of the sensor node	0.25 m/s
F_A	0.001
F_R	0.2
Sensing range (R_s)	5 m
Communication range $(R_c = 2R_s)$	10 m
Uncertain range in sensor detection $(R_e < R_s)$	2 m
α	1
β_1	1.5
β_2	1.5
$d_{th} = \sqrt{3}R_s$	8.6 m
$d_{th\,obs} = d_{th}/2$	4.3 m
$d_{th\,b} = d_{th}/2$	4.3 m
C_{th}	0.7

$$D_{avg} = \frac{\sum_{i=1}^{N}\sqrt{(x(i)_N - x(i)_P)^2 + (y(i)_N - y(i)_P)^2}}{N} \quad (7)$$

where (x_{iP}, y_{iP}) and (x_{iN}, y_{iN}) represent the coordinates of the current location and updated location of sensor node s_i, and N is the number of mobile sensor nodes deployed in the sensing field.

Uniformity is the average local standard deviation of the distance between nodes and the same is calculated as in (8)

$$U_i = \sqrt{\frac{1}{K_i}\sum_{j=1}^{K_i}(D_{ij} - \mu_i)^2} \quad (8)$$

where N is the total number of mobile nodes in the ROI, K_i represent the number of connected neighbors of the ith node, μ_i represent the mean distance among the connected neighbors of the ith node and D_{ij} is the distance between the ith node and its jth connected neighbor. Smaller the U value, more uniformly distributed are the sensor nodes. For performance evaluation, PCVFA is simulated for 50 independent initial random deployments and the average values are taken. We compare PCVFA with two existing algorithms IVFA and VFA proposed in [14]. The other two are algorithms available in the literature which are also applied in similar problems. Therefore, comparing the proposed algorithm with those is only a natural thing to do. Unlike those other algorithms like IVFA and VFA our proposed PCVFA can deal with the existence of multiple obstacles and forbidden zones of different shapes and sizes in the sensing field. The performance summary is documented in Table 2.

From Table 2, it is observed that PCVFA offers better performance under the probabilistic coverage as compared to the IVFA and VFA in all aspects.

5   Conclusion

We studied the area coverage of a randomly deployed mobile sensor network. The proposed approach is a localized self-deployment algorithm for area coverage with and without presence of obstacle. This algorithm works well in the scenarios of the random initial distribution of mobile sensor nodes to improve the probabilistic coverage area with minimal moving energy requirement in the presence of multiple obstacles of various shapes and sizes while maintaining radio connectivity. To prevent the sensor nodes from moving out of the sensing field boundary, a repulsive force is considered which is exerted inward by the sensing field boundary. PCVFA also consider repulsive forces exerted by obstacles to avoid collision with obstacles in the ROI. Simulation results demonstrate that the proposed approach provides better performance compared to the IVFA and VFA for self-deployment of homogeneous sensor nodes in a square shape sensing field in the presence and absence of obstacles.

Table 2 Performance summary for IVFA, EVFA, and PCVFA

Parameters	IVFA			VFA			PCVFA		
Number of sensors (N)	40	30	20	40	30	20	40	30	20
Average initial probabilistic coverage rate (%)	59.50	50.54	38.31	59.50	50.54	38.31	59.50	50.54	38.31
Average final probabilistic coverage rate (%)	95.10	79.85	52.52	94.46	78.04	52.25	96.82	81.77	55.55
Average number of iterations to achieve steady state	> 300	> 300	67	> 300	> 300	43	167	160	50
Average total moving distance (in m)	> 116.22	> 95.32	14.27	> 90.16	> 52.76	9.68	19.25	17.02	8.36
Final uniformity	0.77	0.26	0.04	0.80	0.28	0.12	0.71	0.46	0.29

References

1. Howard A, Matarić MJ, Sukhatme GS (2002) Mobile sensor network deployment using potential fields: a distributed, scalable solution to the area coverage problem. In: Proceedings of 6th international conference on distributed autonomous robotic systems (DARS), pp 299–308
2. Mulligan R, Ammari HM (2010) Coverage in wireless sensor networks: a survey. Netw Protoc Algor 2(2):27–53
3. Heo N, Varshney PK (2005) Energy-efficient deployment of intelligent mobile sensor networks. IEEE Trans Syst Man A Syst Hum 35(1):78–92
4. Zou Y, Chakrabarty K (2003) Sensor deployment and target localization based on virtual forces. In: Proceedings of IEEE INFOCOM, San Francisco, CA, Mar 2003, pp 1293–1303
5. Boukerche A, Sun P (2018) Connectivity and coverage-based protocols for wireless sensor networks. Ad Hoc Netw 80:54–69
6. Li M, Cheng W, Liu K, He Y, Li X, Liao X (2011) Sweep coverage with mobile sensors. IEEE Trans Mob Comput 10(11):1534–1545. Li XY, Wan PJ, Frieder O (2003) Coverage in wireless ad hoc sensor networks. IEEE Trans Comput 52(6):753–763
7. Li S, Xu C, Pan W, Pan Y (2005) Sensor deployment optimization for detecting maneuvering targets. In: Proceedings of 8th international conference on information fusion, July 2005, pp 1629–1635
8. Yang Q, He S, Li J, Chen J, Sun Y (2015) Energy-efficient probabilistic area coverage in wireless sensor networks. IEEE Trans Veh Technol 64(1):367–377
9. Chang R-S, Wang S-H (2008) Self-deployment by density control in sensor networks. IEEE Trans Veh Technol 57(3):1745–1755
10. Bai X, Yun Z, Xuan D, Lai TH, Jia W (2010) Optimal patterns for four-connectivity and full coverage in wireless sensor networks. IEEE Trans Mob Comput 9(3):435–448
11. Al-Karaki JN, Gawanmeh A (2017) The optimal deployment, coverage, and connectivity problems in wireless sensor networks: revisited. IEEE Access 5:18051–18065
12. Farsi M, Elhosseini MA, Badawy M, Arafat Ali H, Zain Eldin H (2019) Deployment techniques in wireless sensor networks, coverage and connectivity: a survey. IEEE Access 7:28940–28954
13. Razafindralambo T, Simplot-Ryl D (2011) Connectivity preservation and coverage schemes for wireless sensor networks. IEEE Trans Autom Control 56(10):2418–2428
14. Xie J, Wei D, Huang S, Bu X (2019) A sensor deployment approach using improved virtual force algorithm based on area intensity for multisensor networks. Math Probl Eng 2019, 9 pp. Article ID 8015309
15. Mei Y, Xian C, Das S, Hu YC, Lu Y-H (2007) Sensor replacement using mobile robots. J Comput Commun 30(13):2615–2626
16. Dhuli S, Gaurav K, Singh YN (2015) Convergence analysis for regular wireless consensus networks. IEEE Sens J 15(8):4522–4531
17. Mahfoudh S, Khoufi I, Minet P, Laouiti A (2013) Relocation of mobile wireless sensors in the presence of obstacles. In: Proceedings of the international conference on telecommunications (ICT), Morocco, pp 1–5
18. Li X, Frey H, Santoro N, Stojmenovic I (2011) Strictly localized sensor self-deployment for optimal focused coverage. IEEE Trans Parallel Distrib Syst 10(11):1520–1533
19. Tuna G, Gungor VC, Gulez K (2014) An autonomous wireless sensor network deployment system using mobile robots for human existence detection in case of disasters. Ad Hoc Netw 13:54–68
20. Adulyasas A, Sun Z, Wang N (2015) Connected coverage optimization for sensor scheduling in wireless sensor networks. IEEE Sens J 15(7):3877–3892
21. Hefeeda M, Ahmadi H (2010) Energy-efficient protocol for deterministic and probabilistic coverage in sensor networks. IEEE Trans Parallel Distrib Syst 21(5):579–593

Artificial Neural Network Based Image Fusion for Surveillance Application

Nirmala Paramanandham, A. Sasithradevi, J. Florence Gnana Poovathy, and V. Rakshana

1 Introduction

Digitalized images are source of information used for problem solving and simplification. Because of the fast evolution of image fusion mechanics, the infrared and visible image fusion had been generally identified for various applications. The infrared sensor notices the radiation, i.e., thermal radiation of the scenario and is found in a smudged background that contains low quality details of an image. In contrast, visible sensors can acquire larger ample of spectral data in order to transmit particular details of the image. Visible images may out-turn in dark and occluded condition in less satisfactory scenes. Henceforth combination of images is advantageous than viewing the input images separately [1].

Image fusion is the technique of integrating the details from many source images into a unique image. The generated image can give more extensive information on that particular scene and is more suitable for successive development tasks than any other origin images. The fused result must meet various specifications such as holding on to all appropriate and required details of origin images. The final fused image holds the enhanced information that will helpful in various applications [2–5]. The infrared images can seize the details of thermal radiation in places where the human eye cannot directly see them [6–8]. Image fusion combines the relevant details of multiple images and it is more suitable to human's visual interpretation. Several

N. Paramanandham (✉) · J. F. Gnana Poovathy
School of Electronics and Communication Engineering, Vellore Institute of Technology, Chennai, India
e-mail: nirmalavp.ece@gmail.com

V. Rakshana
Ramaiah Institute of Technology, Bengaluru, India

A. Sasithradevi
Centre for Advanced Data Science, Vellore Institute of Technology, Chennai, India

© The Author(s), under exclusive license to Springer Nature Singapore Pte Ltd. 2023
K. Kumar Singh et al. (eds.), *Machine Vision and Augmented Intelligence*, Lecture Notes in Electrical Engineering 1007, https://doi.org/10.1007/978-981-99-0189-0_39

fusion techniques are generally used in many applications such as target recognition, image classification, remote sensing, military and concealed weapon detection.

In this work, the input images are decomposed using Gaussian smoothness and joint bilateral filter. The edge and scaling information is utilized for separating the image details from source images. Two different fusion rules are utilized for obtaining the features from the visible and infrared images. The rules in the base layer are used to keep saliency information and detail layer is used for better human perception.

2 Literature Review

Liu et al. [9] suggested an image combination framework that is developed using multi-scale transform (MST) and sparse representation (SR). In this framework, MST is first applied to each pre-registered origin images in order to get low pass and high pass coefficients. These bands are combined using various fusion rules.

Shi et al. [10] proposed a comprehensive, enhanced fusion algorithm based on the smooth-inspired multi-scale decomposition through visual weight analysis. Visual weight maps are determined for each level of the scale of the images. At last, these levels are synthesized with appropriate weights. The resultant image shows the good accomplishment of the fusion algorithm and can easily enhance detailed image information.

Zhao et al. [11] developed a saliency detection algorithm based on pixel values and image decomposition based on information preservation. A weighted least squares filter is used to do multi-scale decomposition of the source images. A saliency map based on pixel values was constructed. By integrating different scales and synthetic weights, the final fused image can be reconstructed. Saliency extraction can well protect and enhance the knowledge and details of the original image. The developed image fusion algorithm yields better results when compared to many techniques that are discussed in the literature.

Lewis et al. [12] developed several fusion algorithms based on average, contrast pyramid, dual tree complex wavelet transform and discrete wavelet transform. These techniques are compared with the area-based image fusion method, which improves flexibility by defining a fusion rule, which makes the task easier. Despite the increased complexity the area-based methods are complex and compared with pixel-based methods, which has various advantages. Ability to handle areas of interest differently depending on various attributes. Wang et al. [13] proposed a methodology based on visual saliency map and weight least squares optimization for overcoming the limitations of traditional fusion techniques. The traditional averaging rule-based techniques, usually fails to utilize the residual low frequency information of the base layer. Therefore, visual saliency maps based on weighted average method are used for base layer fusion. The output combined image can show better appearance and contrast. Fusion of detailed layers based on optimization schemes to overcome the limitations of conventional maximum absolute fusion rules by considering different features of infrared and visible images. Thus, the fused image is more suitable for human visual perception. Yang et al. [14] assessed many multi-resolution transform-based image fusion techniques with various filters and decomposition levels. Performing each multi-resolution transformation, the best decomposition level will be constructed for multi-focus and multi-sensor images. Xing et al. [15] proposed an iterative decomposition method for combining multi-sensor images using various type of filters. By setting the intensity deviation to fuse the detail layers, the regional average energy weighting can be used to get multi-scale decision maps. Enough experiments are introduced to evaluate the fusion performance and experimental outcome validate the performance of this approached method. In this work a method of using ANN technology to fuse infrared and visible images is proposed. In order to obtain good contrast enhancement and well-organized target detection, artificial neural networks can be used to enhance the images.

Shehanaz et al. [16] proposed an optimum weighted average fusion for multisensory medical image fusion. The image decomposition technique being followed is discrete wavelet transform. Minimum loss is incurred while retrieving the original image. This is followed by the application of Particle Swarm Optimization (PSO) in order to calculate the optimum weighted values.

Chen et al. [17] developed an image contrast enhancement approach using artificial bee optimization algorithm (ABC). A new fitness function is also developed to assess the quality of enhanced image. The paper also establishes a parametric image transformation function so that only the optimal parameters used in transformation function are searched by the ABC.

Li et al. [18] developed a method that is based on multi-scale transformation and norm optimization. Pre-fusion image is decomposed using multi-level image decomposition method based on latent low-rank representation to get the base layer of final fused image. To get the detail layer, structural similarity index measure (SSIM) is used to calculate the validity of visible image detail information.

3   Proposed Methodology

The context of multi-scale decomposition iteration is shown in Fig. 1.

The enhanced fused image is obtained using artificial neural network and compared with the existing method. The main endowment of the work is summarized as:

(i)   Fusion performance is improved using multi-scale decomposition.
(ii) By using various filters, the original images are decomposed into four levels. It covers edge retention and scaling perception attributes for separating the structure of the content from the image details.
(iii) Equipped with two layers of rules for combination of base layer and detail layer. Utilizing decision rules, fused image is obtained. The fusion performance is evaluated using quantitative analysis.

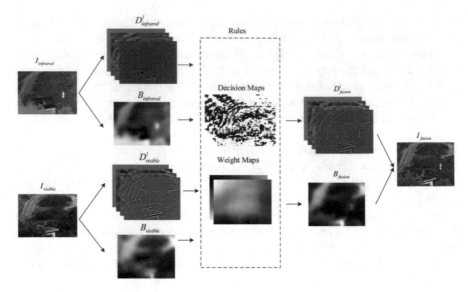

Fig. 1 Image fusion framework

(iv) To obtain the enhanced fused image, ANN is constructed. Given set of images are fused according to the category result of the ANN. Design enough experiments to estimate the performance, including the performance comparison of the existing method to improve the fusion performance with reduced complexity [15]. Experimental outcomes can efficiently evaluate the superior performance of the multi-scale decomposition method.

Artificial neural networks are the collection of connected units and able to learn from data sets. ANN acquires data samples instead of the entire data set to obtain a solution, thereby saving time and money. Artificial neural networks can enhance existing data analysis techniques. The artificial neural network has three layers connected to each other. The first layer consists of input neurons. These neurons send data to the second layer called the "hidden layer", which in turn sends output neurons to the third layer called the "output layer". The structure of ANN [19] is shown in Fig. 2.

Algorithm

(i) Infrared and visible images of the same scene are taken as input images.
(ii) Gaussian filter and Joint Bilateral filters are used for decomposition of the images.
(iii) Rule of base and detail layers takes place in each block of the images and fused image is obtained.
(iv) Neural network is trained using the features that are obtained from the base and detail layers.
(v) By using the trained neural network, the fused image is obtained.

Fig. 2 Structure of ANN [19]

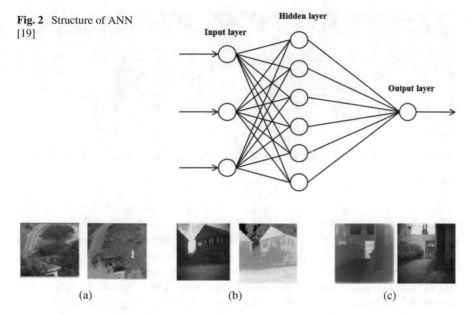

(a)   (b)   (c)

Fig. 3 Few set of visible and infrared images used in experiment (right: visible; left: infrared) **a** 'UN Camp'; **b** 'Marne-02'; **c** 'Kaptein-01'

(vi) Performance is analyzed by evaluating the parameters metrics from the fused image.

4 Experimental Results

The experimental results are explained more detailed step by step. The experiment was conducted on a computer equipped with a 3 GB memory requirement and a 1.87 GHz CPU. Some of the source images that are used in the experiment is shown in Fig. 3 [20]. The function fitting neural network is shown in Fig. 4.

Figure 5 shows some of the fused images obtained through proposed method. To evaluate the performance, quantitative analysis using various parameters [1, 21–26] has been done across set of images and the obtained results for few set of images are listed in Table 1. From the objective and subjective analysis, it is well-known that the proposed method achieves better fusion quality while reducing complexity.

5 Conclusions

This work proposed a framework for fusing visible and infrared images using multi-scale decomposition and iterative methods based on ANN. Joint bilateral and

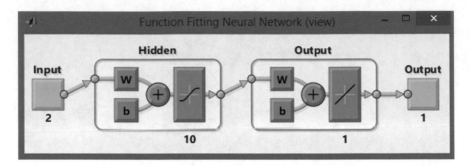

Fig. 4 Function fitting neural network

Gaussian smoothness filters are utilized for decomposing the images for preserving detailed information from the source images. The decomposed layers are combined based on the fusion rule. Using the Gaussian and Laplacian filters, saliency map was obtained. Further, a guided filter is utilized for finding the final weighing factors. ANN is utilized to generate the enhanced fused image. The proposed framework has been widely measured on various publicly available dataset. From the experimental results, it is concluded that better results can be obtained through the implemented technique.

Fig. 5 **a** Infrared image, **b** visible image, **c** fused image

Table 1 Quantitative analysis

Quantitative parameters	Proposed method			
En	6.7601	7.4408	7.3508	7.6326
QE	0.0710	0.1906	0.1356	0.0632
Xc	0.9999	0.9999	0.9999	0.9999
MSE	0.0867	0.2716	0.1046	0.0641
SNR	10.6179	5.6602	9.8042	11.9298
x-p	0.8973	0.4733	0.5548	0.3460
BRISQUE	47	47	47	47
IFC	4.3376	4.6692	4.5784	6.4057
B_NOISE	44.27	45.90	40.61	43.96
MI	0.9192	0.9590	1.713	1.9164

References

1. Paramanandham N, Rajendiran K (2018) Swarm intelligence based image fusion for noisy images using consecutive pixel intensity. Multimed Tools Appl 32133–32151
2. Pan L, Xie M, Ma Z (2008) Iris localization based on multi-resolution analysis. In: 2008 19th international conference on pattern recognition, pp 1–4
3. Zhou Z, Wang B, Li S, Dong M (2016) Perceptual fusion of infrared and visible images through a hybrid multi-scale decomposition with Gaussian and bilateral filters. Inf Fusion 30:15–26
4. Zhang Y, Zhang L, Bai X, Zhang L (2017) Infrared and visual image fusion through infrared feature extraction and visual information preservation. Infrared Phys Technol 83:227–237
5. Zhu P, Ma X, Huang Z (2017) Fusion of infrared-visible images using improved multi-scale top-hat transform and suitable fusion rules. Infrared Phys Technol 81:282–295
6. Zhao J, Chen Y, Feng H, Xu Z, Li Q (2014) Infrared image enhancement through saliency feature analysis based on multi-scale decomposition. Infrared Phys Technol 62:86–93
7. Budhiraja S, Sharma R, Agrawal S, Sohi BS (2021) Infrared and visible image fusion using modified spatial frequency-based clustered dictionary. Pattern Anal Appl 24:575–589
8. Zhang H, Ma J (2021) SDNet: a versatile squeeze-and-decomposition network for real-time image fusion. Int J Comput Vis 129:2761–2785
9. Liu Y, Liu S, Wang Z (2015) A general framework for image fusion based on multi-scale transform and sparse representation. Inf Fusion 24:147–164
10. Shi Z, Xu J, Zhao J, Xin Q (2015) Fusion for visible and infrared images using visual weight analysis and bilateral filter-based multi scale decomposition. Infrared Phys Technol 71:363–369
11. Zhao J, Zhou Q, Chen Y, Feng H, Xu Z, Li Q (2015) Fusion of visible and infrared images using saliency analysis and detail preserving based image decomposition. Infrared Phys Technol 56:93–99
12. Lewis JJ, O'Callaghan RJ, Nikolov SG, Bull DR, Canagarajah N (2007) Pixel level and region-based image fusion with complex wavelets. Inf Fusion 8(2):119–130
13. Ma J, Zhou Z, Wang B, Zong H (2017) Infrared and visible image fusion based on visual saliency map and weighted least square optimization. Infrared Phys Technol 82:8–17
14. Li S, Yang B, Hu J (2011) Performance comparison of different multi-resolution transforms for image fusion. Inf Fusion 12(2):74–84
15. Xing C, Wang Z, Meng F, Dong C (2018) Fusion of infrared and visible images with Gaussian smoothness and joint bilateral filtering iteration decomposition. IET Comput Vis 13(1):44–52
16. Shehanaz S, Daniel E, Guntur SR, Satrasupalli S (2021) Optimum weighted multimodal medical image fusion using particle swarm optimization. Optik 231:166413. https://doi.org/10.1016/j.ijleo.2021.166413

17. Chen J, Yu W, Tian J, Chen L, Zhou Z (2017) Image contrast enhancement using an artificial bee colony algorithm. Swarm Evol Comput. https://doi.org/10.1016/j.swevo.2017.09.002
18. Li G, Lin Y, Qu X (2021) An infrared and visible image fusion method based on multi-scale transformation and norm optimization. Inf Fusion 71:109–129. ISSN 1566-2535. https://doi.org/10.1016/j.inffus.2021.02.008
19. Yang CC, Prasher SO, Landry JA, DiTommaso A (2000) Application of artificial neural networks in image recognition and classification of crop and weeds. Can Agric Eng 42(3):147–152
20. https://figshare.com/articles/TNO_Image_Fusion_Dataset/1008029
21. Paramanandham N, Rajendiran K, Narayanan D, Indu Vadhani S, Anand M (2015) An efficient multi transform based fusion for multi focus images. In: IEEE ICCSP 2015
22. Paramanandham N, Rajendiran K (2017) Infrared and visible image fusion using discrete cosine transform and swarm intelligence for surveillance applications. Infrared Phys Technol. https://doi.org/10.1016/j.infrared.2017.11.006
23. Ma J, Ma Y, Li C (2019) Infrared and visible image fusion methods and applications: a survey. Inf Fusion 45:153–178
24. Zhang Q, Guo B-L (2009) Multifocus image fusion using the nonsubsampled contourlet transform. Signal Process 89(7):1334–1346
25. Li S, Kang X, Hu J (2013) Image fusion with guided filtering. IEEE Trans Image Process 22(7):2864–2875
26. Atyali RK, Khot SR (2016) An enhancement in detection of brain cancer through image fusion. In: 2016 IEEE international conference on advances in electronics, communication and computer technology (ICAECCT), pp 438–442

Experimental Result Analysis of Extreme Learning Machine with Various Activation Functions: An Application in Credit Scoring

Diwakar Tripathi, Y. C. A. Padmanabha Reddy,
Shailendra Kumar Tripathi, B. Ramachandra Reddy,
and Ram Kishan Dewangan

1 Introduction

In arising nations like India where per-capita income is generally low when contrasted with developed nations, the greater part of the populace relies upon minor or huge funds from monetary foundations to achieve their monetary prerequisites. The conventional process for attaining financial support from monetary foundations in the early days encompasses an extensive documentation, by which it results a slow verification process and it involves a huge manual effort. In this way, a credit scoring framework by utilizing AI and ML for handling the credit applications can be accomplished faster. Statistical or machine learning techniques are applicable for the determination of risk associated with credit products and credit scoring [18]. According to Thomas et al. [24], "Credit scoring is a set of decision models and their underlying techniques that aid credit lenders in the granting of credit" [25]. Based on criminal behavior and omission, it attempts to preserve the impact of the characteristic of

D. Tripathi (✉)
Indian Institute of Information Technology Sonepat, Sonepat, Haryana, India
e-mail: diwakarnitgoa@gmail.com

Y. C. A. P. Reddy
B V Raju Institute of Technology, Medak, Telangana, India

S. K. Tripathi
Government PG College Satna, Satna, Madhya Pradesh, India
e-mail: shailendrat027@gmail.com

B. Ramachandra Reddy
National Institute of Technology Jamshedpur, Jamshedpur, Jharkhand, India
e-mail: brreddy@iiitdmj.ac.in

R. K. Dewangan
Department of ECED, Thapar Institute of Engineering and Technology, Patiala, India
e-mail: ram.kishan@thapar.edu

different applicants. The foremost motive behind the credit scoring is for signifying a credit aspirant as a credible or non-credible for applied credit product. It is not a solitary-step progression, and various financial institutions are applying it in various steps which vary time to time and financial institution to institution such as first for new candidate applied for a credit product, second for existing customer to analysis their behaviors, third as grouping to existing customer on the basis of their behavior [5, 20]. In this study, our focus is on application scoring which is applied at the time of submission of application for new product by an aspirant and its credibility is calculated on basis of aspirant's social, financial and other data collected [20, 26]. It helps in "calculating and reducing credit risk", "making managerial decisions" and "cash flow improvement" [5, 20] and directly affects profitability of credit industries by identifying the non-credible aspirants. Currently, credit scoring is not only restricted to credit industry, but some other industries such as Telecom, real estate are also implementing the credit score prediction model to analyze the customer behaviors. Therefore, AI can provide an assistance for providing the insides about non-credible aspirants and on solving the problem of manual credit scoring.

Several investigators have employed several classification approaches such as "Support Vector Machines (SVM)" [4, 29], "Decision Trees (DT)" [3], "Artificial Neural Networks (ANN)" [21], "Bayesian Networks" [6] and statistical methods such as "Discriminant Analysis" [1], "Logistic Regression" [23], "Probit Regression" [7] for an emergent model for precise credit risk assessment. Li et al. [14] and Van Gestel et al. [28] have presented a credit scoring model for loan appraisal using SVM and least squares SVM, respectively. Similarly, Xiao and Fei [32] have applied SVM with optimum parameter selection approach. Various ANN-based approaches for credit scoring are presented on articles [13, 27, 30, 31]. Luo [17] has offered a relative assessment of classifiers such as KNN, DT, SVM and MLP for credit score prediction model and found that KNN has achieved the best outcomes. Blanco et al. [2] have employed various statistical approaches such as Quadratic Discriminant Analysis (QDA), Linear Discriminant Analysis (LDA), Logistic Regression (LR) and MLP techniques and later determined that outcomes attained by MLP are the best among other utilized statistical approaches. Saia and Carta [22] have projected a method for credit scoring by considering the difference between local and global maximum entropies with motive to classify a new instance without training to any model (cold start) with the past default instances. Form the experimental results as are projected, it is visible that its performances are better than Random Forest-based approach for the same.

Artificial Neural Networks (ANNs) are influential classification approach because of its information processing and learning ability by recognizing composite nonlinear associations between input and output [9]. Generally, most of the ANNs use a feedforward learning approach which results to additional time to train (optimization of weights) the model. As, ELM as a classification tool with single-hidden layer feedforward neural networks and its analytically determination of the output fascinated the consideration by various researchers on various domains than other traditional gradient-based learning algorithms [8]. Studies such as [11, 12, 16] demonstrated that ELM's classification performance is somewhat superior to other classifiers. As it involves a large number of neurons in its various layers such as input and hidden and its performance somewhat depends on same and activation function, so main focus of this study is to apply ELM to the credit risk assessment model and assess the impact of activation function and number of neurons on ELMs.

Rest of the study is organized as follows: Sect. 2 presents brief introduction of ELMs, Sect. 3 presents experimental results and discussion of results against various activation functions with various set of neurons, and later, conclusion is presented on the basis of experimental outcomes in Sect. 4.

2 Related Work

ELM as emergent technology which overwhelms some challenges is confronted by other neural network as it uses generalized single-hidden layer feedforward networks (SLFNs) which need not to be trained alike other neural network. The main focus of ELM is that the hidden layer as SLFNs needs to be tuned by applying random computational weights to the neurons at hidden layer. ELM [10, 12] is a three-layer architecture for classification as shown in Fig. 1; in this architecture, each layer consists of specific neurons, and neurons of a layer are completely associated to its next layer's neurons. Primarily, weight matrix and biases at hidden layer are arbitrarily adjusted. Far ahead, weights between hidden and output neurons are assessed on the basis of preceding weights, biases and data samples. As ELM architecture supports SLFN, recursive weight optimization is excluded. ELM training comprises two phases: first phase as "random feature map" and the second phase resolves "linear equations to obtain hidden-weight parameters".

The comprehensive step-by-step approach of ELM (as ELM training is a two-step process and third is output estimation) is summarized in subsequent three phases [19]:

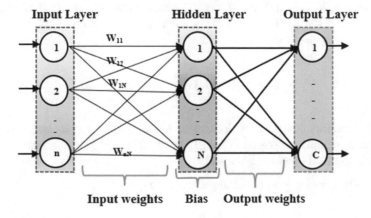

Fig. 1 Architecture of ELM

Phase 1: Primarily, indicate the "input weights W" and "hidden layer biases β" arbitrarily with n and N numeral of neurons at input and hidden layers correspondingly.

$$W = \begin{bmatrix} W11 & \cdots & W1N \\ \vdots & \ddots & \vdots \\ Wn1 & \cdots & WnN \end{bmatrix}, \quad \beta = \begin{bmatrix} \beta1 \\ \vdots \\ \beta N \end{bmatrix} \tag{1}$$

Phase 2: Further, calculate "hidden layer output matrix H" as in Eq. 2 by utilizing W and β as are defined in Eq. 1, where M represents number of data samples and f represents activation function.

$$H = \begin{bmatrix} f(W1 * X1 + \beta1) & \cdots & f(WN * X1 + \beta N) \\ \vdots & \ddots & \vdots \\ f(W1 * XM + \beta1) & \cdots & f(WN * XM + \beta N) \end{bmatrix} \tag{2}$$

Phase 3: Next, calculate the output weight b matrix using Eq. 3, where "H^+ represents the Moore–Penrose generalized inverse matrix of H" and is calculated as defined in Eq. 4.

$$b = H^+ T \tag{3}$$

$$H^+ = \begin{cases} \left(HH^T\right)^{-1} H^T & \text{when } H^T H \text{ is nonsingular} \\ H^T \left(HH^T\right)^{-1} & \text{when } HH^T \text{ is nonsingular} \end{cases} \tag{4}$$

Further, all three phases of ELM as are described earlier can be mathematically represented in Eq. 5 [19]. With M, distinct training samples are a set of Xi and Ti, where Xi and Ti signify the feature vector and target class of ith training sample. N, bi, βi and f are same as described earlier.

$$\sum_{i=1}^{N} bi * f(Wi * Xj + \beta i), \quad 1 \leq j \leq M \tag{5}$$

Further, authors in article [11] have extended the ELM and presented "equality-constrained optimization-based faster ELMs" as faster ELM-I and faster ELM-II, and details are as follows in Eqs. 6 and 7:

ELM-I: When the samples in training dataset are quite less,

$$b = H^T \left(\frac{I}{C} + HH^T\right)^{-1} T \tag{6}$$

ELM-II: When the samples in training dataset are quite high,

$$b = \left(\frac{I}{C} + H^T H\right)^{-1} H^T T \tag{7}$$

where i denotes an identity matrix which corresponds to neurons in hidden layer and C denotes regularization coefficient.

3   Results and Discussion

This section presents comparative result analysis of ELM, ELM-I and ELM-II with various activation functions such as "Sigmoid (Sig)", "Sine (Sin)", "Hard Limit (Harlim)", "Triangular Basis Function (Tribas)" and "Radial Basis Function (Radbas)" in terms of computational time (as C. Time which is total time of training and testing), classification accuracy and G-measure (as are defined in Eqs. 8 and 9) in four credit scoring datasets, and detailed description about the dataset is tabulated in Table 1. All datasets utilized in this study are real-world credit scoring dataset obtained from "UCI Machine Learning Repository [15]" and having two classes: first for approved (credible) and second for not approved (non-credible) samples. Australian and Japanese datasets are of credit card applicants' samples, where German dataset is of loan applicants' samples.

$$\text{Accuracy} = \frac{CC + CN}{CC + CN + NN + NC} \tag{8}$$

$$G\text{-measure} = \sqrt{\frac{CC}{CC + NC} * \frac{NN}{CN + NN}} \tag{9}$$

where CC represents the actual credible and predicted as credible samples, NN represents the actual non-credible and predicted as non-credible samples, CN represents the actual credible and predicted as non-credible samples and NC represents the actual non-credible and predicted as credible samples by the classifier.

Table 1 Description of credit scoring datasets

Credit dataset	Instances (Class-1/Class-2)	Features (categorical/numerical)
Australian	307/383	6/8
Japanese	307/383	9/6
German categorical	700/300	13/7
German numerical	700/300	0/24

In this study, as authors have utilized ELM for credit score classification problem, and its performances depends on activation function and number of neurons in hidden layer. So, various activation functions such as Sig, Sin, Harlim, Tribas and Radbas have been utilized with different set of neurons such as 50, 100, 150, 200, 250, 300 and 350 which are considered with ELM, ELM-I and ELM-II. For comparative analysis, mean of tenfold cross-validation of twenty iterations with respective neuron sets (as mentioned earlier) is considered. And, results are depicted in Figs. 2, 3, 4 and 5 with respective dataset. From Figs. 2, 3, 4 and 5, it is visible that Sig with ELM gets better accuracy with a smaller number of neurons. Overall, it can be summarized as most of the cases with different set of neurons and activation function Sigmoid have the better performances with ELM, ELM-I and ELM-II.

Further, for comparative analysis, mean of tenfold cross-validation of twenty iterations by considering the different set of neurons is tabulated in Tables 2, 3, 4 and 5 in terms of computational time, accuracy and G-measure. The results of Australian dataset as are in Table 2 show that ELM with Sigmoid has the best performances in terms of accuracy and G-measure with ELM, and it has compromised computational time. Similarly, with ELM-I and ELM-II, it has improved the accuracy and G-measure. Overall, with Australian dataset, ELM-II has the best performances as compared to ELM and ELM-I. Further, with other datasets as tabulated in Tables 3,

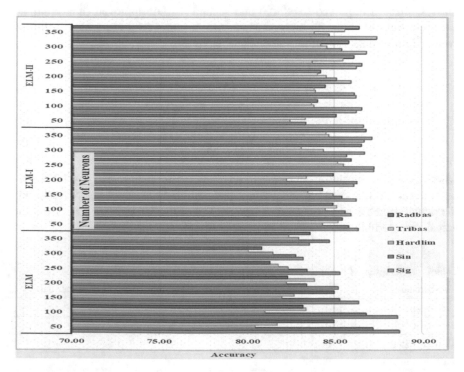

Fig. 2 Comparative accuracy graph of ELMs by considering various set of neurons and activation functions in Australian dataset

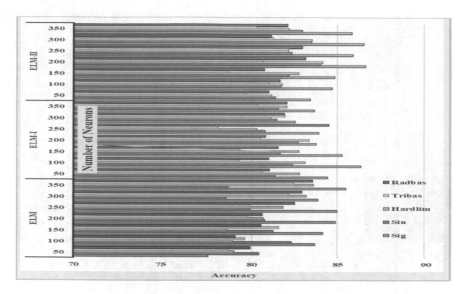

Fig. 3 Comparative accuracy graph of ELMs by considering various set of neurons and activation functions in Japanese dataset

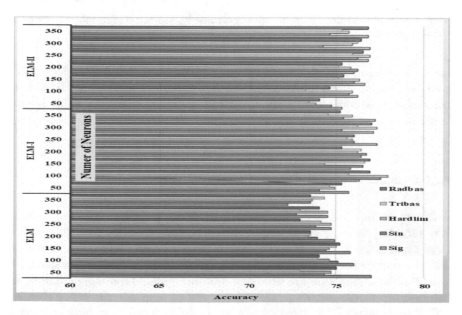

Fig. 4 Comparative accuracy graph of ELMs by considering various set of neurons and activation functions in German categorical dataset

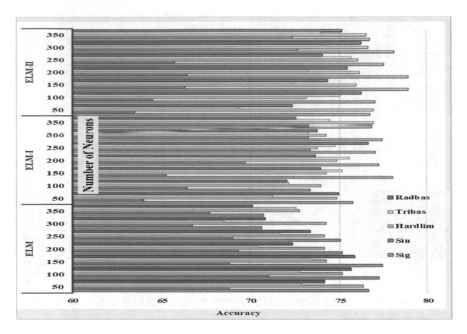

Fig. 5 Comparative accuracy graph of ELMs by considering various set of neurons and activation functions in German numerical dataset

4 and 5, we find the similar performance improvements as for Australian dataset. So, from the depicted values in Tables 2, 3, 4 and 5, it can be concluded that ELM-II is better options for credit scoring data classification and Sigmoid is the best activation function.

4   Conclusion

In arising nations like India, the greater part of the populace relies upon funds from monetary foundations to achieve their monetary prerequisites. The conventional process for attaining financial support from monetary foundations needs an extensive documentation and it results a slow verification process. In this study, we have presented an application of ELM on credit scoring. ELM is a single-hidden layer feedforward and non-iterative model which is getting trained in single-step process. ANNs' performance is subjected to activation function, weights and biases allocated to neurons. In the literature, a range of activation function is available, but from the performance's perspective, performances of these activation function on ELMs are not clear. So, in this study, we have considered various activation functions, namely: Sig, Sin, Hardlim, Tribas and Radbas. Further, we simulated the model with different set of neurons to assess the effectiveness of activations' function with ELM and its some variants such as ELM-I and ELM-II on four credit scoring datasets. From

Table 2 Performance of ELMs with various activation functions on Australian dataset

Function	C. Time	Accuracy	G-measure
Sig	0.072	86.56	86.47
Sin	0.074	85.79	85.67
Hardlim	0.065	80.98	80.75
Tribas	0.063	82.34	82.19
Radbas	0.073	83.16	83.10
ELM-1			
Sig	0.032	86.71	86.33
Sin	0.029	86.23	86.12
Hardlim	0.021	84.49	84.31
Tribas	0.026	84.15	83.81
Radbas	0.031	84.93	84.67
ELM-2			
Sig	0.034	86.79	85.90
Sin	0.031	85.39	85.28
Hardlim	0.022	84.54	84.49
Tribas	0.021	84.17	83.87
Radbas	0.025	85.79	85.69

Table 3 Performance of ELMs with various activation functions on Japanese dataset

Function	C. Time	Accuracy	G-measure
Sig	0.077	82.32	82.51
Sin	0.084	80.33	80.79
Hardlim	0.070	80.90	81.07
Tribas	0.068	79.59	79.44
Radbas	0.075	81.04	81.53
ELM-1			
Sig	0.028	84.67	84.88
Sin	0.031	82.45	82.91
Hardlim	0.031	82.34	82.75
Tribas	0.024	79.93	80.78
Radbas	0.026	81.46	81.51
ELM-2			
Sig	0.025	85.19	85.77
Sin	0.030	82.38	83.01
Hardlim	0.018	82.48	83.18
Tribas	0.019	80.16	83.29
Radbas	0.024	81.93	82.23

Table 4 Performance of ELMs with various activation functions on German categorical dataset

Function	C. Time	Accuracy	G-measure
Sig	0.191	75.23	64.66
Sin	0.197	67.32	60.32
Hardlim	0.167	74.19	59.76
Tribas	0.205	71.73	52.04
Radbas	0.208	73.88	61.64
ELM-1			
Sig	0.041	76.51	64.69
Sin	0.038	67.85	58.99
Hardlim	0.028	74.92	62.23
Tribas	0.027	73.53	57.21
Radbas	0.035	73.92	60.70
ELM-2			
Sig	0.036	77.91	65.92
Sin	0.036	67.25	59.91
Hardlim	0.034	75.26	61.73
Tribas	0.029	73.33	58.97
Radbas	0.029	74.57	56.12

Table 5 Performance of ELMs with various activation functions on German numerical dataset

Function	C. Time	Accuracy	G-measure
Sig	0.191	75.23	64.66
Sin	0.197	67.32	60.32
Hardlim	0.167	74.19	59.76
Tribas	0.205	71.73	52.04
Radbas	0.208	73.88	61.64
ELM-1			
Sig	0.041	76.51	64.69
Sin	0.038	67.85	58.99
Hardlim	0.028	74.92	62.23
Tribas	0.027	73.53	57.21
Radbas	0.035	73.92	60.70
ELM-2			
Sig	0.036	77.91	65.92
Sin	0.036	67.25	59.91
Hardlim	0.034	75.26	61.73
Tribas	0.029	73.33	58.97
Radbas	0.029	74.57	56.12

acquired simulation effects, it is ascertained that Sigmoid activation function offers better performances with three ELM-based models as ELM, ELM-I and ELM-II. From outcomes of ELM, ELM-I and ELM-II, it is observed specifically toward to classification accuracy, and ELM-II is more representative and displays enhancement in the performances.

References

1. Altman EI (1968) Financial ratios, discriminant analysis and the prediction of corporate bankruptcy. J Financ 23(4):589–609
2. Blanco A, Pino-Mejías R, Lara J, Rayo S (2013) Credit scoring models for the microfinance industry using neural networks: evidence from Peru. Expert Syst Appl 40(1):356–364
3. Brieman L, Friedman J, Olshen R, Stone C (1984) Classification and regression trees. Wadsworth, Belmont, CA. Google Scholar
4. Cortes C, Vapnik V (1995) Support-vector networks. Mach Learn 20(3):273–297
5. Edla DR, Tripathi D, Cheruku R, Kuppili V (2018) An efficient multi-layer ensemble framework with BPSOGSA-based feature selection for credit scoring data analysis. Arab J Sci Eng 43(12):6909–6928
6. Friedman N, Geiger D, Goldszmidt M (1997) Bayesian network classifiers. Mach Learn 29(2–3):131–163
7. Grablowsky BJ, Talley WK (1981) Probit and discriminant functions for classifying credit applicants—a comparison. J Econ Bus 33(3):254–261
8. Han F, Yao HF, Ling QH (2013) An improved evolutionary extreme learning machine based on particle swarm optimization. Neurocomputing 116:87–93
9. Haykin SS (2001) Neural networks: a comprehensive foundation. Tsinghua University Press
10. Huang GB, Wang DH, Lan Y (2011) Extreme learning machines: a survey. Int J Mach Learn Cybern 2(2):107–122
11. Huang GB, Zhou H, Ding X, Zhang R (2012) Extreme learning machine for regression and multiclass classification. IEEE Trans Syst Man Cybern Part B (Cybern) 42(2):513–529
12. Huang GB, Zhu QY, Siew CK (2004) Extreme learning machine: a new learning scheme of feedforward neural networks. In: 2004 IEEE international joint conference on neural networks, 2004. Proceedings, vol 2. IEEE, pp 985–990
13. Lee TS, Chiu CC, Chou YC, Lu CJ (2006) Mining the customer credit using classification and regression tree and multivariate adaptive regression splines. Comput Stat Data Anal 50(4):1113–1130
14. Li ST, Shiue W, Huang MH (2006) The evaluation of consumer loans using support vector machines. Expert Syst Appl 30(4):772–782
15. Lichman M (2013) UCI machine learning repository. http://archive.ics.uci.edu/ml
16. Liu N, Wang H (2010) Ensemble based extreme learning machine. IEEE Signal Process Lett 17(8):754–757
17. Luo C (2018) A comparison analysis for credit scoring using bagging ensembles. Expert Syst e12297
18. Mester LJ et al (1997) What's the point of credit scoring. Bus Rev 3:3–16
19. Miche Y, Sorjamaa A, Bas P, Simula O, Jutten C, Lendasse A (2010) OP-ELM: optimally pruned extreme learning machine. IEEE Trans Neural Netw 21(1):158–162
20. Paleologo G, Elisseeff A, Antonini G (2010) Subagging for credit scoring models. Eur J Oper Res 201(2):490–499
21. Ripley BD (1996) Pattern recognition via neural networks. A volume of Oxford graduate lectures on neural networks, title to be decided. Oxford University Press. http://www.stats.ox.ac.uk/ripley/papers.html

22. Saia R, Carta S (2016) An entropy based algorithm for credit scoring. In: International conference on research and practical issues of enterprise information systems. Springer, pp 263–276
23. Steenackers A, Goovaerts MJ (1989) A credit scoring model for personal loans. Insur Math Econ 8(1):31–34
24. Thomas LC, Edelman DB, Crook JN (2002) Credit scoring and its applications: SIAM monographs on mathematical modeling and computation. University City Science Center, SIAM, Philadelphia
25. Tripathi D, Edla DR, Cheruku R, Kupplli V (2019) A novel hybrid credit scoring model based on ensemble feature selection and multilayer ensemble classification. Comput Intell 35(2):371–394
26. Tripathi D, Edla DR, Kuppili V, Bablani A (2020) Evolutionary extreme learning machine with novel activation function for credit scoring. Eng Appl Artif Intell 96:103980
27. Tsai CF, Wu JW (2008) Using neural network ensembles for bankruptcy prediction and credit scoring. Expert Syst Appl 34(4):2639–2649
28. Van Gestel T, Baesens B, Suykens JA, Van den Poel D, Baestaens DE, Willekens M (2006) Bayesian kernel based classification for financial distress detection. Eur J Oper Res 172(3):979–1003
29. Vapnik V (2013) The nature of statistical learning theory. Springer Science & Business Media
30. West D (2000) Neural network credit scoring models. Comput Oper Res 27(11):1131–1152
31. West D, Dellana S, Qian J (2005) Neural network ensemble strategies for financial decision applications. Comput Oper Res 32(10):2543–2559
32. Xiao WB, Fei Q (2006) A study of personal credit scoring models on support vector machine with optimal choice of kernel function parameters. Syst Eng Theory Pract 10:010

Automatic Detection and Classification of Healthy and Unhealthy Plant Leaves

Reeya Agrawal, Anjan Kumar, and Sangeeta Singh

1 Introduction

Indeed, agriculture depends on the bulk of the population in India. Agricultural productivity depends heavily on the Indian economy. India is currently the second-largest agricultural producer in the world. The primary crop is the land of Jowar, wheat and maize of India, which has about 210 million ha [1]. Tomatoes, bananas, sapota, raisins, and oranges are the most popular fruits. Sugarcane, cotton, squid, and groundnuts are the primary economic crops. Cultivation depends on irrigation, soil quality and temperature, and crop losses occur without these. Diseases are the most significant crop every year, and disease control is challenging. This is why fitness, unhealthy identification and agricultural disease detection are important factors [2]. Many diseases affect crops and plants as meteorological conditions continue to develop. If proper precaution is not taken in this area, it has severe repercussions for plants and affects quality, quantity, and productivity [3]. It is essential to identify plant health or diseases using any automated technology. It removes a large-scale monitoring task in big farms and early places symptoms of health problems on plant leaves. Identifying big seed farms using any automatic method minimizes their functioning and identifies illnesses that occur on crop leaves in the early stages is described in [4]. The computerized approaches for detecting conditions in the plant offer numerous advantages. The suggested method may be extended to aid farmers in the early identification of plant disease, which can avert a reduction in output of around 50%. It can also be utilized by ordinary people when they buy fresh green vegetables [5].

R. Agrawal (✉) · A. Kumar
GLA University, Mathura, India
e-mail: Agrawalreeya0304@gmail.com

R. Agrawal · S. Singh
Microelectronics and VLSI Lab, National Institute of Technology, Patna, Patna 800005, India
e-mail: sangeeta.singh@nitp.ac.in

© The Author(s), under exclusive license to Springer Nature Singapore Pte Ltd. 2023
K. Kumar Singh et al. (eds.), *Machine Vision and Augmented Intelligence*, Lecture Notes in Electrical Engineering 1007, https://doi.org/10.1007/978-981-99-0189-0_41

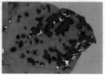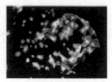

Fig. 1 Different forms of leaves as decay day by day

2 Literature Review

The diagnostic mechanism is obvious and involves a comprehensive interpretation and the application of scientific procedures (i.e. symptom and sign recognition). The proper diagnosis and categorization of leaf diseases are essential to prevent loss of farming. Symptoms in all vegetable diseases include notable leaf symptoms, which impair colour, structure or function when infected with the pathogen [6].

Infectious Illness Symptoms: Aphids, white tongues, leafhoppers. These insects are the common carriers of this disease. It might be scraped, bent or stunted in this leaf.

Bacterial Disease Symptom: Several serious vegetable illnesses are caused by pathogenic microorganisms. Small pale dots are signs.

Fungal: Late fungal blight. Fungal conditions. It first occurs on lower, older blades, treated water, like grey-green patches.

The first step is to process the picture entry beforehand. The first step is to process the picture entry beforehand. In the K-mean clustering, the segmentation of damaged leaves is already imagined [7]. However, K-mean clustering continued to segment. The suggested system comprises hierarchical segmentation clusters with fewer iterations and more efficiency. It takes less time to learn how to classify disease [8]. The primarily green pixels are masked according to these threshold values after segmentation. Vector machine classification assistance is trained. The hierarchical clustering technique needs less repetition, as seen in [9]. Figure 1 shows different forms of leaves as they decay day by day.

3 Proposed Model

The healthy and unhealthy plant leaf detection model includes the loading of the dataset, which is divided into the testing and training phase in the ratio of eighty and twenty [10]. The next step is feature extraction from the image. It is done by initializing the CNN model and adding three convolutional layers with their respective max pool layers to reduce the dimensionality by keeping all the essential features [11]. Furthermore, the Flattening and Compiling of the model is done, and then the

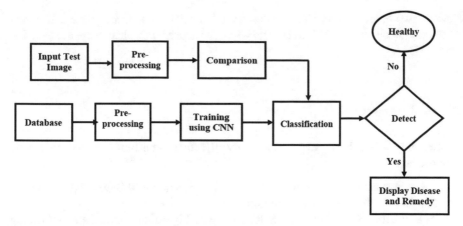

Fig. 2 Proposed system architecture

images are reshaped to fit into the model, and the model gets trained successfully. Afterwards comes the testing phase, where the image is loaded into the model, and predictions are made [12].

The working algorithm of the model is described below:

- Step 1: Load—Image Dataset.
- Step 2: Apply Training Sequence.
- Step 3: Feature Extraction.
- Step 4: CNN-based feature learning network.
- Step 5: Test the data against the test samples.
- Step 6: Output (Fig. 2).

3.1 Machine Learning

Machine learning is an artificial intelligence (AI) technique that allows systems to automatically learn and increase experience without special programming [13]. Machine learning aims to develop computer programmers that access and utilize data for their goals. The learning process starts with insights or data like examples, direct contact or training [14] to find information patterns and strengthen future decision-making based on the criteria.

3.2 Decision Trees

Decision trees are a kind of master learning where data is always divided by a particular attribute (what the input is and the corresponding output in the training data). Two people will clarify the tree, namely decision nodes and leaves. The final effects or decisions are the leaves. And when the data are breached, there are decision nodes [15].

3.3 Naive Bayes

Naïve Bayes is a basic yet unexpectedly effective algorithm [15] for predictive modelling.

- The Naïve Bayes algorithm is a controlled, theorem-based Bayes algorithm used for classification problem resolution.
- They are mainly used in text classification with high-dimensional data for training purposes.
- The Naïve Bayes classifier is one of the simplest and most effective classification algorithms fast-learning machines can quickly predict. It is a classifier that predicts the likelihood of an item.
- Spam, dynamic analysis, and classification articles are some of the most common instances of the Naïve Bayes algorithm. Choose the best hypothesis with machine learning, which is all about. In a classification problem, it's possible that our hypothesis (H) could be the class to give a new piece of data (D) to solve it. It's easy to pick the most likely hypothesis based on what we already know about. It helps us figure out how likely a hypothesis is based on the things researchers already know. Users can find this out in the Bayesian theorem.
- $(P (D|H) * P (H)) P (H)/P (D)$.
- $P (H|D)$ is the hypothesis probability given D. This is called the posterior probability.
- Since hypothesis H was true, $P (D|H)$ is the probability of D data.
- $P (H)$ is the likelihood of hypothesis H. This is called the prior probability of H.
- $P (D)$ means data likelihood (regardless of the hypothesis).
- The afterlife of $P (H|D)$, from previous probability $P (H)$ with $P (D)$ and $P (D|H)$, can be shown to be interesting.

3.4 Convolutional Neural Network

These are the building blocks of neural networks and what makes them work. It is called a convolution when users filter input to make it more interesting. They can automatically learn a lot of files simultaneously, right from a training dataset. This is a big deal because convergence neural networks can know many files simultaneously. These kinds of things are essential when it comes to predictive modelling. There are a lot of very complicated functions that can be found in input pictures all over the place [16].

Healthy Leaf   **Unhealthy Leaf**

Fig. 3 Healthiness of leaf

Fresh   **Old**

Fig. 4 Freshness of vegetables

4 Evaluation of Result

The technology used to recognize plant leaves is the convolutional neural network (CNN). The proposed approach is helpful to identify plant diseases accurately and input to demonstrate whether or not they are healthy, whether they are fresh or not and to which plant they belong. Figure 3 shows the healthiness of the leaf, Fig. 4 shows the freshness of vegetables, and Fig. 5 shows the random leaf and leaf belonging to the tulsi plant [17–19].

5 Conclusion

This study presents a model to determine whether a leaf is healthy or not (whether there are some kinds of plant illnesses) using different machine learning techniques

Random Leaf   **Belongs toTulsi Plant**

Fig. 5 Identification of plant with the help of leaf

to identify and classify diseases. Many systems utilize a dataset including pictures to determine if a leaf is healthy or not. Improved quality pictures lead to better model analysis. Quality and quantity can be enhanced by detecting illnesses at an early stage. Due to lack of time, additional modules were left on a more profound analysis model. The pictures show the present and future model results. Some problems were presented while using this as the background noise effect in the submitted image of a leaf.

References

1. Urva P (2021) Detection and classification of grain crops and legumes disease: a survey. Spark Light Trans Artif Intell Quant Comput 1(1):41–55
2. Alessandrini M et al (2021) A grapevine leaves dataset for early detection and classification of esca disease in vineyards through machine learning. Data Brief 35:106809
3. Appalanaidu MV, Kumaravelan G (2021) Plant leaf disease detection and classification using machine learning approaches: a review. Innov Comput Sci Eng 515–525
4. Yarak K et al (2021) Oil palm tree detection and health classification on high-resolution imagery using deep learning. Agriculture 11(2):183
5. Singh J (2021) Automated disease detection and classification of plants using image processing approaches: a review. In: Proceedings of second international conference on computing, communications, and cyber-security. Springer, Singapore
6. Parraga-Alava J et al (2021) LeLePhid: an image dataset for aphid detection and infestation severity on lemon leaves. Data 6(5):51
7. Abed SH et al (2021) A modern deep learning framework in robot vision for automated bean leaves diseases detection. Int J Intell Robot Appl 1–17
8. Kalwad PD et al (2022) Apple leaf disease detection and analysis using deep learning technique. In: Information and communication technology for competitive strategies (ICTCS 2020). Springer, Singapore, pp 803–814
9. Rao US et al (2021) Deep learning precision farming: grapes and mango leaf disease detection by transfer learning. Glob Transit Proc. In: International conference on computing system and its applications (ICCSA-2021)

10. Mattihalli C, Gared F, Getnet L (2021) Automatic plant leaf disease detection and auto-medicine using IoT technology. In: IoT-based intelligent modelling for environmental and ecological engineering. Springer, Cham, pp 257–273
11. Panigrahi KP et al (2020) Maize leaf disease detection and classification using machine learning algorithms. In: Progress in computing, analytics, and networking. Springer, Singapore, pp 659–669
12. Sambasivam G, Opiyo GD (2021) A predictive machine learning application in agriculture: cassava disease detection and classification with imbalanced dataset using convolutional neural networks. Egypt Inform J 22(1):27–34
13. Shruthi U, Nagaveni V, Raghavendra BK (2019) A review on machine learning classification techniques for plant disease detection. In: 2019 5th international conference on advanced computing & communication systems (ICACCS). IEEE
14. Rajesh B, Vishnu Sai Vardhan M, Sujihelen L (2020) Leaf disease detection and classification by decision tree. In: 2020 4th international conference on trends in electronics and informatics (ICOEI) (48184). IEEE
15. Khan MA et al (2020) An automated system for cucumber leaf diseased spot detection and classification using improved saliency method and deep features selection. Multimed Tools Appl 1–30
16. Singh A, Kaur H (2021) Potato plant leaves disease detection and classification using machine learning methodologies. IOP Conf Ser Mater Sci Eng 1022(1). IOP Publishing
17. Qayyum A et al (2020) Securing machine learning in the cloud: a systematic review of cloud machine learning security. Front Big Data 3
18. Tabeidi RA et al (2021) Smart computer laboratory: IoT based smartphone application. In: The international conference on artificial intelligence and computer vision. Springer, Cham
19. Ghazal TM, Alshurideh MT, Alzoubi HM (2021) Blockchain-enabled internet of things (IoT) platforms for pharmaceutical and biomedical research. In: The international conference on artificial intelligence and computer vision. Springer, Cham

Assistive Technology for Blind and Deaf People: A Case Study

Kondaveeti Aashritha and V. M. Manikandan

1 Introduction

Visually impaired people are the people who are completely blind or partially blind [9]. Blindness is described as the inability to see, and it can also refer to vision loss that isn't be rectified using contact lenses or glasses. Complete blindness means that the person cannot see anything and cannot see light; the term "blindness" usually refers to complete blindness. Individuals with "partial blindness," on the other hand, have severely limited vision.

According to World Health Organization (WHO), visual impairment affects 285 million individuals worldwide [9]. Among them, 39 million individuals were blind; 246 million people have low vision. According to the Information from World Blind Union (2009), there are more than 160 million blind and partially sighted people in the world [13]. The number is expected to be doubled by the year 2020 [2]. According to a fact sheet published by the World Health Organization in October 2017, there were 6 million blind people and 217 million people with low vision in the world [3]. Developing countries are abode to about 90% of the world's visually impaired individuals. The reason for vision impairment includes cataract, trachoma, glaucoma, and also, deficiency like "Vitamin A" which leads to night blindness, onchocerciasis, leprosy is a disease carried on by bacterial *Mycobacterium leprae*. It usually affects the body's colder areas such as the eyes, nose, earlobes, hands, feet, testicles, and so on.

The eyes are a person's primary sense organ. It is commonly recognized that losing one's vision results in a loss of independence, communication, and human contact, as well as a reduction in mobility. We could say that the majority of information in our environment is inaccessible to the blind, and visually impaired leads to limiting their independence because knowledge and understanding are linked with freedom.

K. Aashritha · V. M. Manikandan (✉)
SRM University-AP, Amaravati, Andhra Pradesh, India
e-mail: manikandan.v@srmap.edu.in

© The Author(s), under exclusive license to Springer Nature Singapore Pte Ltd. 2023
K. Kumar Singh et al. (eds.), *Machine Vision and Augmented Intelligence*, Lecture Notes in Electrical Engineering 1007, https://doi.org/10.1007/978-981-99-0189-0_42

We may claim that the majority of this data is unreachable to the blind and visually impaired, restricting their autonomy because access is synonymous with liberty. A single glance of the external world would be adequate to create us realize how optical almost all of the facts in our habitat is; lots of signs specify the ways or possible hazards, and we can also say that all of these important facts are unreachable for the visually impaired individuals, and also, restricting their autonomy because the availability of critical facts signifies choice and freedom. It is natural for sighted peers, family members to be overly eager to help the visually impaired individual. Blind people may complete a task more slowly, but it does not indicate they are incapable of doing so.

Helping the visually impaired without first inquiring or being inquired may make them feel helpless rather than independent. When one is visually challenged, work takes on a whole new meaning. Given the shortage of accessible occupations and workplaces, it is understandable that hiring a visually impaired individual could be seen as a risk for a company. Visually impaired people's confidence and emotional well-being are harmed as a result of this. Not just the aforementioned issues, but several others visually impaired individuals face in their daily lives. Given the afore-mentioned considerations, it is not unexpected that having a vision handicap often implies being alone. Blind and low vision people are frequently isolated due to a lack of emotional support at diagnosis facilities, limited access to activities and information, social stigma, and unemployment.

Hearing problems, deafness is the inability to hear sounds completely or partially. Hearing loss is the inability to hear noises, whereas deafness is the inability to interpret speech even when sounds are magnified. Hearing loss is divided into four categories. "Mild Hearing Impairment" means that a person can only discover sounds among 25 and 29 dB; "Moderate Hearing Impairment" means that a person can only discover sounds in the middle of 40 and 69 dB; "Severe Deafness" means that a person can only hear sounds among 70 and 89 dB; "Profound Deafness" means that a person cannot hear sounds beneath 90 dB. Most individuals with profound deafness are completely deaf and cannot hear anything at any volume.

Hearing loss is quite common, with one out of every five people experiencing some form of hearing impairment [15]. According to the World Health Organiza-tion (WHO), about 5% of the global population or 430 million individuals require hearing therapy, and it is anticipated that over 700 million people will have disabling hearing loss by 2050. In low and middle-income nations, about 80% of people having debilitating hearing loss survive. Hearing loss becomes more common as individuals get older, with over 25% of persons over the age of 60 suffering from debilitating hearing loss.

Hearing is a critical ability in an emergency. The ability to hear warning sounds, receive messages, instructions, and information, as well as sustain outbound commu-nication, is critical to an individual's ability to respond in dangerous situations [10]. There are so many causes of hearing impairment which include heredity disorders, genetic disorders, parental exposure to disease, noise which means loud noises partic-ularly prolonged exposure either in the workspace or recreationally damage the deli-cate mechanism inside the ear. Certain diseases can also cause hearing impairment which includes chickenpox, jaundice, mumps. Aging can also be a problem for hearing impairment.

Hearing loss has a profound impact on one's quality of life. People who suffer from hearing loss may experience depression. Because hearing loss can make conversation difficult and generate feelings of loneliness in certain people. Public announcements, sign language, and lip-reading misunderstanding, as well as hearing loss in emergencies and while traveling, are all big obstacles. The ability to detect sounds of impending danger, receive signals, instructions, and information, and sustain outbound communications are all essential to a person's ability to react in a perilous circumstance.

As life becomes more abundant, the need for human well-being has increased in proportion. As a result, not only normal individuals but also physically challenged persons have become increasingly interested in the quality of life. People with impairments, particularly the visually impaired and hearing impaired, face several challenges daily while doing ordinary tasks and traveling through unfamiliar environments. One of engineering's objectives is to make human's lives better. Consequently, there is a pressing need to develop and design assistive technology to address all of the current issues. Assistive technology allows people to be more independent in their everyday duties and improves their overall quality of life.

2 Various Technologies to Assist Blind and Deaf People

Blind people and deaf people face numerous hurdles in their daily lives. From studying a manual to strolling and from listening to loved ones to traveling, for each blind and deaf person, there are several impediments, respectively. There are numerous techniques accessible to help them to take on the obstacles they encounter. A review of these actions will provide insight into the current frameworks. The following are some of the ideologies.

For visually challenged people, an AI-based assistance system has been proposed. The concept is executed using an android smartphone app that relies on speech recognition, currency recognition, e-books, and chatbots. The software can detect items in the environment using voice commands and perform a content analysis to detect contents in paper documentation. Google's cloud APIs, on the other hand, are a fundamental part of Google's cloud platform enabling users to quickly amalgamate every single thing from memory access to machine learning-based image analysis into their app. All cloud APIs have a basic JSON REST interface and may be accessed straight from client libraries. The Google cloud API mostly uses chatbot clients for sight and dialogue flow. It is utilized for speech recognition in addition to transcribing written materials. A Web-Hook is an HTTP callback: an HTTP POST occurs once a direct notice was sent through HTTP POST in response to a request. A Web application using Web-Hook sends a message when a request is made. Object identification, dynamic and vocal entry and reply, location recognition, textual assessment, and response accuracy for this suggested system are between 80 and 90%. As a multilingual application, this system failed [9].

A novel model that can be used as a traveling aid for the visually impaired was presented in another study. This approach was created to supplement traditional navigation methods like white cane and guide dogs. Two stereo cameras and a portable computer for analyzing environmental data make up the system. This system's objective is to detect static and dynamic objects in the surroundings and convert them into auditory signals. The user sees the audio image of the environment, the volume of objects, moving object direction and trajectory, its distance relative to the user, and free routes in the range of 5–15 m using stereophonic headphones. The acoustic signals are a short train of delta sounds externalized in an anechoic room using non-individual head-related transfer functions. Users were able to manage and maneuver the system safely in both known and unfamiliar environments, according to the results of the experiments [1].

Another prototype describes a navigation tool for the visually impaired who have difficulty while walking. This smart walker not only assists with walking but also allows blind people with mobility issues in regard to agility concerns to minimize hurdles. Using existing robotic techniques, the system detects both favorable and unfavorable barriers like curbs, stairs, and pits within the earth and sends barrier location awareness via haptic feedback. Preliminary tests show that this smart walker can safely explore both indoor and outdoor environments [13].

Another example is obstacle detection in a real-time framework meant to warn blind persons of impending danger and aid humans in securely navigating interior and outdoor spaces using a smartphone device. Interest points defined based on a grid of images are used to detect static and dynamic objects, which are then monitored using the multi-scale Lucas–Kanade algorithm. They also established an approach for classifying objects. They used the HOG descriptor with the BoVW retrieval framework to show how this combination can be utilized to classify objects in video streams [11].

Another prototype is a smart assistance for blind people using Raspberry Pi. This is an optical character recognition (OCR) system, which is a branch of computer vision and a subclass of artificial intelligence. The Raspberry Pi is used in optical character recognition (OCR) to convert optically scanned frames of printed or handwritten text into audio output. OCRs for a variety of foreign languages have previously been developed and are in use. To extract the moving object region, this method employs a Gaussian-based background subtraction algorithm. An Ada Boost model learns gradient properties of stroking orientations and dispersion of corner points to develop a text localization and Tesseract technique. The text characters in the localized text sections are then translated to binary and recognized using off-the-shelf optical character recognition software. To assist blind users, the discovered textual symbols are stated aloud. The performance of the suggested text localization algorithm. The text file's text codes are processed on a Raspberry Pi device, which identifies characters using the Tesseract algorithm and Python programming, and the audio output is listed once the process is finished [4].

Another one is the development of an ultrasonic cane as a traveling aid for visually impaired persons. This cane can identify obstacles in the air and on the ground, as well as potholes (drop-off). The ultrasonic impulses are collected in an Arduino micro-controller, categorized, and control signals are wirelessly transferred to a receiver maintained in a shoulder pocket. Another Arduino micro-controller controls the receiving device, which controls three speaker panels (worn around the chest) and an LED panel. The device has a range of 5–150 cm and can be used by blind persons as a navigation aid. The device was capable of producing auditory warnings to inform users of the position of the obstacles. The capacity of the suggested technology to identify impediments is expected to enable blind people with safe mobility [2].

Another example is the implementation of stereovision as a navigation aid for blind people. This system is made up of three parts: a headphone, the digitized video camera, and the solitary computer. The difficulties of conveying depth information from a single camera, which is critical for navigation, started with the invention of a stereo vision system with two cameras. A rule-based stereo matching approach is applied to the segmented images. The disparity is calculated using the matching features. Focal length and distance information can be combinedly used to estimate the size of the objects. In the final processed image, the distance information is represented by four gray levels: white, light gray, dark gray, and black. For the blind person, the structured coded sound is then employed to cover the placement of the image in the visible plane. To indicate distance information, the spoken sound is used [14].

A wearable healthcare IoT device-based on deep learning for AI-enabled hearing assistance automation is introduced in [15]. In this prototype, a http app has been developed which uses Google's online speech synthesis service to transform obtained conversations into text, which is then displayed to deaf people on a micro-display attached to the spectacles, allowing and assisting good chat with the general public. In addition, a *urban emergency predictor* is created using a deep learning model, Inception-v4, with transfer learning to identify alarming signals, such as horn sound and fire alarm, and texts are generated to notify potential users, to raise alert of traffic or dangerous circumstances. Before being integrated into an AI-based IoT application, Inception-v4 was trained on a consumer desktop. The program initiatives system's sound recognition and classification accuracy was 92% with real-time performance, according to the experimental findings [15] (Fig. 1).

Another prototype is a mobile deaf-to-hearing communication aid for medical diagnosis. A deaf-to-hearing communication tool designed for a mobile phone is utilized in this prototype to facilitate semi-synchronous conversation between a deaf person and a hearing person who cannot sign. Deaf persons who have access to mobile phones have become accustomed to communicating with both hearing and deaf people through short messaging services. However, because most deaf persons have limited literacy skills, they choose not to communicate using writing. The prototype employs interpreted sign language and English communication. The mock-up is designed to assist deaf people in communicating their medical conditions to a doctor in person. Prerecorded sign language videos for deaf people and English text for hearing doctors are used to create the prototype. Instead of playing the video in

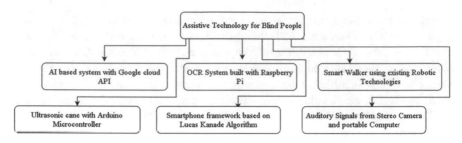

Fig. 1 Classification of assistive technologies for blind

a third-party media player, the interaction on the mobile phone was done inside the phone's browser utilizing video streaming. The purpose of the design was to present the system from a computer-based prototype on a mobile phone [5].

Another variant was a learning aid on the mobile phone to support deaf people learning computer literacy skills. The goal is to allow deaf people to learn at their own pace, reducing reliance on a teacher and allowing weaker students to be helped [6]. We looked at the dynamics of the classroom and instructional approaches to figure out how information is transmitted. A prototype was created for this utilizing South African Sign Language movies that were organized according to the format of pre-existing classes. Its technical goal was to put the prototype on a mobile device and connect the output lesson content from the authoring tool to a sequence of signed language movies and pictures, allowing the deaf people to teach themselves computer literacy skills. The prototype successfully allowed deaf users to study at their own pace by eliminating their reliance on teachers, according to the results of user testing [6].

Another example was a new approach to sound visualization for deaf assistance using mobile computing, which depicted crucial dynamic sound features and recognized sound icons in an easy-to-read format. The MFCC sound characteristics were used to express robust discriminant aspects of sound to easily visualize general sounds. To make the system more usable for the users, input sound was classified and related to the visualization system. To recognize short sound occurrences, each time frame of the sound is subjected to the KNN classification method. Furthermore, the input sound is buffered and transmitted to the dynamic time wrapping (DTW) classification method, which was created for dynamic series classification. Both classifiers work at the same time, and the visualization model receives their classification results. The system was designed based on interviews with five deaf people who tried the system, and the system was evaluated based on their interactions with the system [7].

Another prototype was HospiSign which is an integrated gesture tool for the deaf. For deaf people, sign language is the most natural form of communication. In this model, a computer vision-based method for identifying gesture language is used to provide an interactive communication interface for hospitals called HospiSign. The interface directs deaf visitors to address problems and convey their reason for visiting in sign language without the need for a translation. The system consists

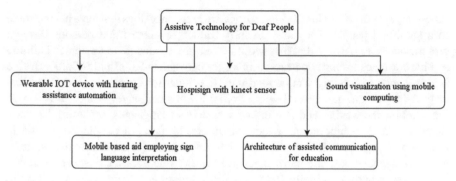

Fig. 2 An overview of assistive technologies for deaf

of a computer, a touchscreen panel for visualizing the interface, and a Microsoft Kinect v2 sensor for capturing the users' answers. To recognize isolated signals in a structured activity diagram, HospiSign employs dynamic time wrapping-based classifiers. Usability tests were performed to assess the intended interface, and it was discovered that the software was capable of aiding its consumers in live time with remarkable accuracy [8].

Another model is Assisted Communication for Education (ACE), an infrastructure for deaf and blind interaction. Conveying difficulties are always present in the lives of deaf and blind people. Utilizing automated solutions to aid fluid communication between people speaking different languages and using multiple communication channels could help impaired students become more socially integrated. The ACE architecture includes virtual sign, a sign language translator, as well as additional components that enable translation between symbol and spoken languages in live time using image processing techniques. Any sign language can be supported by this design. This also allows deaf people from many countries to participate. By integrating voice recognition text to speech, the blind architecture may be linked, allowing for greater involvement of people from other communities. This enables bidirectional communication over a variety of various communication routes [12] (Fig. 2).

3 Various Technologies Available in the Market to Assist Blind and Deaf People

The need for human well-being has increased in proportion to the richness of life. Inventors came up with some rather solutions to help the blind and deaf. Some of them are discussed in this.

Many visually challenged people use a white cane as a walking aid. It not only allows users to scan their environs for impediments or direction markers, and that also aids viewers in recognizing a blind person and taking appropriate measures. It ranges in price from \$20 to \$60. Guide dogs are assistance dogs that have been trained to assist blind people. They are specially trained to guide blind persons through circumstances or barriers that they would otherwise be unable to navigate. Training a guide dog takes around two years and charges between \$45,000 and \$60,000. Braille is a sequence of dots that can be read with the fingertips by persons who are blind or have low vision. In the usual sense, braille is not a language. Instead, it is a code that enables the writing and reading of a variety of languages, including English, Spanish, Arabic, Chinese, and a slew of others. Millions of people use braille in their native languages all across the world, and it gives everyone access to literature. Most college textbooks are more expensive than Braille books. Converting just five chapters of a book into braille, which is the standard arrangement, can cost up to \$15,000. However, once you have it, braille reproductions cost around 5% of the original price, or about \$500.

To prevent getting lost, many people learned to read by dragging their fingers across the paper. This intuitive gesture can assist blind and visually impaired persons in interpreting printed text using a ring-like gadget around a finger that can identify and read-aloud text. The ring uses an algorithm developed by MIT Media Lab researchers to recognize words, which are then given to software that reads them aloud. As the user navigates his or her finger over the page, the device sends out signals in the form of audio or oscillate, avoiding inadvertent line changing. The ring now requires a connection to a computer that interprets and reads the text, but its makers are already working on a version that might run on a smartphone.

Iris Vision is a visual enhancement, wearable low vision aid that has been approved and registered by the FDA as a Class-1 medical device. It is currently one of the top vision enhancement, wearable low vision aids on the market. It is made up of Samsung's VR headset and the latest smartphone, and it is meant to help those with limited vision, such as macular degeneration and other degenerative eye disorders like diabetic retinopathy, cataracts, and albinism. It can cost up to \$2950 per unit. It has a number of features. Electronic glasses consist of a smartphone-mounted VR headset that collects photographs and provides the viewer with a magnified view of the objects. It has a field of view of up to 70°, which is one of the widest in the business. The controls and settings in this are highly configurable and user-friendly. Different modes for different types of legal blindness or a visual impairment, such as "Scene Mode," "Bubble View Mode," "Bi Optic Mode," various modes with color variations for reading help, such as "Reading Line Mode," "TV Mode," and so on. It is another exclusive function based on modern OCR techniques that allow the gadget to read aloud the desired text to you.

Another product available in is MyEye2, which consists of a light-attachable camera installed on a pair of glasses for legally blind people. It is designed to help people with limited vision read better, but it is also useful for a variety of other tasks like barcode scanning, face recognition, and product identification. The price per unit is \$3500. It has several features. It can let you read text from any type of surface. Automatic page detection is included, as well as the ability to read several languages and color detection. It also reads selected text using gestures, requiring only finger-pointing in the direction of the text. Face recognition, barcode identification, and product identification are all supported.

Jordy is another model. Jordy is a connected, portable low vision solution for persons with low vision. It assists people with daily activities like as reading, writing, and recognizing faces in a variety of settings. It can be worn on your head and provides you with glasses-like vision. Each unit costs roughly $2500. Tactile controls provide a user-friendly experience and assist vision-impaired users in observing their environment. Powered by a battery, with the help of a docking station, it may also be used as a CCTV camera. Through the use of a cable box, it is possible to watch television.

This is a prototype of one pair of electronic spectacles that will assist visually impaired and legally blind people in seeing. These are battery operated, and the battery is connected to the device through a cord. This implies you will have limited movement and will need to monitor the battery's charge. The price per unit is $5950. It has many features. Head-mounted goggles are used to display video. With a field of view of 35°, it is designed to help people with visual acuities close to 20/200. Customizable clinical settings are available, as well as optical character recognition.

Nu Eyes is a cutting-edge gadget that consists of a pair of smart electronic spectacles. It is light and can be controlled wirelessly using a controller that comes with the glasses or with a set of voice commands. It ranges in price from $5995 to $6195. It has the following features: lightweight, wirelessly operable, and capable of being used to watch television. Variable magnification from $1\times$ to $12\times$ is available, as are a variety of color and contrast choices, as well as barcode and QR scanning options (Table 1).

If one has hearing loss, hearing aids will most certainly be a huge benefit in daily life. A normal hearing aid costs $373. However, there may be times when hearing aids are insufficient. In that scenario, a slew of assistive listening devices was on the scene to assist deaf people. Assistive listening devices are available in a surprising number of varieties these days. A few of these gadgets are meant to work with a particular hearing aid; some are stand-alone devices that can be beneficial even if you don't wear hearing aids. Smartphones are increasingly being used as assistive listening devices on their own, particularly when combined with contemporary Bluetooth-enabled hearing aids.

Table 1 List of product with their prices which are available in the market for blind people

S. No.	Product name	Price (per unit)
1	White cane	$20–$60
2	Iris Vision	$2950
3	My Eye2	$3500
4	Jordy	$2500
5	Electronic spectacles	$5950
6	Nu Eye	$6195

Amplified phones are designed particularly for people who suffer from hearing loss and permit to customize the volume as required to catch the speech. These devices do not require the usage of hearing aids. They can help you hear high-pitched sounds that people with hearing loss often miss. The ringtones on these phones could be increased, making sure you don't lose a call. Phone manufacturers are required to make phones that are consistent with hearing aids. This incorporates iPhones and android cellphones. Acoustic or telecoil coupling is commonly used in hearing aid compatible phones. Acoustic coupling collects and enhances audio from both the mobiles and the environment. Telecoil coupling necessitates the presence of a telecoil in your hearing aid, a specific function that only the phone signal is picked up for amplification. People with advanced hearing loss prefer telecoils in hearing aids because background noise during phone calls will be blocked out. They are particularly helpful for people who talk on the phone a lot or use other telecoil-based ALDs like public induction loops. Additionally, apps on phones can behave as their own ALDs. For instance, caption apps can provide speech to text conversion.

The majority of ALDs help you listen, but some also help you stay connected to whatever is happening over you and enhance your security. These devices use magnified sounds, visual indications, and even feelings to warn you to sounds in the surroundings. Various instances of warning gadgets are as follows: It contains vibrating alarm clocks to help you get your day started on time. The sonic alert clock uses audio signals and vibrations to wake you up. Doorbell alarms cost $272.00 and employ lighting to notify you of someone who is at the entrance. It can also be stored in a central location in the house and will warn you to a phone call or a buzzing doorknob via a text or a flashlight. It costs around $105.78.

Fortunately, there are smoke alarms designed specifically for the deaf. Some of these devices are marketed independently, while others are included in a system that detects both fire and carbon monoxide. Many have abnormally loud warnings and bright flashlights, depending on the scenario. There are also bed-vibrating smoke detectors with a component that can go beneath the pillow or mattress and shake you awake to notify you of a fire, depending on its power. Other smoke detector alarms employ technology to detect existing smoke detectors and respond with a much louder, lesser sound which is more prone to wake people up. Certain gadgets shock people awakened though the digital display warns FIRE and turns to orange. It will cost at least $640.91.

Hearing-impaired parents can't always determine if their newborns are crying since regular baby monitors don't always emit enough sound. Vendors are already producing transmitters and receivers which can sense a child's cry and relay the data to a chief alarm system. It will set at least $63.95. People with hearing loss may be ignorant of a dangerous storm because they are unable to hear the sound of thunder or see the flash of lightning. Furthermore, some people do not watch or listen to television or the radio. Weather warnings provide advance notification of impending storms or other potentially severe weather events in several situations. A weather warning transmitter can be used alone and in conjunction with additional warning devices such as strobes or bed shakers, depending on your needs and preferences. It costs as little as $20 and as much as $165.

Table 2 List of products with their for deaf people

S. No.	Product name	Price (per unit)
1	Hearing aid	$373
2	Smoke alarms for deaf	$6409
3	Baby monitors for deaf	$105
4	Cochlear implant	$1000–$50,000
5	FM/DM system	$2500
6	IMEHD's	$30,000–$100,000

Though not a novel system, an FM or DM system is a durable and really quite efficient wireless technology that creates it simpler to understand whatever people are speaking in crowded places like schools or public events. The speaker speaking next to the public uses a broadcaster microphone, while the hearing aid user uses a receiver. Through the FM technique, the voice command is directly supplied to both hearing aids. While wearing it, you can choose between entirely shutting out background noise or permitting an ace blend of voice and some sound in the backdrop. In schools, these technologies are commonly employed to assist hearing-impaired kids. They assist students in reaching their academic outcomes, but they are also beneficial to grownups in a variety of contexts. An FM bundle, which contains the transceiver and ear-level detectors and its possible price is $2500.

A cochlear implant is a surgically implanted digital tool that electrically stimulates nerves inside the internal ear to offer usable listening to sensations. Currently, cochlear implants include two primary components: A microphone, a sound processor, and a transmitter system for external use make up the external component. The electronic circuits that receive signals from the external system and send electrical impulses to the inner ear are included within the internal component, which is made up of an implanted receiver and electrode system. With insurance, the cost will range from $1000 to $50,000.

Implantable middle ear hearing devices (IMEHDs) serve to improve sound transmission to the internal ear. The IMEHDs are tiny infix devices that are usually attached to one of the middle ear's tiny bones. IMEHDs vibrate and move the middle ear bones directly when they receive sound waves. This causes sound waves in the inner ear, which aids with hearing detection. Sensorineural hearing loss is the most common condition for which this device is utilized. It expects a cost between $30,000 and $100,000 (Table 2).

4 Challenges and Future Research Scope

This section describes obstacles and potential research areas in this domain. A few feasible technological solutions have emerged that have social or economic impacts and improve blind and deaf people's lives. Basic challenges, such as being able to evacuate independently of the world still need to be addressed. Researchers and technicians are clearly essential to address the needs of the target group. But, the nature, scale, complexity, and variety of problems faced by the visually impaired and hearing impaired to reach acceptable solutions must be understood first. The task is made more difficult by the fact that the target group is heterogeneous in terms of blindness, deafness, age, gender, culture, and talent.

Sensory replacement holds a lot of promise for visually impaired and blind people who want to improve their vision. Sensory replacement devices have been in development in controlled conditions in laboratories for many years, but they have yet to be adopted for public use. In the development of appropriate equipment and interfaces for the visually impaired and blind, computer vision combined with assistive technology has had a lot of success recently. Image description, cognitive mapping, mobile computer vision, eye-free wearable devices, and video description are all types of computer vision. Navigation and wayfinding, particularly in unfamiliar indoor environments, has long been a problem. There aren't any established technologies that can meet this need. When visually impaired or blind people are in an unknown facility, it can be perilous, and smartphone-based ETAs, indoor wayfinding technology, sensory substitution devices, obstacle detection systems, and other technologies can help.

To reach a larger proportion of the deaf population, information should be transmitted through multiple channels. Cell phones, for example, can be used to communicate risk and receive and transmit information. Light and vibration are crucial components for new technology.

The sign language translation on TV and Internet broadcasts should be expanded, given in a slow and straightforward manner, and included in all emergency transmissions.

5 Conclusion

This article provides an in-depth examination of numerous technology and tools to assist blind and deaf people. People who have trouble in speaking, typing, writing, remembering, pointing, seeing, hearing, learning, walking, and many other activities can benefit from assistive technology. The purpose of this article is to provide a concise summary of visually impaired individuals who were completely blind or partially blind, hearing impaired who have total or partial inability to hear sounds and causes of visual and hearing impairment. Because the eyes and ears are the primary sense organs, persons who have problems with them confront a wide range of physical and emotional difficulties, like crossing the street, chatting to loved ones, traveling, reading books/academics, hearing traffic alerts, and dealing with insults and sympathy in society. From various citations, this study cites different inventions like AI-based systems with cloud API, auditory signals from stereo cameras and portable computers, smart walker, smartphone-based, OCR system built with Raspberry Pi, ultrasonic cane with Arduino microcontrollers, wearable IoT device with hearing assistance automation, mobile-based aid employing sign language interpretation, sound visualization using mobile computing, HospiSign with Kinect sensor, the architecture of assisted communication for education. This article also lists the numerous tools and technologies available on the market, along with their features and pricing.

References

1. Dunai L, Fajarnes GP, Praderas VS, Garcia BD, Lengua IL (2010) Real-time assistance prototype—a new navigation aid for blind people. In: IECON 2010—36th annual conference on IEEE industrial electronics society, Nov 2010. IEEE, pp 1173–1178
2. Kumar K, Champaty B, Uvanesh K, Chachan R, Pal K, Anis A (2014) Development of an ultrasonic cane as a navigation aid for the blind people. In: 2014 international conference on control, instrumentation, communication and computational technologies (ICCICCT), July 2014. IEEE, pp 475–479
3. Li B, Munoz JP, Rong X, Chen Q, Xiao J, Tian Y et al (2018) Vision-based mobile indoor assistive navigation aid for blind people. IEEE Trans Mob Comput 18(3):702–714
4. Manonmani A, Masilamani A, Lavanya M, Sellakumar S (2020) Smart assistant for blind people using Raspberry Pi 3. Int J Psychosoc Rehabil 24:3711–3724
5. Mutemwa M, Tucker WD (2010) A mobile deaf-to-hearing communication aid for medical diagnosis
6. Ng'ethe GG, Blake EH, Glaser M (2015) SignSupport: a mobile aid for deaf people learning computer literacy skills
7. Samra AAA, Alhabbash MS (2016) Sound visualization for deaf assistance using mobile computing. J Eng Res Technol 2(2)
8. Süzgün M, Özdemir H, Camgöz N, Kindiroğlu A, Başaran D, Togay C, Akarun L (2015). HospiSign: an interactive sign language platform for hearing impaired. J Nav Sci Eng 11(3):75–92
9. Swathi M, Shetty MM (2019) Assistance system for visually impaired using AI. Int J Eng Res Technol (IJERT). ISSN 2278-0181
10. Tannenbaum-Baruchi C, Feder-Bubis P, Adini B, Aharonson-Daniel L (2014) Emergency situations and deaf people in Israel: communication obstacles and recommendations. Disaster Health 2(2):106–111
11. Tapu R, Mocanu B, Zaharia T (2013) A computer vision system that ensure the autonomous navigation of blind people. In: 2013 E-health and bioengineering conference (EHB), Nov 2013. IEEE, pp 1–4
12. Ulisses J, Oliveira T, Escudeiro PM, Escudeiro N, Barbosa FM (2018) ACE assisted communication for education: architecture to support blind & deaf communication. In: 2018 IEEE global engineering education conference (EDUCON), Apr 2018. IEEE, pp 1015–1023
13. Wachaja A, Agarwal P, Adame MR, Möller K, Burgard W (2014) A navigation aid for blind people with walking disabilities. In: IROS workshop on rehabilitation and assistive robotics, Sept 2014, vol 13, pp 13–14
14. Wong F, Nagarajan R, Yaacob S (2003) Application of stereovision in a navigation aid for blind people. In: Fourth international conference on information, communications and signal processing, 2003 and the fourth Pacific Rim conference on multimedia. Proceedings of the 2003 joint, Dec 2003, vol 2. IEEE, pp 734–737
15. Young F, Zhang L, Jiang R, Liu H, Wall C (2020) A deep learning based wearable healthcare IoT device for AI-enabled hearing assistance automation. In: 2020 international conference on machine learning and cybernetics (ICMLC), Dec 2020. IEEE, pp 235–240

Trustworthiness of Customer Reviews of E-Commerce Portal Using Supervised and Semi-supervised Machine Learning Techniques

Ritesh Prasad, Sitikantha Chattopadhyay, and Shiplu Das

1 Introduction

The world is moving rapidly toward digitization where we compare and buy most of our requirements ranging from small to large sitting at home and pay with just few clicks. In current COVID-19 pandemic situation, online access has increased drastically. Even people from rural areas are taking the benefits of Internet. We are buying groceries item, clothing, electronics, and many more using online portals and also paying using different online payment options like Internet banking, UPI, e-wallet, etc. Hence, buying a good product at a reasonable price is very much needed. The online portal gives the facilities where the people can give their feedbacks after buying in the form of reviews and ratings. These reviews and rating are helpful for others at the time of making decision for a purchase. As these reviews are playing an important role in taking decision, it gives an opportunity to the people to promote or demote a product by writing biased reviews and may influence buyer's decision. Figure 1 is an example from Amazon, a popular e-commerce company, showing the same review which is copy pasted by different users at different time frame, representing the high possibility of being fake or biased. Reviews also help a company to modify the products for betterment based on the feedbacks given by the customers [1].

More use of online portals results into more reviews and gives a huge opportunity to explore the views and opinions for classification problem. In the era where data plays an important role, these reviews can be explored for many applications. At one side, the e-commerce is growing exponentially; on the other side, this give a challenging task to check the quality of the data as anyone can write anything. Any user can write false or biased reviews, called as spam reviews [2].

R. Prasad · S. Chattopadhyay (✉) · S. Das
Department of CSE, Brainware University, Barasat, West Bengal, India
e-mail: sitikantha.1984@gmail.com

© The Author(s), under exclusive license to Springer Nature Singapore Pte Ltd. 2023
K. Kumar Singh et al. (eds.), *Machine Vision and Augmented Intelligence*, Lecture Notes in Electrical Engineering 1007, https://doi.org/10.1007/978-981-99-0189-0_43

Fig. 1 Example of fake review

Basically, there are three types of spam reviews [3, 4]:

Type 1: false reviews to mislead or influence in a biased way
Type 2: product name-based reviews
Type 3: reviews in form of advertisements or with no opinions.

This paper is based on Type 1 reviews from e-commerce portal Amazon of two products categories—software and cellphones and accessories. The reviews of two categories have taken for checking their trustworthiness, as a classification problem with two classes—trusted and not-trusted.

2 Related Works

Earlier research has been started considering the duplicate review on the basis that the same review has been used for different products, by the same user or by many, ignoring the actual perspective for the product using similarity score of the reviews [3, 5]. Focused to classify whether a review can be trusted or not with a motivation that false review may affect the status of the product to a great extent in the business. In [3, 6], focused was mainly on rating and its deviation from the average rating for the product [7, 8]. Proposed a method which calculate a score for the spammers on the basis of rating behavior and similarity among reviews. Thereafter, a subset of reviewers is generated which was later among one feature of being non-trusted review. They used supervised techniques and human evaluator also to class labeling. Results showed that top few reviewers have wrote a large number of reviews in a small time period which is not common among common users [9–11] Added the sentiments of the reviews to get more accurate result. Classification has proven to be a difficult task because of huge imbalanced nature of data [12]. Applies decision tree and Naïve Bayes algorithm on restaurant customer reviews because of its probabilistic behavior, after preprocessing of reviews and creating model using Weka machine learning tool [10]. Has worked on review's sentiments of e-commerce site using term frequency-inverse document frequency (TF-IDF) which calculated the occurrence of selected words [13]. They have tokenized as preprocessing task and used Naïve Bayes classifier for their experimental results [14].

3 Proposed Method

In this paper, logistic regression and support vector machine are used which gives a promising result as compared to the gold standard dataset which was created and labeled by the human evaluators. The motivation for using these two algorithms is their approaches. Logistic regression uses a probabilistic approach for predicting the categorical dependent variables and estimates the relationship among dependent and independent variables and represents the probability of a category using a linear function and helpful in our case of binary classification. Support vector machine follows a non-probabilistic approach using patterns of the taken samples. The model then assigns class to a new sample. Non-linear mapping is also possible if the samples are not demarcated linearly. A complex quadratic programs arise which get solved using sequential minimal optimization (SMO). It divides a big problem into small sub-problems and solve analytically. This paper also uses the concept of co-training which is also a semi-supervised technique and very helpful in the case where labeled data are very less in number. Here, labeled data are used for training the model and tested on large unknown samples. The full feature sets are divided into two views and considered two classifiers are generated for each feature subset. The instances with high confidence score are added to the training set of the other making it a strong model to check the unknown samples. Samples are exchanged between two classifiers till a saturation point is achieved where the performance is not increasing. This also emphasize the weightage of each feature in determining the performance of any specific category (Fig. 2).

Reviews are taken where 1580 reviews are labeled, gold standard data, out if which 1160 reviews are used for training the model, and the remaining are used for testing. The generated model is used our labeled data of two categories from Amazon.

The reviews are available in the format— <product id> <product title> <product price> <user id> <user name> <helpful vote> <rating> <review time> <review title> <review body>. The labeling is done on basis of helpfulness votes, number of users finds a review helpful and rating of 3 and above, where 1 is low and 5 is high [15]. For building a classification model, many features are considered, and class is assigned based on helpfulness votes. The features used are length of the review title, length of review body, rating, its deviation from average rating of the product, number of feedbacks, number of helpful feedbacks, and polarity which defines the sentiments of a review [16]. It is based on the fact of higher possibility of a review being non-trusted if there was a low rating with positive sentiments. The results are measured in the terms of precision, recall, F-measure, and accuracy using Weka tool.

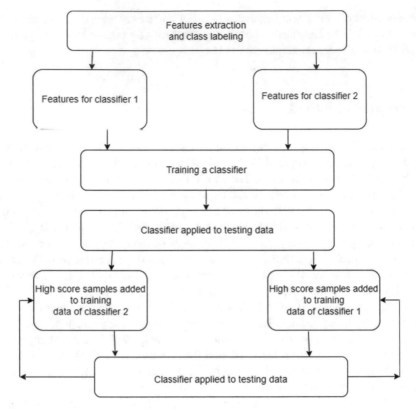

Fig. 2 Working methodology of co-training

4 Experimental Results

The training samples of the gold standard dataset are used to create the model using the two algorithms—logistic regression and SMO. The model is tested using 10 folds cross validation technique and on prepared test set. The results are shown in Table 1.

Table 1 shows all the performance parameters—precision, recall, F-measure, and accuracy from Weka on test set and 10 folds cross validation of gold standard dataset using the model created by the selected training samples of the same gold standard

Table 1 Accuracy analysis

Classifier	Precision	Recall	F-measure	Accuracy (%)
Logistic regression (tenfold)	0.66	0.66	0.66	65.89
Logistic regression (test set)	0.71	0.60	0.61	60.24
SMO (tenfold)	0.63	0.63	0.63	63.30
SMO (test set)	0.70	0.60	0.61	60.00

set. The accuracy is around 60% using both the methods—logistic regression, and SMO, which is lesser than our proposed model.

Another model is trained using the proposed hypothesis discussed in Sect. 3 and tested on the same test set of gold standard dataset. The new proposed model gives a promising better results (65–66%). Hence, the new model is applied to the selected two categories. The results are shown in Table 2.

Table 2 shows all the performance parameters—precision, recall, F-measure, and accuracy from Weka. The model is created based on the proposed methodology and tested on the test set of gold standard dataset which gives better result as earlier by around 5%. Hence, the model is also tested on the selected two product categories which also give a promising result with the both probabilistic and non-probabilistic approaches.

In Fig. 3, the two classifiers with different set of features are trained and tested accordingly. In category software, the classifier 2 is giving better results as compared to classifier 1 that signify the importance of features of classifier 2 with the specific category.

Table 2 Accuracy comparisons

Category	Classifier	Precision	Recall	F-measure	Accuracy (%)
Gold standard test dataset	Logistic regression	0.76	0.65	0.64	65.40
Gold standard test dataset	SMO	0.75	0.69	0.65	66.01
Cellphones	Logistic regression	0.82	0.81	0.80	81.67
Cellphones	SMO	0.79	0.80	0.79	79.76
Software	Logistic regression	0.82	0.82	0.81	82.14
Software	SMO	0.79	0.80	0.79	79.52

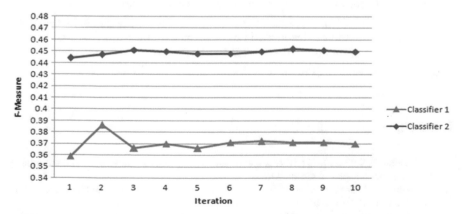

Fig. 3 Comparison of classifier 1 and classifier 2 of software category

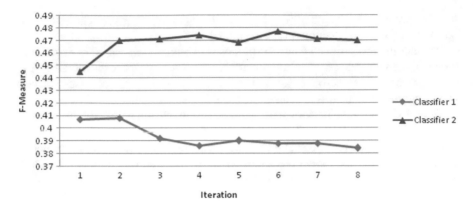

Fig. 4 Comparison of classifier 1 and classifier 2 of cellphones and accessories category

In Fig. 4, the two classifiers with different set of features are trained and tested accordingly. In category cellphones and accessories, the classifier 2 again is giving better results as compared to classifier 1 that signify the importance of features of classifier 2 with the specific category.

5 Conclusions and Future Work

In this paper, we have reported our work on checking the trustworthiness from the customer reviews. We have investigated supervised and co-training methods for finding a promising result in our task of detection of trusted and not-trusted products reviews. We have implemented a set of features and train a model with logistic regression and support vector machine. We evaluated our model for the product reviews of cellphones and accessories and software from Amazon dataset.

In future work, more promising features can be added to increase the performance of our model. Even more categories can be checked with the same features to check the effectiveness of the used features set. Automatic methods for feature selection may be investigated to exploring effective and relevant sets of features.

References

1. Hemmatian F, Sohrabi MK (2017) A survey on classification techniques for opinion mining and sentiment analysis. Artif Intell Rev
2. GuangJun L, Nazir S, Khan HU, Haq AU (2020) Spam detection approach for secure mobile message communication using machine learning algorithms. Secur Commun Netw
3. Sultana N, Palaniappan S (2020) Deceptive opinion detection using machine learning techniques. Int J Inf Eng Electron Bus 12(1)

4. Gangavarapu T, Jaidhar CD, Chanduka B (2020) Applicability of machine learning in spam and phishing email filtering: review and approaches. Artif Intell Rev 53(7)
5. Karim A, Azhari A, Belhaouri SB, Qureshi AA, Ahmad M (2020) Methodology for analyzing the traditional algorithms performance of user reviews using machine learning techniques. Algorithms 13(8):202
6. Keyvanpour M, Zandian ZK, Heidarypanah M (2020) OMLML: a helpful opinion mining method based on lexicon and machine learning in social networks. Soc Netw Anal Min 10(1):1–17
7. Tanwar P, Rai P (2020) A proposed system for opinion mining using machine learning, NLP and classifiers. IAES Int J Artif Intell 9(4):726
8. Zhang M, Fan B, Zhang N, Wang W, Fan W (2021) Mining product innovation ideas from online reviews. Inf Process Manage 58(1):102389
9. Mitra A (2020) Sentiment analysis using machine learning approaches (Lexicon based on movie review dataset). J Ubiquitous Comput Commun Technol (UCCT) 2(03):145–152
10. Sari PK, Alamsyah A, Wibowo S (2018) Measuring e-Commerce service quality from online customer review using sentiment analysis. J Phys Conf Ser 971(1):012053
11. Sánchez-Núñez P, Cobo MJ, De Las Heras-Pedrosa C, Peláez JI, Herrera-Viedma E (2020) Opinion mining, sentiment analysis and emotion understanding in advertising: a bibliometric analysis. IEEE Access 8:134563–134576
12. Varudharajulu AK, Ma Y (2019) Data mining algorithms for a feature-based customer review process model with engineering informatics approach. J Phys Conf Ser 1267(1):012013
13. Liang R, Wang JQ (2019) A linguistic intuitionistic cloud decision support model with sentiment analysis for product selection in Ecommerce. Int J Fuzzy Syst 21(3):963–977
14. Smys S, Haoxiang W (2021) Naïve Bayes and entropy based analysis and classification of humans and chat bots. J ISMAC 3(01):40–49
15. Da'u A, Salim N, Rabiu I, Osman A (2020) Recommendation system exploiting aspect-based opinion mining with deep learning method. Inf Sci 512:1279–1292
16. Kumar R, Pannu HS, Malhi AK (2020) Aspect-based sentiment analysis using deep networks and stochastic optimization. Neural Comput Appl 32(8):3221–3235

Computer Graphic and Photographic Images Classification—A Transfer Learning Approach

Sasithradevi A., S. Shoba, Chanthini Baskar, and S. Mohamed Mansoor Roomi

1 Introduction

With the advancement in digital imaging and 3D rendering software, it has become more complex to differentiate the original photographic images (PG) and system generated computer graphic (CG) images. Traditional photographic images were used as the faithful proof of real-time events. Nowadays, people share images, videos, and ideas with others using public data communication medium. Whereas, CG images have several advantages in augmented reality, computer gaming applications, and many more. However, highly realistic CG images are used illegally in some cases like criminal investigation, academic publications, and many more, which causes serious threat to the society and individual. Due to the availability of large number of rendering software and hardware devices for producing CG images, mishandlers have facilitated to use them in illegal occasions. Recently, forensic community has proposed so many techniques to distinguish CG and PG images. Most of the existing techniques focus on hand crafted feature selection for classification of CG and PG images. Before extracting the features of the images, preprocessing will be done using techniques such as RGB to gray scale conversion [1], transform domain techniques [2], and high pass or low pass filters [3]. The existing techniques for feature extractor can be broadly classified as hand crafted features and deep learning-based convolutional neural network (CNN) methods [4].

A. Sasithradevi · C. Baskar (✉)
School of Electronics Engineering, Vellore Institute of Technology, Chennai, India
e-mail: chanthini.baskar@vit.ac.in

S. Mohamed Mansoor Roomi
Department of Electronics and Communication Engineering, Thiagarajar College of Engineering, Madurai, India

A. Sasithradevi · S. Shoba
Centre for Advanced Data Science, Vellore Institute of Technology, Chennai, India

© The Author(s), under exclusive license to Springer Nature Singapore Pte Ltd. 2023   561
K. Kumar Singh et al. (eds.), *Machine Vision and Augmented Intelligence*, Lecture Notes in Electrical Engineering 1007, https://doi.org/10.1007/978-981-99-0189-0_44

Handcrafted feature extractor involves statistical characteristics in most of the works in the literature. The characteristics such as color, edges, variance, mean, and skewness are used as the features of the images. Geometry-based feature extraction was also performed for feature extraction [5]. Transform domain-based approaches were also used in few works [6]. But, most of these techniques depend on the human intervention which leads more processing time on larger dataset and minimal feature extraction. To overcome the shortcomings of the handcrafted feature extraction, deep CNN-based methods have provided better performance.

CNN-based methods are used for more precise and optimal feature selection. Well-established CNN architectures were also used in many approaches such as AlexNet [7], GoogleNet [8], and other techniques which were also used. Most of the recent works on image classification have reported CNN combined with other classification methods such as SVM [9], attention networks [10], transfer learning-based approaches, and many other.

2 Literature Review

The classification of CG and PG images is highly complex due to similar visual properties of both the images. They cannot be easily differentiated using human visual system, but the generation of the CG and PG images is different. So, the inherent properties are used to differentiate them. The classification of CG and PG images is reported in many works in the literature.

Michael Haller et al. designed an augmented reality framework using photorealistic representation and non-photorealistic representation techniques. Using the developed system, photorealistic virtual scenes can be created easily and which poses very good quality including dynamic behavior, shadow capture, and other features of the images [11]. Tian-Tsong Ng et al. proposed a hand crafted feature selection based on the geometry of the input image. The proposed method utilizes the physical image generation method for image classification. This method used gamma correction property of photographic image for identifying real-time image and the sharp structures in computer graphic images. The classification accuracy is 83.5% [12]. Later, Tian-Tsong Ng et al. introduce an image classification technique for distinguishing CG and PG images using a online system. In the developed system, a passive blind system was developed for tampering identification in images. The system mainly used three different techniques for image classification, namely geometry, wavelet, and cartoon method [6].

In addition, machine learning techniques were also incorporated for performing fusion and bagging techniques to overcome the effects induced on the images because of size reduction. The developed system also achieved a very fast processing time over existing methods and also achieved a overall accuracy of almost 82% [6]. An automatic classification of CG and PG image by using Adaboosting learning algorithm. The system has implemented by using histogram feature and color moment feature. Rong Zhang et al. introduce to differentiating CG from natural images using visual dictionary on image edges. First, image edge patches will be processed and projected as seven dimensional sphere. Then, a visual dictionary is constructed by key sampling points according to Voronoi cells. Finally, employ an SVM classifier for image classification. The classification accuracy is 90% [13].

A software system developed to generate highly precise and accurate multimedia content. It may be hard for humans to differentiate the real and CG images. To address this issue, geometry-based approach was developed using face asymmetry information. Based on the experimental results, this information can be used as the hint for classifying CG and PG images but requires other tools for more precise classification. State-of-the-art approaches can be used along with developed system to improve the accuracy. The classification accuracy is 89.25% [14].

YingdaLv et al. investigate the perceptual differences between PG and CG images. In this work, fractal dimension-based bling identification technique was proposed for classifying CG and PG images. Initially, the image is changed from RGB to HSV, and fractal dimensions are extracted from the HSV image. Then, the gradient image was used for calculating the fractal dimensions, and finally, global fractal and PEM fractal dimensions were calculated. The system has achieved an overall accuracy of 96% [15]. Olivia Holmes et al. have conducted a psychophysical experiments for determining human intelligence in identifying the CG and PG images without applying any techniques. The finding of the experiment was like it has become more difficult to differentiate CG and PG images using naked eye compared to last 5 years.

A deep CNN method was proposed for differentiating CG ad PG image using RNN. During the preprocessing, color space transformation was used to extract the luminance properties of the images. By using this technique, irrelevant information is avoided for classifying CG images. Yao et al. [16] have developed a system based on sensor pattern noise (SPN) and deep CNN for classifying the CG images. As a step for preprocessing, all the images are clipped into patches and then fed into the CNN-based model. Finally, a three stage high pass filter is used for removing the low-frequency components without affecting the image quality.

Even though there are many work reported in the literature to distinguish between CG and PG images using handcrafted features and CNN-based methods, still, new methods are being evolving for image classification. As an initiative, in this work, transfer learning approach is used for classification, and the performance of GoogleNet is estimated for CG and PG image classification.

3 Proposed Methodology

Discriminating the computer graphic images from the photographic image is really a difficult task for the human. The reason is that the statistical properties are different for computer graphic compared to the photographic images. Automatic classification plays a major part for these kinds of images. The existing machine learning classification algorithm proposed uses different transform-based methods to classify the image which leads to less accuracy. The deep learning models in the current

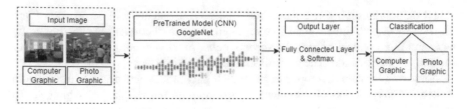

Fig. 1 Proposed framework for CG/PG classification

world have been proved in many applications in the role of classification and prediction. The proposed system uses convolutional neural network architecture which is a proven one for image processing and computer vision applications. The CNN uses large dataset and does not require any handcrafted features to process the data. The advantage of CNN is that it learns the features on its own from the input data fed. The general architecture of CNN contains three layers: (1) convolutional layer (2) pooling layer, and (3) fully connected layer. The first two layers perform the operation of feature extraction, and the third layer does the job of classification. The proposed framework is shown in Fig. 1.

The input to the proposed system uses Columbia dataset [12] with 2000 number of samples each 1000 with computer graphic and photographic images. This work uses a pre-trained CNN model, named GoogleNet, [8] for classification purpose. The architecture of the GoogleNet is as follows:

3.1 GoogleNet

One of the most popular models of CNN is GoogleNet. The GoogleNet architecture was developed by Google in collaboration with different universities. This architecture is quite different from the existing architectures like AlexNet [7] and VGGNet [17] because of the insertion of inception layer. The GoogleNet contains 22 layers of combination of layers such as input layer, convolution, pooling, inception, average pooling, fully connected layer, softmax, and classification layer. It is illustrated in Fig. 2.

3.2 Convolution Layer

The convolutional operation contains different filter sizes of $1 \times 1, 3 \times 3, 5 \times 5$, and 7×7. This network initially starts with a convolution of 7×7 filter size followed by the reduction of 3×3 filter size in the later stages. It is known that the computational cost and time taken to train the neural network are large. So, a 1×1 convolution is

Fig. 2 Architecture of
GoogleNet designed for
CG/PG classification

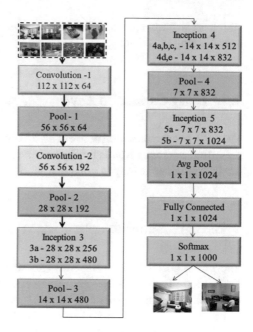

added before 7×7 and 3×3 in order to reduce the computations and the network dimension.

3.3 Pooling

The max pooling operation is followed by the convolution to extract the low-level features like points, edges, sharpen, and smoothening. In this network, after the first convolution layer, a 3×3 filter with a size of stride 2 is fed to the second convolution layer. Similarly, three max pooling operations are performed in this architecture in between various layers to reduce the dimension and to extract the important information of features

3.4 Inception

The interesting and different layer in GoogleNet is the inception module. This layer is the breakthrough in neural network field particularly in CNN architecture. In this network, we used version of 3, 4, and 5. The network uses 3a, 3b inception module in version 3 followed by max pooling operation. In version 4, we used 4a, 4b, 4c, 4d, and 4e inception module followed by max pool. The inception module 5 also contains the subdivision of 5a and 5b layers. In total, there are 9 inception modules which are linearly stacked. The average pooling is connected to the inception for fine smoothening of features.

3.5 Fully Connected Layer

The fully connected neural network uses a dimension of $1 \times 1 \times 1024$ hidden units to the softmax activation units for linear classification. The classification layer classifies finally the image belong to computer graphic or photographic images.

4 Experimental Results

The prime goal of this work is to classify the given images as CG or PG using GoogleNet. To validate the performance of the GoogleNet, we used benchmarks called photo realistic [18] and Colombia University Dataset [12]. The total number of images in each category is 1000. These PG images are gathered from different scenarios like house, living area, natural scenery, human, fruits, flowers, animals, birds, car, and buildings. CG images include house, living room, insects, animals, birds, human, flowers, metals, car, sea, table, and sculpture. The pre-trained model is validated using metrics like precision, recall, and accuracy. The pre-trained network is analyzed for different folding ratio of training and testing. The training parameter for GoogleNet is chosen as, #Epochs = 6, initial learning rate = 0.001, validation frequency = 5.

The pre-trained GoogleNet model is trained for two cases like dataset with augmentation and without augmentation. The proposed method is implemented in MATLAB with deep learning libraries and GPU. The input layer, fully connected layer, and classification layer of the pre-trained model were modified to make it suitable for CG and PG classification problem. The performance of GoogleNet is shown in Fig. 3.

It is evident from figure z that the accuracy of the network was 50% at the initial stage, and later, it reached 70% at the end of the first epoch. Also, the rise is higher only in epoch 1 when compared to others. Apart from epoch 1, others show a gradual rise in accuracy. Similarly, the loss is also minimized to certain extent in epoch 1. At the end of epoch 6, the training loss is 0.4%.

The confusion matrix for the pre-trained GoogleNet model is shown in Fig. 4. It shows that the testing accuracy is 90.4% and 82.1% for CG and PG image classification, respectively. The performance of GoogleNet is analyzed for different folding ratio as well as augmentation. The results are enlisted in Table 1.

It is mandatory to compare the performance of GoogleNet with other pre-trained model. We have chosen the well-known VGG18 model to assess the capability of GoogleNet. The comparison of training accuracy is shown in Table 2.

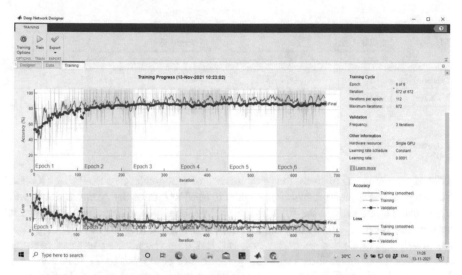

Fig. 3 Performance of GoogleNet for CG/PG classification

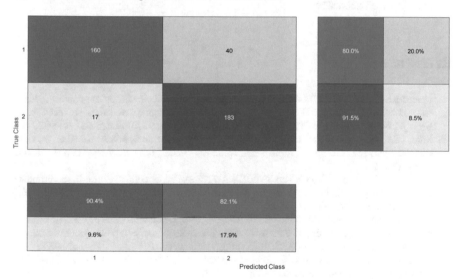

Fig. 4 Plot of confusion matrix

Table 1 Performance of the GoogleNet in CG/PG classification

Model	80:20 Ratio		70:30 Ratio	
	No augmentation	With augmentation	No augmentation	With augmentation
GoogleNet	88%	90.4%	85.3%	87.6%

Table 2 Performance comparison

Models	80:20 Ratio		70:30 Ratio	
	No augmentation	With augmentation	No augmentation	With augmentation
GoogleNet	88.75	90.625	88.33	90.42
VGG18	83.125	84.375	83.33	86.25

5 Conclusion

This paper attempted to study the performance of GoogleNet in classifying CG and PG images. The transfer learning approach is used to reduce the computational and time cost. The initial and the final layers of the GoogleNet are modified to make it appropriate for the CG/PG classification task. The learned weights of the GoogleNet are transferred to the designed network, and it is trained with the proposed training parameters. GoogleNet shows superior performance compared to VGG18 network. The futuristic approach is to use deep fusion features and attention model to enhance the classification accuracy.

References

1. Meena KB, Tyagi V (2019) Methods to distinguish photorealistic computer generated images from photographic images: a review. In: Advances in computing and data sciences, vol 1. Springer Nature Singapore Pte Ltd., pp 64–82. https://doi.org/10.1007/978-981-13-9939-8_7
2. Meena KB, Tyagi V (2019) A copy-move image forgery detection technique based on gaussian-hermite moments. Multimed Tools Appl 78:33505–33526. https://doi.org/10.1007/s11042-019-08082-2
3. Ni X, Chen L, Yuan L, Wu G, Yao Y (2019) An Evaluation of deep learning-based computer generated image detection approaches. IEEE Access 7:130830–130840. https://doi.org/10.1109/ACCESS.2019.2940383
4. Quan W, Wang K, Yan D-M, Zhang X, Pellerin D (2020) Learn with diversity and from harder samples: Improving the generalization of CNN-based detection of computer-generated images. Forensic Sci Int Digit Investig 35:301023. https://doi.org/10.1016/j.fsidi.2020.301023
5. Lyu S, Farid H (2005) How realistic is photorealistic? IEEE Trans Signal Process 53:845–850. https://doi.org/10.1109/TSP.2004.839896
6. Ng T-T, Chang S-F, Hsu J, Xie L, Tsui M-P (2005) Physics-motivated features for distinguishing photographic images and computer graphics. In: Proceedings of the 13th annual ACM international conference on multimedia—MULTIMEDIA '05. ACM Press, New York, New York, USA, p 239. https://doi.org/10.1145/1101149.1101192
7. Krizhevsky A, Sutskever I, Hinton GE (2012) ImageNet classification with deep convolutional neural networks. In: Pereira F, Burges CJC, Bottou L, Weinberger KQ (eds) Advances in neural information processing systems. Curran Associates, Inc.
8. Szegedy C, Liu W, Jia Y, Sermanet, P, Reed S, Anguelov D, Erhan D, Vanhoucke V, Rabinovich A (2015) Going deeper with convolutions. In: 2015 IEEE conference on computer vision and pattern recognition (CVPR). IEEE, pp 1–9. https://doi.org/10.1109/CVPR.2015.7298594

9. Peng F, Shi J, Long M (2014) Identifying photographic images and photorealistic computer graphics using multifractal spectrum features of PRNU. In: 2014 IEEE international conference on multimedia and expo (ICME). IEEE, pp 1–6 (2014). https://doi.org/10.1109/ICME.2014. 6890296

10. He P, Li H, Wang H, Zhang R (2020) Detection of computer graphics using attention-based dual-branch convolutional neural network from fused color components. Sensors 20:4743. https://doi.org/10.3390/s20174743

11. Haller M (2004) Photorealism or/and non-photorealism in augmented reality. In: Proceedings of the 2004 ACM SIGGRAPH international conference on virtual reality continuum and its applications in industry—VRCAI '04. ACM Press, New York, New York, USA, p 189. https:// doi.org/10.1145/1044588.1044627

12. Ng T, Chang S, Hsu J, Pepeljugoski M (2005) Columbia photographic images and photorealistic computer graphics dataset. 1–23

13. Zhang J, Williams SO, Wang H (2018) Intelligent computing system based on pattern recognition and data mining algorithms. Sustain Comput Inform Syst 20:192–202. https://doi.org/ 10.1016/j.suscom.2017.10.010

14. Dang-Nguyen D, Boato G, De Natale FGB (2012) Discrimination between computer generated and natural human faces based on asymmetry information. In: 2012 Proceedings of the 20th European signal processing conference (EUSIPCO), pp 1234–1238

15. Lv Y, Shen X, Wan G, Chen H (2014) Blind identification of photorealistic computer graphics based on fractal dimensions. In: Proceedings of the 2014 international conference on computer, communications and information technology. Atlantis Press, Paris, France. https://doi.org/10. 2991/ccit-14.2014.67

16. Yao Y, Hu W, Zhang W, Wu T, Shi Y-Q (2018) Distinguishing computer-generated graphics from natural images based on sensor pattern noise and deep learning. Sensors 18:1296. https:// doi.org/10.3390/s18041296

17. Nguyen HH, Tieu NDT, Nguyen-Son HQ, Nozick V, Yamagishi J, Echizen I (2018) Modular convolutional neural network for discriminating between computer-generated images and photographic images. In: ACM international conference on proceeding security. https://doi. org/10.1145/3230833.3230863

18. Photographic computer graphic image database. www.%0Airtc.org. Accessed on 10 Aug (2015)

Hybrid Methods for Increasing Security of IoT and Cloud Data

Kunal Mahajan, Sunil Kumar, and Dilip Kumar

1 Introduction

Cloud computing provides an on-demand delivery of various kinds of services via the Internet. It allows us to access and maintain the hardware as well as software resource that we own remotely, i.e., the resource can be controlled from anywhere in the world and from almost every available platform. It increases resource sharing and organizations of various sizes can host their Websites and application on cloud servers of third-party service provider without worrying about all of the internal workings. Depending on the organization's needs, they can choose from various types of services that exist over the cloud. There are 3 basic categories [1].

1.1 Infrastructure-as-a-Service (IaaS)

Provides its users with the infrastructure they desire. The user/organization can build on the infrastructure as per their needs. It provides its users the least level of abstraction from the technicality of the cloud when compared to the other cloud services.

K. Mahajan · S. Kumar (✉) · D. Kumar
Department of Computer Science and Engineering, National Institute of Technology, Jamshedpur, India
e-mail: 2018rscs016@nitjsr.ac.in

K. Mahajan
e-mail: 2021pgcscs11@nitjsr.ac.in

D. Kumar
e-mail: dilip.cse@nitjsr.ac.in

© The Author(s), under exclusive license to Springer Nature Singapore Pte Ltd. 2023
K. Kumar Singh et al. (eds.), *Machine Vision and Augmented Intelligence*, Lecture Notes in Electrical Engineering 1007, https://doi.org/10.1007/978-981-99-0189-0_45

1.2 Platform-as-a-Service (PaaS)

Provides its user with a basic platform on which they can deploy their applications. Here, the user need not manages the underlying infrastructure of the cloud, i.e., the basic requirements like operating system are already setup.

1.3 Software-as-a-Service (SaaS)

Provides its users with the complete product. It is managed by the cloud service provider itself. Users can access the application by connecting the cloud using their Web browser. There is usually not even the need of installing the software. This makes it very easy to perform upgrade and also allows vast reach to the application since the only requirements are Web browser and Internet connection [2].

IoT devices are physical objects that connect wirelessly to the Internet. IoT devices consist of long range of useful applications. Security cameras wirelessly connected to the server, smart wearable devices for tracking the health activities, weather monitors, intelligent refrigerators, optical sensors for automatically turning on the lights, etc. They usually transfer data over the Internet or they may also communicate using Bluetooth if the central operating machine is nearby.

Depending on the device, it may gather various kinds of data as per requirement. But all of the IoT devices require connectivity for data transfer to the central system since they do not possess the computation power to analyze the data. The central system collects data from various IoT devices and then analyze it.

With all the data being transferred over the data, it is an essential requirement to maintain the confidentiality as well as integrity of the data [3]. The integrity of the data can be checked by computing hash of the data and sending that over to the receiver side who will match the received hash with the hash of the received message. The hash functions are generally very fast and can be implemented efficiently on low performance device very easily. To maintain the confidentiality, it is required that the data needs to protected against unauthorized access. This means that only the authorized parties should be able to access it. This is usually done by encrypting the data before sending it over the network.

Essentially, the sender converts his/her message into an unintelligible cryptic form which is then sent to the receiver over the communication channel. The receiver, by some means, is able to convert the encrypted data back into the original message. Even if an adversary is passively listening over the communication media, they will only be able to get a hold of encrypted data. Without the secret keys, no one other that the authorized parties will be able to decrypt the cipher data back into its original form. Cryptographic techniques have been used for well over centuries. "Caesar cipher" was used by Julius Caesar to communicate with his generals. Essentially, each character of the message was shifted by a fixed number of spaces to yield a new alphabet. There could be only 25 other possible shifts of any ciphered English alphabet, and it will take only fraction of seconds to break the cipher.

Encryption can be done by either symmetric or asymmetric technique. In symmetric, we use same key for both encryption and decryption. AES is one of the most popular symmetric encryption techniques. It is a block cipher which takes fixed length of data as input at a time and performs various substitution and transposition rounds on the data. Blowfish is another symmetric block cipher. It consists of 16 Feistel-like iterations and works on a fixed block size of 8-bytes at a time. The key size can vary anywhere from 4 to 56 bytes. Symmetric encryption techniques are usually faster, but the shared secret keys must be known to both communicating parties in advance. So, there is a problem of sharing the secret key. The issue with symmetric algorithms is that if the adversary finds out the secret key, then they will be able to decrypt every message sent from either of the communicating party. So, the symmetric key is the single point of failure.

Asymmetric key encryption uses two keys, such as one for encryption and other for decryption. It allows the sender to make one of their key public and keep the other private. Anyone can encrypt the data with sender's public key, and only sender will be able to decrypt it with the corresponding private key. Asymmetric key-based algorithm usually lacks in time efficiency because they are based on exponential and modulo operations, and they are costly to perform. RSA is well-known asymmetric encryption algorithm. It is based on the fact that finding the factors of large number, which is a product of two prime numbers, is very hard. The computed numbers are thousands of bits long. The key size in RSA is usually more than 3072 bits. The strength of the encryption increases with the key size. But this leads to increase in computation power required for the encryption and decryption. Also, the amount of data that can be encrypted in a single round of RSA needs to be smaller than the key size.

This is the general motivation for using ECC. It is based on elliptic curve discrete logarithm problem (ECDLP) which is much harder problem to solve. ECC is able to provide the same cryptographic strength as an RSA-based system with much smaller key size. A 160-bit ECC key has same equivalent strength as a 1024-bit RSA key. Smaller key is also easily manageable, and for an IoT-device with limited storage, it makes large difference.

Here, a hybrid encryption technique is used where both symmetric as well as asymmetric encryption algorithms are used. The system is capable of encrypting any type of multimedia data (text, images, etc.) and provides the same (or even) better security while remaining time and space efficient.

1.4 Organization of the Paper

Apart from the introduction, related work is done in (Sect. 2). Existing cryptography algorithms are described in (Sect. 3). The proposed hybrid approach is shown in (Sect. 4). Results and implementation are done in (Sect. 5), and the conclusion is in Sect. 6.

2 Related Work

2.1 Implementation of Text Encryption Using Elliptic Curve Cryptography

ECC works by mapping the characters to affine points on the elliptic curve. This paper proposes a new technique where the ASCII values of all the characters in the data are combined which is then passed as input to the algorithm. The algorithm then converts the received data into smaller groups of fixed size. Padding is performed if necessary. The data groups are then finally converted into big integers (of base 65,536 or as per requirements). Using point multiplication and point addition, the cipher text is generated. So, there is no need to map individual characters to the curve.

2.2 Data Security in Cloud Computing Using Various Cryptography Algorithms

The paper describes a hybrid approach for securing the data over the cloud. The proposed technique uses a combination of a symmetric encryption (AES) and an asymmetric encryption (ECC) algorithm to encrypt and decrypt the data. The data is first encrypted with AES using the key generated by elliptic curve algorithm. The encrypted data is then encrypted with ECC public key. During decryption, the data is decrypted firstly with ECC private key of the receiver and then with AES.

2.3 Design and Implementation of Hybrid Encryption Algorithm

The paper proposes a hybrid encryption technique using two symmetric key algorithms, namely AES and Blowfish. Both algorithms use their own unique key. The keys are first expanded so as to get the partial keys that will be used in various rounds of encryption and decryption. The data is first encrypted with the AES using the expanded AES key. Then, the encrypted data is further encrypted again with Blow-fish using the expanded Blowfish keys. These two layers of encryption make the cipher text more difficult to estimate and hence increases the security.

2.4 Evaluating the Performance of Symmetric Encryption Algorithms

The paper provides an analysis of various symmetric encryption algorithms that are available for use. Various algorithms use different mechanism for encryption and decryption which has direct effect on the strength of the cryptographic algorithm. Complex operation does not necessarily mean stronger encryption. The paper analyzes AES, DES, 3-DES, and Blowfish on text and image files. The results show that AES is the fastest, and Blowfish is second in terms of both encryption and decryption time. 3-DES is the slowest among all for both encryption and decryption.

2.5 Hybrid AES-ECC Model for the Security of Data Over Cloud Storage

Cloud storage has been a rapidly growing industry over the past few years. The data of various organizations as well as users is stored on the cloud servers. This provides the user easy access to data from anywhere in the world. However, with the ever-growing demand, there is a need to keep all of that data secured. The encryption algorithm should be fast, and it should have less computation needs. It also needs to be high security since data on the cloud might be sensitive. The article proposes a way of encrypting the data which is stored over the cloud. A hybrid approach is used where the data is encrypted using the ECC key as the secret using the AES algorithm. Combining the smaller but strong keys of ECC with the faster albeit secure AES algorithm results in an efficient encrypting algorithm containing the characteristics of both techniques.

2.6 Dual Encryption Model for Preserving Privacy in Cloud Computing

The paper proposes another way of using hybrid technique to encrypt and decrypt data that is to be communicated over the cloud. The symmetric algorithm used for encryption is AES. It will be used for encrypting the data which is to be communicated. The proposed algorithm also uses ECC. The secret AES key is encrypted with the public ECC key of the receiver. Both the encrypted AES key and the encrypted data are sent over to the receiver or to the cloud. When decryption, the encrypted secret key is decrypted using the ECC private key, which will then be used to decrypt the ciphered data.

3 Various Encryption Algorithms Used

Advanced encryption standard (AES), Blowfish, and elliptic curve cryptography are used in the proposed methodology they are explained:

3.1 Blowfish

Blowfish is a symmetric key block cipher consisting of key-dependent substitution-boxes. It has a 64-bit block size and a variable key length which can be anywhere between 32-bits to 448 bits and consists of 16-round Feistel cipher. Key expansion is done by breaking the key into a set of subkeys arrays: one P-array containing 18 32-bit subkeys and four 32-bit S-boxes [4]. The P-array and all the S-boxes are initialized with values derived from the hexadecimal digits of pi so they have no obvious pattern. The input key is XORed with all the P-entries in order. The key bytes may be cycled; in case, the key is smaller. An eight byte zero-block is then encrypted with the Blowfish algorithm initially. The first 32-bits of key are XORed with P1 and second 32-bits with P2. Newly generated values replace the old values of P1 and P2. The values are then encrypted with the new values of P1 and P2, and the cipher generated after encryption replaces P3 and P4.

This process is repeated 521 times to calculate all the subkeys required during various rounds of encryption as well as initializing the values of S-boxes. Figure 1 shows the encryption procedure of the Blowfish algorithm. Once all the subkeys have been generated, a block of 64-bits of data is taken as input which is then split into two halves. Left half of data is XORed with the subkey of the particular round, and the data is then passed on to a F-function which perform substitution using S-boxes. The resulting data is then XORed with the remaining half of the input data. The left and right half are then swapped, and the process repeats for a total of 16 rounds. The resulting left half is XORed with the P[18], and the right half is XORed with P[17]. Note that swapping is not performed in the last round. During decryption, the subkeys are generated in reverse order. Rest of the algorithm is same as encryption.

Blowfish is a fast block cipher-based. The only issue with the algorithm is that the key generation requires a lot of pre-processing which is equivalent to encrypting text of 4 KB. However, both encryption and decryption are very fast. The slower key generation makes the algorithm suitable for protection against dictionary attacks. The idea is that if the key to be generated takes large amount of time, then it will be harder for an adversary to quickly try all possible combination of words in hope for finding the key.

Fig. 1 Working of blowfish algorithm [5]

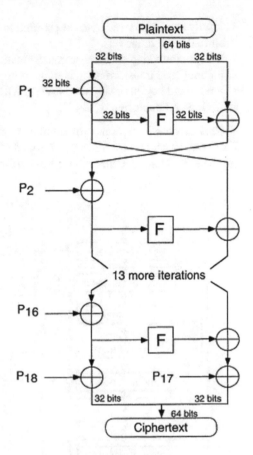

3.2 AES Algorithm

The advanced encryption standard is a variant of Rjindael block cipher instead of Feistel network. It works with a fixed block size of 128 bits, which is subject to encryption with keys of length 128, 192, or 256-bits [6]. Using the AES key schedule, the secret key is expanded into a group of subkeys that will be used for different rounds in the algorithms. It operates on 4×4 column-major order array of bytes, i.e., 16 bytes of data are taken as input by the algorithm at a time. In each round, the input bytes are XORed with the 1st round key. Then for each encryption round, the following operations take place as follows:

- Byte substitution is done by using the predefined and fixed S-boxes. All of the 16 input bytes are replaced by their corresponding values in the S-box.
- Shift row is done where each of the row byte is shifted to left cyclically by a certain number. The first row remains the same. Second row bytes are shifted to

left by one. Third row bytes are shifted to the left by two, and last row bytes are shifted three to the left.

- Mix columns step does linear transformation on all the bytes of matrix column by column. The transformation is done multiplying each column by a fixed matrix.
- Add round key step takes the bitwise XOR of the resultant bytes with the subkey for the particular round (Fig. 2).

This process is repeated for number of rounds depending on the size of key. There are 10 rounds for 128-bit, 12 rounds for 192-bit, and 14 rounds for 256-bit key. The mix columns operation is not performed in the last round. For decryption,

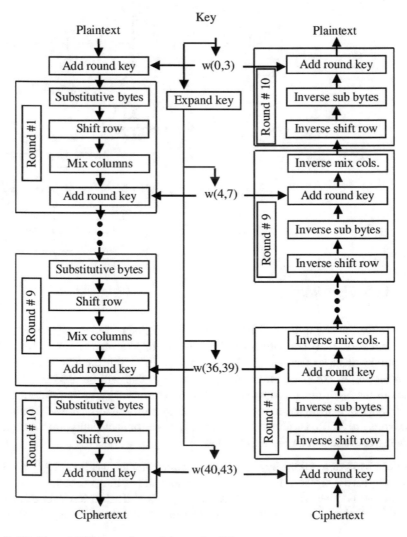

Fig. 2 Working of AES encryption and decryption [7]

the operation order in each round is reversed. This requires different algorithms to be implemented for encryption and decryption, unlike Feistel cipher where same algorithm can do both encryption as well as decryption. Unlike Blowfish, AES does not require heavy pre-processing for key generation. The byte substitution step in the algorithm is responsible for "confusion" which makes it difficult to find the relation between the encrypted data and plaintext. Shifting rows and mixing columns are responsible for achieving "diffusion" which means that even a slight change, like flipping a bit, will lead to drastic change in the cipher text known as avalanche effect. The AES algorithm provides excellent confusion as well as diffusion.

AES also requires very little pre-processing for key expansion. It is also faster in encryption and decryption than almost every symmetric [8] as well as asymmetric cipher. It is also very light on hardware as well as software. These are some of the reasons why AES is pretty much ubiquitous worldwide.

3.3 Elliptic Curve Cryptography

Neal Koblitz along with Victor Miller discovered the ECC in 1985. An elliptic curve, with two variables, over a field K is non-singular cubic curve such that $f(x, y) = 0$. An elliptic curve is defined by an Eq. 1 of the form:

$$y^2 = x^3 + ax + b \tag{1}$$

Using point doubling as well as point addition, any point P (x, y) on the elliptic curve can yield the resultant point P' (x', y') as explained below:

Figure 3a shows the elliptic curve addition in which a straight line is formed by joining the two points (P & Q) that are to be added. The negative equivalent of the point at which the straight line intercepts the curve is taken which is the final result [9]. For point doubling, simply the tangent of the point is allowed to fall on the curve, and the negative equivalent of the point where the tangent intercepts the curve is the result. The great advantage of ECC is that even a smaller key is stronger than a comparatively larger RSA key [10]. The strength is based on the fact that solving the discrete logarithmic problem on an elliptic curve with respect to a publicly known base point is a hard problem [11]. The public key of the ECC is the base point on the curve, while the private key is just an integer describing the number of dots. The keys in the ECC system are not interchangeable. The security and speed lie in the fact that it is very easy to compute a final point if the base point and the number of dots that occur are known. However, given the base point and the end point, it is very hard to compute the number of dots that were taken to get there.

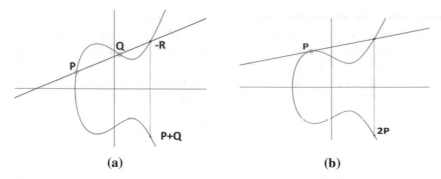

Fig. 3 **a** Point addition, **b** point doubling

4 Methodology and Proposed Hybrid Approach

The proposed model makes use of 3 cipher technologies, namely AES, Blowfish, and ECC, which were described above. The algorithm can work on any type of multimedia data. This is done by pre-processing the data into a suitable form. Symmetric keys are exchanged using ECC, and data is ciphered using the two symmetric encryption algorithms. Various steps performed during the proposed method have been described as follows:

4.1 Pre-processing the Multimedia Data

- Multimedia data is first encoded in Base64 form.
- Using various compression algorithms, the encoded data can be compressed so as to decrease the space requirement.

4.2 Key Generation and Exchange

Symmetric keys can be randomly generated. For added security, the two symmetric keys will be generated by different communicating parties, i.e., suppose Alice and Bob want to communicate over the Internet, Alice can generate Blowfish symmetric key while Bob can generate AES symmetric key. For key exchange, the sender will simply encrypt the key using the ECC public key of the receiver [12]. The receiver will be able to decrypt using their ECC private key.

4.3 Encryption of Multimedia Data

Figure 4 shows the working of the hybrid encryption algorithm. For the sake of simplicity, the sender has generated both the symmetric keys.

- Data from the pre-processed stage is encrypted with AES algorithm.
- AES encrypted data is encrypted again with Blowfish algorithm. This is the final ciphered data which will be transferred over the Internet.
- Randomly generated AES and Blowfish keys are encrypted with ECC public key of the receiver. The keys are piggy-backed with the data.

Fig. 4 Hybrid encryption approach

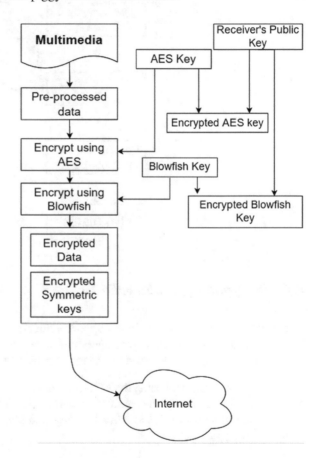

Fig. 5 Hybrid decryption approach

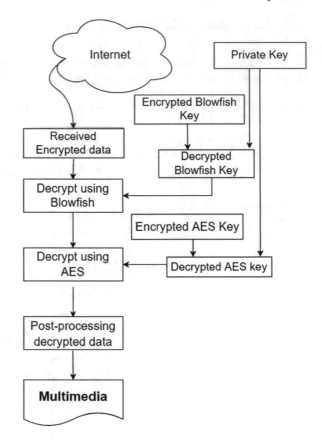

4.4 Decryption of Multimedia Data

The decryption process works in the opposite direction as shows in the following Fig. 5. The receiver will receive the encrypted data along with the encrypted keys. The followings steps are executed on the receiver side for decryption:

- The keys are decrypted using the ECC private key.
- Using the Blowfish key, the received encrypted data is decrypted.
- It is then further decrypted with the AES key, and finally, post-processing is done on the decrypted output.

4.5 Post-processing on Decrypted Data

- Here, the data is decompressed if it was compressed earlier in the pre-processing phase.
- The data is then Base64 decoded to get the original multimedia back.

5 Implementation Results

For the test procedures, multimedia data in form of images was used. Since the hybrid algorithm uses multiple encryption algorithm, the expected time for encryption/decryption is assumed to increase. However, the security also increases. The storage requirements by the algorithms are almost negligible other than the memory required to store the keys. Compared to RSA, the space required will be less because of the small key size used by all the algorithm. By using the technique of pairing up ASCII value as input to ECC, there is a significant decrease in the amount of time used for keys encryption with ECC.

RSA uses complex exponential and modulus operations for encryption. Also, the size of data that can be encrypted by RSA is bounded by the size of key. Key size also determines the strength of RSA. But larger key causes high computation necessity for small size of data as the data has to be padded. For encryption with RSA, multimedia needs to be split into smaller parts, where each individual part is smaller than the size of key. This may lead to increase in size of the encrypted file as the individual encrypted parts of the multimedia need to be merged into a single file to transfer them over to receiver. 3-DES is symmetric technique which uses DES algorithm thrice on the data. Usually, there are 3 separate keys (K1, K2, and K3). The data is first encrypted with K1 then decrypted with K2 and finally encrypted with K3. Process is inversed on the receiver side. If K1 and K3 are identical, then the resulting variant is known as 2TDES. If all of the keys are same, then the algorithm is identical to DES. Even though size of individual key size is 64-bits, every 8th bit is used as parity decreasing the effective key strength. For the tests, 3-DES was used with all keys being unique. So, it has an effective key strength of 168 bits. The sum total of all the keys used by the method is lesser than the RSA key. 3-DES has smallest key size among three, but the encryption strength is also the least. Key strength is not the same as key size. For example, DES uses a 64-bit key of which 8 bits are used for parity. So, the effective key strength depends on only 56 remaining bits.

Table 1 describes the number of keys as well as the effective strength of keys used by each of the algorithms.

Figure 6 shows the time taken by RSA, 3-DES, and proposed hybrid model for encryption of multimedia data in the form of images of various size.

It can be seen that RSA performs the worst among the three because of the higher computational needs. 3-DES performs better than RSA. The proposed hybrid

Table 1 Comparison of various algorithms

	RSA	3-DES	Hybrid
No. of keys	1	2 or 3	3
Key strength	3072 bits	112 if K1 = K3 168, if keys are unique. This has been used for tests	256-Bits AES key 32–448 bits Blowfish key 256-Bits ECC key
Encryption strength	Strong	Medium	Strongest

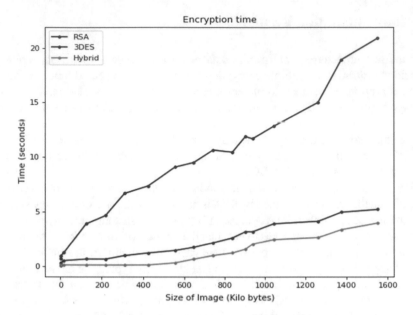

Fig. 6 Depicts the encryption time of multimedia files of various size using hybrid algorithm

method is fastest among the three because both AES and Blowfish that were used for encrypting the data are significantly faster algorithm because of their symmetric nature and the ECC, being an asymmetric encryption method, is slower than both but it is only used to encrypt the keys that are comparatively smaller in size and hence does not affect the performance much.

Figure 7 shows the decryption time of all the three algorithms for decrypting the files of various size. The results clearly show that RSA performs the worst, while the hybrid model is the fastest. Also, the proposed method is space efficient which is a desirable property for both the cloud and IoT devices.

Table 2 summarizes the result of the tests by showing the encryption/decryption time of the various methods used.

6 Conclusion

The current implementation has been tested on various multimedia. The results show that this method is very fast for smaller files. Most of the IoT devices gather sensory information, and the data is not of significantly large size. The larger files can be compressed before encryption which will decrease the time consumed by the algorithm and also save space. AES is usually implemented at hardware level and is very fast encryption algorithm. Blowfish is very fast at software level as it uses Feistel block. For encrypting the symmetric keys, ECC is used which is albeit slow but is

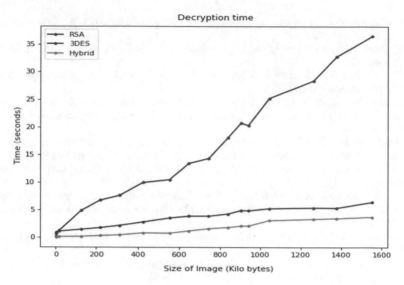

Fig. 7 Depicting the decryption time of multimedia files of various sizes using hybrid algorithm

Table 2 Comparison of encryption and decryption time of proposed methods

	RSA	3-DES	Hybrid
Average encryption time	9.192	2.156	1.161
Average decryption time	14.79	2.41	1.45
Computational power required	High	Medium	Low

very secure and allows secure key exchange. A combination of all of these provides the proposed method with all the desirable properties of an encryption algorithm. For protecting the integrity of the data, hash of the multimedia using SHA-256 or other hashing function can be calculated. This hash can then be transferred over to the receiver either encrypted or as plaintext where the hash of the received data will be matched with it. Other than IoT and cloud services, the implementation can also be used for communication over the Internet by various devices by minor tweaks to the algorithm so as to make them work on various different platforms.

References

1. Rehman S, Talat Bajwa N, Shah MA, Aseeri AO, Anjum A (2021) Hybrid AES-ECC model for the security of data over cloud storage. Electronics 10:2673
2. Agrahari V (2020) Data security in cloud computing using cryptography algorithms. Int J Sci Dev Res
3. Sarmila KB, Manisekaran SV (2019) A study on security considerations in iot environment and data protection methodologies for communication in cloud computing. In: 2019 International

Carnahan conference on security technology (ICCST), 2019, pp 1–6. https://doi.org/10.1109/CCST.2019.8888414

4. El_Deen AET (2013) Design and implementation of hybrid encryption algorithm. Int J Sci Eng Res 4(1)

5. Hemeida F, Alexan W, Sadek S (2019) Blowfish-Secured audio steganography. https://doi.org/10.1109/NILES.2019.8909206

6. Sharma S, Chopra V (2016) Analysis of AES encryption with ECC. In: International interdisciplinary conference on engineering science & management, India, Dec 2016, pp 195–201

7. Wadday A, Wadi S, Mohammed H, Abdullah A (2018) Study of WiMAX based communication channel effects on the ciphered image using MAES algorithm. Int J Appl Eng Res 13

8. Abd Eliminaam DS, Abdual Kader HM, Hadhoud MM (2010) Evaluating the performance of symmetric encryption algorithms. Int J Netw Secur 10(3):213–219

9. Iyer S, Sedamkar RR, Gupta S (2016) A novel idea on multimedia encryption using hybrid crypto approach. Procedia Comput Sci 79:293–298. https://doi.org/10.1016/j.procs.2016.03.038

10. Mahto D, Yadav D (2017) RSA and ECC: a comparative analysis. Int J Appl Eng Res 12:9053–9061

11. Miller VS (2000) Use of elliptic curves in cryptography. In: Advances in cryptology-CRYPTO'85 proceedings, vol 218. Springer, pp 417–426

12. Singh LD, Singh KM (2015) Implementation of text encryption using elliptic curve cryptography. Procedia Comput Sci 54:73–82

13. Nithiya C, Sridevi IIR (2016) ECC algorithm and security in cloud. Int J Adv Res Comput Sci Technol (IJARCST) 4(1):24

14. Abroshan H (2021) A hybrid encryption solution to improve cloud computing security using symmetric and asymmetric cryptography algorithms. Int J Adv Comput Sc Appl 12(6)

15. Ghallab A, Mohammed S, Mohsen A (2021) Data integrity and security in distributed cloud computing—a review. https://doi.org/10.1007/978-981-15-7234-0_73

16. Kumar Y, Munjal R, Sharma H (2011) Comparison of symmetric and asymmetric cryptography with existing vulnerabilities and countermeasures. Int J Comput Sci Manage Stud

17. Kumar S, Dhanamalar M, Ayshwarya B, Bora A, Jegatheesh G (2021) A novel algorithm to secure big data iot system. Des Eng (Toronto) 997–1011

18. Sharma S, Singla K, Rathee G, Saini H (2020) A hybrid cryptographic technique for file storage mechanism over cloud. https://doi.org/10.1007/978-981-15-0029-9_19

Abstractive Text Summarization with Fine-Tuned Transformer

Venkata Phanidra Kumar Siginamsetty and Ashu Abdul

1 Introduction

In this Internet era, data is generated from multiple sources on a day-to-day basis. So, it is necessary to provide a cleaner way to summarize the content based upon the data available in the input document [1]. Extractive [2] and abstractive summarizations [3] are the two forms of summarizations. The extraction of key information or sentences from a text file or source document is referred to as extractive text summarization. The meaningful summary is constructed from the input document using abstractive summarization, which takes into account the material's context. We used a custom scraped IndiaToday dataset,[1] which consists of the title, the short summary, and the original full text related to that news. The other datasets used are CNN/DailyMail data [4] and Inshorts dataset,[2] which consists of news articles and associated short highlights. These datasets illustrate a variety of summary approaches, from highlights to one-sentence summaries.

In this paper, we choose abstractive text summarization (ATS) because it will provide meaningful information to the users. It will provide the summary to the end- users by using out-of-vocabulary (OOV) [5]. We use fine-tuned transformer to generate a more meaningful summary from the input document. In this approach, we have modified the residual connection layer with parametric rectified linear activation unit (PReLU) [6]; in this way, we are attaining a better ROUGE score. The encoder and decoder are the two sub-sessions of the transformer model. A multi-head attention network (MHA) and a pointwise feedforward network are used in the encoder (PFFN). Similar to the encoder, the decoder consists of two MHA and one PFFN. The

---

[1] https://github.com/funnyPhani/Research-day-code-SRM.

[2] https://www.kaggle.com/shashichander009/inshorts-news-data

V. P. K. Siginamsetty · A. Abdul (✉)
Department of Computer Science and Engineering, SRM University, Amaravati, AP, India
e-mail: ashu.a507@gmail.com

© The Author(s), under exclusive license to Springer Nature Singapore Pte Ltd. 2023 587
K. Kumar Singh et al. (eds.), *Machine Vision and Augmented Intelligence*, Lecture Notes in Electrical Engineering 1007, https://doi.org/10.1007/978-981-99-0189-0_46

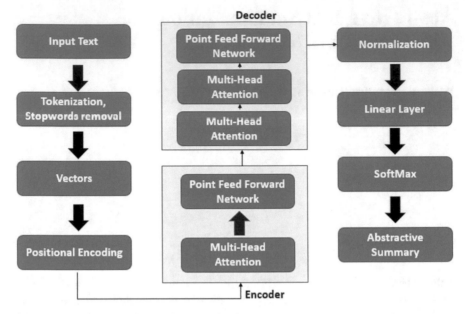

Fig. 1 Proposed fine-tuned transformer architecture

self- attention (SA) weights calculation is also very fast because the normalization takes place. Updating the PReLU activation function and normalization increases the speed of calculating attention weights. The generated summary will have OOV, and it will add more insights to the end users. The candidate document and the reference document will be having a high ROUGE score [7]. By this approach, we are proving a better summary to the user, and by this way, we are reducing the time constraint of the document for understanding. The proposed fine-tuned transformer is done on the PFFN network by updating the activation function (Fig. 1).

To outline our accomplishments, they were as follows: (1) In PFFN, we fine-tuned the existing transformer. (2) We used custom scraped data such as the IndiaToday dataset. Hereunder are the remaining sections: We addressed the existing research effort in Sect. 2 and its limitations. Our proposed methodology and workflow are discussed in Sect. 3. Section 4 analyzes the proposed work for the existing system. Finally, in Sect. 5 we provide the conclusion of our proposed approach.

2 Related Work

In this section, we are going to see the methodologies available to handle the text summarization task. It is necessary to generate the summary of a document; by using this, we can convey the same amount of information to the user within less amount of time. It is [8] of two types extractive and abstractive summarizations. In extractive summarization, only the important sentences are given more importance, and those important sentences are decided by the linguistic and statistical features of paragraphs.

The limitation to this approach is that it is not going to generate a meaningful summary to the end user. To address this issue [9, 10], abstractive summarization comes into the picture. It is accomplished by employing powerful natural language algorithms to provide a concise and understandable summary for end users. In earlier research, the summarization was done based on the word count, phrase frequency, [11] and key features present in the document. The issue with this approach is we are not considering the important information; we are using the word count function to get the more appropriate reputed words from the input document which is not going to solve the actual summarization task. In 1969, [12] they used the structural syntax, which is the combination of work frequency with a position of the word. By this approach, we are solving some extent of the summarization task.

In the current era, the summarization is done by using advanced natural language techniques such as encoder–decoder, recurrent neural networks (RNNs) [13], long short-term memory (LSTM) [14], sequence-to-sequence (S2S) model [15], and transformer models [16]. In [17], researchers used the RNN to generate the summary. The issue with this approach is the training the RNN is too difficult. Which may leads to the vanishing and exploding gradient problems difficult to stack multiple RNN cells. If we use the RNNs, it is more difficult to reach the global minima [18]. To address the issues in the RNN, researchers proposed the LSTMs, which consist of the memory cell in the architecture. However, the LSTMs are prone to the overfitting problem (issue with a low bias and a high variance). To overcome the issues in the LSTMs, researchers proposed the S2S networks with attention functions [19]. The S2S networks consist of the encoder–decoder-based LSTMs with attention functions. The attention functions help the S2S networks to overcome the overfitting problem. But, the S2S networks lack the mechanism to preserve the long-term dependencies presented in the input.

In [20], the researchers proposed the usage of the transformers to overcome the limitations of the S2S networks. The transformer is an encoder–decoder based on the pointwise feedforward neural networks with a multi-head attention mechanism. The transformers use the rectified linear activation unit (ReLU) as the activation function. As per the definition of the ReLU function (i.e., $\max (0, x)$), the negative weights are equated to 0. Thereby, the transformers fail to reach global minima leading to an increase in the convergence time. To overcome these issues, we propose a fine-tuned version of the transformer with PReLU as the activation function.

3 Approach

In this proposed approach, we are using abstractive summarization because it will be more meaningful, and it will be a shorter version of the input document. In this approach, we fine-tuned the transformer, which consists of both the encoder–decoder models. In the encoder phase, it consists of multi-head attention (MHA) and pointwise feedforward network (PFFN). Let, IT represents the input text obtained from the user. We preprocess the IT by tokenizing and removing the stopwords from the IT. After preprocessing the IT, we use the Word2Vector algorithm to obtain the word embeddings, WT from the IT. Later, we extract the positional encodings, PEs from the WT. The PEs are calculated based on sin and cos functions, but here, the positional encoding is used to specify the position of the word in the sequence of inputs $\{pv1, pv2, pv3, \ldots, pvn\}$, so, the ordering of the context is not going to change. The even position of the word is calculated by (2 m), whereas the odd positioning of the word is calculated by (2 m + 1), and along with these, we choose the m dimension because the model is to easily learn to attend by relative position (pos), whereas dm where d is the depth of the model,

$$PE(pos, 2m) = \sin\left(pos/d^{(2m/dm)}\right),$$
$$PE(pos, 2m + 1) = \cos\left(pos/d^{(2m/dm)}\right). \tag{1}$$

Here, PE (pos, 2 m) is used for calculating PE for the even position of the words. Whereas, PE (pos, 2 m + 1) is used to calculate the odd position of the words. Then after PEs are added to the vectors, the data passes through the encoder model. In the encoder, it consists of two phases such as the first is multi-head attention and the second is pointwise feedforward network. In the first phase, we assume query (P), key (Q), and the value (R). Here, Q^t represents the transpose. The operation is as follows:

$$MatMul(P * Q^t). \tag{2}$$

The self-attention, SA(P, Q, R), is the product of SoftMax activation function and the R as follows:

$$SA(P, Q, R) = SoftMax\left(MatMul(P * Qt)/\sqrt{\dim PQ}\right) * R. \tag{3}$$

The next phase of the encoder is the residual connection (RC) layer. We pass the output of the self-attention to the RC. It will normalize the weights of the self-attention network,

$$RC = Norm(SA(P, Q, R)). \tag{4}$$

The RC operation is then passed to the PFFN. It is the main part of the architecture; in this network, the vectors pass through the linear layers with PRELU as an activation function. The main objective of taking PRELU as an activation function is as follows: In backpropagation, if we consider RELU and if the weights are negative, then there might be no weight updating. So, dead neurons might take place if we consider ReLU max (o, x) as an activation function. To avoid these issues, we fine-tuned the

Fig. 2 Pointwise
feedforward network

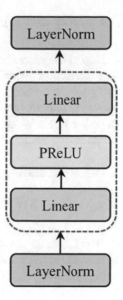

transformer with the PRELU function in the PFFN (Fig. 2).

$$PFFN = RC + \sum_{i=1}^{n} (Linear + PRelU + Linear)_n + RC. \qquad (5)$$

$$f(yi) = \begin{cases} yi, & yi > 0 \\ ai.yi, & yi \leq 0 \end{cases}$$

PReLU Function

In the above function $f(yi)$, αi is the hyperparameter, and we can set the αi value to 0.01. In the same way, we have the decoder network, and it will take the input as the encoder's output. It consists of multi-head attention and a pointwise feedforward network. The workflow of these networks is the same in encoder, but the only difference is that it takes the input as decoder's output and self-attention weights are calculated. Later on, the output is passed through the RC layer, to normalize the self-attention weights. The output of the self-attention is passed as input to the PFFN. Finally, we attain the abstractive summary of the given input. The summary, which is generated by our proposed network, is more meaningful, and it is the short version of the original document. By fine-tuning the transformer, the generated abstractive summary is more meaningful to the user.

3.1 OOV Generation

On top of the generated abstractive summary, OOV generation is taken into account. The words that occur less frequently in the datasets are labeled as OOV. Then, the OOV words are converted into vectors (Voov). Later on, we convert the generated summary into vectors (Gv). The comparison engine will compare each Gv with all the other Voov. We use the cosine similarity (CS) engine; it works based on the cos function. It measures the similarity vectors in the OOV corpus,

$$\text{CS}(G_v, V_{oov}) = \cos(\theta) = (G_v.V_{oov})/(\||G_v\|x\|V_{oov}\|).$$

$$\text{OOV} = \begin{cases} \text{Replace,} & S > 0.85 \\ \text{Nochang,} & S < 0.85 \end{cases} \tag{6}$$

The CS value can range from 0 to 1. If the CS is one, the text is similar, and if it is zero, the text is not similar. Each word in the resulting summary will be compared to every term in the OOV corpus. Replace the word if the CS is more than 0.85; else, leave it alone. The ROUGE score of this proposed network is good compared to the traditional transformers.

4 Experimental Results

In this section, we evaluate the performance of the proposed approach. In Sect. 4.1, we describe the datasets used for the evaluations. Whereas in Sect. 4.2, we discuss the evaluation results in comparison with the S2S approach [21] and traditional transformer approach [16].

4.1 Datasets Description

In our proposed solution, we have used three datasets as CNN/DialyMail, Inshorts, and a custom dataset known as IndiaToday. The description of these data is shown in the Table 1. The CNN/DailyMail dataset consists of articles and their corresponding highlights, i.e., a few highlights will provide a brief overview of the article. We pre-processed the content in the data accordingly to our approach. We preprocessed the data by removing the stopwords, special characters, symbols, and URLs present in the input. It contains an average summary length of 45.70 words and 3.59 sentences.

The Inshorts dataset consists of articles and their corresponding highlights, i.e., a few highlights will provide a brief overview of the article. We preprocessed the content in the data accordingly to our approach. We preprocessed the data by removing the stopwords, special characters, symbols, and URLs present in the input.

Table 1 Datasets descriptions

Dataset	Avg doc words	Length sentences	Avg words summary	Length of the sentences
CNN/DailyMail	760.50	34.54	45.70	3.59
Inshorts	653.74	29.57	54.75	3.78
IndiaToday	800.47	31.54	58.31	4.42

It contains an average summary length of 45.70 words and 3.78 sentences. Similarly, the IndiaToday dataset is custom scraped data, and the main objective of this dataset is to add a few more variants of articles. By this approach, the results of the ROUGE are doing good. We preprocess the data, which includes the processing steps like tokenization, stemming, and handling special characters. It contains an average summary length of 54.75 words and 4.42 sentences.

4.2 Results

By using the fine-tuned transformers, the results are doing good. The input data is passed through the data preprocessing pipeline. In this pipeline, tokenization is applied to the input document. Later on, stopwords are removed from the document, and the special symbols are removed from the input document. The short summary is generated by passing the data to the fine-tuned transformer model. In this paper, we use the recall (β), precision (α), and F_1-score ($F1$) metrics as the ROUGE-N score metrics to evaluate the performance of the proposed fine-tuned transformers. Here, ROUGE-N refers to the overlapping of the n-gram (n words) between the referenced summary and the generated summary. The recall (β) relates to how the system summary recovers or captures the majority of the reference summary. The β represents the number of words that overlap (Ov) to the total number of words in the reference summary (rfs) as,

$$\beta = O_v/\text{rf}_s. \tag{7}$$

The β will indicate accuracy in terms of the referenced summary. Whereas the α signifies the accuracy in terms of the generated summary. The α represents the number of words that overlap (Ov) with the total number of words in the system summary (ss) as,

$$\alpha = O_v/s_s \tag{8}$$

Similarly, the $F1$ measures the overall accuracy of the proposed fine-tuned transformers based on the referenced summary and the generated summary. F_1 refers to the weighted average of recall and precision metrics as,

Table 2 ROUGE scores table

Approach	ROUGE		
	ROUGE-1	ROUGE-2	ROUGE-3
S2S LSTM network	$\alpha = 0.40$	$\alpha = 0.47$	$\alpha = 0.68$
	$\beta = 0.47$	$\beta = 0.51$	$\beta = 0.71$
	$F1 = 0.52$	$F1 = 0.58$	$F1 = 0.73$
Transformer model	$\alpha - 0.75$	$\alpha - 0.78$	$\alpha - 0.81$
	$\beta = 0.78$	$\beta = 0.79$	$\beta = 0.82$
	$F1 = 0.81$	$F1 = 0.82$	$F1 = 0.84$
Proposed model	$\alpha = 0.81$	$\alpha = 0.85$	$\alpha = 0.91$
	$\beta = 0.85$	$\beta = 0.89$	$\beta = 0.93$
	$F1 = 0.91$	$F1 = 0.92$	$F1 = 0.95$

$$F1 = 2 * ((\alpha * \beta) / (\alpha + \beta)). \tag{9}$$

We evaluate the accuracy of the proposed fine-tuned transformers based on the ROUGE-1, ROUGE-2, and ROUGE-3 metrics in comparison with the S2S approach [21] and traditional transformer approach [16] as shown in the Table 2.

In the first approach, researchers used the S2S LSTM network [21]. It is a kind of encoder–decoder-based model. The workflow of this approach is as follows; the input text is passed to the encoder network at each timestamp. It will process the information and collect the contextual information including the input text at each timestamp. The S2S decoder is an LSTM network that analyzes the entire target phrase word by word and predicts the next word in the sequence based on the preceding word. The start and end tokens are added to the decoder before fetching the information. As a result, researchers developed a self-attention mechanism, which is used in the transformer model, to overcome these concerns. Rather than looking at the complete sentence, it will guess the term by looking at a few select portions of the input phrase. The transformer model [22] is an encoder–decoder network that incorporates MHA and PFFN into its architecture. The use of the RELU activation function in the network is a shortcoming of this approach. The number of negative inputs that will result in gradients is zero [23]. The problem with this method is that it forces the encoder to turn the full input phrase into a fixed-length vector. Only shorter input sentences will work with this method. Furthermore, memorizing excessively long words into fixed-length vectors is too tough for the encoder. The S2S LSTM [24–26] model gave a ROUGE score with the α of 0.68, β of 0.71, and $F1$ of 0.73. The transformer model gave a ROUGE score with the α of 0.81, β of 0.82, and $F1$ of 0.74. When compared to existing models, our proposed model produced better outcomes. The ROUGE metrics of our model are better. The ROUGE-3 of our proposed fine-tuned transformer has a α of 0.91, β of 0.92, and $F1$ of 0.95. Precision, recall, and $F1$-score are the ROUGE scores, which determine the performance of our suggested technique, which is based on a fine-tuned version of the transformer

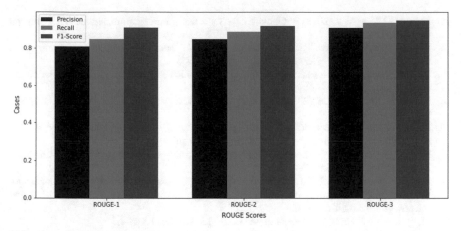

Fig. 3 Fine-tined transformer ROUGE score

model. So, the results are doing good compared to other approaches as shown in the above-mentioned (Table 2). Figure 3 depicts the outcomes of the proposed model.

5 Conclusion

When compared to extractive summarizing, abstractive text summarization is one of the more difficult undertakings. With a brief version of the text, abstractive summarization can provide a more meaningful summary to the user. To obtain better outcomes, we offered a fine-tuned version of the transformer. The proposed model improves the accuracy of the ROUGE score compared to the other approaches like the S2S approach and and transformer approach. The final summary generated by this approach consists of a smaller number of words compared to the other approaches. In this way, we can claim that fine-tuned transformer did the abstractive summarization task with a better ROUGE score.

References

1. Inderjeet M, Maybury MT (2001) Automatic summarization. John Benjamins Pub. Co.
2. Rafael F, de Souza Cabral L, Lins RD, Pereira e Silva G, Freitas F, Cavalcanti GDC, Lima R, Simske SJ, Favaro L (2013) Assessing sentence scoring techniques for extractive text summarization. Expert Syst Appl 40(14):5755–5764
3. Ramesh N, Zhou B, Gulcehre C, Xiang B (2016) Abstractive text summarization using sequence-to- sequence RNNS and beyond. arXiv preprint arXiv:1602.06023
4. Hermann KM, Kocisky T, Grefenstette E, Espeholt L, Kay W, Suleyman M, Blunsom P (2015) Teaching machines to read and comprehend. Adv Neural Inf Process Syst 1693–1701

5. Mahnaz K, Wang WY (2018) Wikihow: a large scale text summarization dataset. arXiv preprint arXiv:1810.09305
6. Bing X, Wang N, Chen T, Li M (2015) Empirical evaluation of rectified activations in convolutional network. arXiv preprint arXiv:1505.00853
7. Yew LC (2004) Rouge: a package for automatic evaluation of summaries. In: Text summarization branches out, pp, 74–81
8. Deepali K, Mahender CN (2016) A review paper on text summarization. Phil Trans Roy Soc London 5(3)
9. Rajman M, Romaric B (2005) Text mining: natural language techniques and text mining applications. In: Data mining and reverse engineering, pp 50–64
10. Erkan G, Radev DR (2004) LexRank:graph based centrality as salience in text summarization. J Artif Intell Res Res 22:457–479
11. Fan W, Wallace L, Rich S, Zang Z (2005) Tapping the power of text mining. J ACM Blacksburg
12. Elhadi MT (2017) Extractive summarization using structural syntax, term expansion and refinement. Int J Intell Sci 7(3)
13. Larry R, Jain LC (2001) Recurrent neural networks. Des Appl 5:64–67
14. Hochreiter S, Schmidhuber J (1997) Long short-term memory. Neural Comput 9(8):1735–1780
15. Pramod V, Chattha MA (2020) A survey on knowledge integration techniques with artificial neural networks for seq-2-seq/time series models. arXiv preprint arXiv:2008.05972
16. Vaswani A, Shazeer N, Parmar N, Uszkoreit J, Jones L, Aidan N, Gomez L, Polosukhin I (2017) Attention is all you need. Adv Neural Inf Process Syst 30
17. Hanin B (2018) Which neural net architectures give rise to exploding and vanishing gradients? arXiv preprint arXiv:1801.03744
18. Shrestha A, Mahmood A (2019) Review of deep learning algorithms and architectures. IEEE Access 7:53040–53065
19. Miller D (2019) Leveraging BERT for extractive text summarization on lectures. arXiv preprint arXiv:1906.04165
20. Tinghuai M, Pan Q, Rong H, Qian Y, Tian Y, Nabhan NA (2021) T-bertsum: topic-aware text summarization based on bert. IEEE Trans Comput Soc Syst
21. Tian S, Keneshloo Y, Ramakrishnan N, Reddy CK (2021) Neural abstractive text summarization with sequence-to-sequence models. ACM Trans Data Sci 2(1):1–37
22. Siwar A, Abbès SB, Hantach R, Calvez P (2021) Automatic text summarization using transformers. In: Iberoamerican knowledge graphs and semantic web conference, pp 308–320
23. K. Cho, B. V. Merrienboer, C. Gulcehre, F. Bougares, H. Schwenk, and Y. Bengio, "Learning phrase representations using rnn encoder-decoder for statistical machine translation," CoRR, abs/1406.1078, 2014.
24. Kuchaiev O, Ginsburg B (2017) Factorization tricks for LSTM networks. arXiv preprint arXiv: 1703.10722
25. Hochreiter S, Schmidhuber J (1997) Long short-term memory. Neural Comput 9(8):1735–1780
26. Cheng J, Dong L, Lapata M (2016) Long short-term memory-networks for machine reading. arXiv preprint arXiv:1601.06733

Music Generation Using Deep Learning

Dinesh Reddy Vemula, Shailendra Kumar Tripathi, Neeraj Kumar Sharma, Md. Muzakkir Hussain, U. Raghavendra Swamy, and Bhagya Lakshmi Polavarapu

1 Introduction

Automating music generation is a computer-based generation of music using machine learning (ML) algorithms. Ongoing interest and improvement in machine learning prodded scientists to investigate the possible applications of ML in creative fields like music. We all know that music is an art. It is concerned with combining instrumental or vocal sounds which is great thing to form as it shows emotional expression, usually consistent with cultural standards of melody, rhythm, and in most Western music, harmony. Whether it is straightforward folk song or complex electronic composition, it belongs to an equivalent activity which is music. If we consider music in a nutshell, it is just combination of different instrumental notes [1]. So, with this idea, we come up with this work as music generation using neural networks. These days, neural networks play a vital role and are used to improve all aspects in our lifestyle including apparel recommendations, text generations, language translations, etc. We present how to use recurrent neural networks for generating melodies. We need to understand what music is and what it is composed of. It is mainly of notes and chords as shown in Fig. 1.

D. R. Vemula (✉) · N. K. Sharma · Md. M. Hussain · B. L. Polavarapu
CSE, SRM University, Amaravati, AP, India
e-mail: dineshreddy.v@srmap.edu.in

S. K. Tripathi · U. R. Swamy
Government PG College, Santa, Madhya Pradesh, India

N. K. Sharma · Md. M. Hussain · B. L. Polavarapu
CMR Technical Campus, Hyderabad, Telangana, India

© The Author(s), under exclusive license to Springer Nature Singapore Pte Ltd. 2023
K. Kumar Singh et al. (eds.), *Machine Vision and Augmented Intelligence*, Lecture Notes in Electrical Engineering 1007, https://doi.org/10.1007/978-981-99-0189-0_47

Fig. 1 Representations of keys on the PIANO

Note: It is the sound produced by one key.

Chord: It is the sound produced by two or more keys parallely.

Octaves: It is the sound produced by repeated patterns. Generally, it contains seven white and 5 black keys.

"The term pitch tells highness or lowness of a sound. A, B, C, D, E, F, G are seven notes in music. Octaves contain set of notes from A to G. Octaves direct pitch range in which the notes are in" [2]. For example, A7 contains high pitch whereas A1 has deeper sound and lower pitch. A piano keyboard contains 88 keys and seven octaves. A key(note) forms the basis for music in the piece. That means if a piece is played in key of F, then the note F will be the base of the music. A chord is a harmonic set of frequencies that are played parallely [2].

2 Literature Review

Before moving into our model architecture, it is important to study what the existing workings were and on what tools and technologies they were been supported. It is also very important to understand the basics of music because that will be involved in the scope of our research. Different kinds of neural networks we observed that have been used for generation of music in previous papers:

1. Feed forward
2. RNN using LSTM
3. RNN using gated recurrent unit (GRU)
4. Bidirectional RNN
5. Autoencoder
6. Transformer
7. Generative adversial network (GAN).

From past decade, music composition is implemented in several different ways. Before shifting to neural networks, we have a rule-based systems where string rewriting grammar produces a simple note sequences. Riffology algorithm by Langston which uses randomness in algorithm but shifted to machine learning and neural networks because of capability to produce complex melodies. In 2002,

Schmidhuber firstly generated music using LSTM [3]. He generated music of blues genre using guitar dataset by having his own format for data representation. In 2016, Walder performed using LSTM's and addressed probabilistic modeling of music data [4]. He started with music rhythm of predefined and made the network to notes and pitches from it. In 2017, Skuli along with LSTM used keras for music generation [5]. This was improved by Walder and Lim in 2018 to produce more structured music [6]. The pieces have fixed time, and no varying duration was the drawback. Douglas Eck, Jurgen Schmidhuber compared the music generation models of regular RNN and LSTM and found that RNNs are suffering with lack of global structure whereas LSTM makes use of local structure in melody and predicts global chord structure [7]. But, this works only for less challenging compositions. In this work, we are using LSTM, but the data encoding part is different and also differs in activation function, layers like drop out layer and note range. And also, we are not using GAN because it was too unstable to produce meaningful output. This model has unstable training between two networks.

In this paper, we are looking for the possibility of high performance using LSTM RNNs and bidirectional LSTM RNNs and to observe the differences in their performance where the output will be in abc-notation.

3 Dataset

In data construction, we construct the data with essential features required by neural networks. Appropriate preprocessing of data should be done. We are going to prepro-cess the data by generating batch-sgd to feed into char-RNN. We are not using normal sgd here as it may lead to vanishing gradient problems because of high sequence lengths. After feeding the models with data, evaluation will be done with some sort of metrics such as accuracy and f1-score. One of the most challenging and important tasks while training models is choosing the right dataset, and the way we train the model with data directly impacts our output. As this is music generation, we should choose the any of the music representations.

Different types of music representations:

1. sheet-music
2. abc-notation
3. MIDI (Musical Instrument Digital Interface)
4. Mp3-audio files.

We choose our data in abc-notation. This abc-notation is the simplest notation, and it will be just in the form of alpha-numeric characters. Brief view on abc-notation is shown below:

Part1:

F:1

T:The Legacy melody

S:6/8

L:1/8

R:melody

K:G

Part2:

FGF ABA I fgf gab I FGF ABA I d2A AFD I

FGF ABA Ifgf gab I age edB I 1 dBA AFD :I 2 dBA ABd I:

efe eBd I dAB Bad I efe eBd I gBd BAd I

efe eBd I d2d dfe I gef eBdI1 dBA Bad :I2 dBA AFDI]

Lines within the part1 of the tune notation, it begins with a letter and then it is followed by a colon indicates various aspects of the tune like index.

(F:)- if there are more tunes in a file

(L:)- default note length

(S:)- time signature

(R:)- type of tune

(T:)- title

(K:)- key.
Lines following the key designation represent the tune.

Those alpha-numeric sequence is our actual music where as other fields such as index, title, and type of tune are considered as meta-data. It is very flexible and easy to convert music representation from abc-notation to sheet-music or vice-versa [8].

4 Proposed Methodology

There are three important tasks involved in methodology:

1. Data construction
2. Feeding the models with data
3. Training phase and generation phase (evaluation).

Before diving into different models, let us get insights on "what is a character-level RNN" where we are going to use char-RNN in our models.

A char-RNN is a character-level RNN, is trained to predict the next character when we feed the model with sequence of characters. Suppose if we give $c(i)$ character, it should be able to predict the $c(i + 1)$ character when we trained the model using few sequences. So finally, this char-RNN will learn the patterns in provided input sequences and output the most probable outcome of next possibly occurring character. This char-RNN is a many-many type of network where it generates output corresponds to each input. This char-RNN is extremely useful in these kinds of models; as we mentioned above, music is sequence of characters, and this char-RNN is going to learn the patterns in the sequences provided as input and generate the meaningful output sequence which turns out to be a decent music.

4.1 LSTM RNN

A recurrent neural network belongs to a type of neural network (NN) that remembers information about a sequence. For every single element of a sequence, they perform the same function where the output is based on previous computations, and hence, they are called recurrent. Whereas in traditional neural networks, outputs are independent of previous computations [5]. But, RNNs suffer from memory lose where it cannot remember the context from way back whereas LSTMs are specialized RNN and have certain multiplicative gates that allow it to capture or retain the more memory. Since we are having the sequence of characters as our input, it is very crucial task to store the memory without vanishing gradient problem. So, we are using LSTM RNNs in this work presented in Fig. 2. It is very useful to solve problems like where the network has to remember information for a long period of time as it is the case in text and music generation.

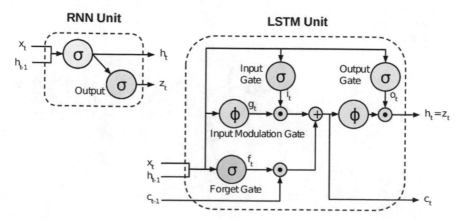

Fig. 2 Architecture of the LSTM RNN

4.1.1 Approach

High-level architecture of the model looks as follows shown in Fig. 3:

We use many-many RNN shown in Fig. 4 where for every input token, a output token will be generated. This is a multi-class classification model, where at last we predict the most possible outcome (character) among all unique characters.

Here, to produce a character-level model to predict the next note in a sequence, we use a 3-layered LSTM RNN. Also, we use a dropout layer to avoid the over fitting if the dataset is small. We set up an embedding matrix that maps each token to a learned vector representation. A sequence of tokens in a piece is then joined into an inventory of embedding vectors which forms the time sequence input that is given into the LSTM. Over all the tokens, the output of the LSTM is fed into SoftMax layer whenever step compared to the particular note played at that particular step that corresponds to the cross entropy error of our predictions.

Our architecture allows the user to line various hyperparameters like hidden unit size, number of layers, learning rate, sequence length, and batch size. We just clip our gradients to stop it from exploding. We also anneal our learning rate once we see that our training error is slowly decreasing. We generate music by feeding a brief seed sequence into our trained model. By the output distribution from SoftMax, we generate the new tokens and feed the generated tokens back to our model. For considering the final output, we choose the token having maximum predicted probability from the SoftMax distribution.

Fig. 3 High-level architecture of the proposed model

Fig. 4 Multi-class classification using many-many RNN

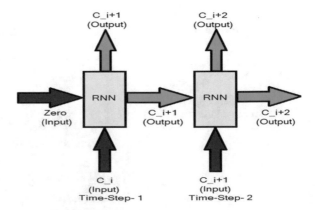

4.2   Bidirectional LSTMs RNN

We know that LSTM RNN will work well, but we are going to experiment with bidirectional RNN in further work and see how this bidirectional RNN really makes improvement compared to simple forward RNNs. We will compare the performance of bidirectional LSTMs to a traditional LSTM.

Bidirectional LSTMs are very useful for sequence classification problems, and they can improve the model performance of such problems as they are extension of LSTMs shown in Fig. 5. Instead of training one LSTMs, bidirectional LSTMs train two on the input sequence where the input sequence must be available in all time-steps [2]. By taking the first input sequence as it is and second input sequence as reverse copy of the first input sequence can provide additional context to the network and end in faster and even complete learning on the matter. To keep it in simple terms, bidirectional recurrent neural networks are really just concatenating two independent RNNs. This structure allows the networks to possess both forward and backward information about the sequence at all steps. This type of RNN can learn the meaning of context better. While analyzing the texts, this bidirectional LSTMs works better. For example, "a minute ago" and "a minute creature" are two different sentences whereas minute is same word but differs contextually. In these cases, bidirectional LSTMs can work well as it is learning from both forward and backward.

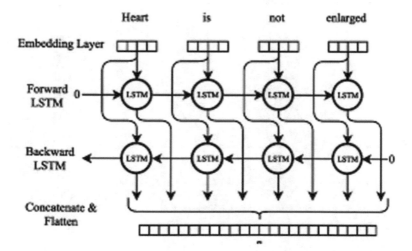

Fig. 5 Flow of the bidirectional LSTMs

4.2.1 Approach

High-level architecture of the model looks as follows:

Bidirectional LSTMs have 3 hidden layers, 1 input and 1 output layers. In implementation, we use Tensorflow where input and output layers are implemented using matrix operations and tensors. Input layer–it has batch size and input dim. It is implemented by sequences of tensors. Here, batch size is 100, and each input is considered as a single note, so we take input dim as 1. Hidden layer 1—this layer consists of 512 hidden units. Each unit has forward and backward LSTM cells where forget-bias is 0.1 (Fig. 6).

Hidden layer 2—this layer consists of 512 hidden units. Each unit has forward and backward LSTM cells where forget-bias is 0.1. Drop probability of 0.2 is added on dropout. Hidden layer 3—this layer consists of 512 hidden units. Each unit has forward and backward LSTM cells where forget-bias is 0.1. Output layer—it is produced by the inclination grid and yield of past layer and with the network duplication of weight framework. Model architecture will be same as the LSTM RNNs, but instead of LSTM, we use Keras bidirectional LSTM (Fig. 7).

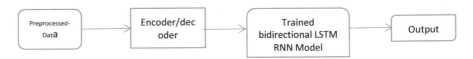

Fig. 6 High-level architecture of the model

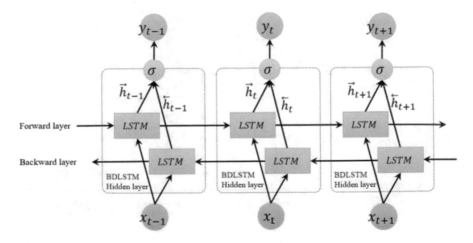

Fig. 7 Details of hidden layers of the model

5 Results and Analysis

After training the models LSTM and bidirectional LSTM, the models are ready for prediction. The uniqueness of our project is the output which will be in abc-notation. From each input character, the proposed model generates corresponding probability using softmax layer. From all those probability values, we choose the character with highest probability as next character and again that chosen character is given back to the model for feeding. This concatenation of output character continues until music of some length is generated. We will give first character and length of the music as input.

The result is as follows:

1. Which epoch number weight you want to load into the model (10, 20, 30, …, 90). Small number will generate more errors in music: 2
2. Enter any number between 0 and 86 which will be given as initial character to model for generating sequence: 10
3. Enter the length of music sequence you want to generate. Typical number is between 300 and 600. Too small number will generate hardly generate any sequence: 580.

MUSIC SEQUENCE GENERATED:

"D"e2B Bed|"E"c2d a2G|"Am"B2A "f7"P2G|"G"G3 -G2:| P:B|:A|"G"BGD "D7"G2A|"G"BGB dBd|

"D"DEF AGF|"G"GBd g2a|"G"g2d "D7"c2BP:B

d|"G"dBd gfg|"C"e^de g2e|"F"dBA "D7"ABA|"G"G3 G2:|

Open the following link and Copy Paste the above generated abc-notation music output is given in order to play like the below attached image. https://www.abcjs.net/abcjs-editor.html

ABC Notation

```
[abcjs engraver="{ staffwidth: 300 }"]
X:1
K:A
A2A2e2e2|f2f2e4|
[/abcjs]
```

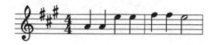

Table 1 Results of LSTM for music generation

	Epoch	Loss	Accuracy
0	1	3.020182	0.184570
1	2	2.151111	0.394531
2	3	1.909831	0.447266
3	4	1.730417	0.515625
4	5	1,618421	0.534180
5	6	1.560469	0.535156
6	7	1.504703	0.549805
7	8	1.459398	0.569336
8	9	1.396415	0.576172
9	10	1.366401	0.584961

Table 2 Results of bidirectional LSTM for music generation

Epoch	Loss	Accuracy
1	0.731297	0.836914
2	0.155229	0.972656
3	0.098093	0.984375

For LSTM:

After running 9 epochs, we are getting an accuracy of 58% where the loss has been decreased as shown in Table 1.

For Bidirectional LSTM

After running 3 epochs, we are getting accuracy of 98% as shown in Table 2. Comparing both the models, bidirectional LSTM is having more accuracy. Figure 8 presents accuracy of the proposed and LSTM models for increasing epochs.

Fig. 8 Epoch versus accuracy of the proposed and LSTM models

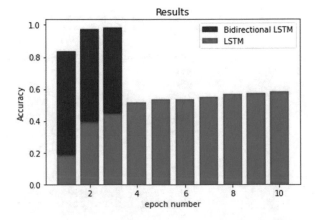

6 Conclusion

We sought to explore the models LSTM and bidirectional LSTM to generate music where we observed that bidirectional LSTM was better and has more accuracy. This bidirectional LSTM obtains the conditional probability from pitch dimensions and time and can effectively explore the complex relationship in music we will be experimenting in further work. This problem can be extended with multi-instrument music generation by experimenting with other music datasets. And also adding start & end encodings can generate more melodious music.

References

1. Briot JP, Pachet F (2020) Deep learning for music generation: challenges and directions. Neural Comput Appl 32(4):981–993
2. Dong HW, Hsiao WY, Yang LC, Yang YH (2018) Musegan: multi-track sequential generative adversarial networks for symbolic music generation and accompaniment. In: AAAI conference on artificial intelligence, vol 32, no 1
3. Walder C (2016) Modelling symbolic music: beyond the piano roll. In: Asian conference on machine learning. PMLR, pp 174–189
4. Skúli S (2017) How to generate music using a LSTM neural network in keras. www.shorturl.at/ezFO4
5. Wang J (2016) Deep learning in music. Stanford University
6. Eck D, Schmidhuber J (2002) A first look at music composition using lstm recurrent neural networks. Istituto Dalle Molle Di Studi Sull Intelligenza Artificiale 103:48
7. Heines JM (2016) Converting MIDI notes to ABC notes in pencil code. ACM inroads 7(2):84–84
8. Schuster M, Paliwal KK (1997) Bidirectional recurrent neural networks. IEEE Trans Signal Process

Breast Cancer Classification Using ML on WDBC

Akhilesh Kumar Singh

1 Introduction

Breast cancer, together with oral, cervical, lung, stomach, and colorectal cancer, accounts for 49% of all new cancer cases. Breast cancer is the leading cause of cancer in today's climate. In the year 2018, around 27.7% of the newly diagnosed cancer cases in women were breast cancer cases. The rise of data science and machine learning [1] is proving to be a tremendous help in the realm of medicine. Its capability to contribute to the decision-making process of medical professionals contributes to its success in the stated sector. These solutions certainly need a few resources, but the value they bring is unparalleled. With the unfortunate rise in cancer cases, the newly collected data can be used to enhance clinical and medical research. Previous studies have explored how machine learning can provide better results, benefiting this critical cause by classification of two cancer tumor types with the help of ML approaches on WDBC [2] to provide a favorable outcome. In this paper, we describe a somewhat different approach to the subject, using some new approaches to improve efficiency and present a fresh viewpoint. These methodologies, all of which were used for our categorization work, are described in Sect. 4. Also, the results for all of the methods and techniques in this project are blocked out in Sects. 5 and 6 with a summary of their performances.

A. K. Singh (✉)
GLA University, Mathura, Uttar Pradesh, India
e-mail: akhilesh.kumar@gla.ac.in

© The Author(s), under exclusive license to Springer Nature Singapore Pte Ltd. 2023   609
K. Kumar Singh et al. (eds.), *Machine Vision and Augmented Intelligence*, Lecture Notes
in Electrical Engineering 1007, https://doi.org/10.1007/978-981-99-0189-0_48

2 Related Works

ML for categorization and prognosis of breast tumor type [3] by Rane et al. has proposed a paper and stated "by presenting several machine learning algorithms: N-Bayes, random tree forest, artificial neural networks, KN-neighbor, support vector machine, and D-Tree with WDBC dataset [2] that is extracted from a digitized image of a breast mass. Further, they segregated the dataset into 2 parts which were used to train and then test the models which they built using those six ML algorithms later out of which the best performing model is used by them for an HTML page."

Gokhale's Ultrasound Characterization of Breast Masses mentioned "[4] a technique where they discovered that physicians had recognized as observed how breast cancer develops if certain cells grow irregularly. Abnormal cells reproduce as well as scatter more quickly than healthy tissue and continue to accrue, creating a lump or mass which may cause discomfort. A cell may move quickly from the tissue of the breast to the body fluid nodes as well as distinct regions from their system. Various factors can directly contribute to the high risk of cancer in women, like their standards of living or style of living, excessive weight, harmful emissions, and past cancer cases in their bloodline family, etc. As with the advancement in the medical sciences, cancer victims can be treated and rescued in cases where an early diagnosis is responsible for the detection of cancer. They have utilized several classifiers which were provided by the machine learning in their study: the NB-classifier, the KNN-classifier, support vector machine, artificial neural network, and random tree forest classifier. It has been demonstrated that linear sympathetic image creation and concurrent blending enhance the picture's pixel-to-pixel ratio and clarity of resolution. In past, USG's EEG technique had previously surfaced to be somewhat effective. According to preliminary findings, which have observed escalation in precision and clear prognostic numbers of USG of the portrayal of lump mass in the breast? The comparative contrast of solidity and audial defiance which contrary with the nearby tissue of the breast is what makes a lesion evident on mammography or USG."

Fred stated that "in published research in respect of unearthing the cancer tumor in breast [5]: using the dataset which was collected during the fine-needle tests and later used for evaluation of cancer if present [2]. Six machine learning techniques are utilized in this work to identify cancer. The GRU-SVM model is used to diagnose the trite cancer type. GRU-SVM, linear regression, multilayer perceptron, nearest neighbor, soft-max regression, and support vector machine on the formerly mentioned breast cancer dataset [2] examining categorization correctness, responsiveness, and meticulousness of figures. The mentioned dataset is made up of characteristics calculated via pictures of fine-needle aspiration assessment done to the mass blob. The used dataset was partitioned in the following manner: to check the correctness and data fed to instruct the model, 30% and 70%, respectively. According to findings, formerly mentioned algorithms of machine learning executed effectively for the binary division or grouping task, i.e., finding out the sample data belong to which of the subset. A rotation-elimination technique such as cross-fold K used for ratification may be taken into account which concretes the valid conclusions made.

Employment of thus strategies may just not merely enlighten more accurate estimation for prognosis correctness assessment, rather make it easier in the selection of pivotal fervent data points for the used machine learning algorithms."

Li and Chen's mentioned "work, effectiveness estimation for ML approaches [6] ways in which prognosis for cancer is done, employed two datasets. This study initially accumulated data from the dataset with blood cells, inclusive of one hundred and sixteen fellows alongside nine determinants, whereas the dataset of white blood cells, which includes six hundred and ninety-nine fellows alongside eleven determinants. The raw data of the WBDC dataset were preprocessed, yielding information with six hundred and eighty-three fellows alongside nine determinants accompanies, with the result, an indexcounter demonstrating in which class the fellow sample contributors fall. Following examining the precision, the F-measure creation and the ROC curve for the formerly mentioned classifier model, the outcome laid out the fact that RF was designated as the principal classifier model for this paper. The consequence, of the verdict for this research, can be used by specialists to determine the class of tumor. The above research has several shortcomings that shall be covered in future investigations. For example, while certain indices have yet to be discovered, this study only gathers information on 10 qualities throughout this trial. The lack of data affects the accuracy of the outcomes."

L Applications of Machine Learning stated that "in Breast Tumor identification [7] Yue and Wang's Prediction. With their research, the duo was able to throw light on various approaches to get to the problem also at the same time we are able to share their perspective on the functionality of the task of cancer predictions by analyzing data from the benchmark database WBCD. ML approaches have demonstrated an extraordinary capacity to further enhance categorization and forecast correctness. Regardless of the point which was that the approaches used have found great success with white blood cell data, the implementation and employment of unripe and advanced algorithms are still needed. Categorization correctness was an important fact to be taken care of for the formation of true standards but still was not an alone job regardless. Every approach grasps unique characteristics to be taken into account still requiring multiple ways of implementation. Even though ANN oppressed cancer detection for a long period, now it is evident that the new ML approaches are finding their ways into new smart medical system to bring more value for medical officials."

3 Proposed Model

3.1 Existing System

Traditionally, the prognosis for cancer tumor in the breast along with the typecasting for cancer tumor which falls under the category of benign or malignant was done by various medical procedures like:

Breast-Examination

The physician would examine the breasts and lymphoglandula under armpits to check if there are any lumps or abnormalities. Feature extraction from the audio (MFCC, Chroma, etc,) has been done.

Mammogram

These are like radiograms the region to be tested. They require examination of whether there is breast cancer or not. If any issues are found, the doctor may ask the patient to take a diagnostic mammogram to check for further abnormalities. For the detection of breast cancer, mammogram enhancement is very important [8].

Breast Ultrasound

Ultrasound uses sound waves to produce images.

Biopsy

Parting specimen for cellule testing.

MRI

Blood tests, CT scans, and PET scans are also done to check for breast cancer.

3.2 Proposed System

In the proposed system, we plan on using existing data of breast cancer patients which have been collected for several years and run different machine learning algorithms on them. These algorithms will analyze the data from the datasets to audit the chances of the patient having a cancerous tumor, and it will also tell us if the tumor is fatal or non-fatal, i.e., treatable. It is done by taking the patient's data and mapping it with the dataset [2] and auditing the changes if there are any patterns found with the data. If a patient has breast cancer, then instead of taking more tests to check whether the cancer is malignant or benign, ML can be used to predict the case based on the huge amount of data on breast cancer. This proposed system helps the patients as it reduces the amount of money they need to spend just for the diagnosis. Also, if the tumor is benign, then it is not cancerous, and the patient doesn't need to go through any of the other tests. This saves a lot of time as well (Fig. 1).

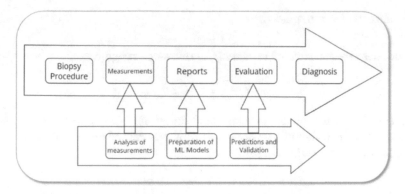

Fig. 1 Data flow

4 Methodology

4.1 Dataset

The Wisconsin Diagnostic Breast Cancer (WDBC) dataset [2] was used to feed data to machine learning algorithms for them to distinguish or prognosis of breast cancer. It is the selection of chosen attributes that enables it to become more adequate for analysis. It includes characteristics extracted from a picture of the lump in the breast on which the FNA test was done. The features corresponding to the cell nuclei within the images are as follows (Fig. 2).

There are 569 data points in the dataset.

212—malignant, 357—benign as:

(1) Smoothness, (2) fractal-dimension, (3) concavity, (4) symmetry, (5) perimeter, (6) texture, (7) area, (8) compactness, (9) radius, and (10) concave points. Together with this for every data point: (1) "worst" or largest (mean of the three largest values) computed, (2) mean, and (3) standard error, hence, making it a complete 30 feature set.

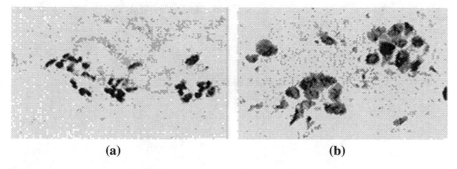

| (a) | (b) |

Fig. 2 Digitized images of FNA: **a** Benign, **b** Malignant [2]

4.2 Dataset Preprocessing

The dataset was standardized to avoid false relevance assignments.

$$z = (X - \mu)/\sigma \qquad (1)$$

In Eq. (1), the feature that is being standardized is X, μ denotes average, and σ denotes standard deviation. The standardization was carried out with the help of the StandardScaler of sci-kit-learn [9].

4.3 Machine Learning Algorithms

The machine learning (ML) algorithms employed in this study are discussed in this section.

Logistic Regression

The term "logistic regression" refers to an expansion of the term "linear regression." Logistic regression alternative yet effective directed machine learning approach toward two-class application, i.e., while resultant is categorical. One major distinction between "linear regression" and "logistic regression" would be the scale which is limited to 0 and 1 in the case of logistics. A better way to describe logistic regression would be to say that "it is similar to linear regression but for classification difficulties." A logistic function is used to represent a single outcome for logistic regression. Also, there is no need for a linear relation among variables in the case of logistic regression [10] (Fig. 3).

$$\ln\left(\frac{p}{p-1}\right) = b_0 + b_1 X \qquad (2)$$

Fig. 3 Relation among a single independent x and a single output with a range from 0 or 1

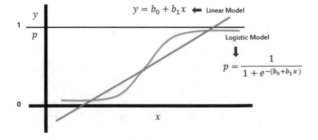

Fig. 4 A decision tree [12]

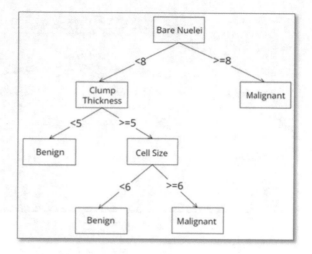

Decision Tree

Decision trees [11] embody a supervised classification approach as being very popular among the profound ML algorithms available for regression as well as categorizing tasks. Some of the reasons which make it more favorable over other algorithms are that it is very easy to understand the inner workings, which further makes it easier to implement. It tries to approach the given task as a human as it tries to comprehend and understand the scene as we do. D-Tree works on a tree, itself as their node representing any feature, each connection representing any criterion, so child nodes represent the outcome subclass. The aim is simply to establish a tree network with data points or features as input and every external node giving out a distinct outcome (Fig. 4).

Random Forest

Random forests [13], also known as random decision forests, are a common ensemble method for modeling classification and regression tasks. In the case of a random forest, the model builds a whole forest of random uncorrelated decision trees to arrive at the best feasible answer. By selecting only, a subsample of the feature space at each split, random forest seeks to eliminate correlation issues. Essentially, it intends to decorrelate the trees and trim them by imposing a node split halting criterion (Fig. 5).

When compared to a single tree classifier, random forest shows a considerable boost in performance. It produces a lower generalization error rate than AdaBoost, but it is more noise resistant.

Keras Sequential Model

Keras [14] is a small and simple high-level Python deep learning package that runs on top of TensorFlow. It enables the building of neural network layers while attending to the nitty-gritty aspects of tensors, their forms, and their mathematical nuances.

Random Forest Classifier

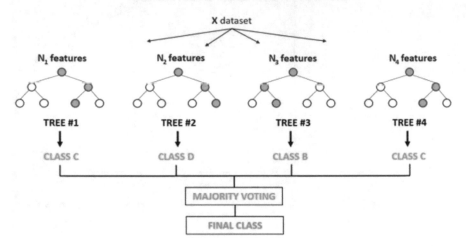

Fig. 5 Random forest classifier [13]

TensorFlow must be the Keras back end. Keras may be used for deep learning applications without having to interface with the more sophisticated TensorFlow. There are two types of frameworks: sequential APIs and functional APIs. The sequential API is built on the concept of a layer sequence; this is the most popular usage of Keras and the simplest component of Keras. The sequential model may be thought of as a layer-by-layer stack.

Support Vector

The given or provided data can be classified into two categories using the SVM "Support Vector" machine learning method. Trained on a set of data that is already divided into two categories and builds the model when first trained. An SVM algorithm's job is to figure out which group a new data point fits in. As a result, SVM is a non-binary linear classifier. In addition to classifying objects, the SVM algorithm needs to have as wide a margin as possible between the objects on the graph [15] (Fig. 6).

KNN

KNN [16] is a data classification algorithm that looks at the data points around the data point to determine which group the data point belongs to. An algorithm that looks at a point on the grid and tries to determine if it is in group A or B looks at the state of nearby points. The range is arbitrary, but the point is to sample the data. If most of the points are in group A, then the data point in question is likely to be A instead of B and vice versa. KNN is an example of a "lazy learner" algorithm because it does not pre-model the dataset. The only calculation performed is when

Fig. 6 SVM hyperplane

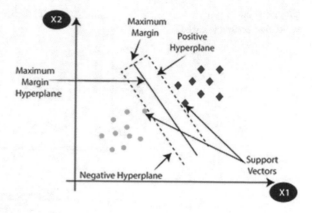

Fig. 7 KNN classifiers

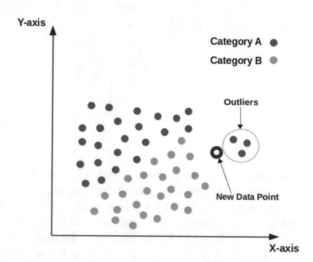

a neighbor of the data point is asked to query. This makes it very easy to implement KNN in data mining (Fig. 7).

5 Results and Discussion

All the results are based on the test results which we collected from our implementation of previously outlined algorithms in Sect. 4. All the conclusive data include precision, which is a simple calculation of true positive divided by the total number of positive outcomes made by the model, recall, which is a ratio that evaluates the overall set of possible positive predictions produced from all potential positives, the F1 score is used to express the balance between precision and recall and support—the amount of correct reply which falls within the class.

Fig. 8 Training and
validation accuracy and loss

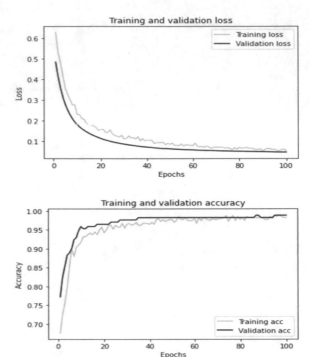

Among other ML approaches with a standout test accuracy ≈of 98.83%, the
sequential model [17] came out as the best among the other three. Figure 8 graph
illustrates training (measures performance on the training dataset) and validation
(measures performance on the validation dataset) accuracy, as well as the training
and validation loss, which reflect how well the model matches training and fresh data.
With the addition in the size of sample data, the unpredictability for every allotment
will decline to become "leptokurtic."

6   Conclusion

A complete comparison of six breast cancer classification machine learning methods
which are logistic regression, decision tree classifier, random forest classifier, KNN,
SVM, and Keras sequential model are performed. In this classification task, the
Wisconsin Breast Cancer Diagnostic Dataset is divided into 70% for training and
30% for testing. These features are based on images of breast masses used in the
FNA test. The parameters used to train the model are manually selected. In this
classification task, all of the above models provide over 90% test accuracy. With a
standout accuracy score, Keras sequential model has given around 98% accuracy
which is followed by an accuracy score of around 97% for both linear regression and

random forest classifier. All presented ML algorithms exhibited high performance on the binary classification of breast cancer, i.e., determining whether a benign tumor or a malignant tumor. Consequently, the statistical measures on the classification problem were also satisfactory.

References

1. Ibrahim I, Abdulazeez A (2021) The role of machine learning algorithms in diagnosing diseases. J Appl Sci Technol Trends 2(01):10–19
2. Blake C, Keogh E, Merz CJ (1998) UCI repository of machine learning databases. Department of Information and Computer Science, University of California, Irvine. http://www.ics.uci.edu/~mlearn/MLRepository.htm
3. Rane N, Sunny J, Kanade R, Devi S (2020) Breast cancer classification and prediction using machine learning. Int J Eng Res Technol 9(02):576–580
4. Gokhale S (2009) Ultrasound characterization of breast masses. Indian J Radiol Imaging 19(03):242–247
5. Li Y, Chen Z (2018) Performance evaluation of machine learning methods for breast cancer prediction. Appl Comput Math 7(4):212–216
6. Yue W, Wang Z, Chen H, Payne A, Liu X (2018) Machine learning with applications in breast cancer diagnosis and prognosis. Designs 2(2):13
7. Sathish D, Kamath S, Rajagopal KV, Prasad K (2016) Medical imaging techniques and computer-aided diagnostic approaches for the detection of breast cancer with an emphasis on thermography-a review. Int J Med Eng Inf 8(3):275–299
8. Singh KK, Bajpai MK (2019) Fractional order Savitzky-Golay differentiator-based approach for mammogram enhancement. In: 2019 IEEE international conference on imaging systems and techniques (IST), pp 1–5
9. Saikia T, Kumar R, Kumar D, Singh KK (2022) An automatic lung nodule classification system based on hybrid transfer learning approach. SN Comput Sci 3(4):272. https://doi.org/10.1007/s42979-022-01167-0
10. Schober P, Vetter TR (2021) Logistic regression in medical research. Anesth Analg 132(2):365
11. Ali J, Khan R, Ahmad N, Maqsood I (2012) Random forests and decision trees. Int J Comput Sci Issues (IJCSI) 9(5):272
12. Jeyasingh S, Veluchamy M (2017) Modified bat algorithm for feature selection with the Wisconsin diagnosis breast cancer (WDBC) dataset. Asian Pac J Cancer Prev: APJCP 18(5):1257
13. Gupta I, Sharma V, Kaur S, Singh AK (2022) PCA-RF: an efficient Parkinson's disease prediction model based on random forest classification. arXiv preprint arXiv:2203.11287
14. Manaswi NK (2018) Understanding and working with Keras. In: Deep learning with applications using python. Apress, Berkeley, pp 31–43
15. Rejani Y, Selvi ST (2009) Early detection of breast cancer using the SVM classifier technique. arXiv preprint arXiv:0912.2314
16. Yigit H (2013) A weighting approach for the KNN classifier. In: 2013 International conference on electronics, computer and computation (ICECCO). IEEE, pp 228–231
17. Gulli A, Kapoor A, Pal S (2019) Deep learning with TensorFlow 2 and Keras: regression, ConvNets, GANs, RNNs, NLP, and more with TensorFlow 2 and the Keras API. Packt Publishing Ltd.

Kappa: A Measure of Classifier Goodness for Diabetic Retinopathy Using EfficientNet

Akhilesh Kumar Singh and Neeraj Gupta

1 Introduction

In various western countries, diabetes mellitus is the main reason for blindness among specific age groups. Diabetes mellitus is the reason behind diabetic retinopathy. DR affects various developed countries also. In the human eye, there is light-sensitive tissue, i.e., called the retina, when damage occurs in the blood vessels of the retina then DR will occur. It is a diabetes problem due to which disturbances can occur in the eyes. Initially, diabetic retinopathy may not affect our eyes. Or it may be possible that simply minor vision problems can arise. But, finally, it may lead to blindness. The person who has Type 1 and Type 2 diabetes DR can affect those people largely [1]. Suppose that if this diabetic retinopathy will be detected at an early stage, then we can save millions of diabetics from losing their eyesight. DR is also called the silent killer because it will be detected only at its last stages, and from this stage, it is very difficult to treat this disease. DR can be treated only when it is in the early stages. So, it is essential to detect DR at an early stage with the help of regular screening. To reduce manual effort, it is highly required to perform the task of screening automatically. When any human body gets affected by DR, then blood vessels that can help in nurturing the retina will start leaking liquid. In Fig. 1a, we have shown a normal retina with its blood vessels segmentation while in Fig. 1b we have shown retina having DR with its blood vessels segmentation.

Outpouchings of the retinal capillaries are microaneurysms. In Fig. 2, it is represented in red color dots. Localized retinal hemorrhage or edema is concluded due to their improvised absorbency and might escape or exploit. Arisement of microaneurysms is the root cause of retinal microvasculopathy in any status. Located in

A. K. Singh (✉) · N. Gupta
GLA University, Mathura, Uttar Pradesh, India
e-mail: akhilesh.kumar@gla.ac.in

N. Gupta
e-mail: neeraj.gupta@gla.ac.in

© The Author(s), under exclusive license to Springer Nature Singapore Pte Ltd. 2023
K. Kumar Singh et al. (eds.), *Machine Vision and Augmented Intelligence*, Lecture Notes in Electrical Engineering 1007, https://doi.org/10.1007/978-981-99-0189-0_49

(a)

(b)

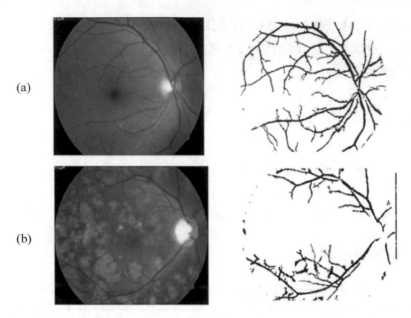

Fig. 1 a Normal retina and its blood vessels segmentation, **b** retina having DR with its blood vessels segmentation

the retina, firm exudates are glittering white or cream deposits and are fine-edged. Congregation of fluid is denoted by them in the retina. Given seeming neighboring to the macula center, sight-threatening is denoted. Microaneurysms are mostly sighted with them. Pacified to their locus within the retina, abundant forms and dimensions are might grasped by hemorrhages. Dot hemorrhages are the excessively usual DR hemorrhages. Arising from the facile capillary mesh of the retina, minuscule-looped desultory hemorrhages are these, yellow/white skin-deep retinal detriments with gauzy feathery extents are cotton wool spots. Because of focal ischemia, regions of dropsy inside the retinal nerve fiber mound are indicated by them.

Commonly, in 3 months, these are naturally settled. Novel mutilations can evolve in distinct regions assuming the elementary ischemic disarray persists. In the convergence between retinal hemorrhages and microaneurysms, it predominantly develops. Retinal microvasculopathy is depicted through them. Figure 2 shows these mutilations along with the anatomy of the retina. When we want to find the agreement of two raters while using nominal scores, then Cohen's kappa [2] and weighted kappa [3] may be used. If we are interested in nominal categorical ratings [4], then the unweighted kappa statistic is used. It is widely used in medical research for measuring the agreement in ordinal rating. In comparison to unweighted kappa, weighted kappa is used to measure agreement in ordinal discrete rating. The reason behind this is it takes into account distances in rating among raters [5]. The range for weighted and unweighted kappa is lying between − 1 and 1. One of the main drawbacks of this kappa statistic is that it is sensitive to the marginal probabilities.

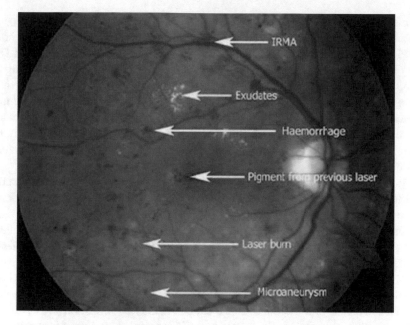

Fig. 2 Various lesions of the retina

In this paper, we have elaborated on our work on the efficient detection of diabetic retinopathy with the help of the EfficientNet model. Our experimental result shows that as we move from $B0$ to $B5$ then accuracy is going to be increased and almost reach to excellent result.

This paper is organized as follows: Sect. 2 elaborates on various related work that is done previously. It articulates diabetic retinopathy, Cohen kappa, and various types of kappa measures. It also includes work done previously on contrast enhancement, deep neural network, ConvNet accuracy, and ConvNet efficiency and model scaling. In Sect. 3, we have described the methodology of our work. Section 4 describes the Result and Discussion. Finally, Sect. 5 describes the Conclusion of the work.

2 Related Works

2.1 Diabetic Retinopathy

Mann, K. S. et al. proposed a method of segmentation of blood veins in the retina using the techniques of ANN, which is required for early detection of eye disease; the author has used the supervised approach for detection purposes. Finally, the author concluded that employing ANN they have got a good result. This method can be utilized to predict the DR at a primary phase in human eyes. However, the drawback of this method is that it operated only on a standard database [6] of images. For the analysis of retina images, the authors GeethaRamani et al. [7] have devised some novel methods. In this paper, the author uses both the concepts called IP and DM. Tang et al. [8] proposed a method using Gabor wavelet transforms for filtering the blood vessels using supervised classification techniques. Abdallah et al. [9] have given a novel method for segmenting the blood vessels which were having similar dimensions. Gang et al. [7] proposed a method using the Gaussian curve techniques for retinal blood capillaries and utilized it for retina blood vessel detection. The authors have given the Gaussian filtering approach which was based on the modified second-order filter.

Aslani et al. [10] developed a hybrid approach that utilized feature extraction for blood vessel detection. For classifying the blood veins/capillaries, preparation of text in the pattern of the dictionary was given by Zhang et al. in their research paper presented in [11]. For segmenting of the blood capillaries using mathematical models along with k-means clustering using was proposed by Hassana et al. in [11]. Using an identification scheme that was based on the characterization of the blood veins (including the shapes, areas, and unwanted regional volumes near the retina) was put forward in their research paper by Sinthanayothin et al. [12]. For the detection of the fine and coarse blood capillaries, the ant bee colony optimization and FC-means cluster method was used by Vermeer et al. in [13] from which they could detect the disease.

2.2 Cohen Kappa

Suppose we have to sort M items into n mutually exclusive groups. For this, we have two judges, then how can we measure the degree by which two judges will agree on sorting M items into n mutually exclusive groups. Here, in this scenario, a "judge" might be a specific person or a group of people who is capable of sorting the M items together. You can also say that a judge can be a non-human agency, like a computer program or diagnostic test that is capable of sorting based on specific criteria. When this type of problem arises, then kappa [14] will be used to measure the degree by which two judges agree in their corresponding sorting of M items into n mutually exclusive groups. When we say that the value of kappa is 1, it means that two judges reached to a perfect agreement, while when the value of kappa is 0, it means under independence agreement is equal to that expected. Finally, the value of kappa is negative when what we expected by chance is not occur in the agreement, i.e., agreement is less. When the data are ordered and categorical, then weighted kappa is widely used.

Simple Unweighted Kappa

In 1960, J. Cohen proposed the novel and simple version of kappa which is known as the unweighted kappa coefficient. The kappa coefficient (κ) will be defined in Eq. (1), which is as follows:

$$\kappa \equiv \frac{p_o - p_e}{1 - p_e} = 1 - \frac{1 - p_o}{1 - p_e} \tag{1}$$

where p_o = proportion of units which agree, = accuracy, p_e = proportion of units for expected by chance agreement. The common range for kappa values is defined as follows:

Range of values	Interpretation
$\kappa < 0.4$	Poor kappa value
$0.4 < \kappa < 0.75$	A good kappa value
$\kappa > 0.75$	An excellent kappa value

To demonstrate, the concept of kappa, assume that A and B, is judges for two clinical tests, and they are engaged independently to sort each of $M = 100$ items into one or the other of $n = 3$ diagnostic groups. A cross-tab of the sorting which is observed is shown on the left side of Table 1, whereas on the other side of the table we have demonstrated the cell frequencies that will occur by chance. Here, observed marginal totals are given. Here, in bold red color, the scenario of both the cells of the table representing the similarity of two tests is represented.

Consider the example as shown in Table 1, the observed no. of concordant items is 70, and the chance expected no. is 41. Hence, the surplus of observed over expected is $70 - 41 = 29$. Correspondingly, the chance expected no. of non-concordant items

Table 1 Cross-tab of cell frequencies for observed and chance data

		B 1	2	3	Total				B 1	2	3	Total
	1	44	5	1	50			1	30	15	5	50
A	2	7	20	3	30		A	2	18	9	3	30
	3	9	5	6	20			3	12	6	2	20
Total		60	30	10	100		Total		60	30	10	100

Observed Concordant Items:

count = 70

proportion = .70

Observed Concordant Items:

count = 70

proportion = .70

Table 2 Cross-tab of cell frequencies for observed and chance data

		B			
		1	2	3	Total
	1	44	5	1	50
A	2	7	20	3	30
	3	9	5	6	20
Total		60	30	10	100

		B			
		1	2	3	Total
	1	30	15	5	50
A	2	18	9	3	30
	3	12	6	2	20
Total		60	30	10	100

is $100 - 41 = 59$. Therefore, Cohen's kappa for this example is calculated as the ratio of the former to the latter, i.e., $29/59 = 0.4915$.

Weighted Kappa

In the scenario where the categories are simply nominal, then we can use Cohen's simple unweighted coefficient. When there is a scenario where classes are ordinal means class 2 embodies more than class 1, and class 3 embodies more the class 2, then it is advantageous to consider absolute concordance which is represented as the red font in the example as well as relative concordance that is represented as the black font in the example. When we are considering the relative concordance, then the cell which is present in the matrix row is according to the rule that it should be nearer to the concordant items (Table 2).

To demonstrate the weighting process, let us consider 3. In this table, first row represents observed frequencies. Consider that we had enough reason to accept that the distance between classes 1 and 2 is approximately identical to the distance between class 2 and class 3. Hence, in this scenario, cell $A1B2$ would lie at a distance of 1 unit from cell $A1B1$. Here, we have considered that the distance is relative. Similarly, cell $A1B3$ would be at a distance of 2 units from cell $A1B1$. Similarly, the concept would be applied to all the rows of the available matrix which is shown in Table 4. Therefore, the maximum potential distance between any two classes will be $n - 1$ with n ordered classes and equal imputed distances between consecutive classes. Here, in this present example, this value is calculated as 2 (Table 3).

The weight for any particular cell provided that the weight is linear then the following formula is defined for calculating the weight of a specific cell which is shown in Eq. (2).

$$\text{weight} = \frac{|\text{distance}|}{\text{maximum possible distance}} \quad (2)$$

Table 3 Cross-tab for the first row in observed frequencies

		B		
		1	2	3
A	1	44	5	1

Table 4 Resulting distances

		B		
		1	2	3
A	1	0	1	2
	2	1	0	1
	3	2	1	0

In another scenario, if the derived weight is quadratic, then the weight for a particular cell is defined by the following Eq. (3).

$$\text{weight} = 1 - \frac{(\text{distance})^2}{(\text{maximum possible distance})^2} \tag{3}$$

For this specific ex., it will give the resulting sets of weights for the cells which are shown in Table 5.

To illustrate how kappa is being calculated, we will show you how to calculate kappa with the present example. Here, in this scenario, which is shown in Table 6, now each of the frequency values will be divided by M. Here, the value of M is 100. This is done to transform it into a proportion.

Now, multiply each gray cells which is present in the observed table by the proportional of the linear weight of the cell. After that sum the outputs over all the nine cells. The result will be

$$P_{\text{observed}} = 0.8$$

Applying the same process for the nine gray cells in the "Chance Expected," table will yield

$$P_{\text{expected}} = 0.62$$

Table 5 Resulting set of weights for the cells in linear and quadratic weight

Linear						Quadratic				
		B						B		
		1	2	3				1	2	3
	1	1	.5	0			1	1	.75	0
A	2	.5	1	.5		A	2	.75	1	.75
	3	0	.5	1			3	0	.75	1

Table 6 Proportions of cross-tab of cell frequencies for observed and chance data

Proportions											
(i)		Observed				(ii)		Chance Expected			
		B			Total			B			Total
		1	2	3				1	2	3	
	1	.44	.05	.01	.50		1	.30	.15	.05	.50
A	2	.07	.20	.03	.30	A	2	.18	.09	.03	.30
	3	.09	.05	.06	20		3	.12	.06	.02	.20
Total		.60	.30	.10	1.00	Total		.60	.30	.10	1.00

When we consider linear weighting, then the kappa coefficient will be calculated as

$$\text{kappa}_{LW} = \frac{P_{\text{observed}} - P_{\text{expected}}}{1 - P_{\text{expected}}}$$
$$= \frac{0.8 - 0.62}{1 - 0.62}$$
$$= 0.4737$$

When there are quadratic weights, then we will apply the same process and get the following value.

$$\text{kappa}_{LW} = 0.4545$$

Weighted kappa coefficients are difficult to interpret because it is less accessible to natural understanding as compared to the simple unweighted coefficient.

Proportions of Agreement

We can also calculate the proportion of agreement without the help of kappa between the two judges within each of the k categories separately. Consider the example which is shown in Table 1 again. Here, Judges A and B contracted on a total of 44 items that are belonging to class 1. There are some items on which Judge A and Judge B are not agreeing. In this particular example, there are 6 additional items in class 1 with which B did not agree for Judge A, whereas for Judge B, there were 16 additional items in class 1 with which A did not agree. Therefore, the proportion of agreement for class 1 is calculated as:

$$\frac{44}{(44 + 6 + 16)} = 0.6667$$

In the same way, the proportion of class 1 agreement to be expected by simply chance is calculated as:

$$\frac{30}{(30 + 20 + 30)} = 0.375$$

And when the observed marginal totals are given, then a maximum possible proportion of agreement is calculated as:

$$\frac{50}{(50 + 0 + 10)} = 0.8333$$

The final result of the maximum possible proportion of agreement is shown in Table 7.

2.3 Contrast Enhancement

Through prosaic pictures, like creatural renderings or lifelike facsimiles, histogram equalization (HE), a conventional disparity refinement has a sensible interpretation [15]. The discrepancy of a ringer is accelerated overall from hither approach nigh outstretching the right periodic vehemence estimates. However, existing kin in unvarying zones undergoes discordance elaboration. Adaptive histogram equalization (AHE) is a denizen generic rendition of HE. Histogram equalization in which

Table 7 Maximum possible proportion of agreement

		B			
		1	2	3	Total
	1	50	0	0	50
A	2	0	30	0	30
	3	10	0	10	20
	Total	60	30	10	100

apiece histogram before substitute facsimile abides articulated adaptive method for the candor estimates ere pictures to be allocated, and AHE is built and is applicable for the improvement of local contrast before a picture and to articulate additional particulars [16]. A substantial advancement in squelching scuttlebutt and ameliorating fluctuations has been ascertained by much of the AHE algorithms. The amelioratement effect upon torrid dingus rather than backdrops could be advanced by the hybrid cumulative histogram equalization (HCHE) [17]. The gap adjustment histogram equalization can be used to solve the athwart enrichment issue and mollify the accentuated deprivation issue in the murk zones of the image [16]. To subdue this error which remains akin through the universal histogram equalization due to the dilating scuttlebutt in moderately analogous zones, contrast limited adaptive histogram equalization (CLAHE) was propounded. With standard histogram equalization, CLAHE can overbear the amid amplification afore scuttlebutt problem latent analogous zone of facsimile. Working on tiles, the puny areas of the facsimile, and calculating numerous histograms, apiece chording to a singular segment of the facsimile and harnessing them to allocate the weightlessness estimates of the facsimile is the main difference between CLAHE algorithm and standard HE [18, 19, 20]. CLAHE refinement algorithm could be wrought in different hues like RGB, YIQ, HSI, and so on. The color space is well-defined in the form of red, green, and blue constituents in the RGB color components. All three components are monochrome intensity images. RGB archetypal is a flawless implement for color generations while capturing images via color video cameras or displaying them on a colored monitor screen. [21]. In the RGB color model, it is all the triconstituents can be individually applied with CLAHE. The conclusion of the RGB full-colored image is obtained by coalescing the R, G, and B individual components. [22]. There is a high grade of a likeness among these triconstituents due to which this RGB color space is not appropriate for assay and processing portraying but is well fitted for the display of colored facsimiles. YIQ, another set out in which three constituents make up the facsimile data: these are (Y) luminance, (I) hue, and (Q) saturation. This first constituent, (Y) luminance, portrays grayscale data, and chrominance or color information is made up of the other two constituents [23]. In expressions of the (H) hue, (S) saturation, and (I) intensity, colors are designated by the HSI color model. The term intensity is the foremost depiction of white and black. The hue and saturation level does not make a difference while the valuation is at maximum or minimum leveled intensity. [22]. Taking advantage of humanoid color-response features and detachment of grayscale data from colored data, so that the same signals are used for both the white and black sets and the colored ones of HIS AND YIQ. It is to be beheld that hue ought not to be changed for each pixel for the contemplation of improving a colored facsimile. When a change occurs in the hue, then the color too gets altered, thereby perverting the facsimile. Improving the visible caliber of a facsimile by not altering it for the enhancements of its image is coveted by everyone [24].

2.4　Convolution Neural Networks

Artificial neural networks are widely utilized in medical imaging tasks. A special category of neural networks which is known as convolution neural networks (CNN) produces outstanding results in the classification task. They have used automatic extraction of features and do the classification task. In handwritten character recognition, they have already proved themselves amazingly great. Deep neural networks [25] are too much robust as if a few features are not present in the test data then the approach such as drop outsteps support the network to yield accurate results. Beside this in deep CNN activation function ReLUs has been introduced. Other activation functions like tangent and sigmoid have been used with traditional ANNs, but they vanish at the extreme points. Finally, with the help of multiple layers in deep neural nets, they could be efficiently worked on GPUs.

Convolutional neural networks (CNNs) are a kind of deep neural network. It utilizes the backpropagation approach to training the multilayer feed-forward neural network. CNN automatically detects and extracts the features from the images [26, 27]. CNN's different layers have extracted both high-level and low-level features. The final layer of convolutional neural networks is known as a final fully connected layer; it has been utilized for suitable tuning of the network.

At each layer of convolution, unique features are extracted, by using a sliding window approach on the full image at various positions of the image. The same training weights have been used by feature maps at different positions. These layers use weight sharing concepts, which require a fewer number of weights as compared to fully connected networks.

EfficientNet Model

Google recently published a paper for a newly designed convolutional neural network (CNN) called EfficientNet [28], which set new records for both accuracy and computational efficiency. The different scaling methods and their comparison are shown in Fig. 3. The AutoML MNAS framework has been utilized in EfficientNet for optimizing both the efficiency and accuracy (FLOPS). The architecture of EfficientNet uses the mobile inverted bottleneck convolution (MBConv). It is analogous to MnasNet and MobileNetV2. However, it is a little larger due to an improved FLOP. The baseline network is scaled up to generate the model known as EfficientNet [28]. In terms of CNN, there are three scaling dimensions: The first one is the depth which is described as how deep our network is. It is concerned with the number of layers in the network. The second one is width, which describes how much wide our network is. It is also equivalent to the number of channels in the convolution layer. The last one is a resolution which is defined as what is the resolution of the image which is passed to the CNN. Now, in the following section, a detailed explanation of these scaling is given.

Width Scaling (w)

This type of scaling is used when we want to keep our small. It is shown in Fig. 3b [28]. With the help of a wider network, we will be able to capture a more fine-grained image. It is also easier to train a small model.

Depth Scaling (d)

The most common way of scaling a network is scaling by depth. By adding or removing the layers in the network, we can scale up or scale down the network as shown in Fig. 3c [28]. Sometimes it is considered that when a network is going to be deeper, then more complex features can be captured.

Resolution (r)

In high-resolution images, the features are more fine-grained, and this is the reason why high-resolution images should work better. When we have a complex task like object detection, we will use image resolutions like 300×300, 512×512, or 600×600. This scenario is shown in Fig. 3d [28].

From the above three types of scaling, we can conclude that when we scale up any dimension of the network, i.e., width, depth, and resolution then it improves accuracy, but for bigger models, the accuracy gain diminishes as shown in Fig. 4 [28].

3   Methodology

In this paper, we have used medical images (APTOS 2019) and EfficientNet. EfficientNet was introduced by Google AI, and this is a new method on ImageNet. It is recommended for the classification task. EfficientNet is a family of image classification models. EfficientNet is too much smaller as compared to other models. The main building block of EfficientNet is the mobile inverted bottleneck MB Conv. This was the first time announced in MobileNetV2.The main advantage of EfficientNet is that it scales more efficiently by making a balance network among depth, width, and resolution. This is the reason behind the better performance of EfficientNet.

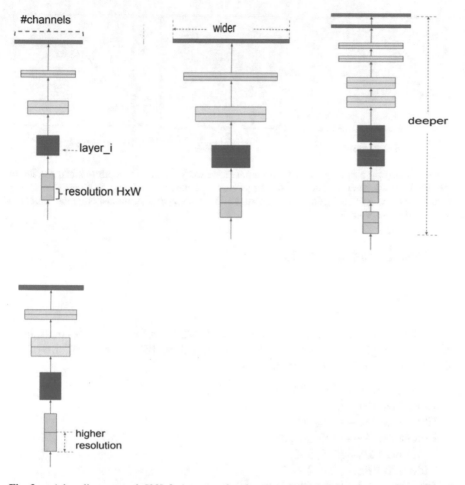

Fig. 3 a A baseline network [28]. **b** A conventional scaling that only increases one dimension of the network which is width [28]. **c** A conventional scaling that only increases one dimension of the network which is depth [28]. **d** A conventional scaling that only increases one dimension of the network which is resolution [28]

The EfficientNet model group contains 8 models. It starts from $B0$ and ends at $B7$. Every subsequent model number refers to variants. With each variant, there are more parameters, and there is higher accuracy.

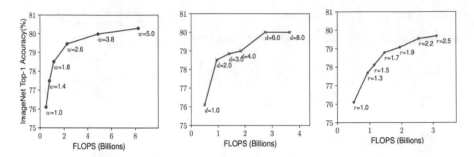

Fig. 4 Scaling up a baseline model with different network width (*w*), depth (*d*), and resolution (*r*) coefficients. Larger networks with a larger width, depth, or resolution tend to attain higher accuracy, but the accuracy gain rapidly saturates after reaching 80%, demonstrating the limitation of single dimension scaling

4   Results and Discussion

4.1   Dataset

In the dataset, we have 3662 train images and 1928 test images. There are total 5 classes of images, which are labeled as 0, 1, 2, 3, 4, and 5. The original size of the image from the EfficientNet paper is as follows:

EfficientNet*B*0—(224, 224, 3)
EfficientNet*B*1—(240, 240, 3)
EfficientNet*B*2—(260, 260, 3)
EfficientNet*B*3—(300, 300, 3)
EfficientNet*B*4—(380, 380, 3)
EfficientNet*B*5—(456, 456, 3)
EfficientNet*B*6—(528, 528, 3)
EfficientNet*B*7—(600, 600, 3).

4.2   EDA (Exploratory Data Analysis)

First of all, we have examined the labels of our datasets. This is shown in Fig. 5.

Now, we will see how the images are looking before preprocessing. Here, in our dataset, there are five labels. This is shown in Fig. 6.

After preprocessing the images using the CLAHE method, same image is looked as shown in Fig. 7.

In the EfficientNet model group, a total of 8 models are defined from *B*0 to *B*7. When we move from *B*0 to *B*7, the number of the parameter, as well as the accuracy of the model, is also increased. In Table 8, we have shown a total of 6 attributes based on which we have compared the various EfficientNet model, i.e., from *B*0 to

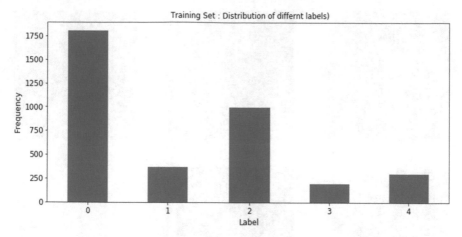

Fig. 5 Label distribution of a dataset

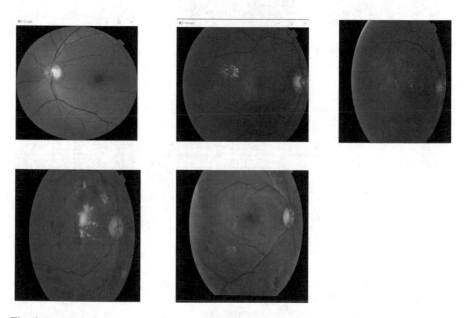

Fig. 6 Images before preprocessing

*B*7. In the table, we have specified the total parameters that are available when we are modeling the network. Trainable parameters are those parameters that are solved by the solver. Non-trainable parameters are those parameters that are not trained with the help of gradient descent. These parameters do not require training. These parameters are not updated and optimized during the training phase. In the last part of Table 8, we have shown the Cohen kappa score which is again segregated for two values, i.e., training and validation.

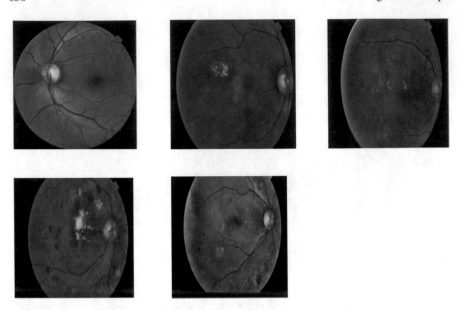

Fig. 7 Images after preprocessing using CLAHE

Table 8 Comparison of various model parameters

Model	Total parameters	Trainable parameters	Non-trainable parameters	Cohen kappa score	
				Training	Validation
EfficientNet B0	4,052,126	4,010,110	42,016	0.82495	0.77395
EfficientNet B1	6,575,232	6,513,184	62,048	0.82958	0.86364
EfficientNet B2	7,768,562	7,700,994	67,568	0.88123	0.85136
EfficientNet B3	10,783,528	10,696,232	87,296	0.926175	0.89276
EfficientNet B4	17,673,816	17,548,616	125,200	0.94176	0.90125
EfficientNet B5	28,513,520	28,340,784	172,736	0.95192	0.91902

In Fig. 8, we have shown in the form of a chart the total parameter in comparison to the trainable parameter. From the graph, we can analyze that almost a large amount of parameters are used as trainable parameters.

In Fig. 9, we have shown the result of various kappa scores for various EfficientNet models from B0 to B5.

5 Conclusion

From the above experiment, we can conclude that when we move from B0 to B5 the accuracy will be increasing, i.e., Cohen kappa score for training and validation is

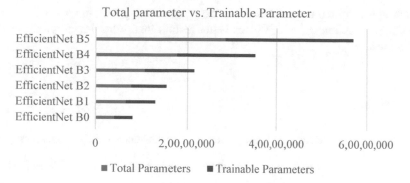

Fig. 8 Total parameter vs trainable parameter in various EfficientNet models

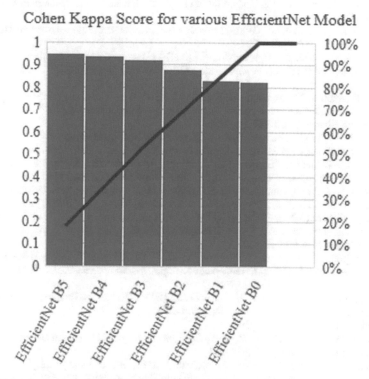

Fig. 9 Cohen kappa score for various EfficientNet models

approaching 1 means perfectness. As we have discussed earlier that when the Cohen kappa value is greater than 0.75, then it is considered an excellent value. In our experimental result, it is about 0.95 for training and 0.92 for the validation which is considered an excellent result when we apply the model $B5$. Even when we have applied $B0$, then we have got a result for training is 0.82 and for validation is 0.77

which is considered a good result. In the preprocessing technique, we have used the CLAHE technique, which gives better results than other image preprocessing techniques.

References

1. https://www.mayoclinic.org/diseases-conditions/diabetic-retinopathy/symptoms-causes/syc-20371611
2. Cohen J (1960) A coefficient of agreement for nominal scales. Educ Psychol Measur 20(1):37–46
3. Cohen J (1968) Weighted kappa: nominal scale agreement provision for scaled disagreement or partial credit. Psychol Bull 70(4):213
4. Kraemer HC, Periyakoil VS, Noda A (2002) Kappa coefficients in medical research. Stat Med 21(14):2109–2129
5. Fleiss JL, Levin B, Paik MC (1981). The measurement of interrater agreement. Stat Med Rates Proportions 2(212–236):22–23
6. Mann KS, Kaur S (2017) Segmentation of retinal blood vessels using artificial neural networks for early detection of diabetic retinopathy. AIP Conf Proc 1836(1):020026. AIP Publishing LLC
7. GeethaRamani R, Balasubramanian L (2016) Retinal blood vessel segmentation employing image processing and data mining techniques for computerized retinal image analysis. Biocybern Biomed Eng 36(1):102–118
8. Tang S, Lin T, Yang J, Fan J (2015) Retinal vessel segmentation using supervised classification based on multi-scale vessel filtering and Gabor wavelet. J Med Imaging Health Inf 5:1571–1574
9. Abdallah AJ, Undrill PE, Cree MJ, Olson JA, McHardy KC, Sharp PF, Forrester JV (1998) A comparison of computer-based classification methods applied to the detection of microaneurysms in ophthalmic fluorescein angiograms. Comput Biol Med 28(3):225–238
10. Aslani C (1999) The human eye: structure and function. Sinauer Associates, Sunder-land
11. Zhang L, Fisher M, Wang W, Hassana C, Boyce JF, Cook HL, Williamson TH (1999) Automated localization of the optic disc, fovea and retinal blood vessels from digital color fundus images. Br J Ophthalmol 83(8):902–910
12. Sinthanayothin C, Boyce JF, Williamson TH, Cook HL, Mensah E, Lal S, Usher D (2002) Automated detection of diabetic retinopathy on digital fundus images. Diabet Med J 19(2):105–112
13. Vermeer KA, Vos FM, Lemij HG, Vossepoel AM (2004) Model based method for retinal blood vessel detection. Comput Biol Med 34(3):209–219
14. http://vassarstats.net/kappaexp.html
15. Wang Y, Wang H, Yin C, Dai M (2016) Biologically inspired image enhancement based on Retinex. Neurocomputing 177:373–384
16. Zimmerman JB, Pizer SM (1988) An evaluation of the effectiveness of adaptive histogram equalization for contrast enhancement. IEEE Trans Med Imaging 7:304–312
17. Lin CL (2011) An approach to improve the quality of infrared images of vein-patterns. Sensors 11:11447–11463
18. Zuiderveld K (1994) Contrast limited adaptive histogram equalization. Academic Press Inc.
19. Pisano E, Zong S, Hemminger B, DeLuca M, Johnston R, Muller K, Breuning M, Pizer S (1998) Contrast limited adaptive histogram equalization image processing to improve the detection of simulated speculations in dense mammograms. J Digit Imaging 11:193–200
20. Jintasuttisak T, Intajag S (2014) Color retinex image enhancement by Rayleigh contrast limited histogram equalization. In: International conference on control, automation and systems, vol 10, pp 692–697

21. Abuturab MR (2015) Multiple color-image authentication systems using HSI color space and QR decomposition in gyrator domains. J Mod Opt 12:1–16
22. Gonzalez RC, Woods RE (2010) Digital image processing, 3rd edn. Prentice-Hall
23. Lal S, Narasimhadhan AV, Kumar R (2015) Automatic method for contrast enhancement of natural color images. J Electr Eng Technol 10(3):1233–1243
24. Naik SK, Murthy CA (2003) Hue-preserving color image enhancement without gamut problem. IEEE Trans Image Process 12:1591–1600
25. Bengio Y et al. (2007) Greedy layer-wise training of deep networks. In: Advances in neural information processing systems, pp 153–160
26. Kaggle Inc. (2015) Diabetic retinopathy detection, vol 2016. Retrieved from https://www.kaggle.com/c/diabeticretinopathydetection. Accessed on 1 Sep 2016
27. http://www.ces.clemson.edu/~ahoover/stare/. Accessed on 1 Jan 2018
28. Tan M, Le QV (2019) Efficient net: rethinking model scaling for convolutional neural networks. arXiv preprint arXiv:1905.11946

Classification of Lung Nodule from CT and PET/CT Images Using Artificial Neural Network

Malho Hansdah and Koushlendra Kumar Singh

1 Introduction

Cancer is a disease caused by an uncontrollable division of cells that spreads into the surrounding tissue. The cancerous cell grows in the body and feeds on another cell. They can also form tumors that damage one immune system. Lung cancer is the result of the uncontrolled growth of cells in lung tissues [1]. Lung cancer is considered one of the most common types of cancer among all types of cancers. Lung cancer accounts for 1.38 million cancer deaths per year worldwide, and it is the major cause of cancer death among both men and women. Lung cancer is one of the deadliest cancers as the five-year survival rate is only 18.6%. The goal of this research is to detect the presence of tumor cells in the lung. The task is to classify the tumor cell type and based on that detect the presence of lung cancer in patients. The CT and PET/CT scans of lungs with suspicion of lung cancer of patients who underwent standard-of-care lung biopsy are used for classification. This research work aims to use methods from deep learning and use the artificial neural network to build an accurate model to classify the lung cancer type in patients. An accurate model could speed up the process of cancer screening and correct classification of lung cancer type. This study will help in early detection and improve the survival rate. CT and PET scan images have been given as input to the model, and the model classifies the input image into one of the four classes or categories as squamous-cell carcinoma, large-cell carcinoma, adenocarcinoma, and small-cell carcinoma [2]. Adenocarcinoma is the most common type of lung cancer among all the types. This type of cancer is mostly seen in people who never smoked. Squamous cell carcinoma starts in a squamous cell. They are found in the center of the lung. It is linked to patients who have a history of smoking. Large-cell carcinoma type can be present

M. Hansdah (✉) · K. K. Singh
Machine Vision and Intelligence Lab, Department of Computer Science and Engineering,
National Institute of Technology Jamshedpur, Jamshedpur, Jharkhand 831014, India
e-mail: malhohansdah777@gmail.com

in any part of the lung. They grow and spread quickly which makes them difficult to treat. Small-cell carcinoma is like large-cell carcinoma and is also called oat cell cancer. This type of lung cancer spreads and grows faster in the body than the other type [3].

The purpose is to build an artificial neural network model that can be used to detect the presence of tumor cells and classify them into the four major classes. Artificial neural networks (ANNs) provide better techniques, which solve classification problems. ANN is a mathematical model that is based on the organization and functional features of natural neural networks [4]. The neural network has input, output, and hidden layers. Hidden layers provide weights to the input and produce output using activation functions. The model will go through three levels: training, validation, and testing. First, the model will be trained on the dataset; then, it will be validated on unseen data. The optimizers used are Adam and RMSprop.

2 Literature Review

Deep artificial neural networks are applied in various fields of pattern recognition and classification problems, especially convolutional neural networks (CNNs) which are one class of models [5]. Deep neural networks have shown better performance in classification problems. Convolutional neural networks (CNNs) have been used in lung cancer classification and detection. Nasser et al. proposed an approach in the lung cancer field and built a lot of models based on neural networks for classification, prediction, and diagnosing [6]. Authors also developed an ANN-based model to detect the cancerous and non-cancerous tissues present in the lungs. The symptoms used for detection of lung cancer are yellow fingers, anxiety, wheezing, coughing, shortness of breath, swallowing difficulty, etc. [6]. Kashf et al. also developed classification models for various problems based on artificial neural networks [7]. Ali et al. worked on deep reinforcement learning for lung nodule detection. They have also focused on the early detection of lung nodules in CT scan images. The training result yielded an accuracy of 99.1% [8].

Senthil and Ayshwarya have used a computer-aided classification method for lung cancer prediction [9]. Based on an evolutionary system, they used a combination of architectural evolution with weight learning using a neural network and particle swarm optimization is implemented [9]. They proposed different variants and hybridized them with an evolutionary algorithm. Mhaske et al. proposed a deep learning technique for lung cancer detection [10]. They have applied a 3D multi-path VGG-like network in combination with U-Net for prediction. Their model has achieved an accuracy of 95.60%. Islam et al. have combined ResNet, AlexNet, and VGGNet together for classification [11]. From this literature survey, we can conclude that deep learning techniques give good results. Qiam and Guirong used the expectation maximization (EM) algorithm for lung nodule segmentation. Their objective was to improve the rate of early detection of lung cancer nodules. The EM algorithm is an effective method for parameter estimation of incomplete datasets using the maximum likelihood method (ML). Due to the lack of data used in this study is not satisfactory [12]. Li et al. in their work combined the chaotic ant colony algorithm for lung nodule detection and recognition [13]. The model effectively removed the interferences such as cross-shaped and strip-shaped blood vessels and achieved accurate detection and recognition of lung nodules. They have achieved reduced false-positive rates for whether the correct nodule is detected and recognized [13]. Saikita et al. proposed a hybrid transfer learning-based model to detect primary lung cancer [14].

In this research work, we have developed a model for the classification of cancerous tissue in the lungs. The model is evaluated with two optimizers, Adam and RMSprop optimizer with ANN. The result from both optimizers is compared. The data are divided into four classes: small-cell carcinoma, adenocarcinoma, squamous-cell carcinoma, and large-cell carcinoma [2].

3 Objective

The aim is to use the available CT and PET scans and classify the type of tumor cells using deep learning techniques and comparing various available techniques. The primary goal is to build a model that takes a CT scan image as input, processes it using intelligence, and successfully brings out the result from the image. The DICOM images are converted into jpeg format using ONIS software. This work aims to develop an artificial neural network-based model for the correct classification of tumor cells in CT scan data for early detection of lung cancer type with better accuracy. Early detection can increase the possibility of survival rate of cancer patients. There is a possibility of variance in results by different radiologists as one may classify the region as a tumor cell and the other may not. Hence, automated methods reduce inter-radiologist variance. Automated methods have also shown comparable accuracy with manual interpretation.

4 Dataset and Method

4.1 Dataset

The proposed work is validated with large-scale CT and PET/CT dataset for lung cancer diagnosis [2]. This dataset consists of DICOM images of lung cancer with XML annotation files that show the tumor locations. The dataset is provided by The Cancer Imaging Archive (TCIA) [15]. The images in the dataset are obtained from patients who may or may not have lung cancer and who underwent standard-of-care lung biopsy and PET/CT. Images were grouped based on tissue histopathological

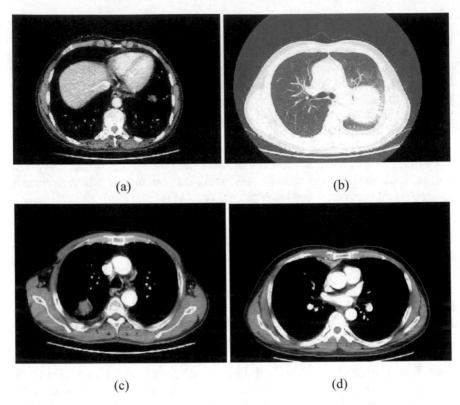

(a)   (b)

(c)   (d)

Fig. 1 a Adenocarcinoma, **b** large-cell carcinoma, **c** small-cell carcinoma, **d** squamous-cell carcinoma

diagnosis. Data are divided into 4 classes: adenocarcinoma, squamous-cell carcinoma, large-cell carcinoma, and small-cell carcinoma. The input images of the CT scan of the lung are shown in Fig. 1.

The window width of the images is 350 HU and level of 40 HU. The CT scan slice interval varies from 0.625 (about 0.02 in) to 5 mm (about 0.2 in). Every study included one CT volume, one PET volume, and fused CT and PET images. Annotations of each tumor location have been done by academic radiologists who have expertise in the lung cancer field. The total number of participants participating in this study was three hundred fifty-five. This makes the dataset a particularly useful resource for developing algorithms for medical purposes. The annotations were captured by the LabelImg. The detailed description of the actual dataset is shown in Table 1.

Table 1 Dataset descriptions

Image statistics	
Modalities	CT, PT
Number of participants	355
Number of studies	436
Series	1295
Total number of images	251,135
Image size (GB)	127.2

4.2 Proposed Methodology

The proposed model consists of five stages, namely data collection and preprocessing, data splitting, training, testing, and validation. The first step is data collection. We have used open-source data from The Cancer Imaging Archive (TCIA) as discussed in the earlier section [15]. All the images are in DICOM format. The images are downloaded and converted into the required jpeg format. The conversion of DICOM images is performed using open-source software ONIS. Data preprocessing is one of the most important steps in machine learning. Each input image has been processed and labeled into four categories: adenocarcinoma, squamous-cell carcinoma, large-cell carcinoma, and small-cell carcinoma in the data collection and preprocessing stage. The excess region was cropped from the images so that the model could work on the region of interest. Normalization is also performed on the training and validation data during preprocessing. Data splitting has been performed by dividing the whole dataset into three categories: training, validation, and testing. The split-folder Python module is used to split our data into training, validation, and testing data. Training data are 80% of the total data. Validation data and testing data will be 10% of the total data. The division of images into three sets is shown in Table 2.

The workflow of the proposed model is shown below in Fig. 2.

We have used an artificial neural network algorithm to build our model. Artificial neural networks perform better in analyzing the dataset, extracting features from

Table 2 Subset of dataset

Class	Images for training	Images for validation	Images for testing	Total image
Adenocarcinoma	1905	238	239	2382
Small-cell carcinoma	1553	194	195	1942
Squamous-cell carcinoma	1187	148	149	1484
Large-cell carcinoma	476	59	61	596
Total	5121	639	644	7104

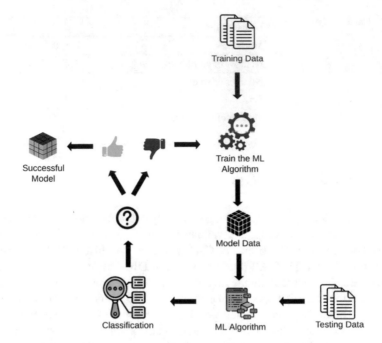

Fig. 2 Flow diagram of proposed model

them, and performing classification. An artificial neural network is nothing but a collection of neurons that are responsible for creating layers. These neurons are also called tuned parameters. The output from each layer is passed to the next layer, and various nonlinear activation functions are used that help in the learning process. The architecture of ANN is shown in Fig. 3.

Fig. 3 Architecture of ANN

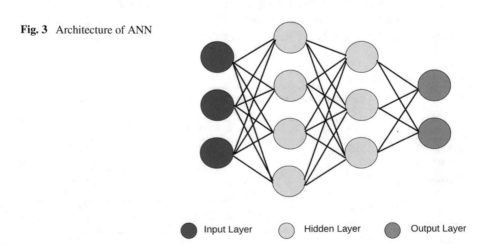

Table 3 Summary of the proposed model

Layer	Output shape	Parameters
input_1 (InputLayer)	[(None, 128, 128, 3)]	0
flatten (Flatten)	(None, 49,152)	0
dense_3 (Dense)	(None, 12)	589,836
dense_4 (Dense)	(None, 8)	104
dense_5 (Dense)	(None, 4)	36
Total parameters: 589,976		
Trainable parameters: 589,976		
Non-trainable parameters: 0		

The proposed model has a total of 5 layers: one input layer, three hidden layers, and an output layer. The first layer is the input layer which is the entry point into the neural network. The input shape is in a 3-dimensional array that is $128 \times 128 \times 3$. The input shape is 128×128 and 3 denotes the number of filters used. The next layer is a flattened layer. Flattening is applied to convert the previous multidimensional data into a 1-dimensional (1D) array or single vector so that 1D data can be given to the next layers as input. A total of 49,152 elements are present in the input tensor after flattening. The next three layers are dense layers. Dense layers are deeply connected with their previous layer also known as the feed-forward neural network. The first dense layer has 12 units, and the next dense layer has 8 units, units representing the output shape of the layer. Total parameters for the first and second layers are 589,836 and 104, respectively. Parameter numbers for a dense layer are calculated using Eq. (1). The last dense layer is also called the output layer. Its shape is (None, 4). Since our problem is to classify the images into four types of lung nodules, the unit value is kept at four. It means the last layer outputs four values per sample in the batch. The proposed model summary is shown in Table 3.

$$\text{Parameters} = \text{output\_channel\_number} \times (\text{input\_channel\_number} + 1) \quad (1)$$

5 Results and Discussion

The data used by our proposed architecture are collected from a large-scale CT and PET/CT dataset [2]. All the CT scan images were from patients who may have lung cancer. Data are divided into 4 classes: adenocarcinoma, squamous-cell carcinoma, large-cell carcinoma, and small-cell carcinoma. A sequential model is used for the machine learning process. In this model, 2 hidden layers are applied. The total parameters present are five lakh eight nine thousand nine hundred seventy six. All the parameters are trainable. To supply weights, ReLU and Sigmoid activation functions are used. Keras library with TensorFlow at the back end is used for the ANN model in Python 3.6.9. For calculating results, performance parameters such as accuracy metrics and categorical cross-entropy loss are used. Adam and RMSprop optimizers are used in the proposed model [16]. In the proposed model with the Adam optimizer, the accuracy achieved is 99.06%, and the loss is 13.09%. The results are compared for different epochs in Table 4. It has been observed that in the proposed model with RMSprop optimizer the testing accuracy is nearly 100%, and loss is 2.26 in the case of 20 epochs. When Adam is used as an optimizer with 50 epochs, the accuracy is also nearly 100%, but the loss is 4.35%. ReLU and sigmoid activation functions have been used for both cases. The results are shown in Table 5. When we increase the number of epochs, the loss is going to increase, and also, overfitting problem comes into the picture.

The graph of model accuracy on training data and validation data with Adam optimizer is shown in Fig. 4a. The x-axis and y-axis are epochs and accuracy, respectively. Similarly, the plot of model loss on training data and validation data is shown in Fig. 4b. X-axis and Y-axis are epochs and loss. The accuracy and loss curve with the RMSprop optimizer is shown in Fig. 5. The comparison of results with existing approaches is shown in Table 5.

Table 4 Results with different optimizer and activation functions

Model	Optimizer	Activation function	Accuracy (%)	Loss (%)	Epochs
ANN + sequential	RMSprop	ReLU, sigmoid	96.09	10.80	10
ANN + sequential	Adam	ReLU, sigmoid	99.06	13.09	10
ANN + sequential	RMSprop	ReLU, sigmoid	99.8	2.26	20
ANN + sequential	Adam	ReLU, sigmoid	99.6	4.35	50

Table 5 Comparison of results with existing models

Authors	Dataset	Technique	Accuracy (%)	Loss (%)
Ibrahim et al. [6]	Survey lung cancer	ANN	96.67	< 1
Saikia et al. [14]	Lung-PET-CT-Dx	Transfer learning	98.70	–
Ali et al. [8]	LIDC-IDRI	Deep reinforcement learning	64.4	–
Senthil and Ayshwarya [9]	Lung cancer dataset (UCI)	Feed-forward backpropagation neural networks	97	–
Mhaske et al. [10]	LIDC-IDRI	3D multipath VGG-like network	95.60	38.77
Experiment	Lung-PET-CT-Dx	ANN + RMSprop	96.8	2.26
Proposed model	Lung-PET-CT-Dx	ANN + Adam	99.6	4.35

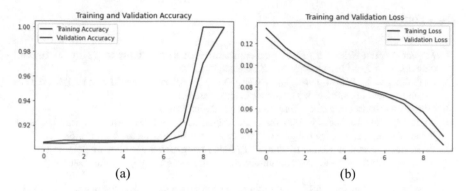

Fig. 4 **a** Training and validation accuracy curve, **b** training and validation loss curve (Adam)

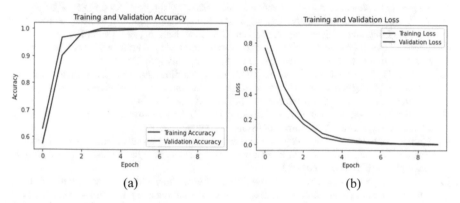

Fig. 5 **a** Training and validation accuracy curve, **b** training and validation loss curve (RMSprop)

6 Conclusion

The ANN architecture is used to build the model. The proposed artificial neural network model can perform the classification of lung cancer into four categories. The proposed model is validated with DICOM images of lung cancer. The proposed approach has ANN architecture which uses a sequential model. Artificial neural networks perform better in analyzing the dataset, extracting features from them, and performing classification. The comparison of our result is performed with the already presented work. The proposed model with Adam optimizer is tested and validated on CT and PET/CT scans; the total validation accuracy achieved is 99.6% with a loss of 4.35%. This will be extremely useful to the radiologists and will reduce the inter-radiologist variance while manually classifying the type of lung cancer nodules through the CT scans.

References

1. Marouf A, Abu-Naser SS (2018) Predicting antibiotic susceptibility using artificial neural network. Int J Acad Pedagogical Res (IJAPR) 2(10):1–5
2. Li P, Wang S, Li T, Lu J, HuangFu Y, Wang D (2020) A large-scale CT and PET/CT dataset for lung cancer diagnosis. In: The cancer imaging archive
3. https://www.cancer.org/cancer/lung-cancer/about/what-is.html
4. Afana M, Ahmed I, Harb B, Abu-Nasser BS, Abu-Naser, SS (2018) Artificial neural network for forecasting car mileage per gallon in the city. Int J Adv Sci Technol 124:51–59
5. Prakashbabu P, Ashok Kumar D, Vithyaa T (2019) Lung cancer detection model using convolution neural network and fuzzy clustering algorithms. Int J Comput Trends Technol (IJCTT) 67(11)
6. Ibrahim MN, Abu-Naser SS (2019) Lung cancer detection using artificial neural network. Int J Eng Inf Syst (IJEAIS) 3(3):17–23
7. Kashf DWA, Okasha AN, Sahyoun NA, El-Rabi RE, Abu-Naser SS (2018) Predicting DNA lung cancer using artificial neural network. Int J Acad Pedagogical Res (IJAPR) 2(10):6–13
8. Ali I, Hart GR, Gunabushanam G, Liang Y, Muhammad W, Nartowt B, Kane M, Ma X, Deng J (2018) Lung nodule detection via deep reinforcement learning. Front Oncol
9. Senthil S, Ayshwarya B (2018) Lung cancer prediction using feed forward back propagation neural networks with optimal features. Int J Appl Eng Res 318–325
10. Mhaske D, Rajeswari K, Tekade R (2019) Deep learning algorithm for classification and prediction of lung cancer using CT scan images. In: 5th International conference on computing, communication, control and automation (ICCUBEA), pp 1–5
11. Islam MT, Aowal MA, Minhaz AT, Khalid A (2017) Abnormality detection and localization of chest X-rays using deep convolutional neural networks. arXiv
12. Qian Y, Guirong W (2014) Lung nodule segmentation using EM algorithm. In: Sixth international conference on intelligent human-machine systems and cybernetics, pp 20–23. https://doi.org/10.1109/IHMSC.2014.13
13. Li J, Zhao H, Yang Y (2020) Detection and recognition of lung nodules in medical images using chaotic ant colony algorithm. In: 12th International conference on measuring technology and mechatronics automation (ICMTMA), pp 517–522. https://doi.org/10.1109/ICMTMA50254.2020.00117
14. Saikia T, Kumar R, Kumar D et al. (2022) An automatic lung nodule classification system based on hybrid transfer learning approach. SN Comput. Sci 3(272). https://doi.org/10.1007/s42979-022-01167-0
15. Clark K, Vendt B, Smith K, Freymann J, Kirby J, Koppel P, Moore S, Phillips S, Maffitt D, Pringle M, Tarbox L, Prior F (2013) The cancer imaging archive (TCIA): maintaining and operating a public information repository. J Digit Imaging 26(6):1045–1057
16. Kumar Singh K, Kumar S, Antonakakis M, Moirogiorgou K, Deep A, Kashyap KL, Bajpai MK, Zervakis M (2022) Deep learning capabilities for the categorization of microcalcification. Int J Environ Res Public Health 19(4):2159. https://doi.org/10.3390/ijerph19042159

An Efficient and Secure Cluster-Based Cooperative Data Transmission for Wireless Ad Hoc Networks IOT Environment

Surya Narayan Mahapatra and Binod Kumar Singh

1 Introduction

In the past few decades, wireless communication has become increasingly important in many applications due to the large demand for connectivity and wireless access [1]. In this, ad hoc networks gained widespread attention in the wireless communication community and a typical IoT application. These networks are widely used in many applications related to the military, emergency services, disaster relief, sensor systems, etc. Although ad hoc networks possess several advantages, there are some challenges and need an improvement in certain characteristics. In most cases, energy is one of the major concerns that cause to suffer from unsuccessful communication. Several approaches are presented earlier to enhance the energy consumption and prolong the network lifetime [2–5]. The energy utilized by the transmitter is proportional to the distance toward the reception side [6]. Hence, for long-distance communication, transmission failure leads to the loss of the packets and needs a large amount of energy for retransmission. As a result, reducing the energy utilization of the nodes is one of the challenging issues in the design of the IoT-enabled wireless ad hoc networks. Security is also a significant issue in upgrading the vast spectrum of IoT applications. The security challenges may arrive in all the layers of the IoT application, such as the sensing layer, network layer, middleware layer, and application layer [7]. The attacks such as routing, spoofing, and DoS attacks primarily affect the network layer.

Cooperative communication is cost-effective and alternative to MIMO systems that achieve spatial diversity gains, increase throughput, minimize retransmission

S. N. Mahapatra (✉) · B. K. Singh
Department of Computer Science and Engineering, National Institute of Technology,
Jamshedpur 831014, India
e-mail: snmahapatra0205@gmail.com

B. K. Singh
e-mail: bksingh.cse@nitjsr.ac.in

latency, and mitigate channel impairments for land distance transmissions [8–11]. In cooperative communication, the intermediates nodes are combined with the sender and receiver at the physical (PHY) or MAC layer to enhance the network's coverage and throughput.

2 Related Work

In wireless ad hoc networks, the cooperative communication with the relay selection sends the data packets via the relay node focuses on improving energy consumption. A proper design of cooperative MAC is necessary to exploit the advantage of energy consumption and assumes trusted routing of packets among the devices. Figure 1 shows the overview of the techniques for the successful data packet transmission broadly classified into two categories (i) optimal relay selection-based MAC protocols, (ii) security-based MAC protocols. Previous protocols were proposed to attain single-objective orientation, and the relay selection back off process has been proposed to enhance the throughput performance and energy efficiency. Some of the recent works in cooperative communication are discussed in Table 1.

Liu et al. [18] proposed a cooperative MAC protocol with rapid relay selection (RRS-CMAC) that aims to select the relay when the sender and receiver data rate

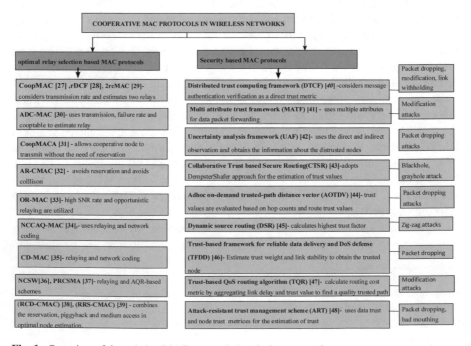

Fig. 1 Overview of the existing MAC protocols in wireless networks

Table 1 Summary of cooperative MAC protocols in wireless communication

Author name, paper ref. no. and year	Technique	Features	Advantages	Drawbacks	Simulation tool, metrics used
Mahmud et al. [12], 2019	$RD^2 C$	Uses the data rates concept to decrease the time delay	Recommend s to select the relay node from midst region	Energy utilization is high	OMNeT + + -Throughput, relay selection delay, energy consumption, and packet error rate
Kakria and Aseri [13], 2019	EDMRS	Uses residual energy and queue size to estimate relay	Back-off timer is used to select from multiple relay nodes	Does not ensure optimal node relay selection	NS2-Throughput, packet transmission delay, end-to-end delay, and energy efficiency
Chen et al. [14], 2019	Improved Authentication Protocol	Communication is carried after verification by trusted party	Minimizes the time required for authentication	Prone to offline identity guessing attack	Embedded device (smartphone—iPhone 6s), cost consumption. Attack analysis
Jiang et al. [15], 2019	IoV model-based blockchain model	Classify the data blocks based on blockchain	Secure storage	Fails during high traffic conditions	MATLAB-average delay time, average number of retransmission, average throughput, blockchain transaction delay
Zhong et al. [16], 2018	CPPA	Change of password and identity by the user at any moment	Reduces the communication overhead	Requires high computing power	Communication, and computation overhead
Epiphaniou et al. [17], 2018	Key generation model	Integrates the scatter mobility and 3D scattering attributes	Turbo coding is used for error correction	Packets drops occur	Execution time, entropy, secret bit extraction rate, bit mismatch rate
Schweitzer et al. [18], 2017	Improved OLSR	Optimization is done by 1-hop neighbors rule	Minimum hop required	Possibility of attack is high	NS3-percentage of dropped packets with movement and without movement

is minimal. The selection is based on the three stages such as rate differentiation phase, priority differentiation phase, and contention resolution phase. The first stage determines the higher-level data rate from all the candidate nodes. The selected nodes are then passed to the next phase, where the node with higher piggyback performance is found. Finally, k-round contention resolution selects the optimal relay with a high data rate to improve the cooperation efficiency and reduces reservation overhead.

However, if various candidate nodes possess the same data level, then the multiple selection of relay node is possible, leading to packet collision.

Liu et al. [19] discussed a power-optimized cooperative MAC (PO-CMAC) protocol that chooses the relay node to optimize the energy consumption during packet transmission. This protocol selects the cooperative node to be placed with the one-hop transmission region between the source and destination. Here, transmission occurs in a two-fold process, i.e., from sender to relay and from relay to destination. To balance power consumption in the network, a lifetime-extended transmission power optimization (LETPO) method is used to calculate the optimal transmission power based on linear programming and a greedy algorithm. Then, the selection process determines the relay node based on the cooperative link quality estimation. However, during non-uniform traffic load condition, there is a low energy consumption at the nodes.

Wu et al. [20] discussed a joint relay selection and power control approach that aims to choose the best relay node to maximizes the throughput in the wireless system. Here, the relay network consists of a sender; multiple relay nodes work on decoder and forward (DF) manner and a recipient, where each relay node has a finite-size battery and a data buffer for storing the harvested energy and the receiving the data. In this, the relay node is estimated based on the statistical knowledge derived from the energy arrivals and channel-state levels of the intermediate nodes. Next the selected relay nodes decide time slots and the power level and based on the present condition of battery energy and queue data. However, the computational complexity of the system is higher. Zhang et al. [21] proposed an energy-efficient cooperative MAC (EECO-MAC) uses the power-adjustable back off model that determines the optimal cooperative node. In this, two frames such as helper to send (HTS) and cooperative clear to send (CCTS) and an additional field is included in the frame which indicates the required minimum transmission power. In this approach, a back off scheme is used that combines the space and time back off mechanism to enhance the throughput. During failed transmission, the transmission power is increased, and the contention window size is doubled for the next transmission. Although two back off scheme is used, the power and network delay is increased during transmission.

Mahmud et al. [12] proposed a reliability-based distance-aware data rate adaptive cooperative MAC that estimates the relay node based on the reliability factor in IoT-enabled wireless ad hoc networks. The relay selection starts from the center region between the source and destination where upper and lower distance threshold limits are utilized to adjust the selection window. Initially starts the search from the center region and if an optimal relay is not found, the selection continues for the primary, secondary regions. However, the energy utilization is not balanced properly among the sensor nodes.

Chen et al. [14] proposed an improved authentication protocol that aims to reduce the online guessing attack and computation time in the vehicular ad hoc networks. Initially, every vehicle should be registered to the trusted party once, and a smart is provided at the registration phase. Then, the trusted authority verifies whether its identity has been registered or not. Next, the user inserts a smart card to obtain secure communication with the vehicular network. However, when the number of registered users increases, then the computation time for issuing the certificate also increases.

Jiang et al. [15] presented a blockchain model based on the characteristics of the Internet of Vehicles (IoVs) to enhance security. In this model, the blocks created by means of the vehicles are transmitted to the network via the neighbor nodes or by 4G network. Here, the neighboring nodes are determined as the nodes for some blockchain in the roadside system in which the vehicles selected for the data communication. A random back off time is used for the transmission, and if retransmission reaches the threshold limit, then the cellular network is utilized for the transmission process. In this, a lag time stamp range is designed where the block sent by IoV has the hash function of the previous blockchain. Thus, the verification is performed by jointly considering the several blocks, and the data corruption affected in the particular node is avoided. However, this model fails when many vehicles and traffic issues occur among the vehicles.

3　Contribution of the Paper

- To provide an energy-efficient long-distance transmission between wireless devices in IoT environment through a proposed cooperative medium access control protocol for multi-hop wireless networks.
- To improve the throughput by successful data transmission to the border line destination using cooperative relay and ensure secure delivery of messages from the source to the destination by effective routing by means of relay node selection.
- To avoid alteration of the transmitted message by a malicious user on the network and to authenticate the users and all the nodes that participate in the long-distance communication by a secured mechanism.

4　Methods

Consider an ad hoc network with multiple transmission ranges defined in IEEE 802.11 b PHY/MAC layer LAN standard. RTS, CTS, and ACK are the control packets of the MAC layer that have the frame headers for exchanging control information such as SNR, residual energy, distance, trust, and reliability. The system model considers a typical energy-limited multi-hop cluster-based cooperative MAC protocol design for efficient transmission. Figures 2 and 3 illustrate the proposed approach and the transmission structure in relay node selection for ad hoc networks in an IoT environment.

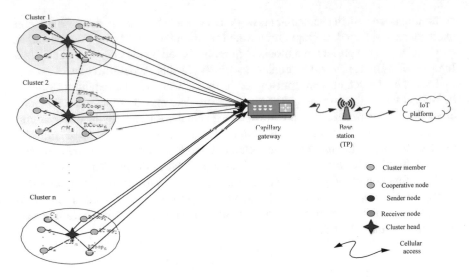

Fig. 2 Illustration of the proposed approach

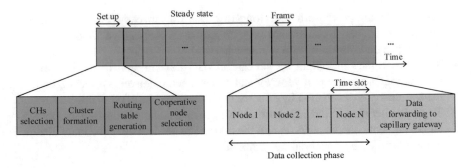

Fig. 3 Transmission structure of the proposed relay node estimation

4.1 Multi-Hop Cluster-Based Optimal Cooperative MAC (MCOC-MAC) Protocol Transmission Procedure:

4.1.1 Setup Phase

In this stage, all node present in network will send their location, and residual energy to the gateway in turn gateway will utilize this information to find best possible path.

This stage consists of the 3 steps, namely CHs selection, cluster formation routing table generation, and relay node selection.

To avoid overhead in transmission, the algorithm chooses the best suitable relay node by satisfying the fitness function threshold value of node with in cooperation of cooperative forwarding.

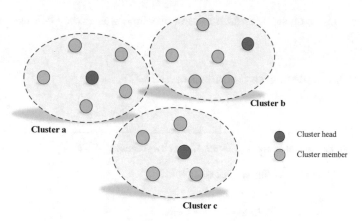

Fig. 4 Cluster formation

A relay node search optimization (RESO) technique depicts that the selection of cooperative nodes in the routed path from source to destination. Every iteration node will update its fitness value and report to the CG by send message (Fig. 4).

CHs selection (step 1) →	Cluster formation (step 2) →	Routing table generation (step 3) →	Relay node selection (step 4)
In this step, first a cluster head (CH) will be selected based on the algorithm which is running capillary gateway. Based on the information of individual node, CH will be selected	After selection of CHs, the cluster will be formed	Based on the routing algorithm which running the capillary gateway, the routing table will be generated	Finding best suitable relay node to transmit the data to the destination CH of source node will find nearest CH to route the packet to the destination node. And finally, CH of destination node will calculate the transmission rate in the cluster

4.1.2 Condition of Relay Node Selection

1. Node density (ND), transmission information history such as SNR, residual energy, reliability, and distance are the factors which will decide the successful transmission and based on the predefined threshold value, the cooperative transmission will take place in the network, and the rate of transmission should be lower than the predetermined value.
2. For the cooperation from other relay node, the destination node should be in communication range. The broadcasted message from a node to all the nodes

present in the cluster with information of which cluster they belongs, is sent to the CH.

4.1.3   Relay Node Search Optimization (RESO)

Initialize a set of nodes (Cluster1, Cluster 2), position p, $Best_{fit}$ = Infinitive.

While the stop condition is not satisfied

        For each node do

        Calculate the fitness value

        If $Fit_i < Best_{fit}$ then

        $Worst_{fit} = fit_i$

        $X_{Best} = X_i$

        End If

        Compute the mass using

        Determine its K neighbors

s   *End For*

End While

Select the best node as relay node

Where

Fit*i* represents the fitness function of the node which will help to decide the find nodes by in the cluster to participate to routing date packets.

Bestfit represents the best node which you carry the transmission.

*X***best** represents the best suitable position of a node in the network.

4.1.4   Steady-State Phase

In this phase, use of time division multiple access (TDMA) technique will help to analyze the duration and number of frames used in a particular iteration. Frames used in this phase are less compared to previous stage.

4.1.5   Data Collection Phase

In the data collection phase, the source assigned to the nearby CH makes the transmission by means of a selected relay node. From the selected node, the data collected from the source are forwarded to the capillary gateway and then reach the destination.

4.1.6   Multi-Hop-Based Cooperative MAC Transmission

When the number of relay nodes is estimated on the source and destination side, then multi-hop transmission occurs in packet transmission. This transmission will further reduce the nodes' energy utilization, and an efficient routing path is established to make an effective transmission.

4.2   Blockchains-Based Trust Management System in the Ad Hoc IoT Environment

Blockchaining is a decentralized approach to overcome the issues such as insecure data storage. Blockchain-based public key infrastructure is more suitable for the identity verification and securely store data (Fig. 5).

4.2.1   Registration Phase

In this phase, all nodes will imposed with unique ID and node number; it will stored in the capillary gateway (CG) before registered in the network. If unique ID and node number are matched during registering for initial verification, then accessing will takes place; otherwise it will terminate the process. After this process, CG will initiate a request message to the trusted authority (TA) for the registration of that

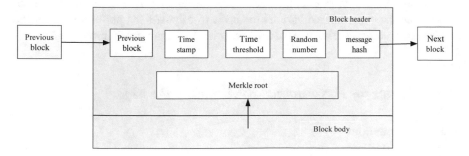

Fig. 5 Blockchain structure

node which is willing to participate for the data transmission or will participate as relay node while transmitting the data.

For security purpose, a random symmetric key (RSK) will be generated by the node which again sent to CG. For encryption purpose, TA will send a public key for encrypting the RSK.

To get a public key certificate, public key (PUBK), private key (PRIK) from the TA, CG will send unique ID, number, and the encrypted RSK to TA. So that while warping the registration phase, CG will issue these constraints to the node. Hence, by this process, all the nodes will get corresponding keys for secure transmission.

4.2.2 Transmission Phase

For secure transmission from source to destination, CH will play major role such as it will first verify the public key (PUBK), private key (PRIK) while a nearest node of the cluster willing to transmit. And it if all the keys are matched, then based on the RESO algorithm, CH will choose best relay node to transmit the data. After verification, CG will get source node certificate from the relay node through CH. While selecting a relay node trust, SNR, residual energy, distance reliability are considered as major factors while selecting a rely node through RESO algorithm.

Every relay node or local agent will broadcast the messing by performing hashing on the message by SHA 256 function. This message has been added after verification and added to the blockchain. And every nodes update its local copy of blockchain. In this, every block will consist of hash, previous hash, index, and its time.

4.3 System Evaluation Metrics

To evaluate the performance of our model, there are certain parameters which can be useful. Mainly the communication in WANET impacted by heavy energy consumption, delay in transmission and in routing which affects the lifetime of the node in the network which eventually effects the throughput of the system. Different researchers have considered various methods to calculate the performances of the system comparing existing one for advancement in technology improvement.

4.4 Metrics for Performance Evolution of the Model

4.4.1 Throughput

This metric will help us to understand number of successful transmission from sender to distention received through proper channel by selecting appropriate relay node based on our model. Throughput expressed in kilobits per second (Kbps).

Mathematically, it is expressed as follows:

$$\mathbf{Throughput} = \frac{8 \times \text{bytes received}}{\text{Time}} \times 1000\text{kbps} \qquad (1)$$

4.4.2 Energy Consumption

After transmitting date and before transmission of date from a node, the amount of energy left out or simply the change in energy level in the node is nothing but energy computation of the node. This will help us to understand the effectiveness of the system. Mechanical equation for the energy computation expressed as follows:

$$\text{Energy consumption} = \sum_{j=1}^{N} \text{initial}(e_j) - \text{final}(e_j) \qquad (2)$$

where, initial(e_j) depicts the initial energy **and** final(e_j) depicts final energy after transmission.

4.4.3 End-to-End Delay (*E-E* delay)

For transmitting the data from one node to another node in the network, certain delay can be raised due to unpredictable nature of the network. The amount of time taken for each successful transmission of the data is calculated to find the end-to-end delay in the network.The equation to specify end-to-end delay is given as,

$$E - E \text{ delay} = \frac{\sum_{j=1}^{N} t_i - t_f}{N} \qquad (3)$$

where *ti* denotes initial time, *tf* denotes final time, and N is the number of nodes.

5 Expected Outcome

The simulation will be carried out in MATLAB platform to show the effectiveness of the proposed method. The ad hoc network topology is based on the IEEE.802.11b PHY/MAC standard, which offers a data rates of 11, 5.5, 2, and 1 Mbps with the distance of 48.2, 67.1, 74.7, and 100 m, respectively. In the PHY layer, IEEE 802.11b standard uses Industry, Science and Medical (ISM) band of 2.4 or 5 GHz frequency along with direct sequence spread spectrum (DSSS), and in MAC layer,

Table 2 Parameter setting

Parameter	Value
MAC header size	272 bits
PHY header size	192 bits
RTS pkt	352 bits
CTS/ACK pkt	304 bits
Data rate for MAC header	1 Mbps
CW min	31 slots
CW max	1023 slots
Retry time	6
Initial power	10 J
Transmit power	281.8 mW
Receive power	1 mW

the CSMA/CA protocol is used. The control packets of the MAC layer can be transmitted at a constant rate of 1 Mbps. Consider a three hops routing scenario (three clusters in one routing path). The simulation settings are listed in Table 2.

Throughput, energy consumption, average end-end delay, execution time, and relay selection delay are the metrics used to simulate the result. Further, the proposed research work will be compared with the existing state-of-the-art approaches. Further to refer towards our more comparative evaluation with the existing models such as fitness function multipath distance vector of ad hoc network found on demand (FF-AOMDV) [22] have used the fitness function to find the routing path in the network, AOMDV [23] have been presented as a modified version of AODV; AOM routing with maximization of life (AOMR-LM) [24] gives an authentic stamp as better model compare to others. These existing protocols have been choose due the inherent capability. We expect that our model will give better performance than the existing one.

References

1. Ju P, Song W, Zhou D (2013) Survey on cooperative medium access control protocols. IET Commun 7(9):893–902
2. Zhang X, Guo L, Wei X (2013) An energy-balanced cooperative MAC protocol based on opportunistic relaying in MANETs. Comput Electr Eng 39(6):1894–1904
3. Chavan AA, Kurule DS, Dere PU (2016) Performance analysis of AODV and DSDV routing protocol in MANET and modifications in AODV against black hole attack. Procedia Comput Sci 79:835–844
4. Wang W, Wang H, Wang B, Wang Y, Wang J (2013) Energy-aware and self- adaptive anomaly detection scheme based on network tomography in mobile ad hoc networks. Inf Sci 20(220):580–602
5. Choi HH, Lee HG, Lee JR (2014) A new energy-aware source routing protocol for maximization of network lifetime in MANET. IEICE Trans Inf Syst 97(2):335–339

6. Fotue D, Labiod H, Engel T (2012) Controlled data collection of mini-sinks for maximizing packet delivery ratio and throughput using multiple paths in wireless sensor networks. In: 2012 IEEE 23rd international symposium on personal, indoor and mobile radio communications-(PIMRC). IEEE, pp 758–764
7. Lin J, Yu W, Zhang N, Yang X, Zhang H, Zhao W (2017) A survey on internet of things: architecture, enabling technologies, security and privacy, and applications. IEEE Internet Things J 4(5):1125–1142
8. Laneman JN, Tse DN, Wornell GW (2004) Cooperative diversity in wireless networks: efficient protocols and outage behavior. IEEE Trans Inf Theory 50(12):3062–3080
9. Niu H, Zhu N, Sun L, Vasilakos AV, Sezaki K (2016) Security-embedded opportunistic user cooperation with full diversity. Wireless Netw 22(5):1513–1522
10. Liu P, Tao Z, Panwar S (2005) A cooperative MAC protocol for wireless local area networks. In: IEEE international conference on communications, ICC 2005, vol 5. IEEE, pp 2962–2968
11. Zareei M, Islam AM, Vargas-Rosales C, Mansoor N, Goudarzi S, Rehmani MH (2018) Mobility-aware medium access control protocols for wireless sensor networks: A survey. J Netw Comput Appl 15(104):21–37
12. Mahmud MT, Rahman MO, Hassan MM, Almogren A, Zhou M (2019) An efficient cooperative medium access control protocol for wireless IoT networks in smart world system. J Netw Comput Appl 1(133):26–38
13. Kakria A, Aseri TC (2019) An efficient distributed multi-hop relay supporting (EDMRS) MAC protocol for wireless sensor networks. Wireless Pers Commun 1–5
14. Chen C, Xiang B, Liu Y, Wang K (2019) A secure authentication protocol for internet of vehicles. IEEE Access 7:12047–12057
15. Jiang T, Fang H, Wang H (2019) Blockchain-based internet of vehicles: distributed network architecture and performance analysis. IEEE Internet Things J 6(3):4640–4649
16. Zhong H, Huang B, Cui J, Xu Y, Liu L (2018) Conditional privacy-preserving authentication using registration list in vehicular ad hoc networks. IEEE Access 6:2241–2250
17. Epiphaniou G, Karadimas P, Kbaier Ben Ismail D, Al-Khateeb H, Dehghantanha A, Choo KR (2018) Nonreciprocity compensation combined with turbo codes for secret key generation in vehicular ad hoc social IoT networks. IEEE Internet Things J 5(4):2496–2505
18. Schweitzer N, Stulman A, Margalit RD, Shabtai A (2017) Contradiction based gray-hole attack minimization for ad-hoc networks. IEEE Trans Mob Comput 16(8):2174–2183
19. Hatzivasilis G, Papaefstathiou I, Manifavas C (2017) SCOTRES: secure routing for IoT and CPS. IEEE Internet Things J 4(6):2129–2141
20. Wu Y, ping Qian L, Huang L, Shen X (2017) Optimal relay selection and power control for energy-harvesting wireless relay networks. IEEE Trans Green Commun Netw 2(2):471–81
21. Zhang X, Guo L, Anpalagan A, Khwaja AS (2017) Performance of energy-efficient cooperative MAC protocol with power backoff in MANETs. Wireless Pers Commun 92(3):843–861
22. Ladas A, Deepak GC, Pavlatos N, Politis C (2018) A selective multipath routing protocol for ubiquitous networks. Ad Hoc Networks. 77:95–107
23. Pathak G, Kumar K (2017) Traffic aware load balancing in AOMDV for mobile Ad-hoc networks. J Commun Inf Netw 2(3):123–30
24. Taha A, Alsaqour R, Uddin M, Abdelhaq M, Saba T (2017) Energy efficient multipath routing protocol for mobile ad-hoc network using the fitness function. IEEE access. 5:10369–10381
25. Gkantsidis C, Rodriguez PR (2005) Network coding for large scale content distribution. In: Proceedings IEEE 24th annual joint conference of the IEEE computer and communications societies, vol 4. IEEE, pp 2235–2245
26. Liu K, Chang X, Liu F, Wang X, Vasilakos AV (2015) A cooperative MAC protocol with rapid relay selection for wireless ad hoc networks. Comput Netw 14(91):262–282
27. Liu K, Wu S, Huang B, Liu F, Xu Z (2016) A power-optimized cooperative MAC protocol for lifetime extension in wireless sensor networks. Sensors 16(10):1630
28. Shamna HR, Lillykutty J (2017) An energy and throughput efficient distributed cooperative MAC protocol for multihop wireless networks. Comput Netw 24(126):15–30

Printed in the United States
by Baker & Taylor Publisher Services